MICRO
SCRIBE
OLOGY

The
BIBLICAL
AUTHOR^ITY
OF THE
Prophetic
SCRIBE

MICRO
SCRIBE
OLOGY

The
BIBLICAL
AUTHORITY
OF THE
Prophetic
SCRIBE

TIFFANY BUCKNER

Microscribeology
The Biblical Authority of the Prophetic Scribe
by Tiffany Buckner

© 2019, Tiffany Buckner
www.tiffanybuckner.com
info@anointedfire.com

Published by Anointed Fire™ House
www.anointedfirehouse.com
Cover Design by Anointed Fire™ House

Author photograph by Dominique 'Chevon' Doyle
www.sochevon.com

Edited by:
Vanessa Hunter
Glenda Giles
Melanie Sanders Stewart
Jose Juguna

ISBN:
ISBN-13: 978-0-9993380-8-7
ISBN-10: 0-9993380-8-0

"Before I formed you in the womb I knew you, and before you were born I consecrated you; I appointed you a prophet to the nations."

JEREMIAH 1:5

Acknowledgments

To my beautiful mother, Alice Buckner. Thank you for always supporting me in my endeavors. You've sincerely taught me the value of hard work. I've never seen you quit anything or even take a day off! No matter what life has thrown at you, you've always managed to make the best of it. I honor, love and miss you dearly! There's so much I want to say to you, but I'll just have to wait to see your beautiful face again. Rest in Christ and I'll see you again, Mom.

To my dad, Gerard Buckner. Thank you for encouraging me in all things. Our long talks always gives me a better sense of who I am. I love you.

To my leaders, Apostle Bryan and Patrice Meadows. Words cannot express how much I love and honor you! Thank you for leading me, pushing me and praying for me. You have sincerely changed my perspective on life, and I'm excited about doing life with you!

Table of Contents

Introduction...XIII
Note from the Author...XVII

Scribeology...1
Good Scribe, Bad Scribe.. 2
Pride: The Enemy of the Scribe... 5
The Micro World of the Scribe... 6

Prophets & Scribes (Officers of the Law)...13
Prophetic Scribes... 16
Authority 21
The Power of Fasting and Prayer.. 27

The Authority of Words...39
The Doorkeepers of Wisdom... 50
How Words Affect Us.. 53
Your Relationship with Words... 61
The Marriage of Words... 63
Startup Exercise (Activation).. 69

Your Right to Write...71
Writer's Block... 72
Mature Revelation... 76
Metrons... 78
Understanding Your Right to Write.. 79
Writer's Block Exercise.. 83

The Author's Pace...87
The Weight of Responsibility... 91
The Speed of Obedience.. 99
The Talent Exercise... 103

The Author's Voice...105
The Authority of the Scribe.. 111
The Words of the Scribe.. 115
Silence of the Saints.. 124
Goliath Exercise... 128

Understanding Your Commitment..131
A Writer's Pledge... 134
A Writer's Commitment... 135

Understanding Your Role..141

Understanding Your Level...149
Measuring Your Impact.. 161
Measuring Your Impact Exercise.. 162
Mountain or Midget?.. 165

Faith that Moves Mountains...173

Counting the Cost of Leadership..**181**

    What is a Leader?..197

    Seed Time, Harvest and Coverings..202

    Seeds Have Coverings..205

    Activation..211

What's Your Range?..**213**

    Plagiarism: The Literary Version of Lip Syncing..216

What's Your Rank?..**219**

    Impersonating an Officer..221

What's Your Peak?..**229**

    Leading Readers Astray..237

    The Peak of Revelation..243

What are You Offering?..**249**

    Give Them Something They Can Use..255

From Layers to Levels..**259**

    The Importance of Identifying Your Level..266

    How to Identify Your Level..268

    From Fact to Revelation..269

    Iron Sharpens Iron..273

    From Revelation to Revelation..275

What's Your Depth?..**279**

    Is Deep Calling You?..287

    Who's Calling You Deep?..289

    Depth Exercise..293

Who Summoned You?..**297**

Writer's Hypoxia..**307**

Writer's Warfare..**311**

    Levels of Warfare..317

    Sometimes, it's Not Warfare..320

Currents..**323**

Understanding Authorship..**343**

    Understanding Authority..348

    Kingdom Protocol for Writers..351

    Understanding Authorization..359

The Literary Process of Creation..**371**

    Building Your Vocabulary..379

    Revealing Your Creativity (Activation)..383

    Creative Revelation..384

The Weight of the Scribe..**389**

    A Scribe's Digestive System..391

    Satan Sifts Scribes..395

    Satan Robs Scribes..400

The Weight of Your Words..406

The Laws of Authorship..**415**

The Practical and the Spiritual Laws of Authorship...............................420
Exercising Kingdom Authority..431
The End is the Beginning..433
The Writing is on the Wall...441
Deliverance for the Scribe..447

Scribal Deliverance...**453**

Delivering Scribes from Legalism...454
Woe to Ungodly Scribes...460
A Prescription for Freedom..469
Driving Scribes out of Caves...479

Microscribeology..**493**

How to Build Your Skills as a Writer..514
Keys to a Successful Writing Career...517
Ready. Set. Activate...523
No More Excuses...529

Introduction

In May of 1977, Thomas Bertram "Bert" Lance popularized the idiom, "If it ain't broke, don't fix it." Mr. Lance briefly served under President Jimmy Carter as Director of Office of Management and Budget. Mr. Lance is not accredited as being the original author of this idiom; it is believed that the quote was a Southern proverb that had been circulating around in the American South before he popularized it. Since then, this quote has been echoed on the seven mountains of societal influence, which are:

- Religion
- Family
- Education
- Government
- Business
- Media
- Arts & Entertainment

Imagine each mountain stood side-by-side, all surrounded by parking lots and beautiful shrubbery. Imagine that you could walk through the double doors of each mountain into a huge, beautifully decorated foyer area. There, you'd see an electronic directory that helped you to find the area of the mountain that you were looking for. Because of the size of each mountain, there would be buses, tour guides and all types of restaurants. If you walked into the Mountain of Religion, you'd see people of every race, ethnicity and tongue. You'd see women wearing everything from hijabs to bonnets to lace-front wigs. You'd see men wearing long robes, two or three-piece suits, turbans and kippahs. If you walked into the Mountain of Family, you'd see people of every race, creed, socioeconomic class and age, all headed towards or away from their homes. You'd see judges and pastors performing wedding ceremonies, and not too far away from that section, you'd see a section for marriage counselors and divorce attorneys. You'd see doting fathers standing in nurseries, peering through the glass at their newborn children. You'd also see mistresses sneaking through the windows of the mountain, performing illegal transactions, hoping that one day, they'll be able to legally enter into the mountain as wives. You'd also see domestic violence officers taking the reports of men and women with black eyes and bloody noses. In the Mountain of Education, you'd see people of all ages and intelligence quotients headed towards their classrooms. You'd see nerds and you'd see bullies. The Mountain of Government would get the most noise complaints. Republicans, Democrats, Libertarians and people from all political parties would be passionately detailing why they believe their views are better. You'd see city police officers, state patrolmen, FBI agents and CIA agents all rushing out of the mountain, jumping into their cars and heading over to one of the other mountains of influence. Of course, the list goes on.

On the walls of every mountain, you'd see hieroglyphics, drawings and words written in every language known to man, all pointing people towards a specific world. In every mountain, you'd see the words that Mr. Bert spoke; they'd be written in varying languages. "If it ain't broke, don't fix it!" Nevertheless, in every one of these mountains, on the very top floor and the bottom floor, you'd find the offices of the scribes. These floors would be in shambles, and you wouldn't find many construction workers on them making any of the needed repairs. Nevertheless, these floors would be the busiest floors on any given mountain, filled with ambitious scribes eager to share their views. Why is the scribe's office in such disarray? The answer is simple. Because every mountain is formed by words, and words shape the worlds that we live in. For this reason, anytime Satan sends workers into any of these mountains, he assigns them to the top and bottom floors. His workers disguise themselves as angels of light and make their way towards the elevators, hoping to intercept any writer who's headed towards his or her next level. When these elevator doors open months or years later, you'd witness women holding up their left hands, trying to get a better look at the engagement rings their "angels" have just given them. You'd see men with child support papers and criminal records, and you'd see women with restraining orders and pregnancy tests. You'd see elevators stopping and starting again; you'd see elevators falling and crashing into the abyss below. You'd also see elevators rising to the top. From those elevators, you'd hear the agonizing sounds of tortured angels who've failed their demonic assignments. You'd witness those elevator doors opening every other floor, and you'd watch in amusement as demons are cast out of those elevators in a process called deliverance. In short, some scribes will rise to the top and become the men and women God has designed them to be. They'll resist temptation and go on to write some of the most powerful books ever written. Then again, some scribes will fall into the mouth of temptation, never to rise again.

Microscribeology is a detailed breakdown of the scribe's world, on both the natural and spiritual side of the plane. This book will give scribes all around the world the tools they'll need to repair the office of the scribe and to restore the integrity back to it.

You'll come to learn:
- the spiritual side of writer's block.
- why you've gone under attack every time you've started writing your book.
- the temptations that many writers face and how to overcome them.
- the varying levels of writing and how to determine which level you write on.
- and much more.

Microscribeology will forever change the way you see the world of the scribe and the way you see yourself as a scribe.

Note from the Author

Dear Bestseller,

First and foremost, let me thank you for purchasing Microscribeology. I believe that many of you are about to go on a journey that will catapult you into your ministry or career as a writer, and for this reason, you need to understand how to navigate your way around the writer's world. In this world, there are many pits, ditches and levels, all of which are filled with writers from every walk of life. And of course, just like any warm-blooded writer, you want to reach the top; you want to write tomorrow's best-seller, and you want to continue writing books that impact the world.

I've written over forty books (to date). I've also written and published close to three hundred articles and several songs, four of which are currently circulating. What this means is, I am a writer to the core. I'm not just someone who's written a few books; writing has engraved itself in my DNA. It's no longer something I do; it's who I am. I live in a world of words—a world where every storm is nothing but a shower of words, some of which are highlighted. Like most writers who live in this world, I take whatever words the Lord highlights and I chew them, breaking them down until they become revelation. While I may not be experiencing this in the natural realm, this is truly how I envision my world to be. With that said, welcome to my world.

In Microscribeology, you will find yourself venturing off into the depths of wisdom, where you'll come to better understand your role and assignment as a scribe. You will also find a lot of practical knowledge in this book. In other words, it's not so deep that you won't be able to understand it, and it's not so practical that you won't be able to glean from it. I am absolutely confident that this book will be one of the most insightful books you'll ever read about the office of the scribe. So, take your time and enjoy every word and chapter that the Lord highlights for you. And again, thank you for purchasing Microscribeology. I pray that it blesses you.

Tiffany Buckner

Scribeology

This may sound cliché, but this is truly a scribe's world. But before we visit the world of the scribe, let's check out a few interesting facts.

- There is no definite number of words in the English language, however, the Oxford English Dictionary currently has over 170,000 English words listed that are in use, with more than 47,000 of those words being obsolete.
- The average adult has a vocabulary that extends anywhere between 20,000 to 35,000 words.
- Upon entry to college, the average young adult's vocabulary consists of 10,000-12,000 words.
- The average adult's *active* vocabulary is roughly around 5,000 words, meaning that the average adult's passive vocabulary is larger than their active vocabulary. Our passive vocabulary are the words that we understand, but don't necessarily use.
- A college professor's vocabulary can be as extensive as 80,000 words.
- The average woman speaks roughly around 20,000 words a day, whereas, the average man speaks roughly around 7,000 words a day. This may be because, according to the Amen Clinic in Newport Beach California, women's brains are more active than men's brains. *And yes, that's the actual clinic's name!*
- Authors tend to use twice as many words in their writings than they do in their normal day-to-day speech.
- More than 80% of Americans say they want to write a book, but of that number, only 10% actually follow through.

What do these numbers tell us? First, the average English speaker only understands 11 to 20% of the English language, with more than half of those words being passive or unused. Next, we come to understand that the world of authorship is so intimidating that 90% of the people who aspire to write never do. Lastly, if we write twice as many words as we speak, this could only mean that the average male author's book will consist of roughly 14,000 varying words, whereas, the average female author's book will consist of roughly around 40,000 varying words. These facts are important to note because they help us to better understand the world of words and how we use them.

What determines how many words are active in our vocabularies? A few of the determining factors include, but are not limited to:

1. Our personal environments. These are the people we surround ourselves with.
2. Our work environments.
3. Media (what we watch on television and listen to on the radio).
4. The books we read.
5. The amount of time we study each day.

Good Scribe, Bad Scribe

There's light and there's darkness. There's evil and there's good. There's love and there's hate. There's up and there's down. There's left and there's right. There are wheat and there are tares. There's Isaac and then there is Ishmael. For every good thing, there is something on the opposite side of the spectrum. It goes without saying that Satan has set out to pervert everything that God has created. For this reason, there are good people in the world and there are bad ones, just as there are good scribes as well as bad ones.

First and foremost, who were the scribes of old? Most of us know them as one of the sects who were partly responsible for Jesus' crucifixion. For this reason, we have ascribed a negative connotation to the word scribe. But before we discuss the New Testament scribes, let's get a better understanding of the ones in the Old Testament. Historically, scribes were men who copied legal documents, the Torah and other manuscripts. They were educated men who were well-versed in matters of the Old Testament law. They also kept records (business, historical and judicial) for kings, nobles and the towns they lived in, and there was typically (at least) one scribe per city.

One good scribe that we'll talk about in this study is named Ezra. First, let's examine a note given to him by the king of Persia.

Copy of Note King Artaxerxes Gave to Ezra, the Scribe (Ezra 7:12-26)

"Artaxerxes, king of kings, to Ezra the priest, the scribe of the Law of the God of Heaven. Peace. And now I make a decree that anyone of the people of Israel or their priests or Levites in my kingdom, who freely offers to go to Jerusalem, may go with you. For you are sent by the king and his seven counselors to make inquiries about Judah and Jerusalem according to the Law of your God, which is in your hand, and also to carry the silver and gold that the king and his counselors have freely offered to the God of Israel, whose dwelling is in Jerusalem, with all the silver and gold that you shall find in the whole province of Babylonia, and with the freewill offerings of the people and the priests, vowed willingly for the house of their God that is in Jerusalem. With this money, then, you shall with all diligence buy bulls, rams, and lambs, with their grain offerings and their drink offerings, and you shall offer them on the altar of the house of your God that is in Jerusalem. Whatever seems good to you and your brothers to do with the rest of the silver and gold, you may do, according to the will of your God. The vessels that have been given you for the service of the house of your God, you shall deliver before the God of Jerusalem. And whatever else is required for the house of your God, which it falls to you to provide, you may provide it out of the king's treasury.

"And I, Artaxerxes the king, make a decree to all the treasurers in the province Beyond the River: Whatever Ezra the priest, the scribe of the Law of the God of Heaven, requires of you, let it be done with all diligence, up to 100 talents of silver, 100 cors of wheat, 100 baths of wine, 100 baths of oil, and salt without prescribing how much. Whatever is decreed by the God of Heaven, let it be done in full for the house of the God of Heaven, lest his wrath be against the realm of the king and his sons. We also notify you that it shall not be lawful to impose tribute, custom, or toll on anyone of the priests, the Levites, the singers, the doorkeepers, the temple servants, or other servants of this house of God.

"And you, Ezra, according to the wisdom of your God that is in your hand, appoint magistrates and judges who may judge all the people in the province Beyond the River, all such as know the laws of your God. And those who do not know them, you shall teach. Whoever will not obey the law of your God and the law of the king, let judgment be strictly executed on him, whether for death or for banishment or for confiscation of his goods or for imprisonment."

"In ancient times the Scribes were Jewish officers who performed duties which included various kinds of writing, but when the Jews returned from Babylonian captivity, the *soferim* or Scribes were organized by Ezra into a distinct body. These Scribes became the interpreters and copyists of God's law. Among these duties, they copied the Pentateuch, the Phylacteries, and the Mezuzoth. (Deuteronomy 6:9)." (Credit: bible-history.com/ The Scribes: Jewish Leaders in the New Testament)

First off, who was Ezra? He was one of the most prominent scribes in the Bible. Known as Ezra, the Priest and Ezra, the Scribe, Ezra was bilingual; he was well-versed in both Aramaic and Hebrew. He was an instructor of the law of God and a scholar. A descendant of Aaron, the High Priest, Ezra was a knowledgeable leader of Jewish law and he was a devout and humble man. We first see him come on the scene in chapter seven of the Book of Ezra. During that time, the Jews were still in the process of returning to Jerusalem from their exile in Babylon. Ezra returned to Jerusalem with a group of exiles in 457 B.C. He'd been sent back to Jerusalem by the king of Persia (King Artaxerxes) to teach the laws to any of the Jews who were unlearned. Nevertheless, when Ezra arrived in Jerusalem, he found that many of the Jews had intermingled with the pagans and had even married non-Jewish women. This grieved Ezra who, after having heard the report, "tore his hair from his head and beard," ripped his garment, fasted and sat in astonishment for hours on end. Later that day, he rose up and went before the Lord, interceding on behalf of the Jews. In short, we see that Ezra was a noble, passionate and godly man, even though he was a scribe. He is an example of a good scribe.

In the Old Testament, the scribes were legal jurists or lawyers. They transcribed the Old Testament Law and taught their interpretation of the Law to their students. Presumably, some scribes were Pharisees, but there is no evidence that any of the scribes were Sadducees. They were the printers of their day, often drafting land deeds, divorce decrees, loans, marriage contracts and many other legal manuscripts. Just like their Old Testament brethren, they were very educated and respected by the Jews. Unlike the Sadducees, most Pharisees believed in the Resurrection, just as they believed in demons, angels and the supernatural world. Nevertheless, one of Jesus' rebukes to them is found in Matthew 19:4. They'd decided to test the Lord by asking Him about divorce; this is because, once again, they were well-versed in the Law. In Matthew 19:4, He starts off His response with, "Have you not read?" Again, these were men who made a life from copying and studying the Torah. Like the legalists of today, many scribes studied to appear intelligent and they studied to be right; they had no desire to preserve the spirit behind the Law. They simply loved the attention, prestige and honor they received from men. Of course, these scribes, along with the Pharisees and Sadducees sought to have Jesus killed. These were the bad scribes. Even to this day, there are many authors who are well-versed in the English language, but in relation to love, they are absolutely bankrupt. They do not have the heart of God; they simply want the praise of men. This doesn't mean they are not called by God to write for Him; it means that they have been perverted by the enemy.

Pride: The Enemy of the Scribe

One of the most effective snares that the enemy sets for the scribe is called pride. You see, anytime a man enters an arena where he can stand out from the rest, he has to *intentionally* and sometimes *aggressively* humble himself. Think of it this way: in the Earth realm, we don't have to struggle to walk in an upright position because of gravity, so when we walk, we aren't so driven by intentionality as we are by instinct. Sure, we have to intentionally stand to our feet and take the necessary steps in the direction we want to go in, however, walking is not a struggle for most of us. Howbeit, when astronauts enter the world of microgravity, they have to be intentional about their walks. What was once easy for them suddenly becomes a struggle, so they have to grab onto or push against a surface to rotate their bodies in an upright position. The same is true for people who find themselves in a place or space in time where they stand out from the crowd. Spiritually speaking, gravity is different in this realm; the individuals have to *intentionally* and *aggressively* humble themselves repeatedly; that is, until they are mature enough to walk upright.

In 1 Corinthians 8:1, the Bible tells us that, "knowledge puffs up," meaning, with knowledge comes pride. This doesn't happen sometimes; knowledge and pride are a package deal, but it's important for you to eat the knowledge, but spit out the perversion that came with it. When you sit down to write your book, you can expect Satan to tempt you with pride. This is similar to what happens midways through a deliverance session. Demons will tempt the deliverance minister with pride; the minister may find himself or herself bombarded with thoughts like, "Look at what you did. You're powerful!" In other cases, the demons will attempt to offend the minister; this way, the minister becomes defensive and prideful. If pride enters the minister, the power of God will lift because according to the Bible, God resists the proud. The minister has to *intentionally* and oftentimes *aggressively* resist this temptation to follow through with the deliverance. After the deliverance session is finished, it is not uncommon for the person or people who received ministry to repeatedly thank the minister. In this moment, it is important for the minister to do like the astronaut; he or she has to grab onto a surface, *intentionally* and *aggressively* turning himself or herself around so that the minister can remain upright. This means that the minister can thank the person or people, however, it is important that the leader not allow the individual(s) to praise and/or give the credit to him or her. The glory has to be returned to God.

The point is, you will be tempted by pride. This is why it takes the average Christian author one to five years to finish a book that could have and should have been finished in a matter of a month or two; this is the modern-day equivalent of what the Israelites did when it took them forty years to complete what should have been an eleven-day journey. Any author who falls into the pride-trap has fallen into the same snare that the scribes of old fell into.

Matthew 15:14: Let them alone: they be blind leaders of the blind. And if the blind lead the blind, both shall fall into the ditch.

The Micro World of the Scribe

When we hear the word "micro," we understand that it means very small or low in quantity. In some cases, it refers to a world not seen by the naked eye — for example, the word of bacteria, fungus and other microorganisms. Of course, to see microorganisms, we would need a microscope. What then is MicroScribeology? MicroScribeology is the in-depth examination of the scribe's world. You see, in every world, there are things seen and unseen, but when it comes to the world of the scribe, we often focus on the obvious. We rarely give our attention to the spiritual side of writing. This is because writing has long been seen as a response to an author's desire to do nothing more than write a book, and while this is true for some authors, the reality is, the world of authorship is governed by principles, laws and authorities. Since the average author-to-be is unaware of this fact, it is not uncommon for people to go charging into this world without any knowledge of or regards for these laws. The end result is, a lot of authors end up enduring some pretty remarkable warfare every time they attempt to write their books.

First and foremost, let's establish this truth: warfare does not always immediately manifest itself as an unpleasant event. There is a form of (micro) warfare that often goes undetected for a season. Good examples of this include, but are not limited to:

- a single woman exchanging numbers with a handsome man who, by all accounts, is nothing more than a weapon formed against her or vice versa.
- a budding entrepreneur hiring what appears to be the most qualified secretary he's ever come in contact with, not realizing her love-hate relationship with men and her history with extortion.
- the flashing sign on a doughnut shop signaling that fresh pastries are available and hot, but what isn't seen is the long-term effects of eating such foods.
- reality television and its effects on our society.
- a compliment out of season. While we all love to be complimented, the truth is, some people are not mature or stable enough to receive praise. For this reason, a single compliment is enough to send them tumbling into the pit of destruction that pride has dug for them.

With that being said, some of the warfare that the authors experience isn't always unwelcome (at first), for example, the sudden reemergence of an ex or an old friend. Think about biological warfare. Google defines "biological warfare" as: the use of toxins of biological origin or microorganisms as weapons of war." US National Library of Medicine National Institutes of Health reports the following:

> *"During the past century, more than 500 million people died of infectious diseases. Several tens of thousands of these deaths were due to the deliberate release of pathogens or toxins, mostly by the Japanese during their attacks on China during the Second World War. Two international treaties outlawed biological weapons in 1925 and 1972, but they have largely failed to stop countries from conducting offensive weapons research and large-scale*

production of biological weapons. And as our knowledge of the biology of disease-causing agents—viruses, bacteria and toxins—increases, it is legitimate to fear that modified pathogens could constitute devastating agents for biological warfare."
Reference: US National Library of Medicine National Institutes of Health/ Friedrich Frischknecht/ 2003).

Biological warfare is the use of unseen weapons such as viruses, gases and pathogens. If humans are using biological warfare, why is it that we expect all warfare from the demonic world to be evident and/or sensed? Why do we think that the devil fights fair? This deception has caused many believers to mistake warfare for blessings and to mistake opportunities for problems. For example, most of us would think that getting fired from a job is warfare when, in truth, it may be the unraveling of an answered prayer. Think of it this way. Imagine that you are in war in the Middle East and half of your team is cities apart from you. You receive a message from them, stating that they're out of food and they can't leave where they are because the city is surrounded by terrorists and militants. The woman who brought you the message is a Middle Eastern woman who is against what her government stands for, so she's standing in as a spy. Now, you have to send her back to the men with the food and weapons they'll need to get out of that city. Would you have her openly toting around guns and ammo? Of course, not! After all, you don't want her to end up dead, nor do you want the position of the men compromised. Lastly, you don't want the weapons to fall into the wrong hands. For this reason, you'd think of a clever way to get her to smuggle the food and the weapons into the city. God does the same! Sometimes, when we're outside of His will, He will send us a problem, hoping that we'll unwrap it and pull the opportunity out of it. Again, this means that many problems are nothing but messages disguised as messes!

"A microbiologist (from Greek μῑκρος) is a scientist who studies microscopic life forms and processes. This includes study of the growth, interactions and characteristics of microscopic organisms such as bacteria, algae, fungi, and some types of parasites and their vectors."
(Reference: Wikipedia)

SCRIBEOLOGY

Scribes are very much like microbiologists. We study what people ordinarily do not and cannot see. How so? We don't just see words; we dissect them. We mentally dissect everything in our world; sometimes, we do this immediately while, at other times, we do this gradually. This means that we can best be described as Microscribeologists.

Before we go forward, let me introduce you to four new words so you can better understand your role as a scribe.
Scribeology: The study of scribes and their worlds.
Scribeologist: Someone who studies the minds, processes and worlds of the scribe.
Microscribeologist: Someone who studies the minds, processes and worlds of the scribe in depth, often going beyond the surface to explore the spiritual or unseen world of the scribe.

We also need to understand an already established word and world, and it is the world of etymology. Oxford Dictionaries defines the word "etymology" this way: the study of the origin of words and the way in which their meanings have changed throughout history. Next, there's anthropology, which Merriam Webster defines this way: the science of human beings especially: the study of human beings and their ancestors through time and space and in relation to physical character, environmental and social relations, and culture.

Every God-appointed scribe is a Scribeologist or a Microscribeologist, meaning, we study other scribes. Every God-appointed scribe is an etymologist, meaning, we study words and the history and culture behind them. Lastly, every God-appointed scribe is an anthropologist, meaning, we study people, cultures and history. This is how we can easily differentiate a God-appointed scribe from a self-appointed one. Self-appointed scribes talk more about themselves than anything; their books are nothing but in-depth studies of themselves and their perceptions of themselves, laced with pockets of wisdom and quotes that belong to other people. This means that the people who read their books don't come out wiser; they come out soul-tied, confused or disgusted. Please understand that soul ties aren't limited to sexual relationships, after all, the soul is comprised of the mind, will and emotions. Soul ties are formed when trust and/or agreements are established or in traumatic situations. Self-appointed authors seek to gain their readers' trust or admiration; this way, the readers will agree with their assessments of themselves.

Every scribe has a depth of perception, meaning, we break words down on different levels. To one scribe, the word "understand" is limited to its definition. Merriam Webster's Dictionary defines the word "understand" this way: to grasp the meaning of. This is a surface-level teacher. Surface-level teachers rarely venture beyond the obvious, meaning, they teach what should be evident to others. So, a surface-level scribe may say, for example:

"To understand something means to grasp or grab onto the meaning of it. It means to study the subject in a way that allows you to teach it to others."

Nevertheless, a more in-depth scribe will write an entire paragraph, chapter or book using a single word. For example, when exploring the word "understand," an in-depth scribe may say:

"To understand something means to stand under it. You'll notice that the word understand is comprised of two words: under and stand. Merriam Webster's dictionary defines the word 'under' this way: in or into a position below or beneath something. Merriam Webster's dictionary defines the word stand this way: to support oneself on the feet in an erect position. So, the word 'understand' can be defined this way: To stand upright or in position under a person, theory, doctrine or thing. It means to submit or reverence through agreement. You don't have to like something or someone to understand it or them; you simply need to agree with or acknowledge the power behind that person or thing. For example, we all 'understand' that snakes can be dangerous creatures, especially the poisonous ones, and while we do not submit to snakes, we acknowledge their capabilities. In other words, we won't go charging into a snake pit just because we have dominion over all of God's creatures. No! We stand under an umbrella called wisdom, and this umbrella keeps us balanced; it helps us to make sound decisions. The Hebrew word for 'under' is 'tachath' and according to NAS Exhaustive Concordance, it means: underneath, below, instead of. The Hebrew word for "stand" is '`amad' and it means to endure, stand still, take a stand or to hold one's ground. Again, in summary, this means to hold one's position or submit to a theory, person or doctrine. So, the next time you tell a person that you understand him or her, what you're really saying is you either agree with what the person is saying, or you are acknowledging the power or abilities of the subject at hand. Again, this does not mean that you agree; it means that you have a firm grasp on the subject and the speaker does not have to go more in-depth. Abram didn't necessarily agree with Sarai when she told him to go and sleep with Hagar, nevertheless, he submitted to her words, and as a result, a wild child was born by the name of Ishmael. David didn't necessarily understand why his first son with Bathsheba had to die, but after the boy passed, he got up and ate."

You can clearly see the differences between both teachers. One teacher didn't venture outside of his or her comfort zone, whereas, the other teacher broke the word "understand" down, conducted research on the word and gave examples of it. Again, every scribe has a depth in which he or she teaches, and the great news is, there is a market for both teaching styles. Some people don't like in-depth teaching; they want the news, the basics and the hard facts. These people are more emotional than they are logical. They don't want to understand processes, laws or compositions; they simply want the summary. Nevertheless, people who want to understand things in depth are more tuned into the logistics and legalities surrounding a matter; such people are more logical in their approach because they like to draw their own conclusions. These people are more logical than they are emotional, and the ones who venture out too deep into a matter can easily become legalistic, meaning, they'll extract and submit to the laws and principles behind a theory and ignore the spirit behind the matter. A good example of legalism is this: imagine that you hire a babysitter to keep your three-year old son. You tell the babysitter that your son is lactose intolerant, and for this reason, he cannot consume any dairy. While you are away, the babysitter notices that three-year old Jason is asleep, so she decides to take a much-needed nap as well. An hour later, Jason wakes up hungry. He quietly gets off the couch and makes his way to the kitchen. From there, he opens the refrigerator and sees a Ziploc bag filled with red peppers. They are Carolina Reapers, which are the hottest peppers in the world; they are two hundred times spicier than jalapenos. He grabs the bag, opens it and stuffs one of the peppers into his mouth. Seconds later, the babysitter is awakened by the most piercing scream she's ever heard. She races to the kitchen, only to find an overturned bag of peppers and little Jason running around the kitchen screaming and fanning his mouth. His face is bloodshot red and it's obvious that he's eaten one of the peppers. The babysitter calls 911 and the operator asks her if there is any bread in the home. There isn't. The operator then tells the babysitter to give Jason a glass of milk, since milk is known to wash away the oils found in hot foods. The babysitter tells the operator that Jason is lactose intolerant and she's been informed by the parents that he isn't to have any milk. The operator insists, nevertheless, the babysitter won't move from her position. Instead, she hands Jason a cold glass of water, only making the pain more intense. Jason suffers until the paramedics finally come. What happened here is the babysitter was legalistic. She could have told Jason to gargle the milk and spit it out or she could have allowed him to drink it but asked the paramedics to bring something to combat the lactose intolerance before it flared up. Nevertheless, the boy was left to suffer the greater of two evils because the babysitter focused more on the rules than the boy himself. This is because there is no love in legalism, only laws and penalties. The little boy made a mistake, but because of the babysitter's legalism, he had no access to grace and mercy.

In this book, you will come to better understand and respect your depth as a teacher and a scribe. Additionally, you'll come to get a more in-depth view of the spiritual world, especially as it regards to scribes.

Prophets & Scribes (Officers of the Law)

Prophets and scribes. We all know a little bit about both officers, however, in the Old Testament, the two often operated independent of one another. So, before we can discuss the modern-day prophet and the modern day describe, we have to take a brief stroll through time to look at both of these offices; this way, we can better understand what it means to be an author.

The Hebrew word for prophet is "nabi," and it means "to bubble up." Nabi also means "to declare." Two other words used in the Old Testament for prophet are "roeh", which means "to perceive," and "hozeh", which means "to see" or "to perceive." Hozeh is used to reference musicians, and it can be used to reference a king's advisers as well. It also means one who has insight. For the sake of this study, we will be discussing the term "nabi" as it relates to the office of the prophet.

There has been much debate amongst theologians regarding the identity of the first prophet mentioned in the Bible. Some argue that Adam was the first prophet, others argue that it was Amos, while some teachers focus on the first mention of the word prophet, which has been officially attributed to Abram. Your interpretation would be subject to your understanding of the prophetic mantle. First and foremost, a prophet is a mediator. Another word for mediator is the word "medium." Because the word "medium" has been largely associated with witches, it has picked up a negative connotation in the body of Christ, nevertheless, the word "medium" means "a go between." For example, your soul is what connects your body to your spirit; it is your medium. Jesus is our Mediator. 1 Timothy 2:5-6 says it this way, "For there is one God, and one mediator between God and men, the man Christ Jesus; Who gave himself a ransom for all, to be testified in due time." A prophet is the mouthpiece of God; he or she is a mediator between the voice of God and man. A sorcerer is also a medium, only the sorcerer is a go-between or mediator between mankind and the demonic world. With that being noted, God spoke directly with Eve. Before the fall, she could hear from God clearly, so there was no need for Adam to mediate. Mediation was needed after mankind fell away from God, but before then, Adam and Eve held the same rank. Eve was demoted because she'd been deceived by the

the enemy, and in return, had deceived her husband. In God's judgment of Eve, He said in Genesis 3:16, "... thy desire shall be to thy husband, and he shall rule over thee." The word "rule" comes from the Hebrew word "mashal" and it means to have dominion, have authority over, to govern.

The first mediator we witness in the scriptures is Noah, even though he did not warn the people of the Earth about the impending flood; he did as God instructed him and saved his family. Nevertheless, the first mention of the word "prophet" can be found in Genesis 20, which reads, "And Abraham journeyed from thence toward the south country, and dwelled between Kadesh and Shur, and sojourned in Gerar. And Abraham said of Sarah his wife, She is my sister: and Abimelech king of Gerar sent, and took Sarah. But God came to Abimelech in a dream by night, and said to him, Behold, thou art but a dead man, for the woman which thou hast taken; for she is a man's wife. But Abimelech had not come near her: and he said, Lord, wilt thou slay also a righteous nation? Said he not unto me, She is my sister? And she, even she herself said, He is my brother: in the integrity of my heart and innocency of my hands have I done this. And God said unto him in a dream, Yea, I know that thou didst this in the integrity of thy heart; for I also withheld thee from sinning against me: therefore suffered I thee not to touch her. Now therefore restore the man his wife; <u>for he is a prophet,</u> and he shall pray for thee, and thou shalt live: and if thou restore her not, know thou that thou shalt surely die, thou, and all that are thine. Therefore Abimelech rose early in the morning, and called all his servants, and told all these things in their ears: and the men were sore afraid." (Genesis 20:1-8).

God told Abimelech that Abram was a prophet, which tells us that the term had likely already been in circulation and was largely understood, even in a pagan land. Of course, it's not advantageous for any of us to know the who's who of prophets, what's important is that we understand the role of a prophet. Again, a prophet is a mediator; he or she conveys the heart of God to His people. In regards to Adam being a prophet, the truth is, Adam, in a sense, is more like Enoch in reverse, whereas Adam walked with God and was cast out of His presence into the realm of the Earth, but Enoch walked with God and was taken out of the Earth into the everlasting presence of God.

Next, let's look at the word "scribe." The Hebrew word for scribe is "sopher" or "sofer" and it means "to count" or "one who counts." The scribes of old had to literally count each letter of the Torah as they copied it. For the most part, scribes were nothing but the copyists or better yet, the manual printers of their day. They took what the prophets said and preserved each word by transcribing it.

There are 71 mentions of the word "write" in the Bible (34 mentions in the Old Testament, 37 mentions in the New Testament). The very first time we see this word is in Exodus 17, when the Israelites were in the wilderness, having escaped from the bondage of Egypt. They were in a place called Rephidim and they'd just defeated a group of people called the Amalekites. During the battle, Moses went to the top of a mountain, and every time he would hold up the rod of God, the Israelites would prevail, but every time he would grow weary and lower his hand, the Amalekites would prevail. Aaron and Hur, who were atop the mountain with Moses, would hold up his hand whenever he got weary. Eventually, they sat Moses on a large rock, and Aaron went to one side of Moses to hold his hand up, while Hur was on the other side holding his other hand up. Israel defeated the Amalekites and God wanted to make sure that the victory was recorded so that future generations would come to see His faithfulness. Exodus 17:14 reads, "And the LORD said unto Moses, Write this for a memorial in a book, and rehearse it in the ears of Joshua: for I will utterly put out the remembrance of Amalek from under Heaven."

The next time we see the word "write" is in when God inscribed the Ten Commandments onto a couple of stone tablets. Once again, Moses was atop a mountain. Writing always served four purposes; they are:
- Keeping a record of the victories God had given the Israelites.
- Giving the law to God's people.
- Recording the many judgments of God as a warning to God's people.
- To keep a record of the prophetic words that God spoke through His prophets.

It is important for us to understand and remember that prophets released the heart of God, and even transcribed those words, but scribes would preserve those documents, copying them letter by letter to ensure that not a single word was lost. As times changed, different types of scribes began to emerge, including the Royal

Scribe and the Temple Scribe. Royal Scribes worked for kings and queens, copying and writing the royal decrees released from the throne. They also kept records of every law and decree made. And then, there was the Temple Scribes who copied, preserved and defended the Torah and the Tanakh. They also served as lawyers, journalists, accountants, judges and so much more.

Today, we are Royal Scribes because we work for the King of kings and the Lord of lords. Additionally, we are Temple Scribes because we copy and preserve the Word of God, sharing it with His people. Even though we don't necessarily copy the Torah letter for letter anymore, we do share one of the many translations of the Bible, both Old and New Testament. Lastly, many of us are Prophetic Scribes. Our assignment is to be sensitive to God's voice and transcribe whatever He shares with us. This means that we bring it from one realm to the next.

Prophetic Scribes

Again, we often operate as both Royal Scribes and Prophetic Scribes. Many Christian books are not prophetic in nature; instead, they are the experiences of the scribe. For example, the biblical prophet, Ezekiel, *recounted* a moment when he had to eat a scroll. "And he said to me, 'Son of man, eat whatever you find here. Eat this scroll, and go, speak to the house of Israel.' So I opened my mouth, and he gave me this scroll to eat. And he said to me, 'Son of man, feed your belly with this scroll that I give you and fill your stomach with it.' Then I ate it, and it was in my mouth as sweet as honey" (Ezekiel 3:1-3/ESV). Here, we witness the Prophet Ezekiel testifying about an experience he'd had.

YOU HAVE TO EAT EVERYTHING YOU INTEND TO SERVE GOD'S PEOPLE!

Another word for "testify" is "recount" or "remember." Again, one of the translations for the word "scribe" is "sopher" and it means *to count*. Ezekiel *recounted* a moment when he had to eat a scroll. The prefix "re" means again. Most modern-day Prophetic Scribes *recount* their experiences, sharing their testimonies with their readers. In these testimonies, they detail their struggles and victories; this not only helps the reader to get free, but it helps the writer to get a mountaintop view of the trial he or she has endured. "And they overcame him by the blood of the Lamb, and by the word

16

of their testimony; and they loved not their lives unto the death" (Revelation 12:11). What does this mean? It is the job of the prophetic scribe to:

- Testify
- Prophesy
- Edify and Exhort
- Witness or Confirm
- Judge

Let's look at all of these points:

Testify

Our experiences, while personal, are not our own. Experiences are like water. Water has to move or flow in order to:

1. Sustain life.
2. To produce power. In the natural realm, flowing water produces what is called Hydel Power Generation.
3. To reduce bacterial growth, thus, allowing the water to be safe for both animals and humans.
4. Reduce the population of disease-carrying mosquitoes.
5. Flowing water fertilizes the ground around it.

Of course, Prophets have to move on (forgive) in order to flow correctly. When Prophets don't testify, like stagnant or standing water, they become bitter. Our assignment is to forgive, heal and share; this is the cycle of the prophetic scribe.

John 7:38: He that believeth on me, as the scripture hath said, out of his belly shall flow rivers of living water.

Psalm 81:10: I am the LORD thy God, which brought thee out of the land of Egypt: open thy mouth wide, and I will fill it.

Understand this: living water is water that gives life.

Prophesy

Most scribes do not like to prophesy. As a matter of fact, this is one of the leading causes for writers' block. You see, the average scribe wants to share his or her own experiences, but when the scribe is given the charge to prophesy in his or her book, most authors refuse to do so because they fear being wrong, they fear the opinions of others and they fear backlash. Nevertheless, as scribes, this is a function we absolutely cannot ignore, after all, we release life through our words.

Ezekiel 37:1-10: The hand of the LORD was upon me, and carried me out in the spirit of the LORD, and set me down in the midst of the valley which was full of bones, And caused me to pass by them round about: and, behold, there were very many in the open valley; and, lo, they were very dry. And he said unto me, Son of man, can these bones live? And I answered, O Lord GOD, thou knowest. Again he said unto me, Prophesy upon these bones, and say unto them, O ye dry bones, hear the word of the LORD. Thus saith the Lord GOD unto these bones; Behold, I will cause breath to enter into you, and ye shall live: And I will lay sinews upon you, and will bring up flesh upon you, and cover you with skin, and put breath in you, and ye shall live; and ye shall know that I am the LORD. So I prophesied as I was commanded: and as I prophesied, there was a noise, and behold a shaking, and the bones came together, bone to his bone. And when I beheld, lo, the sinews and the flesh came up upon them, and the skin covered them above: but there was no breath in them. Then said he unto me, Prophesy unto the wind, prophesy, son of man, and say to the wind, Thus saith the Lord GOD; Come from the four winds, O breath, and breathe upon these slain, that they may live. So I prophesied as he commanded me, and the breath came into them, and they lived, and stood up upon their feet, an exceeding great army.

Also note that you don't have to be a prophet to prophesy. King Saul wasn't a prophet, nevertheless, there were two occasions where he'd come into the presence of prophets and began to prophesy.

1 Samuel 10:11: And it was so, that when he had turned his back to go from Samuel, God gave him another heart: and all those signs came to pass that day. And when they came thither to the hill, behold, a company of prophets met him; and the Spirit of God came upon him, and he prophesied among them. And it came to pass, when all that knew him beforetime saw that, behold, he prophesied among the prophets, then the people said one to another, What is this that is come unto the son of Kish? Is Saul also among the prophets?

1 Samuel 19:19-24: And it was told Saul, saying, Behold, David is at Naioth in Ramah. And Saul sent messengers to take David: and when they saw the company of the prophets prophesying, and Samuel standing as appointed over them, the Spirit of God was upon the messengers of Saul, and they also prophesied. And when it was told Saul, he sent other messengers, and they prophesied likewise. And Saul sent messengers again the third time, and they prophesied also. Then went he also to Ramah, and came to a great well that is in Sechu: and he asked and said, Where are Samuel and David? And one said, Behold, they be at Naioth in Ramah. And he went thither to Naioth in Ramah: and the Spirit of God was upon him also, and he went on, and prophesied, until he came to Naioth in Ramah. And he stripped off his clothes also, and prophesied before Samuel in like manner, and lay down naked all that day and all that night. Wherefore they say, Is Saul also among the prophets?

Edify and Exhort

Edifying and exhorting others are selfless acts that have to be provoked by both love and empathy. As a Publisher, I've seen many books that were written with well-intentions, but the scribes who wrote them forgot that they were supposed to be helping people. When this happened, the scribes focused more on entertaining and impressing their readers than they did on instructing them. In short, the scribes stopped leading and started rambling. A way to visualize this is to imagine Moses splitting the Red Sea, but instead of leading the people across it, he stops and grabs the rod of God with both of his hands. Suddenly, his frown is interrupted by a disturbingly wide grin as he begins to tap dance and use the rod he's carrying as a dancing stick. The people would be lost, afraid and in imminent danger. Moses had to not only strike the water and split the sea, he had to lead the people to the other side of the it, and then through the wilderness. His assignment wasn't just to lead them from Egypt; his assignment was to lead them to the promised land. Your assignment isn't just to lead people out of a mindset, but you also have to lead them to a new perspective. Always remember that readers need three things to flourish: instruction, wisdom and encouragement; without this trio, a book is nothing but a lifeless body of text.

1 Thessalonians 5:11: Wherefore comfort yourselves together, and edify one another, even as also ye do.

Romans 12:6-8: Having then gifts differing according to the grace that is given to us, whether prophecy, let us prophesy according to the proportion of faith; or ministry, let us wait on our ministering: or he that teacheth, on teaching; or he that exhorteth, on exhortation: he that giveth, let him do it with simplicity; he that ruleth, with diligence; he that sheweth mercy, with cheerfulness.

Witness and Confirm

We are witnesses that Jesus Christ is Lord and that He died for our sins, and was raised up from the dead on the third day. Even though we didn't witness this physically, we are witnesses in the spirit that these events took place. This witness is through faith. Additionally, we have witnessed the glory of God manifesting itself in our lives. We believe, in faith, that Jesus Christ is the Son of God. We not only witness and confirm these things, we help to shove the mountains of doubt out of the paths of God's people, and we hush the winds of doctrine at the top of the mountains.

In the biblical days, a law or decree could not be established unless it had been established by two or more people (see Deuteronomy 19:5 and 2 Corinthians 13:1). In short, a prophetic scribe has to believe the words that he or she is releasing.
Acts 1:8: But ye shall receive power, after that the Holy Ghost is come upon you: and ye shall be witnesses unto me both in Jerusalem, and in all Judaea, and in Samaria, and unto the uttermost part of the Earth.
Isaiah 43:10: Ye are my witnesses, saith the LORD, and my servant whom I have chosen: that ye may know and believe me, and understand that I am he: before me there was no God formed, neither shall there be after me.

Another way to look at the word "witness" is from a legal standpoint. A witness testifies against a criminal and helps to exonerate an innocent man or woman. Just like the biblical prophets, we are lawyers, but our courtroom isn't in the realm of the Earth. We weigh matters spiritually and take them before the Courtroom of Heaven.

Judge

When we think of a judge, we think (once again) of a courtroom. Additionally, many believers think that being a righteous judge means judging people when, in truth, God wants us to judge the matters of the heart. He wants us to judge the speck and not the person with the speck. You see, when we judge the speck in a person's eye, it will only be because we've first judged and cast it out of our own eyes. For example, if I judge fornication to be nasty and ungodly, I won't participate in it. If and when I come across a person engaging in it, I'll love the person, but judge the sin; this is the only way I can effectively minister to the person. If I judge the person as nasty and ungodly, the evidence of my heart will come out in my tone and mannerisms. This would either offend the person or cause the fornicator to feel judged, condemned, dirty and without hope. If I judge fornication, however, I can separate it from the person, point out its filth and redeem the soul for the Lord. I can then show the person that the fornication is an attack against his or her character, destiny, body, offspring and finances. Once I convince the fornicator to renounce the fornication, the person will then become an ex-fornicator, meaning he or she has broken up with the sin and is now exercising holiness.

Prophetic scribes also judge matters, for example, a woman finds herself struggling with whether or not she should take the father of her son to court. A prophetic scribe's job is to exegete the scriptures and help her to find the answer to the matter. This means that we don't give our opinions, but instead, we tell people what God has already said in regards to whatever it is that they're struggling with.

Author^{ity}

Again, the prophetic scribe must:
- Testify
- Prophesy
- Edify and Exhort
- Witness or Confirm
- Judge

This means that every scribe has a measure of authority. It also means that, like any office where rank is observed, not everyone has the same measure of authority. Because most authors are unaware of this, they unintentionally sabotage their books by trying to write outside of their metron (measure of rule/authority). Consequentially, many authors end up enduring everything from excessive warfare to bondage. To better understand this, let's take a look at how physical wars were fought.

1. War breaks out between two nations.
2. One nation advances, pushing the other nation back until the other nation

succumbs to the sword, retreats or surrenders.

3. Victorious nation goes into the defeated nation's campsite and/or region and begins to loot, taking every valuable thing for themselves.

4. Victorious nations (in some instances) will bind and imprison the survivors, especially those of notable rank. In other instances, they'll slaughter them.

This is what warfare looks like. When we're writing for the Kingdom of God, we are initiating war; this is why many readers endure warfare when they start writing. Our goal is to destroy the works of the enemy; we all know this, but most people don't realize that when they begin to write books designed to free God's people, they have to address what's binding the people. "But no one can enter a strong man's house and plunder his goods, unless he first binds the strong man. Then indeed he may plunder his house" (Mark 3:27/ ESV). When you're dealing with a strong man, you're dealing with a stronghold. Google defines a (physical) stronghold this way: "a place that has been fortified so as to protect it against attack." In the days of old, nations would build high walls around themselves to protect themselves from an attack. They would then post men around and on those walls to guard the city from an attack. Most nations had an elaborate set of tools to use against any nation that dared to engage them in warfare. Nevertheless, this did not stop other nations from attacking them. Let's say, for example, that a lot of Israelites had been taken into captivity in a war, but the rest of the Israelites had escaped and survived the attack. One day, the survivors decide that they want to rescue the ones who have been taken into captivity. So, the free men, devise a plan, put on their (whole) armor (of God), secure their armor with the belt (of truth), slip on their war shoes and fit their feet with the gospel of peace, and make their way towards the fortified city. This is a picture of evangelism. As they begin to come into the view of the military surrounding the city, a few of the soldiers start sounding off a makeshift alarm, and from there, they start firing darts. The surviving Israelites hold up their shield (of faith) and continue towards the fortified city. This means they are exercising their authority. Finally, the surviving men arrive at the wall and begin to use the sword (of the Spirit) to cut down the strongmen. As they advance, the warfare intensifies and before long, they've managed to defeat the men around the city and on the wall, but there are still skilled soldiers in the city. But now, they have to begin to tear down the wall. They tear it down enough to where they can enter in, and then, they proceed into the city and begin to fight with the soldiers from within. They're not interested in defeating every single soldier in the camp; instead, each man is looking for the king (strongman). Once he's caught, the other soldiers have no choice but to surrender. So, as they fight their way through the city, a few of the Israelite soldiers manage to defeat the men protecting the outside of the castle, and as they make their way in, they defeat the men from within. Finally, they find and bind the king; they take him into captivity and the warfare ceases. The Israelite army will then find the cells holding their brethren and begin to set them free. This is a picture of deliverance. Now, the city is taken, the soldiers are either dead or bound, and there is a calm. Nevertheless, the wall (pride) still has to be addressed, otherwise, some of the surviving noblemen will go and partner with and submit to another nation. That nation will be far stronger than the defeated nation and it will come in and establish itself behind that wall. This is what writing a book looks like, only the strongman is a spirit and the stronghold is a mindset. The mindset secures that demonic spirit's position, so to change the mind, the author must first get close to the bound person by gaining their trust. They have to get past all of the darts that come their way from within that person; these darts are pride, offensive words and every other form of resistance that the person can put up. Once they've gained the person's trust, they have to poke a hole in the person's reasoning; they have to get past the person's pride. Now, they don't have to pull the wall down in its entirety; the author, evangelist or deliverance minister just needs enough room to get into the city and the castle so they can address the strongman. The strongman is oftentimes rejection; a few others include: fear, anger, shame, addiction. Once the strongman is bound, the minister can minister to the bound soul and bring him or her out of bondage. After this, they have to teach the once bound soul to pull down the wall they've built. With this being noted, do you understand why you endured the warfare you endured when you tried to write your book the first time? Writing isn't just a physical act; it is declaring war against a mindset. You can't address the mindset without first addressing the stronghold. Google's second definition for stronghold is "a place where a particular cause or belief is strongly defended or upheld." You are addressing the beliefs of a person. Nowadays, people are bound in their minds and evangelists have to first get past their outer defenses before they can poke a big enough hole in the person's belief system (wall), thus, allowing an apostle, prophet, teacher or pastor to get in. Next, you have to get into the castle to bind the king (strongman). This is where the prophet and/or the teacher comes in. 1 Corinthians 14:24-25 reads, "But if all prophesy, and there come in one that believeth not, or one unlearned, he is convinced of all, he is judged of all: And thus are the secrets of his heart made manifest; and so falling down on his face he will worship God, and report that God is in you of a truth." The prophet's job is to open up a big enough space (moment) to get the apostle, pastor and teacher into the castle (heart). The teacher can also perform this function by repeatedly addressing the man's heart; this takes time, dedication, patience and love. In short, the prophet opens a small window or a moment, but the teacher (if given the time) opens a door. Next, the apostle's job is to address and bind the king (strongman), since the strongman is lodged in and supported by the belief system (apostles deal with systems and regional matters). Think about Elijah and Jehu. Elijah was a prophet, and once he was able to turn the hearts of the Israelites away from Baal and back towards God, he had exhausted his measure. But kings and queens were the equivalent of apostles (if they were good) or principalities and rulers (if they were evil). For this reason, Elijah panicked when Jezebel threatened to take his life. He went on the run and hid himself in a cave. To deal with Jezebel, God raised up the equivalent of an apostolic authority. He brought Elijah out of his cave, had him to anoint Elisha as a prophet, and give him his mantle. Elisha picked up where Elijah left off, and he went and anointed Jehu as king. The minute Jehu became king over northern Israel, he was endowed with apostolic authority; he could now address a queen. Keep in mind that Elijah, the prophet, had already turned the hearts of Israel back to God. This is what cleared the way for Jehu to confront the ruling spirit and principality. Jehu went to Jezebel's castle and had her cast down; in the deliverance ministry, this is the equivalent of casting out a demon.

Once the strongman is bound, the pastor leads the bound soul out of his or her prison. The teacher then deals with the wall; this way, the person doesn't end up bound again. The person is then fortified with a new belief system and a multitude of counselors. This is the effective execution of power and authority. With that being said, what capacity will you be operating in as an author? This is important to know and note. Also, please note that not everyone is personally gifted with an apostle or a prophet (see Ephesians 4:11), nevertheless, there is rank in the Kingdom of God. Demons recognize and respond to rank. For this reason, regional matters are still dealt with apostolically, meaning even though you may not be pastored by an apostle, there is likely an apostle fighting for your region. And even though you may never come in contact with an actual prophet, every believer who has the Holy Spirit should be able to prophesy.

Ephesians 4:11-16: And he gave some, apostles; and some, prophets; and some, evangelists; and some, pastors and teachers; For the perfecting of the saints, for the work of the ministry, for the edifying of the body of Christ: Till we all come in the unity of the faith, and of the knowledge of the Son of God, unto a perfect man, unto the measure of the stature of the fullness of Christ: That we henceforth be no more children, tossed to and fro, and carried about with every wind of doctrine, by the sleight of men, and cunning craftiness, whereby they lie in wait to deceive; But speaking the truth in love, may grow up into him in all things, which is the head, even Christ: From whom the whole body fitly joined together and compacted by that which every joint supplieth, according to the effectual working in the measure of every part, maketh increase of the body unto the edifying of itself in love.

Officer	Function	Authority
Evangelist	Advance against a mindset and get past the first wall.	Save a soul.
Prophet	Deal with matters of the heart; get into the castle where the strongman is.	Open up the soul.
Apostle	Deal with regional matters; bind the strongman.	Deal with legal issues regarding the soul.
Pastor	Tear down what's remaining of the old wall.	Teach and cover the soul.
Teacher	Build a new wall.	Fortify the soul.

When you know your capacity and authority as an author, it'll be a lot easier for you to write and finish your book. Not only that, but it'll be easier for you to write books that people actually want to read — books that change lives and set people free. This is because you'll be more strategic when you write, whereas, a large number of authors are random teachers, rambling on and on about every matter that pops up in their heads.

Every believer has a measure of authority, but it is important for us to personally know how far our metron (measure) extends; this way, we won't try to address, for example, regional matters when we're called to deal with the issues in our communities. The question you have to pose to yourself is: what measure of authority do I have and how will this be conveyed in my book?

Mark 3:13-15: And he goeth up into a mountain, and calleth *unto him* whom he would: and they came unto him. And he ordained twelve, that they should be with him, and that he might send them forth to preach, And to have power to heal sicknesses, and to cast out devils.

Mark 10:8: Heal the sick, cleanse the lepers, raise the dead, cast out devils: freely ye have received, freely give.

The Power of Fasting and Prayer

Matthew 17:19-21: Then came the disciples to Jesus apart, and said, why could not we cast him out? And Jesus said unto them, Because of your unbelief: for verily I say unto you, If you have faith as a grain of mustard seed, you shall say unto this mountain, Remove from here to yonder place; and it shall remove; and nothing shall be impossible unto you. But this kind goes not out but by prayer and fasting.

In the previous section, we discussed the function and authority of every five-fold gift. We came to understand that each officer has a measure of authority and jurisdictional rule, for example, the evangelist cannot do the job of the apostle and the prophet cannot do the job of the teacher. Every officer is a member of the body of Christ, and every member has a function. Think about our own natural bodies. Our eyes function differently from our bladders. Our bladders can't see and our eyes aren't connected to our kidneys. Nevertheless, every organ in our bodies work together in what we call a system. Google defines the word "system" this way:

1. a regularly interacting or interdependent group of items forming a unified whole.
2. a group of body organs that together perform one or more vital functions.
3. a group of related natural objects or forces
4. a group of devices or artificial objects or an organization forming a network especially for distributing something or serving a common purpose

In a system, all things work together for a common purpose. For example, the human body as a whole is a system, however, the body is comprised of a series of systems, all of which work together. They include the skeletal system, the respiratory system, the digestive system, the reproductive system, the nervous system and so on. All of these systems work independently, even though they are interdependent, meaning, they work in tandem with the body's system for our survival, comfort and to allow us to function in our purpose. The same is true for those of us in the body of Christ. Romans 8:28 says it this way, "And we know that all things work together for good to them that love God, to them who are the called according to his purpose." God designed us to work together towards a common goal. What is that goal? To destroy the works of the enemy.

Let's revisit the wall that surrounds a city where our brethren are bound. Inside of that city, there is a castle, and inside of that castle, there is a prison. Inside of that prison are the lost, the backslidden, and the double-minded. We learned how each five-fold minister helps us to get past that wall, get into the castle, free our brethren and destroy both the city and the wall altogether. Amazingly enough, if we are sensitive to the voice of God, we can start this process with the stroke of a pen. But, let's just say that you stay in a region where there are no apostles and/or prophets. What can you do if every church in your region is religious, for example, the church leaders are all adorned in long robes, wearing elaborate miters, and carrying long staffs, but not one of them has ever cast out a demon? The answer is simple: fast and pray. Fasting opens a window in time or a moment where, instead of charging through a wall to save a soul, you can strip yourself of your flesh and go straight through that wall and into the presence of the King of kings. Fasting allows you to go into the courts of Heaven and fight the case there. When we fast, we intentionally make ourselves weak. Remember what the Lord said in 2 Corinthians 12:9. He said, "For my strength is made perfect in weakness."

It is important for the scribe to fast. For example, the biblical scribe, Ezra, the scribe, proclaimed a fast after the Israelites had been freed from Babylon. The purpose of this particular fast was for protection. Ezra 8:21-23 reads, "Then I proclaimed a fast there, at the river of Ahava, that we might afflict ourselves before our God, to seek of him a right way for us, and for our little ones, and for all our substance. For I was ashamed to require of the king a band of soldiers and horsemen to help us against the enemy in the way: because we had spoken unto the king, saying, The hand of our God is upon all them for good that seek him; but his power and his wrath is against all them that forsake him. So we fasted and besought our God for this: and he was entreated of us." Here, Ezra is acknowledging two ways that he could deal with any enemy who rose up against the Jews: he could ask a pagan king for natural help or he could fast and petition the King of kings for supernatural help. Another example is Queen Esther. After having learned about Haman's plot to destroy the Jews, Esther proclaimed a three day fast for the Jews. Esther 4:15-16 reads, "Then Esther bade them return Mordecai this answer, Go, gather together all the Jews that are present in Shushan, and fast ye for me, and neither eat nor drink three days, night or day: I also and my maidens will fast likewise; and so will I go in unto the king, which is not according to the law: and if I perish, I perish." To get a better understanding, let's review the story.

Esther, the newly elected Queen of Persia, had survived a rough life.

- Her family, along with the king of Judah, Jeconiah, had been taken into captivity by King Nebuchadnezzar some decades earlier. They had been taken from Jerusalem to Babylon.
- Mordecai and Esther were amongst the Jews who had not returned to their homeland of Jerusalem as commanded by Isaiah and Jeremiah.
- She'd lost both parents at a young age and had to be raised by her older cousin, Mordecai.
- At the tender age of fourteen, she was taken to a pagan king's castle (King Xerxes' also known as King Ahasuerus) to pretty much audition for the role of being his wife.
- Before Esther could even adapt to her new role, a wicked man by the name of Haman was promoted into the role of the king's visor. Haman decided that he wanted to kill all of the Jews in Persia simply because Mordecai, Esther's uncle, had not given him obeisance.
- Going into the inner court to speak with the king could get her killed, but keeping quiet regarding the matter could cost all of the Jews in Persia their lives. She had to wrestle with fear and the understanding that one wrong move from her could provoke a Jewish genocide of epic proportions.

Now faced with this dilemma, Esther knew that she needed the help of YAHWEH. This is because the matter in itself was legal. Esther 3:8-15 reads, "And Haman said unto king Ahasuerus, There is a certain people scattered abroad and dispersed among the people in all the provinces of thy kingdom; and their laws are diverse from all people; neither keep they the king's laws: therefore it is not for the king's profit to suffer them. If it please the king, let it be written that they may be destroyed: and I will pay ten thousand talents of silver to the hands of those that have the charge of the business, to bring it into the king's treasuries. And the king took his ring from his hand, and gave it unto Haman the son of Hammedatha the Agagite, the Jews' enemy. And the king said unto Haman, The silver is given to thee, the people also, to do with them as it seemeth good to thee. Then were the king's scribes called on the thirteenth day of the first month, and there was written according to all that Haman had commanded unto the king's lieutenants, and to the governors that were over every province, and to the rulers of every people of every province according to the writing thereof, and to every people after their language; in the name of king Ahasuerus was it written, and sealed with the king's ring. And the letters were sent by posts into all the king's provinces, to destroy, to kill, and to cause to perish, all Jews, both young and old, little children and women, in one day, even upon the thirteenth day of the twelfth month, which is the month Adar, and to take the spoil of them for a prey. The copy of the writing for a commandment to be given in every province was published unto all people, that they should be ready against that day. The posts went out, being hastened by the king's commandment, and the decree was given in Shushan the palace. And the king and Haman sat down to drink; but the city Shushan was perplexed."

Again, the matter in itself was legal. King Xerxes had signed a decree legalizing the genocide of the Jews in Persia. The king was the highest ranking official and decrees could not be reversed. For example, a king could not make a decree and then change his mind. The moment a decree was released, it had to be carried out. In short, it meant that the matter could only be addressed in the courtroom of Heaven. Scared for her life and the life of her people, Esther proclaimed a three day fast. During this time, the Lord intervened, turning the king's heart all the more. When Esther went before the king, alongside Haman, she pointed out the evil visor's plot, highlighting the fact that she was a Jewish woman. This upset the king and he had Haman hanged on the very gallows he'd created for Mordecai. Nevertheless, the story doesn't end there because the evil decree was still in place to be carried out in the month of Adar (March by the Gregorian calendar). But to offset the decree, the king had to release a new decree. For this, he had to call in his scribes once again. Esther 8:7-14 details the turn of the tide in the Jews' favor; it reads, "Then the king Ahasuerus said unto Esther the queen and to Mordecai the Jew, Behold, I have given Esther the house of Haman, and him they have hanged upon the gallows, because he laid his hand upon the Jews. Write ye also for the Jews, as it liketh you, in the king's name, and seal it with the king's ring: for the writing which is written in the king's name, and sealed with the king's ring, may no man reverse. Then were the king's scribes called at that time in the third month, that is, the month Sivan, on the three and twentieth day thereof; and it was written according to all that Mordecai commanded unto the Jews, and to the lieutenants, and the deputies and rulers of the provinces which are from India unto Ethiopia, an hundred twenty and seven provinces, unto every province according to the writing thereof, and unto every people after their language, and to the Jews according to their writing, and according to their language. And he wrote in the king Ahasuerus' name, and sealed it with the king's ring, and sent letters by posts on horseback, and riders on mules, camels, and young dromedaries: Wherein the king granted the Jews which were in every city to gather themselves together, and to stand for their life, to destroy, to slay, and to cause to perish, all the power of the people and province that would assault them, both little ones and women, and to take the spoil of them for a prey, Upon one day in all the provinces of king Ahasuerus, namely, upon the thirteenth day of the twelfth month, which is the month Adar. The copy of the writing for a commandment to be given in every province was published unto all people, and that the Jews should be ready against that day to avenge themselves on their enemies. So the posts that rode upon mules and camels went out, being hastened and pressed on by the king's commandment. And the decree was given at Shushan the palace."

Keep in mind that there were no apostles in that day. Esther wasn't just fighting Haman; she was fighting a principality that was over that region, but to do this, she had to enlist the help of the Lord. During the fast, Esther was granted apostolic authority. In the beginning, she couldn't just barge into the inner courts; she would have had to be summoned, otherwise, she could be killed. This was equivalent of the Tabernacle of Moses where only the high priest could go into the Inner Courts. Nevertheless, once Jesus was crucified, the veil was torn and now, we can all go before the King of kings and the Lord of lords at will. We don't need a high priest since Jesus is our High Priest. The fast opened a window for Esther to go before her husband; this small window of time allowed her to step outside of the traditional protocol and petition with her husband. During this window of time, Esther went into the inner courts and obtained favor from the king. He extended his golden scepter to her, which allowed her to approach him. Before Esther could open her mouth, the king said, "What wilt thou, queen Esther? And what is thy request? It shall be even given thee to the half of the kingdom." In this, the king offered Esther a measure of authority or jurisdictional rule. How you handle the authority given to you will determine how far you'll go as a writer and teacher. Esther could have easily said, "Haman is trying to kill my people. Grant me the right to kill him and everyone who hates the Jews and I'll be satisfied." Nevertheless, Esther was engaging a principality in warfare, and warfare has to be strategic if it is to be effective. She pretty much asked her husband on a date with Haman as a third wheel. Once on that date, Esther still didn't tell her husband what she wanted. Instead, when the king once again offered to give her anything she wanted, up to half of his kingdom, she simply asked for another date with him and Haman. The king obliged and it was on the second date that Esther told her husband about Haman's plot. Esther 7:1-6 reads, "So the king and Haman came to banquet with Esther the queen. And the king said again unto Esther on the second day at the banquet of wine, What is thy petition, queen Esther? And it shall be granted thee: and what is thy request? And it shall be performed, even to the half of the kingdom. Then Esther the queen answered and said, If I have found favor in thy sight, O king, and if it please the king, let my life be given me at my petition, and my people at my request: For we are sold, I and my people, to be destroyed, to be slain, and to perish. But if we had been sold for bondmen and bondwomen, I had held my tongue, although the enemy could not countervail the king's damage. Then the king Ahasuerus answered and said unto Esther the queen, Who is he, and where is he, that durst presume in his heart to do so? And Esther said, The adversary and enemy is this wicked Haman. Then Haman was afraid before the king and the queen." Of course, we know the rest of the story. Haman was hanged, the king released a new petition, giving the Jews the legal right to defend themselves against their enemies and the Jews were saved.

Here are a few points regarding fasting:

Fasting is voluntarily afflicting yourself; it is intentionally weakening yourself so you can tap into God's strength.

Fasting allows us to access windows of time where we are granted a measure of jurisdictional rule that we ordinarily don't walk in. For example, demons come in ranks, and for this reason, we must know our own rank in the spirit before we go charging up against a demonic spirit. This is evidenced in Matthew 17:14-21, which reads, "And when they were come to the multitude, there came to him a certain man, kneeling down to him, and saying, Lord, have mercy on my son: for he is lunatic, and sore vexed: for ofttimes he falleth into the fire, and oft into the water. And I brought him to thy disciples, and they could not cure him. Then Jesus answered and said, O faithless and perverse generation, how long shall I be with you? How long shall I suffer you? Bring him hither to me. And Jesus rebuked the devil; and he departed out of him: and the child was cured from that very hour. Then came the disciples to Jesus apart, and said, Why could not we cast him out?And Jesus said unto them, Because of your unbelief: for verily I say unto you, If ye have faith as a grain of mustard seed, ye shall say unto this mountain, Remove hence to yonder place; and it shall remove; and nothing shall be impossible unto you. Howbeit this kind goeth not out but by prayer and fasting." In this, the disciples of Jesus wanted to better understand why they hadn't been able to cast the demon out of the young boy. Jesus gave them two reasons: for one, they didn't have a certain measure of faith. Notice here that Jesus spoke of the size of the mustard seed; He said "a grain." He then contrast that grain with a mountain, stating that if the disciples only had faith as a grain of mustard seed, they could speak to the mountain (giant, principality) and tell it to be to be removed (get out) to yonder place (tell it where to go), the mountain (giant, principality) would have to obey. The second reason was, "This kind," referencing the demon, only went out by fasting and prayer. This means that the demon was of great rank. The disciples were in training; they were not yet apostles, and even then, apostles still have to fast to come against certain princes or principalities. Let's look at the chart once again to see how Esther walked in every one of these roles.

Officer	Function	Authority	Esther
Evangelist	Advance against a mindset and get past the first wall.	Save a soul.	"Likewise, ye wives, be in subjection to your own husbands; that, if any obey not the word, they also may without the word be won by the conversation of the wives." 1 Peter 3:1 "For the unbelieving husband is sanctified by the wife, and the unbelieving wife is sanctified by the husband: else were your children unclean; but now are they holy." 1 Corinthians 7:14

Prophet	Deal with matters of the heart; get into the castle where the strongman is.	Open up the soul.	"Now it came to pass on the third day, that Esther put on her royal apparel, and stood in the inner court of the king's house, over against the king's house: and the king sat upon his royal throne in the royal house, over against the gate of the house. And it was so, when the king saw Esther the queen standing in the court, that she obtained favour in his sight: and the king held out to Esther the golden sceptre that was in his hand. So Esther drew near, and touched the top of the sceptre." Esther 5:1-2
Apostle	Deal with regional matters; bind the strongman.	Deal with legal issues regarding the soul.	"Then Esther the queen, the daughter of Abihail, and Mordecai the Jew, wrote with all authority, to confirm this second letter of Purim. And he sent the letters unto all the Jews, to the hundred twenty and seven provinces of the kingdom of Ahasuerus, *with* words of peace and truth, To confirm these days of Purim in their times *appointed*, according as Mordecai the Jew and Esther the queen had enjoined them, and as they had decreed for themselves and for their seed, the matters of the fastings and their cry. And the decree of Esther confirmed these matters of Purim; and it was written in the book." Esther 9:29-32
Pastor	Tear down what's	Teach and cover the	"And Esther spake yet again before the king, and fell down at his feet, and

| | remaining of the old wall. | soul. | besought him with tears to put away the mischief of Haman the Agagite, and his device that he had devised against the Jews. Then the king held out the golden sceptre toward Esther. So Esther arose, and stood before the king, And said, If it please the king, and if I have found favour in his sight, and the thing seem right before the king, and I be pleasing in his eyes, let it be written to reverse the letters devised by Haman the son of Hammedatha the Agagite, which he wrote to destroy the Jews which are in all the king's provinces: For how can I endure to see the evil that shall come unto my people? or how can I endure to see the destruction of my kindred? Then the king Ahasuerus said unto Esther the queen and to Mordecai the Jew, Behold, I have given Esther the house of Haman, and him they have hanged upon the gallows, because he laid his hand upon the Jews. Write ye also for the Jews, as it liketh you, in the king's name, and seal it with the king's ring: for the writing which is written in the king's name, and sealed with the king's ring, may no man reverse." Esther 8:3-8 |
| Teacher | Build a new wall. | Fortify the soul. | "On that day did the king Ahasuerus give the house of Haman the Jews' enemy unto Esther the queen. And Mordecai came before the king; for Esther had told what |

			he was unto her. And the king took off his ring, which he had taken from Haman, and gave it unto Mordecai. _And Esther set Mordecai over the house of Haman._" Esther 8:1-2

As a reminder, every officer has an office, and every office has an administration and a measure of jurisdiction. Every officer runs the race until he or she reaches the end of his or her metron, and from there, the officer passes the baton to the next officer. That officer runs to the end of his or her own season and metron, and then, passes the baton to the next officer. Of course, the race isn't for the swift; it's for those who will endure until the end. In fasting, we are granted the ability to temporarily execute the roles and walk in the authority of whatever office we need to walk in to complete our assignment. What is our assignment? To destroy the works of the devil. This means we can't fast for our will to be done; we fast for God's will to be done. It was not the will of God that the Jews perished at the hands of Haman, so He raised up Esther.

Scientists have found some physical benefits to fasting as well; they include:
- Fasting controls blood sugar by reducing insulin resistance.
- Fasting enhances the health of our heart.
- Fasting boots our metabolism.
- Fasting promotes healthy weight loss.
- Fasting lowers blood pressure.
- Fasting has been proven to slow down the effects of aging.
- Fasting has been proven to prevent cancer.
- Fasting boosts the function of the brain and prevents neurodegenerative disorders.
- Fasting helps to fight inflammation in the body.
- Fasting supports the production of healthy collagen in the skin.

Of course, this is just a short list of the benefits of fasting.

As an author, it is important for you to fast when you write. Of course, you don't have to do this every time you write, but if your book is designed to help set God's people free, it is better if you fast. If you don't, you haven't sinned (of course), but fasting will help you to circumvent what could have been a long, tedious and otherwise draining process.

Again, as a scribe, you have a measure of authority. When authors go beyond their jurisdictional limitations, they end up enduring warfare that many of them are not equipped to handle. With that being said, it is important for you to know who you are in Christ. If you're called to any of the five-fold offices, it is important for you to know which office you're called to. If you're not a five-fold officer, it is important for you to be sensitive to the voice of God; this way, you won't try to enter someone else's metron and start teaching. God uses systems because He is a God of order. God established rank because He is a God of order. Everything that God does is done for a reason, and it works in tandem with something else to accomplish its purpose.

The Authority of Words

Word	Definition	Credit
Micro	small, very small, or on a small scale	Collins Dictionary
Scribe	a: an official or public secretary or clerk b: a copier of manuscripts writer; specifically journalist	Merriam Webster
Ology	A subject of study; a branch of knowledge.	Oxford Dictionary

"Sit. No. Give me paw. Down. Up. Get out the street. Come here." These are just a few of the commands I've successfully taught my dog. And he's not the only dog I've managed to train. Before Milo, I had two Siberian Huskies—one named Xavier and the other named Rogue (obviously named after X-Men characters, but that was not my doing). Xavier was two years old when I got Rogue and I'd already trained him to sit, lie down, speak (howl), dance, etc. How did I, a woman who is not a dog trainer, manage to train three rather large dogs? It's simple. I read a book and I exercised the dominion (authority) that God gave mankind in Genesis 1:26. If I can be honest, most of what I'd learned had not come from the book I'd read; instead, it had come from my experiences with animals, especially dogs. You see, I have always been an animal lover to the core, and it is my love for animals that legalizes my authority with them. Authority without love is abuse. When I coupled knowledge with that love, I learned to communicate with another species. We see this all the time. Some people have learned to communicate with dolphins, gorillas and many other animals by simply combining love, authority, words and sounds. Words are individual alphabets that come together to form a sound. When we properly release that sound consistently, we learn to communicate with people (and creatures) who are familiar with that sound or we can help them to grow familiar with that sound. We release words as individual sounds, but the hearer takes the words in and it forms a picture in his or her mind. For example, if you tell your child to pick his shoe up off the floor, he won't study each individual syllable and sound that comes out of your mouth. Instead, because he's familiar with your voice and he's heard that command before, his eyes will search the room until he sees the shoe you're speaking of. He will then pick the shoe up so that his action matches the picture that has formed in his mind. When you released the command, you had a picture of a clean room. You had to then ruminate that picture (break it down) and spit it out as individual words. When he took the command in, he had to swallow the words and let them form a picture in his mind. This is how the world of words work.

"Woe unto you, scribes and Pharisees, hypocrites! For ye devour widows' houses, and for a pretense make long prayer: therefore ye shall receive the greater damnation" (Matthew 23:14). In this scripture, we see the Lord addressing two prominent figures of that day: scribes and Pharisees. In this study, we will focus on the scribes.

The Greek word for scribe is "grammateus" and it means:
1. a clerk, scribe, esp. a public servant, secretary, recorder, whose office and influence differed in different states.

2. in the Bible, a man learned in the Mosaic law and in the sacred writings, an interpreter, teacher. Scribes examined the more difficult and subtle questions of the law; added to the Mosaic law decisions of various kinds of thought to elucidate its meaning and scope, and did this to the detriment of religion. Since the advice of men skilled in the law was needed in the examination in the causes and the solution of the difficult questions, they were enrolled in the Sanhedrin; and are mentioned in connection with the priests and elders of the people. See a Bible Dictionary for more information on the scribes.

3. a religious teacher: so instructed that from his learning and ability to teach advantage may redound to the Kingdom of Heaven.

(Reference: Bible Study Tools/ Lexicons/ Greek/ Grammateus)

The word "grammateus" is where we get the word "grammar". Grammar is defined by Britannica Dictionary this way: "rules of a language governing the sounds, words, sentences, and other elements, as well as their combination and interpretation." So, basically, a scribe was a word-master by profession. Scribes studied the Law and transcribed it. They were educated men who were passionate about ensuring that their fellow brethren upheld every letter of the Law. Nevertheless, they grafted many man-made traditions into the Law, and many of them made the mistake of ignoring the spirit behind the Law. Matthew 23:23 reads, "Woe unto you, scribes and Pharisees, hypocrites! For ye pay tithe of mint and anise and cummin, and have omitted the weightier matters of the law, judgment, mercy, and faith: these ought ye to have done, and not to leave the other undone." What is the spirit behind the Law? The answer is obvious: love. Again, authority without love is abuse, and when it is exercised by humans against humans, it also becomes witchcraft.

If you walk down the book aisle at any given retail store, you can easily see (in that moment) that you are surrounded by words. Each book is a compilation of published thoughts designed to teach or demonstrate a point. Honestly, every book on the market is nothing but a summon of sorts, whereas it urges its readers to take a side on any given subject. Readers start off as students, but if they read enough books, they'll eventually become teachers of whatever it is that they've been studying. A book about mysticism, which we know to be witchcraft, details the beliefs of the people involved in it, along with what the author claims to be the benefits of mysticism. A woman with a broken heart may read such a book in her attempt to circumvent the healing process. When she starts reading the book, she's nothing but a student of mysticism. The author has invited the reader into his or her world, and the student will eat the words in that world. As the student begins to ingest and digest what she's read, she will eventually share that information with a heartbroken co-worker who may be going through a contentious divorce. In short, the student has become the teacher. Therefore, a book is nothing but a gathering of minds, with the author being the authority behind the book. Additionally, you don't have to go down the book aisle to see the effects of words. Everywhere you go and almost everything you see started off as a word. For example, if you go into the shoe section of any given store, every shoe in that section started off as a thought. Oftentimes, it started as an image in the mind of a person. It had not yet been born into the realm of the Earth, so the people who imagined those shoes had to act as scribes. They had to inscribe (draw), transcribe (transfer thoughts into written format) and describe (break down each thought into details) what they'd imagined. This is the process of the scribe. Nevertheless, every scribe is driven by something. One man's design is motivated by his love for money, another man's design is motivated by his love for the creative process, one woman's design is motivated by her rejection and another woman's design is motivated by her love for people. Each of these scribes have exercised a measure of authority, and as a result, they were able to pull ideas from the realm of thought and cause those ideas to manifest as tangible items. Through a series of legal and creative processes, they were able to take what was not seen and cause it to come to pass. This is exactly how faith works. As a matter of fact, stop and look around you. You won't find a single thing that did not start off as a word unless, that is, you're looking at a painting or something drawn.

You are a word spoken. Sure, God formed man from the dust of the ground, breathed life into him and man became a living soul, but when God spoke to Adam, he gained his identity (legal ability to respond). Another interesting truth is, every man is a world held together or broken apart by words, for example, when you were born, your parents attached a word to you; this word is called a name. Your name would be the way others identified you; it is the very word that legalized you as a citizen of the country you lived in. Having that name legalized your ability to be called and your right to respond.

It was the words spoken that convinced one woman that she was beautiful enough to run for Miss America. All the same, it was the words spoken to another woman that drove her into an asylum where she is bound by a straitjacket. Interestingly enough, the straitjacket itself started off as a thought that became a word, and then, found itself in the realm of the Earth being used to bind folks who were hearing voices. The point is, almost everything we see, hear, smell, touch and taste is a manifestation of words. Of course, we know that Jesus is the Living Word of God, the Bible is a book filled with words, all of which come together to help us better understand who God is and what He expects of us. The King James Bible has a total of 783,137 words in it, all of which can be summed up into one Word: Jesus.

Jesus is the Word of God transcribed. God described His Word in the Bible, but He transcribed His Word in the flesh. The prefix "trans" means to cross. In the Kingdom, it means to cross one realm to another. The word "scribe," of course, means a copyist or writer. In the Kingdom, it means a prophetic writer, so when Jesus became flesh, He crossed over to our realm; what God spoke simply materialized in human form.

Hebrews 4:12 (ESV): For the word of God is living and active, sharper than any two-edged sword, piercing to the division of soul and of spirit, of joints and of marrow, and discerning the thoughts and intentions of the heart.

John 1:1 (ESV): In the beginning, the Word was with God and the Word was God.

John 1:14 (ESV): The Word became flesh and dwelt among us and we have seen His glory.

Colossians 1:13: Who hath delivered us from the power of darkness, and hath *translated* us into the kingdom of his dear Son.

How did God translate us into the Kingdom of His dear Son? First, let's look at the word "translate." Google defines "translate" this way:

1. move from one place or condition to another.

God translated us, meaning, He transferred us from one state of being to another using His Word.

Isaiah 55:11: So shall my word be that goeth forth out of my mouth: it shall not return unto me void, but it shall accomplish that which I please, and it shall prosper in the thing whereto I sent it.

Why would God translate or, better yet, save people who've repeatedly rebelled against Him—people He has referred to as stiff-necked, rebellious and stubborn? It's simple. He loves us. God is the very essence of love; it is not just what He does, it's who He is (see 1 John 4:8). This means that every word God speaks or has spoken is released in love because it has been released by Love. He is the Author and Finisher of our faith, and one of the lessons you will learn in this book is—we can only release what we are. What this means is that God's authority is provoked by His very own identity: Love. Additionally, what this tells us is that any person who has authority but no love is, quite frankly, a murderer and a witch. Power has to be provoked by love if it is to be legal; any power or authority that is illegal is called witchcraft. Witchcraft is nothing but perverted power or mismanaged authority. Witchcraft doesn't abort the laws of the Kingdom; it simply offends and breaks them. Witchcraft, just like godly authority, is nothing but the release of words; it is nothing but criminal activity in the realm of the spirit.

1 John 3:15 (ESV): Everyone who hates his brother is a murderer, and you know that no murderer has eternal life abiding in him.

Proverbs 29:2 (ESV): When the righteous increase, the people rejoice, but when the wicked rule, the people groan.

An author is a person who not only publishes words; an author changes minds, laws and lives with the words he or she speaks. The word "authority" comes from the word "author," meaning an author is a person who exercises his or her authority, be it God-given, self-appointed or demonically driven. Authors (or scribes) do this by releasing words as facts. These words enter in through the eye gates of man and ultimately find their way into each reader's heart, thus provoking the reader to think, reason and behave like the author. A godly author is driven by love; this is what legalizes the scribe's authority, but a self-appointed author is driven by selfish ambition. All the same, a demonically driven author is motivated by hate, rejection, hurt or desire. The scribes that Jesus rebuked were not inspired by love; instead, they loved the praise of man. They loved being seen as intellectually superior to their fellow Jews. They loved the black and white letters on the pages of the Torah so much that they crucified the transcribed or, better yet, Living Word of God when He manifested in the realm of the Earth.

This world is divided into zones. First, there is the equator, which is an invisible line that divides the Northern hemisphere from the Southern hemisphere. Next, there is the Prime Meridian, which divides the globe into Eastern and Western hemispheres. Each hemisphere is divided up into continents, and every continent is broken into blocks that we call countries. Each country has borders that divide it from its neighboring countries. Sometimes, these borders are marked by signs; other times, they are marked by specific landmarks or mountains. In each country, there are regions that are marked by what we call boundaries. In the United States, each state is separated by a state line and divided up into cities, all of which have city limits. Every boundary, border, or frontier has its own laws, cultures, religious beliefs and so on. American cities are divided up into three zones: industrial, commercial and residential. The residential zones are divided up into neighborhoods, and every neighborhood is separated by socioeconomic class, culture and sometimes race. In every neighborhood, there are homes and every person who owns or lives in each of those homes has rights to a certain measure of land. In every neighborhood, there are invisible, common sense rules that the residents expect one another to abide by, but these rules vary by socioeconomic class. Neighborhoods with the highest crime rates are the ones where a large number of the residents have no respect for or understanding of rules or boundaries. For example, in poverty or below poverty-stricken areas, it is not uncommon for the residents to blast their music. Albeit unwelcome, the lyrics and the bass from the radio invade the homes of other residents. Nevertheless, in middle class to wealthier areas, the residents tend to be more considerate of one another. This honor undoubtedly has provoked the heavens to open over certain neighborhoods, just as dishonor has closed the heavens over other neighborhoods. Please understand that God loves honor and He detests dishonor.

Romans 13:1-7 (ESV): Let every person be subject to the governing authorities. For there is no authority except from God, and those that exist have been instituted by God. Therefore whoever resists the authorities resists what God has appointed, and those who resist will incur judgment. For rulers are not a terror to good conduct, but to bad. Would you have no fear of the one who is in authority? Then do what is good, and you will receive his approval, for he is God's servant for your good. But if you do wrong, be afraid, for he does not bear the sword in vain. For he is the servant of God, an avenger who carries out God's wrath on the wrongdoer. Therefore one must be in subjection, not only to avoid God's wrath but also for the sake of conscience...

1 Peter 2:17-19 (ESV): Honor everyone. Love the brotherhood. Fear God. Honor the emperor. Servants, be subject to your masters with all respect, not only to the good and gentle but also to the unjust. For this is a gracious thing, when, mindful of God, one endures sorrows while suffering unjustly.

Every land, region and neighborhood is guarded by a wall of words; when the people agree, those words are established either as laws, whether those laws become the laws of the land or the invisible, unspoken laws of honor. When a wall is repeatedly dishonored, famine, disease and crime enter into a region and begin to take over. Again, this is the difference between what is referenced as a good neighborhood versus a bad one. The same is true for countries. In many third-world countries, there are laws, but those laws are oftentimes broken by the people in high governing positions. In other words, the governments are corrupt. Additionally, every country has a prominent religion, and every religion is divided up into sectors and separated by what we call "belief systems." There are 4,200 religions in the world, with one of those religions being Christianity. There are more than 33,000 denominations in Christianity, all of which are separated by belief systems. Every line of demarcation mentioned was established by words and is enforced by words. When one religion infringes upon the beliefs of another religion, offense, conflict and rumors of war break out. This means that it is absolutely okay, as a Christian, for me to preach against homosexuality, fornication, abortion and everything the Holy Bible teaches against. Nevertheless, I don't have the right to walk into a mosque and insist that everyone there listen to my views. All the same, a gay man or promiscuous woman has no right to stop me from preaching the whole gospel of Jesus Christ. The only rule in this is, I have to respect their views and they have to respect mine. Where there is no respect, state, federal and moral laws are broken.

If I break a law in my state, I could find myself being arrested. While the officer is binding me, he'd release words at me; he'd read me my Miranda Rights. He'd toss me into a jail and I'd have to go before a judge or jury who would then determine what the next season or next few seasons of my life would look like. The judge would release words, all of which, would be recorded by the Court Clerk and published in the court's records. The officers of the law would then enforce those words and do whatever it is that the judge has commanded them to do with me. Nevertheless, I have rights that have been granted by the U.S. Constitution, therefore, the judge's power cannot trespass against my rights. If I was judged to be guilty and thrown into jail, I would still have rights; these are the invisible boundaries established by words and enforced by laws. If my rights are violated, I could sue whomever it is that violated them. The point I want to make is, as an author, you have to respect boundaries. You cannot barge into any topic just because you've had a powerful conversation or two with a friend of yours regarding that topic. For example, you should NEVER touch the pulpit with your words if you've spent your life in the pews. It doesn't matter who you see standing on the pulpit and what that person is guilty of, it is our job, as Christians, to pray. Why is this? Because anytime a man or woman crosses a boundary without permission, that person will always end up bound. Consider these stories:

"A 58-year-old Louisiana man was arrested while trying to cross the border

from South Korea into North Korea, according to the Korean Ministry of Defense in South Korea. The man was apprehended by South Korean police after crossing the Civilian Control Line just outside of the Demilitarized Zone between North and South Korea. The Civilian Control Line, south of the DMZ, was drawn in 1954 to protect military operations in the DMZ.

According to the South Korean Yonhap News Agency, a villager in the region discovered the man and reported him to the military in the region.

The man, whose identity has not been released while an investigation is underway, reportedly arrived in South Korea three days ago and told investigators he attempted to enter North Korea for "political purposes."
(Reference: ABC News/ American man arrested attempting to cross into North Korea/ Sarah Kolinovsky)

"On March 31st, Andrew Tahmooressi, a decorated United States Marine who served two tours in Afghanistan, made the mistake of taking one bad turn – and the chain reaction to that turn has set off an international furor.

According to Tahmooressi's mother, Jill, earlier that day her son crossed into Tijuana, Mexico, on foot, leaving his car parked on the California side of the border. After dinner with friends, he walked back to the U.S. at about 10:30 p.m. He got into his car and entered the ramp he believed would take him onto the I-5 freeway leading north back to San Diego.

What happened next has become a sore point in diplomatic relations. After crossing the San Ysidro checkpoint into Mexico, Tahmooressi was stopped by law enforcement officials there and charged with possession of three firearms: a 12-gauge shotgun, a .45 caliber pistol, an AR-15 and 400 pieces of ammunition. All were legally registered in the U.S."
(Reference: Fox News/ Border Crossing Where Marine Entered Mexico By Mistake Difficult To Navigate/Rebekah Sager)

In the aforementioned stories, we see examples of two men illegally crossing borders into another country. One man did it intentionally; the other man wasn't aware of the fact that he'd crossed a border. Nevertheless, the consequence was the same. As writers, we don't have the luxury of making excuses because our books will outlive us. Read that again. <u>Your book will outlive you</u>, meaning it will either bless or poison another generation.

As you can see, we were created by the Word and our worlds (collectively and individually) are nothing but words. Our worlds are nothing but the words we've spoken over ourselves, the words we've spoken over others and the words we've allowed others to speak over us. Laws are nothing but words that have been established by people who've been given the authority to establish and enforce them. Kingdom laws are established by God. When the laws of the Kingdom are exercised and honored in the realm of the Earth, we experience miracles, signs and wonders. When Kingdom laws are broken, we experience droughts, famines, wars, outbreaks and so on, either individually or corporately. Matthew 18:18 (ESV) reads, "Truly, I say to you, whatever you bind on Earth shall be bound in Heaven, and whatever you loose on Earth shall be loosed in Heaven." The New Living Translation says it this way, "I tell you the truth, whatever you forbid on Earth will be forbidden in Heaven, and whatever you permit on Earth will be permitted in Heaven." This is why the enemy (Satan) works diligently to get certain laws passed (gay marriage, abortion, tolerance of witches). Now, the NLT version isn't exactly correct when it says "permitted" because no one in Heaven is married, having sex or playing with tarot cards; what this simply means is, the officers of Heaven (angels) will not arrest (bind) what we have given permission to exist in our lives! This answers the age-old question, "Why does God allow so much bad in the Earth?" He allows us to determine the laws of our own individual worlds! "Can two walk together, except they be agreed?" (Amos 3:3). This is a principle of deliverance. If a person is demonically bound, the deliverance minister knows to look for and attempt to nullify the agreement between the bound soul and the devil binding the person.

We speak it and it is so! The point is, words have immeasurable power and ability. We often take them for granted, not realizing that all too often what we call depression is nothing but a wall of words that we have released over ourselves or have allowed someone else to release into our lives. In short, we have drawn a line of demarcation and prohibited our joy from crossing that line until some event has been fulfilled or disallowed in our lives. Nevertheless, we are the ones who have the power to say what goes and what is not permitted in our lives! As authors, our assignment is to exercise our God-given authority and not our perceived authority.

Ambition and entitlement will always cause authors, inventors, teachers and the like to violate the laws of the spirit realm, thus, causing them to be mentally arrested (bound). A bound mind is tossed into a prison that we refer to as a stronghold. This is why it takes some authors five years to write a single, one-hundred-page book! It's not that they can't write; the problem is, they are not familiar with Kingdom principles or they do not respect them. For this reason, they keep venturing outside of their metrons with their pens. The minute you cross a boundary illegally, whether it be in the natural or the supernatural realm, you will find yourself bound. Understand that the word bound is found in the word boundary; it simply means you've gone too far!

Every jurisdictional boundary, be it natural or dimensional, is secured by an invisible wall of words, and these boundaries can oftentimes be sensed, even by writers as they write. Every boundary established or permitted by Heaven is guarded by angels, and these angels are often referred to as doorkeepers. Doorkeepers, also known as gatekeepers, protect what's on the inside of any given dimension. For example, the Bible speaks of the doorkeepers that guard the Garden of Eden. It reads, "He drove out the man, and at the east of the garden of Eden he placed the *cherubim* and a *flaming sword* that turned every way to guard the way to the tree of life" (Genesis 3:24). When we write fictional, cultural or any books that deal with things above the surface of the Earth, we are writing horizontally; these books are easy to write. Nevertheless, when we start writing self-help books or any books that deal with the paradigm (mind) of a man, we are writing dimensionally. When we do this, we have to obey the laws of the spirit realm, for example, you should never write about anything you have not overcome. You can't teach a man to free himself if you are bound. This is why Matthew 7:1-2 says, "Judge not, that ye be not judged. For with what judgment ye judge, ye shall be judged: and with what measure ye mete, it shall be measured to you again." These verses are not telling us that we can't judge matters righteously. This scripture is dealing with hypocrisy. This is why these verses are followed up with Matthew 7:3-5, which reads, "And why beholdest thou the mote that is in thy brother's eye, but considerest not the beam that is in thine own eye? Or how wilt thou say to thy brother, Let me pull out the mote out of thine eye; and, behold, a beam is in thine own eye? Thou hypocrite, *first* cast out the beam out of thine own eye; *and then* shalt thou see clearly to cast out the mote out of thy brother's eye."

Psalm 84:10 (ESV): For a day in your courts is better than a thousand elsewhere. I would rather be a <u>doorkeeper</u> in the house of my God than dwell in the tents of wickedness.

John 10:1-3 (ESV): Truly, truly, I say to you, he who does not enter the sheepfold by the door but climbs in by another way, that man is a thief and a robber. But he who enters by the door is the shepherd of the sheep. To him the <u>gatekeeper</u> opens.

The Doorkeepers of Wisdom

2 Kings 12:9 (ESV): Then Jehoiada the priest took a chest and bored a hole in the lid of it and set it beside the altar on the right side as one entered the house of the LORD. <u>And the priests who guarded the threshold put in it all the money that was brought into the house of the LORD.</u>

Every valuable thing has to be guarded. For example, we know that there is a flaming sword that guards the way to the Tree of Life. The same is true for wisdom. The Bible says that wisdom is "too high" for a fool (see Proverbs 24:7), meaning, it is out of a fool's reach; it is in the treasury of the Lord, set aside for the sons and daughters of God. In short, a foolish or unsaved man cannot freely access the heart of God; this is outside of his metron because he does not value the things of God. He has no inheritance with God, therefore, he can't just walk past the doorkeepers of revelation and take whatsoever he wants. All the same, the children of God must also respect these gatekeepers; we can't just barge into matters that don't concern us and start giving our opinions. Again, every good and valuable thing is protected. This is a lesson that King Uzziah learned the hard way.

Proverbs 8:11: For wisdom is better than rubies; and all the things that may be desired are not to be compared to it.

Proverbs 16:16 (ESV): How much better to get wisdom than gold! To get understanding is to be chosen rather than silver.

2 Chronicles 26:16-23: But when he was strong, his heart was lifted up to his destruction: for he transgressed against the LORD his God, and went into the temple of the LORD to burn incense upon the altar of incense. And Azariah the priest went in after him, and with him fourscore priests of the LORD, that were valiant men: And they withstood Uzziah the king, and said unto him, It appertaineth not unto thee, Uzziah, to burn incense unto the LORD, but to the priests the sons of Aaron, that are consecrated to burn incense: go out of the sanctuary; for thou hast trespassed; neither shall it be for thine honor from the LORD God. Then Uzziah was wroth, and had a censer in his hand to burn incense: and while he was wroth with the priests, the leprosy even rose up in his forehead before the priests in the house of the LORD, from beside the incense altar. And Azariah the chief priest, and all the priests, looked upon him, and, behold, he was leprous in his forehead, and they thrust him out from thence; yea, himself hasted also to go out, because the LORD had smitten him. And Uzziah the king was a leper unto the day of his death, and dwelt in a several house, being a leper; for he was cut off from the house of the LORD: and Jotham his son was over the king's house, judging the people of the land.

Now the rest of the acts of Uzziah, first and last, did Isaiah the prophet, the son of Amoz, write. So Uzziah slept with his fathers, and they buried him with his fathers in the field of the burial which belonged to the kings; for they said, He is a leper: and Jotham his son reigned in his stead.

2 Chronicles 26 talks about King Uzziah's prideful attempt to burn incense to the Lord. He went into the Lord's temple and the priests went in after him. During that time in history, there was always a priest standing at the door of the temple. His goal was to simply guard the temple, which means that King Uzziah charged past the doorkeeper. The priests rebuked the king, meaning, they used their words and their authority, but he became angry. Anger is the evidence of pride and the precursor of judgment. Leprosy broke out on the king's forehead and the priests cast him out of the temple. This is the price of not respecting the laws and the doorkeepers.

As you write, you will have those moments where you'll sense a wall of words protecting whatever information you're trying to access, or you will have those moments where you'll find yourself going outside of your self-imposed comfort zone. When this happens, it is important to pray and/or fast until you feel a release to go forth. You may be venturing off into matters that you have not been summoned to or matters that you have no true understanding of. This is like trying to defend yourself in a court of law when you have absolutely no knowledge of the law. People who do this are oftentimes narcissistic and prideful, and just as they are bound in the soulish and spirit realm, they will find themselves bound in the natural realm by court-appointed officers. To sum it up, as a scribe, author, writer, journalist, blogger or whatever title you wear, it is important that you familiarize yourself with Kingdom laws, and even more importantly, that you respect those laws. It is also important that you respect the doorkeepers of any given realm. As an author, I've written 40 books to date, over two hundred articles and numerous blog posts, not because I'm smart (that word is subjective), but because I've learned to respect the office of the scribe in the very same way I've learned to respect the laws of the land. When Jesus rebuked many of the Old Testament scribes, it was because they lacked the love and respect needed to effectively lead His sheep, nevertheless, they were a sect of leaders in that era who loved the praise of man. They were authoritative men who'd mastered the art of speaking and writing, but in the love arena, they were unlearned and bankrupt. This meant they were guilty of violating the very laws that they had been charged to uphold.

Don't just write the book, love God's people so that you are careful with what you put in your book. Writing is the exercising of authority; it is establishing laws in your life, and enticing others to embrace those same laws. This is why, as a Christian author, you should make sure that every book you write not only lines up with the Word of God, but that it exhorts, edifies and frees God's people. You may have the authority to write, but this does not mean you have the right to write about anything you want to write about. Every keystroke is an advancement towards, past and into a specific realm or dimension. Make sure that you have been invited into every world you type yourself into and that you enter that world in the right way. For example, in many Muslim countries, women are required to wear a hijab and cover their bodies from head to toe. I'm an American woman. Sure, in America, I'm free to wear whatsoever I want, but if I travel to a Muslim country, I have to respect the laws of that land, otherwise, I could easily end up bound or worse. The point is, there is a dress code (dimensionally, dress codes are mindsets and measures of knowledge) that we must have when approaching certain doorkeepers. If we ignore all warning signs and proceed past those doorkeepers, we will walk through the wall of words (boundaries, limitations and laws) that guard that realm. We'd then find ourselves tossed into rooms with other would-be authors whose conversations mirror our own. We'd hear them saying, "I've been writing my book for four years now and I just can't seem to finish mine either!"

Matthew 22:11-14: And when the king came in to see the guests, he saw there a man which had not on a wedding garment: And he saith unto him, Friend, how camest thou in hither not having a wedding garment? And he was speechless. Then said the king to the servants, Bind him hand and foot, and take him away, and cast him into outer darkness; there shall be weeping and gnashing of teeth. For many are called, but few are chosen.

How Words Affect Us

Most of us remember that old adage that we song as kids. Whenever someone said something bad about us, we'd proudly respond, "Sticks and stones may break my bones, but words will never hurt me." We believed this with all of our hearts, after all, our parents would often tell us that even Jesus was talked about. They'd prepare us for this harsh world by helping us to understand that being the butt of jokes, the subject of rumors, and the target of jealous bullies was almost inevitable. We'd prove that our parents' words had not fallen on deaf ears when we lean into our enemies' faces and sing the "sticks and stones" song. We'd then proudly march into our homes and excitedly tell our parents that we'd finally faced our miniature Goliaths. This meant that we were well on our way to become stable adults—or did it?

While the "sticks and stones" song may have been encouraging and even cute, the lyrics were all lies. Words do hurt people, however, words are powerless until they are considered and/or believed. Think about the discussion that Eve had with Satan in the Garden of Eden. Satan had absolutely no power to force Eve to do anything; he could not perform witchcraft on her, after all, to do so, he'd need a witch. Witches use their words to perform their witchcraft. Nevertheless, Satan simply used words similar and contrary to what God had told Eve. He told her that if she'd eaten from the Tree of the Knowledge of Good and Evil, she'd become as a god or, better yet, she'd become like God Himself. In short, she wouldn't need YAHWEH anymore because she'd be His equivalent or close to it. According to Satan, Eve would ascend the ranks of spirituality, causing every mystery to reveal itself to her. She'd become a force to be reckoned with. When Satan released those words, they flew around Eve's head and buzzed in her ears like mosquitoes, meaning, they stood outside of her. The next move belonged to Eve. She could reject them, which means that she would have cast them down, bringing them into captivity to the knowledge of God, or she could let them fly into her ears and enter her belief system. Unfortunately, we know how that story ends. Eve opened herself up to the lie and those words got tangled up into her DNA, after all, we are what we believe (see Proverbs 23:7).

In this image, we see a man who has become a myriad of words, many of which conflict with one another. He's many things to many people, but what manifests in his life is the direct result of what he believes.

One of the words that we see in his being is the word "Scribe." We also see that he's a creative and intelligent man. There are many words that got tangled up within him, many of which conflict with one another, making it hard for him to effectively and consistently use his talents. He should be writing his book, but there is a war going on within him that keeps him in the trenches of depression. He should be rich right now, but the hatred in him makes it difficult for him to push through the haunting memories of past events; he also has trouble getting past fantasies of revenge. The success he craves is centered around his rejection, and for this reason, writers' block meets him every time he touches a keyboard. For his healing to take place, and his gifts to be maximized on his

	journey, he has to: 1. Get past a few things. 2. Get over a few things. 3. Push through a few things.

The words in him include, but are not limited to:

Words of Affirmation	Words of Conformation
Love	Hate
Honor	Dishonor
Happy	Frustrated
Scribe	Addict
Musician	Confused
Friend	Pretentious
Son	Fearful
Father	Rejection
Prophet	Gossiper
Mathematician	
Christian	Pervert
Creative	Double-Minded
Simple	Complicated
Helpful	Selfish
Democrat	Conservative
Loyal	Crazy
Nice	Angry
Intelligent	Stupid
Sane	Prideful
Gentleman	Troubled
Brother	Predator
Dancer	Victim

Introvert	Vagabond
Lonely	Broke
Boisterous	Wasteful
Inventor	Thief
Entrepreneur	Employee
Husband	Adulterer
Mastermind	Quitter
Peacemaker	Suicidal
Driven	Foolish
Best Friend	
Handyman	Ex-Con
Good Listener	Desperate
Stepfather	
Volunteer	
Blogger	
Musician	
Runner	
Philanthropist	
Vegan	

As we can see, the man has become many things to many people. His battle is not external; it comes from within. The words of affirmation category reflect the good that has been spoken into his life by God and by a few of the people he's encountered. The words of conformation (not to be confused with confirmation) are the words that were released into his life by the wrong people. Because he did not address those words, but instead, believed them, they became a part of his being. For this reason, any time he attempts to be the mega gift God has designed him to be, a conflicting word burdens him down, making it hard for him to remain faithful to the process of creation. In the moment when he should be producing books, inventions, music and every other creative gift that he possesses, he finds himself battling with depression, false doctrine and addiction. To ensure that he does not write the book, the enemy then begins to send broken women his way— women who are void-filled, soul-tied and anxious. This is an attack against his finances. Remember, everything that appears to be good isn't always what it seems; somethings that appear to be a blessing or some form of relief are nothing but warfare wearing its prettiest costume. This is the struggle that many creatives face, especially during the seasons when they are the most fertile (spiritually). Just as a woman has a season (each month) where she is the most fertile, most creatives have seasons where they are their most creative. It is in these seasons that the creative experiences the worst warfare, whether it manifests itself as a problem or a glamorous solution to a problem.

In this image, we see a woman who is also a myriad of things, some of which are good, and some that are not so good.

Every good thing in her is at war with every bad thing in her, and vice versa. Here's the deal. Our hearts are like Rubik's Cubes. There are many sides of us that are turned away from God. All too often, what we believe to be warfare is nothing but God trying to get us to turn our hearts around. This lifelong process is easy for God to do, however, He requires that we do it ourselves, after all, He has given us the tools and the time needed to repent.

Just like her male counterpart, this woman's life has been plagued by issues like unforgiveness, addiction, a need for approval and chronic sadness. Amazingly enough, it is these issues that will invite people into her life—people who are like-minded and just as (if not

more) bound as she is. So, while she may have the assignment of the scribe, there are many things within her that keeps her from trusting in the gift that God has given her. These words (or voices) are louder (to her) than the voice of God. The next chart will spell out the words that are at work in her.

Words of Affirmation	Words of Conformation
Loving	Hateful
Approval	Disapproval
Joy	Misery
Author	Procrastinator
Encourager	Nag
Evangelist	Alcoholic
Friend	Enemy
Daughter	
Mother	Murderer
Sister	
Intercessor	Gossiper
Historian	Unforgiving
Christian	Religious
Creative	Pervert
	Confused
Extrovert	Rejection
Confident	Double-Minded
Republican	Negative
Loyal	Prideful
Excited	Bitter
Sweet	Selfish
Intelligent	Idolater

Fearful	Pretentious
Driven	Needy
Weary	Depressed
Rich	Unstable
Beautiful	Insecure
Sexy	Oversexed
Proverbs 31 Woman	Victim
Singer	Slanderer
Dancer	Lonely
Blessed	Desperate
Entrepreneur	Slave
Engaged	Soul-Tied
Mastermind	Ex-Wife
Philanthropist	
Driven	Complicated
Motivated	Foolish
Stepmother	Quitter
Volunteer	Suicidal
Blogger	Desperate
Runner	
Peacemaker	
Vegan	Contentious

As we can see, she is a lot of things, many of which conflict with one another. This is what makes it hard for her to be as creative as she was designed to be. Sure, she's talented, but she's also unstable.

James 1:8: A double minded man is unstable in all his ways.

In many of our churches, we love to confess, "I am everything that God says I am!" While this statement is true, it is also incomplete. How so? God gave us the power of will and the freedom to exercise that will; this is why we call it "freewill." So, while we all have everything that God has spoken over us, we have yet to become many of those things, meaning, we have not allowed the words of God to override the lies we've been told. For this reason, who we are and who we've become, while trapped in the same being, are not one and the same. We are an accumulation of words, many of which conflict with one another. This is what causes the battle between the ears. Therefore, while God may call us blessed, loved, forgiven and wealthy, we have yet to activate those words through faith. So, when the enemy sends someone to tell us that we are accursed, hated, forgotten and broke, we repeatedly meditate on those words, causing them to swell within us. After this, we begin to walk in the lies. This is what starts the war within. God's words and man's words begin to battle with one another. Sure, we'd love to stand on top of our religious pedestals and scream, "God's words are sovereign, so what you say about me does not matter!" We think by quoting these words that a power is released into the air, and that power will pull down the words of our enemies. Nevertheless, most spiritual battles are not fought outside of us; they are fought within. Think about that self-elevated co-worker who makes your job miserable. In truth, she's not your problem. She only has the power that you give her, especially if you're doing your job, coming to work on time and going above and beyond your call of duty whenever you can. Any anxiety that stems from that incident is not the result of her running into the manager's office and giving the manager an evil report concerning you. No. The real battle is, you either believe some of what she's saying about you or you fear that your manager will believe her words. For this reason, you've mentally left the day you're in and started imagining the damage she has the potential to do in the future. You've imagined yourself being terminated from your job and losing everything you'd worked hard for. This imagination is scary. But the imagination that provokes pride, rebellion and revenge is the one of her being rewarded for her evil works. You've imagined her being promoted and living a stress-free life, laughing at all of the evil she's done with no punishment for her crimes in sight. This is the imagination that opens the door for hatred to come in, and this all stemmed from one meeting she had with your manager. So, her words got tangled up in your belief system, and those words gave birth to other words. You may have found yourself thinking, "How could I have been so stupid to trust her?" Now, in the midst of every word that God has spoken over you, the word "stupid" has entered the mix, along with a few other words. When these words go to war with one another, we experience what we call warfare. Deliverance isn't just the casting out of demons; it's the casting down of words. Any words that are not cast down eventually have to be cast out. As scribes, we pour out of our hearts, which is the very core of our being. Out of the abundance of the heart, the mouth speaks. Out of the abundance of our hearts, we also write! For this reason, we have to be careful with who we grant access to our hearts; this is why God told us in Proverbs 4:23, "Keep thy heart with all diligence; for out of it *are* the issues of life." A man (or woman) who does not keep his heart is like a city without walls. "He that hath no rule over his own spirit is like a city that is broken down, and without walls" (Proverbs 25:28).

Your Relationship with Words

What if I were to tell you that you're nothing but a pile of dirt? Would you be offended? Of course. Most people would, even though we know that God formed Adam from the dust of the ground. Since we know that dirt is filthy, we often try to disassociate ourselves from it. We bathe and/or shower daily in an attempt to wash away any loose dirt from our skin. As a matter of fact, we don't like to be dirty, even though we are but a pile of breathing dust.

Mountains are piles of dirt and rock that have converged to form one of the largest and most stubborn landmarks in the world. This statement is not offensive to any of us. Howbeit, we are piles of dirt and we can be stubborn. It goes without saying that this statement can be regarded as offensive. Think about it this way. Every dust particle on a mountain is a single letter that has been tossed onto the mountain by a gust of wind. It had nowhere to go—it hadn't found a place to call its own. It hasn't helped to bed a tree or create a garden. It wasn't used to cover up the bodies of the many men and women whose time on Earth has expired. Instead, it got caught up in the wind, and it found itself resting on some level of a mountain. The same is true for you.

You are an arrangement of letters that have all converged to form words, and those words came together to form the person that is you. When God breathed life into you, you became a living soul. In other words, you received your personality. Have you ever noticed that perfume, when sprayed on multiple people, doesn't smell the same on each person? This is because the pH balance of each individual's skin is different. Hormones also play a vital role in how a scent smells on an individual. This explains why we all have our own unique personalities. Every dust particle that came along to form us is a letter or a word, so when God breathed life into us, He breathed life into everything He's ever said about us. Of course, Satan came along, tempted us into sin, and once we bit into the lie, he started throwing rocks on us and at us. These rocks were used to weigh us down and to bring us down. Many of these rocks made impact—they embedded themselves into us, and for this reason, we are constantly being delivered from the lies Satan told us and the lies he managed to store in the hearts of our ancestors—lies that have traveled from generation to generation through a stream that we call our bloodline. Nevertheless, God had already breathed life into one of the words in our structure, and that word is "perseverance." Eventually, God sent the Rock, Jesus Christ, Himself to deliver us from every lie, curse and death sentence that the enemy managed to engrave in our DNA.

1 Corinthians 10:4: And did all drink the same spiritual drink: for they drank of that spiritual Rock that followed them: and that Rock was Christ.

Psalm 18:2: The LORD is my rock, and my fortress, and my deliverer; my God, my strength, in whom I will trust; my buckler, and the horn of my salvation, and my high tower.

Matthew 16:18: And I say also unto thee, That thou art Peter, and upon this rock I will build my church; and the gates of hell shall not prevail against it.

Psalm 118:22: The stone which the builders refused is become the head stone of the corner.

So now, what if I were to tell you that you were nothing but a pile of dirt? It sounds less offensive now that you understand what dirt is. Now, your assignment is to find the many letters and words piled up on the Mountains of Influence, partner them up with other words and create books that will help to shape the minds and worlds of every person who reads your books. These words cannot contradict the Word of God. Any arrangement of words that come together to contradict what God said is a lie, and every person who publishes, speaks or promotes those words is a liar.

Bringing words together is like trying to fit a bunch of shapes into their corresponding pegs or trying to piece together a puzzle. Some words simply cannot and/or should not be matched. For example, witches match words together to form curses, while we (as believers) are tasked with taking what God has already said, bringing His Word into our hearts, and meditating on His Word until it forms a picture of His will. We then decree and declare what He's said into the atmosphere. When we do this, we are releasing the winds of change. When we come together with other believers in unity and we all release the same sound, we create heavy gusts of winds, tornadoes and even hurricanes in the realm of the spirit. These high winds come together to destroy every lie and mountain that the enemy has erected; they rearrange the thoughts of people, and they bring families back together. This is how we are to relate to words.

It goes without saying that Satan has his own winds, and they are called the doctrines of demons. These piles of words are spoken into the atmosphere by unbelievers and backslidden believers, and then carried around the world through the pipelines of culture, media and false religion. And while these winds are high, they are not powerful enough to move a man or woman who is grounded in God's Word. In summary, your assignment as a scribe is to bring people together and to divide the enemy's camp. We do this using words because we are but a pile of words.

The Marriage of Words

We've all heard the quote, "To thine own self be true" by William Shakespeare. This quote came from a play he'd written called Hamlet and had been spoken by a character in the play who he named Polonius. Today, this quote is one of the most widely known phrases in the Western world and is used on all types of memorabilia. People are even getting tattoos bearing this quote. Nevertheless, every single word in this quote is older than William Shakespeare himself. He didn't invent a single word in that phrase. He simply married the right group of words together and the quote took off from there.

Around one thousand new words are added to the dictionary each year, with many of them being derivations of other words. This is because English speakers are expressive people, plus, we simply need more words to cover all the new inventions, discoveries and findings that emerge each year. However, it's not the new words that garner the most attention; it is oftentimes the marriage of words that are largely understood. For example, look at some of the quotes below:

"The journey of a thousand miles begins with one step." ~Lao Tzu

"If you're always trying to be normal, you will never know how amazing you can be." ~Maya Angelou

"Always be a first-rate version of yourself, instead of a second-rate version of somebody else. " ~Judy Garland

"Anytime God is hiding Himself, He's initiating a seek." ~Apostle Bryan Meadows

"Nothing strengthens authority so much as silence." ~Leonardo da Vinci

"Nothing in all the world is more dangerous than sincere ignorance and conscientious stupidity." ~Dr. Martin Luther King, Jr.

"The supreme art of war is to subdue the enemy without fighting." ~Sun Tzu

"I have not failed. I've just found 10,000 ways that won't work." ~Thomas A. Edison

"The greatest tragedy in life is not death, but a life without a purpose." ~ Dr. Myles Munroe

All of these quotes came from great minds. What do they have in common? It's simple. Each author used words that already existed; they simply brought the right words together and these phrases were powerful enough to dislodge ungodly thoughts and thinking patterns from the minds of many. When the right words link up, revolutions and revivals break out.

Have you ever witnessed a toxic marriage? For example, have you ever seen an angry, violent woman married to a two-timing man? If you happened to be their neighbor, you wouldn't have any peace because the couple would fight almost every day. The sound produced by that marriage would be loud and profane. If you have seen a marriage like this, you've come to understand the difference between holy matrimony versus plain ole matrimony. That angry, violent woman may get divorced from her two-timing husband, get remarried, and suddenly start behaving like a normal, calm wife—or she could end up remarrying a calm, soft-spoken man, and because of her trust issues, unforgiveness and anger, the sound produced by that marriage would mirror the sound produced in her first marriage. Of course, this isn't to promote divorce in any way; my point is, when the right things, people and words come together, they will produce the right sound, but when the wrong people come together, the sound of chaos will go forth from them and it will echo from one generation to the next. When the wrong people come together, the sound that is produced is profane. The same is true for words. When the wrong words come together, both profanity and curses are formed, but when we marry the right words together, a sound is produced that will shake up the kingdom of darkness and shatter the works of the enemy.

Marrying the wrong words together is just as catastrophic as two of the wrong people linking up, whether romantically or platonically. For example, as we can see in this image, the man does not stop being an addict, dishonorable, selfish, frustrated, fearful and everything that he is just because he's now soul-tied to the woman. Of course, the same is true for the woman. She doesn't stop being the product of rejection, a nag, a procrastinator, unforgiving and everything else that she is just because she's now in a relationship. Instead, the two become one, and every single issue they have converge to create a not-so-quiet storm.

As an author and a scribe, you have to marry the right words in your book if you want to produce the right sound. When the right words come together, a bestseller is born. When the wrong words come together, people are bound. I've seen books that read like this:

> *"He said he would call me back, but I was like whatever. I'm tired. People do what they want to do. I just went to sleep and decided to tell my daddy how I felt in the morning. It is what it is. You know how people are. But I wasn't about to worry about that man anymore. Heck. I want some ice cream."*

Of course, this is not an actual quote from anyone's book; it's just an example of the types of books I've come across. Now, get this—people who write like this genuinely believe they have bestsellers on their hands. You'd be amazed at how many people wrote books, all the while, planning to quit their jobs and retire. They hadn't conducted any research or taught their readers a single lesson; all they did was vent. This is because there is a grave misunderstanding of what it means to be an author. Authors aren't just people who write sentences that make sense; we have to marry the right words together. These words create a sound that sets the captives free. These words create sounds that are powerful enough to save lives.

Of course, the million-dollar question is, "How does one marry the right words together?" The same way two people marry one another and that's through what we call a relationship. Relationships are built on like-mindedness, experience and agreement. What initially attracts two people together, outside of their natural, physical attraction to one another is like-mindedness. What links people together is experience. What keeps people together is agreement. As a matter of fact, the most commonly cited reason for divorce in America is "irreconcilable differences," meaning the couple could not seem to agree, despite their many attempts to do so. This brings to mind one of the rules of writing, which is—you should never have two negative words in a single sentence or clause. For example, "I don't have no kids," is improperly written. The correct way to write this is, "I don't have any kids." You can say, however, "I don't have any kids <u>because</u> I'm not married." Even though the words "don't" and "not" are both negative, the sentence has two clauses. The same is true in math. When two negative numbers are added together, they create an even greater negative. For example, look at this problem: $-8 + (-4) = -12$. Let's say that Mary married Bob and she had a negative balance of eight dollars in her account, whereas, Bob had a negative balance of four dollars. Once the two got married, their debt became a unit, meaning, they now owed $12 to their prospective banks. This means that to marry the right people or the right words, we need one or two positives. For example, if Mary married Bob and she had a surplus of eight dollars in her account, whereas Bob owed his bank four dollars, Mary could pay off Bob's debt to the bank, leaving the couple with a surplus of four dollars. This isn't much, but it's better than owing the bank.

To marry the right words together, you have to draw from your experiences, the experiences of others and your vocabulary. But you have to first convert your negative experiences into a positive, meaning, you have to draw the revelation from those experiences. To do this, you have to forgive the people who've hurt, abandoned, rejected and/or persecuted you. When you choose to do this, God will give you insight into what you've experienced. Let's revisit the example of the anger, bitter woman who'd found herself married to and eventually divorcing a two-timing man. In order for her to draw wisdom from this experience, she has to be willing to forgive her ex and she has to look beyond his faults to see her own. You see, what destroyed their marriage is on the surface for everyone to see, but if she wants to break the cycle, she has to dig beyond the obvious. While digging, she may find that the only reason she married the guy was because her father rejected her, which caused her to become an angry and aggressive woman. Her ex was attracted to her dominant ways, even though he didn't agree with or understand the whole concept of monogamy. If she goes beyond her experience, she can dig up generational curses in her bloodline, demonic agreements and every sabotaging spirit operating in her life. From here, she will receive revelation and she's able to marry the right words together to explain her poor choices and her deliverance. Love draws the right words together just as love draws the right people together.

What have you taken from your life's experiences? What about the experiences of others? I can draw from my experiences and write either of the two quotes:

- "People can be ungrateful. If God sends a mentor into your life, don't let stupidity cause you to become familiar to the point where you end up sabotaging your blessing!"

Or I can write ...

- "Never become best-friends with your assignment. Bring people only as close to your heart as their hearts can handle."

Do you see the difference between both statements? The first statement paints me as angry and immature, plus, it would be the evidence that I haven't learned the lesson behind the offense. Nevertheless, the second statement shows compassion and maturity. It shows that I am no longer pointing fingers at the assignment, but at myself. Which of these statements do you believe would be better received? The second one, of course! The first statement is a rant; the second statement is a set of instructions. When people don't extract the lesson behind the storms they've endured, they rant, murmur and complain, but when people forgive their enemies and take accountability for their share in their own hurt and/or disappointment, wisdom meets them at the gate of their repentance.

The right words come when we have the right mind. Let's revisit the quotes.
> *"The journey of a thousand miles begins with one step." ~Lao Tzu*
> *"If you're always trying to be normal, you will never know how amazing you can be." ~Maya Angelou*
> *"Always be a first-rate version of yourself, instead of a second-rate version of somebody else. " ~Judy Garland*
> *"Anytime God is hiding Himself, He's initiating a seek." ~Apostle Bryan Meadows*
> *"Nothing strengthens authority so much as silence." ~Leonardo da Vinci*
> *"Nothing in all the world is more dangerous than sincere ignorance and conscientious stupidity." ~Dr. Martin Luther King, Jr.*

"The supreme art of war is to subdue the enemy without fighting." ~Sun Tzu
"I have not failed. I've just found 10,000 ways that won't work." ~Thomas A. Edison
"The greatest tragedy in life is not death, but a life without a purpose." ~ Dr. Myles Munroe

You can see each one of the authors' experiences in their quotes. Read each quote and try to imagine what each author had to endure to extract such revelation. Now imagine what each author would have written if they had not taken the lesson behind their experiences.

As you can see, the marriage of the right words has absolutely nothing to do with our intellect. You can sit in your seat and think for hours on end, only to come up with nothing but a bunch of pointless phrases. Nevertheless, if you draw from your experiences, you can pull out a bunch of words. If you mix love and forgiveness with that experience, you'll know which words to link together to create an experience for the reader that will change his or her life.

Startup Exercise (Activation)

Before we go any further, let's do an exercise.

1. Write your name on a word document (you can use Microsoft, OpenOffice or whatever word program you have). If you don't have access to a computer, write on the cover of a notebook.
2. On that same page, write your book's title just above your name. If you're using a notebook, write your book's title on the cover of the notebook.
3. On the next page, write between three to ten headers in your table of content. If you can write more, please do so.
4. Skip down about ten pages and then write, "The End" on the last page. If you're using a notebook, on the last page of your notebook, write "The End."
5. What you're doing is initiating the start of your book. What you've just done is exercised your authority.

Your Right to Write

The Bible is a compilation of 66 books written by 35 or more authors (some of the books' authorship are still being debated). The men of old who wrote the Bible are authors; this goes without saying, however, the term "author" back then wasn't viewed in the same way as we see it today. The men were seen as Messengers of God (Prophets) and the works they authored were not seen as "their books". The Jews understood that the messages came from God, and for this reason, they took them seriously enough to create and establish laws from them.

First and foremost, let's establish this: you do not have to be a prophet to write a Christian book, but you should be prophetic! What does this mean? In the book of Acts, we see an interesting turn of events taking place. We get to witness (through the power of words) the day of Pentecost. Acts 2:1-4 (ESV) details this momentous day. It reads, "When the day of Pentecost arrived, they were all together in one place. And suddenly there came from Heaven a sound like a mighty rushing wind, and it filled the entire house where they were sitting. And divided tongues as of fire appeared to them and rested on each one of them. And they were all filled with the Holy Spirit and began to speak in other tongues as the Spirit gave them utterance."

After explaining to the men of Judea what they were witnessing, Apostle Peter went on to remind them of what the prophet Joel had spoken. Acts 2:17-18 (ESV) reads, "And in the last days it shall be, God declares, that I will pour out my Spirit on all flesh, and your sons and your daughters shall prophesy, and your young men shall see visions, and your old men shall dream dreams; even on my male servants and female servants in those days I will pour out my Spirit, and they shall prophesy." In other words, prophets are not the only believers who have the right (or command) to prophesy; prophecy is the language of the believer! So, can every believer prophesy? Yes! If the believer has the Holy Spirit, he or she should be able to prophesy. The next question then is—do all believers prophesy, and to this, the answer is a resounding no. There are many reasons for this, with one of them being the distance between the believer's heart from God's heart. In Matthew 15:8-9 (ESV), God said, "This people honors me with their lips, but their heart is far from me; in vain do they worship me, teaching as doctrines the commandments of men." In other words, some people have God's Spirit, but not His heart. They submitted themselves for salvation, but they did not submit themselves for deliverance. Consequentially, some find it very hard to write Christian books, so they end up settling for God-inspired books, meaning, the words that they publish were inspired by what they've heard other believers say, what they've read and what they've experienced as believers. Others simply stop writing because of writers' block.

Writer's Block

Google defines "writer's block" this way: *the condition of being unable to think of what to write or how to proceed with writing.* To better understand this phenomenon, let's focus on the word "think." To think is the ability to navigate one's mind from one thought process to another. It is the ability to recall an event; it is the ability to remember a face, a place or a conversation. The word "remember" comes from the prefix "re", which means *again*, and the word "member", which means *something or someone that is a part of a larger unit.* Therefore, to remember something is to take its members (details) and put them back together *again* in your mind. This means you have to form a picture of the event in your mind; to explain it, you would have to break down the picture into individual words and serve them to others. With that being said, to remember something, you will have had to first experienced it, otherwise, you will have to put it back together based on someone else's recollection of the event. This means you will form a picture, not only based on someone else's memory, but the picture you form will be laced with your life's experiences, beliefs and assumptions. For some people, writer's block is simply their inability to put together a sentence, paragraph or a book because they've heard more than they've experienced, meaning, their information is secondhand. Now, God does not mind us sharing secondhand information if we know and understand the spirit behind the matter. Nevertheless, when we share stories for any other reason than to give God glory and help His people, we'll add details to the stories to liven them up. Simply put, we'll start lying. In truth, writer's block is oftentimes the result of a believer who wants to tell the story, but does not want to understand God's heart in relation to the matter. For this reason, God blocks the writer from accessing relevant information pertaining to what he or she is *inspired* to write about. Such believers will pray and ask the Lord to help them with their books, but He will not respond. Why is this? James 4:3 (ESV) helps us to understand this; it reads, "You ask and do not receive, because you ask wrongly, to spend it on your passions." The passions that God speaks of here are what we refer to as selfish ambitions, ungodly desires and the lusts of our flesh. Again, remember there are gatekeepers charged with keeping ambitious authors from wandering outside of their metrons. These angels cannot and will not stop a person; their assignment is to simply block the doors to whatever revelation the author-to-be is not mature enough to access. This is oftentimes what some authors refer to as writers' block. The author has an idea of how smart he or she wants to sound, but can't seem to access the words, information or revelation needed to make his or her book read a certain way. Nevertheless, a persistent author can get past these doorkeepers, after all, the angels of God cannot intrude upon the will of a human being. If an author pushes past a door after having been warned, the author will wander off into a region of thought that he or she is not mentally equipped for. Please understand that to get to revelation, you will oftentimes go through warfare.

Luke 12:48 (ESV): Everyone to whom much was given, of him much will be required, and from him to whom they entrusted much, *they* will demand the more.

There's a word we use in relation to patterns of ungodly thinking and destructive behaviors and this word is "stronghold." Google defines "stronghold" this way:
1. a place that has been fortified so as to protect it against attack.
2. a place where a particular cause or belief is strongly defended or upheld.

A stronghold can be good *or* bad. A good, or better yet, godly stronghold is when our minds are so filled with the Word of God that the enemy cannot effectively penetrate them. This is called the shield of faith. Ephesians 6:16 (ESV) reads, "Above all, taking the shield of faith, wherewith ye shall be able to quench all the fiery darts of the wicked." The fiery darts of Satan are mental attacks and accusations; they are nothing but words released that are designed to kill, steal and destroy. A bad, or better yet, demonic stronghold occurs when a believer's mind is so filled with lies that it becomes difficult for the bound soul to hear the truth. Bound people are oftentimes very defensive or, better yet, easily offended because every truth released, in their opinions, is an attack against their beliefs. The point is, writer's block (for believers) is:

1. a believer's inability to access the vault (wisdom) of God because of the distance between his or her heart from God's heart.
2. A believer's inability to access certain details because of lack of experience.
3. A believer's inability to access certain details because of the believer's metron (more on this later in the book).
4. A believer's inability to access the vault (wisdom) of God because the believer is demonically bound.
5. A believer's inability to access information because the revelation has not yet matured within the believer.

Queen Esther had limited access to her husband, King Xerxes, and only the high priests were allowed to go into the Holy of Holies. This means that:

- Every valuable thing is guarded, including revelation.
- Writer's block is not always demonic. Sometimes, it's an author's attempt to illegally access revelation that the author has not been granted access to or share a revelation that the author has not ruminated. Revelation has to be digested before it is shared.

To access the wisdom of God, we have to be patient, repentant, humble and willing. We cannot access what we do not respect, for example, Queen Vashti lost her crown when she lost respect for her husband. Dishonor cost her dearly. Queen Esther had to take a lesson from her predecessor and understand that, even though King Xerxes was her husband, she did not have free roam of the castle. He was valuable to Persia, so he was guarded, and anyone who tried to access him illegally would have been blocked and, in some cases, killed. But Queen Esther had been fasting. She understood honor, so she put on the right garments before going into the king's chambers. Esther 5:1-3 reads, "Now it came to pass on the third day, that <u>Esther put on her royal apparel</u>, and stood in the inner court of the king's house, over against the king's house: and the king sat upon his royal throne in the royal house, over against the gate of the house. And it was so, when the king saw Esther the queen standing in the court, that she obtained favor in his sight: and the king held out to Esther the golden sceptre that was in his hand. So Esther drew near, and touched the top of the sceptre." Notice here that she put on her royal attire before approaching the king. This means that before going into the king's courts, Esther took off whatever it was she had been wearing so that she could put on her royal attire. Consider Matthew 22:11-13, which reads, "And when the king came in to see the guests, he saw there a man which had not on a wedding garment: And he saith unto him, Friend, how camest thou in hither not having a wedding garment? And he was speechless. Then said the king to the servants, Bind him hand and foot, and take him away, and cast him into outer darkness; there shall be weeping and gnashing of teeth." We see here that what we wear is a demonstration of honor, just as it can be evidence of dishonor. In the writers' world, we wear our mindsets and our belief systems. Sometimes, we attempt to approach revelation looking for confirmation and not information, meaning, we have a set of beliefs that we are unwilling to move away from, so we set out to confirm what we believe, instead of testing it. When this happens, authors will always run into writers' block because they won't honor the wisdom behind the vault. To break this, the author has to study and show himself or herself approved, pray and ask for insight and the author must open himself or herself up to receive a truth that does not match whatever it is that he or she believes.

We have to prepare to receive whatever information it is that we're seeking, but we can only do this if we're open to receiving it. For example, I preached against tithing, calling it Old Testament and unscriptural for the modern-day believer. I was passionate about my belief, nevertheless, one day, God answered a nine-year-old prayer of mine. That prayer was for Him to send me to the church He'd assigned me to. I'd spent nine years studying and teaching from home. When I got the confirmation I needed that God had indeed planted me in Embassy Church, one of the first discomforts I had to deal with was hearing my Apostle preach for what I'd preached against. I struggled to make the tithing confession and I gave whatever number I felt God was telling me to give. I joined the mentorship program, and one day, I sent my Apostle a long email, asking a lot of questions, and in that email, I told him about my beliefs in regards to tithing. We emailed back and forth a couple of times before deciding to do lunch. Before I decided to communicate my beliefs with him, I'd told myself that I would be open to his views. As I drove towards the restaurant we'd agreed to go to, I knew that I wasn't going there to change his mind. I didn't prepare a long speech, write down a bunch of scriptures or rehearse what I'd say. I just went with the intent to learn. I decided that if I still didn't understand or agree with him by the end of the meeting, I'd just have to pray and study more. I knew I wasn't going to leave my church, so I'd reconciled in my mind that there was a possibility that I wouldn't understand his point. Thankfully, this wasn't the case. He explained tithing to me in a way I'd never heard it explained and from then on out, I became a tither. The point I'm making is, it would have been dishonorable for me to email him and even ask for a second of his time if I wasn't willing to hear and consider what he would say. I could not have accessed new information if I'd only gone looking for confirmation. Again, this is why many writers suffer through writers' block. When writing a book, you'll find that many of your beliefs are going to be challenged. Nevertheless, you have to welcome the challenges in your pursuit of the truth. If you are more concerned with sounding right than you are with being right, pride will block you from receiving new information.

Mature Revelation

I record a lot of messages using my voice recorder. When I'm done, I'll plug the recorder in, download the message and edit it. For a long time, I would receive some measure of revelation on any given subject, and because it was good to me, I was anxious to release it. So, I would grab my voice recorder and began to share with others what God shared with me. The majority of those recordings were never released; I had to delete them because the revelation was not yet mature. How do you know when revelation has matured? The answer is simple—when you have matured in the revelation. Every line of reasoning is considered a region. In every region of reason you enter, you will enter as a baby and have to grow into it and eventually out of it. You will never mature in reasoning because reasoning involves logic, so your ability to mature in revelation is determined by your ability to overcome every logical argument that dares to rise against the Word of God. 2 Corinthians 10:5 (ESV) reads, "We destroy arguments and every lofty opinion raised against the knowledge of God, and take every thought captive to obey Christ." The word "argument" in this scripture comes from the Greek word *pithanologia* and, according to Strong's Concordance 4086, it means "persuasive speech." A persuasive speech isn't necessarily a conversation you are currently involved in, nor does it have to be an external conversation. Persuasive speech can be much of what you were taught in school (theory of evolution, big bang theory, etc.), or it can be your own line of reasoning that, of course, is a regurgitation of what you've been taught or what you've experienced.

In every region of reasoning you're in, God can get information to you. This information is called knowledge. Knowledge, when it comes from God, gives us access to truth. John 8:31-32 (ESV) reads, "So Jesus said to the Jews who had believed him, "If you abide in my word, you are truly my disciples, and you will *know* the truth, and the truth will set you free." What are they being set free from? Strongholds, of course. They are being set free from ungodly patterns of thinking that led to destructive behaviors and ultimately to hell. This means that salvation is threefold:

1. Saving one's soul from eternal damnation.
2. Delivering God's people from the powers of darkness (demonic deliverance).
3. Renewing the mind.

Mature revelation is a renewal of one's mind; it is overcoming logic with the truth.

After God gets information to the believer in the form of knowledge, it is up to the believer to turn that knowledge into understanding. It goes without saying that knowing something is not the same as understanding it. To understand means to stand under or submit to the information; it means to receive it as truth. There are many people who teach messages that they don't necessarily understand or believe because of logic. For this reason, they cannot teach those messages in detail, nor can they explain them. They attempt to understand knowledge using logic, but logic always filters the truth, taking away its potency until it becomes nothing but a series of words that can be stretched or condensed to fit into the believer's limited perception. When believers have not matured in revelation, they will always run into a wall called writer's block. Understanding, on the other hand, means to have insight regarding a matter or, better yet, be granted the ability to see the spirit or heart behind a matter. You cannot receive understanding without sacrifice.

Anytime I attempt to grab my voice recorder and record a message that has not yet matured, I get to a place in the message where I don't know where I'm going with it or where I am in it. Getting lost is a sign that you are treading on unfamiliar territory.

For example, I moved to Eberbach, Germany in 2009, and almost immediately upon moving there, I started going for walks around my neighborhood. In the beginning, I did not know where I was going, so I would make it a point to remember certain landmarks as I passed them by. It didn't take me long to remember how to navigate around my neighborhood without having to overthink it. The same is true with revelation. If I have to overthink something I'm teaching, it could only mean the revelation isn't yet mature because I don't yet know how to maneuver my way through it, therefore, I'll try to maneuver my way around it.

Proverbs 4:7 tells us the cost of understanding; it reads, "Wisdom is the principal thing; therefore get wisdom: and with all thy getting get understanding." The NIV translation reads this way, "The beginning of wisdom is this: Get wisdom. <u>Though it cost all you have</u>, get understanding." The point is, there is a price tag behind understanding; you will never be able to enter revelation (the revealing of God's heart on a matter) without first getting understanding. To get understanding, you have to give up your old line of reasoning so that you can overcome logic; this will allow you to replace facts with truth.

Metrons

A metron is a unit of measure; it can represent jurisdictional authority and it can represent any form of limitation. Every region has an authority, whether that region is a physical location or a series of beliefs. Oftentimes, writer's block is nothing but a writer attempting to leave his or her own metron and enter a measure of understanding that he or she has not been cleared to enter. This is usually the result of writers' ambition—a writer's desire to garner wealth, notoriety or to get revenge on someone who's hurt or rejected the writer. Any attempt by a scribe to exit his or her own metron will always be met by writer's block, but this barrier does not prohibit the writer from exiting his or her metron; it's more of a warning. Writers who do not adhere to this warning are often met with inexplicable and almost unbearable warfare. Please understand that even though God gave us authority over unclean spirits, we need knowledge to challenge some of them. In short, we need to know what type of demon we're fighting, how it entered in, what legal rights it has, and the proper process to cast it out. This is why Jesus' disciples could not cast the demon out of the young epileptic boy (see Matthew 17:14-20). The spirit in the young boy could only be cast out through prayer *and* fasting (see Mark 9:29). Nevertheless, the disciples didn't initially know this, so they challenged a demon that they weren't prepared for. Did they have authority over it? Yes, but authority without knowledge is like a toy gun.

Understanding Your Right to Write

One of the greatest strongholds to hit the church is the belief that we (as believers) have the right to say whatever we want, when we want to say it, about anyone we choose to speak about. In Psalms 105:15, God says, "Touch not my anointed ones, do my prophets no harm!" Amazingly enough, this verse was addressed to kings who, at that time, had the greatest measure of authority outside of God. If God told kings not to touch His anointed, who are we to think that we are exempt from this rule? The Bible was not written for the unbeliever; it was written for the believer. In other words, when God gave the command to not touch His anointed, He was speaking to us—the church! This rule even applies if an anointed man or woman of God falls into the snares of sin. We can restore them and judge righteously, but we do not have the right to blast them.

Galatians 6:1 (ESV): Brothers, if anyone is caught in any transgression, you who are spiritual should restore him in a spirit of gentleness. Keep watch on yourself, lest you too be tempted.

YOU HAVE THE RIGHT TO REMAIN SILENT!

Every time a scandal breaks out in a church, social media starts becoming the virtual pulpits for unauthorized believers to speak on what they do not understand. Many people want to give their opinions regarding the scandals and the people involved, but very few are willing to encourage the fallen believers and pray for them. What this means is that a large number of believers lack knowledge in regards to their rights; they lack understanding as it relates to boundaries. It also means that a lot of believers unwittingly participate in dishonor. Remember, the word "bound" is found in the word "boundaries," therefore, believers who go outside of their metrons almost always end up bound. Anything you dishonor, whether it be a platform, metron, anointing or wealth, you disqualify yourself from. Our rights are our jurisdictional limitations. Anytime we go outside of our jurisdictions without clearance, we open ourselves for curses. To be blessed means to be empowered to prosper; to be cursed means to be empowered to fail or to become impotent. To be impotent means to be without power. This is why there are so many believers who are powerless—they've given way to dishonor. Think of it this way. A municipal judge who lives in and judges matters in Atlanta, Georgia has absolutely no power in Philadelphia, Pennsylvania. If he were to put on his robe in a Pennsylvania courtroom and sit in the judge's seat, he'd immediately be arrested. More than likely, he'd be sent for a mental evaluation. He could not judge matters outside of his jurisdiction and neither can we.

As believers, we have a right to write, but it's important for us to know what we can and cannot write about. For example, if you've never been granted the responsibility of pastoring a church, it is unwise to speak against someone who is. The reason is, there are somethings you may not understand because your perspective is subject to your metron. If a story breaks that details a cursing, fornicating pastor who's been arrested in a crack house, we can all understand that the pastor is in sin and should not be behind a pulpit. Nevertheless, our assignment is to restore that person. Galatians 6:1 (ESV) says it this way, "Brothers, if anyone is caught in any transgression, you who are spiritual should restore him in a spirit of gentleness. Keep watch on yourself, lest you too be tempted." Does that mean we ought to restore him or her to the pulpit? The answer is simple—if the pulpit wasn't ours to give to them, it's not ours to take away. In every given region, God has prophets to personally address those who have fallen; that is, if the people do not have godly council. God will determine how the matter is handled, but our responsibility is to pray for and encourage those who have been hurt by the scandal. Taking to social media to humiliate and condemn the person is the same as going outside of your jurisdiction. This brings us to our rights as writers.

Whatever we are not authorized to say, we are not authorized to write. It is very important for a writer to understand his or her own measure of authority. This is the place where the writer can clearly hear God's heart; this is the region where writer's block does not exist. Just as God told the Jews He would bring them to a land flowing with milk and honey, our promised lands are the regions in which our blessings flow.

It is the place where there is no obstruction between our hearts and God's heart; it is the place where our hearts merge, and His thoughts become our thoughts, His ways become our ways. This is the place where we have the right to write, not what we want to write, but what God gives us to write.

I've seen many books come across my desk that were filled with bitterness and dishonor. These books were written by authors who did not understand their rights, nor did they understand that they have the right to remain silent. One of the most important lessons I've learned in my writing career is—if you want God's endorsement on your book, be His messenger. This means you are to write what He tells you to write and refrain from writing anything that demeans or dishonors another person, especially a believer. People who understand their rights and their limitations are authors who can write books in as little as a few days, up to a few months. There is no blockage between them and God's heart. God can trust them with the revelation He shares with them. He does not block such writers, and when the enemy gets in the way, the Lord will often instruct the writer to testify their way through the attack. Revelation 12:11 reads, "And they have conquered him by the blood of the Lamb and by the word of their testimony, for they loved not their lives even unto death."

As believers, we all have a right to write, but we don't have the right to write about everything. The best way to choose a topic to write about is to ask yourself these questions:

- **What have I overcome?** Attempting to write about something that you haven't overcome will almost always prove to be disastrous. When readers pick up a book, they are oftentimes looking for a solution to a problem, whether that problem is they want to start a new career, understand the gift of prophecy, find out why they're not yet married or find out how to cast out a demon. People who talk about problems, but don't offer solutions often find their books getting a lot of negative feedback and reviews. This is because readers don't pay to hear authors rant; they pay to receive directions out of a mindset, relationship or situation. Be careful that you do not treat your readers like they are your personal friends. Remember, your book will either be a map to freedom or a religious maze.

- **What did I learn from every event, relationship or warfare I've overcome?** Every time I come across a person who is still blaming someone from his or her past for his or her present situation, I know I've come across a bitter and bound soul. In every good and bad situation, there is revelation, but one thing you'll come to learn is that revelation is a circle that always leads you back to yourself, meaning, it takes away your ability to cast the shadow of blame on others, regardless of what they've done. For example, a divorced woman can say that her ex-husband had an affair, and that affair was the reason they're divorced, but if she receives revelation, she'll be able to trace her divorce back to herself. You see, the problem could have been that she unequally yoked herself with an unbeliever, even though God tells us not to do this. Or the problem could have been that she was mistreating her husband and withholding sex from him every time he didn't do what she thought he ought to do. In this, both the husband and wife are wrong, and it's up to each party to take accountability for what they did wrong. You will always know when revelation is mature because, again, it will always lead you back to yourself.

- **What am I most knowledgeable about; for example, what can I talk all day about?** We all have our triggers; for example, I can talk for hours about relationships, authorship, demonology, entrepreneurship, branding, pets and forgiveness. For this reason, I can easily write a book on any of these given topics and be finished with the book within a few days to a week. This means that these subjects are within my metron (jurisdiction), but it does not mean I have full roam of each subject. I understand entrepreneurship on a certain level, but there are districts in this subject that I am yet to venture into. I understand relationships, but there are some districts on this topic that I am yet to explore. For example, I can't talk about what it's like to be married for twenty years. Speak on what you're most knowledgeable about.

- **On what topic is my advice sought the most or what do my friends and I have in common?** Personally, most of my friends are entrepreneurs, authors and ministers. When my entrepreneurial friends call me, they are oftentimes discussing something that's going on in their businesses—normally something relating to branding or marketing. When my author friends call me, they are oftentimes talking about their books or plans regarding marketing their books. Lastly, when my minister friends call me, they are oftentimes talking about deliverance or some form of paganism that has crept into the church. This means they have identified my metron and vice versa. I call them when I'm in their jurisdictions and need answers, encouragement or to be pointed in the right direction.

Understanding your strengths is the same as understanding your metron. Acknowledging your weaknesses is the same as acknowledging your personal boundaries. Writers who understand these principles normally excel in the world of writing, but writers who wander around in other people's metrons, trying to write about what they do not understand, are ambitious souls who unwittingly open themselves for attacks and negative reviews.

Don't abuse your right to write. Lean your heart close to God's and move with Him. This will make writing a whole lot easier and it'll help you to finish your books in a matter of days, weeks and months.

Writer's Block Exercise

Write between one to two pages of text in your book. After you're done, answer the following questions.

Question	Your Answer
How long did it take you to write each page?	
Would you say that your book is a good idea or a God idea?	
Are you passionate about the subject of your book?	
What is your imagined outcome? List your dominant thoughts in regards to the outcome	

you desire.	
What inspired you to write your book?	
When you're writing, what are the thoughts that distract you the most?	

These questions are important because they often go right to the heart of writers' block.

- If it took you a long time to come up with the content with those pages, chances are, you're either writing the wrong book or writing the right book in the wrong season.
- If your book is a good idea, you will have to conduct a lot of research to get the content, which means, you won't be able to tap into your personal knowledge and experiences as much as you would had the book been a God idea.
- The Bible says that when Jesus saw the multitudes, He was moved with compassion because they fainted and were scattered abroad like sheep without a shepherd. If you're not passionate about the subject, chances are, your book is a good idea and not a God idea.
- If your (dominant) imagined outcome is earning extra income, conducting interviews and building a platform for yourself with your book, God won't partner with you. This is because He loves His people and He's not interested in creating celebrities; He's interested in raising up laborers. Writers' block is often the result of an ambitious author trying to access revelation without the password: love.
- Statistics have shown that women are more likely to start their businesses after having witnessed their friends start their own businesses. In short, women are often driven by inspiration when entering the marketplace. The same is true in relation to authorship. Many women are inspired to write after having seen someone else announcing or promoting his or her book. It's okay to be inspired by others, but it's more important to be moved by love. Again, if your dominating thoughts are centered around yourself, God won't partner with you.

- If your dominating thoughts are washing the dishes or finishing up another project, it is better to complete those projects and then return to your book. Oftentimes, writers' block is nothing but the result of a series of thoughts invading your mind at one time.

The Author's Pace

"Be still, and know that I am God. I will be exalted among the nations, I will be exalted in the Earth!" (Psalm 44:10)

Pace yourself! This is one of the hardest commands to give to a writer, after all, we want to flow at the speed of revelation. For this reason, it is easy for aspiring authors to sit down and start books, only to abandon their projects, promising themselves that they'll finish them at a later date. As authors, we'll continue to update our manuscripts until we finally lose interest in what we have written. Why is this? It's simple. We are ever-evolving creatures who feed on the wisdom, knowledge and understanding given to us in every season of life. But just like the food we buy, most of the information from our previous seasons will eventually expire. This doesn't mean the revelation wasn't good or true; it simply means that we've moved past it as we've made our way from milk to meat, and then from meat to meat. A book that we started writing in 2016 won't be as intriguing to us in 2018 because we are continuously evolving and maturing. With that being said, books that are not completed within a specific time-frame more than likely will never be completed because the content of the books will no longer inspire the author. Again, this is because the information is expired, and just like with all things released into the Earth, God will likely give that revelation to someone else to share. This is to ensure that His voice is repeatedly heard and respected within the Earth realm.

The less revelation an author receives, the more still that author is required to be in order to hear from God. Hearing less isn't always a punishment; sometimes, it simply means that God is no longer speaking to the writer in the place in which the writer first heard His voice. It means that God is requiring the writer to take a journey in Christ Jesus, learning more about Him and seeking His face all the more. This is why God said in Jeremiah 29:13, "And ye shall seek me, and find me, when ye shall search for me with all your heart." There are three important notes that we have to take from this verse of scripture and they are:

1. We have to seek the Lord. No one can find Him for us; we have to seek Him for ourselves by ourselves.

2. God hides Himself. This is why He said we have to find Him.
3. We have to seek the Lord with our whole hearts, not a part of our hearts.

What's interesting is that God required many of His patriarchs to travel, but the question is, where were they going? Each person had an assignment and they didn't always know what they were pursuing outside of the will of God. When God spoke to Abram, He told him, "Go from your country and your kindred and your father's house to the land that I will show you" (Genesis 12:1). God didn't tell Abram the name of the land; He simply told him to leave his country and family and pretty much just follow His voice to a land that He would (eventually) show him. This was indeed a faith walk on Abram's part. This meant that Abram had to leave everything that had a piece of his heart, except for his wife, slaves and personal belongings. He had to pursue God with his whole heart, only being led by His voice.

Every destination represented a place of peace or a stillness in the sojourner's life. After their escape from Egypt, God promised the Jews that He would bring them to a land flowing with milk and honey. This land represented a place of reward and rest. As authors and aspiring authors, we are also taking journeys, only we aren't walking across deserts and climbing mountains; our pens are our legs, and we have to overcome the obstacles of fear, shame, lack of knowledge, lack of funds, public scrutiny and everything that threatens to stand in our way. Nevertheless, just like any sojourner, we have to pace ourselves. How does an author pace him or herself? It's simple. Authors have to be sensitive to God's voice; we lay our heads on the Father's chest so that we can hear what He is saying. But to hear God's heart, we have to spend time alone with Him.

Truly God-submitted authors write as God speaks. Now, let's get one thing straight before we delve deeper into this mystery. Not every (potential or actual) author who waits two or three years to finish his or her book is actually moving with God's voice, even though many claim that they are. Some authors move at the rate of their insecurities, while others are competitive writers. People who are competitive will constantly keep deleting pages and paragraphs every time they come in contact with a book that reads better than theirs, so they can never move forward with writing. They are always abusing their backspace keys and spending way too much time trying to come up with the perfect arrangement of words. The point is, some authors don't move with God's voice; they are led astray by every other voice they hear.

An author's pace is determined by what moves the author. If the author is moved by the Word and has absolutely no fear of the enemy, the author will advance far and fast into his or her book. Authors who have not mastered abandoning seasonal comfort zones always take longer to write their books. All too often, the storms of life have to come and drive them out of those comfort zones every time God gives these authors a set of instructions.

The comfort zone represents what's behind the author, but the unknown is what the author finds himself or herself venturing towards. Fear of the unknown is the number one reason that authors don't finish their books. Believe it or not, many authors actually fear becoming well-known, best-selling authors. They are afraid of wealth and all that comes with it, so they take their times and write, hoping to release a book that does well enough to bring in some extra cash flow, but they will not put too much effort into doing any research, conducting interviews or doing anything that would cause their books to garner too much attention. Just as they hate sticking out in a crowd, they work to ensure that their books don't stick out in a library. In other words, their comfort zones have become well-decorated prisons. As authors, we have to always remember that our journeys have nothing to do with us; they have everything to do with winning souls for the Kingdom of God. Additionally, many authors fear wealth because they are unsure what it would do to their families. This is especially true for married couples. I've seen many cases where, for example, one spouse does not offer support to the other spouse when he or she is writing, but will instead distract and threaten the spouse until the would-be author puts his or her pen away. This not only slows the author's pace, but stops the author in his or her tracks. Of course, the spouse who interfered with God's will is being driven by several spirits, which include:

1. Fear
2. Fear of rejection
3. Rejection
4. Fear of abandonment
5. Jealousy

6. Control (Witchcraft)
7. Jezebel
8. Variance
9. Paranoia
10. Double-mindedness

Of course, this is a short list of demonic personalities that may be present with the interfering spouse. For example, a husband will find himself bombarded with thoughts like, "If she became an author, she'd think she's better than me." A wife may find herself overwhelmed with thoughts like, "If I let him write his book, women will start taking notice of him and he'll become prideful. That book would ultimately destroy our marriage because he doesn't know how to behave himself around women right now and he's broke!" Now granted, these fears likely aren't true, but to the interfering spouse, they are genuine threats. What's happening in these cases is the devil is threatening the interfering spouse from a place within the spouse's heart that is not fully transformed or fully submitted to God. In short, that spouse needs deliverance, but until this happens, the would-be author won't have the encouragement, peace or support that he or she needs to quickly finish his or her book. I've heard stories of spouses threatening to leave their marriages and a few cases of spouses actually leaving simply because their significant others had decided to write books. And honestly, it isn't a male thing or a female thing; I've seen this happen on both sides of the spectrum. Of course, this is demonic, but this is a real issue in many Christian homes.

As authors, one of the things we have to repeatedly remind ourselves of is this—our books were not given to us so that we can become media sensations. When God gives a book to an author, He has given the author a means to save His people. Nevertheless, one of the deceptions of the enemy is to make authors think that their books are all about making them famous. When authors see their assignments as tickets to wealth and fame, they will not write in love, but they will put too much of their personalities into their books in an attempt to win over the hearts of their readers. Think of it this way: the author is tap-dancing on the pages of what would be, could be and should be a love letter from God to His people. In other words, the author's over-the-top personality becomes a distraction. In some cases, the thought of fame and fortune deters the author. When this happens, the spirit of procrastination takes over and the author makes finishing the book a low priority. Eventually, God has to take the revelation He wanted to share with that author and give it to someone who is more faithful because there are certain people who that book is supposed to reach at a certain time.

The Weight of Responsibility

"For it will be like a man going on a journey, who called his servants and entrusted to them his property. To one he gave five talents, to another two, to another one, to each according to his ability. Then he went away. He who had received the five talents went at once and traded with them, and he made five talents more. So also he who had the two talents made two talents more. But he who had received the one talent went and dug in the ground and hid his master's money. Now after a long time the master of those servants came and settled accounts with them. And he who had received the five talents came forward, bringing five talents more, saying, 'Master, you delivered to me five talents; here, I have made five talents more.' His master said to him, 'Well done, good and faithful servant. You have been faithful over a little; I will set you over much. Enter into the joy of your master.' And he also who had the two talents came forward, saying, 'Master, you delivered to me two talents; here, I have made two talents more.' His master said to him, 'Well done, good and faithful servant. You have been faithful over a little; I will set you over much. Enter into the joy of your master.' He also who had received the one talent came forward, saying, 'Master, I knew you to be a hard man, reaping where you did not sow, and gathering where you scattered no seed, so I was afraid, and I went and hid your talent in the ground. Here, you have what is yours.' But his master answered him, 'You wicked and slothful servant! You knew that I reap where I have not sown and gather where I scattered no seed? Then you ought to have invested my money with the bankers, and at my coming I should have received what was my own with interest. So take the talent from him and give it to him who has the ten talents. For to everyone who has will more be given, and he will have an abundance. But from the one who has not, even what he has will be taken away. And cast the worthless servant into the outer darkness. In that place there will be weeping and gnashing of teeth.'"

The Hebrew word "talent" is "kikkar" and it can be defined as "a measure of weight or money" (Reference: Strong's Concordance, 3604). A talent is also a gift that is passed from one individual or generation to the next; it can be inherited or passed down. In the parable of the talents, the talent was passed down from the master to the servants, but two of the servants actually used their talents. The unfaithful and slothful servant buried his. Why did he bury his talent? His excuse was, "I knew you to be a hard man, reaping where you did not sow, and gathering where you scattered no seed, <u>so I was afraid</u>, and I went and hid your talent in the ground. Here, you have what is yours." Again, fear is what stops people from starting or finishing their books. There is no excuse that the Lord will accept when He has given us the power, the gift, the ability and the means to carry out an assignment, but we choose to bury our talents. It doesn't matter if we plan to bury them for a season or forever, God expects us to take what He's given us and multiply it.

Let's consider the weight of a talent. In the biblical days, a single talent weighed roughly 75 pounds. Again, one servant had been given five talents, meaning, that servant was responsible for carrying around 375 pounds! He then doubled those talents, meaning, he had to cart around 750 pounds! Another servant had been given two talents, meaning, he had to manage 150 pounds. When he doubled those talents, he found himself responsible for carting around 300 pounds! The wicked and slothful servant, on the other hand, had been given a talent which weighed 75 pounds, but instead of managing what he had been given, he relieved himself of the burden. This means that their master had given each man a measure of responsibility. The two faithful servants went out and increased their responsibilities. The unfaithful servant decided to bear the title of a servant without actually serving. This is what a lot of authors are doing in this very hour! Let's face it —writing is a huge responsibility, and with it comes more responsibilities. Why is this? Luke 12:48 answers this question for us. It reads, "For unto whomsoever much is given, of him shall be much required: and to whom men have committed much, of him they will ask the more." The measure of a servant's heart is shown in how much that servant is willing to serve.

Now, think about the pace of an author carting around 375 pounds of responsibility. This could easily slow the author down, however, as we can see in the parable of the talents, it did not affect the servant's pace because when his master returned, the servant had doubled his load. The servant who moved at the slowest pace was the one who'd lightened his load by burying his talent. This is because greater responsibility only serves to increase our strength, our endurance and our drive. Nevertheless, procrastination chains us to our fears and our comfort zones.

Luke 12:48 (ESV): Everyone to whom much was given, of him much will be required, and from him to whom they entrusted much, they will demand the more.

A gold talent, on the other hand, was believed to be around 110 pounds, which was the typical weight of a man. This suggests that the parable of the talents was symbolic of us taking on the responsibility of helping others. Think of it this way. One man had been given five talents, another received two and the slothful servant received one. Let's compare this with evangelism and/or exhortation. One man had the responsibility of saving or encouraging four others, including himself, making the weight of his responsibility a total of five people. Another guy had been charged with saving one other soul, along with pastoring his own soul and working out his own soul's salvation. The unfaithful servant was given the responsibility of managing and controlling himself, but instead of pushing past offense, rejection, abandonment and whatever problems he had, he decided to bury himself in drugs, partying, promiscuity or depression. He saw his problems as God's responsibility, meaning, he did not try to free himself. Instead, he could often be heard saying, "God knows my heart. When He's ready to set me free, He will." When the master came back, he found the man who'd been given the responsibility of pastoring four other souls, along with himself, running a church of nine members. When he checked on the guy who'd been charged with helping one other soul, along with himself, He found him in the company of three other people, spreading the gospel. When He checked on the last guy, He couldn't find him in His will. Just like the moment God called out to Adam in the Garden of Eden and asked him where he was, the unfaithful servant was passed out drunk in a seedy hotel, naked and lying next to a woman who was not his wife. In short, the man could not manage himself, let alone, help someone else out of their mess!

Genesis 3:9-11 (ESV): And the LORD God called unto Adam, and said unto him, Where art thou? And he said, I heard thy voice in the garden, and I was afraid, because I was naked; and I hid myself. And he said, Who told thee that thou wast naked? Hast thou eaten of the tree, whereof I commanded thee that thou shouldest not eat?

An author's pace determines the measure of rule that God will give each individual author. Even though a talent, biblically speaking, was currency, it also represented gifting, responsibility and jurisdiction. When God trusts you with a responsibility, it is unwise to bury that responsibility, even for a spouse. Mark 16:17 reads, "And these signs shall follow them that believe; In my name shall they <u>cast out</u> devils." What does this have to do with the author's pace or marriage? It's simple. Sometimes, the weight that an author carries around is the burden of bondage, whether the author himself or herself is bound or the author's spouse is bound. In short, before the author can effectively exercise his or her authority in the outside world, the author must first exercise his or her authority at home. This means the author should seek deliverance, take himself or herself through deliverance and then proceed take his or her spouse through deliverance. This is the servant with two talents. Once the author can effectively cast out the in-house demons, God will entrust him or her to cast out the demons outside of his or her zip code. This is what Psalm 55:22 means when it says, "<u>Cast thy burden</u> upon the LORD, and he shall sustain thee: he shall never suffer the righteous to be moved." In the book, "Pigs in a Parlor," author Frank Hammond detailed the moment he took his wife and fellow co-author Ida Mae Hammond through deliverance. He said,

> *"We realized that demons were responsible for certain tensions between ourselves. One day, when we were at home by ourselves, we decided to minister to one another in these areas. As I called for the demons to release her, she was thrown to the floor and evil spirits began to speak through her. One demon made a direct accusation against me. I know that I was guilty of what the demon accused me. It put me under such condemnation that I could not proceed with her deliverance. It was necessary for me to confess my sin, ask her forgiveness and have her cast the demon out of me before I was able to continue with her ministry. This bonded us with love and forgiveness, and shut the door on any further interference from the enemy."*
> *(Reference: Pigs in a Parlor/ Should I Be a Deliverance Minister/ Frank and Ida Mae Hammond)*

As with all leaders, it is vital for spouses to minister deliverance, not only to themselves, but to one another. When spouses are too proud or too ashamed to minister to one another, they are usually driven apart or bound together by demonic forces. God's desire is for us to cleave, but two people who are bound to one another are often bound by one another, not through love, but through fear. This means that the marriage slowly becomes a toxic environment where nothing is produced but conflict. This also means that the spouses begin to weigh one another down; the spouses essentially become one another's burdens.

Your burden is anything that weighs you down and slows down your pace. You cast your burden upon the Lord through prayer, fasting and making whatever sacrifices God tells you to make. For example, one of the authors I worked with had to deal with threats from her husband of nearly two decades while she wrote her book. He was tormented by the idea of her becoming a published author, not because she had the potential to hurt him, but because he'd already damaged their marriage with his affairs. The thought of her self-worth being rebuilt scared him so much that he'd mentally tortured her while she was writing the book and even after she'd finished it. Nevertheless, she'd made up her mind to do as God told her to do and let Him deal with her husband. I've seen this happen many times. She'd done well in following the Lord, but the one thing she had neglected to do was chase the enemy out of her house. How is this done? James 4:7 gives us a principle of deliverance; it reads, "Submit yourselves therefore to God. Resist the devil, and he will flee from you."

While the author had successfully finished her book, she'd admittedly argued with her husband every time he'd offended or threatened to leave her. You see, her responsibility wasn't just to write the book; her responsibility was to also deal with what was manifesting in her home. Her job was to take authority over every ungodly force that was coming against her. So, how does one submit themselves to God, after all, you can't take a grown man or woman through deliverance who doesn't want to be free, right? Understand this: most bound people don't know that they are bound; they think they are protecting their marriages when, in truth, they are forcing or attempting to force their spouses to bury their talents. The Bible said that her responsibility was:

- To submit herself to God and resist the devil; this way, the devil would flee

(see James 4:7).
- Not let the sun set on her wrath, neither give PLACE to the devil (see Ephesians 4:27).
- Submit to her husband (consistently) and win her husband with her conversation (see 1 Peter 3:1-2).

To increase your pace, you have to walk in your God-given authority. Consistency is key. Your pace as an author has nothing to do with your speed, after all, this race isn't given to the swift. Her job was to overcome her own flesh. This was her first talent. This means that when the enemy came through her husband to slow her down or attack her altogether, she was supposed to:

1. Restore her husband with the spirit of meekness.
2. Submit herself to God and resist the devil; this way, the devil had no choice but to flee from her.
3. Not let the sun go down on her wrath, neither give place to the devil.
4. Submit to her husband (not his demons).
5. Win him with her behavior.
6. Cast her burden (husband) upon the Lord. This is done through prayer and fasting.
7. And if the unbeliever wanted to depart after all this was done, let him depart.

Let's address number four. A lot of women today don't realize the authority behind submission. Let's look at it from a natural standpoint and then from a supernatural standpoint.

Scenario: Imagine that you are a married woman, fulfilling an assignment given to you by God to write a book. Your husband happens to be a believer, but isn't necessarily submitted to God outside of a few Sunday service visits, and he doesn't like the idea of you writing. He doesn't say this directly, but he goes out of his way to convince you that you're not smart enough to write a book, and when you decide to write anyway, he starts torturing you with his words. He starts staying out late again and talking excessively about divorce. You try to do the Christian thing and ignore him, but you soon realize that he's making the atmosphere become so weighty with negativity that you find it hard, if not impossible, to finish a sentence when he's around. He deletes your rough draft, but thankfully, you have a spare copy on an external hard drive. He then starts being critical of everything you do, everything you say and even how you breathe. You've been married to him for many years so you don't want to give up on your marriage. You reason within yourself that everything will go back to normal as soon as you finish the book, but things keep escalating while you're writing. It gets so bad that you find yourself battling with anxiety. Nevertheless, your mind is made up that the two of you are not going to divorce, so you argue with him every time he starts behaving immaturely.

Natural Response: You repeatedly step away from your computer to argue with him, and during a couple of those heated battles, you've said things that seemed to have sent him into an emotional tailspin. The damage seems irreparable, so reason would suggest that you stop writing and deal with the issues that are forming in your marriage. You do this on and off for several years, all the while, stealing every moment you can utilize to write your book. Every time you stop writing, things seem to get better, but when you start writing again, he suddenly finds fault in everything you do. Determined not to let him control you, you write all the more when your husband is being argumentative, but when he's acting like the loving husband that he has the potential to become, you stop writing. This is because you want to maintain the atmosphere of peace and it almost feels as if your husband is rewarding you for not writing. Do you see how the tables have turned here? In this, the enemy is just provoking you to spend your energy. By the time you try to write, you're going to either be too tired, too frustrated or too pride-filled to write. Always remember that the enemy is strategic. His goal is to either stop you from writing the book or provoke you to write it in the wrong spirit.

Supernatural Response: You have had to repeatedly step away from your computer to bind up every spirit in your atmosphere, even taking the time out to tell your husband that you love him, before retreating into your bedroom to pray. You won't argue with your husband; instead, you answer his questions lovingly and ask him what he needs to make him feel better as a husband. He goes on a long rant about you not cooking as much, the children being too noisy and you not seeming to care about the marriage anymore. You apologize to your husband, even though you know that everything he's saying is not true. You then commit to cooking more often, ensuring that the children aren't as noisy (with his help, of course) and you commit to being more in tune with him. Understand this: what you've done is addressed every lie and now, he has nothing else to accuse you of. He then responds,

"Everything seems to have gone downhill ever since you started writing that book of yours! That book can wait! Your family is falling apart and you seem to be too stupid or too blind to see this! I make enough money to take care of our family, so if money is the issue, I'll get another job! Put the book down and take care of your family!" Sure, it's easy to get offended with this, but if you understand that you're dealing with a spirit, you can better address it. You explain to him that it's not about the money—you simply want to help others. When he's being argumentative, you don't answer him; instead, you go into your prayer closet and begin to summon the angels of God to deal with every spirit operating in your marriage. One night, you take the time out to write your husband a long love letter, and in this letter, you don't mention any of the issues he's been having. You simply tell him how amazing of a husband he is. You pray over the letter, fold it up and place it in his work boots. The next day, as he's getting dressed for work, he finds the letter. What you have done is separated your husband from the spirit operating within him. You see, it's easy to argue with him, especially since he's a willing vessel of the enemy, but believers must take authority over the enemy. On his way to work, your husband's heart begins to ache when he thinks about all the things he's put you through. He calls you and says, "I'm thinking about taking off early today so you and I can go hang out. Is that okay with you?" You happily agree. Later, when he comes home, he starts apologizing for his behavior, and it is then in that moment that he will take his first step towards deliverance. He will name his demons! For example, he may say, "I apologize. I guess I've just been feeling insecure lately, thinking that if you become some big shot author, you would think you were too good for me. I guess I just got scared; that's all." You'd be amazed at the power of submission! In that moment, he has just identified five spirits: lying spirit, rejection, fear of rejection, fear of abandonment and the spirit of fear. In that moment, you can ask your husband if you can pray with him, and more than likely, he'll say yes. Utilize that opportunity to take him through deliverance! You see, in order to address an issue, you have to put a name to that issue. What you've just done is similar to what the patriarchs of old did. You took a journey through a wasteland and you kept calling on the name of Jesus when all hell broke loose in your life. For this reason, the spirits were addressed and your marriage was left intact. This is what godly authority looks like. You absolutely cannot be an author if you are afraid to exercise your authority. "Submit yourselves therefore to God. Resist the devil, and he will flee from you" (James 4:7).

Just remember this: processes cannot be rushed, but they do have to be consistent. This means that if a demon tries to attack your pace while you are on assignment, consistently attack that demon while it is on assignment. Move at the speed of God's voice. Oftentimes, He may tell you to stop writing for a few days, weeks or months, and then again, there will be times when He will tell you to write your way out of a storm. Either way, if you believe God has called you to authorship, you have to first exercise your authority in your personal life before you can address God's people. This means that you must first learn to carry 75 pounds without complaining or quitting before God will trust you with 375 pounds!

The Speed of Obedience

Romans 13:1-7: Let every soul be subject unto the higher powers. For there is no power but of God: the powers that be are ordained of God. Whosoever therefore resisteth the power, resisteth the ordinance of God: and they that resist shall receive to themselves damnation. For rulers are not a terror to good works, but to the evil. Wilt thou then not be afraid of the power? do that which is good, and thou shalt have praise of the same: For he is the minister of God to thee for good. But if thou do that which is evil, be afraid; for he beareth not the sword in vain: for he is the minister of God, a revenger to execute wrath upon him that doeth evil. Wherefore ye must needs be subject, not only for wrath, but also for conscience sake. For this cause pay ye tribute also: for they are God's ministers, attending continually upon this very thing. Render therefore to all their dues: tribute to whom tribute is due; custom to whom custom; fear to whom fear; honor to whom honor.

The word "obedience" is defined by the Online Etymology Dictionary this way: "submission to a higher power or authority." In short, obedience is only rendered when we recognize that there is a higher authority; it is only demonstrated when we recognize and honor rank. Of course, God is the highest authority; He is Sovereign, meaning, He is the Supreme Ruler. To be obedient means to give obeisance to a higher authority, distinguishing that individual as being of greater rank than ourselves or others. For example, Ephesians 6:1 reads, "Children, obey your parents in the Lord: for this is right." Titus 3:1-2 (ESV) reads, "Remind them to be submissive to rulers and authorities, to be obedient, to be ready for every good work, to speak evil of no one, to avoid quarreling, to be gentle, and to show perfect courtesy toward all people."

In these scriptures, we get to see God's heart towards order. If you read the Bible from cover to cover, you'll see that God is very passionate about honor and obedience, after all, honor is order and order is a reflection of honor. If I lived with my mother and I kept my room clean, I would be demonstrating honor. It doesn't matter if she kept the rest of the house in disarray, I would be demonstrating honor by keeping the room she entrusted me with clean and in order. I'd be demonstrating maturity along with honor if I took the time to clean the rest of the house without complaining. Even though I'm an adult, I would still have to obey her while living in her home. If she told me to clean her room, even though this could and would seem unfair to me, I'd have to obey her. My age means nothing if I'm living under someone else's roof. In order for me to be promoted to my own home, I have to honor the place that I'm in. People who think they can dishonor a platform and then grace that same platform are delusional; whatever you dishonor, you disqualify yourself from. Should you stand in that place, you will be courted by the same dishonor that you once gave birth to.

But why are we talking about honor and obedience? It's simple. Many authors do not honor God enough to obey Him. Let me explain. All too often, authors edit what God tells them to write, because they fear backlash. *What will my family say? What will my friends say? Will I appear to be unlearned to those who know the Bible more than I do?* In truth, our assignment is to obey God; that's it and that's all. Adam and Eve fell because of disobedience. God told them not to eat from the Tree of the Knowledge of Good and Evil, but they disobeyed Him and ate from the tree anyway. For this reason, they were no longer able to dwell with God. We will always lose access to whatever and whomever it is that we dishonor. When we mentally debate with ourselves about what we should include and/or exclude from our books after God has instructed us about what He wants us to write, we are debating with God. We are attempting to obey God our own way, all the while, pacifying our need to remain in good-standing with certain people or, at minimum, under their radar. Disobeying God is always centered around the author's determination to hold on to his or her comfort zone. Understand this: God does not care about our comfort zones; He cares about us. So, writing will take you outside of your comfort zone; it will stretch and challenge you.

There are three things that trigger favor, and they are:
1. Obedience
2. Responsibility
3. Submission

(Reference: Apostle Bryan Meadows/ Revival Culture)

Obedience, of course, is obeying God and obeying the people He's placed in charge over us (ex: parents, authorities) and around us. Mount Machapuchare, a mountain located in the Himalayas, is off limits to climbers for religious reasons. A British team led by Lieutenant Colonel Jimmy Roberts climbed to within 492 feet of the summit via the north ridge, but they did not complete the climb, since they'd promised the authorities of that region that they would not set foot on the actual summit. Since then, the mountain has been declared sacred, and is now closed to climbers. Even though Lieutenant Colonel Jimmy Roberts more than likely didn't share in the locals' beliefs, he and his team had to obey the authorities of that region. When we enter the world of writing, we don't have the luxury of writing what feels right to us. In truth, God will often stretch you to write things that are uncomfortable to share and revelation that may not be largely received within your circle. The sooner we obey God, the faster we will receive the revelation we'll need to complete our books. All too often, authors take anywhere between a year to a decade to complete a single book simply because they want to superimpose their own visions over the books that God has given them to write. When this happens, most authors will endure writers' block because God won't allow them to access the revelation they'll need to complete their books.

Another extension of honor is writing down the visions and ideas that God gives you. For example, in 2014 or 2015, I would have sudden flashes of beautiful, what I believe to be never-before-seen pieces of jewelry. They were very extravagant pieces, but because I've never designed jewelry before, nor did I have any interest in designing jewelry, I would just marvel at the vision, repeatedly think about the pieces and then go to sleep. I didn't write down what I saw so I forgot the details of what I'd seen. This happened for a while before the visions suddenly stopped. Why did they stop? It's simple. I didn't honor what God was showing me. When God gives you a vision, it's not for you to marvel at; there is an assignment attached to that vision. The visions started back around 2017 or early 2018, and again, they are always very abrupt and very detailed. Nowadays, I not only see flashes of jewelry, but I oftentimes see unique pieces of clothing. Even though I'm not (currently) in fashion design, that was an interest of mine when I was younger, I get downloads from Heaven of unique pieces of clothing and jewelry. As an adult, I've never had an interest in that world. Howbeit, I have an assignment there, even though I'm not one hundred percent clear on what it is God will have me doing, outside of introducing the images to someone who can actually design them. Nevertheless, I recently started writing down the visions and I'm excited about someday entering that chapter of my life. Why did God give me those visions? It's simple. Because He knows He can trust me with them, even though I've ignored them in the past. I allowed my lack of knowledge in regards to the world of fashion to almost cost me a talent. Remember, in the parable of the talents, the master took the talent from the unfaithful servant and gave it to the faithful one. Nowadays, I can say that I have a better understanding of Matthew 13:12 (ESV), which reads, "For to the one who has, more will be given, and he will have an abundance, but from the one who has not, even what he has will be taken away." This is because the one who has is obedient with what he or she has been given. When Charles Babbage received a vision of a computer in the early 19th century, do you think he understood what he'd seen, given the fact that nothing even resembling a computer was on the market? Nevertheless, he went forth with his vision, and today, almost every American has a computer in his or her home. Do you think that Antonio Meucci understood the vision he'd had of a talking telegraph (telephone) in 1849? Sure, Alexander Graham Bell is credited with being the inventor of the telephone, but the original idea came from Antonio Meucci. Even though there is still a lot of controversy surrounding the invention of the telephone, one thing is for sure—the telephone, like every other invention, started off as an idea in a person's mind. When it came in as an idea, it was intimidating. Nevertheless, the inventor decided to take a risk and that risk paid off well.

God has given you a vision; write it down and make it plain. If you are a faithful scribe, God will give you many ideas, including witty inventions, strategies and solutions. This is because an obedient soul is like a healthy intestine; there is no blockage or obstructions, so everything flows as it should. God is not going to waste time trying to explain why He told you to write what He told you to write, just as He didn't stop to address my confusion regarding the visions I kept having. I've learned that God will tell us to do a thing just to see if we trust Him enough to do it, even though we don't understand the assignment. The people who fully obey, albeit rare, often acquire tremendous success in life and in ministry; they are blessed coming in and blessed going out. The people who either disobey God or try to manipulate His instructions to fit their agendas don't go very far in life or in ministry. They are the souls who end up having more potential than they have power.

"The graveyard is the richest place on Earth, because it is here that you will find all the hopes and dreams that were never fulfilled, the books that were never written, the songs that were never sung, the inventions that were never shared, the cures that were never discovered, all because someone was too afraid to take that first step, keep with the problem, or determined to carry out their dream."
(Reference: Les Brown)

"The wealthiest place in the world is not the gold mines of South America or the oil fields of Iraq or Iran. They are not the diamond mines of South Africa or the banks of the world. The wealthiest place on the planet is just down the road. It is the cemetery. There lie buried companies that were never started, inventions that were never made, bestselling books that were never written, and masterpieces that were never painted. In the cemetery is buried the greatest treasure of untapped potential."
(Reference: Dr. Myles Monroe)

The Talent Exercise

1. Every person is a talent. How many people are you (effectively) responsible for?
2. How many responsibilities have you picked up at your job, in your family, in your church or in your community?
3. Since you are a talent, have you buried yourself to help others?

The Author's Voice

"Who shall ascend the hill of the Lord? And who shall stand in his holy place? He who has clean hands and a pure heart, who does not lift up his soul to what is false and does not swear deceitfully. He will receive blessing from the Lord and righteousness from the God of his salvation. Such is the generation of those who seek him, who seek the face of the God of Jacob" (Psalm 24:3-6/ESV).

The word "hill" is synonymous (biblically speaking) with the word mountain. Both are derivations of the Hebrew word "har." Mountains were important in the Bible because this is where God often met with the patriarchs of old, plus, many great things occurred on mountaintops. Noah's ark rested on Mt. Ararat after the flood that destroyed every living thing, except for Noah, his family and the animals he brought with him onto the boat (see Genesis 8:4). Abraham was commanded to sacrifice his son, Isaac, in Genesis 22. He took him on Mt. Moriah, but an angel of the Lord intervened. Isaac was saved and a ram was sacrificed in his place. Moses would often ascend Mt. Sinai. It was there that he received the Ten Commandments (see Exodus 34). Moses saw the Promised Land from Mt. Pisgah, Jesus was transfigured on a mountain (believed to be Mt. Hermon or Mt. Tabor), and Jesus ascended into Heaven from Mt. Olivet (also known as the Mount of Olives). As we can see, mountains were used as meeting places between God and man.

Mountains often represent boundaries, borders and problems. Ascending a mountain meant the climber had to exhaust himself, endure sudden changes in air pressure, and possibly come in contact with dangerous animals like mountain lions, coyotes, red wolves, snakes and so on. Additionally, the climber risked falling to a sudden death. As a matter of fact, many mountains are littered with the human remains of climbers who either died after falling or people who'd succumb to the elements. It is not uncommon today for climbers to request that their remains be left in the place in which they'd fallen should they perish.

What is the holy place? Exodus 3:1-5 (ESV) describes an encounter Moses had with God. It reads, "Now Moses was keeping the flock of his father-in-law, Jethro, the priest of Midian, and he led his flock to the west side of the wilderness and came to Horeb, the mountain of God. And the angel of the Lord appeared to him in a flame of fire out of the midst of a bush. He looked, and behold, the bush was burning, yet it was not consumed. And Moses said, 'I will turn aside to see this great sight, why the bush is not burned.' When the Lord saw that he turned aside to see, God called to him out of the bush, 'Moses, Moses!' And he said, 'Here I am.' Then he said, 'Do not come near; take your sandals off your feet, for the place on which you are standing is holy ground.'" Was this mountain the holy place that Psalms 24:3 spoke of? Of course not. The holy place is wherever God is. Wherever He decides to meet a person, that place is holy. "Then the Lord said to him, 'Take off the sandals from your feet, for the place where you are standing is holy ground" (Acts 7:33).

As Christian writers, it is important to understand that writing is a process of ascending and descending—it is meeting with God to hear His heart and then, transcribing what He's taught us. It is becoming a solutionist: a person who not only talks about problems, but one who provides solutions. It is becoming an extension cord that connects man with Heaven. This is why writing for the Kingdom is not something we should take lightly. It's more than just book signings, photo shoots and television interviews; it is a letter from God to His people—or it can be a letter from the author's heart to God's people. If it is a letter from the author, for example, a testimonial, a fictional book or a book full of the author's opinions, it can be a godly book (if the author has the heart of God), or it can be a demonic binding tool disguised as a Christian book, written to ensnare God's people (if the author is demonically bound). A good example of an ungodly book is a book detailing the hurts and betrayals the author has suffered through. The book becomes ungodly when it does not give God the glory, but is instead used as a tool to expose, hurt and humiliate others. Sadly enough, in this day and age, there are many Christian authors using their books as venting tools. The problem with (air) vents is that they transfer air from one source to another. The vents in our homes take the outside air and bring it inside after cooling or heating it, of course. A venting author simply transfers to or better yet, shares his or her pain or anger with the readers. This is called transcribing as well, however, the scribe's heart is perverted with pain and therefore, the author isn't transferring godly words to his or her readers; the author is simply sharing his or her burden with the readers. This leaves readers feeling frustrated, depressed and hopeless because what the author did was make an ungodly impartation. Remember that the word "trans" means to cross, therefore, when an author vents, what the author is doing is causing his or her pain to cross over into the author's life. This doesn't mean the reader will be plagued by the same situation; it simply means that the reader will be burdened with the author's issues. Understand the power of words. A burden is nothing but a mountain of words and worries that a person is carrying. When authors vent, they take their burdens (words and worries) and share them with their readers. This means that the author is being used by the enemy to further oppress people.

The Bible is comprised of 66 books. Every author had his own personality, story and unique experience with God, all of which played an important role in the author's writing style. Every author was a prophet or a disciple; this is how he was able to hear the heart of God and express it to God's people. Nowadays, most believers who have stories to tell about their lives and experiences genuinely believe that God wants them to write a book or several books for His people. It goes without saying that this is not true. The prerequisites of writing for God include, but are not limited to:

1. **Salvation.** How can we write for God if we don't have His heart, don't believe what He's said and cannot hear from Him?

2. **Assignment or Permission.** Matthew 22:14 reads, "For many are called, but few are chosen." Jesus had many disciples, but He only chose 12 to be apostles (see Luke 6:13). There is God's perfect will and there is His permissive will. An author can write from His perfect will, meaning, the author was specifically given an assignment by God to write a particular book. Then again, an author can write from His permissive will, meaning that even though God did not specifically tell the author to write a book, the author has decided to do so. This is acceptable if the book gives God the glory and sets the captives free. Do you remember how Jesus responded when John said that they'd seen a man casting out demons in His name and they'd tried to stop him from doing so? Mark 9:39-40 answers this question for us. It reads, "But Jesus said, "Do not stop him, for no one who does a mighty work in my name will be able soon afterward to speak evil of me. For the one who is not against us is for us." Even though the man who was casting out the demons was not in

God's perfect will, the Lord still *permitted* him to continue casting out demons. This is an example of His permissive will.

3. **Knowledge.** God has called many people to write, but there are various levels of writing, just as there are various offices in the five-fold ministry. It can be emotionally and spiritually devastating to both authors and their readers if the authors write what's in their hearts, instead of what's in God's heart. Jeremiah 17:9 reads, "The heart is deceitful above all things, and desperately wicked: who can know it?" We cannot teach what we do not know. People who lack knowledge and take up the charge to write, end up writing their readers a prescription for bondage.

4. **Understanding.** Knowledge and understanding are not one and the same. To know something does not equate to understanding it. Knowledge is everywhere; it is freely accessible to anyone who wants and reaches for it. To receive understanding, however, a person has to intentionally seek it and be willing to make whatever sacrifices he or she needs to make in order to advance more into the heart of God. Proverbs 4:7 reads, "Wisdom is the principal thing; therefore get wisdom: and with all your getting get understanding." To get understanding, we have to be willing to make an exchange; we give up our old beliefs, relationships and lifestyles the moment God reveals His heart to us; that is, if what we're believing or building does not match His blueprint for our lives. Knowledge is nothing without the illumination of revelation and the delivering power of understanding. For example, many people know that fornication is wrong, but do not understand why. Understanding answers the why. Without understanding, people reject knowledge and essentially perish.

5. **Repentance.** Anytime we go before the Lord, we have to repent; we can't just barge into His presence and begin to download what's in His heart. An author who has not repented will not hear from God and will therefore, write books that are filled with the fruit of the flesh. Remember, the high priest in the biblical days had to make atonement for his sins and the sins of the people. Jesus is our atonement; He exchanged His life for ours, but this does not excuse us from sin. When Jesus taught His disciples to pray, He told them to say the following words, "Our Father which art in Heaven, Hallowed be thy name. Thy kingdom come. Thy will be done in Earth, as it is in Heaven. Give us

this day our daily bread. *And forgive us our debts, as we forgive our debtors.* And lead us not into temptation, but deliver us from evil: For thine is the kingdom, and the power, and the glory, forever. Amen." Jesus told them to ask for forgiveness, all the while, forgiving others for their sins against them. Any author who has not forgiven is an author who has not truly repented for his or her sins. This means that the author is a scribe for Satan.

6. **Discerning of Spirits.** As believers, we hear many voices—some of which impersonate the voice of God. If we cannot discern who is speaking to us, we should not convey what we've heard to God's people. 1 John 4:1 reads, "Beloved, do not believe every spirit, but test the spirits to see whether they are from God, for many false prophets have gone out into the world."

7. **Deliverance.** When Paul and Silas had been thrown into prison, an earthquake shook the doors of their cell open. This meant they could freely come out of their cell, but they chose not to. They waited until they'd received an apology from the people who'd placed them in bondage. This is to say that even though Jesus came to set the captives free, a person has to intentionally walk out of bondage. Just like there are many well-spoken people in prison who write letters to their loved ones, there are many well-spoken believers who write books while in bondage. If we don't know how to discern what spirit is talking to us, we will become mouthpieces for the enemy.

8. **Love.** 1 Corinthians 13:8-10 (ESV) reads, "Love never ends. As for prophecies, they will pass away; as for tongues, they will cease; as for knowledge, it will pass away. For we know in part and we prophesy in part, but when the perfect comes, the partial will pass away." 1 Corinthians 13:13 (ESV) finishes this statement with, "So now faith, hope, and love abide, these three; but the greatest of these is love." Where there is no forgiveness, there is no love. Where there is no deliverance, there is no love. Where there is no salvation, wisdom, knowledge, understanding or repentance, love is absent. A writer who does not have God's heart does not have love and therefore cannot set the captives free, but will instead be used by the enemy to bind God's people. This is why God didn't use every Christian with a testimony to write one of the books of the Bible. He used people who had His heart, people who intentionally sought after His voice. He used people who had ears to hear and a desire to hear what the Spirit of the Lord was saying. He's still the same

today as He was yesterday. It is important to Him that we not only hear His voice, but that we have His heart for His people.

As writers, our assignment is simple: to set the captives free, but we can't do this if we're bound. Our voices aren't our own. When we speak, our readers should hear God. When we decide to write, we decide to become teachers of God's people. In other words, we are applying for the right to lead God's people through our writings. This is no small matter in the eyes of God. As a matter of fact, it is a dangerous thing to mislead God's people. In Matthew 18:5-6 (NASB), Jesus warns us this way, "And whoever receives one such child in My name receives Me; but whoever causes one of these little ones who believe in Me to stumble, it would be better for him to have a heavy millstone hung around his neck, and to be drowned in the depth of the sea." Please understand that a little one isn't just a child; a little one is anyone who is considered a babe in Christ. There are two types of leaders: the ones who lead people to Christ and in Christ, and then, there are the ones who lead God's people astray. Always remember that Jesus is our Shepherd, and as such, one of His duties is to protect the sheep He's leading, even if that means leaving the 99 to find the one who got lost. If we're the ones leading them astray, we have become wolves with good intentions and God won't excuse us because of our intentions; He will deal with and respond to our fruit.

Your voice is unique to you. It is a unique variation of sounds that converge to create your vocal fingerprint. Sure, many of us have similar-sounding voices, but no two people have the same voice. Our voices are as unique as our fingerprints, and just as we have an audible voice, we also have a writer's voice. The writer's voice is the manner in which we write. It is our own unique style; it is what distinguishes us from most writers. When readers read a book, they assign a voice and personality to the author based on what they've read. After reading one or more of an author's books, most avid readers will become familiar with, not just the author's voice, but the magnitude of power that flows through the author. This is why most readers prefer to read certain books while on the go and read others while at home in a relaxed state. The ones they read while relaxing are oftentimes in-depth and requires them to meditate on some of the book's content. In this, the readers have come to recognize the potency of each writer. Realizing that one writer's messages require time and deliberation to digest, the readers determined what state of mind they should be in before opening each author's books.

The Authority of the Scribe

Scribe: a member of a learned class in ancient Israel through New Testament times studying the Scriptures and serving as copyists, editors, teachers, and jurists.

    2 a: an official or public secretary or clerk.

      b: a copier of manuscripts.

(Reference: Merriam Webster)

The Hebrew word for "scribe" is "sopher," (also known as sofer) and it means: enumerator, secretary, scribe (Reference: NAS Exhaustive Concordance). In short, a scribe or author is a Kingdom secretary. The word "scribe" is synonymous with the term "wise men." A scribe creates a portal between the past and the present; this is a form of transcribing. Another form of transcribing is taking a written set of instructions from one realm to the next. "The LORD gave me the two tablets of stone written by the finger of God; and on them were all the words which the LORD had spoken with you at the mountain from the midst of the fire on the day of the assembly" (Deuteronomy 9:10).

The magnitude of power a scribe releases is determined by the depth of knowledge and height of revelation that the book holds. Power isn't always determined by what is said, but the ability to move readers can also be the aftermath of how something is said. For example, two professors can teach the same message, but receive different results. One professor is better at delivering and summarizing (describing) the message than the other. Additionally, the magnitude of an author's words is determined by the distance between the author's message and the reader's experiences. In short, how relatable is the author to the reader? Let's consider earthquakes. There are different types of earthquakes, all of which produce different types of movements. For example, one earthquake produces a jolting-like movement, while another is reported to produce more of a rolling sensation—like a ship at sea. The reason for this is, earthquakes produce different types of waves. The following was taken from the University of Wisconsin Eau Claire's website: "There are four different types of earthquakes: tectonic, volcanic, collapse and explosion.

1. A tectonic earthquake is one that occurs when the Earth's crust breaks due to geological forces on rocks and adjoining plates that cause physical and chemical changes.
2. A volcanic earthquake is any earthquake that results from tectonic forces which occur in conjunction with volcanic activity.
3. A collapse earthquake are small earthquakes in underground caverns and mines that are caused by seismic waves produced from the explosion of rock on the surface.
4. An explosion earthquake is an earthquake that is the result of the detonation of a nuclear and/or chemical device."

(Reference: University of Wisconsin Eau Claire/ Types of Earthquakes and Faults)

The way an earthquake feels is determined by the type of earthquake it is, how far the person experiencing it is from the epicenter, and where the person is standing or what the person is standing on. The same is true for the author/reader relationship. The manner in which a book's content moves any given reader is determined by how distant or close the person reading it is to the writer's experience, meaning, how relatable is the author's story from what the reader is experiencing or has experienced. Additionally, a book's potency is determined by where the reader is standing or what he or she is standing on. In other words, does the reader want to hear the whole truth and be free, or is the reader looking for another way to justify staying angry, hurt or ignorant? (Note: the word "ignorant" comes from the word "ignore" and it simply means that, even though knowledge and truth are present, a person chooses to ignore it in favor of another report.)

Every author's voice has a magnitude in the realm of the spirit. Every author's voice has a measure of reach in the natural and in the spirit. For example, our audible voices can be measured in hertz (range). The average human voice ranges from 80- to 250-hertz, but there are some people who (when excited) have vocal ranges of 3000-hertz. This means someone with a louder voice has more vocal reach. Nevertheless, an author's voice is not heard; it's felt. An author's faith will determine the pitch of his or her words in the realm of the spirit, after all, a faith-filled author will speak in the confidence and authority of Jesus Christ. The more faith an author has, the more reach that author's voice will have. To better understand the long arm of faith, let's visit the story about the faith-filled Centurion in Luke 7. "Now a centurion had a servant who was sick and at the point of death, who was highly valued by him. When the centurion heard about Jesus, he sent to him elders of the Jews, asking him to come and heal his servant. And when they came to Jesus, they pleaded with him earnestly, saying, 'He is worthy to have you do this for him, for he loves our nation, and he is the one who built us our synagogue.' And Jesus went with them. When he was not far from the house, the centurion sent friends, saying to him, 'Lord, do not trouble yourself, for I am not worthy to have you come under my roof. Therefore, I did not presume to come to you. But say the word, and let my servant be healed. For I too am a man set under authority, with soldiers under me: and I say to one, 'Go,' and he goes; and to another, 'Come,' and he comes; and to my servant, 'Do this,' and he does it.' When Jesus heard these things, he marveled at him, and turning to the crowd that followed him, said, 'I tell you, not even in Israel have I found such faith.' And when those who had been sent returned to the house, they found the servant well."

The Centurion man understood that he didn't need Jesus at his home physically in order for a miracle to happen. He understood that impartation doesn't always involve touch; impartation can be activated anywhere faith has been activated. What he did that day was to stand in the gap for his servant. Remember, in a few biblical passages, Jesus told others, "Your faith has made you whole." (Note: Jesus is the living Word, so when He spoke to people, no scribe was needed. He prescribed an action to couple with their faith and watched as their faith made them whole. A pill is powerless unless it's ingested; in other words, faith without works is dead). Nevertheless, in this particular passage, Jesus was granted access to the ailing servant through the Centurion's faith! This means that the Centurion stood in as an intercessor. Your readers will hang onto your words, looking for whatever it is they believe they need, whether it's healing, deliverance, peace, restoration or clarity. Your range (ability to reach them) will often be an important part of their processes. This means you should never discount the words that God put into your mouth to speak and into your heart to write. These words serve as anchors for drowning people. They aren't just well-written words on a page, designed to make you sound smart; they are literary life jackets for many of your readers. Think of it this way: a large number of people are drowning in a lake and Heaven sends a strategy to an inventor to help pull as many people out of that lake alive as possible. The inventor rushes into his laboratory and looks at all of the materials he's got. He has some solid and very durable material, but he reasons with himself that the material is not that attractive. He knows that the media will be at the lake, and even though he wants to save the people, he also wants to look good doing it. He sorts through all of his resources and comes across another material that isn't that durable, but it is attractive. He reasons with himself that he could easily market the new life jackets a lot better because the plastic-like material can be easily painted. He gets his team together, shows them the blueprint and they immediately begin making the new life jackets. After this, they rush to the lake wearing their attractive uniforms. Every man and woman jumps on his or her jet ski and rushes out to help the others. Because they'd chosen to use jet skis, each man and woman can only rescue one person at a time, so they rush onto the lake and start pulling people up one by one. They toss the flimsy life jackets to the rest of the people. The 24 employees manage to save 24 people before a huge wave surfaces and drowns the rest. Their life jackets were no match for the wave. This is what it looks like to Heaven when an author is more concerned with sounding intelligent and marketing himself or herself, as opposed to helping the many souls out there who are drowning in sin, hurt and debt. Sadly enough, in this day and age, authors seem to be putting more emphasis on the foolish things of this world as opposed to genuinely loving God's people.

Again, the patriarchs of old climbed mountains to have an encounter with God, but as authors, we pray until we hear back from God. God feeds us with one chunk of revelation, and we have to take that revelation and chew it until it becomes many words. We then take those words and publish them. Our readers will then take those words and feast on them. This is the process of ascending and descending. We ascend in prayer, fasting and worship. We then take what God has shared with us and transcribe it. Notice the word "scribe" is in the word "transcribe." The word "trans" means, "to cross." Think of the word translate. It simply means to cross language barriers so that two or more people can communicate. To transcribe is to cross barriers between God and man, thus, allowing God to communicate with His people. The prefix "de" means down. In short, the word "describe" can be translated this way: a scribe must bring and break down the revelation that God has shared with him or her. In other words, you must become Heaven's translator. To break down revelation, you must chew it until you are able to describe it in a way that your readers can consume it. This means that if you're writing a book and it's hard to understand, it may not be your season to write that book. You may have to chew on the revelation a few more weeks, months or years until you understand it so thoroughly that you can describe it to a baby. This is what God did with Jesus! He first sent His Logos (written) Word, and before long, His written Word manifested in the flesh. This was Jesus' process of descending to ascend.

The Words of the Scribe

Genesis 3:23-24: And the LORD God said, Behold, the man is become as one of us, to know good and evil: and now, lest he put forth his hand, and take also of the tree of life, and eat, and live for ever: Therefore the LORD God sent him forth from the garden of Eden, to till the ground from whence he was taken. So he drove out the man; and he placed at the east of the garden of Eden Cherubims, and a flaming sword which turned every way, to keep the way of the tree of life.

Genesis 11:1-9: And the whole Earth was of one language, and of one speech. And it came to pass, as they journeyed from the east, that they found a plain in the land of Shinar; and they dwelt there. And they said one to another, Go to, let us make brick, and burn them thoroughly. And they had brick for stone, and slime had they for mortar. And they said, Go to, let us build us a city and a tower, whose top may reach unto Heaven; and let us make us a name, lest we be scattered abroad upon the face of the whole Earth. And the LORD came down to see the city and the tower, which the children of men builded. And the LORD said, Behold, the people is one, and they have all one language; and this they begin to do: and now nothing will be restrained from them, which they have imagined to do. Go to, let us go down, and there confound their language, that they may not understand one another's speech. So the LORD scattered them abroad from thence upon the face of all the Earth: and they left off to build the city. Therefore is the name of it called Babel; because the LORD did there confound the language of all the Earth: and from thence did the LORD scatter them abroad upon the face of all the Earth.

Mark 16:14-16: Afterward he appeared unto the eleven as they sat at table, and rebuked them for their unbelief and hardness of heart, because they believed not them who had seen him after he was risen. And he said unto them, Go you into all the world, and preach the gospel to every creature. He that believes and is baptized shall be saved; but he that believes not shall be condemned.

In Genesis 3, after the fall of mankind, God drove Adam and Eve out of paradise. Some people believe paradise was in Heaven, while others believe it was on the face of the Earth, but the truth of the matter is, at that time, there was no separation of Heaven and Earth, after all, Heaven is dimensional. It's not a physical place; it is the atmosphere of perfection—a place where sin does not exist. It is a state of being, a state of mind; it is the very atmosphere of God. It is the mind of God manifested. "Heaven is not up; Heaven is all around us" (Apostle Bryan Meadows). So, when God drove Adam and Eve out of paradise, He simply evicted them from His presence. Remember what Satan told Eve when he deceived her. God told Adam and Eve not to eat from the Tree of the Knowledge of Good and Evil. He told them that *when* they did this, they would surely die. He didn't say "if". God used the word "when," after all, He knows the beginning from the ending because He is Alpha and Omega, the Beginning and the End. When Satan approached Eve in the Garden of Eden, he said to her, "Ye shall not surely die: For God doth know that in the day ye eat thereof, then your eyes shall be opened, and ye shall be as gods, knowing good and evil" (Genesis 3:4-5). Satan told Eve a partial truth; he told her that her eyes would open and she'd know good from evil. This part was true, after all, the name of the tree that they'd been commanded not to eat from was The Tree of the *Knowledge* of Good and Evil. The Bible goes on to tell us that Eve bit into the fruit and she gave some of it to her husband, Adam, who also bit into the lie. From there, their eyes were opened and immediately, their sin-conscious awakened. They realized that they were naked, and for this reason, they made themselves aprons from fig leaves. When God called out to Adam, He didn't find him in His will; instead, Adam and Eve both hid themselves from God. This means that their perspective of God had changed. The first question God asked Adam was, "Where are you?" This means that He could no longer locate Adam in holiness. He no longer found Adam to be in agreement with Him. "Can two walk together, except they be agreed?" (Amos 3:3) Once Adam fell out of agreement with God, he got evicted from the peace that surpasses all understanding. He shifted between two worlds mentally and spiritually, and found himself having to work towards what once came easy for him. This is similar to an heir of a fortune being evicted from his parents' house and cut out of their will because of the poor choices he keeps making. He suddenly finds himself without his parents' resources; he suddenly finds himself having to build his character from the ground up so that he could learn to respect his parents and everything they've built. Sure, his parents still love him and want the best for him, but they simply came to the realization that their sons' free roam of their finances and resources was only serving to destroy him one bad choice at a time. So, they had to give him what we call tough love. Without his parents' resources, the now fallen heir finds himself in a world unlike the one he once took for granted. He now has to work to pay his bills, and he soon discovers that most bill collectors are without mercy. As his character is built, he begins to better understand his parents and he begins to see their wealth from another perspective. He realizes that his parents' wealth is not just free money to do with as he pleases; it is the fruit of their blood, sweat, tears and sacrifices. It is the fruit of sleepless nights, broken promises and shattered dreams. As his mind changes, he begins to come back into agreement with his parents. Slowly, he begins to produce fruit of his own. All of what he'd learned in his parents' house had not been lost or forgotten. When he found himself having to endure the struggles of life without the funds or connections to fix those problems, he had no choice but to reach into the one thing he'd once taken for granted. He had to reach into his belly and pull out his father's knowledge and his mother's instruction. Reconciliation between the man and his parents isn't physical, after all, they never stopped being his parents. Reconciliation, for them, is mental; the son came into agreement with the parents, and when they saw him building his own integrity, career and family, the parents reinstated their son to their will.

In Genesis 8, God destroyed the Earth with a flood because man had become increasingly evil or, in layman's terms, man had become all the more separated from God in their hearts. "This people draweth nigh unto me with their mouth, and honoureth me with their lips; but their heart is far from me" (Matthew 15:8). In Genesis 9, the first sin after the flood was recorded. The Bible tells us that Noah planted a vineyard, and when that vineyard sprung up, Noah turned grapes into wine and had gotten drunk off that wine. After this, he'd fallen asleep naked in his tent. His son, Ham, saw the nakedness of his father, and instead of covering him, he went and told his brothers. This means that Ham attacked the platform (position) of his father by attempting to expose him. For this reason, when Noah woke up, he cursed Canaan, who was the son of Ham. After Noah's death, we see three races of people developing, and they were the Japhetites, the Hamites and the Semites. Nevertheless, they all still spoke one language. They were still walking as one people, one race and one culture, but each group had been named after their fathers, and they carried their father's blessings and/or curses. In short, both good and evil people dwelt together; there was no separation. Some theologians believe that Genesis 11 is really an extension or flashback of sorts of Genesis 10. They believe that the Japhetites, Hamites and Semites were named or divided only after they attempted to build the Tower of Babel together in Genesis 11. Nevertheless, there is no biblical evidence of this. Each tribe had been named after his father (obviously). Howbeit, the tribes lived, walked, worked and reasoned together. This is how we got to Genesis 11, whereas, God confused the language of man because the Bible says "the whole Earth" was of one language, meaning again, there was no separation of the Japhetites, Hamites and Semites. All of mankind walked together. They began to reason among themselves and decided that they didn't want to spread out across the Earth and do what Adam had been commanded to do. What was man's assignment? "Therefore the LORD God sent him forth from the garden of Eden, to till the ground from which he was taken" (Genesis 3:23). Mankind's job description hadn't changed; sin had not exempt man from his initial responsibility. Adam had initially been created to keep the Garden, but after he was evicted from paradise, his job was to still till the ground; he just had to do it from a different perspective (region of thought) or dimension. He now had to gather fruit from the sweat of his brow.

When the people decided to build the Tower of Babel, they were simply choosing not to spread out and do the work that had been commanded of them. They tried to illegally regain access to Heaven. Amazingly enough, this showed how separated they were from God in their thinking because they still believed that Heaven was a physical place, so they tried to build upward when, in truth, Heaven is not a few thousand kilometers above the clouds. Heaven is found in a changed heart; it is around us, and when we get saved, Heaven starts growing within us. It gets bigger and bigger in our bellies as we come back into agreement with God. Let's revisit

Genesis 11. Because the people were as one person, they didn't know the difference between good and evil; whatever one man suggested, everyone else would agree with. For this reason, the wheat had to be separated from the tares. God confused man's language and scattered them throughout the Earth.

In Matthew 13, Jesus shared the parable of the tares with His disciples. The story goes this way, "Another parable put He forth unto them, saying, The Kingdom of Heaven is likened unto a man which sowed good seed in his field: But while men slept, his enemy came and sowed tares among the wheat, and went his way. But when the blade was sprung up, and brought forth fruit, then appeared the tares also. So the servants of the householder came and said unto him, Sir, didst not thou sow good seed in thy field? From whence then hath it tares? He said unto them, An enemy hath done this. The servants said unto him, Wilt thou then that we go and gather them up? But he said, Nay; lest while ye gather up the tares, ye root up also the wheat with them. Let both grow together until the harvest: and in the time of harvest I will say to the reapers, Gather ye together first the tares, and bind them in bundles to burn them: but gather the wheat into my barn."

In Matthew 16, we find Jesus rebuking His disciples and then giving them a command to go out and preach the gospel. In this, He is pretty much telling them to bind the tares (unbelievers) and gather the wheat (good fruit/ believers) into His barn (church). Whereas, the language of man had once been confused, Jesus was in the process of reconciling us to the Father by first gathering us (believers) together in thought. Once we believed that Jesus Christ is the Messiah and once we believed the Word of God, we could then begin to gather together corporately in thought and in body. After all, when the Jews were separated from the Gentiles, there were many wicked leaders. These men (the scribes, Sadducees and Pharisees) brought God's people together only to lead them astray. For this reason, God found Himself having to confuse their languages all over again, but this time, He didn't change their tongues; He separated His people (wheat) from the tares by confirming what He'd already spoken. He sent His Son into this Earth, and those who believed upon Him were saved, meaning, the mental/ spiritual veil that once separated them from God was torn. The ones who did or do not believe upon the name of Jesus would be cast into the fire. Jesus didn't just preach to the Jews, He ministered to the Gentiles who'd been scattered across every region of thought. He offered salvation to the people inside and outside of the twelve tribes of Israel, including the Canaanites. He gathered all men in thought, and men who think together build together.

Most of the scribes who lived when Jesus physically walked the Earth wanted Him dead. You see, by gathering the people of God in thought, Jesus was scattering them abroad, sending His people (once again) to till the ground, but this time, the fruit that Jesus wanted them to bring back was men. He was dividing the wheat from the tares, thus making it easier to differentiate the two. Realizing that their positions of nobility and their wealth were both being threatened, the scribes, Sadducees and Pharisees conspired to have Jesus killed. After Jesus' crucifixion, buildings began to spring up all over Israel. They weren't as high as the Tower of Babel; instead, they were wide buildings where the Apostles would gather to reintroduce God's people to Heaven the right way. The gospel of Jesus Christ taught men to ascend mentally and spiritually into the presence of God, after all, God is Spirit. Those seated under the voices of the apostles learned that they could not access God with the works of their hands; they had to go down to go up. In other words, they had to accept Jesus Christ as their Lord and Savior. They also had to get baptized; this symbolized the going down of the old man and the resurrection of the new one. After this, they had to ascend into God's presence through humility (the bowing of the body and soul) and worship (the bowing of the spirit man). But none of this could be done without the Word of God; none of this would be done without the words of men. God needed and still needs people to spread the gospel of Jesus Christ. He still needs us to gather what was once scattered and to scatter what was once bound together by familiarity, fear and sin.

Nowadays, the harvest is still plenteous, just as the laborers are still few. As laborers for Christ, our job isn't to just write books, take pictures, and teach people of a like mind. Our job is to gather the lost and bring them back to God. We introduce them to the Word of God one word at a time. Our pens and our keyboards are our mics and our books are our platforms. No man can hear the words that are behind our exclamation points, nor do they quiver when we use bold fonts and capital letters. In short, it's not by our devices that men return to Jesus; we usher them back to Him with the Word of God. We also get their attention with our testimonies. As scribes, our God-given assignment is to till the ground. The ground (dirt), in the scriptures, represents the flesh of a man. It is to teach man to get his flesh under subjection so that the fruit of the Holy Spirit will begin to emerge from his life. One man plants a seed, another one waters it, but it is God who brings the increase. The seeds planted are words spoken and words written. It was through words that Satan led mankind astray, and it is by the Word that God reconciles man to Himself. What God is doing through teachers and scribes is inviting us back into the mindset that we were once evicted from. He has to do this by evicting every lie that Satan told us—every lie that we've inherited from our parents, grandparents and ancestors.

As a scribe, it is important to note that you are a liar (see Romans 3:4), and your heart is deceptive (see Jeremiah 17:9). Nevertheless, you've been washed clean of your sins through the blood of Jesus, even though you are still in the process of having your mind renewed. You are still ascending in thought. This is why it's important for you to tune into God's heart to get the content for your book. God often communicates with us through pictures or thoughts. We see the picture of what we want, what we can have and what we do not want. When this happens, a desire is formed. We then find two roads in front of us, both promising to lead us to that picture. One road is called Conformation and the other is called Transformation. "And be not _conformed_ to this world: but be ye _transformed_ by the renewing of your mind, that ye may prove what _is_ that good, and acceptable, and perfect, will of God" (Romans 12:2). The road Conformation is short and broad; it appears to be a shortcut to the promises of God, plus, on that road, we have plenty of company. Additionally, we can relate to many of the people on that road. The road of Transformation, however, is long and narrow. It is a rather lonely road to travel and there seems to be no end to it. On the road of Transformation, we find ourselves weary and constantly hearing messages that tell us not to faint or give up. As we journey down this road, many of the pictures we were chasing suddenly become distant memories as our hearts change. On this road, our perspectives are changed. On this road, we find many signs and wonders, but little relief. Nevertheless, we continue to build towards the pictures we want to see come to pass—the pictures that have yet to pass away. They, in a sense, become our personal, temporary heavens. We die (to ourselves) on the road of Transformation. We are resurrected on the road of Transformation. After our resurrections, we are then given the command to turn around and start chasing souls more than we were chasing the pictures that once enchanted us. These are the crossroads that many believers find themselves at because many of the images don't pass away, meaning, it is the will of God for us to have them. After having traveled towards our desires for so long, we find ourselves wanting to continue chasing the desires of our hearts, however, the road towards lost souls appears to take us in the opposite direction. Now, the money you wanted to build your dream house with has to go towards building a church. Now, the time you wanted to rest and relax now has to go towards writing a book. Howbeit, in all of this, God promises us that if we seek His Kingdom and all of His righteousness first, He will add all of "these things" to us (see Matthew 6:33). What are "these things"? They are our needs and desires; they are the pictures that managed to survive our journeys. Sometimes, to find our way to the Truth, we have to lead others to the truths that we know. Again, we do this with words and through demonstrations.

A scribe's words are the pieces of the scribe that he or she has chosen to share with others. They are the testimonies and knowledge acquired through the scribe's journey. In his own words, a scribe describes his encounters with God. With his words, a scribe leads the people of God to a conclusion. Understand this: a thought or a mental picture is nothing but a starting point, but the conclusion or manifestation of that thought is every man's destination. The space between the starting of the ignition and the destination is called the journey. On this road, there are many signs, with some of them being images while others are words. Every sign is not for you. For example, the stop sign on the other side of the highway is not for you if you're heading in a different direction. Sure, you can see the sign, but this doesn't mean you have to stop. The sign that reads "No U-Turn" is only there for the people who want to make u-turns; it is not for you if you plan to keep straight. The same is true in the realm of the spirit. Every prophecy released in a corporate setting may not necessarily be for you. Your assignment isn't to describe another man's journey; your assignment is to tell the people of God about Jesus and to share your personal journey to Him with them. After all, just like on any given freeway, there are many people on the same road that you're on, heading in the same direction, some of which are driving towards the same image. After you've arrived at a conclusion (destination), your assignment is to lead others to that same conclusion or to warn them so that they will turn around (repent). You do this with the words you choose; you do this through the revelation and testimonies you are willing to share with God's people.

Imagine this: Every mindset is a cage; some people have huge cages, while others have small ones. Some people can't even move around in the cages they've boxed themselves into. Every man's cage represents his reality, his way of thinking. In every cage, there is a Goliath. If you were to peer into these cages, you'd see people doing different things with their Goliaths. You'd witness one man fighting with his Goliath and winning. You'd witness another man being pummeled by his Goliath. You'd see a woman lying with her Goliath, while another guy is slowly morphing into a Goliath. Every man's diet consists of words, and the words that a man eats will determine the size of the cage he finds himself in and the position of his Goliath. Let's imagine that the people in these cages are your readers and you've been given the task of feeding them. Your assignment is to help them outgrow the cages they're in. Your words are the food that you use to feed each man. You start off by giving the man light food; this is the Word of God mixed with your experiences and the revelation God has shared with you. As each man grows, you pull a little more of yourself out so that the man can enjoy the Word of God at one-hundred proof. As you pull yourself out more, you pay attention to every man's reaction. In one cage, you see a man vomiting while his Goliath holds the barf bag; this means he can't ingest or digest the Word without some practical words (testimonies, parables) behind it. In another cage, you witness a woman lying next to her Goliath, trying to force feed him the Word of God. This means that she hasn't fully consumed the Word; she still believes she can save a man who doesn't want to be saved. In another cage, you see a man holding his Goliath's severed head. This means that he's outgrown the cage he's in, and it's time to place him in a larger cage. Understand this: one man's freedom looks like bondage, while another man's bondage looks a lot like freedom. What this means is, you can't be fooled by the fact that some men have become best friends with their Goliaths. You have to focus on teaching the Word of God in a way that your readers will understand. Your goal is to lead them to the measure of freedom you've received. You do this while eating the revelation that's being dropped into your cage. What you're doing is enlarging your territory through revelation and then sharing that revelation with everyone who's willing to peel back the pages of your book. No one should read your book and remain the same. As a matter of fact, as each person reads your book, their cages will start to shake. The magnitude of this earthquake will match the power of the words you've released, coupled with the amount of those words that they've consumed. This shaking is often mistaken for warfare when, in truth, it's the dismantling of demonic principles. For example, let's revisit the woman lying with her Goliath. As she reads your book, Goliath will begin to manifest his ugly ways. No longer will he play the doting boyfriend, but what's on the inside of him will reveal itself. What that woman will do is either keep reading the book and then taking in the Word of God at full proof, thus dislodging Goliath from her bedroom and her life, or she will close the book and Goliath will go back to impersonating a gentle giant. This is the power of a scribe's words. It is for this very reason that we cannot take our assignments lightly. Our assignment is to go into the world and preach the gospel. As scribes, we cover more ground with our words than we do with our feet.

Silence of the Saints

In my writers' classes, I often warn my students about the dangers of doors that have not fully been closed. These doors are the bridges that link their presents and their futures to their pasts; these doors allow what we call familiar spirits to enter, reenter or freely roam around in their lives, finances and relationships. Imagine, for example, you have a neighbor who can legally walk into your home at any given moment. The neighbor walks in, walks past you and heads straight into your kitchen, ignoring your presence altogether. He then reaches into your refrigerator and pulls out a few items. He makes himself a few sandwiches and then proceeds to head upstairs into your bedroom, where he makes himself comfortable before turning on your television set. He turns up the volume on the television so loudly that you have trouble hearing anything. When you walk into the room, you find him stretched out on your bed naked and howling. He's defecated on your brand new comforter, drawn profane images all over your walls, broke out the windows and is now wearing your most expensive jewelry. Would you be silent? Of course not! For most of us, he wouldn't have gotten too far past the living room door. Nevertheless, as offensive and disgusting as this picture is, it is a clear depiction of what demons do when they have access to our hearts because of doors that have not been properly shut. This is a picture of a personal Goliath. Let's revisit the scene. Would you date the guy? Would you lie next to him and ask him to share your own food with you? Believe it or not, many people do this; in short, they date their Goliaths. Let me explain.

I can't tell you how many women I've met who've started writing books, only to stop writing because they started dating. In some cases, a Goliath from their pasts reentered their lives, and because they had not fully forgiven their former lovers (the men bound by the Goliath) or repented of their fornications with the Goliath, that devil was able to put on its favorite costume (the flesh of their exes) and reenter their lives. It was then able to restart an unfinished conversation. From there, it appealed to the very same voids it had once appealed to or even created. It began to flatter, distract and romantically control them, all the while, enlarging and magnifying their voids. I've seen cases where women who had been walking strongly in the Lord suddenly reentered fornication when their exes returned to their lives. Of course, this is because they never truly repented of fornication, which means they were still there; they were still in the ungodly mindsets their exes had once abandoned them in. This is why that same spirit was able to locate, flatter and entice them back into the ditch God had once pulled them out of. These women then chose becoming girlfriends over becoming authors. Remember, the word "authority" comes from the root word "author," so in short, the women relinquished their authority to become some man's slave or, as we say in the western world, lover. All the same, I've seen women re-engage their Goliaths while dating men they've never dated before. In other words, they started courting the same demon in different men. They put their pens away and let the devil start writing on their hearts. He was able to pacify them by appealing to a void. A void is an empty room in the heart that has not been filled with the Word of God and the glory of God. It is a dark room; it is where demons hide and abide. For deliverance to be thorough, the light of revelation must come into that room, and from there, the Goliath hiding in it will be exposed and have no choice but to give back or restore whatever it has stolen. Proverbs 6:30-32 says it this way, "Men do not despise a thief, if he steals to satisfy his soul when he is hungry; but if he be found, he shall restore sevenfold; he shall give all the substance of his house. But whoso committeth adultery with a woman lacketh understanding: he that doeth it destroyeth his own soul."

The goal of the enemy is not just to bind the woman and stop her from writing, it is to use her to do further damage to the man who's entered or reentered her life as well. You see, fornication, according to 1 Corinthians 6:18, is a sin against one's own body, meaning, the woman becomes her lover's drug of choice. She allows him to abuse himself with her body, and she abuses herself with his body. Nevertheless, if you come across a woman who has abandoned her assignment to be entertained by romance, that woman will almost always say that the nature of her relationship is evangelism. Such souls will rarely admit to being soul tied, desperate and obsessed with marriage and motherhood. Once their Goliaths have once again abandoned or hurt them, they'll start their books again, only to hear another knock on their hearts. Do you see why so many men and women take their books to their graves? Satan knows how and when to silence a saint, especially if she keeps climbing into the closet with her skeletons. Please note that even though I referenced women, this is also applicable to men.

Which Goliath has Satan used to silence you? Is it a job that takes up large chunks of your time and peace? Is it the mother or father of your children? Or could it be that you are the Goliath in your own life?

If you were to walk into a nursing home today and speak with all of its residents, you would find men and women who should have written books long ago. They are treasure chests of wisdom who alone possess the key to the wisdom and experiences stored in their hearts. They have not shared those keys with anyone, and for this reason, they are preparing to take what they know to their graves with them. They'd hold you up for hours on end, detailing the stories of their lives. They'd tell you about their many trials, mistakes and regrets, and they'd also smile as they boasted about their victories. If you tell them that they should have written many books over the course of their lives, some of them would stare off into nothingness and say, "Yeah, I wish I had." What silenced them? After all, they won't mind sharing the stories of their lives with you. They were silenced by lust, ambition, opportunity, culture, fear and condemnation; many of them had been silenced by relationships or distracted by the problems that arose in those relationships. Many of them had been silenced in the workplace or by their parents. Sadly enough, some of them had even been silenced by their own children. Goliaths come in a variety of shapes, ages, colors, nationalities, responsibilities and positions. We've all been trained to think that a person who openly opposes us is an enemy, but this isn't always the case. An enemy is anyone who opposes your God-given assignment, whether openly or privately. Many of the people in nursing homes have married, bedded, worked for and even raised their Goliaths. The problem with most saints is, they think a Goliath has to be a loud, obnoxious person who is publicly trying to destroy them or their ministries when, in truth, a Goliath is oftentimes a Delilah. Delilah didn't openly or publicly criticize Samson; she privately plotted against him, while publicly acknowledging herself as his wife. She ran her fingers through the same locks that she told the Philistines to cut off. She'd stared into the same eyes that the Philistines would gouge out. She made love to the same body that she was assigned to assassinate. The point is, a Goliath or an enemy isn't always obvious; some of the most effective enemies are the ones who say, "I love you." The worst of them (yes, there are levels to enemies) are the ones who genuinely believe they love you. Think about two of David's greatest enemies: Goliath and Saul. Which one do you think was the worst? The answer is obvious; it was Saul, of course. This is because Saul was king over David and Saul believed that he loved the little shepherd boy when, in truth, he hated his potential. Any person who loves you, but hates your potential is an enemy of your future. Additionally, David had to endure Saul for several years, whereas, Goliath was just a pop quiz.

The enemy has many weapons that he uses to silence God's people, most of them being other people. If you're going to be successful at anything in this life, whether it is writing a book or a series of books, starting a business or raising a family, you have to open your mouth and address your Goliath. You shouldn't entertain the giant, even if he is gentle. Remember, the weapon of the scribe is the Word of God, but the thrust of that weapon is called obedience. Every time you strike a key, you are pushing against a wall of limitation—you are pushing up against your next level. Nevertheless, you have to keep striking that key until the wall comes down and your Goliath is no more.

Exodus 14:13: And Moses said unto the people, Fear ye not, stand still, and see the salvation of the LORD, which he will shew to you today: for the Egyptians whom ye have seen today, ye shall see them again no more for ever.

Goliath Exercise

This exercise is designed to help you identify your Goliath so you can stop identifying with your Goliath. Follow the instructions below and make sure that you're completely honest with yourself.

Step One: Open a document on your computer or use a sheet of notebook paper.

Step Two: Create a document like the chart below.

Age Range	Goliath (Villain)	Present or Past	Revelation
5-9	*Example:* Rejection	Past	Dad leaving wasn't my fault. He was fighting his own demons, so I forgave him and now, we have a pretty solid relationship.
10-14			
15-19			
20-24			
25-29			
30-34			
35-39			
40-44			
45-49			

Step Three: For every age range posted, list your Goliath(s) from those seasons. Please note that a Goliath doesn't have to be a person. It can be a series of challenges, for example, depression, obesity, fear or so on.

Step Four: Determine whether the Goliath is still present or not. Note: The presence of a comfort zone does not equate to the absence of a Goliath. Some people just learn to live with their giants.

Step Five: List what you took from each storm and how it has shifted the direction of your life. How did the storm affect your reasoning?

The purpose of this exercise is for you to not only locate yourself, but to locate your Goliath. You see, there are far too many people living with Goliaths that should have been slayed several decades or generations ago. Again, many people are married to their Goliaths, working for their Goliaths, paying child support to or collecting child support from their Goliaths, and the list goes on. If you don't identify what's chasing you, you'll never stop running.

Understanding Your Commitment

The Earth has five layers, with the fifth layer (the inner inner core) being a new discovery. This layer is pretty much still considered speculation, even though scientists believe they have enough evidence to prove its existence.

The Earth's layers are very similar to the Tabernacle of Moses. Please see the chart below.

Layers of the Earth	Tabernacle of Moses	Ascension Process	Man
Crust	Gate/ Entrance	Enter	Body
Mantle	Outer Courtyard	Sacrifice/Cleansing	Mind
Outer Core	Outer Courtyard	Praise	Soul
Inner Core	Holy Place	Worship	Man's Spirit
Inner Inner Core	Holy of Holies	Encounter	God's Spirit

Crust: The crust of the Earth is the surface of the ground. It is what covers the mantle; it is the layer we walk and live on. The crust is equivalent to the body of mankind. It is the outer shell, the part that people see. God told us in Romans 12:1 to present our bodies a living sacrifice, holy and acceptable onto God which is our reasonable service. Of course, this is how we begin our ascension into the presence of God.

Mantle: The mantle of the Earth is the hot layer just beneath the crust. It can be compared to the mind of a human, since it is the part we do not see (even though it's in constant movement), but are directly affected by. Additionally, it is similar to the outer court of the Tabernacle of Moses. It served as an entrance to the Holy Place. This is where the Brazen Altar (the place priests had to give their initial sacrifice) was found.

Outer Core: The Outer Core for a person is the entrance of his or her heart (this is why God told us to guard our hearts, for out of it pours the issues of life). The outer court that surrounded the Holy Place was oblong in shape and surrounded by thick (fine) white linen, supported by bronze posts. This setup looked like a large privacy fence.

The outer core has a magnetic pull 50 times the pull of the Earth's magnetic field. This means that even though it's not seen, it has the power to draw (or influence) the masses. Outer core writers are oftentimes the ones who don't get the recognition or notoriety that they should, nevertheless, their pull (influence) is more potent and long-lasting than the writers on the surface-level, as well as many mantled writers. The outer core can be compared to the heart (soul) of a man because it is where most of our movements take place. Of course, the heart of a man is the man's outer court and the gate to his holy place. Remember, the Holy Place is the place where the Menorah (lampstand), Table of Shewbread and the Altar of Incense were found.

Most Holy Place	Scripture
Menorah/ Lampstand	Psalm 11:105 (ESV): Your word is a lamp to my feet and a light to my path.
Table of Shewbread	Matthew 6:11 (ESV): Give us this day our daily bread. Matthew 4:4 (ESV): But he answered, "It is written, "Man shall not live by bread alone, but by every word that comes from the mouth of God." Matthew 26:26 (ESV): Now as they were eating, Jesus took bread, and after blessing it broke it and gave it to the disciples, and said, "Take, eat; this is my body."
Altar of Incense	2 Corinthians 2:15 (ESV): For we are the aroma of Christ to God among those who are being saved and among those who are perishing, to one a fragrance from death to death, to the other a fragrance from life to life.

Psalm 22:23 (ESV) reads, "Yet you are holy, enthroned on the praises of Israel." This

level is where we praise God. We praise Him with our knowledge of Him, but when we enter the realm of worship, true worship comes from the most intimate places in our hearts; it comes from our understanding or revelation of Him.

Inner Core: The inner core is the second least understood part of the Earth. It is believed to be as hot as the sun. What's interesting about the sun is that it's very similar to the Son of God, Jesus Christ. For example:

- When the sun rises, darkness flees.
- The sun's glory is too much for us to look upon.
- The sun has a very strong magnetic field.
- Scientists believe that someday the sun will consume the Earth.
- The sun is far bigger than the Earth.
- The sun is a huge star.
- The Earth orbits the sun.

The inner core can be compared to the Holy Place because it is similar to man's spirit. After we've bypassed our own thoughts, sacrificed our flesh and received a new heart and a new mind (soul), we will penetrate the most intimate part of ourselves: our spirit man. This is the place that no man has seen, but we know exists, even though scientists try hard to debunk this truth. When we initially start worshiping God, we worship from our intellect (our mind, will and emotions), otherwise known as our soulish man. Nevertheless, worship is a process of ascension. If we repent, shed our own agendas and surrender our very being to God, we will witness our spirit man taking over. This is when we begin to praise God outside of our intellect; this is when we no longer care for the things of the world or the opinions of the people around us. This is where our spirit gets involved and the sound of our praise lowers itself and becomes worship as we enter our most intimate place.

Inner Inner Core: The inner inner core is still a new discovery for scientists, but it goes without saying, it's been here all along. Because there is little known about the inner inner core; it is difficult (from a factual standpoint) to compare it with the Holy of Holies, nevertheless, I believe this is no accident on God's part. You see, in the Old Testament, only the High Priest could enter the Holy of Holies. This part of the temple was a mystery to most men. Nowadays, Jesus is our High Priest. Because He died for our sins, the veil is torn and we now have access to the presence of God. Hebrews 4:14-16 (ESV) reads, "Since then we have a great high priest who has passed through the Heavens, Jesus, the Son of God, let us hold fast our confession. For we do not have a high priest who is unable to sympathize with our weaknesses, but one who in every respect has been tempted as we are, yet without sin. Let us then with confidence draw near to the throne of grace, that we may receive mercy and find grace to help in time of need."

Lastly, the inner inner core can be compared to God's Spirit. This is the Holy of Holies within the believer; this is the place that the enemy cannot enter or possess. Understand that evil cannot *stand* in the presence of God. Pure worship leads us into an authentic encounter with God.

Philippians 2:10-11: That at the name of Jesus every knee should bow, of things in Heaven, and things in Earth, and things under the Earth; And that every tongue should confess that Jesus Christ is Lord, to the glory of God the Father.

A Writer's Pledge

As scribes, we must understand that our assignment isn't to lead readers into our presence, nor is it to showcase our wit and charismatic personalities. We are acting as priests, leading believers to the Most High Priest. We are delivering manna to the people in the wilderness. We are Elijah's ravens; we are the doves who bring hope to Noah. We are the Moses' of our generation, commanding Pharaoh to let God's people go, and when he refuses (as he will), we are the ones who lead God's people to freedom with our words. You see, we take the Word of God and chew it, and then, we feed it to our readers so they can digest it better. This process is called rumination. The word "ruminate" is defined by Google as, "chew the cud." The word "cud" is defined by Google this way: "partly digested food returned from the first stomach of ruminants to the mouth for further chewing." When we decide to write, we become parents, big brothers, big sisters, aunts and uncles. Sometimes, we temporarily become our readers' pastors, especially if they do not have a church home. We aren't just entertaining them with words; we are leading them with words. This is why we have to be careful that we do not lead God's people astray. Always remember that

Jesus will leave the 99 to recover one lost sheep, even if that sheep was led astray by an ambitious believer. We must make a pledge within ourselves that we will be careful with the words we teach and the way we teach them. One of the things I've discovered about writing is that, like life, the flesh is always warring with the Spirit, even competing with God for the pen. This is why we fast, pray, confess and surrender; and then, we repeat this process again and again.

You must not only understand the importance of writing godly, revelatory books that help to deliver, empower and encourage God's people, but you must also understand what you're going to experience as you delve into the many realms of revelation. What I've found is many aspiring writers never finish the books they'd started because they simply did not understand the resistance, warfare, emotions and changes they'd experienced when they started writing. Additionally, many did not understand Kingdom protocol and therefore, they legalized the warfare they experienced the minute they decided, not just to write, but what they were going to write about.

A Writer's Commitment

Three words that describe commitment are: responsibility, faith (or trust in the natural realm) and faithfulness. Without these three, there can be no commitment. Understand that the word "responsibility" comes from the word "response." When I have faith in something or someone, I'll respond by taking on more responsibility. For example, if I take a free painting class and I learn to paint, I can take the knowledge that I've acquired, start my own gallery, start my own paint class and proceed to make money from my new skill. Then again, I could say "thank you" to the teacher by taking on more responsibility in what the teacher is building. If I chose to take the knowledge and begin to build my own business with it, I have dishonored my teacher. How so? After all, many would reason that the teacher freely taught me, and once his or her job was done, I was free to do whatsoever I pleased with my new skill. And while this is a fact, it does not excuse me from the responsibility to show honor. Let's look at the story of the lepers. Luke 17:11-19 reads, "And it came to pass, as he went to Jerusalem, that he passed through the midst of Samaria and Galilee. And as he entered into a certain village, there met him ten men that were lepers, which stood afar off: And they lifted up their voices, and said, Jesus, Master, have mercy on us. And when he saw them, he said unto them, Go shew yourselves unto the priests. And it came to pass, that, as they went, they were cleansed. And one of them, when he saw that he was healed, turned back, and with a loud voice glorified God, And fell down on his face at his feet, giving him thanks: and he was a Samaritan. And Jesus answering said, Were there not ten cleansed? but where are the nine? There are not found that returned to give glory to God, save this stranger. And he said unto him, Arise, go thy way: thy faith hath made thee whole."

In this story, we see one of the (former) lepers responding to what Jesus had done for him. The other nine went on with their lives, never taking the time out to go back and thank the Lord for healing them. For this reason, ten lepers were healed, but only one was made whole. The word "whole" comes from the Hebrew word "shalem" and it simply means "complete." Philippians 1:6 reads, "And I am sure of this, that he who *began* a good work in you will bring it to completion at the day of Jesus Christ." In this, we come to understand that a good work can be started in us, but never completed because of our choices. Another example of a man responding to His deliverance is told in Mark 5. Mark 5:2-13 tells the story this way, "And when he was come out of the ship, immediately there met him out of the tombs a man with an unclean spirit, Who had his dwelling among the tombs; and no man could bind him, no, not with chains: Because that he had been often bound with fetters and chains, and the chains had been plucked asunder by him, and the fetters broken in pieces: neither could any man tame him. And always, night and day, he was in the mountains, and in the tombs, crying, and cutting himself with stones. But when he saw Jesus afar off, he ran and worshipped him, And cried with a loud voice, and said, What have I to do with thee, Jesus, thou Son of the most high God? I adjure thee by God, that thou torment me not. For he said unto him, Come out of the man, thou unclean spirit. And he asked him, What is thy name? And he answered, saying, My name is Legion: for we are many. And he besought him much that he would not send them away out of the country. Now there was there nigh unto the mountains a great herd of swine feeding. And all the devils besought him, saying, Send us into the swine, that we may enter into them. And forthwith Jesus gave them leave. And the unclean spirits went out, and entered into the swine: and the herd ran violently down a steep place into the sea, (they were about two thousand;) and were choked in the sea."

In this story, we witness deliverance taking place. Deliverance is an act of love. Jesus undoubtedly had compassion for the man who was bound, and instead of focusing on his outer appearance, Jesus spoke to the spirits that were in him, commanding them to come out. This was Jesus responding in love because of love.

Every great conversation involves more than one response. After having been set free, the man responded to Jesus, asking if he could travel with Him. Mark 5:18-20 reads, "And when he was come into the ship, he that had been possessed with the devil prayed him that he might be with him. Howbeit Jesus suffered him not, but saith unto him, Go home to thy friends, and tell them how great things the Lord hath done for thee, and hath had compassion on thee. And he departed, and began to publish in Decapolis how great things Jesus had done for him: and all men did marvel."

What we've witnessed was a free man responding to the One who'd set him free. He wanted to walk alongside Jesus and spread the gospel, but Jesus told him to stay in his country and share the gospel there. Thankfully, the man did this, and the scripture tells us that he began to "publish" in Decapolis the great things Jesus had done for him, and all the men marveled. Thanksgiving isn't just the verbal giving of thanks; it is assuming responsibility with the person, group or organization that has helped you in one way or another. A man's appreciation can always be measured by the amount of responsibility he is willing to assume with a right heart! The scripture also said he "published" his testimony. The word "publish" comes from the word "public." It simply means to make share or make plain. In short, the man who'd once been possessed by Legion took on the responsibility of evangelism.

One of the reasons it is hard for writers to finish their books is because many lack responsibilities outside of their normal nine to five jobs, parental responsibilities and other standard commitments. Many aspiring authors don't know what it means to commit to something other than what directly affects or affirms them. For this reason, it is hard for many to commit to finishing their books. Writing is not a struggle for a leader with a consistent schedule and a true heart of thanksgiving.

This is because forsaking self is a part of the leader's culture.

One of our commitments as authors is to provide sound doctrine to readers. This doesn't mean that we take the Bible and translate it; it simply means that we have to have what Jesus called an "ear to hear." In other words, we have to be able to hear from God, Himself. Our relationships with God cannot be tainted by selfish ambition, worldly lusts or a desire to please others. Many writers don't realize this, but the minute you decide to write a Christian book, you are affirming and disputing doctrine. If what you write lines up with the Word and heart of God, you are affirming the Word of God. If what you write does not line up with the Word, but leads people away from the truth, you are disputing the Word of God and writing what the Bible refers to as the "doctrine of demons." This is why we have to commit to learning the Word before we try to assume the responsibility to teach the Word. Sadly enough, there are many aspiring writers out there whose remote controls have more fingerprints than their Bibles. These writers are oftentimes ambitious, hurting or both. Please understand that a person who is hurting is going to always look for ways to relieve himself or herself of the pain he or she is in. After having tried talking to and about the people who've hurt them, many aspiring authors feel that their voices are intentionally ignored, so they see writing as a way to platform their pain and be heard. In other words, they take on the responsibility of writing, not because God called them to write, but because they're trying to force whoever it is that hurt them to give them their attention. These people will often disguise their books as Christian books, especially if the people who've hurt them are Christians. This is why one of the most important commitments we can make is to ensure that we are healed of past hurts. We all know that hurt people hurt people. Let's revisit the man at the tombs. While he was demonically bound, it goes without saying that he'd likely hurt many people, especially the ones who had once been closest to him. Jesus came along, set him free and sent him out to preach the gospel. Someone who'd been hurt by the once deranged man when he was bound sees him sharing the gospel in the marketplace one day and decides to get his revenge by telling others what the once bound man had done to him. Can you see how he could potentially be hurting the once bound man and stopping others from receiving their salvation, all because he chose to remain in unforgiveness? This is literally what happens today. People write books and attack folks who are either new creatures in Christ Jesus or on the way to becoming new creations in Christ, whether their journeys are evident or not.

God said that we (His people) perish from lack of knowledge. For this reason, one of our commitments is to get as much knowledge as we can. The more we know, the more we can teach and the more effective our messages will be. When an author is ignorant, the author will take from but not give to his or her readers. How so? The author will collect the money earned from each book sale and take up the readers' time, but the readers won't take much from the books; that is, if they take anything at all. I can't tell you how many books I've seen come across my desk that, simply put, had no peak or revelation in them. They were mountains of sentences stacked on top of one another with no point. They were a maze of words that led readers in circles with no real way out. When we take to the highway each day, just like the other drivers on the highway, we have a destination in mind. A book is supposed to be a journey for the readers as well, but there are many books on the market that lead readers nowhere. Your book should be filled with knowledge; your readers should be smarter after having read your book. There should be a point to your book; the book should climax at some point. Readers should be taken from one point to another until they reach the peak or highest point of the book. One of the greatest injustices that can be done to hard-working readers is that a writer takes their hard-earned money and time, and sells them the writer's unsubstantiated opinion. So, as a writer, make a commitment to not just being the author of a book, but commit to actually making your readers smarter, wiser and better prepared for this journey we call life. When your readers see that you're not just trying to take their money and get their applause, they will give you something far better than a few bucks and a good review; they will give you their respect and loyalty. Relationships have to be reciprocal to work. Make no mistake about it—every time someone purchases a book of yours, you have established a relationship with that person. The content of that book and the intent of the reader will determine if the relationship is functional or dysfunctional.

Remember that you are a literary Moses. Your assignment isn't to march God's people around a mountain, after all, doing so is called confusion. Google defines confusion this way: "the state of being bewildered or unclear in one's mind about something." The Israelites were in the wilderness (bewildered) for 40 years; what was supposed to be an 11-day journey ended up becoming a forty year hiatus. Your assignment isn't to get them to ascend the mountain. You have to commit to teaching them to speak to the mountain in faith until it moves. "For verily I say unto you, That whosoever shall say unto this mountain, Be thou removed, and be thou cast into the sea; and shall not doubt in his heart, but shall believe that those things which he saith shall come to pass; he shall have whatsoever he saith" (Mark 11:23).

Understanding Your Role

Authors have to serve in many roles, oftentimes, in one book. One of the ways to distinguish someone who's called to write versus someone who's ambitious is to pay attention to which roles they operate in while writing. For example, one of the roles of an author is to serve as an unofficial, temporary pastor to those who are not members of the author's church; that is, if the author has a church. This doesn't mean that the author takes the place of the reader's official pastor; it means that the author has taken a leadership role in the readers' life, and as such, is leading the reader with his or her words. There are several roles that a God-established pastor has, including being a shepherd. A shepherd feeds, protects and provides for his sheep. A true shepherd would never expose his sheep to a predator. Writers who are not called to write will expose their readers to false doctrines, demons, their own misguided beliefs, their insecurities, and so on.

True, God-established writers are:
- Swimmers
- Divers
- Historians
- Earthquakes
- Teachers
- Offerings

Swimmers

Like swimmers, authors have depths that they can swim to. Unlike swimmers, authors don't swim in water; we swim in revelation. Swimming is like running track underwater. It's a race against time for those who compete. For those who do not compete, it is a sport and a pastime.

As a writer, you will take your readers from one place to the next, using keystrokes. You will be able to take your readers from one side of knowledge to the next, helping them to stay afloat as they go. You're teaching your readers to swim in the understanding. This is why you have to know who your target market is. Authors who don't know their target audiences oftentimes drown their readers in words that are too rich for them, while others starve their readers of revelation.

Divers

Every diver is a swimmer, but not all swimmers are divers. Diving is more of the gymnastic style of swimming. Divers jump into water; they are judged by what they do above the surface before the leap, as well as what they do underwater. A diver is declared a winner by a panel of judges, whereas, swimmers are judged by the time on the scoreboard.

As a diver, you will take your readers to various depths of knowledge, but before they'll follow you, most people will want to see what you do above the surface in your own life. Can you carry the 110-pound talent that is your own flesh? What about your family? This is especially true for mature believers. Understand this: an author who cannot manage what's on the surface of his or her own life won't be able to safely navigate the depths and heights of revelation.

Some divers don't use diving as a sport; they use it for historical and scientific research. They go to the depths of seas, rivers and oceans, bringing to the surface many historical artifacts, wreckage and information that would have otherwise remained in their watery graves. As a writer, you will do the same. You will dive into the different realms of wisdom, knowledge and understanding, bringing new knowledge, confirmation and/or clarity to the surface. You will introduce and reintroduce your readers to history and help them to understand how so many believers have wrecked their lives and the lives of others. For example, various writers wrote the stories of how so many Jewish kings in the biblical days fell into the traps of Satan (see King David, King Solomon, King Saul, King Ahab, etc.). Many of these kings repented and recovered, while others did not. Scribes had to publish these accounts for us to understand man's history with God.

Historians

Knowledge is power. In truth, knowledge is the treasure chest of wealth. Underneath its lid, you will find understanding, discernment and every good thing this Earth has to offer.

Historians dive into knowledge, attempting to make sense of historical events, old cultures and outdated beliefs. You see, most of the people who lived in and through the events that have shaped our history are deceased. For this reason, we can't ask them what happened in their era; we have to dig for it and we have to make sense of it. This is why historians are like grave-diggers, searching for wealth in unusual places.

As a writer, you will be a historian; the great news is, much of what you unearth no longer requires an archaeologist; it is already on the surface. Now, you simply need to dig through the many books, articles, and of course, the Bible, to pull up facts and truths that many of your readers would never have ventured out to get on their own. You have to rightly divide the word of truth, throwing away information that does not align itself with the Word of God.

Psalm 42:7: Deep calleth unto deep at the noise of thy waterspouts: all thy waves and thy billows are gone over me.

Earthquakes

An earthquake shakes regions, countries, islands and large territories, shifting the land as it releases its power. Earthquakes have been known to divide continents, as well as bring them together. Earthquakes are often sudden, violent movements of the Earth's surface.

As a writer, you will become a natural disaster in the kingdom of darkness. You will expose what's underneath the surface, divide what needs to be divided and bring people together. Every God-established author's book has a certain degree of power. Some move families, others move nations. Then again, this is one of the ways we can distinguish a God-sent author from a self-sent author. Self-established authors only move flesh; they do not change lives—for the better, that is. Nevertheless, God-established authors bring down false religions, rearrange people's thinking and cause revivals to resurface.

Teachers

Many people underestimate the power of words, not taking into account that the Bible itself is a book of words. Jesus is the living Word. We use words to communicate. We see signs all around us; they include store signs, traffic signs, price tags, posters, and so on. Signs tell us where we should go, the speed we need to travel at, what to avoid and so on. Many of us look to the supernatural for help navigating through life, when God oftentimes answers us in the natural realm through words. We must remember that we are manifested words and everything around us is a word manifested.

As a writer, you will change the consistency of words. To teach mature, meat-eating believers, you will take words and form what is called revelation. For babes in Christ, you will break down words so that your readers can better digest them. This is what it means to be a teacher, and again, this process is called describing.

A kindergarten teacher will take the word "stop" and demonstrate what it means through natural movement. She may walk a few steps and suddenly stop walking. This is because the students in her care are still being introduced to words. They understand pictures better, so most of their books are filled with pictures. Their teacher's job is to help them to convert pictures into words. In summary, he or she will teach the children to chew the pictures and spit them out as individual words. A college professor, on the other hand, will take the word "stop" and show the many times that the word could have saved or changed someone's life. This is why it is important for us to know our levels as writers and teachers; this way, we won't write books for college-level saints using sentence structures and words that appeal to new believers, and vice versa.

Offerings

Another way to tell the difference between a God-established writer versus a self-sent writer is by looking at the writer's consistency. Our consistency isn't just a revelation of what we do faithfully; it is a revelation of our own states. It is a revelation of our composition. For example, water cannot flow through a rock because they have different compositions. Water can flow on a rock, under a rock and around a rock, but it cannot flow through it unless, of course, the rock is permeable. Nevertheless, water can flow through water and a rock can break another rock if enough pressure, distance and velocity are placed behind it.

As authors, we cannot feed our readers if we are unable to match (relate to) their composition. For example, a woman who has never been married cannot effectively teach married women how to stay married. She can give some great advice to married women, but she hasn't experienced many of the challenges that married women face daily. This means that if she were to write a book to married women, she would be like a rock thrown into water. Sure, she may cause a splash, but her impact would be short-lived; plus, it wouldn't be big enough to shift nations. An author who happens to be married could write a book to married women and that book could have the effects of an earthquake in the realm of the spirit. It can establish families, re-establish families, empower families, and if it's written by someone who is not ready or sent by God to write, it could destroy families. Again, words are powerful enough to move people, places and things.

As authors, we have to become what we are offering. We offer up our testimonies, our lessons, our hurts, and our histories for others to learn from. We pour ourselves out, trusting that God will refill us and use what we've experienced to help others. One of the most overlooked stories in the Bible is the story of the two prostitutes. **1 Kings 3:16-28 (ESV):** Then two prostitutes came to the king and stood before him. The one woman said, "Oh, my lord, this woman and I live in the same house, and I gave birth to a child while she was in the house. Then on the third day after I gave birth, this woman also gave birth. And we were alone. There was no one else with us in the house; only we two were in the house. And this woman's son died in the night, because she lay on him. And she arose at midnight and took my son from beside me, while your servant slept, and laid him at her breast, and laid her dead son at my breast. When I rose in the morning to nurse my child, behold, he was dead. But when I looked at him closely in the morning, behold, he was not the child that I had borne." But the other woman said, "No, the living child is mine, and the dead child is yours." The first said, "No, the dead child is yours, and the living child is mine." Thus they spoke before the king.

Then the king said, "The one says, 'This is my son that is alive, and your son is dead'; and the other says, 'No; but your son is dead, and my son is the living one.'" And the king said, "Bring me a sword." So a sword was brought before the king. And the king said, "Divide the living child in two, and give half to the one and half to the other."

Then the woman whose son was alive said to the king, because her heart yearned for her son, "Oh, my lord, give her the living child, and by no means put him to death." But the other said, "He shall be neither mine nor yours; divide him." Then the king answered and said, "Give the living child to the first woman, and by no means put him to death; she is his mother." And all Israel heard of the judgment that the king had rendered, and they stood in awe of the king, because they perceived that the wisdom of God was in him to do justice.

In this story, King Solomon was faced with a situation that he'd never experienced. In other words, he had no knowledge of what it felt like to have a child stolen from him, so he could not understand either woman's plight. Where there is no knowledge or understanding, wisdom is needed to judge rightfully. Wisdom is the supernatural knowledge that flows from the heart of God. To receive wisdom, Solomon had to become wise; he had to become the very thing in which he needed to pour out. What does this mean? It means that he had to apply an action. The book of Proverbs is full of instructions on how to become wise and it demonstrates the characteristics of wise men and women. Proverbs 29:11 (ESV), which happens to have been written by King Solomon, reads, "A fool gives full vent to his spirit, but a wise man quietly holds it back." Proverbs 1:5 (ESV) reads, "Let the wise hear and increase in learning, and the one who understands obtain guidance." Proverbs 13:20 (ESV) reads, "Whoever walks with the wise becomes wise, but the companion of fools will suffer harm."

King Solomon had to listen more, instead of speaking. He had to be self-controlled, not giving full vent to his feelings every time his emotions shifted. He could not walk in the company of evil men, nor could he give himself over to much wine. These are some of the actions he executed. When he became wise, he opened himself up for wisdom and was able to pour it out of his own consistency.

As authors, we have to address each readers' experiences on three levels:
- **Knowledge:** The root word of "knowledge" is "know." It means we must have experienced whatever it is that we are teaching or, at minimum, our knowledge has to be established by facts or truths, not speculations. This means that, even though we may no longer be rocks, we can still shatter stony

hearts.

- **Understanding:** Understanding is a revelation of what we know. It is a breakdown of knowledge. A person does not have understanding until he or she can not only retain knowledge, but teach whatever it is that he or she has knowledge of. I can't teach it if I don't understand it. To understand something, I must ruminate it until I'm able to teach it plainly to others.
- **Wisdom:** Wisdom is above knowledge and it surpasses understanding. It is the knowledge of God given to man in a state in which the man can receive and retain it. It is the revealing of a mystery—the illumination of what was once hidden. It is an open invitation into the heart of God.

To pour out knowledge, we have to have knowledge. To pour out understanding, we must first understand or better yet, stand under the knowledge we are pouring out. To pour out wisdom, we must first become wise. Again, as writers, we have to become the very state in which we intend to flow. Think about humans. Our (natural) fathers were first sperm cells before they became men who were able to release sperm cells. They once had fathers; this is what legalized them to become fathers. We can only flow in the state in which we are or what we've been.

Understanding Your Level

It is one accomplishment to understand Kingdom protocol, but it is also just as advantageous for us to understand levels. One of the biggest problems we have nowadays is that many writers don't understand what level they are on as teachers. For this reason, we see an increase of people attempting to write books on subjects they do not truly understand. As a result, many people who are truly called to write abandon their books because of the experiences they had when they attempted to write. As a publisher, editor and writers' coach, one of the most common excuses I hear from aspiring writers is, "I stopped writing because I was going through something at that time." Even when the storm ends, the writer is oftentimes afraid to start back writing. The reason for this is most writers start to notice the correlation between them writing and their warfare. Most people don't understand that before a writer or teacher can produce an earthquake (revival), that writer has to overcome an earthquake of that same magnitude. In other words, the writer or teacher has to be revived. All the same, writing forces writers to stop moving around physically. The author-to-be must sit down and focus, not just on what he or she is writing, but the author must search out his or her heart to obtain knowledge, understanding and memories that will be beneficial to readers. What then happens is, the writer will feel the aftershocks of every earthquake he or she has not yet overcome. These aftershocks are oftentimes mistaken for warfare; they are regrets, memories and experiences the writers have never received closure in.

There are different sounds and movements on every level that we write. Every writer has a level; every writer has a sound, and every writer has a capacity. Your capacity is determined by your measure of faith, and your level is the result of your faith. This means that your ability to move the people of God and shift paradigms, atmospheres, continents, powers, principalities, rulers and Heaven is the direct result of your faith. Your sound, as a writer, isn't your voice; it is the measure of your authority in the realm of the spirit—it is the weight of your words. One way to measure one's voice in the spirit is to note how demons respond to it. Consider how the demon responded to the sons of Sceva when they tried to cast it out of a man. Acts 19:15-16 (ESV) reads, "But the evil spirit answered them, "Jesus I know, and

Paul I recognize, but who are you?" And the man in whom was the evil spirit leaped on them, mastered all of them and overpowered them, so that they fled out of that house naked and wounded."

The demon did not recognize the sons of Sceva, which means they did not pose a threat to the demonic kingdom. Ahab recognized Elijah, even though Elijah was not a king. Saul recognized David, not just by face, but he saw his potential. When Jesus would come in contact with demon-possessed people, He would often command the demons to be silent because they would recognize Him and proclaim who He was. This means that our levels aren't determined by our titles; they are determined by who and what responds to and acknowledges us. One parable that Jesus told was the parable of the wedding feast.

Luke 14:7-11 (ESV): Now he told a parable to those who were invited, when he noticed how they chose the places of honor, saying to them, "When you are invited by someone to a wedding feast, do not sit down in a place of honor, lest someone more distinguished than you be invited by him, and he who invited you both will come and say to you, 'Give your place to this person,' and then you will begin with shame to take the lowest place. But when you are invited, go and sit in the lowest place, so that when your host comes he may say to you, 'Friend, move up higher.' Then you will be honored in the presence of all who sit at the table with you. For everyone who exalts himself will be humbled, and he who humbles himself will be exalted."

One of the lessons to take from this parable is that we should never honor ourselves, but should instead allow others to honor us. This is especially true for writers. If we don't know our level, we'll try to write on someone else's level, only to find ourselves being publicly corrected, scorned and humbled.

The Earth is comprised of mostly iron, nickel and magnesium. Every metal found in the inner core of the Earth is found on the surface (crust). If it wasn't, we wouldn't know the properties of the metal to determine what's on each level, given the fact that mankind has never gone past the Earth's crust. Scientists draw their conclusions about what's in the Earth by measuring seismic waves. What is a seismic wave? Britannica defines it this way:

"vibration generated by an earthquake, explosion, or similar energetic source and propagated within the Earth or along its surface. Earthquakes generate four principal types of elastic waves; two, known as body waves, travel within the Earth, whereas the other two, called surface waves, travel along its surface. Seismographs record the amplitude and frequency of seismic waves and yield information about the Earth and its subsurface structure." (Britannica/ Seismic Wave).

What is an earthquake? USGS explains,

"An earthquake is what happens when two blocks of the earth suddenly slip past one another. The surface where they slip is called the fault or fault plane. The location below the earth's surface where the earthquake starts is called the hypocenter, and the location directly above it on the surface of the earth is called the epicenter.

Sometimes an earthquake has foreshocks. These are smaller earthquakes that happen in the same place as the larger earthquake that follows. Scientists can't tell that an earthquake is a foreshock until the larger earthquake happens. The largest, main earthquake is called the mainshock. Mainshocks always have aftershocks that follow. These are smaller earthquakes that occur afterwards in the same place as the mainshock. Depending on the size of the mainshock, aftershocks can continue for weeks, months, and even years after the mainshock!" (Reference: USGS/ The Science of Earthquakes).

John, the Baptist, was an example of a foreshock. As writers, we are oftentimes foreshocks, warning and/or preparing others for what or who is to come. A mainshock, in the writing or teaching world, is the fulfillment of a prophecy. Jesus was the mainshock that John, the Baptist, spoke of. When He died and was resurrected, He left aftershocks that we are still feeling to this day. Even hell feels those aftershocks! How do we know this? James 2:9 tells us, "Thou believest that there is one God; thou doest well: the devils also believe, and tremble." Additionally, when Jesus' Spirit left His body, the Bible tells us that the Earth shook, meaning, there was an earthquake. Understand this: when the Spirit of God moves upon the Earth, the Earth trembles.

Matthew 27:50-54 (ESV): And Jesus cried out again with a loud voice and yielded up his spirit. And behold, the curtain of the temple was torn in two, from top to bottom. And the Earth shook, and the rocks were split. The tombs also were opened. And many bodies of the saints who had fallen asleep were raised, and coming out of the tombs after his resurrection they went into the holy city and appeared to many. When the centurion and those who were with him, keeping watch over Jesus, saw the earthquake and what took place, they were filled with awe and said, "Truly this was the Son of God!"

Earthquakes are symbolic of a shift. In the natural, an earthquake forms when two plates underneath the Earth's crust move past one another. As the plates rub up against one another, an earthquake ensues. If there's a continent on top of the plates, the collision forms what we know as a mountain or a series of mountains. In the biblical days, God used mountains as meeting places between Him and whomever He'd called to ascend them. He gave Moses the Ten Commandments at the top of Mt. Sinai. He told Abraham to go to the land of Moriah and offer his son, Isaac, on one of the mountains of that land (Mt. Sinai). Of course, we know that God sent an angel to stop Abraham from following through with his son's sacrifice. Jesus' transfiguration took place on a high mountain. When the Israelites murmured and complained, they went in circles around a mountain for forty years, never being able to ascend or move the mountain. So mountains are significant in the Kingdom. When Jesus died, a shift happened in the realm of the spirit. Darkness collided with light and hell could no longer hold many of the saints who'd passed away before Jesus' coming.

The word "mountain" comes from the word "mount," which means to climb or pile up. A mountain is nothing but a pile of rocks and dirt. God created man from dirt (see Genesis 2:27) and the Bible refers to Jesus as the stone in which the builders rejected (see Psalm 118:22, Matthew 21:42, Acts 4:11), a stone of stumbling and rock of offense (Romans 9:33, 1 Peter 2:8), a tested stone and costly cornerstone (see Isaiah 28:16), a choice stone (1 Peter 2:6), a spiritual rock (1 Corinthians 10:4) and the rock on which God would build His church (see Matthew 16:18). So, it's safe to say that most spiritual earthquakes occur when man or flesh has an encounter with God. When God wanted to meet with Elijah, He told him to go and stand on a mountain. 1 Kings 19:11-12 (ESV) reads, "And he said, 'Go out and stand on the mount before the Lord.' And behold, the Lord passed by, and a great and strong wind tore the mountains and broke in pieces the rocks before the Lord, but the Lord was not in the wind. And after the wind an earthquake, but the Lord was not in the earthquake. And after the earthquake a fire, but the Lord was not in the fire. And after the fire the sound of a low whisper." As we can see, the presence of God produced an earthquake. Again, mountains form when two plates move past one another underneath the earth's crust. God passed by Elijah and this produced a strong wind, an earthquake and fire. There is sin in the Earth; we know this. There is bloodshed on almost every inch of ground we step on, and because of this, the Earth trembles in God's presence.

Psalm 104:32: He looks at the Earth, and it trembles; He touches the mountains, and they smoke.

There are writers (and teachers) who produce similar effects in the world's system as well as the body of Christ. Every writer produces an effect similar to seismic waves. A writer's God-given assignment is displayed in:

- **what the writer has overcome** (What has the writer moved past?)
- **the writer's impact** (What has the writer collided with, and what did it form in the writer's life?)
- **the writer's personal life** (Is the writer creating, ascending, circling or avoiding the mountains in his or her life?)
- **the level of impact the writer has on the people** (When the writer writes or speaks, do the people proclaim that God surely is in or with the writer? Who gets the glory—the writer or God?)
- **the level (rank) of the people impacted by the writer's teachings** (Has the writer been granted the authority to confront his or her own Pharaoh or Goliath, or is someone else speaking on the writer's behalf?)
- **the level (rank) of devils that respond** (Does Pharaoh respond to the writer, or is the writer still dealing with Pharaoh's taskmasters?)
- **the amount of people the writer has the ability and/or potential to reach** (How many people are influenced by the writer's voice, and how far does the writer's influence stretch? Is it local or global?)

What the Writer has Overcome

Imagine this: David goes inside his home and begins to write a book about how to overcome Goliath, all the while, Goliath is in his living room forcing David's wife to wash his feet. In order for Goliath to have any measure of authority in David's home, he'd first have to bind David. To overcome something, you must place it beneath you. When two plates collide in an earthquake, one plate rises above the other. The one that goes under is destroyed because it goes into the mantle of the Earth; from there, it is melted down because of the heat. David had to <u>over</u>come Goliath before the story could be written for you and I to read, meaning, he had to place Goliath under his foot. Before decapitating Goliath, David likely placed his foot on the giant's head. The head of a person or thing represents its authority. By cutting off Goliath's head, David demonstrated the dismantling of the Philistines' authority. A writer who has not overcome anything is un<u>author</u>ized, meaning, the writer does not possess or has not demonstrated his or her authority.

The Writer's Impact

In the natural, a tool called a Richter Scale is used to measure the magnitude of an earthquake. The following magnitude scale was taken from Michigan Tech's website.

Magnitude	Earthquake Effects	Est. Number Each Year
2.5 or less	Usually not felt, but can be recorded by a seismograph.	900,000 **(Minor Earthquake)**
2.5 to 5.4	Often felt, but only causes minor damage.	30,000 **(Minor to moderate Earthquake)**
5.5 to 6.0	Slight damage to buildings and other structures.	500 **(Moderate Earthquake)**
6.1 to 6.9	May cause a lot of damage in very populated areas.	100 **(Strong Earthquake)**
7.0 to 7.9	Major earthquake. Serious damage.	20 **(Major Earthquake)**
8.0 or greater	Great earthquake. Can	One every 5 to 10 years

	totally destroy communities near the epicenter.	**(Great Earthquake)**

(Reference: Michigan Tech/ UPSeis/ Earthquake Magnitude Scale)

A writer's impact will always be seen in how people respond to what the writer says. Understand this: everything that occurs in the natural is a response to something in the spirit. So, to measure your level of impact as a writer, you will have to see who or what responds to you. If you're a minor earthquake, for example, the effects of what you write won't be largely felt. It may be felt in your family, but not in your community; or it may be felt in your community, but not your city as a whole. This doesn't mean you're a bad writer; it simply means that the measure of your assignment (right now) is more local or centralized than it is universal. It means that you may, spiritually speaking, have the jurisdictional reach of a city police officer or a state patrolman, but not the reach of a FBI agent. Again, this is okay. A police officer's job is important, and the officer does possess a measure of authority, just like the FBI and CIA both possess a measure of authority. No governmental entity possesses absolute authority except the Kingdom of God. A local cop's authority is not as widespread as that of a highway patrolman or a FBI agent, nevertheless, you will rarely, if ever, hear an officer complaining about this. The reason is, most officers learn to respect their metron or jurisdictional reach, and the ones who don't usually end up jobless or on the wrong side of the law. Jesus was a great earthquake. Apostle Paul was a major earthquake. Elijah was a major earthquake. Abraham was a major earthquake. David was a strong to major earthquake. Moses was a major earthquake. We can measure each man's impact based on the number of people affected by his life and by the duration of the aftershocks.

The Writer's Personal Life

There are some believers who move mountains, believers who ascend mountains, some believers who go around mountains and some believers who are mountains. What's the difference? Those who ascend mountains are the ones who love God, but often go the long way around a problem. In some cases, this means that the believer is somewhat religious, since man no longer has to meet with God at the top of a mountain. Believers who move mountains are the ones who have faith; they are the ones who have personal, intimate relationships with God. The ones who go around mountains are the ones who murmur, complain and gossip because they have little to no faith. They are the followers of religious movements and people; they are the ones who keep trying to make God serve them, rather than them serving Him. For this reason, they find themselves in cycles of defeat, constantly returning to the very thing they thought they'd been delivered from. And finally, there are the ones who are mountains. Mountains not only represent meeting places, but they can represent problems when they stand between a believer and his/her destination (destiny). This is why God said that we can tell a mountain, "Be thou removed, and be thou cast into the sea" (see Mark 11:23). He also said in Mark 9:42 (ESV), "Whoever causes one of these little ones who believe in me to sin, it would be better for him if a great millstone were hung around his neck and he were thrown into the sea." The mountain referenced in Mark 11 is anything or anyone that stands between a believer and his or her assignment. Goliath was a mountain for David. Saul was another mountain David had to overcome. Jezebel was Elijah's mountain. Since he didn't overcome her, God raised up someone who would: Jehu. Instead of commanding that she (Jezebel) be cast into the sea, Jehu had Jezebel's servants to cast her out of her window onto the ground below. Haman was a mountain for the Jews and Queen Esther was the sweet apostolic voice who God raised to move him. Her humility moved God which, in turn, provoked Him to move (or change) the king's heart. The king then (legally) moved against the force that had been moving against the Jews.

Proverbs 21:1: The king's heart is in the hand of the LORD, as the rivers of water: he turneth it whithersoever he will.

With that being said, the measure of a believer's faith or power is demonstrated in his or her own personal life. When David petitioned King Saul to let him fight Goliath, he presented a verbal resume to him. He told the king that he'd killed a lion and a bear with his bare hands (see Samuel 17:26). David was detailing something strong he'd overcome in his personal life. The same is true for a believer. Writers who waste their time talking about their problems, instead of overcoming them are slaves with pens. Remember, the first talent that God gives us is ourselves. We must first overcome our own flesh before we can help others. When David talked about killing a lion and a bear, he was pretty much showcasing his talent. A gold talent weighed 110 pounds; the average male lion weighs in at well over four hundred pounds. The average male grizzly bear weighs around six hundred pounds. David was showing that he had not only learned to manage his own weight, but that he'd faced and overcame problems far bigger than himself.

Level of Impact Writer Has on the People

When Jesus' Spirit left His body, an earthquake ensued and the dead saints began to come out of their graves. Many of the people who saw this miracle proclaimed that surely, He is the Son of God. There are two seasons for every believer and they are: seedtime and harvest. During seed time, there is no fruit, therefore, it is hard for onlookers to determine who a sower is and if the sower is worthy of their attention. During Jesus' time here on Earth, He grabbed the attention of many, so His level of impact was felt throughout all of Israel and abroad. Nevertheless, there were many who refused to believe that He was and is the Son of God, so they opposed Him openly. However, many of them were present when the earthquake took place and they could no longer deny His majesty when they saw the harvest (saints rising from the dead).

A believer's impact is always made evident through sound. If I were to throw a bunch of rocks into a crowd of people, the people impacted would let out sounds. I'd hear a number of varying sounds every time a rock came in contact with a person. My level of impact could be measured by the number of people I hit, but it is more effectively measured by the sounds that are emitted from the people I hit, the force behind my throw and the distance between myself and the people impacted. For example, I can throw a small rock into a crowd and get a faint "ouch." Of course, that "ouch" could be exaggerated, nevertheless, the person impacted would be more offended than they were hurt. The rock would have barely grazed the person it came on contact with. I can throw a few medium-sized rocks into a crowd and not only get a few "ouches," but I'd also hear what was in the heart of each person impacted. For example, I'd likely hear profanity and threats. I could then throw a large rock into a crowd and the sound that would be emitted would likely be louder and it would permeate the atmosphere longer because the person impacted would moan in pain for a period of time. The people surrounding that person would even respond to me with loud sounds and possibly even violence. With that being said, a person's impact will always be made evident through, not just the sounds emitted from the people impacted by that person's ministry, but by the range and longevity of the sounds emitted by the people who were impacted and the people (family, friends) surrounding them.

Level (Rank) of People Impacted

In the writing world, we understand that we have what's called a target audience. These are the people who are most likely to purchase and glean from our teachings. For example, books written to singles are oftentimes not in-depth books; they are designed to reach the crust (surface-level) saints, but books on demonology, legalities and the like are more in-depth and would reach people who rank higher (in the realm of the spirit). Again, there's nothing wrong with surface-level teaching, just as there is nothing wrong with surface-level readers; it's simply a matter of where we are in Christ at any given moment. There are people who, for example, are mantled believers who love to read surface-level books just as much as they love to glean from books that are more in-depth. You can easily get a picture of their ranks based on the content of their libraries and the rank of the people who respond to what they teach.

Level (Rank) of Devils that Respond

We understand that demons come in rank. A few scriptures to consider are Ephesians 6:12, Romans 8:38-39, Colossians 1:16-17, Matthew 17:19-21.
Ephesians 6:12: For we wrestle not against flesh and blood, but against principalities, against powers, against the rulers of the darkness of this world, against spiritual wickedness in high places.
Romans 8:38-39: For I am persuaded, that neither death, nor life, nor angels, nor principalities, nor powers, nor things present, nor things to come, nor height, nor depth, nor any other creature, shall be able to separate us from the love of God, which is in Christ Jesus our Lord.
Colossians 1:16-17: For by him were all things created, that are in Heaven, and that are in Earth, visible and invisible, whether they be thrones, or dominions, or principalities, or powers: all things were created by him, and for him: And he is before all things, and by him all things consist.
Matthew 17:19-21: Then came the disciples to Jesus apart, and said, why could not

we cast him out? And Jesus said unto them, Because of your unbelief: for verily I say unto you, If you have faith as a grain of mustard seed, you shall say unto this mountain, Remove from here to yonder place; and it shall remove; and nothing shall be impossible unto you. But this kind goes not out but by prayer and fasting.

What we learn from the aforementioned scriptures is that there are principalities, powers, and rulers that sit upon the thrones in the heavenlies, exercising dominion over the people they've bound. Some demons are cast out easily; other higher-ranking ones require more than a, "Come out of him you foul spirit," command. They require fasting *and* prayer.

We understand that there are rulers in high places in our government, in Hollywood and in every high place that has not been submitted to God. Let's say, for example, that there was a demon-bound, internationally known media mogul making 39 million dollars a year. That celebrity uses his position to encourage promiscuity, unforgiveness and divorce. Of course, we know that such a character is being used by demons; his heart is nothing but a demonic throne occupied by what we call a strongman. Another media personality rises up. This guy has a radio show that is popular in his city, but his reach is not global. He makes half a million dollars a year and happens to be God-fearing.

One day, the locally known radio personality decides to attack the internationally known media mogul via his radio show. He does this every few days for a year. A year later, the news report that the international mogul is suing another guy for slander. The guy being sued has a company with worldwide influence and he averages 22 million dollars a year. Additionally, he's only attacked the media mogul one time via his blog. Why didn't the media mogul go after the guy who attacked him regularly on his radio show? Why did he, instead, direct his attention to the guy who attacked him one time via his blog? This has everything to do with rank, reach and influence. The small-town radio personality didn't have enough impact (reach) to get the media mogul's attention. The demons in the media mogul don't necessarily feel threatened by the radio jockey. However, the other guy had enough influence and money to put a dent in the devil's plans.

I recently read an article about the President of Tanzania banning young mothers from returning to school. A young woman named Petrider Paul decided to take up the cause and fight to have young women's rights reinstated. She filed a petition on Change.org and has since accumulated close to 56,000 signatures. The population of Tanzania is over 55 million people strong, meaning, the President rules over 55 million people. Fifty-six thousand signatures are just a little more than one percent of the people in Tanzania! What this means is to grab the President's attention, Ms. Paul will need to reach more people (quantity) or reach higher ranking people whose voice the President is or can be intimidated by (quality). God can raise up someone who's financially or socially able to get the President's attention, or He can raise up one or more apostolic voices to deal with the matter in the realm of the spirit.

The point is, ruling spirits will not respond to people who only have enough influence to move small pockets of people unless those people have enough faith to identify, confront and bind them. You can always measure the impact of your writings based on the level of the demon that responds to what you've written.

Amount of People Reached

Now, this one isn't etched in stone or, better yet, this wouldn't be a law. There are some people who have large followings who, if shaken, wouldn't be able to withstand anything greater than a minor earthquake in the spirit. This is because they are, spiritually speaking, the equivalent of a 2.5 earthquake. You see, what moves us is a representation of our ability to move others. How did they get large followings? It's simple. By being bold enough to be controversial. People often mistake contentiousness for boldness. Nevertheless, everyone who is controversial cannot withstand controversy. Many people wait for leaders to fall into sin or for rumors to rise against people in leadership, and when this happens, the controversial ones will try to build "their ministries" around another leaders' fall. This is the Athaliah spirit in action.

2 Kings 11:1-3 (ESV): Now when Athaliah the mother of Ahaziah saw that her son was dead, she arose and destroyed all the royal family. But Jehosheba, the daughter of King Joram, sister of Ahaziah, took Joash the son of Ahaziah and stole him away from among the king's sons who were being put to death, and she put him and his nurse in a bedroom. Thus they hid him from Athaliah, so that he was not put to death. And he remained with her six years, hidden in the house of the Lord, while Athaliah reigned over the land.

People who are bound by the Athaliah spirit wait for others to fall before they attempt to rise up. They will then use that opportunity to further crucify the fallen leader, and use it as an opportunity to attack other leaders. Needless to say, however, people who have this spirit never reign long.

Most writers who have large followings have genuinely impacted their readers by speaking the truth (in love) and taking the time out to help their followers to understand that truth. For this reason, people continue to follow them.

Measuring Your Impact

We must measure our impact as speakers before we can effectively measure our impact as writers. Of course, we don't have to have platforms and microphones to measure our impact. We simply need to look at the people around us and determine what type of impact our words have on their lives. For example, what has your ministry done for your family? Has anyone ever given his or her life to Christ because of you? Has anyone ever repented because of something you said to him or her? Additionally, how many people can say that you've made an impact on their lives? The reason this is important is because ministers make mistakes, especially in the infancy stages of their ministries. In most cases, there is someone holding them accountable and determining how much air-time or face-time they receive in front of fellow congregants. This arrangement is good because new leaders can make their mistakes in a controlled environment where they'll be corrected and sat down if necessary. This limits the amount of damage done by a new leaders' mistakes. Understand that every time we enter a new phase or position, we enter that place as a babe or an unlearned person. Like babies, we will make mistakes as we learn to navigate our way through our new responsibilities. Nevertheless, anyone can write a book, and for this reason, many people publish books that they are not accountable for. This means that a man, for example, who hears what he believes to be a revelatory word from God can publish that word, even though he never took the time out to test the spirit that spoke to him. If his book is read by one hundred babes in Christ who have little to no understanding, he will lead them astray or confuse them with his words. This is why it is important for us to see the impact we have on the lives of the people around us before we try to impact people on a global scale.

Measuring Your Impact Exercise

To measure your impact, write down the names of the people closest to you and ask yourself these questions in relation to them:

1. How has (insert person's name here) been changed by my presence in his or her life?
2. Has (insert person's name here) been changed since I entered his or her life?
3. What level of impact have I had on (insert person's name here) life? What magnitude of an earthquake would I say I've been for him or her? Has (insert name here) life changed dramatically or was the change barely noticeable?
4. How many people's lives were negatively impacted by my attempt to minister to them? This is especially important because if you have not identified your mistakes in ministry, you have yet to correct those mistakes. This means you'll make many of those mistakes in your books where your impact could be greater since books aren't limited to the four walls of a church's building or the confines of a zip code.

When measuring our impact, we should consider and compare the impact that earthquakes have to the impact we've had on the lives we've spoken into. This will help us to better understand who we are writing to when we start writing our books. Let's revisit the earthquake chart to compare our progress.

Magnitude	Earthquake Effects	Our Impact
2.5 or less	Usually not felt, but can be recorded by seismograph.	Impact not felt by others, but is slightly evident.
2.5 to 5.4	Often felt, but only causes minor damage.	Minor changes made to a person's life because of our words.
5.5 to 6.0	Slight damage to buildings	Noticeable changes made to

	and other structures.	a person's life because of our words.
6.1 to 6.9	May cause a lot of damage in very populated areas.	Undeniable changes made to a person's life and relationships. For example, a woman who was once surrounded by ungodly, immoral friends is now friendless (for a season) or is surrounded by godly, moral friends as a result of our ministry.
7.0 to 7.9	Major Earthquake. Serious damage.	A major change was made to a person's life because of our ministry. For example, a man who was once an addict is now drug free; a woman who was once a prostitute is now off the streets, a young man who was once suicidal is now enjoying his new life in Christ.
8.0 or greater	Great Earthquake. Can totally destroy communities near the epicenter.	A person's life no longer mirrors or shows any residue of the life he or she once lived because of our impact on that person's heart.

(Magnitude and Earthquake Effects taken from Michigan Tech/ UPSeis/ Earthquake Magnitude Scale)

A babe in Christ probably won't understand the importance of being accountable with the words he or she writes and the impact he or she has on others. We cannot afford to be reckless with the minds, hearts and souls of God's people. When we come to understand our impact on the lives of the people we've spoken to, it will be easier for us to determine what type of impact we'll have on our readers. Additionally, this will help us to understand *if* we'll impact our readers in any way. Most books aren't written to entertain people; they are written to move people, and if I cannot move anyone with my spoken words, I won't have enough power to move them with my written words. Additionally, if I cannot move people with my spoken words, it can only mean that I, myself have not been moved by them, nor have I been moved by God's Word. In other words, it would not be my season to be a teacher; instead, in that season, it would be more advantageous for me to be a student.

Using the chart below, document the names of a few people who've been impacted by your words. Be sure to list their names in the field that corresponds with the magnitude of your words. Again, the effect is evident in the person's life or if you don't know what effect you've had, you can outright ask the individual.

Magnitude	Earthquake Effects	Impact	Your Impact
2.5 or less	Usually not felt, but can be recorded by seismograph.	Impact not felt by others, but is slightly evident.	
2.5 to 5.4	Often felt, but only causes minor damage.	Minor changes made to a person's life because of our words.	
5.5 to 6.0	Slight damage to buildings and other structures.	Noticeable, but not major, changes made to a person's life because of our words.	
6.1 to 6.9	May cause a lot of damage in very populated areas.	Undeniable changes made to a person's life and relationships. For example, a woman who was once surrounded by ungodly, immoral friends is now friendless (for a	

		season) or is surrounded by godly, moral friends as a result of our ministry.	
7.0 to 7.9	Major Earthquake. Serious damage.	A major change was made to a person's life because of our ministry. For example, a man who was once an addict is now drug free; a woman who was once a prostitute is now off the streets, a young man who was once suicidal is now enjoying his new life in Christ.	
8.0 or greater	Great Earthquake. Can totally destroy communities near the epicenter.	A person's life no longer mirrors or shows any residue of the life he or she once lived because of our impact on that person's heart.	

Mountain or Midget?

Genesis 6:4 (KJV): There were giants in the Earth in those days; and also after that, when the sons of God came in unto the daughters of men, and they bear children to them, the same became mighty men which were of old, men of renown.

Jonah 1:17 (ESV): And the LORD appointed a great fish to swallow up Jonah. And Jonah was in the belly of the fish three days and three nights.

1 Samuel 17:4 (ESV): And there came out from the camp of the Philistines a champion named Goliath of Gath, whose height was six cubits and a span.

Isaiah 27:1 (ESV): In that day the LORD with his hard and great and strong sword will punish Leviathan the fleeing serpent, Leviathan the twisting serpent, and he will slay the dragon that is in the sea.

Throughout the Bible, we see stories about large creatures opposing men of faith. Each creature had to be <u>over</u>come, meaning, it had to be defeated or placed "under" the believer's feet. To be placed under one's feet means to be placed under that person's authority. When judging the serpent who'd deceived Eve in the Garden of Eden, God released this judgment. Genesis 3:14-15 (ESV) reads, "The Lord God said to the serpent (Satan), 'Because you have done this, cursed are you above all livestock and above all beasts of the field; on your belly you shall go, and dust you shall eat all the days of your life. I will put enmity between you and the woman, and between your offspring and her offspring; *he shall bruise your head*, and *you shall bruise his heel*.'" To bruise the snake's head means to disable and control it. One of the most effective ways to kill a snake is to cut off its head. God was saying that to overcome a thing, we must stand "over" it. We have to become a mountain to the very thing that's opposing us.

The Bible rarely, if ever, talks about small creatures posing a threat to the men of God. Instead, every hero had to either come against someone tall in stature, someone great in rank, something that was bigger or more powerful than himself or a large army of people. God uses the height and width of what we can see to demonstrate His sovereignty. One of the most common giants mentioned in the Bible is called a mountain. Mountains, unlike people and animals, do not attack their opponents; they do not make intimidating noises, nor do they have any weapons to boast of. Instead, they represent one of the greatest threats to mankind there is. The threat is—they keep people from moving or migrating beyond a specific region or season. A man faced with a mountain has nowhere to hang his blame but on himself. Sure, he can talk about how it's in his way and how hard it is to climb over, but until he gets the revelation of faith moving mountains, he will repeatedly circle every mountain in his life or he will climb mountains that he was supposed to move.

A man's greatest enemy is anything that stands in the way of his destiny. It would then suffice to say that each large creature mentioned in the Bible represented a mountain, just as our problems today represent mountains of varying heights and strengths. For this reason, every mountain has to be addressed by different measures of faith. Romans 12:3 (ESV) reads, "For by the grace given to me I say to everyone among you not to think of himself more highly than he ought to think, but to think with sober judgment, each according to the *measure of faith* that God has assigned." Romans 12:6 (ESV) reads, "Having gifts that differ according to the grace given to us, let us use them: if prophecy, *in proportion to our faith*." This is to establish two facts:

- One man's giant is another man's midget.
- A reader could have a similar problem as the writer, but the writer's faith and advice won't always be great enough to move the mountains that the reader is facing.

One Man's Giant is Another Man's Midget

I host a writers' class at least twice a year and I always find myself teaching two types of students—the ones who will inconvenience themselves to finish their books and the ones who will inconvenience their God-given assignments to stay in their comfort zones. The process is a giant for most writers; that is, until the ones who are willing to inconvenience themselves receive the revelation of writing. Without fail, they come to see the process for what it is—a trying of their faith. This process separates the true writer from the ambitious soul who has more fantasies about book signings and huge royalty checks than they have revelation. This process is a giant for some, but for the ones who receive revelation, it becomes a midget, meaning, it's not as hard or frustrating as many would make it out to be.

Goliath was a mountain to King Saul, but to David, he was a midget, shrunk by David's faith in God. Sure, in stature, Goliath was considered a giant, but to a man of faith, Goliath had more mouth than he had potential. For this reason, David, a man King Saul, referred to as a "young man" was not intimidated by Goliath's height or weight. King Saul, however, was considered a tall man. As a matter of fact, 1 Samuel 9:2 (ESV) says, "From his shoulders upward he was taller than any of the people." Howbeit, Saul was a coward. The Bible tells us that when he and all of Israel heard the threats being made by Goliath, they were "dismayed and greatly afraid." To King Saul, Goliath was a mountain. Remember, mountains represent nearly immovable fixtures; they are intimidating and can almost appear indestructible. To David, Goliath was a midget. David, through his faith, became a mountain, but because Goliath lacked faith, he didn't realize what or, better yet, who he was up against. David came to him in the name of the Lord, meaning, even though Goliath saw David, he was really in a battle with the Lord.

Writers Faith vs. Readers' Problem

One man overcomes a problem that was threatening his marriage. He follows the advice of God and his marriage is saved. He writes a book detailing what a man should do to save his marriage. His book is powerful and it blesses many men and women, both local and abroad. Nevertheless, another man comes along and reads that same book. He has a similar problem, however, the root of his issue goes way deeper. You see, the author's wife, for example, had an affair, and as painful as this was, he decided to heal with her. During their healing process, he discovers that his wife's affair was a response to him going out of town every other week for his job. He learns that her father did the same thing, and while out of town, he would be having extramarital affairs and creating children with his mistresses. Having seen her mother suffering, the wife vowed to never allow herself to endure that level of pain or betrayal. At some point, she started suspecting that her husband was having an affair, so she called an old friend of hers who had always comforted her with his words. It wasn't long before she found herself curled up in that friend's arms. That woman's giant was that she had not gotten over what her father took the family through. The reader, on the other hand, has a wife who has had multiple affairs. She'd finally settled down to one affair with a co-worker of hers. The reader buys the author's book and tries to apply the same advice to his own marriage, but it doesn't work. Finally, after divorcing his wife, he runs into an older relative of hers who takes the time out to explain to him that his wife's mother and grandmother were both promiscuous. His ex-wife's problem had nothing to do with trauma; it was just in her blood. Sure, she could be delivered, but she would first have to acknowledge where she is and what she is, and then, decide to fall out of agreement with the devil. Additionally, she would have to trace the root of whoredom in her bloodline, and this investigation would likely lead her to the moment in which the spirit of rejection entered into her family.

The author's book was rich with advice and instructions, but the reader didn't need a book on how to save his marriage after an affair; he needed a spiritual warfare manual that detailed many of the spirits his wife was bound by. He needed to understand the power of generational curses, familiar spirits and marine spirits, which are the spirits behind lust, promiscuity, witchcraft and mind control. The author's knowledge was surface-level; it was a revelation of his faith and jurisdictional reach. His faith was big enough to help many men move their mountains, but for the aforementioned reader, it wasn't enough. The author's jurisdiction was surface-level; he was not equipped to tackle spiritual matters. Some issues require much more than a self-help, surface-level book. They require an earthquake—one that goes to the core (spirit) of the matter and produces a volcanic eruption. In layman's terms, sometimes, a problem has to arise and shake up a sinner or backslidden person's life so violently that the person agrees to go through deliverance. During deliverance, the volcanic eruption for the believer is when the strongman and all his henchmen come up and out. Apostle Paul, when judging matters regarding a young man who'd been having an incestuous relationship with his stepmother, instructed the Church of Corinth this way. 1 Corinthians 5:1-5 reads, "It is actually reported that there is sexual immorality among you, and of a kind that is not tolerated even among pagans, for a man has his father's wife. And you are arrogant! Ought you not rather to mourn? Let him who has done this be removed from among you. For though absent in body, I am present in spirit; and as if present, I have already pronounced judgment on the one who did such a thing. When you are assembled in the name of the Lord Jesus and my spirit is present, with the power of our Lord Jesus, you are to deliver this man to Satan for the destruction of the flesh, so that his spirit may be saved in the day of the Lord."

Why would he tell the church to turn the man over to Satan for the destruction of his flesh so that his spirit could be saved? The answer is as simple as it is complicated. Because some people's love for sin is so deeply rooted that mere words and great miracles won't be enough to get them to repent. They are the ones who Jesus spoke of when He said, "Let him who has an ear hear what the Spirit of the Lord is saying..." Quite frankly, they have no ears to hear, meaning, they have shut off their ears to spiritual matters. They don't want to hear anything about judgment or holiness. Their responses are almost always, "God knows my heart."

They tune into conversations that appeal to their lustful desires and their sinful ways. They rarely come to church; they ignore the prophets of God, and when they read their Bibles, they become increasingly tired. When they see miracles taking place, they get excited in that moment and their faith is temporarily recharged, but Satan comes along and tempts them right back into sin. Mark 4:16-19 (ESV) describes them this way, "And these are the ones sown on rocky ground: the ones who, when they hear the word, immediately receive it with joy. And they have no root in themselves, but endure for a while; then, when tribulation or persecution arises on account of the word, immediately they fall away. And others are the ones sown among thorns. They are those who hear the word, but the cares of the world and the deceitfulness of riches and the desires for other things enter in and choke the word, and it proves unfruitful."

Again, one man's mountain is another man's midget, therefore, as a writer, you must understand the size of the mountains that your words will move. This will help you to avoid marketing your book to the wrong audience and maybe even aiding in the destruction of someone's peace, marriage, life and so on. Now, the aforementioned author is not responsible for the destruction of the other guy's marriage because he wrote on his level about an experience he'd endured, and the reader, not understanding the level of warfare he was enduring, purchased the wrong book. However, if the author understood his level and had a disclaimer in the book, this problem may have been avoided. The disclaimer could have helped the readers to understand that some experiences are far more spiritual and require more deliverance, counseling and time to eradicate. With a disclaimer, it is possible that the reader wouldn't have hinged all of his hope on that one book. This is similar to what many medical offices do. If you call their lines, you'll likely get a recording that lists a series of departments. Each department will have a numerical prompt that you have to push in order to access. At the beginning or end of the recording, the operator can be heard saying, "If this is an emergency, call 911." This is because every problem requires a certain level of attention and certain tools to address. This is to keep you, the caller, from hinging all of your hope on that particular office because many offices are not equipped to deal with certain matters. When I had my first miscarriage, for example, I went to the hospital because I didn't know where else to go. The doctor who looked after me was highly agitated that I'd come to the hospital. He wanted to know why I hadn't gone to my OBGYN. The truth was, I didn't have one. I'd just discovered that I was pregnant and I hadn't had time to make an appointment with anyone. The doctor ran a series of tests, and after fussing with me nonstop about coming to the hospital, he referred me to a local Obstetrician. He called the office, set up an emergency appointment for me and sent me on my way, explaining that the Obstetrician had more advanced tools and could deal more with the root of the matter. The hospital, he said, could perform the D&C surgery, but the Obstetrician could help me discover why I'd had the miscarriage in the first place. I was in a place that could help me address the problem, but I wasn't in a place where I could get to the root of it. The doctor at the hospital had faith to deal with emergency matters, but he didn't have the faith or tools to deal my issue. This doesn't discredit him as a doctor, nor does it make him a bad doctor; he simply had to stay in his jurisdiction. He knew what he had the knowledge and tools to address, and the mountain I was facing required more knowledge and more advanced tools.

The point is, the doctor understood his level. He understood that going beyond his metron could have some dire consequences for both him and me. For this reason, he referred me to someone who could help me—someone who was better equipped. As writers, we have to do the same, but we won't be able to do this if we don't know what level we are on.

171

Faith that Moves Mountains

As writers, we have to know what mountains we can move versus which mountains we are not called to or not yet called to address. It is important that you have a disclaimer in your (self help) book that helps the readers to understand your jurisdictional limitations *if* your book deals with highly sensitive matters like marriage, divorce, psychology, health, spirituality, dreams and so on. The reality is, regardless of how traumatic your life has been, you will always come in contact with readers who have far more traumatic stories to tell.

Two noted natural disasters that move mountains are droughts and earthquakes. Both natural phenomena move mountains in a different way. Earthquakes cause mountains to shift and/or shrink, whereas, droughts cause them to rise by causing the land to swell. When a mountain shrinks, it does not move from one territory or another, however, if a mountain moves, it can easily cross a border, thus becoming the property and problem of a specific country. For example, Mt. Everest sits on the borders of Nepal and China. If the mountain moved across China's border, it could easily become the property of China; if it shifted fully into Nepal, it would become the property of Nepal. As of right now, both countries own a specific side of the mountain.

In April of 2015, there was an earthquake in Nepal. The earthquake's magnitude was 7.8, making it a major earthquake. What's even more amazing is that Mt. Everest actually moved an inch southwest. Scientists are even reporting that many of the mountains surrounding Mt. Everest actually shrunk as a result of the earthquake. Mt. Everest didn't move much, but it did move. The mountains surrounding Mt. Everest didn't shrink much, but they did shrink. Even though the earthquake was considered a major earthquake, its impact on the mountains was barely noticeable. What does this mean? It's simple. Faith moves mountains, but there are cases when what our faith has moved is barely noticeable. Needless to say, however, if we note every small movement that takes place, our faith will continue to grow, thus, giving us the ability to make an even greater impact.

A writer's magnitude is determined by what and who the writer moves. The power that a writer unleashes is not in his or her tone, nor is it found in a bunch of exclamation points. A writer's power is his or her faith. 1 Corinthians 13:2 (NIV) reads, "If I have the gift of prophecy and can fathom all mysteries and all knowledge, and *if I have a faith that can move mountains*, but do not have love, I am nothing." Again, faith can be measured. Apostle Paul demonstrated this by saying *"a faith that can move mountains,"* meaning, there are some measures of faith that cannot move mountains. How is it then that some writers believe they can have the power of a 2.5 magnitude earthquake and think they are ready to confront great mountains outside of their jurisdictions? After all, a man's faith is his jurisdiction; he has no authority where he has no faith. Let's revisit the sons of Sceva. The Bible refers to them as "exorcists," which means they'd successfully cast a demon out of someone before. More than likely, they'd cast several demons out using what they referred to as "the Jesus in whom Paul preaches." However, they came in contact with a high-ranking demon who recognized that they didn't have the authority they boasted of or the faith to cast it out. The demon did not recognize the men, but it did recognize the fact that they were out of their jurisdictions. For this reason, the man who was possessed by the demon beat the men and ripped their clothes off them. This was symbolic of them having no covering. A covering represents legally transferred authority. The men ran away naked and ashamed; this was symbolic of them being exposed. The sons of Sceva, like many men who barge into spiritual matters with no revelation, were ambitious souls who had no faith, meaning, they had no power. What they did is similar to a man walking into a house he does not own in the middle of a drug deal and then, telling every person there that he is placing them under arrest. Sure, in the United States of America, we can perform citizen's arrests, however, to do this, we must exercise wisdom and we must have the proper tools (guns, handcuffs). The criminals won't surrender to him just because he's right and they're wrong; they'll put up a fight, and if he has no wisdom, weapons or manpower to protect himself, he will likely find himself buried under his mountain.

If the sons of Sceva were alive today and a part of the millennial generation, could you imagine what types of books they'd write? Like many authors, they'd boast of an authority that they did not have. They'd likely have the intellect and hermeneutics of their father, Sceva, who happened to be a Jewish chief priest. They'd even have the many valuable connections to help their books hit the mainstream market. They'd be astute writers with brilliant book covers and highly engaging book trailers. Nevertheless, their books would be powerless paperbacks filled with right-sounding words but no delivering power.

To understand the level you are on as a writer, you must first understand the level you are on as a teacher. Again, one of the most important questions to ask yourself is, "Who is or has been moved by my words?"

IF YOU CAN'T REACH THE PEOPLE AROUND YOU, YOU'RE NOT READY FOR GLOBAL IMPACT.

This doesn't mean you shouldn't write; it simply means you need to pay attention to the range and impact of your voice, and the sounds emitted by the people who are impacted by your voice. One of the reasons that eighty percent of Christian books flop is because a lot of believers are writing about matters they have little to no revelation about. Think of it this way—if the writers were police officers, many of them would be guilty of traveling outside of their cities' limits, going into other cities, conducting traffic stops and writing tickets when they had no legal backing to do so. None of those citations would hold up in court.

Everything that we see, think or believe has a certain height, even if it doesn't exist in the natural realm. The height of everything that's invisible but real to us is determined by us. The height of a thing is the value or perceived power of it. For example, two women can work at the same company, making the same amount of money, all the while, managing the same amount of debt. Both women can receive a call from the same debt collector, threatening to sue them, take their homes and garnish their paychecks. The woman with faith may deal with the initial worry, but then decide in her heart that God has been good to her all of her life. She reasons within herself that the debt collector, albeit intimidating, is not bigger than her God. For this reason, the debt collector becomes a small issue for her. The minute she exalted God over the debt collector, she submitted herself to God's will. The woman with no faith may panic and start sabotaging every good thing in her life because of the stress. To her, the threat is a whale that's going to swallow her whole. Because of how she perceives the threat, she would cause it to become a giant in her life, and instead of her moving the problem, the problem will begin to move her. This would cause the problem to chase, corner and consume her, not because it was too much for her to bear, but because her lack of faith made it bigger than it was. Whenever we magnify a thing, we empower it. This is why we need to continuously magnify the name of the Lord.

As a writer, it is important for you to ask yourself three questions:
1. What and who has my faith moved recently?
2. What size was the situation (to me) that my faith moved?
3. What was the last thing or who was the last person that moved me?

The goal is to identify your level as a writer; this way, you won't fall into the wrong side of the 80/20 statistic. We all have a measure of faith. It is important for us to identify the measure we have; this way, we'll understand our jurisdictional limitations. Most Christians don't have the faith to move mountains and that's okay. According to Romans 12:3, God has allotted or given each man his *measure* of faith. This means that faith comes in various sizes and every man or woman has his or her own measure. We should not address what we cannot or have not moved. Additionally, we should not tell people how to get over a mountain that we have yet to address.

We all have a spiritual dialect in the realm of the spirit. Our dialects tell others where we've been. A woman can write a book detailing how to survive an abusive marriage, but if she's never been in an abusive marriage, her language (choice of words) and dialect (knowledge, sensitivity) will betray her. Most readers, especially the avid ones, can detect the writer's true voice, and if they sense that the writer is an ambitious, glory-seeking soul who's embellishing or padding a story, they will expose the writer's deception. I've seen book reviews that have crippled or successfully destroyed an author's credibility and his or her writing career. The author's mistake was that he or she wrote about a mountain that was still very much present in the author's life or a mountain the author has never come in contact with.

Mountains represent giant, seemingly immovable landmarks. In the realm of the spirit, mountains represent demonic strongholds, generational strongholds and self-inflicted strongholds. Google's online dictionary defines "stronghold" this way: *a place that has been fortified so as to protect it against attack.* A mental or spiritual stronghold is a belief system that is so strongly embedded that the person who has it will defend it at any cost. The stronghold, in this case, is a series of lies guarded by pride, designed to keep the truth from coming in. This is because every belief has a story behind it and an imagination or desire in front of it. In other words, every belief has a history and what appears to the host to be a promising future. People with ungodly beliefs genuinely believe that the truth is an attack against their identities and their plans. This is why they will defend their beliefs, regardless of how ungodly, unproductive and dangerous they are. This is why strongholds are synonymous with mountains; they are hard, but not impossible, to move. A mountain stands in the way of a person's journey. An ungodly belief stands in the way of a person's life journey. To get over a mountain, the climber has to wear the proper clothing. In the Kingdom, this gear is called "the full armor of God."

Every person has a mountain that stands in the way of his or her destiny. Nevertheless, not every person has the faith to move the mountain that he or she is faced with. Generational strongholds are nothing but mountains that a certain family has repeatedly circled one generation after the other. It means that many people in a particular family have died in the wildernesses of their belief systems. To address the mountain, it is necessary for each man and woman to first build upon his or her faith. Just like faith can be measured, it can also be grown. Faith is grown through hearing (see Romans 10:17) and demonstration (see James 2:17).

As writers, it is important that we learn to identify the mountains in our personal lives and only address the mountains that we have moved or the ones we want to bring down with our testimonies. Revelation 12:11 reads, "And they overcame him by the blood of the Lamb, *and* by the *word of their testimony*; and they loved not their lives unto the death." The word "overcame" means to place something under one's foot. It means to make a bridge or footstool of it. David said in Psalms 110:1 (ESV), "The LORD says to my Lord: "Sit at my right hand, until I make your enemies your footstool." What this means is we can write about a mountain that we have yet to cross if:

- We've repented.

- Prayed to get past the mountain.
- Have the right intentions in regards to writing about the mountain.

We overcome or make a footstool of the enemy through the blood of the Lamb, Jesus Christ, and the power of our testimonies. We should only testify about mountains that we no longer want to face — mountains that we've repented for creating. It is unwise to write about a mountain that you are still in agreement with, meaning, a stronghold you are still embracing. A good example is, I've had a few women to reach out to me, *demanding* that I pray for them and ask the Lord to break the soul ties in their lives. When I asked them why they wanted to be free, they cried out and said that their former lovers had moved on with their lives and they were tired of hurting because of them; they wanted to move on as well. Of course, I had to tell them that they were not repentant for their fornication, idolatry and their sudden desire to call God's name in vain (they didn't want Him; they wanted revenge). Sadly enough, many women who are angry with the men who've forsaken them decide to write books and address the mountains of betrayal, hurt, rejection and abandonment. This seems like a great idea until you consider the fact that they have not addressed the mountains of fornication and idolatry that led them to betrayal, hurt, rejection and abandonment. For this reason, they end up writing books and unleashing earthquakes in the realm of the spirit—earthquakes that move the readers (emotionally), but not the mountains. Additionally, because they were not delivered, they managed to get the attention of every demonic force that was still present in their lives. Always remember that whatever we speak to has the right to respond; when this is done through words, it is called an argument. When it's done by physically, psychologically or spiritually engaging the enemy, it is called warfare.

The point is that many writers go under what they believe to be an attack while writing when, in truth, they are simply attempting to move the wrong mountains. Lastly, even when we do move mountains, as writers, we won't always notice a huge impact, but this doesn't mean that impact hasn't been made. The scientists who conducted studies on Mt. Everest after the earthquake had to do some very thorough, rigorous examinations before they noticed that the mountain had moved an inch. Imagine how difficult it must have been to make this determination. Nevertheless, they took their time, and their findings are now recorded facts that will someday be in our history books. Even slight movement is still movement. Nevertheless, understand that every movement you experience while writing, whether that movement is in your finances, body, family, job or so on, is a representation of a very present mountain in your life. Instead of doing like many aspiring authors do, which is to stop writing, allow every distraction to alert you to the fact that there are unaddressed strongholds in your life. After that, begin to address those strongholds and write about them as you go along; that is, of course, if you truly want to be free. Again, many writers don't want full freedom; some want to address what walks through the open doors of their lives, without addressing the fact that there are opened doors in their lives.

We all have the faith to move mountains, but not everyone's mountain is the same size. One man's mountain is his debt, while another man's mountain is his wealth. Even though it appears that the wealthy man may have an easier life, the truth is, a mountain of wealth with no wisdom to ground it, is an almost unbearable burden. Howbeit, each man can move his own mountain if he allows his faith to become big enough to dwarf it. One woman's mountain is her absent father, while another woman's mountain is her very present father. Even though it appears that the woman with a present father has an easier life, this isn't always true. I've met women who would have been better off if their fathers had been absent from their lives. Howbeit, each woman can move her own mountain if she builds upon her faith. Always remember that just as God has given us all a measure of faith, every man's Goliath is not the same height.

Counting the Cost of Leadership

As a reminder, the Hebrew word for "writer" is "sopher," and it means "to count." In this chapter, instead of using the word "scribe" or "author," I'll be using the word "sopher". This is to help you familiarize yourself with another aspect of your assignment—sacrifice. Hollywood has glamorized authorship. Almost every time an actor is cast as an author on the big screen, he or she is cast as successful, intelligent and attractive. This has caused men and women around the world to write books filled with unusable content for the sake of being called an author. People from every nation and tongue are lusting after the author title, not realizing that there is a cost associated with becoming a world-changer. Sure, many authors these days write countless books, but those books are not designed to shape people's minds or worlds. Instead, they are written to entertain. Then again, many authors write self-help books that don't help anyone. Nevertheless, there is a cost involved with being a sopher—one that has caused many men and women to put away their pens. Understand this—the minute you decide to write a book, you have decided to take a leadership position, after all, you will be leading your readers from one thought to another, one concept to another, and one conclusion to another. In order to lead and/or be a world-changer, you need legal authority, and to receive legal authority, you need love. Now, love isn't a feeling, as the world would have you to believe. It is the heart of knowledge, the fabric of understanding and the product of wisdom. This three-fold cord is passed down from the Father's heart to ours and made stronger through unity, perseverance, prayer and correction. This is why God gave us fathers and mentors.

I was on the phone with a sister in Christ one day, and after listening to me speak for about twenty minutes, she'd found herself on the other end of the line feeling frustrated and discouraged. Initially, she had been excited about an idea she had—an idea that would pretty much launch her into ministry. A seasoned entrepreneur, she saw ministry the same way she saw entrepreneurship. She was focused on numbers and the opportunity to build something new—something she could attach her name to and add to her portfolio. I knew this excitement all too well, but as a minister, I also knew that ministry and entrepreneurship don't involve the same formula. Sure, there's marketplace ministry, but she'd mastered one side of the marketplace and was now interested in ministering to married couples. Normally, when people call me, they get off the line excited about their newfound ideas, but this wasn't the case; at least, not this time. Instead, after listening to me passionately detail what it truly meant to be a minister, she yelled out in frustration, "You're supposed to be encouraging me in this! Now, I don't know if I want to do it anymore!" My response shocked and silenced her. I interrupted her rant with one word, "Good!" I knew she was looking at ministry from a toddler's perspective. At that stage, she was more focused on herself than she was the people whose lives she'd impact, and this is normal, after all, we enter new realms as infants and we have to grow up in them. I went on to explain to her that in business, we can make many mistakes and easily recover from them. I have learned many, many expensive lessons—I've lost tens of thousands of dollars over the years in business, but none of those mistakes had affected anyone other than myself. Nevertheless, in ministry, we can't afford to be playing with people's souls, relationships or lives. We can't replace people's spouses if our advice destroys their marriages, we can't refund peace, nor can we write off someone's suicide on our taxes. No. We are speaking into and affecting the lives of living, breathing people; these are real souls with real problems, serving a real God. When you take on the opportunity to teach God's people, you need to empty yourself of all your selfish ambition so that you can be an effective witness. You have to minister in fear and trembling, questioning your motives every time you grab a microphone or a camera. Matthew 18:6 warns us this way, "But whoever causes one of these little ones who believe in me to sin, it would be better for him to have a great millstone fastened around his neck and to be drowned in the depth of the sea." In other words, God's love for His people runs deep, and He won't write off our mistakes with them "cute." This is the very reason that less than twenty percent of Christian books succeed—a lot of authors don't understand how dangerous it is to approach God's people lightheartedly. You have to chew EVERYTHING you intend to feed His people! If you cannot chew, ingest or digest anything you share with God's people, you're not ready for ministry. Of course, I shared this with my sister and told her to speak more about the matter with her spiritual father.

What was I doing? After all, the world would have us think that I should have congratulated and welcomed her to her next level. Ironically enough, this is exactly what I did, but a congratulation in ministry doesn't sound the same as a congratulations in the marketplace. You see, in the marketplace, we applaud the minister, but in every other extension of ministry, we tell the minister to go somewhere and die to himself or herself. In short, I was preparing her for the journey she was about to take. I could initially hear the excitement and the anticipation in her voice, and as much as I hated to hear that excitement fade, my job as a big sister and mentor was to not only protect her, but to protect God's people from what I could clearly see—her ambition. Sure, I knew that she would make a great minister someday, but at that moment, I also knew that she was a baby in the realm of ministry, and babies are ambitious, reckless and impatient. They like to play on God's altar, instead of lying on it.

I wasn't frustrated, angry or feeling anything negative in my heart. Instead, I felt the intensity of God's love for His people, and while I know she'll be a powerful minister someday, my assignment in that moment was to take the Sword of the Lord and swing it at the head of ambition. I asked her about her goals and helped her to see her blind spots. Her views were one-sided and had been skewed by her experiences in life, so I showed her another perspective. Thankfully, she knows my heart, and while she was frustrated with me, she's known me long enough to know that I meant her no evil. I reminded her that there is safety in the multitude of counselors (see Proverbs 11:14) and encouraged her to call her leader. He's been in ministry for well over thirty years and married for more than forty years. I knew he'd steer her in the right direction. Of course, I encouraged her as well, but my job in that moment was to pull the plug on anything that would destroy her God-given assignment and help her to understand the differences between being in business versus being in ministry.

We enter every new realm as an infant. In the professional world, the corporate word for infant is rookie or beginner. In the church, we refer to new believers as babes in Christ. In marriage, we refer to newly married couples as newlyweds. When an author pens his or her first book, that author is simply referred to as a new author, and the author's book is referred to as his or her debut book. It doesn't matter how seasoned people are in every other realm, the minute they first enter the realm of the sopher (scribe), they have entered into the diaper of that realm. And just like an infant, they will mess up, but anytime you write books, launch ministries or do anything that would affect someone's life, relationship or finances, it is *imperative* that you seek wise counsel and be patient.

YOU HAVE TO BE OFFENDED BEFORE YOU CAN BE STRETCHED.

Correction is the bending of your will. It not only helps you to walk uprightly, it helps you to locate everything that's broken in you.

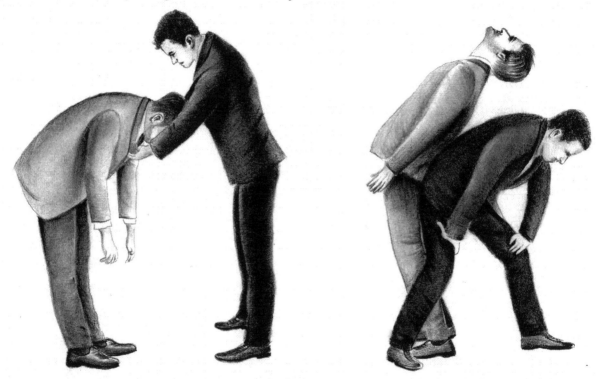

Take a look at the picture above. It is a demonstration of what it looks like to be corrected. In the first image, you see two men—one of the guys has been deformed by sin, and the other guy is his pastor. His pastor's assignment is to help him to walk upright, so he has to put pressure on him. This process requires time and a lot of patience. It can be painful, humiliating and frustrating for both parties, but it will also be rewarding if both men remain committed to the process. In the same image, we see the pastor holding the man up. To do so, he has to bend (or forsake) his own will.

We all need someone who's not afraid to bend, stretch and correct us. We all need someone in our lives who'd risk losing us by telling us the unfiltered, unadulterated and unapologetic truth. Now, of course, I'm not talking about rude, jealous, loveless and prideful people who lack tact. I'm talking about people who genuinely love us and want to see us reach our full potential—people who want to see us do greater exploits than they have. It goes without saying that we often reject these types of people when we are immature because they remind us of the rude, prideful people who've hurt us at some point in our lives. All too often, we've called these people "family" and many of us have called them our brothers and sisters in the Lord. For this reason, we have to receive a new heart and a new mind, after all, the old one has been broken, traumatized, deformed and conformed. According to Matthew 18:3, we must become as *little* children if we want to enter the Kingdom of Heaven. We have to love like we've never been hurt, trust like we've never been betrayed and give like we've never been robbed. This is the heart of a child. Again, you have to be offended before you can be stretched, and you have to be stretched before you can go forth.

In ministry, to be stretched means to be intentionally grown; it means to be tested, corrected and fed. This makes me think about the many times I've bitten into a sugar crystal while chewing gum. Like most people, anytime this happened, I would take the gum from my mouth, hoping that it wasn't contaminated with dirt or any other foreign particle. To see what was in the gum, I would stretch it, and in most cases, I had to stretch it to its breaking point. Once I realized that I'd bitten into a sugar crystal, my peace would return, and if my hands were clean, I'd return the gum to my mouth. This is how God is with us. He brings people into our lives to stretch us; this way, they can see everything that's in us. This is the very heart of correction.

What's your stage as a writer? What needs to be corrected in your heart? Who's correcting you? It's important that you know where you are; this way, you'll know how to intentionally, consistently and aggressively grow your writing talent. In the natural world, we'd pose this question differently. We'd ask, "What's your age," or better yet, "How old are you?" Nevertheless, in the writing world, our natural age is irrelevant, but rather, we are all in different stages. We can compare these stages to the human stages of development.

- Infant
- Toddler
- Kid
- Teen
- Young Adult
- Adult
- Seasoned Adult

Every stage of a writer's development can be measured by the author's:

- Diligence
- Perseverance
- Patience
- Content (Substance)
- Punctuality
- Excellence
- Investment

All of these can all be categorized as fruit, and just like natural fruit, they all start off as seeds. Nevertheless, these seeds don't reflect the author's ability to produce books, because any human being who's learned to read and write can sit down and pen a book. This is the very reason that eighty percent of Christian books flop. Instead, they reflect the author's relationship with God. You see, as we grow in our relationships with God, we assume more responsibilities with Him and we're more intentional about producing books that will help to free His people. In other words, we begin to create books filled with usable content. As we grow in Him, authorship becomes less about us and more about Him. As we grow in Him, authorship becomes less of an opportunity and more of a responsibility. As we grow in Him, we become more strategic, patient and intentional with what we write. A lot of books on the market today are nothing but heaps of words that have no mobilizing power. They don't move the readers forward, and many of them even set their readers back.

New writers are almost always ambitious; that is, unless they've been in ministry for a while. People who are seasoned ministers simply have to learn the ins and outs of authorship, and from there, they will integrate what they've learned in ministry into their books. Nevertheless, authors who've never been in ministry often exhibit the same traits that new ministers exhibit—they still see authorship as an opportunity for themselves, rather than an opportunity for God to exalt Himself. The way you view the office of the scribe has everything to do with your perspective, and your perspective is determined by *where* you are standing (your position) and *what* you are standing on (your foundation). Your position is your belief system; it is the series of beliefs that converge to form your world and shape your decisions, but your foundation is the materials you've used to hold up this world. For example, if you are a believer and you fully trust the Lord, your foundation is the Word of God and your position is where you stand in His Word. Your position in Christ is the distance between your heart and His; it's the space between your will and His will. This is what determines your age in Christ. Without being exhaustive, we can safely summarize that new writers will display less of the fruit mentioned (diligence, perseverance, patience, content, punctuality, excellence and investment) and more of the fruit of their flesh.

Most God-installed authors remain in the infancy of their writing careers up until they've written and published their second or third books. During the infant stage, a large number of authors share their testimonies or speak a lot about themselves in their books. This is normal and it's needed! What the author is doing is called budding. Think about a plant. When it initially comes out of the ground, its leaves are pointed inward towards itself. As it begins to develop, the leaves start pointing outwardly, and from there, the plant and its leaves begin to grow. Truly God-installed sophers (writers) have been rooted in the Word of God and planted in the house of the Lord, so when the sopher picks up a pen to write, we are witnessing God bring forth the increase that He's placed in that author. The author is pushing himself or herself out of his or her hard shell and beginning to show the world the first-fruits of his or her identity. The author is in the process of overcoming the issues that have plagued him or her in the past and helped to shape the author into who he or she is today. Revelation 12:11 reads, "And they overcame him by the blood of the Lamb, and by the word of their testimony; and they loved not their lives unto the death." If an author does not share his/her story in the author's debut book, you will often find the author's story scattered throughout every book that he or she writes.

Counting the Cost of Leadership

When an infant cries, it does so because of an unmet need. This is a survival mechanism that allows the infant to communicate with its parent or guardian. Nevertheless, toddlers usually cry because of an unmet desire. You see, toddlers don't know the difference between a desire and a need, and for this reason, they communicate through grunting, pointing and speaking (if they can speak). When they lack the words to communicate what they want, they will cry, but this is why the parent has to intentionally and consistently teach the baby to express himself or herself through healthy communication. Nevertheless, because the child has become accustomed to using tears and loud noises as his or her mode of communication, the toddler will continue to wail and scream in an attempt to get what he or she wants. This is the stage when most parents begin to discipline their children. The goal is to teach the children to communicate using words, because once the child learns to express what he or she feels, needs, or wants using spoken words, every other (negative) form of communication then becomes manipulation. "Foolishness is bound in the heart of a child; but the rod of correction shall drive it far from him" (Proverbs 22:15). Sure, toddlers do not understand what manipulation is, nevertheless, parents must diligently encourage healthy communication and refrain from rewarding unhealthy communication. The same is true for new sophers. Oftentimes, new writers don't know the difference between testifying versus exposing someone who's hurt them. Of course, this is why we need to have our books inspected by good, godly men and women of God. I can't tell you how many authors I've come across who've had to have their first, second or third books pulled because of the content. The authors matured and realized that they'd written their books when their hearts weren't healthy. One day, they grew up and realized that the information they'd published was toxic, and it was hurting more people than it was helping. This normally happened when someone notable or someone they greatly admired inquired about their books. Realizing that the content of their paperbacks was emotional and unusable, they'd gone out of their way to change the subject. After that, they unpublished their books with the intent of rewriting and republishing them.

When a sopher whines in his or her book, it is because of an unmet need or desire. It goes without saying, publishing your pain is never a healthy way to communicate. Before you can share your testimony, you need to have forgiven the people who've hurt you, plus, you have to take accountability for your role in your own pain. Until a sopher understands this, he or she will not write books filled with usable content.

In the above picture, you witness a woman spitting up or vomiting in her book. This illustration designed to help you understand what it looks like when an author publishes his/her hurt, rejection, offenses and entitlement issues. Many new authors publish their tantrums. While we see this a lot in the infancy stage of a new sopher, it is also common for authors who've written two or three books; that is, unless the authors have:

1. received training from a good, godly writer's coach.
2. already dealt with his/her issues through counseling or coaching.
3. submitted his/her book to a leader to be inspected (accountability).

Toddler sophers are usually very vocal about the fact that they haven't received the support they thought they'd receive when they'd published their debut books. This is because young sophers still deal with entitlement, believing that everyone who knows them should buy their books, if for no other reason than to show their support. Again, this is normal for new authors. Sophers usually grow out of this stage over time.

To summarize this, authors who are in the infancy or toddler stages of their writing careers will oftentimes:

1. take shortcuts to save money, including attempting to edit their own books, hiring anyone who has Photoshop or any paint program to design their covers, attempt to publish their books themselves, etc.
2. take three or more years to finish a single book.
3. write only when they feel like writing.
4. write about their unresolved issues and their enemies.
5. attempt to resolve their issues using their books.
6. overly showcase their wit in an attempt to charm/humor their readers.
7. tell their readers what or how they're feeling at any given moment.
8. tell their readers what they're doing, for example, they'll write, "I just finished a very delicious sandwich (thank you, Lord), but I came back so I could finish telling you what the Lord shared with me. I just hope that tuna fish doesn't come back to haunt me while I'm writing."
9. share every thought they have.
10. share information without breaking that information down for others to understand.
11. share information that has no depth.
12. share information that has no substance.
13. share irrelevant, unusable information. For example, new sophers may say, "It's a cold day in January and I'm waiting for the spring to come so I can show off my weight loss. But that's a whole other subject. Anyhow, the best way to create an extra stream of income is to ..."
14. pile up heaps of unrelated words in an attempt to sound smart. This is the sopher mimicking the voice of someone he or she reveres as "big."
15. are just learning their writers' voice and are still afraid of their own individual voices. For this reason, many sophers in this stage mimic others and will sometimes engage in plagiarism.

Next, there are sophers in the kid stages of their writing careers. Sophers in this stage normally take two years or less to finish their books. And even though their books still contain a lot of content that points back to themselves, their readers will notice that their books' content has started pointing more outwardly. In other words, the writer will give the readers more usable content.

During this stage of the writer's career, a large number of authors, including the ones who are called to write in-depth (third, fourth or fifth level) books still write on the first and second level. The ones who have in-depth knowledge and revelation are often afraid to publish what they know out of fear of being misunderstood, questioned or attacked. They are even afraid to share what they know or believe with their pastors. Again, this is just a stage or a phase, and most sophers who consistently write will eventually grow out of it.

Kid sophers often:
1. have increased page counts. When they were in the infancy stages of their writing careers, many of them wouldn't write anymore than 75-100 pages, but as the author matures, their page count often increases. This is because the author now has started growing teeth and is learning to break revelation down.
2. take one to two years to finish a book.
3. have more in-depth knowledge to share. Again, a lot of what they share points back to themselves, but you'll find that authors in this phase of their writing careers or ministries will conduct some minor research, even though they won't often break their findings down.
4. have phases of consistent writing, followed by months of no writing.
5. are concerned about what others think about their books.
6. will sometimes share their books with their leaders and/or their mentors to ensure they are not publishing heresy.
7. invest more money in their books than they invested in their previous books.

Next, there is a group that can be classified as teen sophers. These writers have learned to conduct research and are more diligent with completing their books. They still demonstrate the characteristics of the kid sopher, but writers in this stage exhibit the following:
1. **Pride:** because they've conducted more research and learned a lot over their

writing careers, teen sophers tend to get puffed up and believe that they do not need mentors. 1 Corinthians 8:1 tells us that knowledge puffs up or, in layman's terms, it causes people to become prideful.

2. **Rebellion:** teen sophers will oftentimes attack their leader or mentor's theology because, during this phase, the sopher is still looking for his or her identity. For this reason, the sopher has likely read a few controversial books, started following leaders teaching a different theology than the one their leaders/mentors are teaching and started hanging around people who are rebelling against what they believe to be traditional church practices. Teen sophers often leave their churches offended and they often write books attacking church movements and leaders that they believe to be crippling the body of Christ.

3. **Puberty:** during puberty, a child's voice often changes. With teen sophers, their tones often change in their books. They are more confident with what they have written, even if their theology has been skewed by false doctrine. During this phase, they begin to sound more like adult sophers and they also begin to sound more like their pastors or their favorite pastors.

4. **Jealousy:** it is difficult for many teen sophers to identify when they are wrestling with jealousy; this is the force that fuels their competitive ways. During this phase, teen sophers usually compare themselves with other leaders, saying or thinking in their hearts that they can do what their leaders or other leaders have done or are doing. In this phase, sophers tend to attack other leaders, especially the ones who have big platforms and prospering ministries. They are always the first to voice their opinions when a leader's actions, sermons or beliefs are publicly brought under question. They almost always tend to side with the world anytime a scandal arises in the church. This is because teen sophers are overly determined to be heard and liked. At this stage of their ministries, they do not understand the value of silence. At this stage in their ministries, they do not understand the value of remaining hidden.

HUMILITY IS SOBRIETY.

During this phase in a writer's career, it is important that the writer remains humble and has two or more people that he or she can trust to inspect the author's belief systems. Sophers need to be corrected; correction is an important part of their development. It is also very important that sophers intentionally, consistently and aggressively humble themselves to ensure that the books they are writing are sound; this is especially true for writers called to write in-depth books. During this phase, sophers and young leaders run the greatest risk of being ensnared by false religions and doctrines because of pride. Teen sophers have a big appetite for knowledge, and this hunger can lead them into some dark places. Again, this is why the Bible says there is safety in the multitude of counselors (see Proverbs 11:14). A lot of people who rant all over social media, especially the ones who rant against leaders, leadership and church practices are teen sophers. I have seen these young leaders break away from their mentors and pastors, only to take to social media and attack the very leaders that they were once trained under. These writers often acquire a lot of followers because of their in-depth knowledge, controversial stances and unwillingness to remain silent when offended, hurt or confused. For this reason, the church loses more would-be leaders during this phase than any other stage. Thankfully, some sophers return to the faith and repent, but sadly enough, many of them never return. Luke 15 gives us an illustration of this in the parable of the prodigal son. It reads:

> "And he said, a certain man had two sons: And the younger of them said to his father, Father, give me the portion of goods that falleth to me. And he divided unto them his living. And not many days after the younger son gathered all together, and took his journey into a far country, and there wasted his substance with riotous living. And when he had spent all, there arose a mighty famine in that land; and he began to be in want. And he went and joined himself to a citizen of that country; and he sent him into his fields to feed swine. And he would fain have filled his belly with the husks that the swine did eat: and no man gave unto him. And when he came to himself, he said, How many hired servants of my father's have bread enough and to spare, and I perish with hunger! I will arise and go to my father, and will say unto him, Father, I have sinned against Heaven, and before thee, And am no more worthy to be called thy son: make me as one of thy hired servants. And he arose, and came to his father. But when he was yet a great way off, his father saw him, and had compassion, and ran, and fell on his neck, and kissed him. And the son said unto him, Father, I have sinned against Heaven, and in thy

sight, and am no more worthy to be called thy son. But the father said to his servants, Bring forth the best robe, and put it on him; and put a ring on his hand, and shoes on his feet: And bring hither the fatted calf, and kill it; and let us eat, and be merry: For this my son was dead, and is alive again; he was lost, and is found. And they began to be merry.

Now his elder son was in the field: and as he came and drew nigh to the house, he heard music and dancing. And he called one of the servants, and asked what these things meant. And he said unto him, Thy brother is come; and thy father hath killed the fatted calf, because he hath received him safe and sound. And he was angry, and would not go in: therefore came his father out, and entreated him. And he answering said to his father, Lo, these many years do I serve thee, neither transgressed I at any time thy commandment: and yet thou never gavest me a kid, that I might make merry with my friends: But as soon as this thy son was come, which hath devoured thy living with harlots, thou hast killed for him the fatted calf. And he said unto him, Son, thou art ever with me, and all that I have is thine. It was meet that we should make merry, and be glad: for this thy brother was dead, and is alive again; and was lost, and is found."

Teen sophers and leaders often believe they are ready to be leaders themselves; this is the very reason that they attack their own leaders. This is especially true for young leaders who have suffered through parental rejection, abandonment, abuse, or addiction in their developmental years. Like their younger counterparts, they often see ministry as an opportunity to become household names, increase their income and gather followers to themselves. They are more likely to create gangs or, if you want to get technical, covens of religious, rebellious young leaders who feel that their voices should be heard and their issues should be *immediately* addressed. Let's consider a pride of lions. Only one out of eight male lions survive until adulthood. There are many factors that contribute to this, but one of the greatest contributors to their mortality is the fact that young males normally challenge the heads of the pride (kings) before they reach adulthood. Male lions usually reach adulthood at the age of three. When lions are between the ages of one and two, they are classified as sub-adults, which is pretty much the human equivalent of a teenager. Around the age of two, most male lions reach sexual maturity, and again, the other males within a pride will normally kick them out. The male lion then runs off by himself or a few of his siblings and cousins will follow him into what is considered no-man's land. No-man's land is a territory that hasn't been claimed by another pride of lions. This is the transitional period for the ousted lion. Nevertheless, he will eventually find his way into the territory of another pride of lions where he will either kill the pride's males or, in most cases, be killed. If the lion successfully kills the king of the pride, he will then kill all of the male cubs. In Christianity, we call this "splitting churches." This animalistic behavior is normally attributed to teen sophers. This is why so many people suffer through what we commonly refer to as "church hurt." Without knowing it, they wander off into the no-man's land of Christianity and begin to attend churches headed up by young sophers who've established their ministries by splitting or destroying other ministries.

Next, we have young adult and adult sophers. We won't be exhaustive with this group, but in summary, young adult and adult sophers are usually the ones who've stuck by their leaders during the infancy stages of their writing careers or have returned, not necessarily to the churches they've left, but to the faith as a whole. In other words, if they fell by the wayside, they've repented. Please understand that many teen sophers start dabbling with false religions, and while many of them still believe in **a** Christ, they often start questioning and customizing **the** Christ so that He can fit into their theologies. Nevertheless, sophers and young leaders who survive the teen years of their assignments normally humble themselves, and it is during these phases that they begin to hear from God more. Young adult sophers can still be relatively rebellious, but they'll usually submit to correction, even though they may cry and question the correction. This is because they genuinely want to please God, and they want to be backed by God in everything they do. They are just at a point in their ministries where they don't necessarily understand everything they're told to do. Adult sophers, on the other hand, have realized that understanding does not come before submission; it can come weeks, months and even years after they've consistently submitted. Nevertheless, they've been in a relationship with God long enough to know that He is in control of their lives, even when they don't understand what He's doing or how He's doing it. Adult sophers have learned and are learning to process their offenses, not giving voice to their feelings every time they are hurt or offended, especially with their leaders. After all, offense is inevitable; it will happen, but whether we grow to become God-led leaders ourselves depends largely on how we respond to offense.

Young adults sophers normally take a year to complete a single book, whereas adult sophers normally take anywhere between three to six months to complete a book.

And finally, there are seasoned adult sophers. These writers are one-of-a-kind. They've survived the rigorous journey to and through adulthood; they've survived their own pride, rebellion and wavering beliefs. They've survived many scandals, survived being attacked by many of the people they've mentored or been mentored by, and they've survived the temptation to just quit and be normal. Seasoned sophers normally write some pretty in-depth books, especially the ones who write on the second to fifth level. You will find brief testimonies in their books, but most of their content is usable and points away from them. They bear the scars left from ambitious teen sophers who believed that they are being manipulated and taken advantage of by the seasoned sophers. Normally very humble, leaders who reach this stage often graduate from writing life-changing books to world-changing books. They acquire sons and daughters who are diligent and faithful—men and women who know the value of walking in peace and unity. In summary, seasoned sophers:
1. normally write two or more books a year.
2. finish their books in one to six months. Some adult sophers can finish their books in a matter of days or weeks.
3. conduct and publish a lot of research in their books to substantiate their views.
4. are accountable with anything controversial that they write.
5. are very confident in what they write.
6. are very humble.

Very few writers arrive at this stage because of pride. Nevertheless, when you come across a seasoned sopher, you've come across a leader who has overcome the very forces that have killed and chased away his or her brethren. They've seen great men and women fall because of pride. To make matters worse, they often have no choice but to stand on the sidelines and watch other powerful men and women self-destruct because of their choices and refusal to repent. All too often, seasoned sophers have to deal with people who repeatedly refuse wise counsel, refuse to sit down for a season or two and refuse to humble themselves or remain humble. And for this reason, they have to stand by as many powerful men and women of God fall by the wayside, after all, no man is exempt from the Word of God. Proverbs 16:18 reminds us this way, "Pride goeth before destruction, and an haughty spirit before a fall."

What is a Leader?

Many leaders will tell you that you don't need a leader. These leaders are in the teens of their ministries. They don't know or value the power of unity or correction because they don't know how to overcome the ambition that has silenced so many of their predecessors. Before you start your writing career, it is absolutely imperative that you make peace with the fact that God did institute and authorize fathers because He is *the* Father. Ephesians 4:11-15 confirms this; it reads, "And he gave some, apostles; and some, prophets; and some, evangelists; and some, pastors and teachers; for the perfecting of the saints, **for the work of the ministry**, for the edifying of the body of Christ: Till we all come **in the unity** of the faith, and of the knowledge of the Son of God, unto a perfect man, unto the measure of the stature of the fullness of Christ: That we henceforth be no more children, tossed to and fro, and carried about with every wind of doctrine, by the sleight of men, and cunning craftiness, whereby they lie in wait to deceive; but speaking the truth in love, may grow up into him in all things, which is the head, even Christ." In Psalm 133:1, David said, "Behold, how good and how pleasant it is for brethren to dwell together in unity!" Lastly, in Genesis 1:26, God said, "Let us make man in our image, *after our likeness.*" So, if any sopher or leader approaches you and questions why you, for example, believe that you have to have a leader, please understand that you have come in contact with someone who's likely been wounded. I've noticed that many of these young leaders have accomplished some great feat (graduated from college, launched successful businesses), and for this reason, they begin to value what they've learned in the secular world more than what they were taught in church. Honestly, many of them begin to see themselves as superior to their own leaders, as well as other leaders because the world's views differs from the church's theology.

For this reason, many young sophers and leaders wander off into universities and never truly return to the faith. Sure, they'll physically return to the church, but they will often use their degrees and what they've learned in the world to split churches and draw followers for themselves. They are the Hams who often expose what they see behind-the-scenes in ministry, but will NEVER expose what they've witnessed within the worldly organizations that they are so proudly members of. Again, like young male lions, they often find themselves wandering around without a covering, looking for another pride that they can attack. They walk into churches and slowly make their way towards the front, and they are the first to cry "church hurt" the minute they are rebuked for their divisive ways. How powerful would it be if our young leaders and sophers would defeat pride in their teen years and walk together in unity?! This would require that they submit to other leaders, and this is why so many of them fail; they don't want to be accountable and they don't want to be told by someone else that they are not ready to launch their ministries or write their books. They want to do what they want to do when they want to do it; this is the evidence of their immaturity.

A popular site for animal lovers called The Dodo gives us a picture of what it would look like if pride could no longer divide the church. In one of its articles, it tells the story of three male lions who refused to be kicked out of their pride. It reads:

"Three lion brothers decided long ago that it was best to stay together. Sirwa, Sayid and Shona lead a pride of 24 lions on the Ol Pejeta Conservancy in Kenya. Theirs is the Eastern Sector Pride, the largest lion pride on the conservancy and the safest—the survival rate of cubs is the highest for miles. The arrangement is highly unusual. 'They have not split from their birth pride as male lions are known to do,' Ol Pejeta told The Dodo. 'They protect the pride as a brotherhood coalition, which is rare. They peacefully share equal dominance, mating rights and pride protection duties with no infighting among them.' With the strong lionesses of the pride, the brothers are raising their families.

'Male lions are notorious for being aggressive and impatient with cubs,' Ol Pejeta said. 'However, our field technician, Chris, reports that the three brothers are extremely gentle with their offspring—Chris has never seen

them lash out at the cubs. Sayid fathers his cubs and defends the pride from intruders with his two brothers—and has the scars to prove it. He is a brother, a father and a peaceful member of the pride. The unusual arrangement shows how unique animals can be, with varying histories and experiences. The pride is truly a force of love and loyalty. Ol Pejeta is a wildlife conservancy of 110,000 acres that seeks to conserve endangered species and promote community development."
(Source: The Dodo/3 Lion Brothers Refuse to Leave Pride, Raise Their Kids Together/Sarah Schweig)

Of course, some people will come along and argue that the three male leaders of the pride are not lashing out against the young, using this to further their beliefs that they should never have to endure correction, and this is not true. Remember, the goal of correction is to bend our will until we stand upright in the image of Christ Jesus. The story details the fact that three rulers are humble enough to dwell together in one pride, sharing equal rights and authority. They are not against one another; instead, they have harnessed the power of unity. Proverbs 3:11 reads, "For whom the LORD loveth he correcteth; even as a father the son in whom he delighteth."

Another group of lions enjoy this same bond, only they are venturing off into other territories slaughtering their competition. They are called the Mapogo lions or the Mapogo brothers. Here's their story:

"'Legend' is a word that is thrown around all too often in this day and age, but the term surmises the reign of the Mapogo lions in the Sabi Sands to perfection. For the last six years or so, this notorious band of brothers has ruled the area with an iron paw. They are true warriors and have proved themselves time after time on the field of battle. During their prime, six of these magnificent specimens patrolled their territory, dispatching all competitors and striking fear into the hearts of all that found themselves in their way.

Legend has it that the Mapogo have been responsible for killing in excess of 40 males, females and cubs as they stamped their authority on their domain.

199

Whole prides have been wiped out in their relentless march for dominance and challengers have been eaten in an act of defiance: a fate almost unheard of in the species of _Panthera leo_. The former warden of the Sabi Sands has been cited saying that he believes them accountable for over 100 lion fatalities although the true number will probably never be known. Never before has the lion population known such a force and it is stories like this that have elevated their exploits to legendary status.

These brothers may have a fearsome reputation but in the world of the lion, they should be seen as the epitomes of what a successful coalition should be. They have been labeled as sadistic and remorseless to mention only a few adjectives assigned to them, but their exploits have ensured safe breeding grounds and stability in an area of unusually high competition. Their success has changed the dynamic of the lion population in this area forever and it is no surprise to me that litters are becoming more and more skewed in favor of male offspring. This is an inevitable outcome as nature attempts to balance the scales and provide a more level playing field.

In recent years, new and equally formidable coalitions have been responsible for whittling down the Mapogo's numbers as territorial lines were drawn in the sand and crossed and repeated battles were waged. The Majingilanes in the north and the Southern Pride males in the south have both had their say in the shaping of the new regime and now all that remains of the mighty Mapogo are two aging specimens known as Makhulu and Pretty Boy.

Since being overthrown by the Southern Pride males, the last of these legends have been sighted regularly on Sabi Sands as they search for new territory or maybe just sanctuary as they live out the remainder of their days. At 14 and 11 years of age, they have surpassed the life expectancy of most male lions and carry the scars of years of conflict on the front line."
(Source: Africa Geographic/The Legend of the Mapogo Lions/Ben Coley)

Sure, the aforementioned story details the power of walking together and conquering territories in unity. Nevertheless, when I read this story, I see a different picture. It makes me think about the many young leaders who wander around as nomads, creating coalitions with other rebels, slaughtering pastors and splitting churches with their words. They are the bloodthirsty Absaloms who were once a part of royal families, only to break away, gather up allies for themselves and return with the intent of slaughtering their fathers and taking over their ministries. Many of them are not interested in establishing physical churches; they simply want followers and allies. Then again, some of them go on to start false religions. They take to social media and repeatedly attack the very leaders who once entrusted them with their platforms. They passive-aggressively attack their leaders by attacking their theologies, and then, a few posts later, will take a moment out to honor the very leaders they are attacking. Sadly enough, many of these young sophers and leaders burden and kill leaders with unrealistic expectations, accusations and whatever devices they can unearth and use against them. To get a better understanding of what this looks like in the realm of the spirit, please review the picture below.

Seed Time, Harvest and Coverings

Many people nowadays are afraid of the word "father". First and foremost, we understand that a father is a covering, but why do we refer to them as such? To understand, let's examine the horticultural world. In this world, a covering is the hard shell that encases a seed, protecting it from the harsh elements and pests; it also keeps it from flying away in the wind. This shell is called a coat or covering. "The purpose of the seed coat is to protect the seed from physical, temperature-related, or water damage. The seed coat also ensures that the plant seed remains in a state of dormancy until conditions are right for the plant embryo to germinate, or sprout" (Reference: Study.com/Seed Coat: Definition & Function).

In Christianity, a covering serves many functions; they are:
1. For the perfecting (maturing of the saints). This keeps us from getting caught up and carried away by the many winds of doctrine.
2. For the edifying of the body of Christ. This helps us to free ourselves and others from the many traps and pests (demons) of the enemy. It also helps us to grow our relationship with God.
3. For the work of the ministry. The goal is reproduction. Our ultimate assignment is to reproduce Christ in others. We become more like Him, and then, teach others to do the same.

GOD USES THE NATURAL TO EXPLAIN THE THINGS OF THE SPIRIT.

You'll notice that every fruit and vegetable has a covering; we refer to this covering as a peel or a shell. It protects the edible, vulnerable interior and helps to regulate the fruit or vegetable's temperature so that it can grow and ripen. 1 Peter 5:8 reads, "Be sober, be vigilant; because your adversary the devil, as a roaring lion, walketh about, seeking whom he may devour." What this scripture tells us is that Satan looks for someone he can devour, meaning, he cannot devour everyone. He is a pest looking for something or someone to snack on. One of the easiest nuts to attack is one without a covering. In the Christian world, a covering is a leader; we all need someone to be accountable to, and of course, you will find many people, including some leaders, who will argue with this statement. Proverbs 11:14 reads, "Where no counsel is, the people fall: but in the <u>multitude of counselors</u> there is <u>safety</u>." Let's highlight two words in the aforementioned scriptures. Satan looks for whom he may **devour**. Where there is no counsel, the people **fall**.

The average height of a fruit tree is 18-20 feet. Why is this? We can safely summarize that God created all things to survive until it's ready to give life (reproduce), meaning, the height of the fruit tree protects the fruit. Nevertheless, many fruit that fall are not ripe. These premature drops are due to environmental conditions, pests and diseases. Some trees, such as peach trees, are known to get rid of their immature fruit; this allows the growing fruit to have access to more water and nutrients provided by the tree. Some plum trees, especially the ones that are less than five-years old, are known to "abort" excessive plums, especially in the summer. Satan comes along and devours or attempts to devour any believer who is not rooted in the Word of God and planted in the house of the Lord. What is the point? If you're a baby writer, it is important that you have someone covering and instructing you; this is where the Bible says you have safety. Despite the many right-sounding arguments that people make, you need a shell or, better yet, a covering. You don't have to use the term "spiritual father" or "spiritual mother," but you do need someone to father you.

1 Corinthians 4:15: For though ye have ten thousand instructors in Christ, yet have ye not many fathers: for in Christ Jesus I have begotten you through the gospel.

Examples of Coverings

- Your body has skin; this is its first covering. Skin protects the body from irritation, blood loss, and it regulates our body temperature.
- Your organs are covered and protected by your skeletal system. If someone argues with the covering theory, tell them to go and donate their skull to science. People know they need their skulls, but for whatever reason, the enemy has convinced them that they don't need a spiritual covering.
- Your house is a covering. It is a hard, outer shell that protects you from the external elements that would otherwise kill you.
- Your car is a covering. Even with convertibles, makers had to include windshields to protect the drivers. Motorcyclists are encouraged to wear helmets, and the ones who don't are more likely to die if they are involved in an accident than the ones who do.

- Your food has a covering. Your fruits, nuts and vegetables grow inside of a covering. When you order fast-food, restaurants will always cover your food before handing it to you. Nevertheless, in most non-fast-food chains, should you choose to eat inside, they will not cover your food since the building itself will serve as your food's covering. Sure, some flies may get in the building, but when and if they do, you have to behave like Abram when he drove the birds of prey away (see Genesis 15:11).
- You cover your body with clothes. You do this because it is the law, of course, and because you have to protect your "sensitive areas" from many of the bloodthirsty pests that wander around looking for something to devour. You also have to protect yourself from perverted, demonized people who can barely handle the sight of a thigh.
- Most of what we purchase is covered either by a box, a jar, a can or a plastic wrapper.
- Most, if not all states, now require drivers to have car insurance. Insurance is referred to as "coverage."
- Our head has a covering; we call this covering hair. Hair serves as a source for heat insulation and cooling.
- Unborn babies grow inside of what scientists refer to as the amniotic sac. This covering protects and nourishes the baby while it grows and develops in the womb.

We see coverings all around us, so how is it that we have allowed the devil to convince us that we don't need fathers? Everything that's valuable is worth protecting, and everything that's worth protecting (our brains, organs, food, spirit) has to be valued to be covered. If Jesus had to have a covering, who are we to think that we don't need one? "But I would have you know, that the head of every man is Christ; and the head of the woman is the man; **and the head of Christ is God**" (1 Corinthians 11:3).

Check out this powerful article about the emerging of butterflies.

"Butterflies go through a life cycle that involves several stages: egg, larva, pupa, and adult. The metamorphosis from a caterpillar into a butterfly occurs during the pupa stage. During this stage, the caterpillar's old body dies and a

new body forms inside a protective shell known as a chrysalis.
Moth caterpillars and many other insect larvae spin silk coverings for the chrysalis. These silk casings are called cocoons. Cocoons can be soft or hard, solid or web-like and any of several different colors or even see-through. Cocoons provide camouflage and additional protection for the chrysalis. Many moth caterpillars will spin their cocoons in concealed locations, such as the underside of leaves, at the base of a tree, or hanging from a small branch.

While some people think of cocoons as a resting place, there's no resting going on inside the cocoon! To the contrary, there's a lot of activity. Inside the cocoon and the chrysalis, the caterpillar is transforming into a new creature. This requires that the old caterpillar body be broken down and turned into something new. Think of it as insect recycling!"
(Source: Wonderopolis/Wonder of the Day #93/What Goes On Inside of a Cocoon?)

The word "covering" comes from the Hebrew word "kasah," which means to conceal. The purpose of a covering is to hide you for a period of time. The goal is to develop you into a mature believer and to keep you from emerging prematurely because of selfish ambition, fear, rejection or anything that would tempt you out of your season of obscurity. A covering helps you to crucify your flesh and all of its fruit (adultery, fornication, uncleanness, lasciviousness, idolatry, witchcraft, hatred, variance, emulations, wrath, strife, seditions, heresies, envyings, murders, drunkenness, revelings).

Seeds Have Coverings

You are a seed. What stage of development are you in? First and foremost, the obvious question is, can you effectively measure yourself? The answer is simple. No, just as you cannot cover yourself, you cannot effectively measure yourself. Someone else has to do this. Again, this is why we need good, godly leaders. 2 Corinthians 10:12 reads, "For we dare not make ourselves of the number, or compare ourselves with some that commend themselves: but they measuring themselves by themselves, and comparing themselves among themselves, are not wise." Ask your leaders/mentors to help you to identify where you are and stretch yourself. Remember, it is when we are stretched that what's on the inside of us will be revealed. This is an intentional and oftentimes frustrating process. Many leaders will teach you, but won't stretch you unless you specifically ask to be developed. You will never know what's in your heart, either good or bad, if you never allow yourself to be stretched. Of course, if you're never stretched, you will never really grow.

Genesis 8:22 reads, "While the Earth remaineth, seedtime and harvest, and cold and heat, and summer and winter, and day and night shall not cease." It is important for us to note that we are all seeds sown, and what we yield will be determined by:
1. what we sow.
2. where we sow.
3. how we sow (God loves a cheerful giver).
4. when we sow.

Consider the parable that Jesus shared in Matthew 13:3-9; it reads, "And he spake many things unto them in parables, saying, Behold, a sower went forth to sow; and when he sowed, some seeds fell by the way side, and the fowls came and devoured them up: Some fell upon stony places, where they had not much earth: and forthwith they sprung up, because they had no deepness of earth: And when the sun was up, they were scorched; and because they had no root, they withered away. And some fell among thorns; and the thorns sprung up, and choked them: But other fell into good ground, and brought forth fruit, some an hundredfold, some sixtyfold, some thirtyfold. Who hath ears to hear, let him hear." Now, let's look at the stages of sophers to get a better understanding.

Classification	Stage of Sopher
Infant Sophers	Seed Stage
Toddler Sophers	Germination
Kid Sophers	Sprout
Teen Sophers	Growth
Young Adult Sophers	Reproduction

Adult Sophers	Pollination
Seasoned Adult Sophers	Spreading Seeds

First and foremost, a leader is a sower. A leader has not finished his or her assignment until the leader duplicates himself or herself (Apostle Bryan Meadows). Now, let's examine the seed that fell:

1. **Some seed fell by the wayside** and the fowls came and devoured them. Fowls, in the scriptures, are symbolic of demonic spirits. In Genesis 15, Abram sacrificed several animals to the Lord, and the scripture tells us that when the fowls came down on the carcasses, Abram drove them away (see Genesis 15:11). And while this is an actual event that took place, it is also a symbolic event. It captures a still shot of what it looks like to be in ministry. While a leader raises up many would-be leaders, the truth is, many of them are led astray by demons and doctrines of demons. The word "wayside" means the side of a road. It depicts a point in a journey, meaning that as the leader leads, many of people following him or her will turn around or turn away.

2. **Some seed fell on stony places** where they had not much earth, and as a result, when the sun came up, they were scorched. Because they had no root, they withered away. When the Bible speaks of a stony place, it is dealing with the spirit of pride. Many believers cannot and will not receive the truth because of their hardheartedness. Then again, many sophers and young leaders enter no-man's land, refusing to be pastored and corrected, meaning, they have no root and no covering. They are not planted in the house of the Lord (see Psalm 92:13), and for this reason, they cannot flourish in every season that they enter. Many leaders lose sons and daughters to pride, some of which hide in stony places (caves). Some of these young rebellious believers will partner up, or better yet, pile up with other hardhearted believers (rebels) and become mountains used by the enemy to either block God's people or bring confusion to them. For this reason, God told us to say to the mountains, "Be thou removed, and be thou cast into the sea." The sea is a body of water, just like we are. The human body is sixty percent water! Remember, Jesus walked on water. What the Lord does is allows anyone who decides to come against a God-installed leader to become a footstool or place

of elevation for that leader. Psalm 110:1 reads, "The LORD said unto my Lord, Sit thou at my right hand, until I make thine enemies thy footstool."

3. **Some seed fell among thorns**, and the thorns sprung up and choked them. To better understand this, we have to familiarize ourselves with the story of Abimelech. Abimelech conspired to have all of his brothers killed, but not before convincing his mother's side of the family that he should be the sole ruler over the family. He had the women to go and speak into the ears of the leaders of Shechem. After he convinced them to make him king, he then went out and killed all of his brothers, except Jotham, who managed to escape. Abimelech killed all of his brothers with a single stone. Again, stones represent hard hearts or, better yet, pride. When Jotham, the surviving brother, heard about Abimelech's ordination, he went and stood atop Mount Gerizim and rebuked the men of that city for making his evil brother king. In that infamous speech, he spoke a parable, referring to his brother, Abimelech, as a bramble. A bramble is a thorny plant. He then cursed the people and fled. God eventually sent an evil spirit between Abimelech and the leaders of Shechem, who then began to conspire against him. Abimelech's end came in the Battle of Thebez after he'd reigned for three years. He had taken most of the city of Thebez before coming to the strong tower of that city to attack it. There, he met his fate. A woman in the strong tower threw down a stone and struck him on the head, crushing his skull. Realizing he was about to die, he told his armor bear to thrust him with his sword so that no one would ever say he had been defeated by a woman. In short, Abimelech had been surrounded by what the Bible refers to as "worthless fellows," to whom the scripture compares with brambles (thorns). Eventually, the people who Abimelech trusted rose up against him, and just as he'd killed his brethren with a stone, he too was mortally wounded by a stone. In short, many leaders lose some of their sons and daughters when those sons and daughters come of age and attempt to assassinate the leaders and/or anyone they've appointed.

4. **Some seed fell on good ground** and brought forth fruit of varying measures —hundredfold, some sixty-fold, some thirty-fold. Consider the parable of the talents. Remember, a gold talent was about the standard weight of a man. In summary, there are men and women of God who will stay the course, allowing

their leaders to take them the full distance that God has assigned them to lead them. These men and women will overcome pride, offense, correction, ambition and every dart/temptation the enemy throws their way. Someday, they too will become fathers and mothers, all bringing in the fruit of their labor which, of course, is the harvest of souls. They will raise up leaders who will also embark on the same journeys they were on. Together, they will defeat the "Mapogo lions" who roam outside of their jurisdictions looking to devour leaders and those who are loyal to them. They are the remnant who will repeatedly show the church (at large) the purpose and power of unity.

Again, this message won't resonate well with some people because they are still dealing with the aftermath of "church hurt." This is because many of the people who've been hurt by "a" church (not "the" church) were very well the victims of a pride of believers led astray by a man or woman who've split or attempted to split a church. The point is, it is important to know where you are as a Sopher; this way, when the temptation arises to walk away or rise up against your leader, you will understand what stage you're in and you will intentionally, consistently and aggressively overcome every spirit that's tempting you. Please understand that there is a season for everything. If God doesn't hand you a platform, a pile of money or a bestseller, please note that it's simply not your season for it. God knows how much you can handle in any given season. After all, every new level of success requires a greater level of sacrifice and comes with a greater level of warfare. Luke 12:48 says it this way, "Everyone to whom much was given, of him much will be required, and from him to whom they entrusted much, they will demand the more."

Classification	Stage of Sopher	Return
Infant Sophers	Seed Stage	
Toddler Sophers	Germination	
Kid Sophers	Sprout	
Teen Sophers	Growth	
Young Adult Sophers	Reproduction	Thirty-fold

Adult Sophers	Pollination	Sixty-fold
Seasoned Adult Sophers	Spreading Seeds	One Hundredfold

Sophers oftentimes start seeing a notable increase in their books' sales once they've past the teen years and have become young adult sophers. Now, this isn't to say that every other classification above young adults will not and do not see a return because many of them do. Nevertheless, their return is often determined by their investment (time and financial). Sophers who successfully deny themselves at any stage will oftentimes see a return on their investments. As sophers enter adulthood, many of them begin to see the fruit of their labor. I've coached hundreds of people, and one of the most common questions I've received from first-time authors is, "What can I do to get more sales? What is the best and most effective way to market a book?" Of course, any and every author wants to know this, and I always tell the author that it takes time. When people don't know who you are, it doesn't matter how good your book is, your book won't reach its maximum potential in sales. To reach more people, you have to market your book on the radio and on every media outlet possible. You have to be consistent at this, even when it doesn't appear to be working. Additionally, you have to continue to put out new material. You can record videos, audio messages and blog posts. The most effective marketing tool is consistency. Some sophers can write twenty or more books and suddenly find themselves on the best-seller's list with their twenty-first book. As God-installed authors, we can't be so focused on success that we miss the lesson in it all. We are all trying to go somewhere, but any successful entrepreneur or author will tell you that the journey can be long and frustrating; it's designed to separate the anxious from the diligent, the ambitious from the loyal and the slaves from the sons.

Please understand it's not about who gets "there" first, wherever "there" is to you. It's about who makes it there in one piece. Many sophers and leaders die in battle, only our battle isn't against flesh and blood. According to Ephesians 6:12, we are wrestling against principalities, powers, the rulers of the darkness of this world, and against spiritual wickedness in high places, even though the enemies that we can see have skin and teeth. The journey to success is long. This is because the majority of that journey is getting us to understand just what success means to God. It's not having a thriving business, a mega church, a big house, the best-looking spouse and two or three children; success, in God's eyes, means to persevere; it means to not give up, even when giving up makes the most sense to you.

Activation

Look at the image below. You see a female sopher (writer) signing a book for one of her readers. She looks well put together, and as a leader, no one knows what she's endured to get her books into the hands of her readers. Nevertheless, the next photo allows us to see the reality of the process.

This is a better depiction of what a true leader and/or sopher looks like once they've completed a God-given assignment. So, your assignment as a sopher is to write a note to your leaders, thanking them for their service. We say this to people who've served in war, but we rarely thank the people who've fought for us in warfare. Don't write anything less than five hundred words. Understand this: God blesses us when we place honor on others.

What's Your Range?

As writers (and teachers), our teachings range from minor to major earthquakes, however, the amount of people we've affected isn't always a representation of our potential. There are many writers who are comfortable shaking people up in the pews, but will not write or teach anything that shakes up the people in the pulpits or the people on the mountains of influence. This doesn't mean they can't teach on those levels; it simply means they're afraid to be as potent as they are, they're questioning what God has given them, or it's simply not their time to teach on those levels. Understand that the word "potent," as defined by Google, means: having great power, influence, or effect. It is the word in which "potential" derives. Google defines "potential" as: having or showing the capacity to become or develop into something in the future. It's also where we get the word "impotent," which means to be absent of power or to lack the ability to produce.

I've met teachers who are potent enough to send shockwaves through every community, country and continent, but they've learned to recognize (and respect) the seasons they're in. They know that the words they have in their bellies are not ready to be released and/or the people of God are not ready to receive such words. It takes a great deal of wisdom, maturity and discipline to have access to Earth-moving power but not use it, and they definitely have it. This means they have the potential (capacity, power, stamina) to release words over time that will disrupt governments, principalities and powers, but they also understand seasons. A wise man knows when to listen, when to observe, when to speak, how to speak and who to speak to.

What's your range? Most singers know this term all too well because every singer has a vocal range. What is vocal range? Wikipedia defines it this way, "Vocal range is the measure of the breadth of pitches that a human voice can phonate. Its most common application is within the context of singing, where it is used as a defining characteristic for classifying singing voices into groups known as voice types" (Reference: Wikipedia/ Vocal Range). Voice types vary from soprano, mezzo-soprano, or contralto, alto (if you are a woman), and a countertenor, tenor, baritone, or bass (if you are a man). Your voice type is a representation of your range or your ability to reach others. For example, one woman's voice is so low that only the people in the room she's in can hear her; another woman's voice is so high that it can be heard two or three houses away.

Your vocal range is the measure of your ability to move and manipulate sound waves. Sound is the energy produced by vibrations. Someone with a higher pitch causes those vibrations to move at a greater speed than someone whose pitch is lower. As a writer, your voice has a distinctive sound and pitch. Sure, people can't *hear* what you're writing, but they can *feel* the potency of your words. This is why, as a writer's coach, I strongly advise people to not overuse exclamation points. New writers often think that exclamation points, especially a lot of them, will cause their words to have the power and ripple effect they felt when they wrote them, not understanding that what moves them may not necessarily move others. An earthquake that hits China will rarely be felt in the United States. Someone in China could write, for example, "We're experiencing an earthquake!!!!!!!!!!" to someone in America, but this won't cause the American to feel the vibrations or understand the fear the writer is experiencing. Instead, the excessive exclamation points would only serve as a distraction or go unnoticed. This means that what is powerful enough to move you may have little to no effect on others. With that said, as writers, we have to be mindful of our pitches when writing. This means that we should not attempt to speak to the lost if we ourselves aren't submitted to God. We should not try to speak to the married if we've never been married. We should not try to speak to the people in the pulpits if we've never owned or rented a pulpit to stand on. Your pitch should always stay in the vicinity of your experience. When you stay within your range, your voice won't crack.

If a singer whose range is, for example, contralto attempts to sing soprano, she would experience what is called voice breaking, otherwise known as vocal cracking. Voice breaking happens when a person's voice is strained. Professional singers learn to stay within their own voice registers, but new, inexperienced singers may attempt to go beyond their vocal range. This is similar to what happens to writers who do not know their range (reach, target audience). They attempt to speak to people they cannot relate to—people they simply cannot reach. Moses had to first escape Egypt before he could lead the people of God out of it. He was raised as Pharaoh's grandson, meaning, he had access to Pharaoh. He didn't have a castle advantage; he didn't sneak into the Pharaoh's chambers in the middle of the night and threaten him. He followed kingdom protocol and requested a meeting with Pharaoh.

When writers use the right pitch, they release a sound that's powerful enough to move the people within their jurisdictions. Think of a singer. A woman with a contralto voice doesn't have to sing soprano to move the crowd. She just needs to sing the right song and be sincere in her worship. When the people's hearts begin to open, God's presence will begin to fall and this is when deliverance starts breaking out. Nevertheless, if she loses focus on her assignment (ushering in the presence of God) and focuses on sounding better than the artist who went up before her, she'll release the wrong sound. As a result, she'll bore, frustrate and even offend the people in the audience. Her jurisdiction is her vocal range. As for writers, our jurisdiction revolves around the people we're called to reach. If we attempt to teach outside of our range (understanding), we'll bore, frustrate, offend and even bind our target audience.

You can discover your range by paying attention to the people who are interested in what you have to say. You can discover your range by paying attention to the voices you are attracted to. What type of friends do you have (see Amos 3:3)? What topics do you speak about the most (see Luke 6:45)? Are you deep (speaking on controversial, underlying issues that most people don't understand or talk about) or are you surface-level (speaking on matters like trends, politics, celebrities, etc.)? Are you calm when people don't agree with you or do you feel the need to make your voice heard? People who take to social media to voice their offenses usually have low pitches because of their little faith, so they try to increase their range by fishing for likes. A good example of this would be when the media began to crucify Joel Osteen for not allowing people who were displaced by Hurricane Harvey to use his church for shelter. When this controversy broke, people who had little to no range took to social media and began to verbally stone Joel Osteen. They didn't wait to see if the reports were true. They saw an opportunity to make their voices heard and they took it because their pitches were so low that they couldn't even reach their own families. The same is true when, for example, a woman took to social media and posted a list of leaders she called false prophets and apostles. She did this because her range (reach) was low, but the spirit operating in her was considered high-ranking. To increase her range, she attacked people who could reach the people whose attention she coveted. This is similar to what kings would do in the biblical times. If a king coveted the land and resources that another king presided over, that king would gather his troops and go to war against that country. His goal was to take what he believed he was entitled to. In some cases, this worked (see 1 Chronicles 5:26), but in others, it backfired (see 2 Chronicles 18:28-34).

As a writer, you will either stay in your range or stray from your range. To stay in your range, you need to accept and make peace with the sound of your voice (both audibly and in written form). You also need to be thankful for the reach God has given you, not coveting another man or woman's followers. You will discover your range simply by speaking. For example, when I speak on matters that God has graced me to speak on, I attract many viewers, but any time I tackle a topic where my pitch is low, my viewer-count will be low. This doesn't mean I'm not graced to speak on certain topics; it can simply mean that it's just not my season to address those matters. So, I pay attention to the sound that draws the people to me, and I pay attention to the sound that repels them from me. Lastly, I pay attention to my voice breaks. A writer's voice breaks when the writer runs out of revelation and starts recycling what they've already taught. For me, it's usually when I use a lot of filler words and I rush through a topic because I'm questioning what little information I do have regarding the matter.

Plagiarism: The Literary Version of Lip Syncing

As an editor, I've edited many books, but the most memorable ones were the ones that were plagiarized. I would find myself editing what felt like the worst books ever written because of poor syntax, misspelled words, misused words and so on. I've edited books where the author wrote on the level of a seven-year-old child (this isn't to condemn the authors; it's to make a point). Suddenly, the book went from elementary to amazing. All of a sudden, the paragraphs started reading as if they'd been written by a very wise (adult) man or woman. When this happens, I know that the author is engaging in plagiarism.

What is plagiarism? Dictionary.com defines the term this way, "An act or instance of using or closely imitating the language and thoughts of another author without authorization and the representation of that author's work as one's own, as by not crediting the original author." In the music world, this would be the equivalent of lip syncing. Authors who plagiarize the text of others do so when their motives for writing a book are ungodly, meaning, they are not receiving revelation from God. This leads them to covet another writer's words and/or writing style. Consider King Saul. When he could not hear from God anymore, he went and inquired of the witch of Endor. Sadly enough, many authors have the ability to write some amazing books, but because of selfish motives and pride, they are not hearing from God. For this reason, they take to Google, looking for blog posts and articles that they can steal. One of the most common devices I've seen works this way: the author will take a few lines from several blogs and articles written by others and mix them together, believing that if he or she doesn't share the entire article or written work of a single writer, his or her deception won't be found out. I've seen cases where the author will even add a little text of his/her own, not realizing that the paragraph reads like it was written by someone battling with multiple personalities. When confronted, most would-be authors want to know how I knew their books were plagiarized, and the answer is simple—the author's range changed. The author went from writing paragraphs that could reach surface-level believers to posting paragraphs that were potent enough to rearrange continents. The author's range *suddenly* elevated from a soft meow to a loud roar. And when the author attempted to reinsert his or her voice, the author's voice cracked because the author was attempting to go outside of his or her metron.

Please understand that staying in your range is necessary if you ever want to become a best-seller. If you search Amazon, you'll find many books with one-star ratings and bad reviews because the authors chose to use voices that were not their own, not realizing that their voices were good enough to reach the people God wanted them to reach. Instead, they coveted another man or woman's audience, not realizing that the shockwaves required to move that audience would tear up the author's life. The minute you release a sound, that sound will first invade your hearing before it reaches your audience. This means that you will experience the same earth-moving power that you are releasing to your audience. For example, if you have the power of a minor earthquake and yet, you attempt to sound and write like someone who has the potency of a major earthquake, you will have to experience the power that you are releasing. When this happens, most authors claim they are going through warfare when, in truth, they are simply feeling the power of the words they've released. This is why it is necessary to write on your level. As writers, we have to respect our own range (reach). When we don't respect our range, we don't respect the people God has given us the ability to reach and this will always translate in our books.

What's Your Rank?

Remember, there is protocol in the Kingdom of God. For this reason, knowing our range is as important as knowing our rank. Amazingly enough, many believers today are unaware of the fact that there is rank in the spirit, just as there is rank (order) in the natural. For this reason, we see an incline of believers attempting to challenge people and spirits who, quite frankly, outrank them. This is why some believers endure heavy opposition. Understand this: when the enemy comes in like a flood, the Spirit of the Lord will raise up a standard (rule, regulation) against him. This scripture shows us the direction of the attack; the enemy *comes in* like a flood. But what happens when a believer *goes out* after a foe that he or she has not been authorized by God to challenge? Let's consider Luke 9:40 (ESV), which reads, "John answered, 'Master, we saw someone casting out demons in your name, and we tried to stop him, because he does not follow with us.' But Jesus said to him, 'Do not stop him, for the one who is not against you is for you.'"

In this story, someone who clearly did not have a personal relationship with Jesus was using His name to cast out devils. He wasn't *trying* to cast out demons; he was *successfully* casting them out. Nevertheless, Jesus did not oppose him. In Luke 9:50 (ESV), He responded by saying, "But Jesus said to him, "Do not stop him, for the one who is not against you is for you." In this, we see that the man who'd gone out was not "sent" by God, however, he was working in alignment with God's will. Additionally, it is the finger of God that casts out demons, meaning, God was in and with him, so the Lord was not opposed to him. Because he was in tune with the heart of God, we can stretch out to say that he knew which demonic cases to tackle and which ones he wasn't equipped to address.

A similar group of men arose who we know as the Sons of Sceva. Acts 19:14-16 (ESV) details their story. "Then some of the itinerant Jewish exorcists undertook to invoke the name of the Lord Jesus over those who had evil spirits, saying, 'I adjure you by the Jesus whom Paul proclaims.' Seven sons of a Jewish high priest named Sceva were doing this. But the evil spirit answered them, 'Jesus I know, and Paul I recognize, but who are you?' And the man in whom was the evil spirit leaped on them, mastered all of them and overpowered them, so that they fled out of that house naked and wounded. "

Why is it that one man was successfully casting out demons in the name of Jesus, but *seven* sons of a Jewish High priest couldn't cast out a single demon? The answer is in the text. They obviously did not believe that Jesus was and is the Christ. They referred to Him as, "... *the Jesus whom Paul proclaims*." This means they went up against a demon with absolutely no faith. Additionally, the Bible refers to them as "exorcists," which means they'd successfully driven out demons before using the name of Jesus. Nevertheless, the demon they confronted on that particular day drove them out because they needed more faith. Why is this? Because the demon likely outranked them. Keep Matthew 17:19-21 in mind. The disciples of Jesus had successfully driven out many demons, but they came in contact with one they could not drive out as easily. Matthew 17:19-21 (ESV) reads, "Then came the disciples to Jesus apart, and said, Why could not we cast him out? And Jesus said unto them, Because of your unbelief: for verily I say unto you, If you have faith as a grain of mustard seed, you shall say unto this mountain, Remove from here to yonder place; and it shall remove; and nothing shall be impossible unto you. But this kind goes not out but by prayer and fasting." Jesus said they couldn't drive the demon out because of their unbelief, coupled with the fact that the demon they were addressing required more than a "*manifest and go*" command. Such a demon is driven out by fasting *and* praying. Why? Because of the rank of the demon. Queen Esther knew she was about to go up against a decree that had been sent out by Haman (a man who represented a principality) and authorized by her husband, King Xerxes, in his ignorance. She couldn't just charge into her husband's office (before the throne) and mouth off about how Haman was conspiring to kill the Jews, after all, doing so could have gotten her killed or dethroned like her predecessor, Vashti. Sure, she was queen, but she still had to obey the law. She had not been sent for, therefore, she had to petition the King of kings before going before her king. For this reason, she asked Mordecai to proclaim a fast.

Esther 4:15-16 (ESV): Then Esther told them to reply to Mordecai, "Go, gather all the Jews to be found in Susa, and hold a fast on my behalf, and do not eat or drink for three days, night or day. I and my young women will also fast as you do. Then I will go to the king, though it is against the law, and if I perish, I perish."

Mordecai was telling Esther to go before the king and plead with him on behalf of the Jews, but initially, Esther refused, fearing for her own life. Mordecai had once acted as Esther's father, having raised her after the death of her parents. He then *sent* her into the king's castle to compete for the role of queen. Once she got into position, he tried to send her before the king, but Esther was under a different authority; she had to abide by a different set of rules. Nevertheless, she realized the urgency of the matter and decided to fast and pray so she could go before the authority who was greater than herself—the king.

Impersonating an Officer

Revelation 2:2 (ESV): I know your works, your toil and your patient endurance, and how you cannot bear with those who are evil, but have tested those who call themselves apostles and are not, and found them to be false.

In most U.S. states, impersonating a police officer is a felony, punishable by fines of one thousand dollars or more and up to five years imprisonment. Remember, the natural is very much like the supernatural. There are people inside and outside of the church who are impersonating officers of the five-fold ministry. These people are not authentic; they are self-proclaimed leaders who've managed to find other people to back their lies. They look like godly leaders, sound like godly leaders and even dress like godly leaders; that is, until they are faced with real warfare. Because they were not sent by God, they do not understand Kingdom protocol, for the most part, and the ones who do understand it have a slight grasp on it or do not respect it. This is why they act, behave and fall into the same snares as the world does.

The word "Apostle" means "sent one." Every apostolic voice in the Bible was sent by a father or a father figure; this was what legalized them. Moses, Abraham, and John the Baptist were sent by God. David was sent by his father to the battlefield, but King Saul sent and legalized him to go up against Goliath. Jehu was called by God, but sent by Elisha, the prophet. Queen Esther was sent into the king's castle by her father-figure, Mordecai. All throughout the Bible, we see examples of people being sent into varying lands and situations to address evil. Sure, believers can and should cast out demons, but one of the things most (authentic) deliverance ministers will tell you is

—don't try to cast out every demon you come in contact with. There will be times when you'll feel like the anointing is lifting; this is usually indicative of God telling us to fast and pray. You need strategies. You need understanding. You may even need to close some demonic-access doors that are open in your own life. Fasting exposes those doors. Esther fasted because she needed to appeal to the authority who was higher than her husband. Sure, she outranked Haman the moment she became queen, but the decree that Haman sent out had been signed (authorized) by her husband, meaning that even if she had confronted Haman and had him killed, the decree would have remained active. She needed to bring down the enemy of the Jews, but she had to follow the chain of command to do so.

What does this mean for writers? It's simple. With your pen, you are to address whatever situations, spirits and mindsets (strongholds) that God leads you to address. Address only what you understand and have overcome. If you address something or someone who outranks you, the enemy won't *come in* like a flood; you will have *gone out* after him, thus, engaging him in a war that you may not yet be prepared for. For example, I don't understand sex trafficking outside of what I've heard and what I've read. I can mildly address the matter, but to come up against that principality, I need to align myself with someone who God has given the tools and understanding needed to properly and strategically confront it. This doesn't mean the person will have had to be involved in the sex trade; it simply means that the person will, at minimum, have received revelation from the Lord on the matter. If I decided to write a series of books on sex trafficking without the permission of God, the enemy would attack me in the areas in which I am ignorant. Then again, I could wait on instructions from God, and if He gave me the green-light to charge up against that principality, I could do so. Again, I'd have to remain prayerful and I'd have to fast throughout the ordeal. Consider David and Goliath. Goliath, at best, represents a high-ranking demon or principality. He was so big that even King Saul was afraid of him. 1 Samuel 17:4-11 (ESV) tells the story: "And there came out from the camp of the Philistines a champion named Goliath of Gath, whose height was six cubits and a span. This means that he was nine feet, six inches tall. He had a helmet of bronze on his head, and he was armed with a coat of mail, and the weight of the coat was five thousand shekels of bronze. And he had bronze armor on his legs, and a javelin of bronze slung between his shoulders. The shaft of his spear was like a weaver's beam, and his spear's head weighed six hundred shekels of iron. And his shield-bearer went before him. He stood and shouted to the ranks of Israel, 'Why have you come out to draw up for battle? Am I not a Philistine, and are you not servants of Saul? Choose a man for yourselves, and let him come down to me. If he is able to fight with me and kill me, then we will be your servants. But if I prevail against him and kill him, then you shall be our servants and serve us.' And the Philistine said, 'I defy the ranks of Israel this day. Give me a man, that we may fight together.' When Saul and all Israel heard these words of the Philistine, they were dismayed and greatly afraid."

In the aforementioned story, we see the enemy coming in like a flood. 1 Samuel 17:1 reads, "Now the Philistines gathered together their armies to battle, and were gathered together at Shochoh, which belongeth to Judah, and pitched between Shochoh and Azekah, in Ephesdammim." Again, this means that the enemy came in because the city of Shochoh belonged to Judah. Goliath was too much to bear for most of the Israelites. He did not outrank King Saul in the natural (King Saul was king of Israel; Goliath was a champion fighter for the Philistines), but he was greater in stature and in skill. David, on the other hand, was apostolic in nature. He had not been ordained king of Israel at that point, but he was being *sent* back and forth by his father to feed his brothers. Remember, the word "apostle" means "sent one." As an apostle of the Lord, David started experiencing what we now call righteous indignation when he heard Goliath challenging the Israelites. Remember, Goliath represents a principality (prince, principal demon), whereas the king of the Philistines represented a ruling spirit. The king of the Philistines' strength was in the principality. David answered the call on his life and decided to address Goliath.

When the sons of Sceva addressed the demon that was in the man who ultimately beat and stripped them of their clothes, the demon responded, "Jesus I know, and Paul I know about, but who are you?" This was the equivalent of the demon asking the guys to show it their badges or what legal rights they had to bind it. They didn't have any because they had not been authorized. This means they were impersonating the anointing, and as such, they started a conversation with a demon that they could not finish. The enemy didn't come in like a flood; the Bible tells us that they went to the guy's house.

The same was true for David. Before David could go up against Goliath, he had to be given the charge (sent) by someone who outranked him (King Saul). It would have been out of order and even foolish for David to rush onto the battlefield and start attacking Goliath (the same is true for writers). First, he underwent the scrutiny of his brothers and then, King Saul sent for him. After he met with King Saul, his abilities were questioned by the king himself. David told King Saul that he'd killed both a bear and a lion with his bare hands, meaning, he was giving his testimony, showing that he had endured and overcome battles that would have killed most men. Lastly, King Saul decided to put his armor on David. This is something we see quite often these days—people trying to teach others to fight an enemy while wearing the same armor that they once trembled in. This armor, which represented the Old Testament, was slowing David down, so he took it off. He grabbed his staff — which was a representation of the apostolic, and five stones, all of which represented the five-fold office (apostle, prophet, pastor, teacher, evangelist). He then went up against what he called the uncircumcised (unsaved, ungodly) Philistine in the name of the Lord. 1 Samuel 17:43-50 (ESV) reads, "And the Philistine said to David, 'Am I a dog, that you come to me with sticks?' And the Philistine cursed David by his gods. The Philistine said to David, 'Come to me, and I will give your flesh to the birds of the air and to the beasts of the field.' Then David said to the Philistine, 'You come to me with a sword and with a spear and with a javelin, but I come to you in the name of the Lord of hosts, the God of the armies of Israel, whom you have defied. This day the Lord will deliver you into my hand, and I will strike you down and cut off your head. And I will give the dead bodies of the host of the Philistines this day to the birds of the air and to the wild beasts of the Earth, that all the Earth may know that there is a God in Israel, and that all this assembly may know that the Lord saves not with sword and spear. For the battle is the Lord's, and he will give you into our hand.'

When the Philistine arose and came and drew near to meet David, David ran quickly toward the battle line to meet the Philistine. And David put his hand in his bag and took out a stone and slung it and struck the Philistine on his forehead. The stone sank into his forehead, and he fell on his face to the ground. So David prevailed over the Philistine with a sling and with a stone, and struck the Philistine and killed him. There was no sword in the hand of David."

THERE WAS NO SWORD IN DAVID'S HAND BECAUSE THE SWORD OF THE LORD WAS IN HIS MOUTH.

He came against Goliath in the name of the Lord. He didn't just go out against Goliath; he was sent, or better yet, authorized. Sure, he volunteered, but he could not take on the assignment until he was sent by someone greater (in rank) than himself. A similar account is found in the story of Jehu versus Jezebel. As we all know, Ahab died in the war against Ramoth-Gilead. Ahab, who was King of Israel, represented a nation and Jezebel represented a principality (principal demon); she was submitted to the ruling spirits of Baal and Asherah. To take down Baal and Asherah, God had to follow His own established rules of rank. In order for something in the natural to be overtaken, it had to be taken down by someone in the natural. Spirits have no authority when they have no authorities to work through. Jesus had not yet come into the Earth (in the flesh), so God dealt with ruling authorities by dealing with the rulers who gave them authority. Ahab was that ruler. The same demons he trusted in were the ones who led him to his death. After he died in the war, the principality (Jezebel) had to be dealt with. Again, God never goes against His own established rules, so He needed someone to take on Jezebel, but before this could happen, the person had to have the rank of Jezebel. He sent out a prophet to anoint a warrior named Jehu as king over Northern Israel (Samaria).

2 Kings 9:1-10 (ESV): Then Elisha the prophet called one of the sons of the prophets and said to him, "Tie up your garments, and take this flask of oil in your hand, and go to Ramoth-gilead. And when you arrive, look there for Jehu the son of Jehoshaphat, son of Nimshi. And go in and have him rise from among his fellows, and lead him to an inner chamber. Then take the flask of oil and pour it on his head and say, 'Thus says the Lord, I anoint you king over Israel.' Then open the door and flee; do not linger."

So the young man, the servant of the prophet, went to Ramoth-gilead. And when he came, behold, the commanders of the army were in council. And he said, "I have a word for you, O commander." And Jehu said, "To which of us all?" And he said, "To you, O commander." So he arose and went into the house. And the young man poured the oil on his head, saying to him, "Thus says the Lord, the God of Israel, I anoint you king over the people of the Lord, over Israel. And you shall strike down the house of Ahab your master, so that I may avenge on Jezebel the blood of my servants the prophets, and the blood of all the servants of the Lord. For the whole house of Ahab shall perish, and I will cut off from Ahab every male, bond or free, in Israel. And I will make the house of Ahab like the house of Jeroboam the son of Nebat, and like the house of Baasha the son of Ahijah. And the dogs shall eat Jezebel in the territory of Jezreel, and none shall bury her." Then he opened the door and fled.

What happened in this story? Elisha, who had been given authority by God, "sent out" one of the sons of the prophets to anoint Jehu as king. This means that the son of the prophet was granted apostolic authority—if but for a moment. He did as he was instructed, but after his assignment was completed—after he'd emptied out the oil, Elisha instructed him to run. This is a message that many modern-day believers can benefit from. Sometimes, God will send us to complete an assignment, but once the anointing has lifted, we'd better flee.

Jehu, by the Word of the Lord, became king of Israel, thus giving him the legal authority to cast her out. Jehu was given equal rank before he could address, not only Jezebel, the woman, but Jezebel, the principality. When Jehu went to her castle, he was a representative of the apostolic. He had been sent to come against her; he didn't just casually decide to write a book and address a principality. Before Jehu could address Jezebel, he had to address some smaller principalities (King Joram, who was king of Northern Israel, and King Ahaziah, who was king over Judah). Why did he address these kings before going up against Jezebel? It's called strategy.

After taking down the two kings, Jehu went to Jezebel's castle and addressed a few of her servants. 2 Kings 9:30-33 (ESV) reads, "When Jehu came to Jezreel, Jezebel heard of it. And she painted her eyes and adorned her head and looked out of the window. And as Jehu entered the gate, she said, 'Is it peace, you Zimri, murderer of your master?' And he lifted up his face to the window and said, 'Who is on my side? Who?' Two or three eunuchs looked out at him. He said, 'Throw her down.' So they threw her down." Why didn't Jehu respond to Jezebel? Why did he address her servants? It's simple. Because you cannot reason with a demon; you can only reason with the people who have been serving that demon. When they threw Jezebel down, this was a picture of deliverance. They were now free from her, but they could not legally throw her down unless someone of equivalent or greater authority gave them the command to do so. Jehu had been anointed as king over Israel, meaning that

Jezebel had been deposed, even though she was still reigning as queen. In the ministry of deliverance, a principality can be deposed, but it still has to be cast down, just like we can fall out of agreement with a thought, but if it rises up again, we still have to cast it down.

Let's revisit Esther's story. She too was going up against a principality, but before she could do so, she had to be elevated to the position of queen. As queen, she outranked Haman, the enemy of the Jews, but her husband's signature gave Haman the legal authority he needed to come up against the Jews. To defeat Haman, Esther had to pray, fast and strategize. Again, she couldn't just charge into the main hall and "expose" Haman, which is what so many believers attempt to do these days. What if they'd had internet and social media at that time? Would it have been a wise move for Esther to "expose" Haman on social media? No, it would have been silly, at best. Not to mention, it could have cost her dearly. Esther needed a Word from the Lord. She fasted, prayed and submitted to wise counsel (Mordecai). To defeat Haman (the principality), she had to speak with the king and get him to release another decree— one that would give the Jews the legal right to respond to their enemies with equal force. She ended up having two meetings with the king and Haman. During the first meeting, she didn't casually blurt out that Haman was trying to kill her people. Instead, she was strategic. She held her peace, waiting for the moment when the Lord would impress upon her heart to reveal the wicked deeds of Haman. God was working on the heart of King Xerxes, so Esther had to wait for the right moment to tell her husband that she was a Jew, meaning that Haman's plot to kill the Jews was also a plot that would affect her. It was during that second meeting that she exposed Haman. She didn't stand on her balcony, call the towns' people together and blast Haman. She exposed Haman to the one who could do something about Haman's plans. Honestly, this is why so many believers who attempt to "expose" leaders go through so much warfare. There is order in the Kingdom of God; you cannot just go charging up against someone who outranks you. Additionally, many believers try to expose good, godly leaders who, quite frankly, haven't done anything but rebuked them. By striking up against someone or something that outranks us, we invite unnecessary warfare into our lives.

Esther didn't bring Haman down; God did. Esther recognized who had the authority to address Haman. What does this mean? This is to help us better understand why so many authors or aspiring authors go through warfare. Many authors attempt to address spirits, people and authorities that they have not been *sent* to address. In the writing world, there are rules, regulations, ranks and restrictions, just as there are in every other world (law, medicine, entrepreneurship, education, etc.). We can't just go charging out against a situation just because we are physically able to do so —just as a police officer whose jurisdiction is limited to, for example, Tampa, Florida cannot (legally) use his badge to arrest a criminal in Ft. Lauderdale, Florida. Sure, the officer has some power in his own region, but in Ft. Lauderdale, his authority is subject to the laws and authorities of that city. For this reason, he would have to call the police in that area to make an arrest or he could make a citizen's arrest. Even if he decided to make a citizen's arrest, he'd have to understand and execute the laws of that region in regards to citizen's arrests.

The point is, it is important for us to understand rank when we start dealing with spiritual matters. Pride will always make a writer believe that he or she can go up against any and everything that *needs* to be addressed, but humility will always give us the wisdom we need to know which wars are ours to fight and which ones are not. We, as Christian writers, should know our jurisdictions. When we better understand this, we will birth out more books and those books will be more effective at destroying the works of the enemy. Even if we are surface-level writers, our pens have enough power in them to destroy the works of the enemy, otherwise, God would not give us the charge to write. Understand this: even if you're a surface-level writer, your assignment is to prepare the ground (hearts of the people) for someone who could go further underneath the surface.

Esther was a true officer because she held the office of the Queen of Persia, even though she was a Jewish woman. King Xerxes was a true officer because he held the office of the king of Persia. Haman was a real problem because he'd been authorized by an authentic officer. To clean up the mess her husband had made, Esther had to make sure that everything she did was authorized; she could not use the fact that she was right and Haman was wrong to justify being out of order.

What's Your Peak?

Every mountain has a peak. The peak (or summit) is the highest point of the mountain. A peak represents the overall destination for most climbers; it is the furthest point in which a person can travel. After a climber has reached the peak of a mountain, he can no longer ascend on that mountain. He has to descend. One interesting fact is that not all mountains have been fully climbed. For example, Machapuchare, a mountain that stands over 22 thousand feet in the Himalayas, is off limits to climbers for religious reasons. Wikipedia.org reports the following:

> "Machapuchare has never been climbed to its summit. The only attempt was in 1957 by a British team led by Lieutenant Colonel Jimmy Roberts. Climbers Wilfrid Noyce and A. D. M. Cox climbed to within 150 m (492 ft) of the summit via the north ridge, to an approximate altitude of 22,793 ft (6,947 m). They did not complete the ascent, as they had promised not to set foot on the actual summit. Since then, the mountain has been declared sacred, and is now closed to climbers."

KNOW YOUR LIMITS!

The climbers knew their limitations. Even though the climbers were British and were not Hindu, they knew they had to respect the government and religion of that region. Had they gone further up the mountain, it is possible that they could have been arrested or worse, killed—if not by the locals, they could have been killed by the unmerciful weather at the top of the mountain. The harsh reality is many mountains are littered with the bodies of people who've perished in the extreme conditions or because of an avalanche. Mt. Everest alone is believed to be the resting place of more than two hundred unclaimed bodies. The reality is, every climber has a limit; not all climbers can reach the peak of a mountain and not all mountains are safe for climbing. It is imperative that every climber knows:

1. His or her physical limitations.
2. The laws of the country that owns any given mountain.
3. If the mountain has ever been climbed.
4. If the mountain can safely be climbed.

WHAT'S YOUR PEAK?

Much like Machapuchare, there are several mountains, especially in Asia, that have never been fully climbed for religious reasons. Locals believe that the mountains are sacred to their gods, and as silly as this sounds to us as Christians, we have to respect their wishes when we're in their region.

Every author has a peak. This isn't just a spiritual jurisdiction, it is the writer's mental limitations. Now, this may not make sense to some, but will be understood by seasoned writers. Writing can be both mentally and physically demanding, after all, the body responds to the report of the mind and vice versa. Just as we all have a spiritual capacity, we all have a mental capacity. Our mental capacity is the amount of knowledge we are able to retain at any given time. This capacity is determined by our level of understanding, after all, you cannot understand what you do not know. This means that knowledge comes *before* understanding, and not the other way around. Think of it this way. 1 Corinthians 10:13 (ESV) reads, "No temptation has overtaken you that is not common to man. God is faithful, and he will not let you be tempted beyond your ability, but with the temptation he will also provide the way of escape, that you may be able to endure it." In this, God is letting us know that we all have a measure of ability and He won't allow us to be tempted beyond our ability to resist temptation. Of course, our capacity is determined by whatever measure of faith we've been gifted with. Additionally, the way of escape isn't always an issue of choice. For example, two almost supernatural abilities of the human body are comas and Dissociative Amnesia. When severe trauma happens to the body, especially the brain, the brain can shut itself down in an attempt to protect itself or the body from further injury. This episode is called a coma.

Next, there's Dissociative Amnesia. WebMD reports, "Dissociative Amnesia occurs when a person blocks out certain information, usually associated with a stressful or traumatic event, leaving him or her unable to remember important personal information. With this disorder, the degree of memory loss goes beyond normal forgetfulness and includes gaps in memory for long periods of time or of memories involving the traumatic event." Both comas and trauma-related amnesia serve as temporary ways of escape. Most victims of violence cannot recall every minute detail of a traumatic event. Undoubtedly, this was and is God's way of protecting the victim.

What's Your Peak?

Most bank ATMs won't allow you to withdraw more than four to five hundred dollars on any given day. Banks place these limitations on ATMs to protect their customers' money and their own money, after all, the average responsible consumer won't spend any more than four to five hundred dollars a day, unless the buyer is making a large purchase. However, a thief will try to spend as much as he or she can, because the thief knows that it's just a matter of time before the debit or credit card has been reported stolen. Additionally, withdrawal limitations protect us, the consumers, from our ability to be immature at any given moment. Let's face it. We're human, and as such, we all have varying degrees of maturity in every given area and in every given season of our lives. This maturity can oftentimes become subject to our emotions when we are dealing with moments of high stress, depression and/or trauma. For example, some of us are very mature when it comes to managing our finances (on normal days), while others are not. Some of us are very mature when it comes to maintaining cleanliness in our homes (on most days), while others are not. Some of us are disciplined when it comes to tithing (on most paydays), while others are not. However, a woman who is good at managing her finances, when faced with a highly traumatic event like a sudden breakup, can suddenly feel the need to engage in retail therapy. *Retail therapy is using shopping or spending as an outlet to relieve one's self of stress, fear, worry or any other negative emotion.* This means that even though she is mature enough to manage the financial measure in which God has given her, her maturity was subject to her life's seasons. In other words, like a Governor can override a judge's judgment, her emotions were able to override or cloud her judgment. We live in a capitalistic and demanding nation where we are repeatedly and oftentimes subconsciously taught that we can fix almost every problem with a credit or debit card swipe. For this reason, most Americans deal with trauma by spending. After spending, most consumers find themselves suffering through what is known as buyers' remorse. Wikipedia defines "buyers' remorse" this way: "Buyer's remorse (or buyer's regret) is the sense of regret after having made a purchase. It is frequently associated with the purchase of an expensive item such as a car or a house. It may stem from fear of making the wrong choice, guilt over extravagance, or a suspicion of having been overly influenced by the seller." Buyers' remorse is usually the result of a person engaging in retail therapy. After the excitement of having purchased something new wears off, the buyer's perspective of whatever it was that he or she purchased becomes subject to the buyer's reality.

WHAT'S YOUR PEAK?

Because some stores and service providers have strict policies regarding what can and cannot be returned, some buyers report their cards lost or stolen in an attempt to recover the money they've spent. This is why most banks place a limit on ATM withdrawals.

Some writers can attest to becoming increasingly tired, disinterested or stressed when attempting to testify about a traumatic event that took place in their lives. Of course, there are many writers who, to this day, haven't recognized the fact that they become frustrated, weary or distracted every time they start writing about something they've experienced or witnessed. This isn't always a demon engaging them in warfare; in some cases, the author has reached his or her peak or limitations. The author's inability to write any further can be the result of the author going too far on any given day or going too far into any given story. The reality is, some traumatic events have to be remembered in segments, because knowing the whole story would be too much to bear for the person who's been traumatized. This is why we recall details in what we refer to as *bits and pieces*. Just as our brains shut down in a comatose state to protect us, our memory banks also allow us to make just as much of a withdrawal as we can bear. Like an ATM, God often places limitations on mental withdrawals.

When I was eight-years old, I witnessed the near death of my then two-year-old sister. My mother was at work and my dad had given my then ten-year-old brother and I permission to go to the community swimming pool. Of course, he told us to take our two-year-old sister with us. So, we got on our bikes and headed to the pool with my sister riding along on the back of my brother's bike.

At the pool, all went well at first. Neither of us could swim, plus, I was shorter than most children my age, so I decided not to get into the water. The pool was huge and had two depths (if I remember correctly): three feet and either six or ten feet. My brother got into the pool, my sister got on his back and off they went, wandering around. Not realizing that there was no divider between the two depths, my brother wandered too far into the pool, suddenly stepping into the deepest part of the pool. I was on the other side of the pool fussing at him when suddenly, both him and my sister went underwater. At first, I thought he was playing around, so I continued to raise my voice at him, threatening to tell our parents. Nevertheless, it didn't take me long to realize that he wasn't playing and both he and my litter sister were in grave danger. Not knowing how to swim, I started screaming at the top of my lungs, and before long, one of the teenagers who volunteered at the pool dove in and rushed to their aid, with another boy diving in right behind him. Seconds later, I watched as my brother emerged from the pool. He was okay—just shaken up, but my sister was nowhere in sight. I panicked all the more and then, the other young man emerged carrying my sister's nearly lifeless body. She was unconscious. They rushed her out of the pool and immediately started pumping her stomach. At first, nothing happened. She didn't respond, so the guys picked her up and rushed her into the building. There, they continued performing CPR on her while we waited for an ambulance. Seconds felt like minutes and minutes felt like hours. I was only eight-years old, but because this was a traumatic event, the images burned themselves into my memory.

Suddenly, my sister started coughing and vomiting up water. A few minutes later, the emergency medical response (ambulance) arrived and my sister was rushed to the hospital. As traumatic as this event was, not just for me, but for my siblings, I learned a very valuable lesson: when we are aware that we are wandering in a place where there are varying depths, we need to always look for the signs that we are leaving one measure and entering another. This is especially true when we are responsible for another person's life. Understand this: when writing a book, you are responsible for the lives affected by the words you write. This means you should never go beyond the peak of what you understand.

First, let me address the obvious. The story I told was personal, appalling and may even seem disjointed from the writing experience. Nevertheless, let me assure you that your words can be just as devastating to the lives of your readers. There are many scriptures in the Bible that detail the power of words. Proverbs 2:16-19 (ESV) reads, "So you will be delivered from the forbidden woman, from the adulteress with her *smooth words*, who forsakes the companion of her youth and forgets the covenant of her God; for her house sinks down to death, and her paths to the departed; *none who go to her come back, nor do they regain the paths of life.*" 1 Kings 13 tells the story of a Judean prophet who'd been given strict directions by God to not go back in the direction he'd come from when he'd come to Bethel. He was also told to not eat bread or drink water while there. While in Bethel, he'd prophesied against a pagan altar that King Jeroboam had built in the city. King Jeroboam wasn't too far away, and when he'd heard what the man prophesied, he pointed towards him and commanded that he be seized, nevertheless, his hand shriveled up. He then pleaded with the prophet to intercede for him. The prophet complied and the king's hand was restored. King Jeroboam then tried to convince the man to have dinner with him, but he refused. He obeyed the Lord and left, heading in a different direction, but the sons of a prophet saw the ordeal and rushed back to tell their father about it. The father then pursued the man, and when he found him, he asked him to come back and have dinner with him. The young man refused, telling the old prophet (as the Bible refers to him) what God had commanded him. Here's the rest of the story as told in 1 Kings 13:16-22 (ESV). "The man of God said, 'I cannot turn back and go with you, nor can I eat bread or drink water with you in this place. I have been told by the word of the Lord: 'You must not eat bread or drink water there or return by the way you came.'

The old prophet answered, 'I too am a prophet, as you are. And an angel said to me by the word of the Lord: 'Bring him back with you to your house so that he may eat bread and drink water.' (But he was lying to him.) So the man of God returned with him and ate and drank in his house.

While they were sitting at the table, the word of the Lord came to the old prophet who had brought him back. He cried out to the man of God who had come from Judah, 'This is what the Lord says: 'You have defied the word of the Lord and have not kept the command the Lord your God gave you. You came back and ate bread and drank water in the place where he told you not to eat or drink. Therefore your body will not be buried in the tomb of your ancestors.'"

As we can see, the words we use can change lives, ruin lives and end lives. That prophet died because he'd trusted in the words of another fellow prophet—a prophet whose words he didn't bother to test. Additionally, the Bible does not refer to the old prophet as a false prophet. As we can see, while at the table, he actually did give an accurate word from the Lord. What does this mean? Even a God-installed prophet can be a deadly prophet when he or she is led astray by ambition. This means the prophet has gone beyond the peak of his or her understanding, wandered outside of God's Word and is now leading others astray with his or her own words. Consider the British climbers who were allowed to climb Machapuchare in 1957. Even though they may have been physically able to go beyond 457 feet, they knew to respect the laws of the land they were in. They had already established how high they would go before they started climbing, so even though they didn't reach the mountain's peak or the peak of their potential, they reached the peak of their agreement with the locals. It was wise of them not to go beyond this point.

My sister trusted my brother to carry her around in the pool. She didn't understand the whole concept of depth, drowning or death. She simply wanted to have fun, but because she'd trusted in the wrong person (at that time), she almost lost her life. We aren't just wandering around in the depths of understanding by ourselves; we are carrying our readers with us. This is why so many authors end up with negative reviews. Many authors are not aware of the fact that they have a target audience, meaning, there are people of a specific gender, race, age group, socioeconomic class, and so on who are most likely to read each author's book. Your target audience has a depth of knowledge and a peak of understanding that they can grasp. If an author takes a newly converted Christian (babe in Christ) and suddenly dips that reader into, for example, deep revelatory conversations, that author runs the risk of drowning the reader. Of course, we know the reader will walk away with his life, but for how long? Think about this: most people who've joined false religions were led astray by words. We can safely say that many of those people likely came in contact with deep Christians who tried to give them meat when they had no teeth to chew it, nevertheless, some smooth-talking, serpent-possessed soul from a false religion walked up to that person and explained his beliefs in a way that the person could understand. Was it the false teacher who led the saint astray? Sure, but he had help in doing so. The believer who nearly drowned the baby Christian was equally as responsible for that believer's entrapment. Think of it this way. If you are drowning, would you resist a Muslim man's attempt to save you? No, you wouldn't. The same is true for people who find themselves in hardships; they'll get any book that looks like it has the potential to pull them out of their chaos. Matthew 18:5-6 (ESV) reads, "Whoever receives one such child in my name receives me, but whoever causes one of these little ones who believe in me to sin, it would be better for him to have a great millstone fastened around his neck and to be drowned in the depth of the sea."

In this scripture, Jesus isn't just talking about little children; He's also talking about babes in Christ. As we can see, Jesus spoke of drowning, depths, burdens (millstones) and seas.

When we hear the word "drowning," we automatically think of water, and rightfully so. Water represents many things in the Bible, including baptism. To be baptized means to be submerged in water. It represents the death of the old man and the rising of the new one. Nevertheless, in the aforementioned passage and scripture, we understand that Jesus isn't talking about baptism, because He did not mention the person rising again. Instead, the millstone represents a weight or, better yet, an anchor. Millstones were large and very heavy stones used to grind grain.

Additionally, a millstone was symbolic of Leviathan—a demonic spirit that the Bible associates with pride. In Job 41:24, God compares the Leviathan serpent (spirit) to a millstone; it reads, "His heart is hard as a stone, hard as the lower millstone." What's interesting is that a millstone was used to kill a wicked and very prideful man named Abimelech who rose to the position of king by killing all but one of his brothers. The Bible says he killed them all on one stone. Biblically speaking, stones represent hardheartedness, stubbornness or pride. Abimelech was eventually killed by a stone—a millstone that is. Judges 9:50-54 (ESV) details Abimelech's last moments; it reads, "Then Abimelech went to Thebez and encamped against Thebez and captured it. But there was a strong tower within the city, and all the men and women and all the leaders of the city fled to it and shut themselves in, and they went up to the roof of the tower. And Abimelech came to the tower and fought against it and drew near to the door of the tower to burn it with fire. And a certain woman threw an upper millstone on Abimelech's head and crushed his skull. Then he called quickly to the young man his armor-bearer and said to him, 'Draw your sword and kill me, lest they say of me, 'A woman killed him.' And his young man thrust him through, and he died."

Abimelech was so proud and so filled with the Leviathan spirit that he could not bear the thought of people saying a woman killed him. For this reason, in his dying moments, he commanded his armor-bearer to thrust his sword through him to ensure that he died with his dignity in place.

Leading Readers Astray

Let's revisit the story of the man who'd been sleeping with his mother or stepmother. This sin was so grievous that Apostle Paul said that it wasn't even named amongst the Gentiles (unbelievers). 1 Corinthians 5:3-5 (ESV) reads, "For though absent in body, I am present in spirit; and as if present, I have already pronounced judgment on the one who did such a thing. When you are assembled in the name of the Lord Jesus and my spirit is present, with the power of our Lord Jesus, you are to deliver this man to Satan for the destruction of the flesh, so that his spirit may be saved in the day of the Lord." Why would Apostle Paul tell the Church of Corinth to hand over a person to Satan for the destruction of his flesh?

1. The man was a member of the Church of Corinth, which means he was saved or he was familiar with salvation.
2. The man in question was sleeping with his mother or stepmother.
3. Even if the man hadn't accepted Jesus Christ as his Lord and Savior, and even if he had stayed under Old Testament law, he would have been killed by the traditional Jews because the crime he'd committed was punished by death under the Law.

Handing him over to Satan was a figurative command. The church wasn't going to pray to Satan, after all, this would be witchcraft. Instead, they were to cut ties with the believer and he would no longer be able to assemble with the congregants. The command was to basically stop covering him—to kick him out of the church. He would then be exposed to the very devil in which he'd been led astray by which, of course, could mean a speedy death for him. But just like many rebellious believers we know, watching his life slowly pass away from him would be enough for that young man to call on the name of the Lord. As cruel as Apostle Paul's words appeared to be, they were actually merciful because:

1. If the man wasn't saved and was just attending church because his parents forced him to do so, Apostle Paul could have easily turned him over to the unconverted Jews. Again, his crime merited a stoning for both him and his mother or stepmother.
2. The man knew his behavior was wrong, which means he was pride-filled and rebellious. This means he was likely bound by the Leviathan spirit. Apostle

Paul was pretty much saying to let that spirit have the man's flesh. Job 41:34 says the following about Leviathan, "He sees everything that is high; he is king over all the sons of pride."

3. Apostle Paul was concerned about the man's soul, which is why he ended his judgment this way, "... so that his spirit may be saved in the day of the Lord."

What does this mean and how does it tie in to Jesus saying it would be better for that man (the one who'd caused a babe to sin) to be cast into the sea with a great millstone around his neck? It's simple. Jesus was being merciful as well. The millstone was likely symbolic; it represented the person being turned over to Leviathan (a servant of Satan) for the destruction of his or her flesh. Proverbs 16:18 (ESV) reads, "Pride goes before destruction, and a haughty spirit before a fall."

A little one who believes in Christ is a believer, albeit immature, which means he or she is easily led astray. Who better to lead a child of God astray than a proud, boastful, self-elected soul whose ambition is bigger than his or her pride? To cause a "little one" to sin is to overwhelm the person. Remember, Isaiah 59:19, which reads, "When the enemy shall come in like a flood, the Spirit of the LORD shall lift up a standard against him." The Greek word for "standard" is kanón, and it means *a rule of conduct or doctrine* (see Strong's Concordance 2583). When Apostle Paul told the Church of Corinth to "turn over such a one to Satan for the destruction of his flesh," he was establishing a rule of conduct. Turning a man over to the enemy was nothing new. Psalm 81:12 reads, "So I gave them up unto their own hearts' lust: *and* they walked in their own counsels." Romans 1:24-27 details another account of God turning people over; it states, "Therefore God gave them up in the lusts of their hearts to impurity, to the dishonoring of their bodies among themselves, because they exchanged the truth about God for a lie and worshiped and served the creature rather than the Creator, who is blessed forever! Amen. For this cause God gave them up unto vile affections: for even their women did change the natural use into that which is against nature: And likewise also the men, leaving the natural use of the woman, burned in their lust one toward another; men with men working that which is unseemly, and receiving in themselves that recompense of their error which was meet. "

As writers, we have to be very careful that we do not allow pride to enter our hearts, otherwise, we will be guilty of leading God's people astray. This includes drowning them in information far too great for them to understand or taking them beyond the borders of our understanding where they can be easily bound by the enemy. Please know that wisdom speaks through the mic of humility, meaning, if you are led by the Spirit of God, you will know how to speak to your target audience. Nevertheless, if you are led astray by pride and ambition, your dominating thoughts will be:

1. Your face on the cover of a book.
2. Getting the best shot of yourself at your book signing.
3. How your enemies will be ashamed and envious when they see your book.
4. How much money you'll make from your book.
5. You holding up a cover of your book on television.

Such thoughts lead writers to harm God's people with their books. This is why we have to be mindful of our thoughts and goals when we decide to teach God's people. Remember, He is the Great Shepherd, and as such, He is very protective over His sheep.

I remember my brother saying that when he started sinking in the pool, my sister fell off his back and grabbed onto one of his legs. Being young and scared, he'd kept trying to shake off her his leg because she was pulling him down. Now, I'm pretty sure had he gotten out of the pool without my sister, he would have tried to get help for her, but in that life or death moment, he could only seem to think of himself. This is why we, as writers, cannot afford to suffocate ourselves with revelation, meaning, we go beyond our depth of knowledge or peak of understanding in an attempt to sound "deep." In other words, it is possible for us to go too far. When a writer writes what he or she does not thoroughly understand, the writer will:

1. **Try to rush to a conclusion.** In swimming, this is called, rushing to the surface too quickly and it can be dangerous.
2. **Lie.** We can't speak the truth if we don't know it.
3. **Plagiarize.** As an Editor, I've seen this many times. Aspiring authors who are more focused on photo shoots than they are on souls will become frustrated while attempting to sound "deep." Realizing that they have no revelation to boast of, they will go online and start copying paragraphs from blogs and

articles. They will then slightly edit those paragraphs, mix them with text they've stolen from other authors and then try to pass the work off as their own.

4. **Write a shallow book about deep matters.** Imagine this: a woman stands at the edge of a cliff. She's wearing a bathing suit and excited about jumping into the waters below. The water looks deep and inviting, so she dives off the cliff and hits her head on a rock. As it turns out, the waters below her were not deep at all. They just looked that way. A man standing at the base of the mountain jumps into the water and swims over to the now unconscious woman. When he reaches her nearly lifeless body, he starts performing CPR. Thankfully, she lives, but the damage that's done to her affects her quality of life. This is similar to what happens when shallow (unlearned) people write books that appear to be in-depth theological books upon first glance, but turn out to be nothing but powerless paperbacks with no substance.

5. **Underfeed the readers.** It is possible to tell the truth but not have enough for the audience you're feeding. For example, have you ever heard someone say another person has outgrown the church he or she attends? What the speaker is suggesting is that the soul in question is not receiving the amount of knowledge or the depth of revelation he or she needs to move through and/or past the season he or she is in. The speaker is suggesting that the person in question is no longer growing and needs a richer diet of wisdom, knowledge and revelation to sustain and elevate him or her. If you don't have enough knowledge to feed the people you are attempting to feed, you will starve them.

My brother knew he couldn't swim, but he didn't pay attention to the signs that were posted up. He wandered from the three-foot side of the pool to the six (or ten) foot side. When asked why, he said he saw other children who appeared to be standing upright; he simply assumed that their feet were touching the bottom of the pool when they were not. This is what happens when we, as writers, stop paying attention to the signs around us and start focusing on the success of other people's books and ministries. Joyce Meyers is a wonderful teacher and I love to hear her speak, however, she does not teach on the same level (depth) as Cindy Trimm. Both women are awesome teachers who've garnered a lot of success in ministry by teaching from their sphere of influence (metron). Joyce Meyers talks a lot about practical matters—things most people can relate to, whereas, Cindy Trimm speaks a lot about spiritual matters—matters most people do not understand. This doesn't mean that one teacher is better than the other; it simply means they teach on different levels. If Joyce Meyers was to take her eyes off Jesus and start focusing on Cindy Trimm's ministry, she'd start sinking and she'd take her followers with her, or she could end up bound if she went beyond the borders of her understanding. Thankfully, she's a wise woman who is content with the measure that God has given her. This is how we must be as writers. We can't look at others and desire their platforms, their audiences and the reactions they get when they teach. Our assignment is to stay focused on Jesus so that we can teach our readers to do the same.

What signs should we, as writers, look out for—signs that indicate we're going further than we should go?

1. **Extreme weariness after writing:** When authors write, we are pouring out of the abundance of our hearts. For this reason, it is normal to feel a little tired after writing, but writers who go too far into revelation usually get tired very quickly. This is because they are drowning (in a sense).

2. **Headaches and neck pains while writing:** Headaches, neck pains and shoulder pains often mean you are messing around in the spirit realm. Headaches usually indicate that we are ascending or have ascended to a new realm. The shoulder represents government, so sudden shoulder pains are often indicative of you messing with legal (spiritual) matters. Understand that demons, for example, use legal premises to justify inhabiting, attacking and oppressing believers. To address them, you have to address the doors (legal rights) they are using. Shoulder pains are okay if you understand what you're teaching, have experience warring against the enemy, there are no open doors to the enemy in your life, and you've experienced this pain before. Nevertheless, it's not okay if it's all new to you.

3. **Seemingly unmanageable warfare:** Remember, demons love legal advantages, so if you charge into an area that you are not knowledgeable about, you've charged into a prison cell of sorts. A simple, "Satan, I bind you," won't suffice when dealing with high-ranking spirits. Believe it or not,

wisdom, knowledge and understanding all serve as protective armors. If I know my rights, I can use that knowledge to navigate the subject I'm teaching, plus, if I am attacked by the enemy, I can easily (and legally) bind him. Ambitious Christians led astray by dreams of grandeur almost always end up bound and under attack. Now, let's understand one thing. The moment you decide to write, the enemy will try to offer up some resistance, and if he can find a way to engage you in warfare, he will. Nevertheless, when the warfare is seemingly unbearable, this normally means that the writer has encountered a Goliath-sized demon and has no understanding of how to take him down.

4. **A sudden disdain for writing:** If every time you start typing a book, you end up under attack or feeling drained, it goes without saying that you'll lose interest in or respect for the writing process. You may even begin to hate it. Writers who venture outside of their metron normally write one or two books in their lifetimes because the experiences they had while writing were terrible, sometimes even traumatic.

5. **Feeling rushed to draw a conclusion:** Again, writers who go too deep in revelation don't truly understand what they're teaching, and for this reason, they will rush towards homeostasis. Google defines "homeostasis" as the tendency toward a relatively stable equilibrium between interdependent elements, especially as maintained by physiological processes." When a person goes into "survival mode," while experiencing a life-endangering event, the person will try to quickly return to the element that he or she felt safe in. This is what happens when authors rush toward the peaks of revelation; they rise too quickly in their attempts to rush to a conclusion. In the swimming world, when a swimmer ascends too quickly, that swimmer runs the risk of catching "the bends." Libretext.org defines "the bends" this way, "The Bends is an illness that arises from the rapid release of nitrogen gas from the bloodstream and is caused by bubbles forming in the blood when a diver ascends to the surface of the ocean to rapidly. It is also referred to as Caisson sickness, decompression sickness (DCS), and Divers' Disease" (Reference: LibreTexts/Chemistry/Case Study/ The Bends/Dhara Shah/UCD)."

Again, going too deep into knowledge and then rushing to a conclusion not only endangers the writer, but it endangers the readers. An example of this is when a writer makes a deep, profound or controversial statement or two, and then, suddenly starts teaching on the surface level again. There is a level between the deep and the surface and writers have to venture through it before they can resurface. For example, if a diver swims thirty feet underwater, he has to go through levels just to resurface. He has to respect each level, venturing through them at a certain speed, otherwise, he risks getting the bends. When writers suddenly start teaching practically after making a few controversial statements, it simply means that writers have no basis, evidence, understanding or substance for whatever it is that they're teaching.

Knowing how far we can venture off into revelation can make the difference between us becoming best-sellers who not only write and sell books, but authors who are reaching the people in our spheres of influence. We'd become effective at teaching God's people, meaning, our words will meet their targets. It's a great accomplishment to be a teacher, but it is a blessing to be an effective one.

The Peak of Revelation

Every good thing has a peak or point. Another word for peak is climax. Google defines "climax" this way: *the most intense, exciting, or important point of something; a culmination or apex.*

The word "climax" comes from the word "climb." To climb means to ascend or move upward while pursuing a particular destination. Anything that can be climbed has a point to it. The point or peak is the highest stationary location on any given object; it is oftentimes the destination of the climber. In the writing world, every book must have a point. The book's title isn't the point or peak of the book; the book's summary is. When a book cannot be effectively summarized, it will be written off by readers and critics as a *pointless* book, also known as a flop.

Every reader is a climber and every climber has a destination that he or she wants to reach. When a book is horizontally written, meaning, it has no climax, it reads like a boring professor who's speaking just to hear himself talk. Needless to say, unlike the professor, as writers, we don't have the luxury of grading our readers; they are the ones who'll be grading what we've written. To avoid receiving bad reviews, it is always important to take your readers towards a peak. Remember, God often revealed Himself on the top of mountains; this is usually where revelation is birthed and understanding is unearthed.

There is a difference between descending and ascending; this is true even while writing. Knowledge is within our reach. We can pick up a book or speak with an elder. Many of us can go online or if we're patient enough, we can study our surroundings. Knowledge is everywhere; it's not hidden, nor does it require a team of scientists to decode or a team of archaeologists to excavate. Like cold air; it travels low and can be heard by anyone who has ears to hear. Nevertheless, knowledge has to be received, and the way we receive knowledge is by believing the information that is presented to us. Understanding, on the other hand, is like heat; it rises, therefore, to get to it, we must ascend. We dive into the depths of knowledge, but we ascend the heights of revelation, and it is there that we receive understanding. Revelation is the lighted path that leads us to understanding.

The word "revelation" comes from the word "reveal." To reveal a thing means to uncover what was once hidden. Proverbs 25:2 (ESV) reads, "It is the *glory* of God to conceal a thing: but the honor of kings is to search out a matter." God covered our sins with the blood of His Son, Jesus Christ. This was for His glory.

The word "reveal" comes from the word "veil." It simply means to unveil or uncover; to illuminate. In the Tabernacle of Moses, there was a veil that separated the Holy Place from the Holy of Holies. During the annual atonement ceremony, the High Priest was allowed to go beyond this veil where he would then enter the presence of God. When Moses would ascend Mt. Sinai, the glory of God would permeate him so much that when he descended, he would cover his face with a veil because his face was illuminated. Jesus took a few of His disciples on a high mountain and there, He was transfigured in front of them. Matthew 17:1-5 (ESV) reads, "And after six days Jesus took with him Peter and James, and John his brother, and led them up a high mountain by themselves. And he was transfigured before them, and his face shone like the sun, and his clothes became white as light. And behold, there appeared to them Moses and Elijah, talking with him. And Peter said to Jesus, 'Lord, it is good that we are here. If you wish, I will make three tents here, one for you and one for Moses and one for Elijah.' He was still speaking when, behold, a bright cloud overshadowed them, and a voice from the cloud said, 'This is my beloved Son, with whom I am well pleased; listen to him.'" As a matter of fact, the book of Revelation is the revealing of Alpha (the Beginning) and Omega (the End). It foretells of what is to come regarding the judgment of God, but it also introduces us to a Genesis moment (the war in Heaven). The end represents the end of ignorance; it is the mystery of God solved once and for all. It is the peak or point of God's earthly sermon to us.

As we can see, God usually reveals Himself in high places and heightened moments. As writers, we must understand that knowledge without revelation is like a wedding with no bride. The two must marry if understanding is to be conceived. Therefore, when we begin to explain certain points in our books, our goal is to help the readers to pace their way through revelation so they can get to understanding. When Jesus took Peter, James and John on a high mountain with Him, they saw Him transfigured; this was the revealing or confirmation of His identity. As a matter of fact, not long before this transfiguration, Jesus asked His disciples a very important question. Matthew 16:13-17 (ESV) reads, "Now when Jesus came into the district of Caesarea Philippi, he asked his disciples, 'Who do people say that the Son of Man is?' And they said, 'Some say John the Baptist, others say Elijah, and others Jeremiah or one of the prophets.' He said to them, 'But who do you say that I am?' Simon Peter replied, 'You are the Christ, the Son of the living God.' And Jesus answered him, 'Blessed are you, Simon Bar-Jonah! For flesh and blood has not *revealed* this to you, but my Father who is in Heaven.'"

In the aforementioned scripture, Jesus tested His disciples' knowledge of Him, but it was Peter who had gotten the revelation of who Jesus was and is. Less than a week later, John, James and Peter were on a high mountain with Jesus when He was suddenly transfigured. Peter already had the revelation, meaning, he had already seen (in the spirit) beyond the veil, but it was on this mountain that he received understanding and confirmation. When he interrupted the meeting between Jesus, Moses and Elijah, the Lord spoke from a cloud and said to him, "This is my beloved Son, with whom I am well pleased; listen to him." This was the moment that Peter received understanding. Sure, he had already accepted that Jesus Christ was the Son of God; He is the Messiah—the Holy One of Israel, however, there was still a few things that Peter did not understand. This is why he interrupted the meeting. God validated Jesus on that mountain, likely removing any residue of doubt that may have been hindering the three men who'd ascended with Him.

The point is, every book should be filled with knowledge, but that knowledge must always come to a head in order for the book to be relevant. Every book must have a climax. Without a climax, readers are left feeling robbed of their hard-earned money and time. Always decide (before writing) what the point of your book is. If you don't know what it is, you may be prophesying in part, meaning, you are only ready to start writing the book, but until you get the rest of the message, you are not ready to publish it, and this is okay. What's important is that you draw a conclusion for your readers and then, help them to reach that conclusion. What's the difference? Every mountain has a peak, but this doesn't mean that every climber has reached the peak. Some people can see it, but don't know how to safely reach it. This is where tour guides come in. As an author, you are a tour guide. You have to layer your book with knowledge and revelation, both of which will serve as guides to help your readers reach understanding. How do you do this? By simply taking every key moment in your book and tying it into your already established summary.

The word "summary" comes from the word "sum." The following definitions were taken from Dictionary.com.
Sum: the aggregate of two or more numbers, magnitudes, quantities, or particulars as determined by or as if by the mathematical process of addition: (ex: The sum of 6 and 8 is 14).
Summary: a comprehensive and usually brief abstract, recapitulation, or compendium of previously stated facts or statements.
Summit: the highest point or part, as of a hill, a line of travel, or any object; top; apex.

Your book's summary is the highest point of it; it is the overall conclusion or the sum total of the message. It is taking previously stated facts and truths and fusing them together to make a point—or it can be the highest point broken down into facts and truths that eventually converge to create a climax. Either way you write it, just make sure that it takes your readers on a journey—a journey that has an overall destination for the readers to reach.

What are You Offering?

One of the problems that believers have today is, there are many people walking around with testimonies they have yet to share. There are many believers who God has given revelation to, but they are withholding those revelations because they want to copyright them (they missed the point of the message). In other words, people tend to forget that revelation is the revealing of a prophecy; it is a message revealed to a person or a group of people for the sole purpose of encouraging, edifying or warning God's people. Nevertheless, when a person receives revelation and decides to keep it, that revelation becomes bitter in that person's belly. Anytime God gives you a Word for His people, you have to pour it upon His people.

Revelation 12:11: And they overcame him by the blood of the Lamb, and by the word of their testimony; and they loved not their lives unto the death.

Let's first establish one thing—you have to become whatever it is that you intend to pour out. In other words, you will be transformed into a drink offering to be poured out before the Lord for the sake of edifying His people. What is a drink offering? ATS Bible Dictionary describes it this way: "A small quantity of wine, part of which was to be poured on the sacrifice or meat offering, and the residue given to the priests, Exodus 29:40; Leviticus 23:18; Numbers 15:5,7. It may have been appointed as an acknowledgment that all the blessings of the Earth are from God, Genesis 35:14" (Reference: Bible Hub/Drink Offering/ ATS Bible).

You are a drink offering. A libation, also known as a drink offering is "a drink poured out as an offering to a deity" (Google.com/Drink Offering). Of course, we know the deity is the only true and living God, Himself. Leviticus 23:13 (ESV) reads, "And the grain offering with it shall be two-tenths of an ephah of fine flour mixed with oil, a food offering to the Lord with a pleasing aroma, and the drink offering with it shall be of wine, a fourth of a hin."

Fine flour: sifted/tested. (Satan asked if he could sift Peter/see Luke 22:31).

Oil: anointing/empowerment. (Kings were often anointed with oil before they took their offices. Anointing oil represented empowerment, <legal> authority and sanctification).

Wine: revelation/new heart (Wine is symbolic of transformation/see Ezekiel 36:26).

You are a grain offering. What was a grain offering? It represented our devotion to God. The goal of the grain offering was to acknowledge God and show one's gratitude.

Jesus offered Himself for us. There are five offering types mentioned in the Bible, outside of the drink offering. The five offering types are: burnt offering, grain offering, peace offering, sin offering, guilt offering. Now, we won't go into the differences between each offering, however, Jesus became every one of these offerings on our behalf. Nevertheless, we have to become drink offerings, to be poured out with Him as an offering to God. What does this mean? It means we have to empty ourselves out of all that does not give God glory and let Him fill us up. It means that we empty ourselves of our own will or, better yet, we give a freewill offering. We have to empty ourselves of our will and fill ourselves with His Word. Filled with Him, we then begin to pour ourselves out to others, sharing our testimonies, wisdom, and revelations. In other words, He empties us of ourselves and fills us up with His Word. We then become vessels of His Word, pouring the revelation He's given us into others.

Imagine this. A man takes a large bottle and heads over to the Atlantic Ocean in Florida. He fills the bottle halfway and then, takes a flight out to California, where he heads over to the Pacific Ocean. He then fills the other half of the bottle with water from the Pacific Ocean. One day, he looks at the bottle and decides to separate the waters of the Pacific from the Atlantic waters. He can't. He's used every straining tool imaginable and come up with every idea he can possibly come up with, but nothing works. Why? Because when two of the same elements (in liquid state) mix, they become one; you cannot divide them. What does this mean for us as writers? We will pour out whatever we've allowed to be poured into us, plus, our state (conditions) change to match our thoughts. Proverbs 24:7 reads, "For as he thinketh in his heart, so is he." Luke 6:45 (ESV) reads, "The good person out of the good treasure of his heart produces good, and the evil person out of his evil treasure produces evil, for out of the abundance of the heart his mouth speaks." In other words, we are offerings, but whatever it is that pours out of us is a representation of our conditions (states).

As You Pour

Just like a glass, you have a certain measure (capacity). Your capacity is the maximum amount of revelation and information you can contain consistently (without forgetting, getting confused or becoming agitated). Agitation is simply a sign that you've reached the end of revelation and the beginning of your flesh; it means that you've exhausted your potential or you're afraid of your potential. Your revelation can never surpass your faith, however, you can receive in-depth revelation in moments of high faith. For example, Esther had to pray and fast before going before the king. It was her humility that kept her from emotionally charging into a situation with a lot to say, but no authority to say it. She didn't have enough understanding to challenge Haman; she wasn't that familiar with legalities or authority. Queens, in that era, were nothing but the kings' wives. They didn't go into battles or involve themselves in legal matters; they simply attended to their kings' needs and produced heirs for them.

Think of yourself as a cup that has a certain amount of wisdom, knowledge and understanding. Revelation is the substance that God uses to finish your sentence. As you begin to write, God will begin to speak. As you empty yourself out, God will pour back into you *if* your motives are right. Needless to say, if your motives are self-centered, God will allow you to empty yourself of the revelation you've stored over the years, and He will not refill you. When this happens, authors begin to become sluggish, agitated and unproductive. Consequentially, pride-filled, self-motivated authors will look for others to blame for their lack of revelation. One of the most common things I've heard prideful authors say is, "You expect me to write an entire book in five weeks and that's too much! I'm gonna take my time and write it as God gives it to me!" This sounds super-spiritual, but here's the punchline: they'd signed up for my five-week writing course, and they knew the course was designed to pull their books out of them in five weeks. Having no understanding to boast on, they found themselves in a complicated position—in the delivery room with stirrups around their ankles, only to discover that they had no revelation to give birth to.

WHAT ARE YOU OFFERING?

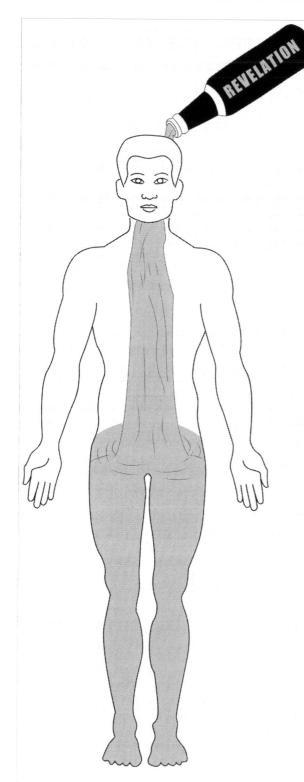

One of the things you should note about the illustration (left) is that even though revelation is being poured into the man, he is not full of revelation. Average writers have ten to twenty percent of their books stored in their hearts when they start writing. The rest of the book comes as God pours revelation into the author. Nevertheless, most authors believe they have enough revelation stored within themselves to easily write and finish their books. After pouring out around twenty pages, they find themselves feeling depleted. Sure, they were filled with knowledge, but on the subject they were writing about, as with all subjects, they didn't have as much revelation as they once believed. They'd simply received a powerful revelation and thought they could build a book around it. Ten to twenty pages into the book, they come to realize that they're empty and in need of more information.

God does this intentionally so the author does not rely on his or her own understanding or memory bank. God wants to be the Author of the author's book; the human author is just there to be the vessel or mic He speaks to His people through. He'll let us take credit by calling ourselves the primary authors as long as He gets the glory. Authors who do not spend much time with God will run out of revelation quickly, and since God resists the proud, they won't be able to get fresh revelation from Him. This is what causes many cases of what is reported as writer's block.

What are You Offering?

Sometimes, writer's block is just God blocking the author from receiving any additional revelation until the author comes to see His vision for the book, instead of the author's vision. All too often, potential authors spend so much time fantasizing about the glory of being an author (photo shoots, recognition, book signings) that they miss the point of authorship. I can't tell you how many aspiring authors I've met who couldn't seem to see past their own reflections and rejection. They wanted to write books to respond to the many people they felt had rejected, abandoned and betrayed them. They fantasized about the wrong things and forgot about the souls who would be harmed by their self-exaltation. They wanted mics, platforms, God's glory, validation and money. Their readers would serve as nothing more than tools to validate their pride, unforgiveness and ungodly beliefs. Some of these writers took my writers' class, hoping that I'd be able to pour into them the revelation that God was withholding from them, and when this did not happen, the pride in their hearts began to manifest. This is no different than a leader waiting for his moment to show the world how smart and deep he is, not considering the many people in the crowd who are broken, suicidal or in need of deliverance. God resists the proud, so writers who try to write themselves into God's glory usually run out of revelation before they've completed their book's first or second chapter.

Anytime I teach a writers' class, I almost always have one student who becomes agitated within the first week of the class. What does this reveal? To me, it says that the student wanted to pour out of his or her head when that student had no revelation in his or her heart. It means that the student has not spent much time with God. It means that the student has not crucified his or her flesh and is likely very carnal. It means that the student's motives for wanting to write a book were self-motivated. Out of the abundance of the heart, the mouth speaks; we understand this, but at the same time, out of the abundance of the heart, the teacher teaches. If a teacher accepts a nine-month position, for example, as a science teacher, but does not understand science, the teacher will run out of fuel within the first few weeks or months of the class's startup. From that point on, the teacher, having no information to give the students, will spend more time yelling at the students than he or she does teaching them. This is because an idle mind is the devil's workshop. Sure, this isn't scriptural, nor do we need scientific backing to substantiate this fact, after all, most of us have children or have been around idle children enough to see that this is true.

The same is true for adults. Bored adults can be destructive, promiscuous and dangerous creatures.

As you pour, you need to pay attention to what comes out of you. Additionally, you need to pay attention to your capacity. How long can you pour out before you reach the belly of your flesh? How deep is the well of your understanding? This will help you understand what level writer you are. Are you a surface-level writer? Are you a mantled writer? Are you an outer or inner core writer? Understand that the deepest part of the Earth is the inner inner core. Once we reach the core of your being, what will we discover? Again, I can always tell when a student has ankle-level revelation based on how he or she responds to the assignment. People who become easily agitated have emptied themselves out within the first few pages of their books. Now, this doesn't mean that they should give up and stop writing. It simply means they need to spend more time in the presence of God than they do watching reality television.

As you pour, you're going to discover things about yourself that you didn't know. For example, if there are some unresolved wounds on your heart, you'll likely find them. Oftentimes, people remember incidents they'd initially forgotten. As you pour, you will better understand which level writer you are (surface-level to inner inner core). Again, remember, just because you write a surface-level book doesn't mean you are a surface-level writer. You may be afraid of revelation (this is common for first-time authors) or you may have chosen a surface-level topic (there's nothing wrong with this). Sometimes, people have to adjust to the water before they're comfortable enough to go deeper into it. The same is true for writers. Sometimes, new writers have to get comfortable pouring out of their abundance (knowledge) before they are comfortable enough to pour out of God's knowledge (wisdom). Truthfully, many new authors are afraid to be too exegetical because they worry that what they're teaching will be written off as heresy. So, they swim in the depths that they feel they can stand in.

As you empty yourself, you're likely going to worry about what people will say, think or assume. You're likely going to worry that your book won't be good enough. You're likely going to worry that you'll unintentionally offend people. You'll probably think that you won't be deep enough or you may be too deep. When writing a book, your heart is on display; your knowledge is on display, and your depth (or fear of depth) is on display, but that's okay. You just have to write past your fears and learn to ignore the backspace key.

Lastly, as you pour out of your abundance, you're going to start feeling empty. You will likely feel drained and want to stop writing. This is not the time to give up. It simply means you have to go outside of yourself to get new knowledge and revelation. You need to spend some time with the Lord, do some research online and maybe even talk to one or two of your wise friends. In other words, you need to be refilled. Many authors decide to stop writing once they run out of revelation, waiting years to receive enough knowledge to look as intelligent as they believe themselves to be. Understand that a book is not sentence behind sentence of deep revelatory truths; a book is practical truths and testimonies, followed by revelatory truths. People who don't understand this will pour text into their books that is completely unrelated to the subject matter just because the text, to them, is revelatory. That's the danger of being a pride-filled writer.

Give Them Something They Can Use

One of the worst things you can do to a reader is give them a book that's filled with unusable content. When I teach my writer's class, I'm always trying to get my students to understand that their readers aren't interested in being their friends. So writing statements like, "That's just how I am. I'm the type of person who'll walk away if you keep hurting me." This is unusable content! The writer is assuming that the reader wants to be his or her friend, and the writer is teaching the readers the roads they'll need to travel to win over the author's heart. Books like these always end up with a few bad reviews and less than one hundred sells.

Look at it this way. When people give you their money, they are giving you their blood, sweat, tears and sacrifices. They've had to work to earn that money. You are also giving them your blood, sweat, tears and sacrifices, but you're giving it to them in a different form. You're giving it to them in the form of wisdom, knowledge and understanding. The goal of the book is to help them ascend to another level, but this will only happen if the content is relevant, true and usable.

To produce usable content, your book must incorporate:
1. Knowledge: Share new information with your readers. This means that you must tell the readers something they didn't initially know.
2. Wisdom: Give your readers insight into old information. In other words, give them revelation.
3. Understanding: Help your readers to better understand one of the many lessons of life.

While you're writing the book, stop after you've completed a chapter and ask yourself this—"Will the readers benefit from the information shared in the last chapter?" If the answer is no, go back and edit or delete that chapter. It's okay to throw away paragraphs, pages and even chapters of content. Every great author has had to do this at some point in his or her life! When I initially wrote *To Hell with Hate*, I didn't have any sense of direction. I just typed out every experience I've had. Once I was finished with the book, I didn't like it. I would find a few paragraphs that were usable, but the rest of it was just me rambling on and on about some of the things I've gone through in life. I knew I wanted the readers to see someone who's overcome hell, and has still chosen to forgive others. In other words, I had a destination in mind, I just didn't know how I was going to get there. I kept looking at chapters of piled up text, hoping that if I read the book again, I'd like it. This never happened. Instead, every time I tried to read it, I became more agitated, frustrated and discouraged than I had been before. Eventually, I realized that I needed to throw away the entire book and rewrite it. I think I kept a few paragraphs, but I threw over one hundred pages away. Why would I do this? Because anytime a writer has no sense of direction, that writer will do what I call "circling the drain." What this means is, the writer has nothing to give the readers, so the writer just goes in circles, constantly sharing the same information using different words. This means that the writer will distract the readers with a bunch of recycled revelation or unusable information.

In order for your book to garner any measure of success, it must be filled with usable content, meaning, the readers should be able to benefit from the information you've shared. The more useful information you share, the more valuable your book becomes. Sure, it's okay to testify in your self-help book—as a matter of fact, I believe that this balances a book out, but make sure that your testimony helps the readers to understand your points. You should never publish random thoughts that are unrelated to the subject matter. This is called fluff and will only serve to agitate your readers.

Once your book is finished, eighty to ninety percent of the content in it should be helpful to your readers. The content should be leading the readers from one revelation to the next. Your book should increase your readers capacity to understand the Kingdom of God. Think of it this way. If you were to open a restaurant, you wouldn't make satisfying your customers' appetites your top priority; you'd first want to appeal to their taste buds. This is because people want to like what they eat. We are often led by our cravings. Our hunger simply tells us that we have room for revelation, but our taste buds tell us where to go to receive this revelation. If you give your readers information can benefit their lives, they'll keep coming back for more. In other words, they'll buy more of your books. Understand this—your readers aren't interested in how smart you are. I tell this to authors all the time because the majority of first-time authors fill their books with words they don't use in their everyday lives. Your readers don't want to think about you while they're reading, unless you've written an autobiography. Your readers want to get what they've paid for—revelation! Remember, they're giving you their time and money; give them content they can use in return.

As a reminder, the Hebrew word for "writer" is "sopher," and it means "to count." In this chapter, instead of using the word "scribe" or "author," I'll be using the word "sopher". This is to help you familiarize yourself with another aspect of your assignment—sacrifice. Hollywood has glamorized authorship. Almost every time an actor is cast as an author on the big screen, he or she is cast as successful, intelligent and attractive. This has caused men and women around the world to write books filled with unusable content for the sake of being called an author. People from every nation and tongue are lusting after the author title, not realizing that there is a cost associated with becoming a world-changer. Sure, many authors these days write countless books, but those books are not designed to shape people's minds or worlds. Instead, they are written to entertain. Then again, many authors write self-help books that don't help anyone. Nevertheless, there is a cost involved with being a sopher—one that has caused many men and women to put away their pens. Understand this—the minute you decide to write a book, you have decided to take a leadership position, after all, you will be leading your readers from one thought to another, one concept to another, and one conclusion to another. In order to lead and/or be a world-changer, you need legal authority, and to receive legal authority, you need love. Now, love isn't a feeling, as the world would have you to believe. It is the heart of knowledge, the fabric of understanding and the product of wisdom. This three-fold cord is passed down from the Father's heart to ours and made stronger through unity, perseverance, prayer and correction. This is why God gave us fathers and mentors.

From Layers to Levels

- Crust (First Level)
- Mantle (Second Level)
- Outer Core (Third Level)
- Inner Core (Fourth Level)
- Inner Inner Core (Fifth Level)

Crust (First Layer)

1. Surface, the layer humans live on. It consists of everything above the Earth's surface; it is what we can visibly see.
2. Is less than one percent of the Earth's volume.
3. Cool, hardened part of the Earth (because of temperature).
4. Three to five miles thick under the ocean (oceanic crust).
5. Is made up of basalt rocks (oceanic crust) and granite (continental crust).
6. Twenty-five miles thick under the continents (continental crust).
7. Temperatures can vary from air temperature (top) to 1600 degrees Fahrenheit (in deepest parts of the crust).
8. The crust is broken into plates (small pieces that float on a plastic mantle, just beneath the crust).
9. When the plates stick and pressure forms, an earthquake ensues. Earthquakes are caused by mantles.

Crust (First Level Writers)

First level writers usually:

1. Write on a level that most people can understand. Surface writers take what's evident and give readers the revelation behind whatever it is that's been obstructing their view.
2. Even though these writers and teachers can reach the large majority of the people with their messages, they carry less than one percent of the revelation that fourth and fifth level writers and teachers carry.
3. Can reach some of the most hardened hearts because they are seen as "down to Earth."

4. Are not shallow writers, but can teach what most believe to be in-depth messages.
5. Are the most common writers or teachers (think pastoral level).
6. Can normally reach the nations.
7. Can range from the most carnal minded teachers (think hip-hop, street style or stripper types) to the most astute teachers.
8. Range in categories, each divided by class, culture, doctrine and religious affiliations.
9. Are moved by the mantled writers.

Mantle (Second Layer)

1. Largest layer of the Earth. The mantle amounts to about 85 percent of the Earth's surface.
2. Is 1800 miles thick.
3. Is made up of very hot, dense rock.
4. The first fifty miles of the mantle consists of thick, solid rock.
5. The next 150 miles of the mantle are made up of very hot, solid rocks.
6. After that, the next several hundred miles (distance unknown) are made up of very solid, sturdy rock.
7. Upper mantle is predominantly solid, but behaves like an aggressive fluid (lava).
8. The rocks on this layer flow like asphalt. Asphalt is used to cover roads and highways.
9. Temperatures on this layer range between 1600 to 4000 degrees Fahrenheit, depending on the depth. The deeper you go, the hotter the temperature.
10. Mantles move the plates under the outer crust.
11. The movement of the mantle is the reason the Earth plates move.

Mantled Writers (Second Level)

Second level writers usually:
1. Affect the largest amount of people by affecting the surface-level writers.
2. Can be pretty deep to the point where they can easily be mistaken as third or fourth level writers if given the right opportunities.
3. Made up of people who've experienced notable hardships—people who can

reach the most stubborn and prideful souls.

4. There are levels of mantled writers (and teachers) with the first level being very rigid, unmovable souls who feed solid words to people who have the teeth to chew them.

5. The second level of the mantle consists of writers (and teachers) who most will say are on fire for the Lord, meaning, they are consistent in their holiness, persistent in ministry, and resistant to outside influences.

6. The third level of mantled writers is where you'll come in contact with writers and teachers who generate a lot of power when they deliver messages. These are the leaders who demons know and fear by name; they are unmovable and uninfluenced by the world.

7. Can easily be mistaken for surface-level teachers when they teach certain messages, but their determination and faith will always distinguish them from writers (or teachers) on the first level.

8. Serve as a covering to others (think Pastor, Prophet or Apostle).

9. Range from well-spoken teachers to people who can best be described as being similar to Moses—people who are not well-spoken, but are largely known for the miracles that come through their ministries.

10. People on this level affect the people on the surface (first) level, so much so that they can cause earthquakes (revivals) to break out.

11. Are the heartbeat of writers and teachers.

Outer Core (Third Layer)

1. Between 4000 to 9000 degrees Fahrenheit, depending on the depth.

2. Is comprised of metals, nickels and iron, all of which are in melted form (lava) because of the heat.

3. Rotates faster than the rest of the planet.

4. Has a magnetic field 50 times the strength of the Earth's magnetic field.

Outer (Soft) Core Writers (Third Level)

Third level writers usually:

1. Are very, very bold and unapologetic teachers.

2. Are people who've survived the harshest of conditions, and for this reason, such teachers will not conform to the norm, regardless of what the cost may

be. As a matter of fact, they unapologetically offend religious traditions.

3. Are the most diligent and unyielding teachers you'll ever come in contact with.

4. May not be the most popular teachers, but their messages are more potent and have more impact than writers and teachers who teach from the first and second level. As a matter of truth, second level teachers receive their boldness from teachers on this level (think iron sharpens iron).

Inner Core (Fourth Layer)

1. So hot that the liquids underneath cannot flow, but are forced to move in place like solid matter.

2. Is as hot as the surface of the sun. Please note that because of the heat, it is impossible for any living thing to get close enough to the sun to touch it.

3. Eight hundred miles thick.

4. Pressure is 45 million pounds per square inch.

5. Density suggests that there is more than metals, nickels and iron on this level. Density suggests that this level is also comprised of gold, platinum, palladium, silver and tungsten.

6. Temperatures can reach up to 9800 degrees Fahrenheit.

Inner (Hard) Core Writers (Fourth Level)

Fourth level writers usually:

1. Cannot and will not teach what they want to teach, but are instead, more spiritual in their approach to ministry (think Elijah).

2. Writers and teachers on this level walk in the authority and power of the Son, Jesus Christ. They are potent in their delivery and can easily cast out the most stubborn of demons.

3. Are the rarest teachers of all.

4. Teach such potent messages that they put pressure on teachers on every level.

5. Are the most mysterious of writers and teachers, but their impact is so great that they don't just sharpen others, they empower them.

6. Can change the state (status) of any and everyone they come in contact with in a matter of minutes.

Inner Inner Core

Of course, we've been taught that the Earth has four layers, but Scientists now believe there is a fifth layer. It is a core inside of the inner core. Geek.com reports the following:

> "Though you may be familiar with the phrase 'molten core,' the reality is that Earth's inner core is actually solid, and it's the outer core that surrounds this enormous ball of heavy metals which remains liquid. A new study from American and Chinese researchers now posits the existence of an all-new region of the Earth, a distinct core within the inner core — an inner inner core.
>
> By studying the propagation of shockwaves from earthquakes around the world, they think they can prove that the iron crystals there are aligned differently than the outer inner core, and that has big implications for our understanding of how the Earth first formed" (Reference: Geek.com/ earthquakes May Reveal New Layer of the Earth: the Inner Inner Core/ Graham Templeton).

The Earth having an inner inner core is no surprise to believers who understand the significance of numbers. Five is the number of grace. Man has five fingers, five toes and five senses. There were five offering types. God created the five-fold ministry, consisting of the apostle, prophet, teacher, pastor and evangelist. So again, it is no surprise that the Earth has five cores Lastly, five is the number used to represent creation.

Since the existence of an inner inner core is still in speculation, there is little to be said regarding the temperature, composition and movements of the inner inner core, but with what we know about the inner core, we can safely assume the following:

1. Solid (extremely hot) matter, possibly solid metal that moves or behaves like a liquid.
2. Is hotter than the surface of the sun, likely as hot as or hotter than the core of the sun.
3. Likely around four hundred miles thick.

Inner Inner Core Writers

Just like Scientists don't have much to say about the inner inner core of the Earth, there isn't much to be said of inner inner core writers outside of speculation. Based on the movements we've witnessed with revivals, the sudden emerging of God-fearing, fire-unleashing leaders, coupled with the increase in evil, we can safely conclude the following about inner inner core (fifth level) writers:

1. They are immovable. Nothing you say or do will change their minds. They live for Christ and have resolved in their hearts to die for Him if necessary. They will not compromise the Kingdom, regardless of what they stand to lose.

2. They are the equivalent of a tsunami. Many people fear earthquakes, but little are aware of the dangers of tsunamis. Tsunamis are large waves often caused by underwater earthquakes. What makes them so dangerous is they are rarely detected, they usually come without warning, and have been known to sweep through cities and islands in a matter of seconds. One of the deadliest tsunamis ever recorded took place in Indonesia in 2004. That tsunami was the result of a 9.1 magnitude earthquake and it claimed over two hundred thousand lives in fifteen countries. Inner inner core writers usually rise without warning (think Elijah). They come preaching a bold word that not only shifts the people, but overturns governments. They are the ones who are hidden, not recognized as notable speakers and leaders, but are instead the Elijahs who send out the Elishas.

3. They aren't a large group of believers. If you come in contact with a leader of this magnitude, you probably won't know how powerful he or she is because they are very humble, and in some cases, very odd.

Earthquakes and Tsunamis

As we discussed earlier, earthquakes can range in strength (magnitude) and will normally last a few seconds. The longest recorded earthquake, however, lasted ten minutes, and again, it was the earthquake that caused the deadliest tsunami in history (2004, Sumatra, Indonesia). The difference between an earthquake and a tsunami is location. Earthquakes shake the earth; tsunamis are displaced waves that result from underwater earthquakes. As of right now, scientists can predict some earthquakes, but predicting a tsunami isn't as easy. The same is true in regards to revivalists. We see leaders emerging all the time, and while this is great news, we must remember that tsunamis are rarely detected until they hit—just like many earth-moving revivalists. No one saw them coming until they emerged and released destruction against the kingdom of darkness with their words. Think about Elijah. Sure, Ahab and Jezebel were fully aware of Elijah's existence, after all, he was potent enough to get the attention of the king, however, Elijah's magnitude and influence had been completely underestimated by the power couple. He wasn't seen as a major threat. If Ahab had known the power that God placed in Elijah, he wouldn't have ever agreed to a showdown between Baal and the Most High God. 1 Kings 18:17-19 (ESV) reads, "When Ahab saw Elijah, Ahab said to him, 'Is it you, you troubler of Israel?' And he answered, 'I have not troubled Israel, but you have, and your father's house, because you have abandoned the commandments of the Lord and followed the Baals. Now therefore send and gather all Israel to me at Mount Carmel, and the 450 prophets of Baal and the 400 prophets of Asherah, who eat at Jezebel's table. So Ahab sent to all the people of Israel and gathered the prophets together at Mount Carmel. "

Ahab didn't know the tsunami that was about to hit; he had no way of preparing himself or his followers for what was about to happen. Of course, if you know the story, Elijah challenged Baal's followers for their double-mindedness. He told them to call on the name of Baal for half of a day. It goes without saying that Baal did not answer because he could not answer. After this, Elijah called the people to come near him; he'd repaired the altar of the Lord and cut up a bull for the burnt offering. He then began to call upon the name of the Lord, and shortly thereafter, fire fell from Heaven and consumed the burnt offering. The people were astonished. The Bible tells us that they fell on their faces and began to proclaim, "The Lord, he is God; the Lord, he is God!" With their hearts turned back to God, Elijah told them to seize the prophets of Baal. Elijah then brought them down to the brook Kishon and killed them. This is an example of a tsunami.

Here are a few interesting facts about tsunamis.
1. The first wave is usually not the strongest; the succession of waves that follow are normally stronger.
2. Tsunamis can travel up to five hundred miles per hour, giving no man in its vicinity enough time to prepare or respond.

3. Tsunamis can travel across entire oceans without losing energy.

How is this information relevant to you as a writer? This information helps us to label the writers and teachers we've encountered, as well as help us to better understand the level at which we write and teach. One of the most common ways the enemy ends the writing careers of authors is by leading some to believe that they can teach on all levels. You see, if I think I'm a level five teacher (inner inner core) and I attempt to speak boldly against something God has not authorized me to come against, I will release a sound that will first interrupt my own life. This would be okay if I'd experienced that quaking before, but if I have not, I will experience situations, emotions and encounters that I've never experienced. In other words, I'd be overwhelmed. Not realizing that the quaking was the result of me trying to write on a level that I have not been called to, I'd try again at some point and experience that same quaking. Eventually, I'd consciously or subconsciously connect the "attacks" with me putting my pen to paper and I'd start procrastinating to write the books God genuinely wants me to write. Now, in this, I wouldn't truly be procrastinating (as many report that they are), I'd simply be too scared to write.

Today, many would-be authors who start and stop writing their books say, for example, "I just didn't have the time; I was too busy," when in truth, the author is just too scared to get back in the ring with the devil. Not realizing it, the author, figuratively speaking, tried to fight Goliath while wearing Saul's armor. Saul's armor was likely too big and too weighty for David, neither had David tested it. Wearing another man's armor could have easily sealed David's fate. The same is true when writing. If you wear a personality that's not your own, you will give the enemy the upper hand.

The Importance of Identifying Your Level

Every writer has a level in which he or she writes and teaches on. It goes without saying that most of us are unaware of our level, and for this reason, we often spend the first few years of our writing careers trying to give solid foods to saints who can barely withstand liquids. It is important for every writer to understand the manner in which he or she flows. This is why the first few years of teaching, ministering and writing are oftentimes centered around the teacher finding his or her own voice. When the teacher finds his/her voice, it is easy for the teacher to find the sheep who can feed from his/her pasture.

Most of us have heard the term, "target audience." When you're an entrepreneur and/or an author, knowing your target audience can make or break your career. The same is true in ministry. When someone says, "Know your target audience," what that person is essentially saying is to know the manner in which you flow or the composition of whatever it is that you're attempting to sell. For example, it would be unwise (and dangerous) to go into a crime-ridden neighborhood and market a bag full of uncut diamonds. The reason for this is, most (if not all) of the people in that neighborhood will not be able to (legally) afford a single diamond in that bag. The end result would be you getting robbed of your wealth (or killed), and the people who robbed you will sell the diamonds for far less than what they are worth. This is because they will not know (1) the value of the diamonds they're selling and (2) the price you had to pay to get those diamonds. Quite frankly, they won't care either way. Additionally, it would be unwise to take a bag of uncut diamonds into a pawn shop because a pawn shop targets buyers who cannot afford or are too frugal to purchase valuable items at market value. So, the person at the pawn shop would offer you thirty percent or less of the bag's value. It would even be unwise (and dangerous) to attempt to sell your diamonds on the black market. Instead, you'd take those diamonds and have them certified with the American Gem Society. After that, you'd get them appraised. Next, you'd market the diamonds to companies like Large Diamond Buyers USA or World Jeweler, Inc. What you're doing here is called "flowing." This means you're taking the necessary steps to ensure you can effectively sell the diamonds you have, and you won't put your life in danger doing so.

As an author, you need to identify whether your writing level is surface (crust), mantle, outer core or inner core. Understanding your voice and your depth can make the difference between you selling ten books or ten million copies of your book. But how can you identify the level at which you write?

How to Identify Your Level

1. **Let your fruit tell you where you are.** Never attempt to determine your own level. If you do so, you'll likely underestimate yourself or you'll start dabbling with pride. Romans 12:3 reads, "For I say, through the grace given unto me, to every man that is among you, not to think of himself more highly than he ought to think; but to think soberly, according as God hath dealt to every man the measure of faith." How do you allow your fruit to determine your status? You simply look for the presence (and state) of the fruit of the Holy Spirit in your life. What state is each of these fruit in: (1) love, (2) joy, (3) peace, (4) patience, (5) kindness, (6) goodness, (7) faithfulness, (8) gentleness, (9) self-control?

2. **Let your friends tell you where you are.** Of course, you don't ask your friends to tell you what level you flow or walk in. Instead, look at their levels and the level of conversations you have with them. Can you flow with the deepest of them? Which ones can you flow with, and which ones do you learn from the most? In many cases, you'll come in contact with people who are deeper than you are, and in those friendships, your assignment is to do more listening than you do speaking. This is because God is trying to change your state of mind. Nevertheless, if you see the state of the teacher, you see the state (or status) in which God is elevating you to.

3. **Pay attention to the state (status) of the sheep God sends your way.** What level of people are more attracted to you? Remember, every layer of the Earth has a magnetic pull. Would you say that the people who are more attracted to you are the crust (level one), mantles (level two), outer core (level three), inner core (level four) or inner inner core (level five) of the Earth? *Please note that the state they arrive in is not their actual status. You will come in contact with people who have the potential to flow on the third level (outer core), but are worldly (walking after the flesh on the surface level).*

4. **Pay attention to the difference your ministry (life, words) makes in the lives of others.** Think of it this way. If you're a third level writer, most of the people who will come your way may start off as a solid

(hardhearted, prideful, judgmental, stubborn), but once they've come in contact with you, it is important for you to note their new composition. Did they change? What type of changes did you notice? Were their lives made better? Did they go from being hardened saints to flowing in the Spirit, or did they stop flowing altogether? *Please note that some people won't change and it won't be because of you. It's because the outer core's temperature changes the deeper you go into it. Some people won't let you lead them into the depths of wisdom, knowledge and understanding, and for this reason, they will walk away unchanged.*

5. **Pay attention to how you feel after ministering.** People who teach on a surface level do not expend a lot of energy, whereas, people who teach on the second, third, fourth and fifth levels can feel a change in themselves after ministering.

From Fact to Revelation

One of the things we must always remember is that facts and truth are not one in the same. Facts are what we can prove in the natural, but truth is the supernatural Word of God. Facts are established through research and evidence; the truth is whatever God speaks. He is the true and living God; He cannot lie and no words He speaks will ever or have ever returned to Him void. So the truth is established by God. With that being said, below you'll find some interesting facts and the truths that we can extract from them. Revelation, on the other hand, is the illumination or revealing of a truth; it is when what was hidden is suddenly revealed. Revelation can be truths that manifest themselves as facts, meaning, they can be tangible or they can be hidden in the realm of faith for only the faithful to see. Jesus spoke many parables to His disciples. He spoke of earthly situations and then He illuminated them with the truth. He told the parable of the prodigal son, the parable of the talents, the parable of the unforgiving servant, and so on. One of the things you'll notice when reading the parables that Jesus told was that He did not illuminate all of them. He explained a few, but with others, He remained mum because He knew the disciples had been given the ability (by God) to understand Kingdom mysteries. One of the parables He illuminated was the parable of the lost coin.

Luke 15:8-10 (ESV): Or what woman, having ten silver coins, if she loses one coin, does not light a lamp and sweep the house and seek diligently until she finds it? And when she has found it, she calls together her friends and neighbors, saying, "Rejoice with me, for I have found the coin that I had lost." Just so, I tell you, there is joy before the angels of God over one sinner who repents."

The illumination or revealing takes place on the last line (Luke 15:10) when He says, " Just so, I tell you, there is joy before the angels of God over one sinner who repents."

Fact	Truth
The crust of the Earth is made up of several elements, including iron and magnesium. A few things we should know about iron is that iron is the fourth most common element in the Earth's crust and is mostly found in the Earth's inner and outer core. Additionally, iron can corrode if it comes in contact with water and oxygen (elements commonly found above the surface of the Earth, but not so much beneath the surface).	Matthew 5:13 (ESV) reads, "You are the salt of the Earth, but if salt has lost its taste, how shall its saltiness be restored? It is no longer good for anything except to be thrown out and trampled under people's feet."

Revelation
Parable of the Foolish Woman

The crust of the Earth is made up of several elements, including iron and magnesium. A few things we should know about iron is that iron is the fourth most common element in the Earth's crust and is mostly found in the Earth's inner and outer core. Additionally, iron can corrode if it comes in contact with water and oxygen (elements commonly found above the surface of the Earth, but not so much beneath the surface).

Next, iron is needed for the survival of living things; for example, it plays a vital role in the production of chlorophyll — the pigment that makes plants green and

Parable of the Foolish Woman
A young and charismatic woman worked as a secretary at a law firm. Studying to be a paralegal, the young woman was bright, driven and inexperienced. She worked alongside another woman who was twenty years her senior. The older woman was also training to be a paralegal and rarely came into the office.

One day, the older woman came to work but didn't appear to be too happy. She greeted the young woman and went directly to her office to sort through some of the cases her boss had given her.

Outside of the office, the young, charismatic woman

is responsible for the absorption of light.

Magnesium, on the other hand, is created in the stars. It is the result of neon and helium fusing together. Even though magnesium is weak, it is often mixed with alloy. When the two are combined, they form a very durable metal that is often used in cars.

could see her co-worker. "Why is she always stressed?" the young woman questioned in her heart. "I come to work everyday and I do my job with a smile. Even when I'm at school, I smile because I love law. Obviously, she hates what she's doing, which means she's in the wrong field." Believing that she had a word of wisdom, the young woman decided to update her blog. The name of her blog post was, *"If You Hate What You Do ... Quit!"*

Three days later, the older woman was promoted in the office to a management position. She smiled as the founders (all lawyers) boasted about her diligence and hard work. Frustrated, the young woman walked out of the room. "I smile everyday," she said to another co-worker. "I've never taken a day off and I come to work in a good mood." Noticing the young woman's attitude, the older woman who'd just been promoted suggested that the managers give her old position to the young woman. They didn't understand her request, but they agreed out of respect for her.

When the young woman learned that she'd been promoted to the older woman's former position, she yelped with joy. She said in her heart that she'd be the best paralegal-in-training they'd ever had. Five weeks later, she turned in her resignation letter. Immediately after taking the new position, the young woman started feeling overwhelmed. The three attorneys who owned the firm not only had her doing paperwork, constantly coming to court and doing all of their research for them, they also

had her running personal errands. When handing her resignation to one of the attorneys, the young woman was shocked to see the grin on the lawyer's face. "You appear to be happy that I'm quitting," remarked the young woman angrily. The attorney did not respond immediately. Instead, he stood to his feet, gently removed the resignation letter from the woman's hand and bid her farewell. When the woman was walking out of the office, the man finally responded. He said, "I read your blog post. You're an experienced writer and now you have experienced the world of a paralegal. What's amazing is, because of your blog post, we tried to take it easy on you. You didn't have the same workload as the former assistant and yet, you complained, did not complete all of the work we gave you, and five weeks later, you're in my office turning in your resignation letter. I believe the lesson you've learned is to never speak about a position you've never held. And by the way, the former assistant did the job while going to school full-time and battling through a very contentious divorce. Nevertheless, she never complained about the workload, she turned the work in on time and she was the one who recommended, against our wishes, that we give the job to you. I wish you well. Oh, and by the way, we don't pay you to smile; we pay you to perform."
The end.

The aforementioned story is a parable; it is designed to demonstrate a point. The point can be summarized this way: never criticize a person in a position you have not held. I could further demonstrate this point through another parable, for example, I can write the parable of a single woman and detail how overwhelmingly frustrated she's become with her married cousin. Noticing that her cousin's marriage is failing, the single and never-before married woman feels anxious to share her opinion. While much of what she says is true, it wreaks of inexperience. I can then tell the story of that same woman being married and show how she responds to the same set of problems with a different man. These two stories demonstrate the same point.

Iron Sharpens Iron

Proverbs 27:17 (ESV) reads, "Iron sharpens iron, and one man sharpens another." When dealing with the crust of the Earth, we are dealing with the surface of the Earth. Iron is the most common element on the face of this Earth. Even though it's mostly found in the inner and outer core of the Earth, it can still be found in abundance on the surface.

In order for iron to sharpen iron (in the natural), it has to be in solid form. Iron in the core (inner, outer) of the Earth is in liquid form, so it cannot sharpen iron. Instead, iron in the depths of the Earth would only change the composition (chemical breakdown) of any metals it comes in contact with. Nevertheless, iron on the surface-level can sharpen iron on the surface-level. What does this mean? One of the most dangerous (and foolish) things for a writer (or teacher) to do is attempt to address, confront or correct a writer (or teacher) who teaches on another level. This is because solid iron cannot relate to the movements of liquidized iron. This is the reasons many leaders have suffered from what we commonly refer to as a "meltdown."

But iron sharpens iron. As a writer, your assignment is to address what you understand and address what is on your level, unless God tells you otherwise. There is much to address on the surface if you happen to be a surface-level writer. Write from your metron and it'll be easier to finish three, four and five books in a year (if that's what you want), versus taking two or three years to finish one book. This is because you'll have to wait for new experiences and new revelation just to write on another level. There are readers who can learn from where you are right now. There are readers who will be sharpened by your works if they are from God.

Many writers who were called to deal with matters on the surface envy those who were chosen to go deeper—people who deal with what we don't see—matters that are spiritual and matters that are mysteries. As a result, they endure what they believe to be warfare when, in truth, they have exposed themselves to another dimension. For this reason, their composition (state of mind) is being shaped and molded so they can effectively minister to the people they are targeting. If they endure these changes without fainting (giving up), which is unlikely, they may be authorized to write on that level. Nevertheless, every man has his own measure of faith, therefore, when people expose themselves to new dimensions without the guidance of the Lord, they almost always faint. Fainting, in the natural, is a response to a lack of oxygen; it is a survival mechanism. People faint, for example, when trying to climb mountains without the proper equipment. This is because the air pressure at the top of the mountain is denser than the air at the bottom. The same is true when dealing with spiritual matters. Fainting (giving up) is a survival mechanism. For example, Elijah fainted spiritually when he ran away from Jezebel and into the wilderness. In other words, he gave up or temporarily lost his mind. He asked the Lord to take his life. The dimension he'd exposed himself to was the dimension of fear. People will almost always faint in fear. Nevertheless, the Lord sent an angel to Elijah and the angel ministered to him. The Lord also gave him his next set of instructions. 1 Kings 19:15-17 (ESV) reads, "And the Lord said to him, 'Go, return on your way to the wilderness of Damascus. And when you arrive, you shall anoint Hazael to be king over Syria. And Jehu the son of Nimshi you shall anoint to be king over Israel, and Elisha the son of Shaphat of Abel-meholah you shall anoint to be prophet in your place. And the one who escapes from the sword of Hazael shall Jehu put to death, and the one who escapes from the sword of Jehu shall Elisha put to death.'"

ELIJAH WAS COMMANDED TO NOT ONLY ANOINT HIS REPLACEMENT, BUT HE HAD TO SHARPEN HIM.

1 Kings 19:19-21 (ESV) reads, "So he departed from there and found Elisha the son of Shaphat, who was plowing with twelve yoke of oxen in front of him, and he was with the twelfth. Elijah passed by him and cast his cloak upon him. And he left the oxen and ran after Elijah and said, 'Let me kiss my father and my mother, and then I will follow you.' And he said to him, 'Go back again, for what have I done to you?' And he returned from following him and took the yoke of oxen and sacrificed them and boiled their flesh with the yokes of the oxen and gave it to the people, and they ate. Then he arose and went after Elijah and assisted him."

Elijah assisted Elisha. This means that he trained and sharpened him. The call was already on Elisha's life. Elijah simply had to act as the audible voice to validate that call. He had to act as a father. Remember, we can only reproduce what we are or where we've been. Additionally, every element has a certain form at every given level. Iron, on the surface-level, does not look, move or behave like iron in the mantle of the earth. This is because of the temperature. Iron on the surface of the earth is solid, but iron in the mantle is mostly liquid. In the core, iron is forced to flow as a solid. If there was a surface-level (true) iron-man who went into the mantle of the earth to minister to the metals there, he would first be melted down so that he can flow with the other metals. No ordinary man could have sharpened Elisha. Please understand that there were many prophets on the face of the Earth during that time. God could have sent any one of them to train Elisha, but He chose Elijah because the mantle that was on Elijah's life was too great for an ordinary prophet. Just like there are five-fold ministry offices, every office has officers. Every officer has a measure of rank. This means that one prophet can outrank another prophet.

From Revelation to Revelation

1. Most third and fourth level writers (and teachers) can flow on all levels. The same is true for some of the writers who are considered in-depth, second level writers or teachers.
2. There are different depths to all levels, especially the second level. One teacher can write (or teach) near the bottom of the first level, whereas,

another teacher can write (or teach) near the surface of the third level.

3. The deeper you are, the fewer people you'll be able to reach (on a personal level); this is because most people are surface-level learners. For this reason, worldly books sell more than spiritual books.

4. Even though you'll reach fewer people (personally), the deeper you are, the greater impact your ministry (books, life, words) will make wholly. This is because, for example, people who teach on the second level (mantle) set the stage for the people who teach on the surface (first) level. What a mantled teacher teaches will move, shape and inspire surface-level teachers. All the same, what a third level teacher teaches will always affect teachers on the second and first level, and so on.

5. Most writers, teachers and ministers can teach at a greater level than the level they are currently teaching on, but are restrained from doing so because of the level the people who follow them are on. For this reason, they can "flow" in conversation with friends, but must give portioned out revelation to the people who follow them. Have you ever heard a leader grunt and groan out of frustration while teaching? This is usually indicative of the teacher wanting to go deeper, but being restrained by God because the people he or she is teaching have not yet reached that level of understanding.

6. As a writer, you can be called to go deeper in your writing, but teach on the surface because of fear, opinions, unforgiveness and offense. This is why God told Ezekiel to not be afraid of the Israelites' faces. Ezekiel 2:6-7 reads, "And thou, son of man, be not afraid of them, neither be afraid of their words, though briers and thorns be with thee, and thou dost dwell among scorpions: be not afraid of their words, nor be dismayed at their looks, though they be a rebellious house. And thou shalt speak my words unto them, whether they will hear, or whether they will forbear: for they are most rebellious."

7. In-depth writers don't like to write on their level because of the pressure involved. They are crushed, stretched and melted down when writing, and for this reason, they often have to be commanded by God to write in-depth materials. They will write surface-level articles, books and the like because doing so does not extract a lot of energy from them, however, they'll often put off writing the deep, controversial books that God has given them.

8. When teaching, you often have to extract the wisdom from the scriptures and

give them to the people in a state that they can receive it in. For this to happen, your state has to be changed and you have to eat what it is you are about to feed God's people.

Ezekiel 3:1-3: And he said to me, "Son of man, eat whatever you find here. Eat this scroll, and go, speak to the house of Israel." So I opened my mouth, and he gave me this scroll to eat. And he said to me, "Son of man, feed your belly with this scroll that I give you and fill your stomach with it." Then I ate it, and it was in my mouth as sweet as honey.

Revelation 10:10: And I took the little scroll from the hand of the angel and ate it. It was sweet as honey in my mouth, but when I had eaten it my stomach was made bitter.

9. A good writer can swim from the level he or she is on to the surface. Please note that it is unwise (foolish) to attempt to go deeper than where you're accustomed to. For example, if you're a mantled writer, it is never wise to try to write or teach like a third level writer. The reason is, the temperatures on each level are different, meaning the state of the teachers on the second level is very different from the state of the teachers on the third level. Attempting to go deeper than the state you've learned to live in will always result in either unnecessary warfare or almost unbearable pressure.

10. If you're deep (wise), that's a good thing, but always bring people to the surface so they can chew what you're teaching them. If you keep them too deep too long, you'll end up drowning your readers.

Levels	Gifts
Crust (First Level)	Teacher
Mantle (Second Level)	Pastor
Outer Core (Third Level)	Evangelist
Inner Core (Fourth Level)	Prophet
Inner Inner Core (Fifth Level)	Apostle

As you can see, I've compared each level of the Earth with the five-fold ministry gifts. What's important for us to understand is, each office has a certain grace. At the same time, each man or woman's grace is not necessarily a reflection of that person's teaching. For example, there are teachers who are more apostolic in their grace, but they are not apostles; they are teachers. If you come across a teacher who is more apostolic than anything, chances are, that teacher is submitted to an apostle and is therefore, walking in his or her grace. Nevertheless, the teacher may be able to teach on the level of an apostle, but not necessarily move on the level of an apostle, meaning, he or she may not be able to address governmental matters in the realm of the spirit. Think of it this way. A city police officer can be the first to report to a crime scene where someone has been murdered. That same officer may be able to boast of having been present on the scene of 125 murders. For this reason, he has learned a lot about investigating murders just from watching the homicide detectives on the scene and from having to go to court in some of those cases. Nevertheless, this knowledge does not make him a detective. He may be able to teach on the level of a new or seasoned detective, but at the end of the day, he's still a uniformed officer. If he tries to go outside of his metron by walking onto the scene a crime and collecting evidence that he's not supposed to touch, he could be reprimanded, terminated and maybe even prosecuted. The point is, just because you notice a grace on your life doesn't mean you are called to the office of that grace. It could mean that you are seated under or following someone who has that grace. So, if you're a teacher with apostolic insight, teach the people the revelation that God has granted you access to. This is how you effectively edify the body of Christ and perfect the saints.

What's Your Depth?

It is very important for us, as writers, to have somewhat of an idea as to where we are as writers. The reason that this is important, again, is to keep us from venturing into topics that we have little to no knowledge or experience of. For example, when I wrote *Top Heavy, Bottom Fed*, I ventured out too far into revelation. How so? I knew enough about holidays to know what to avoid celebrating, but anytime you write a book, you will have to go deeper than what you know. You have to give people facts to validate what you're saying. In other words, you have to conduct a lot of research.

I found myself going deeper and deeper into new knowledge. This resulted in me having a headache the entire time I was writing that book. When diving, the average healthy person can hold their breath up to two minutes. Hyperventilation (holding one's breath) is tied to many drowning deaths. Drowning is the result of Hypoxia. WebMD says this about Hypoxia: "When your body doesn't have enough oxygen, you could get hypoxemia or hypoxia. These are dangerous conditions. Without oxygen, your brain, liver, and other organs can be damaged just minutes after symptoms start. Hypoxemia (low oxygen in your blood) can cause hypoxia (low oxygen in your tissues) when your blood doesn't carry enough oxygen to your tissues to meet your body's needs."
(Reference: WebMD Medical Reference/Hypoxia and Hypoxemia/Reviewed by Melinda Ratini, DO, MS)

I was definitely experiencing what could best be described as Spiritual Hypoxia. I recall the stress and the pain vividly. I was diving into the deep—a place where I had never been and had not been called to in that season. King David says in Psalm 42:7, "Deep calls to deep at the roar of your waterfalls; all your breakers and your waves have gone over me." What does this mean? For me, it meant that I was diving into new knowledge—knowledge that I wasn't necessarily ready for. I was swimming in foreign waters without the proper gear. I wasn't that deep, so it was not wise for me to dive off the peaks of revelation that I'd suddenly found myself on. Now, don't mistake what I'm saying. I was not in sin; I was just in error. This means that I was not utilizing my God-given wisdom. I had not prayed about my decision to write *Top*

Heavy, Bottom Fed. Nevertheless, I dove into new knowledge without having a proper covering (I didn't have a church home at the time). I had no one to help me understand what I was submerging myself in, and I had no one to pour back into me. One of the reasons I'm glad this happened to me is because the revelation I received from the experience is my own. No one can accuse me of recycling charismatic heresy. I went where I wasn't called, and as a result, I endured a lot of warfare. *Top Heavy, Bottom Fed* turned out to be an *amazing* book. What I learned from that experience is that God will allow you to go as deep as you want to go if it gives Him the glory, however, ascending in revelation with no covering (spiritual climbing gear) means that you will experience the pressure associated with going from one realm of understanding to the next and everything that comes with it. Sure, the book can come out amazing (as did my book), but I personally have learned my lesson. I'll go as far as I'm invited by God to go. I won't venture off into revelation that I have not been cleared to enter into.

Revelation is like the five layers of the Earth. It is tall, wide and deep. There is surface revelation, just as there is in-depth revelation. Nowadays, we have a lot of surface writers attempting to dive into knowledge that they are not yet ready to dive into. Think of a diver. When a diver jumps into the sea, he has to follow a certain protocol to ensure his safety.

Taken from Scuba Diver Life (www.scubadiverlilfe.com/ Is Scuba Diving Dangerous/ Credit: DivemasterDennis)	Revelation (How Can We Apply the Wisdom of Diving to Our Writing Careers?)
Unless you have special training to dive in caves or inside wrecks, limit your dives to open water with no overhead environments. That means only dive where you can go directly to the surface, if necessary, without any obstructions.	There are some depths that you shouldn't venture off into unless you've received the proper training, for example, writing books about demonology is better suited for people who've actually confronted and repeatedly cast out demons. To be safe, a writer can talk about his or her experience, for example, with a certain demonic entity and how he or she overcame it, but to go into the depths of demonology would not be

	wise for a person who isn't trained or knowledgeable about the ministry of deliverance.
Again, unless you have specialized training, only dive within recreational limits, which means no deeper than 130 feet (40 m) beneath the surface. Newer divers or those without advanced certification should stay above 60 feet (18 m).	Recreational limits are limitations placed on casual divers, for example. As a writer, you can only dive so deep into knowledge. As I mentioned earlier, only go as far as you've gone. In other words, don't try to be too deep; stay within the confines of your knowledge until or unless the Holy Spirit takes you deeper.
Dive within the limits of your training and experience. All divers should learn and get better with each dive; as you dive more, you'll get better at it. If you're trying something new, like your first drift dive, or first night dive, go with a professional or at least with other divers experienced in the conditions and environment you are about to dive.	Every writer should know his or her limits. For example, if you have never been married, it is not ideal for you to write a book about marriage. Why? Because you have not had on-the-job training as a spouse. Spectating does not qualify divers; it is actually experiencing the temperature of the water, understanding how their bodies respond to the water and knowing their limitations that helps divers to become good at what they do. Additionally, if you're writing about a subject that you have little to no experience in, get the backing of someone who does have experience in that arena. For example, if you want to write a book about demonology, it would be wise to co-write the book with someone who is an experienced deliverance minister or, at minimum, submit the book to a seasoned deliverance minister for proofing.
Maintain good health. A substantial portion of dive accidents, especially those that are fatal, actually relate to a pre-existing disposition to a medical problem such as cardiac failure or other issues. Maintaining good health will substantially reduce your risks when diving.	Please understand that the enemy is looking for any and every open door he can find to attack a writer who has decided to fashion his or her pen as a sword. If you don't properly take care of yourself, the enemy won't necessarily need a door to attack you through; he'll just encourage you to attack yourself. Before starting a career as a writer, it is wise to start some type of exercise

regime because writing involves a lot of sitting down.

Maintain your diving skills by being an active diver. Active divers are safe divers who remember and follow their training and safety rules. If you have been out of the water for six months, a year, or even longer, you should really consider taking a scuba refresher course before resuming open-water diving. At the very least, spend some time in the pool refreshing your familiarity with the equipment and practicing some basic skills, especially buoyancy control.

Of course, authors should continue writing, even after their books are finished. Nevertheless, every author should also continue learning about whatever it is he or she wrote about. The reason for this is, you will eventually come into contact with people who've read your book—people who want you to give them an oral explanation of a particular excerpt from your book. In some cases, you're going to encounter legalistic souls who are knowledgeable about the subject that you spoke on. One thing about legalistic people is they study to be right and not righteous. The point is, keep writing and keep learning.

Dive only with quality equipment, and keep it well-maintained. I'm partial to having my own gear, and making sure it is properly maintained. However, quality rental gear that is well maintained is available in most places. Have your gear serviced regularly, and rinse and store it properly after each dive outing.

The equipment that we, as writers, must wear is called the full armor of God. We maintain this armor through the reading of the Word, meditation on the Word, submission to God, worship and prayer. Ephesians 6:10-18 (ESV) reads, "Finally, be strong in the Lord and in the strength of his might. Put on the whole armor of God, that you may be able to stand against the schemes of the devil. For we do not wrestle against flesh and blood, but against the rulers, against the authorities, against the cosmic powers over this present darkness, against the spiritual forces of evil in the Heavenly places. Therefore take up the whole armor of God, that you may be able to withstand in the evil day, and having done all, to stand firm. Stand therefore, having fastened on the belt of truth, and having put on the breastplate of righteousness, and, as shoes for your feet, having put on the readiness given by the gospel of peace. In all circumstances take up the shield of faith, with which you can extinguish all the flaming darts of the evil one; and take the helmet of salvation, and the sword of the Spirit, which is the word of God, praying at all times in the Spirit, with all prayer and supplication. To that end, keep alert with all perseverance, making supplication for all the saints."

Plan your dive and dive your plan. Proper dive planning and execution will eliminate a substantial level of risk, but no plan is safe unless you follow it. Once you are at a level of experience at which you can independently plan and carry out a dive with your buddy, you have truly arrived as a competent and safe diver. That leads to the next safety rule.

2 Timothy 2:15 reads, "Study to shew thyself approved unto God, a workman that needeth not to be ashamed, rightly dividing the word of truth."

Have a destination in place. Don't just write for the glory of being an author. Ask yourself this: What do I want my readers to take from my book? What is my vision for the many people who will buy my book? In short, don't write on subjects that you have little to no knowledge about. Don't talk about your experiences if you don't have facts and scriptures to draw or back your conclusion. It is also good to have a God-fearing, reliable source to look at what you've written, especially if it's controversial. Proverbs 15:22 says it this way, "Without counsel purposes are disappointed: but in the multitude of counselors they are established."

Always dive with a buddy. I know some of you are solo divers and even have training for that kind of diving, but it is far safer to dive with a competent dive buddy unless you have that special training, plenty of redundant equipment, and always follow specialized safety rules. Diving with a buddy means staying close to each other in case either of you requires assistance. Too many divers forget that.

Of course, as authors, this doesn't necessarily mean that we are to co-author books with others. Most of us will build our writing careers writing solo books, but every now and again, we may co-author or contribute to another book. It is, however, important to know the difference between co-authoring versus being a contributing writer. Knowing the difference can save you from a lawsuit. A co-author shares in the expenses as well as the royalties of a book.

There is normally an equal distribution of the royalties between co-authors. Co-authors are considered one of the authors of a particular book, however, contributing writers simply submit articles to be published in another author's book. This means that the author will retain one hundred percent ownership of that book, in addition to paying one hundred percent of the fees required to publish it and receive one hundred percent of the book's royalties. A contributing writer is not considered an author. Additionally, our dive buddy should be the person or people we're accountable to, for example, our leaders. We should always submit our books to someone who knows more than what we know; this way, we won't accidentally lead others astray.

Do a thorough pre-dive check with your buddy. Too often divers get casual about this. Take a minute to make sure air is turned on, all regulators (even alternates) are working properly, and that any weight belts or pockets are secure. During that check, also learn where releases are on each other's equipment, and look over each other generally to make sure you are both are ready to enter the water. You probably know someone who entered the water having forgotten their fins, or light, or didn't have their air turned on, or they didn't put in their weight pockets. Doing a good buddy check will catch these little annoyances, which can create real safety issues if not corrected before getting in the water.

An author's pre-dive check involves researching books similar to his or her own. Does anyone else have the title you're planning to use, and if so, how many reviews do they have? This is important because it is never wise to give your book the same title as another *popular* book. However, if someone has that same name, but they don't have many reviews and the author is not popular, you can use the book's title without concern. For example, I came up with the title *Sex, Lies and Soul Ties* for one of my books. The moment I heard the title, I was taken aback and excited, nevertheless, I knew to research the title to make sure that I wouldn't be drowned out by someone else's book. Sure enough, another author was using that name (please note that you can't stop people from using the same title that you're using unless your title is unique and you've filed a trademark). Anyhow, the other author's book was eight years old and had two negative reviews.

This told me that I could definitely use the title and do something great with it. Today, I have 22 reviews and my star rating for *Sex, Lies and Soul Ties* is 4.7 out of five stars. It would be unwise for me, however, to write a book and give it the same title as one of Cindy Trimm's books because she is a renowned author who always gets a star rating that ranges from 4.5 to five stars. Also, make sure the information you are giving isn't rehashed information that someone else has given. You can do this by researching similar books on Amazon and opening the preview of the books to look at the Table of Content. Yes, you will talk about the same things from time to time, but you want to make sure that you aren't selling the same dog wearing a different collar.

Follow no-decompression dive limits. We were all trained how to calculate our no-deco limits, and now we all almost always dive with a computer. When your computer tells you it's time to go to shallower depths, go to shallower depths. If you are timing the dive and monitoring depth without a computer, then ascend when you have been at depth for the duration planned. This is really just another way of being sure you plan your dive and dive your plan.

Thoughtco.com defines "no decompression limits" this way: "A no-decompression limit (NDL) is a time limit for the amount of time a diver can stay at a given depth. No-decompression limits vary from dive to dive, depending upon depth and previous recent dive profiles."

What this means for authors is we should know when to bring our readers back to the surface. The surface allows readers to collect themselves and ingest what they've just read. If they're too deep for too long, they'll get confused, agitated, and in some cases, bound. When writing a book, I will often prepare the readers by giving them surface-level wisdom—information they can understand or relate to, and then, I'll take them into the depths of knowledge and the heights of revelation. I keep bringing them back to the surface to understand each pointer before taking them back into revelation. We don't need a computer to time this; we just need to be sensitive to the voice of the Holy Spirit.

Don't feed the animals. Divers know that dangers from sea creatures are minimal, almost non-existent in fact. But these dangers do exist. That danger level increases a bunch if you feed sharks, or eels, or other potentially aggressive sea creatures. Altering the natural behavior of any creature is not a good idea.

Critics can be an author's worst nightmare if they are entertained. Oftentimes, a Christian writer's critics are legalistic, prideful, platform-seeking souls whose wounds are as big as their egos. These are people who study the Bible in their attempt to discredit it or discredit the people who dare to pull revelation from it. They are oftentimes intelligent but foolish souls who, quite frankly, are angry that they don't have the followers they think they are deserving of. For this reason, they browse social media, looking for people who have large followings. They will then monitor those people's pages, waiting for an opportunity to attack them. For example, if a leader unintentionally misquotes a scripture or gives a questionable revelation regarding a scripture, the legalist will see that as his (or her) opportunity to strike. Legalists are more determined to gain followers for themselves than they are to bring down other leaders, but if attacking a leader gives them what they want, they are more than willing to do so. In the world of writing, these are the sharks that you have to look out for. To not feed them means to not debate with them. When an author starts getting a lot of reviews, a legalistic soul will often purchase the author's book so that he or she can also leave a review, but they never plan to leave a positive review. They want to leave an educated, soulish review designed to make themselves look like they have more knowledge than the author on the subject. Never answer them. Always ignore critics because the minute you answer a critic is the very moment that you've gained yourself a loyal, albeit critical, follower.

Is Deep Calling You?

"Deep calls to deep at the noise of your waterspouts: all your waves and your billows are gone over me" (Psalm 42:7 (AKJV).

There will be times when God will call you higher in revelation than you've ever been. There will be times when you'll want to surface from knowledge when God is calling you to go deeper. There will be times when you'll want to quickly draw a conclusion, but God won't let you. We've talked about writers who dive too deep into knowledge, but are not called to that depth. Nevertheless, there are writers who are called to go deeper than they've ever been.

How can you tell you're going deeper without authorization from the Most High God? It's simple. Below are a few signs that you're going into a place God did not call you into:
1. You are motivated by the thoughts of looking or sounding deep (intelligent).
2. You are motivated by thoughts of fame, microphones and platforms.
3. You are motivated by the desire to show up your enemies.
4. Your book presents a platform for you to address or respond to someone else who has a platform.
5. You refuse to be corrected in regards to the content of your book or you won't submit it at all to your leaders.
6. You are motivated by the depth of someone else's book.
7. You don't think about the impact (either good or bad) that your book will have on its readers; you are more concerned with sales and numbers.

Below are a few signs that God is calling you to go deeper:
1. You feel the need to go deeper, even though you may not necessarily want to.
2. You are motivated by thoughts of people being helped, delivered, and empowered.
3. You feel love and compassion when you're writing.
4. You are not comparing your book to another author's book.
5. You are not responding to something someone said or did.
6. You are not moved by ideas of money, fame and mics.

7. You are prayerful about and accountable for what you write.

When God begins to lead you higher into revelation, you'll feel the confines of your intellectual limitations. You'll notice that when you initially started writing, you seemed to be flowing, but you'll come to a point where your knowledge runs out. From there, you are required to pray and trust God. From there, you have to type what God tells you to type, regardless of how disconnected it appears to be from what you've already typed. Once you come to the end of yourself, you've just started your ascension into the very heart of God. For example, Queen Esther could feel her limitations the moment Mordecai told her to go before the king and plead with him on behalf of the Jews. This is why she not only fasted, but told Mordecai to get *all* of the Jews to fast. This was the will of God for her; this was her God-given assignment. The same goes for you. There may be times when you experience tension (headache, pressure, frustration) while writing. This doesn't *always* mean that you've gone *too far*. Sometimes, it simply means you are in a spiritual place, attempting to use your own reasoning. Sometimes, it could mean that you need to fast and pray before going any further, meaning, you have to strip yourself of your flesh so that you can clearly hear from God.

I've found that while writing, it is important that we spend as much time listening for the voice and instructions of the Holy Spirit as possible. If we don't, we'll spend that time worrying and doing a whole lot of pointless research. So when you start feeling the pressure, the best thing to do is take a break and pray. Also, be sure to listen carefully for the Lord's instructions. Take a pen and paper with you so that should the Lord speak, you can write down the revelations without rushing back to the computer.

The deeper you go into revelation, the higher you'll ascend into the presence of God. There will be times when you'll honestly want to stop writing because of the pressure you'll feel during the ascension. This is not the time to stop writing; it simply means that you are shifting to another dimension in Christ. This is something that Christian authors must become accustomed to, otherwise, we'll keep retreating every time we experience the weight of another dimension. This is the very reason most Christian authors take three to four years to complete a book; they are not accustomed to the pressures felt during ascension.

In the presence of God, your knowledge doesn't mean a thing—your intellect is rubbish and your experiences are shallow. You are but clay in the Master's hands; let Him mold you. Some of the deepest, most relevant books came from authors who threw caution to the wind and decided to let God have His way. You see, when writing, you will oftentimes question yourself. "Is this too deep? What if what I'm saying is controversial? What if I unintentionally offend the people I love? What if what I write is considered heresy, after all, I've never heard anyone preach what I'm teaching *or* I've never heard anyone preach it *the way* I'm teaching it? Am I really hearing from God? What will the more seasoned leaders think about my book?" These are just a few of the questions that will haunt you over the course of your writing career. To get past this, you have to learn to ignore every voice (including your own) that makes you question what God is saying to you. Additionally, it is good to have a leader who you can be accountable to. Submit your book to him or her; this way, if there is anything controversial, wrong or not layered enough, your leader can have you revisit it. Proverbs 11:14 (ESV) reads, "Where there is no guidance, a people falls, but in an abundance of counselors there is safety."

To go deeper into knowledge and higher into revelation, you must allow God to lead you outside of your understanding. I don't think this is easy for any author because it feels like you're taking your hands off the wheel of your car and closing your eyes, all the while saying, "Jesus, take the wheel!"

Who's Calling You Deep?

I wrote my first book (*The Gospel Propeller*) while living in Germany in 2009. It was a book written to Christian artists who desired to take their music ministries to the next level and it appealed to artists on a budget. Previously, I'd worked with secular artists, helping to brand and promote their music careers. I'd even managed a couple of artists, spoke often with A & R reps and scouted for new talent. Almost everyone in the music industry can clearly see how fast their careers were taking off, and this was no different for me. I was consistent, determined and I'd started making some really invaluable connections. I could tell that I was on the fast track to success. So when the Lord called me out of working with and for the secular world, I had a lot of knowledge that I thought was going to go to waste. Nevertheless, nearly two years later, after having committed my heart and hands fully to the Lord, He gave me my first book, *The Gospel Propeller*—a book that details what I learned in the music industry. It is a book designed to help Christian artists further their music careers.

When I wrote *The Gospel Propeller*, I wasn't a revelatory writer; I was more of an informational writer than anything. I didn't understand spiritual things and I had no desire to become a "deep" Christian. I simply wanted to please the Lord. So when I wrote my first book, I wrote from my knowledge and my understanding, which were both surface-level. I wasn't much of a reader; I didn't collect books and I barely read articles, so I wasn't inspired to become an author based on what I'd seen someone else do. At that point in my life, I just wanted to use my talents. The more I came to love the Lord, the more I wanted to use my talents for Him. Imagine my surprise when a musician by the name of Dr. John Butler featured my book on his show, entitled *So You Wanna Be a Music Star.* This took me completely by surprise, and to be honest with you, it gave me the motivation I needed to continue writing. It showed me that my self-published book was making an impact. A year or two later, I wrote my third book, but this time, the book was spiritual. It was entitled *The Spirit of Heaviness and All Its Cousins.* What led me to write that book? It's simple. I'd had a spiritual dream and woke up with a lot of revelation. Just like *The Gospel Propeller*, I started and finished *The Spirit of Heaviness and All Its Cousins* in a day or two. After waking up, I started writing and would not stop until I was finished. I published the information on a website, and eventually, I published it in a book. After I was done, I created a cover for my book (just like I'd done the first time) and published it without editing it. A few years later, I pulled and republished each book and both books have done well, especially *The Spirit of Heaviness and All Its Cousins.*

One of the things I noticed was the deeper my conversations got, the more intentional I became when making friends. This afforded me the opportunity to have more in-depth conversations and retain more knowledge. Consequentially, this inspired me to want more knowledge, and as a result, my books became more revelatory and spiritual. What was I doing? I was learning to ascend the ranks of revelation. I wrote for a publication called Examiner (now closed) and I utilized that platform for several years to speak more about spiritual things than I did in my books. Why did I do this? Because I wasn't confident with the knowledge I had, plus, writing for the public allowed me to receive more immediate feedback from readers. I allowed that platform to be training grounds for me; I allowed that platform to show me how deep I really was *or* was not.

I ended up writing over two hundred articles for Examiner alone, and during my tenure as a writer (2010-2015), I came to understand that the word "deep" is subjective. To one reader, I was very deep, but to another, I was a surface-level writer. What this taught me was every reader is a student, which meant that I was taking on the role of a teacher. As a teacher, I had to learn what level I was on so that I could effectively market my writings to people who could benefit from them. Additionally, I had to learn when it was my time to teach versus when I was to be taught. No teacher ever becomes a teacher without first having been a student. I had to stop being a non-reader after I discovered that a large part of a (true) writer's life is spent reading.

Are you called deep, and if so, what level are the people on who see you as being a revelatory speaker or writer? Knowing this will help you find your target market; this is how you sell more books and receive better ratings. Are your friends teachers or students? If they are teachers, what level do they teach on? What type of conversations do you have on a regular basis? Are you outgrowing any of your friendships and are you making new friends? Growth is often seen in, not just who we're connected with, but how often we connect with new people and disconnect from old ones. Growth is tangible and intangible; it can be both seen and experienced.

I remember in 2009, I had a friend who I spoke with everyday. It had been that way for more than 15 years. Our conversations were surface-level; we talked about the past and the present, but we rarely talked about our futures outside of what we hoped we'd have someday. But the more I wrote, the more knowledge I had to seek. The more knowledge I sought, the hungrier I became for more in-depth conversations. Before long, I was making new friends—friends who were more spiritual. I began to sense my appetite for knowledge growing. When I spoke with "deep" people, I found myself speaking less and listening more. I'd been told my entire life that I was overly talkative, however, in the presence of wisdom, I was told that I didn't talk enough. I learned that I'd done like many believers do to this day— I'd stayed in a mindset for so long that I'd mastered it. I could talk on and on about where I was and where I'd been, but I could not talk too much about where I intended to grow (go). There were times when I wanted to have surface-level conversations, and when this happened, I called my old and trusted friend. There were times when I wanted to have more in-depth conversations, and when this happened, I called my new friends. Slowly but surely, my old friend and I began to drift apart. I soon learned that every believer is like a child and every friendship is like a garment. As the believer grows, the garment has to be made bigger. If the garment is not adjusted, it will begin to squeeze the people who are wearing it until it rips under the pressure.

Your communications and friendships will give you a lot of insight into what depth of a writer you'll be. If most or all of your conversations are surface-level, your books will be surface-level. Please understand that even on the surface of the earth (above the crust), there are different levels. You can ascend a mountain or swim in the depths of a sea on the surface. What this means is you can be a deep surface-level writer if you are intentional about learning. You can ascend into revelation or you can create oceans of knowledge for your readers to swim in. This all depends on how much wisdom you seek and how often you seek it. Additionally, it is possible for a person to have knowledge and not have anywhere to exercise that knowledge, as was the case with me. When I opened myself up for more friendships, I heard words coming out of my heart that I'd never truly put much thought into. I found that I had some measure of depth to myself, but I'd never had anyone to share that information with. Just like you can sense the gatekeeper (limitations) when writing, you can sense the gatekeeper when speaking with people. Wisdom will tell you how deep you can go with every given person.

Are you deep, or the better question is: who calls you deep? Are you growing, or the better question is: when was the last time you outgrew a mindset? Growing people have growing friends, not in numbers, but in knowledge. Deep calleth unto deep. When was the last time someone deep (wise) called you? These questions are important if we want to change how we, as Christian authors, are viewed. Eighty percent of Christian books flop because Christian writers rarely challenge themselves and are rarely challenged. No one wants to be seen as a believer who tried to stop another believer from writing a book, especially a Christian book. For this reason, we give ourselves a bad name in the marketplace. Our music isn't mastered and our books aren't edited. We are ambitious and unable to be corrected, so we accept failure in exchange for the privilege of calling ourselves authors. The marketplace belongs to the believer, but we won't be able to dominate it until we learn to assess where we are and seek to go further. When we become correctable, we'll become wiser. Proverbs 9:8 (ESV) reads, "Do not reprove a scoffer, or he will hate you; reprove a wise man, and he will love you."

Depth Exercise

So how does one learn how deep he or she really is, or if that person has any depth at all? The following questions will help you to assess where you are. Be sure to write your answers on a separate sheet of paper.

1. **Are you a leader or follower, not in opinion, but in reality?** In other words, who's following you? A leader *always* has followers. Sure, there are many people who use the world's measuring system to determine whether they have leadership potential, but the truth is being a type A personality doesn't mean you're a leader. It can simply mean you're aggressive and controlling. Look around you and pay attention to the people who are following you. What level are they?

2. **How long do you retain your followers' attention?** Now, this is a tricky question because we all understand that a wise man can have one follower (look at Elijah), however, one of the things you'll come to see is that love is a revelation of depth. The deeper you are, the more attention you can hold. A person who forgives easily and is empathetic will garner more followers than a person who is not. This is because love is a revelation of wisdom. Now, don't get love confused with tolerance. The world tolerates perversion and they call their tolerance love when, in truth, it is not. True love corrects; true love looks at the bigger picture. One of the easier ways to determine how much love you have is to pay attention to, not the number of people who are attracted to you, but your ability to retain those people's attention. I've found that most leaders

with growing churches and growing numbers of followers all have one thing in common—they keep growing in love and in revelation, meaning, they intentionally seek knowledge, understanding and wisdom. This results in them being able to hold their followers' attention, which in turn, results in them garnering more followers. Sure, every leader will experience people walking away from him or her; that's a given, but a leader with God's heart will have more people following after him or her than people walking away.

3. **What type of friends do you have? Are they leaders or followers?** Your friends are a revelation of, not just who you are, but where you are in Christ Jesus. They are also a revelation of where you're going. Amos 3:3 reads, "Can two walk together, except they be agreed?" In other words, our friends are a picture of our character. Sure, we may not agree with everything they do or say, but if they are our friends, there is an agreement somewhere that keeps us connected. Are your friends' leaders? Of course, I'm not just talking about religious leaders; I'm talking about leaders as a whole. Are they entrepreneurs? Leaders attract followers but are attracted to other leaders. Remember the various levels of the earth. Are your friends surface-level, helping to keep you afloat, or do you have some friends who've taken you so deep into revelation that it's changed the state of your mind? Leaders have friends who change their minds, but followers seek to change others, even though they themselves don't want to be changed.

4. **What types of conversations do you have regularly?** Are you talking about people, the past, the present or the future? Are you talking about problems or are you solution-minded? Taking an inventory of your regular conversations will help you to determine what level writer you are or if it's your season to write. What you focus on the most will determine whether it's your season to teach or not. Historians focus on the past, counselors focus on the present, but teachers use history to address the present with the intent of helping their readers to attain a better future. Additionally, we speak out of the abundance of our hearts. In other words, people who are more problem-centered are not mentally or spiritually ready to become authors. Godly books are designed to solve a set of problems in the readers' lives; they should never be written to address a problem with hopes that the readers will figure out a solution. This is why people who believe they are called to expose others are

so focused on the people they want to expose, as opposed to focusing on what their books will do to their potential readers. Their goal is to hurt the people they believe have either hurt them or have the potential to hurt them or their cause. This means that if your conversations are more about problems than they are about solutions, it may not be your season to write. Nevertheless, if you want to help people and you have a set of God-given solutions to deliver to God's people, it may be your season to write.

5. **Do you listen more than you speak when talking with friends?** If most of your conversations start and end with you talking, this could mean that you are either surrounded by people who take from you but do not have the capacity to pour into you or it could mean that you are controlling. Controlling people surround themselves with people they can easily control. A true leader doesn't just surround himself or herself with listeners; a true leader surrounds himself or herself with people he or she loves to listen to. This is a revelation of our maturity and our desire to grow and learn. If you are surrounded by listeners, this could also be a picture of fear manifesting itself in your life. People bound by fear enjoy the comforts of familiarity and are often afraid of people who they cannot relate to. Nevertheless, one of the nutrients needed for growth is called "new." We need new information, new revelation and new people in our lives. We need relationships where we're forced to listen and ask questions more than we speak and make suggestions. We need to be taught, instead of always trying to be the teacher.

6. **Do you see a growth in your life financially, spiritually and socially?** Growth manifests itself in our finances, the level of our warfare and our relationships. Where there is no growth, there is no teacher. Growing is an intentional process that can be uncomfortable and taxing. It can be taxing because, in order to grow, we have to give up something. So, a better question is, what have you sacrificed or when was the last time you sacrificed a mindset, a relationship or anything that was hindering your growth? Growth also manifests itself in our warfare. Many people who believe themselves to be surface-level writers experience high-level warfare because of their rank. We aren't the rank we acknowledge; we are who God says that we are. Some people won't acknowledge, for example, that they have a prophetic call on their lives, however, demons will acknowledge their calls by attacking them

on the very levels they are called to. This is why it is silly to run from your assignment. Most of us have done this, only to find ourselves enduring intense warfare while surrounded by people who could not help or pray us out of the warfare. This is because people who do not acknowledge the call on their lives usually surround themselves with people who are on the level they believe themselves to be on. Ignoring God's voice won't stop the devil from hearing it.

EVERYONE IS DEEP OR REVELATORY TO SOMEONE.

The key is finding the people who can learn from you versus just writing books, tossing them off into a crowd and waiting to see if someone's life is impacted by what you wrote. Additionally, our depths of revelation can change over time—sometimes even overnight if we're intentional about our growth. Obtaining knowledge is a digging process; it is unearthing the information that God has already availed to us and then peeling back (unveiling) the layers to make it more editable and palatable. Understanding is a process of digesting the knowledge you have and growing from it. Additionally, whatever you digest, you can feed to others. Wisdom is the ability to take knowledge and filter it through the Word of God, separating truth from tradition and lies before feeding it to others. Knowledge is obtained, understanding is ascertained, but wisdom is shared.

Who Summoned You?

King Ahasuerus, also known as King Xerxes, was initially married to Queen Vashti. A pagan king, it would seem unlikely that God would send a Jewish woman to be his wife, but He did. As the story goes, King Xerxes held a feast after showing off his wealth for 180 days. On the seventh day of the feast, the intoxicated king summoned his wife, Queen Vashti. She refused to come and this, of course, embarrassed the king. He inquired of his wise men what punishment he should execute upon Vashti for her dishonor. One of the men (a man named Memucan) suggested that the king put Vashti away and give her crown to a woman who was better than her. This sounded like good advice at the time so the king agreed to it. He made it a law that Queen Vashti could not come before him anymore; this was the equivalent of a divorce, even though the queen would remain in the castle, most likely in the concubine's quarters. The Bible goes on to tell us that after the king's anger had dissipated, he remembered Vashti and the decree he'd made. This means that he started feeling regretful and brokenhearted. Seeing the king's pain, the men who attended to him suggested that the king appoint officers to bring all of the beautiful young virgins to the king's harem in Susa. He'd then be able to pick another queen for himself. This petition pleased the king and he went forward with it. This is how we meet Esther.

Esther 2:5-9 (ESV): Now there was a Jew in Susa the citadel whose name was Mordecai, the son of Jair, son of Shimei, son of Kish, a Benjaminite, who had been carried away from Jerusalem among the captives carried away with Jeconiah king of Judah, whom Nebuchadnezzar king of Babylon had carried away. He was bringing up Hadassah, that is Esther, the daughter of his uncle, for she had neither father nor mother. The young woman had a beautiful figure and was lovely to look at, and when her father and her mother died, Mordecai took her as his own daughter. So when the king's order and his edict were proclaimed, and when many young women were gathered in Susa the citadel in custody of Hegai, Esther also was taken into the king's palace and put in custody of Hegai, who had charge of the women. And the young woman pleased him and won his favor. And he quickly provided her with her cosmetics and her portion of food, and with seven chosen young women from the king's palace, and advanced her and her young women to the best place in the harem.

As we can see, all of the beautiful young virgins under the king's province were summoned to come before the king; they were called, but not all of them were chosen to audition for the role as queen. This helps us to better understand Matthew 22:14 which reads, "For many are called, but few are chosen."

There are a lot of writers taking up the charge to minister, even though they have not been summoned by the King of kings. The penalty for going before King Xerxes without being summoned was death; that is, unless the king lifted his scepter to you; this was a picture of mercy. Of course, we're not citizens of Persia and the times have changed drastically since then, but going before God or His people involves a process. We won't die naturally if we go before Him, but He does require that we die to ourselves (flesh). "That no flesh should glory in his presence" (1 Corinthians 1:29).

As writers, we have to know *if* we're called to write, *when* we're called to write and *what* we're assigned to write. You see, there are many writers out there who want to glory in God's presence. They want to minister to God's people, not realizing how delicate of a matter this is. When Vashti refused to come before the king, she proved herself to be unworthy of the crown she so proudly wore. She didn't come *when* summoned.

Growing up, my siblings and I knew to answer our parents the very minute they called us. We didn't have the luxury of waiting a minute or two. *When* we answered was just as important as *how* we answered. This seemed cruel then, but nowadays, this structure has helped to deliver me from the hand of the enemy many times. It takes a great deal of wisdom and maturity to learn when to speak versus when to listen. When Queen Esther had her first meeting with King Xerxes and Haman, her conversation had the power to make or break the breakthrough she'd been petitioning Heaven for.

Esther 5:2-8 (ESV): And when the king saw Queen Esther standing in the court, she won favor in his sight, and he held out to Esther the golden scepter that was in his hand. Then Esther approached and touched the tip of the scepter. And the king said to her, "What is it, Queen Esther? What is your request? It shall be given you, even to the half of my kingdom." And Esther said, "If it pleases the king, let the king and Haman come today to a feast that I have prepared for the king." Then the king said, "Bring Haman quickly, so that we may do as Esther has asked." So the king and Haman came to the feast that Esther had prepared. And as they were drinking wine after the feast, the king said to Esther, "What is your wish? It shall be granted you. And what is your request? Even to the half of my kingdom, it shall be fulfilled." Then Esther answered, "My wish and my request is: If I have found favor in the sight of the king, and if it pleases the king to grant my wish and fulfill my request, let the king and Haman come to the feast that I will prepare for them, and tomorrow I will do as the king has said."

In this first conversation, we see that Esther didn't say much. She let the king eat and enjoy his food, and after the feast, when they were drinking wine, the king asked her to tell him the petition of her heart. Nevertheless, Esther chose her words carefully. Sure, she could have exposed Haman right at that moment, but she couldn't afford to be led by her emotions. She had to wait for the right moment to tell her husband about Haman's plot. Sensing that the moment they were in was not the right one, Esther invited the king and Haman to a second feast to be held the following day. **Esther 7:1-6 (ESV):** So the king and Haman went in to feast with Queen Esther. And on the second day, as they were drinking wine after the feast, the king again said to Esther, "What is your wish, Queen Esther? It shall be granted you. And what is your request? Even to the half of my kingdom, it shall be fulfilled." Then Queen Esther answered, "If I have found favor in your sight, O king, and if it pleases the king, let my life be granted me for my wish, and my people for my request. For we have been sold, I and my people, to be destroyed, to be killed, and to be annihilated. If we had been sold merely as slaves, men and women, I would have been silent, for our affliction is not to be compared with the loss to the king." Then King Ahasuerus said to Queen Esther, "Who is he, and where is he, who has dared to do this?" And Esther said, "A foe and enemy! This wicked Haman!" Then Haman was terrified before the king and the queen.

Esther waited until the king asked her what her petition was before telling him what

Haman was planning to do to her people. She had to choose her words carefully; she had to wait for the right moment to speak. She couldn't just blurt out her petition; she had to wait. When Mordecai told her to plead with the king on behalf of the Jews, Esther told him that she couldn't just barge into the king's chambers; she had to be summoned, otherwise, her life would be in grave danger. Nevertheless, Mordecai helped her to understand the urgency of the matter and she'd risked her life by going before the king when she hadn't be called for. Now, there she was—at a second meeting with the king and Haman, and just like she wasn't supposed to barge into the king's chambers, she knew not to barge into the king's conversation with Haman. She waited until he summoned her words by asking, " What is your wish, Queen Esther? It shall be granted you. And what is your request? Even to the half of my kingdom, it shall be fulfilled." It was then that she spoke; it was then that she sensed the right moment. Her wisdom, humility and conversation were all crucial in saving the lives of the Jews.

Believe it or not, Queen Esther was a representative of the apostolic. As a matter of fact, kings and queens were pretty much the equivalents of apostles in the Old Testament era. Needless to say, some of the kings and queens back then were evil, so instead of acting like apostles, they became what Ephesians 6:12 refers to as "the rulers of the darkness of this world." Howbeit, Queen Esther was a godly woman, even though she was married to a pagan king. Submitting to the king sanctified the king or, better yet, made him holy. 1 Corinthians 7:14 (ESV) reads, "For the unbelieving husband is made holy because of his wife, and the unbelieving wife is made holy because of her husband."

As a representative of the apostolic, Queen Esther had to address what was the equivalent of a principality (Haman). We can see this based on the level of the attack that Haman plotted. He wanted to annihilate an entire Jewish nation because they refused to bow to him. But Esther could not defeat him in the natural; she had to defeat what was in him in the realm of the spirit. She did this by fasting; she did this by prostrating herself before the Most High God. She also had to defeat Haman by submitting to her husband. Esther's humility was her weapon. 1 Peter 3:1-2 (ESV) reads, "Likewise, wives, be subject to your own husbands, so that even if some do not obey the word, they may be won without a word by the conduct of their wives, when they see your respectful and pure conduct."

Authority doesn't always involve screaming at demons; authority has several dimensions. One of the greatest and most potent forms of authority is humility. We see this in Matthew 17 when the disciples could not cast the demon out of a young boy who the Bible refers to as a lunatic. In modern day terms, the young man was deranged. He also is believed to have suffered from what we now refer to as epilepsy. Jesus ended up casting the demon out of the boy and His disciples wanted to know why they'd failed at delivering the young man. Jesus responded in Matthew 17:21 by saying, "However, this kind goes not out but by prayer and fasting." Praying and fasting are extensions of humility. Esther had to win favor with someone who outranked her (in the natural), and that someone was her husband.

The voice of the church is under attack. Is Satan coming after God's influence? Of course! He wants to birth distrust inside and outside of the church, however, the wombs he's using to carry out his attack are the mouths and fingertips of immature believers. Here's how. It's not uncommon for us, as believers, to see something wrong. It is not uncommon for us to see Satan working behind the scenes. However, it is common to see believers attempting to "expose" the people who the devil is working through without exposing the devil himself. Ephesians 6:12 warns us this way, "For we wrestle not against flesh and blood, but against principalities, against powers, against the rulers of the darkness of this world, against spiritual wickedness in high places." What does this mean for us? It means that we have to see past the people if we're going to minister to them. We can't just teach them to see the obvious. As writers and teachers, we have to teach them to open up their eyes to what's seen and unseen. Nevertheless, in this day and age, there are a lot of immature believers who've been led astray by their own selfish ambitions trying to voice their opinions when the King of kings has not summoned them.

I think it was the year 2009 or 2010 when I had a strange dream. In the dream, I was standing with a group of no more than three to five women. We appeared to be in Europe somewhere because we were surrounded by rolling hills. Anyhow, we were all laughing and talking when some man walked up to us. He was dark complexioned and wore dark sunglasses. I didn't know him, but he looked familiar. *(Familiarity in dreams usually represents a familiar spirit).* Obviously, the women were all familiar with him as well because when he walked up, their countenances changed and they all dropped their heads in fear. I watched as he walked up to every woman, taking something out of her hand. None of the women resisted him, nor did they utter a word when he robbed them of what belonged to them. I found myself becoming agitated, and when he walked over to me, he reached into my hand and took my cell phone. Offended, I said something to the effect of, "Oh, so you're just gonna take my phone?!" The guy didn't respond. He just looked at me with an unusually calm expression. Through his calm, I could still see that he was surprised. He hadn't expected me to respond that way. He was used to robbing people at will with no pushback. Nevertheless, there I was inadvertently revealing that I would be a voice that would cry out against him. I then snatched my phone from him and told him I was going to call the police. He responded in the calmest tone I'd ever heard. He said, "Oh, so you're gonna call the cops on me?" When I replied with "yes," he calmly nodded his head. The nod in itself looked threatening. I called the cops, and when they arrived, I could see them from afar handing him some court papers. They didn't arrest him, they just handed him a stack of papers. Of course, I was terrified because that meant he was free to come after me for a season or two. And he did just that. I spent the rest of the time (in my dream) running from the guy, hiding out in the homes of people I knew, all of which turned on me to save themselves. When I sought the Lord about the interpretation of that dream, He told me that the guy, of course, was a familiar spirit. He had been robbing women of the things that rightfully belonged to them, but when he'd come after me, I fought back. Now, that fight cost me a lot of friendships and relationships, but I kept what belonged to me. The court documents or summons represented the fact that the devil would answer for his crimes, but his time to be punished had not yet come.

I wanted to address the enemy right then and there; I wanted him arrested on the spot, but that didn't happen. After he was free to go, I went on the run. Did this signify that I'd run my entire life from the enemy? No. It represented the place I was in during that season of my life. It meant that no one I was affiliated with would be willing or able to deliver me from the familiar spirit I'd been bound by. It was a message to me that I would have to deliver myself; I would have to speak up on my own behalf before I could speak up for the women I'd someday minister to.

WHO SUMMONED YOU?

Eventually, my season came to respond to him. I received my deliverance and then, I was able to minister to other women who were in bondage. The most important lesson in that dream wasn't the fact that the enemy was after me; that was obvious. The lesson I had to grasp centered around two words and they were, "not yet."

Ecclesiastes 3:1-8 (ESV): To everything there is a season, and a time to every purpose under the Heaven: A time to be born, and a time to die; a time to plant, and a time to pluck up that which is planted; a time to kill, and a time to heal; a time to break down, and a time to build up; a time to weep, and a time to laugh; a time to mourn, and a time to dance; a time to cast away stones, and a time to gather stones together; a time to embrace, and a time to refrain from embracing; a time to get, and a time to lose; a time to keep, and a time to cast away; a time to rend, and a time to sew; a time to keep silence, and a time to speak; a time to love, and a time to hate; a time of war, and a time of peace.

The message here is that the "when" will lead you to the "how." If I'd tried to deliver myself in that season, I wouldn't have received the instructions needed to effectively fight the enemy because there was a lot I needed to first learn. I wasn't ready for that level of warfare, after all, I wasn't going to be going up against a small demon. That demon had an entire region scared of it because in my dream, I was running all around the country looking for help, but the people were too afraid to get involved. God was just telling me that the enemy had been charged with his crimes against me because I'd called upon the name of the Lord, however, I had to endure for just a little while longer. When that season ended, God led me to the information and people I needed to obtain my freedom. I was still in the middle of my own personal earthquake. God was in the process of shaking up my life so that He could get me to fully break any and every agreement I had with the enemy. This is because Satan is a legalist who represents himself well in court. Any agreements I had with offense, pride, unforgiveness or generational strongholds would be used against me. I was repentant and finally surrendered to God, but there were some things still in my life that needed to be addressed. God wanted to rig the case in my favor, but before He could, I had to give up my old heart and be cleansed of its residue; this way, when the enemy brought up pictures of the old me, the Lord would render the evidence inadmissible.

Hebrews 8:12 (ESV): For I will be merciful toward their iniquities, and I will remember their sins no more.

Isaiah 43:25 (ESV): I, I am he who blots out your transgressions for my own sake, and I will not remember your sins.

Again, the when is just as important as the how. If Queen Esther hadn't trusted God, she would have become impatient and put the Jews' life in more immediate danger. She would have proved Haman's case for him that the Jews were rebellious and did not honor the king. She had to be prayerful; she had to be strategic. She couldn't afford to be led by her emotions. As writers, we have to learn when to write, what to write and how to write it. Of course, before we do this, we must know if God wants us to write what we're planning to write.

I met a girl a few years ago who had an awesome idea for a book. I was already a published author of around ten or more books and she'd never written a book. She was a dreamer at best. She was a person who had a lot of great ideas, yet she lacked the discipline needed to follow through with any of them. She started telling me her idea for a book and I remember thinking, "Why haven't I ever thought of that?" The next series of thoughts I had were from the enemy. I thought to myself that she wasn't going to carry those ideas out, after all, she reminded me of a lot of people in my family. She had enough ideas to earn her a billion dollars, but she loved her lifestyle and was too committed to her comfort zone to write a book. Nevertheless, I was mature enough to understand that the thoughts I had were not from God. I cast them down immediately and encouraged her to follow through with that book. I told her about the thoughts I'd just had and told her to keep her idea to herself. "Everybody won't be like me," I warned her. She thanked me and agreed.

The book she had wasn't mine to write. It was a great idea and I was confident that it would be a best-seller if she followed through with it, but the idea had been given to her by God. I was intimate enough with Him to know that He wouldn't bless it if I wrote it. The point is we have to know *if* we're summoned to write, *what* we're summoned to write and *when* we're summoned to write. Being obedient to God and sensitive to His voice will determine if we become best-sellers or not. I couldn't take her book idea, after all, doing so would render me a thief. I had to watch a good idea pass me by because I had not been summoned to write that book. Do I regret not writing it? Absolutely not. This is because I've learned to tell the difference between good ideas versus God ideas.

Writer's Hypoxia

Science News for Kids reported the following on their website: "A diver who stays down too long, swims too deep, or comes up too fast can end up with a condition called "the bends." In this case, bubbles of gas in the blood can cause intense pain, even death" (Reference: Science News for Kids/ The Pressure of Scuba Diving/ Emily Sohn).

The result of a diver staying down too long or rising too quickly is called Hypoxia.

"Hypoxia: diminished availability of oxygen to the body tissues; its causes are many and varied and includes a deficiency of oxygen in the atmosphere, as in altitude sickness, pulmonary disorders that interfere with adequate ventilation of the lungs; anemia or circulatory deficiencies, leading to inadequate transport and delivery of oxygen to the tissues; and finally, edema or other abnormal conditions of the tissues themselves that impair the exchange of oxygen and carbon dioxide between capillaries and tissues.

Signs and symptoms vary according to the cause. Generally, they include dyspnea, rapid pulse, syncope, and mental disturbances such as delirium or euphoria. Cyanosis is not always present and in some cases is not evident until the hypoxia is far advanced."
(Reference: The Free Dictionary by Farlex/ Hypoxia).

Hypoxia, in short, simply means to suffocate. How does this relate to the reader or writer's experience? It is very common for authors to drown themselves or their readers by:

1. Going too deep into knowledge.
2. Staying in the mountains of revelation for too long.
3. Ascending the heights of revelation too quickly.
4. Ascending to the surface from revelation too quickly.
5. Staying on the surface-level too long.

Going Too Deep into Knowledge

The word "scuba" as in scuba diver stands for "self-contained underwater breathing apparatus." Diving gear is designed to protect divers, in addition to making their underwater experiences easier and more comfortable.

Writing is about sharing your experiences and what you've learned with others who may be sharing those same experiences or may experience them in the future. It is not uncommon for untrained authors to attempt to write about experiences they've never had and mysteries they have yet to solve. You should never go beyond your knowledge or understanding; you should never go past your experience. Additionally, you need to wear the whole armor of God when addressing spiritual matters. This is your scuba gear.

Staying in the Mountains of Revelation Too Long

Revelation has to be digested, meaning, you will have to explain some of the facts, truths and controversial information that you share. This isn't just for your readers; it's also for you. After all, you will learn as you write. When an author keeps layering revelation with revelation, it is easy for the author to get lost and forget his or her own point. Delirium is one of the signs of Hypoxia. Every writer (and teacher) has experienced delirium at some point.

Ascending the Heights of Revelation Too Quickly

Children are progressively given wisdom, knowledge and understanding because if we were to spell out life for them in our adult terms, they'd become confused, disinterested and depressed. They'd then find people they could learn from, and we all know that, in many cases, the people they would choose to glean from wouldn't necessarily be good role models for them.

Please understand that your readers have a certain age in the Lord. Some are babes in Christ; some are little children, others are servants, and some are mature meat-eating sons. Regardless of where a believer is in Christ, that believer has to be led level by level into revelation; you can't just take people from their bedrooms to the peak of a mountain, suddenly dip them into the depths of a sea and then sit them back on their beds. Every high and low thing has laws that every living thing must abide by in order to survive. Every time we ascend or descend to another level in the natural, we have to adjust to and obey the laws of that level.

Ascending to the Surface from Knowledge Too Quickly

Remember, a scuba diver can experience Hypoxia from coming to the surface too fast. This is called "the bends" in the swimming world. Sure, we want to explain our points to the readers, but the best way to do this is by explaining what we've typed and then breaking down some of the key points. Just like we had to gradually descend into knowledge, we have to gradually ascend into revelation to make our points. This means we must build our messages line upon line and precept upon precept.

Staying on the Surface-Level Too Long

This is especially true for subjects that are normally deep and revelatory. For example, the subject of demonology is not a surface-level topic. If I wrote a book about demonology and deliverance, I couldn't have a book that read like this: "Demons are bad. They are responsible for many of the sicknesses and most of the problems we have in our lives. Demons are evil. That's why they are called devils. They love to see people suffer. When we cry, they rejoice. If given the chance, they'd kill us all. I hate demons. I wish they'd all just go to the fiery pits right now and drown in the fire." That would be a horrible book to read because most of the people who purchase demonology books aren't looking for surface-level information. So, as deep as I can be, if I go to the wrong depth, I can end up sounding like a child. People who buy books on demonology have on their diving and climbing gear and they're ready to dive into knowledge and then ascend into understanding. So if I decided to write a book about demonology, I could write, for example: "One of the greatest travesties to hit the modern day church is the belief that Christians cannot have demons. Such teachings have afforded many evil spirits the opportunities to intrude upon the lives, families, peace and finances of God's people. So first and foremost, let's get one thing straight: a Christian can be oppressed, not possessed, by a demon. What's the difference? It's simple. The word "oppress" means to weigh down a person unjustly; to "possess" means to own, to (justifiably) hijack a person's will. The difference is what's considered legal versus illegal in the realm of the spirit.

Isaiah 59:19 reads, 'So shall they fear the name of the LORD from the west, and his glory from the rising of the sun. When the enemy shall come in like a flood, the Spirit of the LORD shall lift up a standard against him.' We all understand that the Bible was not written for the unbeliever, but for the believer. Please understand the nature of a flood. A flood can carry someone away against his or her will. This means that should the enemy's oppression become too much for a believer to bear, God will raise a standard (regulation, rule) against him."

As you can see in this text, I'm building on key points. I started off at the surface talking about the doctrinal belief that Christians can't have demons. Next, I took two keywords (oppress and possess) and started detailing the differences between the two. Please notice that I didn't take my definitions from online (even though it would have been okay if I had). Instead, I looked up the definition for "oppress" online and one keyword stuck out—that word was "unjustly." The word "unjustly" comes from "just," which, of course, is short for the word "justice." So, I was able to subtly use the Kingdom's justice system to explain my point. I backed up my message with Isaiah 59:19 and I can create an entire chapter surrounding that. This means I didn't stay on the surface, even though you'll also notice that I didn't go as deep as I could have gone. Why not? Because I am swimming. I can't take readers from one depth to another suddenly. I have to gradually take them there. Howbeit, the point is, you cannot keep readers in shallow waters (surface). You have to baptize them in knowledge and then, bring them back up again.

Writer's Warfare

Have you ever taken a stick and shoved it into an ant-pile? If so, what happened? Nine times out of ten, if it was a live pile, a lot of ants started pouring out of the pile, ready to protect their queen. What you experienced was called a response. Not only did the ants respond to your intrusion, but they also responded by rank. You will rarely, if ever, come in contact with the queen ant. What we have to understand, as believers and writers, is that every time we do or say something, there will be a response to our words and our choices. The same is true for writing. Anytime a writer strikes his or her keyboard, the sound of the keys will echo in the writer's ears. Nevertheless, this is the natural response, but there will also be a supernatural response, especially if the writer has not closed every demonic-access door in his or her life. The writer, the moment he or she strikes a key, has stuck a stick into the kingdom of darkness. Feeling threatened, the enemy will respond. To keep this from happening, the writer needs to ensure that he or she is submitted to God and that he or she remains prayerful throughout the ordeal. Additionally, the writer may need to fast.

James 4:7 (ESV): Submit yourselves therefore to God. Resist the devil, and he will flee from you.

Earlier in this manuscript, we briefly discussed the science of sound. Anytime we speak or move, we cause vibrations in the air to move. This is a response to our words or actions and this response usually comes in the form of sounds. When plates under the Earth's crust move past one another, the Earth responds in what we refer to as an earthquake. When an earthquake occurs, the Earth responds by splitting in some places and merging together in others. When a believer says to a demon, "Come out of him in Jesus name," the demon will respond by coming out (in most cases) or by manifesting (in other cases). Sometimes, to get a response, the person needing deliverance has to fast and pray. When we ascend the mountain, our body responds. When we dive into the depths of the sea, our body responds. When we speak to people, they'll likely respond. Every time a sound is made, a response will follow. Every time we execute an act, a response will follow. The same is true for writing. This is why it is unwise for glory-seekers to write spiritual books. The moment they start typing, the enemy that responds will likely respond from within them.

Many believers cripple their writing careers by trying to write on levels they have not lived on. Again, when a surface-level writer dives into the depths of revelation, that writer's state must be changed before he or she can pour out revelation on that level. When this happens, writers normally report that they are going through warfare and are in need of prayer when, in truth, what they're experiencing is not warfare (in many cases). What they're experiencing is the melting down or sifting of who they are. If I teach a deep, revelatory message about fornication and the doors it opens, I'd better be fully delivered from fornication and the demons that came into my life when I was in fornication. If not, as I'm being melted down, whatever impurities that are in my heart will rise to the surface. This is why fasting is necessary. It, in a sense, melts down the flesh, exposing any and every ungodly belief and spirit that's been hiding in the believer's life.

Anytime a metal is melted down, every impurity in that metal will rise to the top. This means that the writers were being hypocritical, whether intentionally or unintentionally. If a writer addresses the subject of unforgiveness and yet has not forgiven, for example, his ex-wife for leaving him, whatever unclean things are burrowing in his life and heart will rise to the surface as he ascends the hills of revelation. Does this mean that we should only teach when we're fully delivered? No. It means that we should teach on matters that we *want* to be delivered from — just as we should teach on the matters that we are delivered from. However, if we have a secret (or flamboyant) sin that we don't want to let go of, teaching about that sin or anything related to it will cause our personal demons to take the mic and give their testimonies.

It is not uncommon for writers to go through warfare while writing their books, just as it is not uncommon for writers to mistake a lovers' spat with the devil for warfare. What's the difference? Warfare involves two enemies; it means that the person under attack is opposed to the one who is attacking him or her. Nevertheless, anytime a believer is double-minded, the Word says that the believer will also be unstable. This instability is the direct result of the demon the believer is in agreement with simply responding to the believer's betrayal. In other words, it's a couple's fight; it's a game of tug-of-war. This tells us, as writers, that we cannot afford to entertain the slightest of sin. Now, this doesn't mean we'll be perfect; what it does mean is we have to be intentional.

But what if you are submitted to God and intentionally living a righteous life? What if, after all of your sacrifices, the enemy is still attacking you every time you try to write? The answer is simple. More than likely, there are some doors open in your life that the enemy is using to come in through. For example, maybe you have rebellious, backslidden friends who are pouring into your heart. Remember, every person we open our lives to will slowly begin to pour into us. For this reason, we spend a great deal of our Christian walk getting delivered from the contaminants we've picked up through association. We're constantly having to be poured out like drink offerings. Needless to say, the more backslidden, rebellious, sin-loving folks we have around us, the more warfare we're going to endure because every single one of those people represents a door. Without sounding callous, I'll venture out to say this: when God has you pouring out into His people through books, spoken words or by your lifestyle, you need to be very mindful of who you allow to pour into you. If you're being contaminated by your friends, family, television or music, and yet, you decide you want to write a book to help God's people, the Lord sees a contaminated vessel who's about to poison His people. It is of no wonder that He will allow so many aspiring authors to go through warfare until they take their pens, shove them into their own ears and inject the revelation they are so eager to share.

Next, warfare comes to show us what doors are open in our lives. For example, God has closed many doors in my life ever since I've started my writers' journey and I think this is true for every (consistent) writer. Most people who write for the Kingdom of God can tell you some strange things they've witnessed while writing (power suddenly going off, missing USB cards, computer suddenly malfunctioning, significant and insignificant others suddenly behaving strangely, unexpected phone calls from old friends and family members, etc.). Some of the incidents appear to be pure coincidence until they became frequent (they would happen every time the writer started writing, but would stop when the writer stopped writing). Of course, an author won't notice this if the author (or writer) isn't consistently writing.

Nevertheless, when authors start working on, for example, their third book and up, they will likely be able to tell you about things that always seem to happen while they were writing—situations that don't normally occur in their everyday lives.

Again, consider the response of the ants in an ant-pile when they are disturbed. They rush out of their hill and grab onto whatever foreign object they find in their pile. If it's a foot, for example, the ants will crawl onto the foot and began to attack the person from the heel up. The person doesn't have to have his or her entire body in the ant's pile to instigate an attack. Even if the person placed a single toe onto the hive, the ants would crawl onto it and begin their ascension, biting the person mercilessly as they climb. The same is true for demonic spirits. If a believer has even a slight investment in the kingdom of darkness, this investment is enough to open the believer up for an attack. For example, if the believer is an unrepentant gossiper, the enemy will have a foothold on that believer and will attack him or her mercilessly—should he or she attempt to write. The attacks should serve as notifications for the believer, signaling that there is a door open in the realm of the spirit that needs to be shut. Of course, this is if the believer wants to be free. If not, the believer will more than likely not finish the book because, just as ants keep ascending and biting until they go into the "intimate place" if not stopped, demons will continue to attack the believer, hitting him or her where it hurts the most until he or she stops writing.

Every writer who (genuinely) writes for the Kingdom of God will create an earthquake in the realm of the spirit when he or she begins to write. This earthquake will affect the writer's life before it shakes up the lives of others. This is why most authors experience a host of emotions when writing. When the writer begins to shake up the spirit realm, there will be a notable response. Now, if the writer has closed all demonic access doors in his or her life, the writer can still experience warfare, but it won't be severe enough to get the writer's full attention. Instead, it could be as minute as coming in contact with a disrespectful co-worker, being falsely accused of something or getting a call from an estranged family member whose hellbent on starting trouble. In most of these cases, the writer won't be moved by the attempted attack because it's external warfare, meaning, the enemy had no way of attacking them from within, so he started attacking them from without. The author will likely brush or laugh off the encounter, giving the enemy no weight in his or her life or book. With that being said, we not only have to pay attention to the response we get when we start writing, but we have to pay attention to the location of the response. Did it come from within (people we are intimately connected to) or did it come from without (people whose opinions of us have no weight in our lives)? If it comes from within, this could signal a breach in our heart's security systems, meaning, someone has access to us who should not have access or, in some cases, the person's access is too intimate. The person is to be ministered to. Giving people intimate access who shouldn't have it can prove to be dangerous.

Friendly Fire

"Friendly fire is an attack by a military force on non-enemy, own, allied or neutral, forces while attempting to attack the enemy, either by misidentifying the target as hostile, or due to errors or inaccuracy.

According to the most comprehensive survey of casualties (both fatal and nonfatal), 21 percent of the casualties in World War II were attributable to friendly fire, 39 percent of the casualties in Vietnam, and 52 percent of the casualties in the first Gulf War." (Reference: Wikipedia.org/ English/ Friendly Fire).

Friendly fire is an unintentional attack from someone who's supposed to be fighting with or for you; in short, such a person is called an ally. In the writing world, friendly fire is oftentimes an author being polluted by someone the author holds dear to his or her heart. For example, an author may have a gossiper, slanderer or complainer who regularly calls him or her. The caller calls to "get something off his/ her chest." This is called transference, whereas, the caller calls to relieve himself or herself. To relieve ourselves, we have to transfer what's in or on us to another source. For example, when a man urinates, he won't absorb his own urine; instead, he will pour it out into a toilet, field or whatever it is he chooses to relieve himself in or on. What he did was transfer his waste into or onto another object. As human beings, this is our nature. We are creatures of waste and treasure. When we are filled with wisdom, we pour out wisdom and we become invaluable to the people who are connected to us. When we are filled with waste (hatred, rebellion, unforgiveness, rejection and the like), we intentionally or unintentionally use people as tools to relieve ourselves.

315

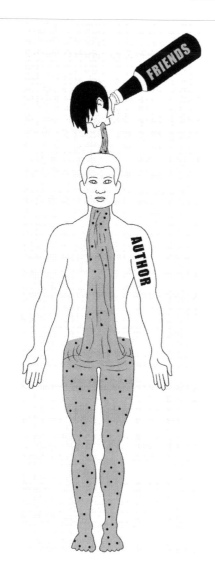

Gossipers pick up burdens that do not belong to them, add more weight to those burdens and then transfer them to other gossipers.

Sadly enough, many believers don't understand the dangers of having gossiping, slandering, complaining friends. These people can be friendly, but when they speak, they release friendly fire. If the polluted person then attempts to write a letter (book) to God's people, being the Protector that He is, God will oftentimes intervene. Again, the author will first come in contact with a stop sign in his or her heart. The stop sign is oftentimes the author feeling empty of revelation and drained every time he or she attempts to write. Nevertheless, if the aspiring author has a lot of revelation stored in his or her knowledge, he or she may attempt to write the book without hearing from the Lord. When this happens, the aspiring author may endure what he or she believes to be warfare when, in truth, it's correction.

Levels of Warfare

One of the things we must understand, once again, is that the impact of our books can be likened to the impact that an earthquake has on a city, state or region. Before we can produce an earthquake in someone else's life, we must have survived, overcome and extracted understanding from an earthquake of that same magnitude or greater in our lives. With that being said, anytime an author decides to pour out of his or her heart, the author will embrace the same earth-moving power that he or she is attempting to release. If the author has been contaminated by friends, family members or associates, every contaminant in the believer's life will begin to surface as the author begins to write. Some of those contaminants are self-inflicted strongholds of the mind, while others are demonic. While this can be considered warfare, in truth, the believer is simply experiencing a moment of revelation and an opportunity to repent. If the author does not recognize this fact, he or she will write the issue off as demonic and proceed to pray against the forces of evil coming up against him or her. This is good, however, there are three levels of warfare, all of which have to be approached differently. They are casting down, casting off and casting out.

Casting Down

The first level of warfare is called "casting down." 2 Corinthians 10:5 details this level of warfare and it reads, "*Casting down* imaginations, and every high thing that exalteth itself against the knowledge of God, and bringing into captivity every thought to the obedience of Christ." By casting down an imagination, you are casting away from yourself an attempt by the enemy to hijack your thought life. This means that the enemy is external and is attempting to enter your heart. This is why God told us to guard our hearts.

To cast down a thought means to resist temptation. For example, let's say someone cuts you off in traffic, causing you to swerve. You blow your horn out of frustration and the driver extends his hand out the window and sends an ugly message to you using his middle finger. The driver then pulls in front of you and proceeds to drive extremely slow, hitting his brakes regularly for no apparent reason. At this moment, you are in the midst of temptation, especially if you're in a rush to get to your destination. In that moment, you will likely be bombarded with a series of ungodly thoughts. You'll want to run the guy off the road, chase him, show him your prized middle finger or do something to let him know that his behavior is unacceptable. How do you fight off this temptation? The following scriptures should give us a better understanding.

Scripture	Explanation
James 4:7 (ESV): Submit yourselves therefore to God. Resist the devil, and he will flee from you.	To submit ourselves to God, we must submit ourselves to His Word, which is His will. To resist the devil, we must resist temptation. To resist temptation, we should not want anything or anyone more than we want God. This means we have to intentionally keep our minds on Christ.
Scripture	**Explanation**
Ephesians 4:26-27 (ESV): Be angry and do not sin; do not let the sun go down on your anger, and give no opportunity to the devil.	This scripture lets us know that it is not a sin to be angry. Of course, we become angry when we meditate on what someone has done to us, but the scripture goes on to tell us that there is a time limit on this process. You have twelve hours to be angry, but you must change your mind before the sun sets.
Scripture	**Explanation**
Romans 12:1 (ESV): I appeal to you therefore, brothers, by the mercies of God, to present your bodies as a living sacrifice, holy and acceptable to God, which is your spiritual worship.	One of the weapons that Satan uses against believers and unbelievers is their bodies. You see, the flesh desires what is contrary to the Spirit and vice versa. To resist temptation, you have to crucify your flesh. You can do this as an act of will, fasting, serving, etc.

Casting Out

The next level of warfare is called "casting out." Luke 4:35 reads, "But Jesus rebuked him, saying, 'Be quiet and *come out* of him!' And when the demon had thrown him down in the midst of the people, he came out of him without doing him any harm." This level of warfare is the result of the believer not guarding his heart, or it can be generational. This means that the enemy has gotten past the believer's imagination, has entered the believer's heart and is also working through the believer's members. In this case, the demon has to be evicted. To evict the devil, the believer has to go through an eviction process called deliverance. The believer can perform deliverance on himself or herself or the believer can allow someone else to perform the deliverance. Either way, if the believer is not delivered before he or she attempts to write, the attack the believer endures will come from within.

Casting Off

To cast off means to take off; it is an act of works. James 4:7 tells us to submit ourselves to God and resist the devil. Of course, when we do this, we're not casting off, we're casting down the temptations and lies of the enemy. But casting off means to receive a new heart and a new mind; it means to submit your workers (limbs) to the will of God. This happens through genuine repentance, which is a turning of the heart. This is the part of deliverance that often goes overlooked, thus, opening believers up for re-infestation. Many believers frequent the altars of their churches because they keep returning to the vomit God delivered them from. After getting the demons cast out, they didn't cast off or cast away the old mind. Instead, they returned to the sins they loved, thus, reopening themselves to demonic infestation. Jesus told us to cast our burdens upon Him; this is an act of casting off. Of course, one of those burdens is worry, and we all know it's a sin to worry. Romans 14:23 reads, "But whoever has doubts is condemned if he eats, because the eating is not from faith. For whatever does not proceed from faith is sin." When David tried to put on Saul's armor, it was a burden to him, so to effectively fight Goliath, he had to cast off or take off the wrong armor and put on the armor of the Lord. Romans 13:12 reads, "The night is far spent, the day is at hand: let us therefore cast off the works of darkness, and let us put on the armor of light."

Sometimes, it's Not Warfare

When an aspiring author's heart is polluted with rejection, hatred, unforgiveness, pride, rebellion, selfish ambition and anything that is unpleasing to God, the author-to-be will not edify God's people, but will instead poison them. It is then no wonder that the individual will endure what he or she believes to be warfare when, in truth, it's just God placing a stop sign in front of the author's heart. If the author runs the stop sign, the author will oftentimes run into other obstacles. We must understand that God will stop at nothing to protect His people from harm. Sure, there are some ungodly books out there disguised as Christian books, but one of the things you'll notice about the majority of them is they don't have many reviews, meaning, God has not and will not promote them. Please understand that God can take away a person's appetite if what's about to be served to that person will harm him or her. Avid readers can look at a poisonous book and feel absolutely no desire to read it, despite how interesting the title and the cover is.

Sometimes, it's not warfare that the author is enduring; it's correction. It is important for us to carefully examine our hearts and motives before attempting to write a letter to God's people in the form of a book. Anytime we write books that will harm God's people, whether intentionally or unintentionally, we are rising up against God and He will respond accordingly. This is why we should always do a self-examination before writing.

Heart Check

When authors or aspiring authors decide to write, they are simultaneously deciding to help their readers with their burdens or they (the authors) will cast their burdens upon their readers. Of course, we know that Jesus told us to cast our burdens upon Him (see Matthew 11:28-30). As Christian authors, our responsibilities are to teach others to sort through their burdens, taking responsibility for their own decisions when necessary and then casting those burdens upon the Lord. Nevertheless, authors who are burdened with hatred, rejection, fear, abandonment, and so on will look to cast their burdens upon their readers. They see their books as an opportunity to grow their alliances; this is especially true if the authors were humiliated by someone they once cared for and are still responding to that pain.

WRITER'S WARFARE

What commonly happens in a situation like this is the authors in question will harden their hearts (become prideful) when the Lord speaks to them internally (via their conscious) or externally (via people). They will be heard making statements like, "No, because this needs to be exposed! People need to hear what these people are doing!" They will find people who agree with their agendas or people who are too afraid to disagree with them. After feeling validated, they will begin to write their books.

Now, here's something to consider—when a person begins to empty himself or herself out, the person will start feeling relieved. Think about a man at a urinal. The more he releases, the better he'll feel because he's transferring what's in him into another source. This is what confuses broken souls who begin writing. They feel a sense of relief as they empty themselves out on paper or on a Word document, not realizing that they are simply sharing (transferring) their burdens to their readers. If I'm walking down the street holding five large grocery bags filled with food, I will feel a measure of relief if someone walked up to me, grabbed a couple of those bags and carried them for me. This doesn't take away the fact that I am burdened; it only means I am now sharing that burden with someone else.

When the warfare comes coupled with the correction, many would-be authors feel betrayed once again. Oftentimes, authors like this will openly criticize God for not protecting them, not realizing that He's protecting His children from them. Please note that just because we're hurting does not give us the right to invite others into our pain. Additionally, a burden that's weighing one person down could kill another person. What does this mean? As authors and aspiring authors, we must be cognizant of the fact that everything we've endured, we were graced to endure. Attempting to cast those life-sized burdens on others can equate to the author pouring out what would be considered a flood in the lives of some of his or her readers. Remember, how God handles floods. Isaiah 59:19 reads, "So shall they fear the name of the LORD from the west, and his glory from the rising of the sun. When the enemy shall come in like a flood, the Spirit of the LORD shall lift up a standard against him." Sometimes, it's not warfare the author is enduring. Sometimes, the Lord has simply raised up a standard to keep a wounded author from wounding others.

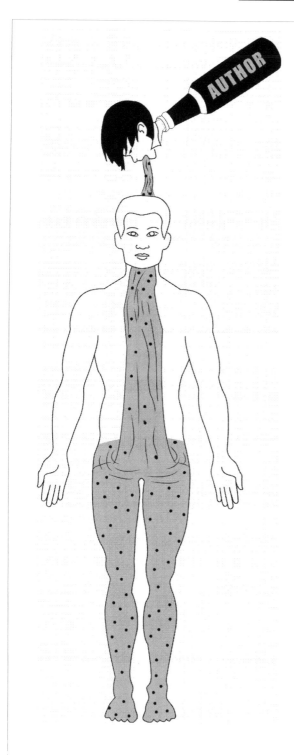

Sometimes, it's Not Warfare

In this illustration, we see the author as a drink offering. The author here isn't pouring out revelation; the author is polluting a reader. It is a well-known fact amongst mature, avid believers that there are some books out that are disguised as Christian books—books that are reported to bring warfare into the readers' lives. These books undoubtedly are the results of demonically bound authors trying to find some way to relieve themselves. They then become vessels used by the enemy to contaminate and bind any person who dares to read their books.

1 Timothy 4:1-5 (ESV): Now the Spirit expressly says that in later times some will depart from the faith by devoting themselves to deceitful spirits and teachings of demons, through the insincerity of liars whose consciences are seared, who forbid marriage and require abstinence from foods that God created to be received with thanksgiving by those who believe and know the truth. For everything created by God is good, and nothing is to be rejected if it is received with thanksgiving, for it is made holy by the word of God and prayer.

Currents

The following information was taken from CDC.org:

- "From 2005-2014, there were an average of 3,536 fatal unintentional drownings (non-boating related) annually in the United States — about ten deaths per day.[1] An additional 332 people died each year from drowning in boating-related incidents.[2]
- About one in five people who die from drowning are children 14 and younger.[1] For every child who dies from drowning, another five receive emergency department care for nonfatal submersion injuries.[1]
- More than 50% of drowning victims treated in emergenFcy departments (EDs) require hospitalization or transfer for further care (compared with a hospitalization rate of about 6% for all unintentional injuries).[1,2] These nonfatal drowning injuries can cause severe brain damage that may result in long-term disabilities such as memory problems, learning disabilities, and permanent loss of basic functioning (e.g., permanent vegetative state)."

(Reference: Centers for Disease Control and Prevention/ Unintentional Drowning: Get the Facts)

Now, we've discussed the dangers of drowning ourselves and our readers, but one phenomenon we have not discussed is called a current. In the natural, a current is a body of water or air moving in a definite direction, especially through a surrounding body of water or air in which there is less movement (Reference: Google/ Current).

A few things to consider about currents are:

1. Currents are mass flows of water.
2. Currents can move along the surface of water or can be deep.
3. They can move water horizontally or vertically.
4. Currents flow both locally and globally.
5. Currents are driven by winds, tides, water density, the rotation of the Earth (Coriolis Effect) and the sun.
6. Currents are affected by the rotation of the Earth, for example, currents in the Northern Hemisphere tend to veer to the right, whereas, currents in the

Southern Hemisphere tend to veer towards the left because of this rotation.

7. Currents play an important role in influencing climates around the world.

For the sake of this study, we will compare ocean currents to the masses or, better yet, the world. Let's revisit the pointers to understand our roles as writers.

1. **Currents are mass flows of water:** What is so powerful that it could gather large amounts of water and carry them in a particular direction? Of course, we know that God can do this, but we must also know that the kingdom of darkness has a measure of power. With that being said, demonic forces or, better yet, the winds of doctrine are powerful enough to move nations against nations, turn mothers against daughters and destroy entire continents. As a writer, you will find yourself going up against the masses when you begin to teach the unpopular truth. Understand this: there are some truths that are widely accepted by the world and the church, but there are some truths that are not welcome. The deeper you dive into the truth, the more resistance you will feel. God alone can determine how much we can bear so with that being said, it is extremely important to make sure He's the force behind you, should you decide to tackle the masses.

2. **Currents can move along the surface of water or can be deep:** In every depth of the ocean, there is a force that moves the water. The surface of the ocean is moved by the wind, but deeper waters are often moved by density. Density is mass per unit volume. In layman's terms, it is a measurement of how much matter is crammed into a particular unit. Water density is determined by the temperature of the water. Hot water is less dense than cool water, so it'll float, whereas cool water will sink under warmer waters. In Revelation 3:16, the Lord says, "So then because thou art lukewarm, and neither cold nor hot, I will spue thee out of my mouth." Of course, we know to spue means to spit. As believers, we are going to come across warm Christians, which are people who are (as we say) on fire for the Lord, meaning, they are fully surrendered to holiness. Then again, we are going to come in contact with cold Christians. These are believers whose faith is dead. They love sin and most of what sin produces for them. They are religious and worldly, performing the ceremonial practices of Christianity, all the while, practicing heathenism. The most common Christian you'll find, however, is

the lukewarm Christian. These are the believers who are not hot, nor are they cold. They've managed to find themselves a place in the middle, whereas, they speak in tongues, cast out devils, and go to church faithfully, all the while, holding onto their worldly lusts. They love the world's music, trends, celebrities and all that the world has to offer. As a writer, the greatest current you will face will come from this body of believers. They will refer to you as "deep" or "religious" when you teach against what they love. You have to decide whether you're ready to face these forces or if you simply want to write a surface-level book that does not receive as much backlash.

3. **Currents can move horizontally (regionally) or vertically (dimensionally):** What moves you as a writer, teacher and believer can come from within or without. The people not directly affiliated with you are vertical currents. They may move up against you, but they don't have the power to move you unless you allow fear to make you dense. Currents that come from within, however, are your own personal fears, your friends and the people you have soul ties with. Additionally, some people are moved by their communities, especially in tight-knit communities where everyone seems to know one another. Lastly, one of the most obvious currents that can come from within are demonic spirits that have somehow found a legal right to inhabit any given believer. When a believer is going through deliverance from demonic bondage, you'll notice (in some cases) that the minister tells the spirits to come *up* ↑ and *out*→. In many of these cases, the believer will begin to vomit. This is a representation of a vertical force. What moves you is determined by how dense you are regarding the topic you're teaching on. For example, it would not be wise to teach against homosexuality if you are struggling with fornication because the force that moves the homosexual is the same force that's moving you. In a situation like this, you'd find yourself avoiding delving too deep into the topic of perversion because you'll feel convicted and hypocritical. Additionally, if you managed to get past the vertical current, you'll still have to deal with the outside forces (people) who will highlight your sins in an attempt to discredit you as a teacher and writer.

4. **Currents flow both locally and globally:** Currents can be trends, mindsets and cultures that are influenced by the media, celebrities and traumatic events. As a writer, it is important for you to identify your target market

before you release your book; this way, you will use the right verbiage, the right amount of pressure and the right level of sensitivity. Understand this: currents that flow locally don't have the same amount of force behind them as global currents. For example, in 2016 and 2017, we saw a large number of videos released showing police brutality towards minorities. During this time, many writers blogged and wrote books about the epidemic of racism in America. Because the matter was not global, it had to be dealt with on a national scale, even though it was addressed by other writers around the world. American writers had to consider many factors before writing their articles, blog posts or books. They had to consider their surroundings (friends, community, and geographical locations) and their intended reach. So, an African American author who was the minority in his or her workplace and lived in a community that was seventy percent Caucasian could not be as "raw" or, better yet, honest as an African American writer who was self-employed and lived in a community that was fifty percent White and fifty percent Black. The reason for this is, the author could have lost his or her job and received quite a few death threats because of the author's views on a very sensitive topic. That same author, however, can address the topic of genocide in Rwanda, Africa and be as honest as he or she is knowledgeable. The point is, as an author, the force of your words has to match your intended impact and your surroundings. Now, this isn't to say that an author who lives in Arkansas and has seen a lot of racism cannot speak against racism; it is to say that if the author decides to come against racism with brutal force, the author must first consider the dangers involved and make the necessary adjustments to prepare for the backlash he or she will receive. "For which of you, desiring to build a tower, does not first sit down and count the cost, whether he has enough to complete it?" (Luke 14:28)

5. **Currents play an important role in influencing climates around the world:** I remember going to France and getting on the Paris Métro. Not long after I got on the train, a group of guys came aboard, some of them wearing their hair in cornrows, with sagging pants and baggy shirts. Being that it was my first time going to France, I was absolutely convinced that the guys were Americans. The guys began to interact with one another; they were all speaking French. It became clear to me that they had been born and raised in

France. Slowly but surely, I began to see the effects of American culture, not just in France, but in most of the countries I visited. What I came to learn is this—what happens in America does not stay in America. We truly are a superpower in more ways than we realize. Whatever we (the church) allow on Earth is allowed in Heaven, and whatever we (the church) loose on Earth is loosed in Heaven. All the same, whatever we (the church) tolerate in America will become the trends and cultures of other nations. If we don't bind what threatens to bind God's people, we will inadvertently loose powers and principalities that will go forth and enslave others. These forces will only increase wickedness in this world, slowly drowning out and opposing the voice of the Christian.

6. **Currents are driven by winds, tides, water density, the rotation of the Earth (Coriolis Effect) and the sun:** As believers, many of the people who will rise up against us will be driven by winds of doctrines or, as the Bible refers to them, "doctrines of demons." You won't hear too much from cold Christians because they couldn't care less what's being taught on the Christian front, but again, one of the biggest waves that will threaten you will be lukewarm Christians who love their sins. These are the people who witness the power of God coming through them (they prophesy and cast out devils), and because of this, they believe that they are not required to uphold the standard of holiness. These believers will have followers who support them because of their miracle-working power. These are the believers who Jesus addressed in Matthew 7:21-23, which reads, "Not everyone that says unto me, Lord, Lord, shall enter into the Kingdom of Heaven; but he that does the will of my Father who is in Heaven. Many will say to me in that day, Lord, Lord, have we not prophesied in your name? And in your name have cast out demons? And in your name done many wonderful works? And then will I profess unto them, I never knew you: depart from me, you that *work iniquity*." Another force that influences currents is the rotation of the Earth. First, let's talk about inertia—the force that causes the Earth to spin. Inertia is the tendency for something to maintain itself or remain unchanged. Scientists believe that the Earth was formed from dust that was spinning, and one of the facts about mass is that it maintains its state of motion unless otherwise moved upon by a greater force. This is called inertia. As believers, some of the

forces you may confront with your writings are powers, principalities, the rulers of this dark world and spiritual wickedness in high places. Now, you won't necessarily see these forces, but you will see them at work through cultures, traditions and widely accepted beliefs. You aren't just challenging mindsets when you decide to write a self-help book, you are challenging ungodly forces. These forces will influence the systems of this world and are largely behind many of the traditions we accept in our churches today. When you begin to address them, you have to be ready for them to respond. Nevertheless, if you are fully submitted to God, He will not suffer your foot to be moved, meaning, He will protect and keep you. He won't allow the pressure of public opinion to become unbearable to you. Understand this: people who fall away from the faith and give in to the world's pressure aren't victims of public opinion; they are men and women who have unaddressed lusts that the devil appealed to. James 1:14 says it this way, "But every man is tempted, when he is drawn away of his own lust, and enticed." Lastly, the currents of this world are affected by the sun, but for believers, one of the greatest currents we'll ever witness is the power of God's Son, Jesus Christ. He isn't just a current trend; He is the first and the last—Alpha (the beginning) and Omega (the end). His name is above every name, which means that every word that rises up against you will fall when you call upon His name. No force is greater than His Word and no power is mightier than His power.

Ocean currents can be divided into two categories; they are warm currents and cold currents. Unlike warm and cold air, the mixing of warm currents with cool currents often does have positive effects. All the same, it's great for us to address ungodly practices, even when we live amongst those who practice them. When warm and cool climates meet, they produce fog. Additionally, scientists have even found that some of the most productive fishing zones are located in places or regions where cold and warm currents meet.

Matthew 4:19: And he saith unto them, Follow me, and I will make you fishers of men.

Matthew 6:16-20: Behold, I send you forth as sheep in the midst of wolves: be ye therefore wise as serpents, and harmless as doves. But beware of men: for they will deliver you up to the councils, and they will scourge you in their synagogues; and ye shall be brought before governors and kings for my sake, for a testimony against them and the Gentiles. But when they deliver you up, take no thought how or what ye shall speak: for it shall be given you in that same hour what ye shall speak. For it is not ye that speak, but the Spirit of your Father which speaketh in you.

If a current can change the weather in any given region, a believer has enough power within himself or herself to change the culture and beliefs of any given region. One of the reasons we don't see this happening very much is because the average believer has unchecked, ungodly desires that the enemy appeals to. If the enemy can't scare a believer away using fear, he will then begin to appeal to the believer's lusts. Lust isn't just an ungodly sexual desire; lust is any desire that is contrary to the will or timing of God. For example, if a woman desires another woman's husband, she is bound by lust. She may not be sexually attracted to him, but she can be attracted to how he treats his wife, how much money he earns, how he looks or how much power he has. Another example of lust is called covetousness, which means to desire what belongs to someone else. For example, a teenage boy can lust after the shoes of one of his peers and this lust could lead him to murder the young man. As believers, the greatest lust that we often have is our desire to become rich. Now, don't get me wrong, it is not a sin to be rich, despite the erroneous misinterpretation of Matthew 10:25 that has led many believers to religiously renounce wealth and embrace poverty. Nevertheless, it is dangerous to desire riches because anything you desire to have can easily become the very lure that Satan uses to ensnare you.
1 Timothy 6:9-10 (ESV): But those who desire to be rich fall into temptation, into a snare, into many senseless and harmful desires that plunge people into ruin and destruction. For the love of money is a root of all kinds of evils. It is through this craving that some have wandered away from the faith and pierced themselves with many pangs.

One of the reasons this desire is a snare is because it will lead and has led many believers to compromise with the world and mix what is godly with what is profane. Before this happens, the believer will convince himself or herself that he or she won't get swept away with the ungodly practices of the environment he or she has to go into to obtain that wealth. But remember that mass will maintain its state of motion unless otherwise acted upon by a greater force. This means that if a believer acquires wealth through sin or compromise, to maintain his or her wealth, that believer will have to continue to sin and compromise with the world. The only two forces that will move that Christian to change his or her mind are: (1). More money or (2). the judgment of God. Of course, we know that God is not going to buy the Christian out of sin, given the fact that His Son has already paid the price for our sins. For this reason, judgment has to hit the Christian where it hurts him or her the most. This is what happened in the story of the rich young ruler.

Matthew 10:17-28 (ESV): And as he was setting out on his journey, a man ran up and knelt before him and asked him, "Good Teacher, what must I do to inherit eternal life?" And Jesus said to him, "Why do you call me good? No one is good except God alone. You know the commandments: 'Do not murder, Do not commit adultery, Do not steal, Do not bear false witness, Do not defraud, Honor your father and mother.'" And he said to him, "Teacher, all these I have kept from my youth." And Jesus, looking at him, loved him, and said to him, "You lack one thing: go, sell all that you have and give to the poor, and you will have treasure in Heaven; and come, follow me." Disheartened by the saying, he went away sorrowful, for he had great possessions. And Jesus looked around and said to his disciples, "How difficult it will be for those who have wealth to enter the kingdom of God!" And the disciples were amazed at his words. But Jesus said to them again, "Children, how difficult it is to enter the kingdom of God! It is easier for a camel to go through the eye of a needle than for a rich person to enter the kingdom of God." And they were exceedingly astonished, and said to him, "Then who can be saved?" Jesus looked at them and said, "With man it is impossible, but not with God. For all things are possible with God."

In this story, we are witnessing a current. A current is whatever force has the ability to move you at any given time. The rich young man was moved or ruled over by his money, meaning, he was a slave to a principality called Mammon. This principality doesn't just rule over the elite; it controls the movements of many believers who are chasing riches. Of course, none of us desire to be poor, but a desire to be rich has to be matched by a desire to do greater things for the Kingdom of God, otherwise, it becomes lust. Again, any lusts that are not brought under submission will become the very tools the enemy uses to seduce believers outside the will of God, where he can pervert and destroy them. As a writer, it is very important for you to determine what forces are behind your desire to write a book and what motivates everything you do, especially in ministry. If this isn't a conversation you have with yourself often, it will be easy for you to get swept away by the desires of this world. Understand this: whatever has the power to move you also has the power to move against you, meaning, the very same current that drives a man can also drown him. In drug usage, we call this overdosing; with alcohol, we call this alcohol poisoning, and with sex, we can call this an incurable sexually transmitted disease. None of us want to believe that we can be taken away by lust, but we can. This is why we have to be honest with God about where we are and ask Him to deliver us, even when our prisons are beautifully decorated comfort zones with high-end amenities.

I was speaking over the phone with a relative of mine one Saturday evening. She was states away from me, and I was in a TJ Maxx store looking at a Michael Kors bag. I liked the purse, but I wanted to be frugal, so I stood in front of the purse for a few minutes, reasoning with myself. I hadn't planned to visit the TJ Maxx store that day; instead, I was on my way to a local restaurant to treat myself to my weekly Daddy/daughter date with the Lord. One of the strongholds in my family is that the women don't know how to be alone; they jump from one relationship to another, often sticking around for ten to fifteen years with men who are not only ungodly, but are poisonous to their destinies. Of course, God had delivered me from this stronghold, and I was out enjoying my freedom from it. While speaking with this relative, I told her that I was looking at a Michael Kors bag that would cost me a whopping $179. Somehow, the conversation took a wrong turn and she started talking about a purse her boyfriend had bought her for around $60. I suddenly realized that she hadn't dined in at restaurants for most of her life (unless she was taken by relatives) and she didn't do much for herself, so a sixty-dollar bag was enough to convince her that she was loved. That's when I realized what God had been doing in my life every time He told me to take myself out to eat. He was disemboweling a demonic current in my bloodline. I was no longer impressed by dinner dates or fancy gifts because God, the Father, had stepped in and was doing all of those things for me. Additionally, He was doing more in me than He was doing (tangibly) for me. Sure enough, a well-to-do ex-boyfriend of mine suddenly rose up and tried to reenter my life, and two things made him an attractive option: (1). he was overly determined to have me and (2). he could have easily become the answer to my financial woes. Nevertheless, these things didn't move me anymore because that current had been stopped altogether.

What happens when a current stops? The following information was taken from Sciencing.com: *If ocean currents were to stop, climate could change quite significantly, particularly in Europe and countries in the North Atlantic. In these countries, temperatures would drop, affecting humans as well as plants and animals. In turn, economies could also be affected, particularly those that involve agriculture. If these effects were to continue, Europe, North Atlantic countries and parts of North America could experience long periods of freezing conditions. However, if ocean currents halted as a result of global warming, these temperatures would also be affected by other aspects of the global-warming phenomenon (Reference: Sciencing.com/ What Happens if Ocean Currents Stop).*

In short, when a current stops, death is inevitable for many. As for me, the old girl died and I'd become a new creature in Christ—a woman who was no longer moved by the winds and currents that moved the women in my family. Before this transformation, I was like the rich young ruler, but my idol was marriage. I'd asked the Lord many times to bless and keep me, but I wasn't willing to give up my idols. Nevertheless, a mass will continue to remain in the same state it is in unless acted upon by a greater force. The greater force in my case is God. He challenged the mass (my beliefs, fears, insecurities, desires) with His Word until every lie, demon, demonic system and ungodly soul tie gave way.

I can't tell you how many aspiring authors I've come across who are driven by the wrong motives. They want affirmation, redemption, revenge, wealth, power, fame and anything they believe will make their lives better. They write their books with no regards to the effects they will have on God's people, and for this reason, they run into what is commonly known as writer's block. Oftentimes, writer's block is nothing but God denying a writer access to His mysteries. In many cases, writers' block is just God protecting His people from those who would devour them. These are the people who will take writers' classes and convince themselves that the rules of the class don't apply to them. If allowed, they'll call, email or message the mentor every day, saying that they don't know what to write. This is because they want the mentor to give in and either write their books for them or tell them what to write. The force driving them is ungodly and this will always become evident when the mentor does not make himself or herself so readily available to them.

Currents don't just represent what moves you as an author; they also represent your ability to move others. Please understand that whatever force is driving you will be the force you use to move others. Nevertheless, as you mature as a writer, you will understand how much of this force to release in any given book. This force represents wisdom, revelation and correction. For example, I have currently written and published 39 books, but every book doesn't have the same amount of revelation. This is because the target market for each book wasn't the same. Some of my books are more likely to be read by new believers or believers who don't understand the spiritual side of life, whereas, other books are written for meat-eating believers. Again, books written about relationships aren't as "deep" as books written about demonology. I do, however, have a book entitled *The Submissive Wife: Breaking the Strong Arm of Jezebel*, which is a book that details the power of submission. This book is seasoned with demonology lessons, so it bridges the gap between those looking for relationship messages and those wanting to better understand the spirit realm. This book has helped believers who once binge-watched relationship messages and attended singles' conferences to understand what the Jezebel spirit is and how it operates. This is what we call progression—introducing readers to a new level of understanding. This means that the readers are growing up or, better yet, maturing. Many of the people who've read this book have been taught that Christians couldn't have demons. Of course, they were taught this at the churches they attend. These precious souls have sat in one service after another demonically bound, confused, weary and frustrated. After reading *The Submissive Wife,* they started seeking deliverance ministries, and many of them have gone through multiple deliverance sessions. The point is, each book I've written has a certain amount of revelation in it, and the amount of revelation released is determined by my target market.

Another current to look at is the electric current. Electricity can gather in one place or flow from one point to another. Stationary electricity is called static electricity, whereas, electricity that moves is called current electricity. Static electricity is often produced by friction. How does this relate to writers? It's simple. Writers can be placed in two categories: stationary writers and flowing writers. Stationary writers are people who haven't moved around a lot and have gotten most of their revelation from watching television, going to church or from their intimate relationships with God. They are very familiar with friction, given the fact that they've endured a lot of it in their personal relationships. Flowing writers, on the other hand, are individuals who've met many people and may have traveled quite a bit. They are the ones who can tell countless stories about their experiences in life. Both writers can be good writers, but there is a notable difference in their writing styles. Stationary writers usually write about what they've gone through or what they've learned. You won't get many personal stories from stationary writers after their third or fourth book; they are message-driven and you won't find too much of their personalities in their books. Stationary writers can be in-depth writers, whereas, flowing writers can take you further in distance than they can in depth. What does this mean? Flowing writers are like electrical currents; they can flow from one subject to another, without losing the point of their message. Their books are filled with their personalities and experiences. It's easy for flowing writers to capture and keep the attention of their readers. Flowing writers are great teachers, but their readers receive more entertainment than they do revelation. This is okay because some readers have short attention spans and wouldn't finish a book written by a stationary writer, given the fact that it's more educational than it is entertaining.

To better understand the difference between a stationary writer versus a flowing writer, think of a ship and think of an anchor. Stationary writers are more like anchors; they don't go very far, but they do reach the depths of revelation and they help to ground some of the strongest men and women of God in the faith. They speak more on revelatory topics like demonology, spiritual legalities and the like. Flowing writers are more like ships. They open our minds to worlds outside of the ones we've grown accustomed to. They speak more on practical matters like money management, relationships, health and character. Both writers need each other. Flowing writers need stationary writers to ground them, helping them to add more depth and revelation to their teachings. Without the stationary writer, the flowing writer would write more about himself or herself than God. Again, flowing writers are personality-driven and they've learned a lot from their experiences in life.

Without the flowing writer, the stationary writer wouldn't be able to reach the nations. How so? Flowing writers not only engage their readers, they open them up to the world of revelation, thus, leaving their readers hungry for more. For example, a woman obsessed with the idea of marriage will likely purchase books written by flowing writers. One book may satisfy some of the questions she has, but it won't necessarily answer all of those questions, which would lead her to another book written by a flowing writer. This book may satisfy a few more questions and give her the courage to wait a little bit longer, but after a while, the effects of that book will wear off. Eventually, the reader will come across a flowing writer who will introduce her to the word "idolatry." Reading this book, the reader will come to realize that her obsession with marriage is idolatrous and is likely rooted in rejection. She'll come to understand why she's been so frustrated, depressed and anxious. Desperate to be free from this, she will start researching topics like idolatry and depression, and will eventually come across reading materials that introduce her to the spiritual side of her desires. Realizing that she may be in need of deliverance, the reader will start researching books and ministries that talk about the spirits she may be wrestling with. This is the process of maturity. At one point, she was flowing from one relationship to another, one book to another and one singles' conference to another, but all of a sudden, she will find herself looking for more wisdom than knowledge. What's the difference between the two? People who seek knowledge are simply wanting information that explains something they are currently facing or wrestling with, but people seeking wisdom are more mature. They want to know the heart of God regarding a matter.

The chart below details the pursuit of information from knowledge-seekers versus wisdom seekers using the Google search platform.

Knowledge Seekers	Wisdom Seekers	Revelation
What's the best eyeshadow color for medium skin?	Is it a sin to wear makeup?	Knowledge seekers are generally not interested in the spiritual side of things.
Why do men cheat?	Why do I attract cheaters?	Wisdom seekers take accountability for their

		actions and results because they are more solution-oriented than they are problem-focused.
How much is a bundle of 16-inch Remy hair?	What is the origin of human hair sold in stores?	Knowledge seekers would prefer to not know a truth if knowing it will put pressure on them to change their lifestyles. Wisdom seekers, like everyone else, hate to make lifestyle changes, but would rather know the truth and change than to live in the bliss of ignorance.
How to know if the man you're courting is the one ...	Signs that the man you're courting is not the one ...	Knowledge-seekers focus more on their current feelings and their immediate goals, but wisdom-seekers are more concerned with their futures.
Can a Christian have a demon?	What are the characteristics of the Python spirit?	Knowledge-seekers will unearth some truth to satisfy their curiosities, but they normally won't get to the core of a matter because they don't like to be seen as "deep." They'd rather stay on the surface, where most people can relate to them.

Knowledge-seekers oftentimes want confirmation, whereas, wisdom-seekers tend to be more concerned with deliverance. As you can see, this is an issue of maturity.

CURRENTS

Stationary writers help to ground readers, giving them the meat of revelation, whereas, flowing writers are the cruise ships of the writing world.

Earlier, we talked about the types of water currents and one of the things we discovered was that currents can move both vertically and horizontally. Stationary writers write vertically, giving readers in-depth information, but flowing writers write horizontally, giving the readers more practical information. Again, both writers need one another. One of the most common mistakes in the writing world occurs when a flowing writer decides that he or she wants to be "deep." Again, flowing writers are like ships, so in order for them to be "deep," they have to sink or, as we discussed earlier, drown their readers. Think of an inexperienced swimmer who doesn't know how long he can stay underwater. He's infatuated with the skill of his brother who can stay underwater for two minutes without coming up for air. He puts on his swimming gear one day and heads out to an ocean near his home. He dives into the depths of the ocean, timing himself as he goes deeper and deeper. Finally, two minutes have passed and he's gone further than he's ever gone in his entire life. Nevertheless, one of the things he did not consider before taking this plunge is the fact that he has to resurface, and this takes time. He becomes stressed under the water and begins to drown. Thankfully, his brother came with him and was able to recover him before he perished.

While at the hospital, the hospitalized brother confesses that envy had been the driving force behind his decision to go deep underwater. "How do you do it?" he asks his frustrated brother. "How do you go underwater for so long without coming up for air?" His brother looks at him and walks out of the room. Five minutes later, he comes back into the room, holding two large bags. In one bag is the hospitalized brother's swimming gear. In the other bag is the other brother's diving gear. "I'm a diver," he says in a calm but firm tone. "You're a swimmer. I've been trained to go into the depths of the abyss, wearing uniforms and lifting items that are oftentimes heavier than I am. I'm trained to hold my breath for long periods of time, but you are not. You can travel large distances without stopping and I admire that, but I'm not going to kill myself trying to compete with you. I go deep; you go far." What the diver is saying to the swimmer is, respect your metron.

CURRENTS

This is what many flowing writers do when they are not yet mature. They write about sensitive subject matters that they do not fully understand, but when they get to the part of their books where they are required to explain what they've been teaching, they become overwhelmed and begin to feel like they're drowning. This is where most flowing writers stop writing, put their books away and tell themselves that they'll finish on a later date. These books are rarely, if ever, completed. Why is this? People who are designed to flow almost always lose interest in unfinished projects because, like electrical currents, they are always on the move. Whatever doesn't move with them will get left behind. Flowing writers are swimmers; stationary writers are divers, which brings us back to water currents. Remember, most people who drown are 14 years old or younger, but before we go further into this, let's discuss the makeup of living things.

Everything that lives and moves is a part of a larger system. Google defines the word "system" this way: *a set of connected things or parts forming a complex whole, in particular.* This means that everything on the Earth is connected. Every system has a function (purpose) and a force that drives it. Ocean currents can be driven by varying forces, including wind, water density and earthquakes. Human beings are complex systems with four limbs, five senses and ten thousand taste buds. Everything in our systems is designed to keep us alive and enable us to provide for ourselves and others. One interruption in our systems could slow us down. Additionally, it can temporarily or permanently disable us. For example, if a person catches an ear infection, that person's balance can become unstable because of a condition called vertigo. That ear infection is powerful enough to throw off the balance of a three-hundred-pound man, stopping him from functioning in his normal day-to-day routine. As a result, he may have to take some time off work which, of course, could result in him receiving less pay and more medical bills. With little to no money to pay the rent, he could easily end up being evicted from his home. That man could end up moving back home with his mother and becoming depressed. Depression and an overly attentive mother could cause him to gain another one hundred pounds, which would affect his self-perception, health, his ability to work and his quality of work. All of this started as an ear infection and could easily lead to his untimely death. The point is, everything is designed to work together, whether good or bad, including flowing writers and stationary writers.

When a flowing writer decides to dive, that writer throws something off balance, not just in his or her life, but in the lives of the people who depend on that writer to help them get from one revelation to another.

Just like the systems of this world, the systems of our bodies and the systems of government, we are multi-faceted creatures with all of our talents representing one of our many faces. Just like it's possible for a human being to lose a leg and still be able to function, it is possible for us to lose one of our many talents or faces and still be able to function. We see this demonstrated in the parable of the talents (see Matthew 25:14-30). The unfaithful (slothful) servant buried the one talent his master had given him and, for this reason, that talent was taken from him and given to the faithful servant. Burying a thing and planting a thing are not one and the same, therefore, the burying of the talent, as depicted in the book of Matthews, represents the death of a thing. It meant that the servant in question had no future plans to use what his master had given him. Nevertheless, dead things decompose and eventually become fertilizer, enabling what's planted to grow. With that being said, a person can be multi-talented; he can be an author, entrepreneur, chef, and inventor. Let's say that he does not respect the author side of himself because a few of his friends are authors and they don't make a lot of money from their books. He can bury this part of himself, meaning he is slaughtering a piece of who he is, or he can drown this part of himself by attempting to be who he is not. This means that he can snuff out his desires to write, and all of a sudden, find himself with little to no interest in becoming an author. In other words, he amputated a part of his system, and even though he can still function, he won't be able to function the way God designed him to function because his system was altered. Satan comes to kill, steal and destroy; we know this, but we must also understand that Satan often kills believers one talent at a time. He loves to do this when we are young and immature in the faith. Why is this? Teenagers are driven by peer pressure, so if you decide to write a book while you're still young in the faith, many of your peers will follow you. Please understand that in the spirit realm, youth is not determined by age; it is determined by your distance from God's heart. Most people who drown (in the natural) are 14 years of age or younger. The same is true on the spiritual side of the spectrum. Most people who drown themselves in revelation are young in the faith.

Proverbs 11:14 reads, "Where no counsel is, the people fall: but in the multitude of counselors there is safety." As a writer, it is absolutely necessary that you are accountable with what you write. Many authors don't finish their books because they go into realms that require a specific part of God's armor. Some realms require what the Bible refers to as the "whole armor of God," meaning, the warrior must be covered from head to toe. Divers and swimmers don't wear the same uniforms, and a multitude of counselors is like a panel of judges, helping you to better understand your limitations. Sure, you may not like the score that's on the scoreboard, but that score helps you to understand your limitations and it keeps you humble.

When flowing authors begin to sink, they get overwhelmed and decide that the writing experience is too much for them. For this reason, many multi-faceted people have buried the author side of themselves, exchanging talents for skills, and choosing to work nine-to-five jobs for the rest of their lives. When this happens, just like any system, the person will slowly begin to kill off every facet of himself or herself until that person becomes what he or she identifies with the most. Again, this is why we all need a multitude of counselors, especially when we decide to take up the charge to write.

As an author, you will be sharing pieces of yourself with your readers. Jesus told us to eat His flesh and drink His blood; we all know that Christ Jesus was and is perfect. When you, on the other hand, write a book, you are going to either feed your flesh and blood to the readers, or you will cause them to eat the Lord's flesh and drink His blood. This simply means to believe upon the Lord to the point where you depend completely on Him to sustain you. This is why He said that man shall not live by bread alone, but by every word that proceeds out of the mouth of God (see Matthew 4:4), He referred to deliverance as the children's bread (see Matthew 15:26), and this is also why the Levitical priests would eat the sin offering (see Leviticus 6:24-27). Jesus is our sin offering. The more you mature in the Lord, the less of your flesh you will feed to your readers. This is when you can actually see yourself slowing down, eventually becoming a stationary writer, going into the depths and heights of revelation to feed your readers. This is when you'll lift up the name of Jesus in your books so much so that the readers will not think about who wrote the book, because they'll be so enamored by the voice of God coming from within the book. Jesus summed it up best in John 12:32 when He said, "And I, if I be lifted up from the Earth, will draw all men unto me."

Understanding Authorship

Author	Authorize	Authority	Authoritative
a.) the writer of a literary work (such as a book). b.) one that originates or creates something.	to endorse, empower, justify, or permit by or as if by some recognized or proper authority (such as custom, evidence, personal right, or regulating power)	a.) power to influence or command thought, opinion, or behavior. b.) a citation (as from a book or file) used in defense or support.	a.) having, marked by, or proceeding from authority. b.) possessing recognized or evident authority: clearly accurate or knowledgeable.

The above definitions were taken from Merriam Webster Dictionary Online.

Taking the posted definitions, we can safely define author as a writer, creator of a literary work—one who empowers and influences people, movements and laws; a person whose knowledge affords him or her the ability to change minds, lives and laws. A changed mind equates to a changed life. Before you (the author) accept the charge to write, you have to start (consistently) exercising your authority in the right way. This is no light matter, especially in the realm of the spirit. This is why so many authors go through warfare the very minute they start outlining or typing out their books. The truth of the matter is, authorship is engaging the enemy in warfare one pen-stroke or keystroke at a time. You are showing others how to break through the enemy's strongholds—strongholds that once held you in captivity. As a Christian author, you will, in a sense, become the literary Moses of your generation, helping to free people who've been bound by their own personal Pharaohs. One thing we should always understand is that we cannot walk into Egypt and not expect to fight. Writing is taking a leadership role. Writing is declaring that you are no longer a prisoner, but are instead a revolutionist sent to rescue God's people.

The Bible mentions two notable authors: one being God, Himself and the other being Satan.
1 Corinthians 14:33: For God is not the *author of confusion*, but of peace, as in all churches of the saints.
1 Timothy 4:1-3: Now the Spirit speaketh expressly, that in the latter times some

343

shall depart from the faith, giving heed to seducing spirits, and *doctrines of devils*; speaking lies in hypocrisy; having their conscience seared with a hot iron; forbidding to marry, and commanding to abstain from meats, which God hath created to be received with thanksgiving of them which believe and know the truth.

Hebrews 5:8-10: Though he were a Son, yet learned he obedience by the things which he suffered; and being made perfect, he became the *author of eternal salvation* unto all them that obey him; called of God a high priest after the order of Melchisedec.

Hebrews 12:2: Looking unto Jesus the *author and finisher of our faith*; who for the joy that was set before him endured the cross, despising the shame, and is set down at the right hand of the throne of God.

The minute a Christian decides to write a book, that Christian has decided to become what can best be described as a drink offering. The Bible tells us that out of the abundance of the heart, the mouth speaks (see Luke 6:45). The same is true for writing; out of the abundance of the heart, an author writes. When a person decides to author a book, that person has decided to have the contents of his or her heart poured out onto paper. Now, this is a good thing if the author's heart is renewed; it's a bad thing if the author is still dealing with the wounds of rejection, pride, hurt, abandonment and the like. Needless to say, authorship is something God takes seriously, after all, He is the Author and Finisher of our faith. We are representatives of Him and as such, He wants to ensure that we represent Him the right way and not the way we think He ought to be represented. In other words, He wants us to understand what it means to be an author, not just by definition, but by roles, responsibilities and expectations.

Author: "mid-14c., auctor, autour, autor "father, creator, one who brings about, one who makes or creates" someone or something, from Old French auctor, acteor "author, originator, creator, instigator" (12c., Modern French auteur) and directly from Latin auctor "promoter, producer, father, progenitor; builder, founder; trustworthy writer, authority; historian; performer, doer; responsible person, teacher," literally "one who causes to grow," agent noun from auctus, past participle of augere "to increase," from PIE root *aug- (1) "to increase."
(Reference: Online Eytomology Dictionary/ author)

Understanding Authorship

As we can see, the word "author" means many things, which include:

- **Father:** A father creates and raises up sons and daughters.
- **Creator:** A creator creates; he or she is not just a builder, but one who provides the building blocks to start building. For example, God created Adam. Adam's body, outside of his organs, was an empty shell; it needed to be inhabited. God then breathed the breath of life into him. This is what established Him as Adam's Father.
- **Originator:** An originator is the first to do a thing.
- **Historian:** A Historian writes and studies history.
- **Promoter:** A promoter promotes or brings attention to something.
- **Producer:** A person who raises a thing from the seed stage, cultivates it through the development stage and brings it to fruition.
- **Builder:** One who intentionally establishes a thing one thought, brick, word or dollar at a time.
- **Founder:** The first to create and acknowledge a thing.
- **Teacher:** One who gathers knowledge, digests it and feeds it to others.

As an author, you will be many things, but in them all, you have to be intentional and knowledgeable. Without knowledge, one cannot speak in authority or to authorities. Passive writers don't sell books because their readers can easily detect their lack of knowledge and confidence. This is one of the reasons traditional publishers reject more than ninety percent of the books that land on their desks. There are a lot of people who want to be authors—people who lack the knowledge to teach and the authority to speak confidently. You will be a father (or mother) to your readers. You will teach history and create history. You will promote your beliefs; this is why they have to line up with God's Word. You will build your books one word at a time. Additionally, you will build up people and tear down mindsets. People who were not called to write build up (ungodly) mindsets and tear down people. You will be a teacher and the CEO of the words you teach. This is why we can't take authorship lightly.

Many would-be authors carry their books to their graves simply because they didn't understand what being an author entails. Talk to the average person who says that God told him/her to write a book long ago, but have yet to do it, and what you'll find is the person thinks being an author is all about promoting himself or herself. People see books as platforms that provide another avenue of income, and for this reason, even though God has placed books in their bellies, He won't induce labor until each individual person comes to understand what being an author encompasses. Why is this? Because if, for example, I think writing a book is about promoting myself and my own agenda, I'll let my personality drown out the voice of God in that book. I'll be too busy trying to show off my bigger than life personality, my intellect and my own understanding to think about the hundreds, thousands, millions or billions of people who may pick up my book needing to hear from God, not me. Therefore, even though I may be pregnant with a book, I have to submit myself to God to deliver that book, otherwise, I risk miscarrying it.

1. God intended for authors to be people of (godly) authority—people of influence. Authors shouldn't be passive, easily influenced or fearful; authors should be authoritative. This doesn't mean you need to have a huge following before God will give you the grace to write; it simply means you need to have the faith to write. It means you need to be steadfast, unmovable, a lover of God and a lover of God's people. It means that you are taking on the assignment of shepherding some of God's people, if but for a season. Your book may temporarily pastor (cover, protect, provide for) people or, if it's written in the wrong spirit, it could lead them astray (expose, scatter, rob). Needless to say, just like there is godly authority, there is ungodly authority. Sadly enough, there are many broken believers who genuinely believe they've been anointed to write books to expose other people, expose leaders, expose movements in the church, etc. This means that they want to use their God-given authority in an ungodly way (in most cases). But of course, some would ask, "What if God told them to expose something that was an abomination to Him?" The answer is simple. God usually has us to expose "some-<u>thing</u>" and not "some-<u>one</u>." You see, if I expose that fornication is wrong and I back it up with scriptures, I wouldn't have to expose, for example, a woman of God who is involved in it. Sure, I could rebuke her and I could even follow the chain of command (speak to her, speak to her leaders), but if she refuses to repent, I still have to follow Kingdom protocol in regards to her. When God wanted to address Ahab and Jezebel, He sent Elijah. When Elijah came before the people, he could not just

oust the wicked couple because the people were under their bewitchment. Instead, Elijah arranged a showdown between Jezebel's false god (Baal) and the one true and living God (YAHWEH). By exposing that Baal was a demon, he exposed the hearts of Jezebel and Ahab.

1 Kings 18:20-40 (ESV): So Ahab sent to all the people of Israel and gathered the prophets together at Mount Carmel. And Elijah came near to all the people and said, "How long will you go limping between two different opinions? If the Lord is God, follow him; but if Baal, then follow him." And the people did not answer him a word. Then Elijah said to the people, "I, even I only, am left a prophet of the Lord, but Baal's prophets are 450 men. Let two bulls be given to us, and let them choose one bull for themselves and cut it in pieces and lay it on the wood, but put no fire to it. And I will prepare the other bull and lay it on the wood and put no fire to it. And you call upon the name of your god, and I will call upon the name of the Lord, and the God who answers by fire, he is God." And all the people answered, "It is well spoken." Then Elijah said to the prophets of Baal, "Choose for yourselves one bull and prepare it first, for you are many, and call upon the name of your god, but put no fire to it." And they took the bull that was given them, and they prepared it and called upon the name of Baal from morning until noon, saying, "O Baal, answer us!" But there was no voice, and no one answered. And they limped around the altar that they had made. And at noon Elijah mocked them, saying, "Cry aloud, for he is a god. Either he is musing, or he is relieving himself, or he is on a journey, or perhaps he is asleep and must be awakened." And they cried aloud and cut themselves after their custom with swords and lances, until the blood gushed out upon them. And as midday passed, they raved on until the time of the offering of the oblation, but there was no voice. No one answered; no one paid attention.

Then Elijah said to all the people, "Come near to me." And all the people came near to him. And he repaired the altar of the Lord that had been thrown down. Elijah took twelve stones, according to the number of the tribes of the sons of Jacob, to whom the word of the Lord came, saying, "Israel shall be your name," and with the stones he built an altar in the name of the Lord. And he made a trench about the altar, as great as would contain two seahs of seed. And he put the wood in order and cut the bull in pieces and laid it on the wood. And he said, "Fill four jars with water and pour it on the burnt offering and on the wood." And he said, "Do it a second time." And they did it a second time. And he said, "Do it a third time." And they did it a third

347

time. And the water ran around the altar and filled the trench also with water. And at the time of the offering of the oblation, Elijah the prophet came near and said, "O Lord, God of Abraham, Isaac, and Israel, let it be known this day that you are God in Israel, and that I am your servant, and that I have done all these things at your word. Answer me, O Lord, answer me, that this people may know that you, O Lord, are God, and that you have turned their hearts back." Then the fire of the Lord fell and consumed the burnt offering and the wood and the stones and the dust, and licked up the water that was in the trench. And when all the people saw it, they fell on their faces and said, "The Lord, he is God; the Lord, he is God." And Elijah said to them, "Seize the prophets of Baal; let not one of them escape." And they seized them. And Elijah brought them down to the brook Kishon and slaughtered them there.

As we can see in this story, Elijah was a man of authority, however, as powerful as he was, he had to follow a system of protocol. The same is true for us as authors. Being an author is much more than having a voice; it's being responsible with the voice that God has given us.

Understanding Authority

Our understanding of authority reveals our maturity or immaturity as believers. Unlike natural aging, spiritual maturity does not come automatically. In the realm of the spirit, growth has to be intentional; you have the responsibility of humbling yourself, all the while, eating, meditating on and believing the Word of God. What does this look like? In every given season that you enter, you enter that season as a "little one" or babe. Imagine that you have been placed in a single room with six feet ceilings. As you grow in the Lord, you'll start to fill the season you're in. Eventually, in the realm of the spirit, you'll grow well beyond six feet tall. This is when you have to intentionally humble yourself. In this season, you are a "great man" or giant. In this season, every "little one" in the realm you're in looks up to you. In this season, you are a leader. Nevertheless, if you do not humble yourself, you cannot stand; if you do not humble yourself, you cannot be promoted to the next level. Being the God-loving, God-fearing soul that you are, you decide to keep looking up to the hills, knowing that your help comes from the Lord, instead of looking down on His people. Eventually, God promotes you out of the season you're in and plants you in another season. Now, you're a babe all over again. Now, you're in a room that has a ten-foot ceiling, plus, that level has many rooms. This allows you to spread out a little more. The danger of this season is, it's easy to get comfortable and choose not to grow beyond that six-foot ceiling, after all, the season you're in is attractive, spacious and it's higher than the seasons you've exited. In this season, you have to continue to humble yourself, feast on the Word of God and extract the revelation in every notable and seemingly insignificant experience you have. Additionally, as you grow, you have to limit yourself to certain rooms or, better yet, amenities in that season. The reason for is this, in order to outgrow a comfortable season, you have to make yourself uncomfortable. After you've grown beyond the ten-foot ceiling, you have to remain humble, assuming the prostrate position in your heart all the more. The greater you get, the more you must bow down and worship the Lord. After you've outgrown and honored that season, God will take you into another one. In your new season, once again, you are a babe. This time, your season has twenty-foot ceilings and just like the babes in the old season, there are people who've mastered the season you're in. These are the people you will look up to and pattern after; this is, until you discover who you are in that season. Once you reach maturity in that season, you will once again become a wise man or woman, meaning, you'll begin to grow until you're well over twenty foot tall in the spirit. From here, people will look up to you, but you must intentionally and consistently bow down to the Lord so they don't worship you. This allows their eyes to remain fixated on the Lord, thus encouraging them to grow in that season until they discover their identities and eventually outgrow that same mindset. Do you see the pattern here? There are many believers who reject knowledge because they do not want to change, which consequentially leads to them not growing. What then happens is, they get stuck in seasons, and from there, they become repetitious and religious. For this reason, they begin to consume God's people because they are not feasting on His Word; instead, they feast on attention, compliments, platforms and some people even feast on negativity. Psalm 53:4 calls them workers of iniquity; it reads, "Have the workers of iniquity no knowledge? Who eat up my people as they eat bread: they have not called upon God." People who get stuck in seasons become familiar with the systems of those seasons and they eventually begin to submit to the strongmen (familiar spirits) of those seasons.

UNDERSTANDING AUTHORSHIP

A person who does not understand or respect authority, if given any, will abuse it. A good example of this would be a manager who repeatedly yells at and micromanages the employees under him. People like this are promoted when their leaders focus more on their potential, gifts or words than they do on their character. Anyone who is given more authority than he or she can manage will end up bound. Imagine a giant man stuck in a small room; he has no room to grow or move. Consequentially, he becomes aggressive, controlling, unstable, insecure and frustrated. Eventually, he himself becomes a strongman. Can you now understand why you've come across some angry and controlling giants who've had the potential to do great things, but weren't humble enough to reach that potential? Ahab was too wicked and immature to have any measure of authority and he repeatedly proved this. He stood by and allowed his wife to falsely accuse and murder Naboth simply because Naboth refused to sell him his vineyard. He threw Micaiah in prison for prophesying the truth to him. He called Elijah a "troubler of Israel" simply because he stood against what Ahab stood for. Lastly, unlike most kings, he turned over the important matters of the kingdom to his bloodthirsty wife, Jezebel. Again, any person who has more authority than he or she can manage will almost always end up in demonic bondage if that person does not resign or, better yet, relinquish that authority. Resignation is not always an admittance of failure; sometimes, it is a person admitting that the responsibilities given to him or her are too much for that person to bear at the moment. God said that He won't put more on us than we can bear, but He never said He would keep us from putting more on ourselves than we can bear, nor did He say He'd keep others from doing the same. People who don't understand authority usually overwhelm themselves with it. Consider a high-powered rifle. The gun has power in it, but that power is released when a person pulls the trigger. A child who does not understand the power behind the weapon, if given the opportunity, may pick up the weapon and fire it. This could result in the child getting hurt or worse, he could kill himself or others trying to handle something that he does not understand. The same is true with writing. However, unlike guns, it is difficult to (immediately) see the effects that an immature writer has on his or her audience.

An author is a person who writes in authority; this is why, once again, passive and passive-aggressive writers don't sell many (if any) books. The tone of a book should always be informative and authoritative (not to be confused with mean); the author should never sound unsure. An author who isn't confident in the message he or she intends to write is not ready to teach that message. Nevertheless, many authors have prematurely written the books that God placed in them because of immaturity. Consider the impatience of children. A young girl discovers a gift that's supposed to be opened on her eighteenth birthday, but she is only ten. Seeing her name on the gift, she begins to plead with her parents, begging them to at least let her see what's in the small box. Her parents give in and the young girl opens the box. Inside it is a set of car keys. These are the keys to her father's barely driven antique Mercedes Benz. Nevertheless, after having seen the keys, the young girl will likely have one of two reactions: either she won't be interested in the car because she's too immature to understand the value of it or she'll plead with her parents to at least allow her to sit behind the wheel. On her thirteenth birthday, she comes back to her parents and pleads with them again; this time, she asks her father to let her take the car for a spin with him in it, of course. He agrees and she illegally drives the car around the corner, but is pulled over for failure to signal. Having no drivers' permit to show, the young girl watches as her father is placed in handcuffs and arrested for endangerment of a child. The truth of the matter is, she was too young to drive and too irresponsible to utilize her gift. Believers are the same way. It is possible to be a mature believer but not be mature enough to write one or more of the books that God has given you. One of the ways to know if you're attempting to open a gift prematurely is to check your message and your tone. If your tone sounds unsure, you've opened the gift prematurely. If your message has no depth, you've opened the gift prematurely. Lastly, if you believe God is telling you to expose someone, chances are, you are opening your gift prematurely. We prophesy in part, but an immature believer hears a part of the message and then tries to publish it.

Kingdom Protocol for Writers

Ephesians 5:11 (ESV): Take no part in the unfruitful works of darkness, but instead expose them.

Ephesians 5:11 is probably one of the most misunderstood, misquoted scriptures in the Bible. In this day and age, there are a lot of believers who not only endure warfare, but step directly into the judgment of God because they do not understand

Kingdom protocol. They believe that they have the right to say what's on their minds and to say it to whomever they want to say it to. They believe that they can grab microphones and address people who outrank them in the Kingdom.

Before we go any further, let's come to terms with the fact that in the Kingdom of God, there is rank and there is protocol, just like there is in the kingdom of darkness. God left King Saul, meaning, He turned him over to a reprobate mind. Nevertheless, David understood that Saul was still king, even after Saul repeatedly tried to take his life. David ran for his life and even had the opportunity to take Saul's life (twice), but he revered God so much that he would not touch the king.

1 Samuel 24:1-7 (ESV): When Saul returned from following the Philistines, he was told, "Behold, David is in the wilderness of Engedi." Then Saul took three thousand chosen men out of all Israel and went to seek David and his men in front of the Wildgoats' Rocks. And he came to the sheepfolds by the way, where there was a cave, and Saul went in to relieve himself. Now David and his men were sitting in the innermost parts of the cave. And the men of David said to him, "Here is the day of which the Lord said to you, 'Behold, I will give your enemy into your hand, and you shall do to him as it shall seem good to you.'" Then David arose and stealthily cut off a corner of Saul's robe. And afterward David's heart struck him, because he had cut off a corner of Saul's robe. He said to his men, "The Lord forbid that I should do this thing to my lord, the Lord's anointed, to put out my hand against him, seeing he is the Lord's anointed." So David persuaded his men with these words and did not permit them to attack Saul. And Saul rose up and left the cave and went on his way.

1 Samuel 26:6-16 (ESV): Then David said to Ahimelech the Hittite, and to Joab's brother Abishai the son of Zeruiah, "Who will go down with me into the camp to Saul?" And Abishai said, "I will go down with you." So David and Abishai went to the army by night. And there lay Saul sleeping within the encampment, with his spear stuck in the ground at his head, and Abner and the army lay around him. Then Abishai said to David, "God has given your enemy into your hand this day. Now please let me pin him to the Earth with one stroke of the spear, and I will not strike him twice." But David said to Abishai, "Do not destroy him, for who can put out his hand against the Lord's anointed and be guiltless?" And David said, "As the Lord lives, the Lord will strike him, or his day will come to die, or he will go down into battle and perish. The Lord forbid that I should put out my hand against the Lord's anointed. But take now the spear that is at his head and the jar of water, and let us go." So David took the spear and the jar of water from Saul's head, and they went away. No man saw it or knew it, nor did any awake, for they were all asleep, because a deep sleep from the Lord had fallen upon them.

Then David went over to the other side and stood far off on the top of the hill, with a great space between them. And David called to the army, and to Abner the son of Ner, saying, "Will you not answer, Abner?" Then Abner answered, "Who are you who calls to the king?" And David said to Abner, "Are you not a man? Who is like you in Israel? Why then have you not kept watch over your lord the king? For one of the people came in to destroy the king your lord. This thing that you have done is not good. As the Lord lives, you deserve to die, because you have not kept watch over your lord, the Lord's anointed. And now see where the king's spear is and the jar of water that was at his head."

What does this mean for us as authors? It simply means that even though we have authority, we have to be careful how we exercise that authority. We have to be responsible with the gifts, assignments and opportunities that God entrusts us with. We cannot use those opportunities to go after people, even when they are clearly in error. Understanding Kingdom protocol will determine whether we become best-selling authors or a pack of disgruntled authors mumbling and complaining in books that no one wants to read.

One of the greatest injustices we've witnessed in the body of Christ is the rising up of people who believe they are called (*or chosen*) to expose leaders. Now, don't get me wrong; God can raise up whomever He wants, but the truth is most, if not all, of these people were not sent by God. They are products of rejection, church hurt, ambition and rebellion. The ones who have been sent by God to expose a demonic system or practice, in many cases, have not received the full assignment yet (we prophesy in part), and for this reason, they hear "expose" and think God wants them to expose a person. This means they are not yet ready to walk out their calling. Anyone who has truly studied the Bible and understands Kingdom protocol can differentiate between a person who was sent to expose a thing versus a person who's just hurt and looking for a way to respond to that pain. Additionally, many ambitious believers attack people who have the platforms that they covet. They believe that exposing the deeds of a person who outranks them will propel them to the next level in ministry. This mindset is demonic, to say the least. This is the same mindset Absalom had when he set out to kill his own father. He wanted to dethrone David so he could take his place. What's amazing is he had what most would consider a justifiable reason for his rebellion. His sister, Tamar, had been raped by his brother, Amnon, and David hadn't done anything about it. He was an angry young man who likely felt that he'd make a better king than his father. He felt entitled to the throne and this mindset led to his untimely demise. Nevertheless, God's hand was on King David, regardless of how many mistakes he'd made during his reign as king. You see, David was a repentant man; he didn't harden his heart when corrected. So while Absalom and the people who allied with him were focusing on David's wrongs, they didn't realize that David had reconciled with God. The Bible called David "a man after God's own heart," nevertheless, we can see many of the mistakes he made. This did not change God's declaration of him. God simply chastened him (and Israel) for his mistakes.

One of the things you'll come to understand about God is He sends people to confront, but He rarely sends people to expose. Noah was clearly wrong. He was lying asleep in his tent, drunk and naked, and his son, Ham, saw this. In that moment, he could have started a rebellion by exposing his father or he could have covered him. He chose to expose his father. Noah's sons Shem and Japheth covered their father. When Noah woke up and realized what had been done to him, he cursed Cain (Ham's son) and blessed Shem and Japheth. Miriam and Aaron spoke against Moses because he'd married a Cushite woman. The Cushites were descendants of Cush (also known as Kush) who were of the lineage of Ham. This means that Moses hadn't followed Jewish tradition when choosing his wife, but this did not change the fact that Moses was chosen by God to deliver God's people. I tell these stories to demonstrate a point—it is dangerous to rise up against God-established leaders, even if they are in error. God is a God of order; He raises people up and brings them down. If they refuse to repent, He will send someone of equal or greater rank to confront them. (Note: the word "apostle" means "sent one). If they still refuse to repent, He sends people to expose the evils they are practicing. He turns the hearts of the people before He executes judgment.

TRULY SENT MEN AND WOMEN OF GOD DO NOT ADDRESS ONE ANOTHER

THROUGH BOOKS, BLOGS OR PASSIVE-AGGRESSIVE FACEBOOK POSTS.

Proverbs 28:1 (ESV) reads, "The wicked flee when no one pursues, ***but the righteous are bold as a lion.***" This scripture makes a clear distinction between a righteous and a wicked man. A lion confronts; it does not roar from a distance. A lion pursues; it does not flee. So, if you believe you've been called to expose someone, please understand Kingdom protocol. The right thing to do before you start that book is spend some time praying and fasting to ensure that you are not another Ham, Miriam or Absalom. Ask yourself the following questions:

1. **Am I at the same rank or greater as the person I believe I'm called to address?** Elijah was not allowed by God to "expose" Jezebel and Ahab; he was sent to expose a demonic system. He was sent to turn the hearts of the people back to God by exposing the god (demon) they were worshiping. After he exposed Baal, Elijah didn't command the people to arrest Ahab because Ahab was established as a king by God. It was not Elijah's place to bind Ahab; he was sent to bind the demons that Ahab had been worshiping. This was done by binding the people who were mouthpieces for those demons (the prophets of Baal). Once Ahab had been rebuked and Baal had been exposed, the next order of Kingdom protocol was judgment. God judged Ahab and allowed a lying spirit to deceive him. He went to war against Ramoth-Gilead and was killed in the war. Ten years later, Jezebel still hadn't repented and God anointed Jehu to kill her and all of Ahab's children. This was God cleansing (delivering) the Jews from the bondage they'd blindly submitted to and the residue of that bondage.

2. **Have I confronted the person?** Elijah confronted Ahab. Matthew 5:23-24 (ESV) reads, "So if you are offering your gift at the altar and there remember that your brother has something against you, leave your gift there before the altar and go. First be reconciled to your brother, and then come and offer your gift." Let's be honest with ourselves. We live in the era of the coward. Many people spend their lives passively and indirectly addressing people with social media statuses when God wanted us to boldly confront them after, of course, we've addressed ourselves. We were never assigned to talk *at* people; God told us to talk *to* them. Additionally, there has to be some level of accountability before we decide to confront people. Do you have a multitude

of counselors and have they heard back from the Lord regarding the matter?

3. **Have I sought wise counsel?** The Bible tells us in Proverbs 11:14 that in the multitude of counselors, there is safety. The Bible also tells us in Proverbs 14:12 (ESV), "There is a way that seems right to a man, but its end is the way to death." This means that there will be times when we are so convinced that we're right that we'll become passionate about our cause, only to later discover that we were wrong. This is why we need a multitude of counselors —not just one person, and definitely not someone who agrees with everything we say. We need a multitude of praying, God-submitted, God-fearing counselors who aren't afraid to rebuke us if we start entertaining demonic thoughts.

4. **Have I submitted to a greater authority?** Sure, God is the greatest authority, but that's not what this question is referencing. Have you submitted to a person who outranks you in the realm of the spirit? In God's Kingdom, there is rank and there is order. One of the most dangerous believers is a person who is the highest ranking authority in his or her own life—a person who can't be corrected by anyone. People who have not submitted to a greater authority almost always believe they are called to confront people in authority. This is because they don't understand Kingdom protocol. Elijah was sent to confront Ahab and bring down Baal; the warfare that followed this confrontation was too heavy even for him. Let's not forget that he was a prophet who called fire down from Heaven. Nowadays, there are a lot of believers who can't manage home-sized warfare who think they are called to confront church, denominational or even global-sized demons. This is the recipe for a straight-jacket. Sure, we do not know who mentored Elijah, but this does not mean that he didn't have a mentor. In the biblical days, prophets were oftentimes trained in private, and in many cases, their teachers aren't spoken of. It is possible that his mentor could have been his father—a man who the Bible does not mention. So, we don't know where Elijah came from; we only know that he was authorized by God to confront Ahab. This was evident in the fact that Ahab saw him as a threat and would go out to meet with him whenever he requested a meeting. If the person you believe you're supposed to confront does not know of your existence or does not acknowledge you, it could only mean that you were not sent to address that person.

5. **Did God send me or am I being led by hurt, rebellion or ambition?** If you continue reading the story of Ahab and Jezebel, you'll discover that Ahab refused to stay repentant, and for this reason, God arranged for him to meet his end. This is because God was (and still is) merciful to the people who were under Jezebel and Ahab's control. Ten years later, God sent Jehu to execute judgment on Jezebel. When Jehu went to the castle, Jezebel tried to scare him into retreating. She looked out her window and said to him, "Had Zimri peace, who slew his master?" (see 2 Kings 9:31). What's intriguing here is that Jehu did not respond to her. He had a job to do. Judgment had already been decreed (legalized) and he was there to carry it out. Instead, he spoke to a few of the people who served under Jezebel. He addressed two or three of her eunuchs. 2 Kings 9:32-33 reads, "And he lifted up his face to the window, and said, Who is on my side? Who? And there looked out to him two or three eunuchs. And he said, Throw her down." Of course, the eunuchs threw her down and she died. This is a picture of true, God-given authority and deliverance. The people had to deliver themselves from Jezebel; they had to grow weary of her evil ways, and when they were, God ordained a new king to confront the wife and the deeds of the old king. One of the ways to know if God sent you is by examining the hearts of the people. Even in the ministry of deliverance, people don't normally get set free until they are weary of their demons. Once their hearts are turned back to God, they begin to cry out and God sends someone to deliver them.

People who believe they were called to expose others almost always use the scenario of Apostle Paul ousting Peter, also known as Cephas. Let's examine the story.
Galatians 2:11-14 (ESV): But when Cephas came to Antioch, I opposed him to his face, because he stood condemned. For before certain men came from James, he was eating with the Gentiles; but when they came he drew back and separated himself, fearing the circumcision party. And the rest of the Jews acted hypocritically along with him, so that even Barnabas was led astray by their hypocrisy. But when I saw that their conduct was not in step with the truth of the gospel, I said to Cephas before them all, "If you, though a Jew, live like a Gentile and not like a Jew, how can you force the Gentiles to live like Jews?"
What can we take from this text?

1. Apostle Paul saw hypocrisy in Peter.
2. Apostle Paul opposed Peter to his face.
3. He saw that this same hypocrisy was being carried out by the other Jews because of Peter.
4. He told Peter (in so many words) how his hypocrisy was affecting his ministry (assignment).

This means that Apostle Paul wasn't "exposing" Peter. He wasn't trying to destroy "his ministry" or embarrass him. He followed a system of protocol and was being accountable by detailing the ordeal. He was an apostle, therefore, he had the right to correct another apostle. Again, there is protocol in God's established kingdom that most believers are unaware of. This lack of knowledge has led many believers to write books, articles and posts designed to right what they believe to be wrong. This is why so many authors endure what feels like unbearable warfare. What they did not understand was this—the minute you start writing, you become an author, meaning, you are exercising your authority. With every keystroke, you are releasing darts into a kingdom. If what you write is good and godly, you are releasing darts into the kingdom of darkness, but if what you write is ungodly, you are releasing darts toward Heaven. Whenever you release darts against a kingdom, you can expect a response from that kingdom. If God is pleased with what you're writing, He'll cover you as you write. But if you begin to exercise unauthorized authority against another believer, whether that believer is in right-standing with God or rebellion, you will entice the enemy to respond through a system we called warfare. It's normal for writers to endure warfare, but God covers and fights for the ones who go to war on His behalf and exercise Kingdom protocol.

There are steps to authorship and one of those first steps (after salvation) is called self-control. Proverbs 25:28 (ESV) reads, "A man without self-control is like a city broken into and left without walls." A city without walls is a city that has no protection from the enemy. Walls represent protection (covering) and boundaries (self-control). Lastly, walls represent jurisdiction. Any foreigner who goes past the walls of an established government without permission is called an illegal immigrant. Every land and government has laws that the illegal immigrant will be subject to the moment he or she enters its jurisdiction. An author with no self-control is a person whose authority has been hijacked or taken away from him or her. In secular terms, we call this incarceration, but in churchosity (church language), we call this bondage.

Sadly enough, bound people do write books that lead others into bondage. This includes bound Christians who believe themselves to be free—people who believe they have the right to say what they want to say to whomever they want to say it. Because they lack self-control, they further bind themselves with their words and choices. The point is, let us ensure that we understand Kingdom protocol before we begin our writing journeys. Do not be led astray by hurt, anger, rejection or selfish ambition. Authorship (authority with a pen or a keypad) is designed to set people free; authority is also used to bind bound people, meaning, to prevent or further prevent any damage being done by them. Understand that even as God-established authors, we still have boundaries; we still have jurisdictions. Boundaries keep us from being bound. When authors begin to understand how far they can go, we'll see an increase of Christian authors actually writing books that impact, influence and change the world and its systems.

Understanding Authorization

It is possible to have authority, but no legal authorization (permission) at any given season. This means that even though you have the authority (as all believers do) to address unclean spirits, you may not be authorized (at this moment) to address all of them. Consider David. When King Saul wanted to kill him, David, like all men, possessed some measure of authority, but he initially could not respond to Saul with deadly force, after all, Saul was king over Israel. Nevertheless, God gave Saul over to David twice, meaning, David was *legally* permitted by God to kill Saul. David wouldn't carry the act out, however, because he feared God. Elijah was permitted to address Ahab, but nowhere in the Bible does it say that God authorized him to kill Ahab, even though he could have on many occasions. Jehu was eventually sent to purge Israel of Ahab's filth (his wife, Jezebel, and their sons). Before he became king of Israel, he was a commander in Ahab's army. This means that he had authority, but he did not initially have authorization (legal permission) from Heaven to confront Jezebel. Once Elisha anointed Jehu as king (the biblical equivalent of apostolic authority), Jehu could address Jezebel because he had the backing of Heaven. In other words, Jehu was able to take Israel through deliverance. Leviticus 18:25 gives us more of a glimpse of what this looks like; it reads, "And the land is defiled: therefore I do visit the iniquity thereof upon it, and the land itself vomiteth out her inhabitants."

Police officers have the greatest amount of authority in their jurisdictions, however, any officer who travels outside of his or her jurisdiction can only make a citizen's arrest. An officer outside of his or her jurisdiction has the same level of power as the citizens in that region. An officer from Atlanta, Georgia has authority, but if he were to travel to Tampa, Florida, his authority is limited or reduced to that of a citizen. How does this relate to writing? It's simple. Writing, like teaching, is an attempt to reach people who have certain mindsets. A person's mindset is his or her region; it's that individual's personal zip code. In order for a leader to reach a mindset, he or she must be familiar with it or be authorized to address it.

Levels of Government	Law Enforcement	Governing Official
County	Sheriff	Board of Commissioners
City (Municipal)	Police	Mayor
State	State Police, Highway Patrol	Governor
Federal	FBI	President

There are laws that govern our nation, just as there are laws that govern the Kingdom of God. The average modern-day believer is not familiar with spiritual laws, and for this reason, the average believer endures warfare that he or she could have avoided. This is why God said in Hosea 4:6, "My people are destroyed for lack of knowledge." Of course, God was referring to the Levitical priests who had *intentionally* rejected knowledge, therefore, causing the people of God to be destroyed. Nevertheless, this passage of scripture is not limited in its reach. Whenever we intentionally reject knowledge, we become willfully ignorant, thus, causing anyone who depends on us to stop growing.

Proverbs 13:20: He that walketh with wise men shall be wise: but a companion of fools shall be destroyed.

A Sheriff is authorized to make arrests in a county; he or she is only authorized to make arrests in a city if the deputy is under contract with that city. A police officer's jurisdiction is limited to the city (in most states); the officer cannot arrest anyone outside of the city limits. State Police officers cannot legally arrest anyone outside of the states they are employed by. The Federal Bureau of Investigation (FBI) covers the entire United States, but their powers are still limited to federal jurisdiction. The following was taken from the FBI's website.

Question: What authority do FBI special agents have to make arrests in the United States, its territories, or on foreign soil?

Answer: In the U.S. and its territories, FBI special agents may make arrests for any federal offense committed in their presence or when they have reasonable grounds to believe that the person to be arrested has committed, or is committing, a felony violation of U.S. laws. On foreign soil, FBI special agents generally do not have authority to make arrests except in certain cases where, with the consent of the host country, Congress has granted the FBI extraterritorial jurisdiction.

(Reference: FBI.gov/ Frequently Asked Questions)

As we can see, each agency has jurisdiction and there are laws and higher authorities that govern their authority. One of the things we must understand is that the legal systems in the United States and abroad are almost a replica of God-instituted Kingdom laws. God uses the natural to explain the supernatural. This is why He often spoke in parables. There is such a thing as jurisdiction in the realm of the spirit. This means, as writers and teachers, it is imperative that we understand our limitations. We cannot (legally) authorize ourselves to write what we want to write, after all, the Kingdom of Heaven is established in order. If we want to understand this order, we simply need to review our own judicial system. For example, in a courtroom, the presiding judge is the highest-ranking official. Lawyers cannot casually approach the judge's bench; they have to ask for permission (authorization) or the judge has to summon them. This is very similar to the legal system that was set up in Persia during King Xerxes' reign. No one could barge into the king's chambers; every person had to be summoned. Barging in could cost the intruder his or her life; that is, if the king did not lift his scepter to the person. In the American court system, a lawyer wouldn't be killed if he or she approached the judge's desk without permission, but the lawyer could be held in contempt of court (charged) and arrested (bound). When this happens, the judge will lift up his equivalent of a scepter; he will lift up his gavel and begin to strike his sounding block with it, thus, alerting the authorities in the courtroom that order needs to be restored. Additionally, if a person was convicted of a crime and sentenced to State prison, the Governor of that State could pardon the person, but the Mayor could not. All the same, there are ministers who have the faith and the knowledge to cast out high-level demons that other deliverance ministers could not cast out. This is all a matter of rank.

WHEN WRITING A BOOK, IT IS IMPORTANT TO UNDERSTAND WHAT YOU ARE AUTHORIZED TO SPEAK ON AND SPEAK AGAINST.

It is important to understand your jurisdiction and the concept of jurisdiction as a whole. For example, the Lord told me in 2015 that I was going to write a book about the Jezebel spirit. He even gave me the title for the book: *Jezebellion*. I wanted to sit down and start writing immediately because I believed I had enough knowledge to start and finish the book. Ambition provoked me. The title enticed me. My imaginations were all over the place. Nevertheless, I could sense a wall. Thankfully, after having authored over thirty books and written well over two hundred articles, I was familiar with that wall. It was a yield sign for me. I understood that it meant it wasn't my time to write that book. I understood that what I was sensing was an angel who was acting as a doorkeeper. This angel was sent to ensure that I didn't lose my life or my mind trying to play around with spiritual things. He was an enforcer of God's law, nevertheless, he had no authority to bind me. His assignment was to warn me. I heeded the warning, pulled down those imaginations and continued to build everything God was telling me to build in that moment to build. God allowed me to have more experiences so I could gather more knowledge about the Jezebel spirit, and two years later, I found myself suddenly having a renewed interest in writing the book. When I started the outline, I didn't feel the limitations anymore. The yield sign was no longer there. I could actually feel God urging me to write it. Instead of feeling something preventing me from writing, I felt a loving force pushing me. This meant it was time. I had finally been authorized to write the book, so I started, completed and published the book in early 2017. If I had started writing before I received permission from Heaven to write *Jezebellion*, I would have endured a lot of warfare. How so? The Jezebel spirit would have attacked me in the areas in which I was ignorant regarding it. Before you approach an enemy, it is important to know your enemy's fighting style, otherwise, he or she will attack you where you are not guarded. I knew a lot about the Jezebel spirit in 2015, but in the two years that God kept me from writing the book, I learned a lot more about that spirit—I learned things I had not known. Where I lacked knowledge, I would have been vulnerable to attack. When I finally did start writing the book, I didn't go under attack because I was no longer ignorant of Jezebel or her devices. In short, you may be assigned to write a particular book, but it's always important to know when you are authorized to begin writing. When you are authorized to write, God will protect you as you write. This does not mean you will avoid going through warfare; it means that the warfare won't be unbearable.

Writing is not only a privilege; it is an honor, but it is also a process that is governed by orders and laws. This means that there is such a thing as criminal behavior in the realm of the spirit.

In the above image, we see two evangelists. One's shirt reads "Evangelist," while the other's shirt reads "Ambitious Evangelist." Both men are traveling outside of their jurisdictions; they could be venturing off into regional matters —matters that are normally addressed by apostles.

The gatekeeper represents a jurisdictional boundary; he can be the enforcer of a city limit, state limit or a border between two governments. Behind the gatekeeper, we see a box that reads "Apostolic Authority." The gatekeeper is holding up a stop sign; he's trying to get the men to back off, however, God gave us free will. This means we have the freedom to obey or disobey Him. In other words, we can actually run that stop sign. This also means that the gatekeeper, as intimidating as he looks, can only warn the men, but he can't stop them from going outside of their jurisdictions. However, in every jurisdiction, there are laws (legal permissions, restrictions), limitations (speed limits, borders) and officials (deputies, wardens, judges). The officials (or officers) of every given jurisdiction are either good or evil. So, a man who has been given apostolic authority has the keys (legal permission to enter and execute authority) in certain jurisdictions. A man who enters this jurisdiction without authorization will not understand how to legally bind everything in that region because he does not understand the laws of that region. This means he can be bound (enslaved), but it would be difficult for him to bind (arrest) certain spirits. Remember, when the disciples could not cast the spirit out of the young lunatic, Jesus didn't say it was impossible for them to bind the demon; He said that it was *because* of their faith that they'd failed. Additionally, *that kind* (referencing the demon) only came out through prayer and fasting. This is similar to our legal system, whereas, Sheriffs (in most states) can only arrest criminals in unincorporated jurisdictions like counties and some incorporated cities (by contract). It is important for us to understand *what kind* of issues we can effectively address in any given season.

One of the men's shirts reads "Ambitious Evangelist." This is because ambition often leads God's people astray. Selfish ambition has caused many writers to be bound when they tried to address matters that were outside of their jurisdictions. The reason they did this was because they wanted to write, for example, on Bishop T.D. Jakes' level, not understanding that he teaches from his metron (measure). When they encountered the gatekeeper (ministering angel), they could feel the resistance; they could feel the pressure, nevertheless, they kept going into a realm that they hadn't been summoned into. The wise retreated, the unwise kept typing until what they were addressing responded to them. They discovered one kingdom law that most people are unaware of and that is—things that outrank you have no (legal) right to come up against you, however, they do have the (legal) right to respond (sometimes with force) when you address them. Goliath most likely would never have noticed David, but once David stepped onto the battlefield, Goliath challenged him. Let's revisit David and Saul's story. Because Saul outranked David, David had no legal right to take Saul's life, but the moment Saul came after David's life, God leveled the playing field. He authorized David on two occasions to respond with equal force; he gave David the opportunity and the right to take the king's life. When King Saul decided to hunt David, he left his jurisdiction and entered a place where his crown and rank didn't matter. Thankfully for him, however, David feared God and was determined not to touch God's anointed. Again, this means that whatever speaks to us, regardless of what rank it is, we have the right to respond to, just as whatever we speak to, regardless of what rank it is, has the right to respond to us. This is why so many ambitious writers end up going through warfare when they start writing outside their metron (jurisdiction).

An easier way to understand the concept of jurisdictions and boundaries is to familiarize yourself with the word "realm." The word "jurisdiction" denotes a horizontal space (since we stand vertically, but live horizontally) in which one has authority. The word "realm" is more associated with the vertical rule. When we think of realms, we think of atmospheres or worlds stacked vertically. Nevertheless, in the realm of the spirit, our jurisdictional lines are not horizontal; they are vertical. We cast imaginations down, our praises go up, we kneel down and we lift up our hands. An apostle in America would still be an apostle in Africa; he or she would still have the same amount of dominion, rank and authority in the realm of the spirit. Needless to say, however, there are different realms in the spirit so regardless of whether the leader is in North America, South America, Africa, Asia, Australia, Antarctica or Europe, there are certain spirits presiding over certain realms that the leader may not be sent to address. This doesn't take away from who the leader is or the call on his or her life; it simply means in that present season, the leader may not have enough knowledge or experience to deal with a certain principality. Knowing what realm to exercise authority over is as important as a police officer knowing when and how to draw his or her weapon.

The Hebrew word for "realm" is "mimshal" (masculine) or "memshalah" (feminine) and it means: dominion, rule, authority or to reign. Remember, in Ephesians 6:12, the Word says one of the forces that we wrestle against is "spiritual wickedness in *high places.*" The Berean Study Bible's translation says we wrestle against "spiritual forces of evil in *heavenly realms.*" A realm represents a kingdom; it is a place of authority. Again, the word "authority" comes from the word "author." An author has a measure of rule, that is, if the author is called by God to write. Just like a leader should not randomly challenge every spirit he comes in contact with, an author cannot write about every realm or address what he or she doesn't understand. We have to write in the realms in which we have dominion, meaning, we've been granted authority over and overcome whatever ruler is in that realm. Consider what the angel sent to help Daniel said to him.

Daniel 10:10-14 (ESV): And behold, a hand touched me and set me trembling on my hands and knees. And he said to me, "O Daniel, man greatly loved, understand the words that I speak to you, and stand upright, for now I have been sent to you." And when he had spoken this word to me, I stood up trembling. Then he said to me, "Fear not, Daniel, for <u>from the first day</u> that you set your heart to understand and humbled yourself before your God, your words have been heard, and I have come because of your words. The <u>prince of the kingdom of Persia</u> withstood me twenty-one days, but <u>Michael, one of the chief princes</u>, came to help me, for I was left there with the kings of Persia, and came to make you understand what is to happen to your people in the latter days. For the vision is for days yet to come."

Here, we have an angel who says that he was held up by the prince of Persia for twenty-one days. Why couldn't he free himself? After all, a lot of people who do not understand heavenly things would argue that we can fight every unclean spirit that dares to challenge us because we're Christians. However, God is demonstrating, through the biblical text, how kingdoms work. The term "prince" of Persia means that the demon was a ruler; it was a principality and had dominion over a certain heavenly realm. It was able to capture one of God's angels as the angel made its way through that realm. It held the angel up for *twenty-one days* because it outranked that angel, so God sent Michael, who the Bible refers to as a "chief prince," to help the bound angel. Please understand that every realm represents a kingdom, and even though we have authority over unclean spirits, we can only exercise that authority in whatever realm God has given us the keys to. A better way to look at this is to consider an earthly kingdom. Even though the king of one country could ally with the king of a neighboring country, he could only exercise his authority in the country that he reigned over. Being in another region didn't change the fact that he was a king; it meant he was not king over the land he was currently in. This is why the enemy can't come in like a flood against a believer. By doing so, God said He would raise up a standard (rule) against him. The word "ruler" comes from the word "rule." So another way to read this text is, God will raise up a ruler against him, just as He did when the prince of Persia withstood the angel. He sent out Michael who was a "chief prince" or ruler.

A lot of aspiring authors make the mistake of trying to address spiritual matters when they have not yet overcome the ruler of the realms they're in. Mark 3:27 (ESV) reads, "But no one can enter a strong man's house and plunder his goods, unless he first binds the strong man. Then indeed he may plunder his house." The "goods" when referencing spiritual things aren't material; the goods are spiritual (wisdom, understanding, revelation). For example, we can receive the wisdom of wealth-building. Sure, we can overcome the enemy by the blood of the Lamb and the word of our testimony (see Revelation 12:11), but to overcome an opponent means that we have to oppose or come against him. In other words, we have to want to be free. For example, a woman who has been engaging in premarital sex, only to have her lover abandon her should not write books about the dangers of premarital sex if she isn't yet delivered from it. You see, in that realm, she's still a slave so the moment she addresses the evils of premarital sex, her ruler will overwhelm her with warfare or he'll tell her what to type. In other words, he will respond to her or through her. This is similar to what Pharaoh did to the Israelites when Moses confronted him, saying to let God's people go. Pharaoh increased their workload. The Jews were slaves in Egypt, therefore, they were in a realm that they did not have dominion over. God delivered them horizontally (He led them out of Egypt), but they refused to be delivered vertically (they still thought like slaves). So, if the woman who's bound by fornication becomes angry with the devil for the ending of her relationship and she decides to write a book about the dangers of fornication, the enemy will increase her burden. He'll likely send another man into her life to deceive and further bind her or he'll send disease into her life. This is because her decision to write the book had nothing to do with her loving God's people. It was centered around her bitterness; she was raising up against her own personal Pharaoh when God wanted to free her altogether. Once she was no longer a slave to fornication, she may have been granted the authorization to write about the dangers of premarital sex. This is why we have to be mindful of our own motives. I've spoken with countless women, for example, who've demanded that I pray for God to break the soul ties between them and their former lovers. They would try to spiritualize their requests by saying, "I know what we did (fornication) was wrong and I've repented for that, but I need to be free from this man! He's moved on with his life, so I want to move on with mine!" Their motives for wanting to be free had nothing to do with them realizing the error of their ways and desiring to please God. It had everything to do with them feeling rejected by their former lovers. To retaliate against the men who'd walked away from them, they wanted to remove themselves emotionally and spiritually from the captivity of an ungodly soul tie, but they didn't want to submit their bodies as a living sacrifice (holy and acceptable) to God, which would have been their reasonable service (see Romans 12:1). This means that they were slaves who didn't want to come out of Egypt physically or mentally; they simply wanted to teach Pharaoh a lesson by refusing to work for a season. If they were to write books against fornication, the prince (or principality) they've submitted themselves to would begin to attack them or attack God's people through them. The point is, yes, we overcome the enemy by the blood of the Lamb and the word of our testimonies, but to utilize the blood, we must do like the Israelites and escape from our Egyptian bondage. We must then place it on the doorposts of our hearts and stay in our dwelling place of righteousness.

The message here is be sure to write what God tells you to write and don't let the enemy tempt you out of your realm (jurisdiction) with ambition. As a writer, you will reach the people in the jurisdiction in which you have authority. If you simply trust the voice that God has given you, you will write books that effectively help, encourage, deliver and empower people. Additionally, your books will convey you as a strong and knowledgeable writer versus just someone who decided to write. Think of it this way. A third-grade math teacher appears intelligent to a bunch of eight-year-old children who are learning multiplication, however, that same teacher may not appear to be so intelligent to a class of sixteen-year-old children who are learning second level trigonometry. In her classroom (jurisdiction), she is a teacher, but in another person's classroom, she is a student or a visitor. It is error to teach deep things from a student's standpoint.

The Literary Process of Creation

The process of creation begins with a single word. God is our Creator; we are His creations, and therefore, we are creative. Genesis 1:1 says, "In the beginning, God created the Heaven and the Earth. And the Earth was without form and void." Every formed thing starts as a problem until it is spoken to.

Genesis 1:3: And God said, "Let there be light." The problem was the Earth was without form and void. For this reason, God had to address the problem by creating a solution. Every solution has to be given a name before it becomes legalized in the realm of the Earth. Everything that God legalizes, He gives a measure of authority to. Genesis 1:5 reads, "And God called the light Day and the darkness Night." One of the first things that should grab our attention with this scripture is that the words "day" and "night" are both capitalized, signifying that they are of great significance. In the English language, we capitalize the names of people, specific places and things. Of course, there is a reason that these words were capitalized, and the reason is, they were granted a measure of authority or rule. Genesis 1:16 speaks of the authority given to the day and the authority given to the night; it reads, "And God made the two great lights—the greater light to *rule* the day and the lesser light to *rule* the night—and the stars." The word "rule" is an authoritative word; it speaks of the authority that God gave to the sun and the moon. It is not legal for the sun to remain in the sky past a certain hour. It has to shift so that the lesser light (the moon and the stars) can rule the night. Google defines "rule" this way: one of a set of explicit or understood regulations or principles governing conduct within a particular activity or sphere. Everything that God created has to abide by the laws He's set in place for it. But before a creation (created thing) can respond to God's voice, it has to first be given a name.

Throughout the book of Genesis, we witness God solving problems and then giving names to the solutions. What was He doing? He was legalizing the solutions; He was using His authority. For example, trademarks, patents and copyrights give us legal rights to the works we create, nevertheless, before we can obtain these legal protections, we have to put a unique name to our creations. The names are what gives us our rights to our inventions. When the inventors of the first home air purifier (Marcus and Klaus Hammes) filed for a trademark, they had to submit a unique name for it and they also had to describe the purpose of the air purifier. Lastly, the Hammes brothers had to distinguish the air purifier from similar items that were already on the market like the already established humidifier. They had to also distinguish it from industrial air purifiers that were already on the market. Basically, they made the government aware of the laws surrounding the air purifier they'd created; they spoke of its jurisdictional authority (rules and limitations). In other words, they spoke of what the purifier could do and what the purifier could not do. In short, they became authors of the very first home air purifier. An author isn't just someone who writes a book, an author is a person who exercises authority in the realm of creation.

The root word of authority is author. Author comes from the Greek word "ktizo", which means to shape, form or make. This means that before we become authors, we have to exercise the authority God has granted us in our own lives. We have to be transformed by the renewing of our minds. In other words, something or someone will begin to shape our thinking. If the Word shapes our thinking, we will walk and write in godly authority. This is called transformation. But if our thinking is shaped by someone or something that is ungodly, we will walk and write in ungodly authority. This is called conformation. Romans 12:2 reads, "And be not conformed to this world: but be ye transformed by the renewing of your mind, that ye may prove what is that good, and acceptable, and perfect, will of God." Another word for conformation is deformation. Remember this principle:

- God formed us.
- Sin deformed us.
- And now, we have to be transformed by the renewing of our minds. After transformation, we face the danger of conformation. In this, conformation is just another extension of deformation.

Ungodly authority can be exercised on three levels and they are:
1. Error
2. Rebellion
3. Witchcraft

The difference between the three is this. When a person teaches from the spirit of error, that person isn't intentionally leading God's people astray. He or she is simply deceived. 1 Timothy 4:1-2 reads, "Now the Spirit speaketh expressly, that in the latter times some shall depart from the faith, giving heed to seducing spirits, and doctrines of devils; speaking lies in hypocrisy; having their conscience seared with a hot iron." A rebel knows the truth, but denies it because of something the rebel has esteemed higher (in his or her heart) than God. A rebel is pretty much a witch with a pacifier. This is why God said in 1 Samuel 15:23, "For rebellion is as the sin of witchcraft, and stubbornness is as iniquity and idolatry." A witch, on the other hand, intentionally leads people astray because of selfish ambition, hatred or unforgiveness. Revelation 2:20 (ESV) reads, "But I have this against you, that you tolerate that woman Jezebel, who calls herself a prophetess and is teaching and seducing my servants to practice sexual immorality and to eat food sacrificed to idols."

Next, God created the heavens and the Earth. The Earth was without form and void. God then had to form the Earth before He turned on the light in it. Later, God formed Adam from the dust of the ground and breathed life into him. This was the representation of God cutting on the lights in Adam. Light represents life, presence and revelation. Right now, your book may have a form, but your words will give life to it. David said in Psalm 119:105, "Your word is a lamp to my feet and a light to my path."

LIGHT WAS CREATED AS A SOLUTION TO A PROBLEM.

The Earth was void, meaning, it was absent of light (revelation, life). Adam was created as a solution to a problem, but after he was created, he did not immediately begin to speak. The Bible says, "There was no man to till the ground." This was the problem that Adam was created to solve. Genesis 2:15 reads, "And the LORD God took the man, and put him into the garden of Eden to dress it and to keep it." After this, God spoke to Adam, telling him which trees he could eat from and the one he was forbidden from eating from.

A few notes to ponder are:
- Adam was nameless in the beginning. He was referred to as man. He wasn't called Adam until he was called, meaning, until he was given his assignment. A

name gives you the legal ability to respond, but an assignment gives you the responsibility of responding.

- One of Adam's first assignments was to name the animals that God brought to him, but he still had not spoken to or addressed God. He addressed his assignment. God brought the animals to Adam to see what he would call them. All too often, writers complain about their assignments and this only causes God to give the assignments to what He refers to as His "faithful servants." Faithful servants don't complain; they serve.

- Without a name, God would not have given Adam the right to name the animals. He could not identify anything until he (1) had an identity and (2) could identify his authority. This is the same principle found in Matthew 7:3-5, which reads, "Why do you see the speck that is in your brother's eye, but do not notice the log that is in your own eye? Or how can you say to your brother, 'Let me take the speck out of your eye,' when there is the log in your own eye? You hypocrite, first take the log out of your own eye, and then you will see clearly to take the speck out of your brother's eye." Here, Jesus is telling us to "name" or "identify" our own strongmen. Without doing this, we cannot properly identify another man (or woman's) strongmen. What the Lord was telling us to do is first exercise our God-given authority over ourselves before we go out and try to exercise it on others. This is the power of identification; it helps us to better understand the significance of a name.

- After naming the animals, God gave Adam rest, and while he was resting, he gave him a responsibility called a wife. He then had to give a name to the solution God had created for him. Adam called her "woman," in Genesis 2, but he had to give her a name in Genesis 3 because the two had fallen. Eve didn't need a name in the Garden of Eden; she was simply Adam's helpmeet, his wife and the daughter of the Most High God. But once they were evicted from the Garden, Adam started referring to his wife as Eve. Eve means "mother of the living." Her name legalized her in the realm of the Earth and distinguished her from every woman who was to be born.

- God forms somethings, but it is not until He speaks to those things that they are transformed, meaning, His supernatural ability called "blessing" is transferred to it. Blessing means empowered to prosper. You can write a book, but God has to write your foreword if you want it to be blessed.

- Adam did not speak until he had to address something he had been given legal authority over. One of the mistakes many authors make today is they attempt to address matters that are outside of their jurisdictional limits. Please understand that you cannot bind what you don't understand; it is knowledge that gives you power over the enemy. "My people are destroyed for lack of knowledge: because thou hast rejected knowledge, I will also reject thee, that thou shalt be no priest to me: seeing thou hast forgotten the law of thy God, I will also forget thy children" (Hosea 4:6).

We were given the ability to reproduce, but we have to be granted the authority to create. To reproduce means to produce again or produce after one's self, but to create means to transcribe or, better yet, pull something out of the realm of the spirit, ruminate it and cause it to materialize. Our ability to pull something out of the spirit realm and break it down into words is called creativity. When we break something down, the process is called description. The prefix "de" means down and the word script comes from the word scribe. A scribe, of course, is a writer. When we break food down in our mouths, the process is called chewing. We chew food until it is broken down enough for us to swallow and digest it. We can only chew a certain measure of food at any given time. This is because the standard size of a human esophagus is 1.5 to 2 centimeters in width. This means that we have to eat our food in portions; the general rule is, if it's too much to chew, it's too much to swallow, and if it's too hard to swallow, it'll be almost impossible to digest. The same is true in the writing world. Readers can only take in so much at any given time. This is why revelation has to be broken down. This is also why people who try to sound intelligent and use far too many complex words often get negative reviews. Information has to be broken down if it is to be stored. Remember this: books are built one word at a time. God told the prophet Habakkuk to write the vision and make it plain. This means we have to take our thoughts, plans, ideas, dreams and prophetic messages and ruminate them until they become words that our readers can understand. What you're doing is transcribing or translating a message. We're taking it from Kingdom language to the language that mankind understands.

In Ezekiel 3, the prophet Ezekiel was commanded to eat a scroll that God had given him. The scroll, according to Ezekiel, was sweet, but then he was told to go to the people of Israel and deliver the words of lamentation and woe. In Revelation 10, Apostle John was given a scroll to eat. He said that it was as sweet as honey, but in his stomach, it became bitter. This means it was good to receive, but hard to deliver. What should we take from this chapter?

1. Writing is a response to God's voice or a response to a problem that God has brought to your attention. Never speak to God's people when God has not spoken to you.

2. A solution is not a solution until you transcribe it, describe it and give it a name. This is the birthing process between Heaven and Earth.

3. Respect the doorkeepers of revelation. Never try to write someone else's book or you may have to deal with the devils in that jurisdiction.

4. Never speak to God's people until you've silently tilled your flesh.

5. Never sit on revelation too long or it'll become spiritual constipation. When this happens, authors find themselves knowing what they want to write about, but can't find the words to get started or to finish what they've started. Anytime a person is constipated, that person needs water and, of course, water represents the Word of God and the Spirit of God.

6. Do not refuse to write whatever it is that God wants you to say, otherwise, you may suffer another form of spiritual constipation. This is when God was once speaking, but suddenly stops because of rebellion. The person who now has trouble hearing from God then begins to turn to other mediums in an attempt to get things moving again.

7. Never address something you haven't been given authority over or in (example: pulpit).

8. Jesus's disciples had to follow Him before they were granted the ability to cast out devils, and some were even given the charge to author books in the Holy Bible. Each man's assignment had nothing to do with the number of years they'd followed the Lord; it had everything to do with the closeness of their walk with Jesus and the level of authority they'd accepted. Walking with Jesus gave them the ability to address demons. Never try to address a demon that you're walking with.

Books are a compilation of words brought together to make a point. Remember, the point of a mountain is the highest part of that mountain. It's the place that most climbers aspire to ascend to. Mountains can have several peaks, all of which generally have their own names, but the overall peak is the highest point of that mountain. In short, your book has to have a point. It can't just be a mountain of words that lead people in circles. Where there is no peak or point, there is only confusion. Sadly enough, many authors take their readers on journeys that lead to nowhere.

Just like books are a compilation of words, words are a compilation of letters and sounds brought together to create an image. For example, when God told Adam to name each animal, He was telling Adam to speak the words that came into his head every time he saw an animal. This is similar to what we have toddlers do. We sit our children down, show them flash cards and tell them to say what they see. When a child says "dog" when what's clearly on the flashcard is a cat, we know that the child is simply still learning, so we'll correct the child and continue teaching him or her. What we're doing is teaching the child to take an image and convert it into words. This is what God did with Adam. He brought animals to Adam to see what he would call them. The Lord even put Adam in a deep sleep, and when he awakened, he saw his wife, Eve. Adam then identified her saying, "This is now bone of my bones, and flesh of my flesh: she shall be called Woman, because she was taken out of Man." Adam described what he saw; he spoke the words that entered his heart. When he spoke those words, Eve was standing in front of him and those words formed an image in her mind, helping her to understand who she was and why she had been created. This is what communication is. We take an image and ruminate it down into words and then we speak those words or write them out. The words then form a picture in the listener or the hearer's mind, thus conveying whatever it is that we desire to have or want to convey. Let's say that you want a new home. You'd get on the phone with your new Realtor and convey to him what you want in your new property. You'd say, for example, "I want a three bedroom, two bathroom house on, at minimum, an acre of land. I want it to be a Victorian style home or a traditional home with an open floor plan, two stories and it must have a pool in the backyard." While you're speaking those words into the Realtor's understanding, those words are forming a picture in the Realtor's mind. The Realtor responds by transcribing what he's heard you say onto his notepad. This means he is transcribing the words from one medium of communication (spoken words) to the next (written words). He will then look at some properties, trying to find a few that match the items on your wish-list. The two of you will continue communicating until your need has been met. After this, you will speak with the Lender, your bank and every person or organization you'll need to follow through with purchasing your home. What you're doing is creating a problem to address a problem and then introducing a solution. How so? Self-help books are generally written to address a problem or a set of problems. A problem isn't always bad; a problem can be, for example, you wanting to write a book. This isn't a bad thing; it's simply a desire or an assignment that has yet to be fulfilled. So, what you'll do is create another problem which is, you'll open a document and start typing. Now, the problem you have is an empty book! Again, all problems aren't bad; some are just opportunities that have not been seized.

Again, books are a compilation of words brought together to make a point and words are a compilation of letters and sounds brought together to create an image. All the same, we are a compilation of words brought together to form a message. Every man is a minister, whether he stands on a pulpit and holds a mic or he stands in his living room, holding his cellphone. Every man is a message. We don't just teach what we believe, we are what we believe (see Proverbs 23:7). This is why it's important for us to receive deliverance regularly and to constantly renew our minds. We teach from the abundance of our hearts; we pour out who we are on paper and we publish our thoughts, essence and issues for others to buy, read and embrace.

An author's closet (in the writers' world) is filled with every word that the author knows and/or understands. This is the place that authors shop for the words they will use in their books. This is why it is important for authors to enlarge their vocabularies. When authors enlarge their vocabularies, they are simultaneously enlarging their territories. How so? The more people you can speak to, the more people your book will reach. A broader vocabulary gives authors the ability to build better books. The moment you realize that you are an author (scribe), you should:

1. Slow down and pay attention to every (good) detail in life.
2. Go far outside of your traditional, cultural and religious comfort zones so that you can enlarge your territory by enlarging your understanding. Authors who speak, teach and reason from a cultural standpoint can only reach the people who are familiar with the author's culture.

3. Shop for words every day. Every time you hear a word that you don't quite understand, look it up and incorporate it into your vocabulary.
4. Hone your skills as a writer by blogging, journaling and/or writing for a publication. This will help to enlarge your vocabulary, stretch your imagination and attract more people to you.
5. Make it a habit of breaking down every word that grabs your attention. You can do this by looking for the Greek and Hebrew translation of that word and also looking for synonyms and antonyms of that word.

Remember, your book isn't about making you an author or creating another stream of income for you; these are just bonuses. Your book is an arrangement of words brought together to solve a common problem. You are a solutionist, not an opportunist. If you embrace the right attitude in regards to your book and you are careful, intentional and protective of God's people, He will market your book for you.

Building Your Vocabulary

First, let's define the word "vocabulary."
*   words used on a particular occasion or in a particular sphere.
*   the body of words known to an individual person.

(Reference: Google's Online Dictionary)

Your vocabulary is a sum total of the words you know and understand. It is more than your vocal ability, it is the way in which you are acquainted with each word. A man's vocabulary reveals a lot about him, which include:

1. His aspirations.
2. His orientations.
3. His agreements.
4. His fears.
5. His limitations.

Aspirations. Every man's reality is his world. A man's world is built by what he believes, and what a man believes has the power to shape his desires. This is what determines what revolves around the man and what the man himself revolves around. For example, a man who wants to dominate the world of business and become a millionaire will often use words that, to most people, sound complex. Many such men and women will speak a lot about statistics and they'll avoid words that they feel will repel the people and connections they want to attract. A man who aspires to be feared in his neighborhood, on the other hand, will use a lot of profanity, plus, he will speak more about violence than anything else. Both men have collected words from the environments they grew up in, the people they've familiarized themselves with and the worlds they aspire to enter or dominate.

Orientations. A man's orientation is how he perceives himself and the world he's in. It is a reflection of his thought-process or, better yet, what he relates to. For example, most men and women identify themselves as heterosexual; this is their orientation. A man who believes that he is a woman born in a man's body will often build a vocabulary that he feels is more suited for women. He'll listen to women speak and collect the words he believes he needs to build his world. He may surround himself with women, if but for a season, just to pick up their words and mannerisms. This is because of how he perceives himself. Your orientation will determine what world you pull your words from.

Agreements. Remember, you are a body of words, and what you attract and/or repel is a reflection of the agreements you've made. For example, a woman who has soul-tied herself to many men has made many agreements. She's told men that she would be with them forever, she'd never leave them, she'd never be with any other men and so on. When her relationship ends with one man, that agreement is still in place. For this reason, she will repeatedly enter relationships, only for them to end. She will collect words from and invest words in every relationship she enters and exits. Before long, her vocabulary will become a mixture of sexually suggestive words, words of hurt, words of rejection, words of fear, flattery and every word she's used to enter relationships, every word she's collected when trying to save a relationship, and every word she's released after the end of a relationship. The same is true for authors. Every author's vocabulary will reveal the agreements that the author has. For example, I speak a lot about honor, excellence and breaking ungodly soul ties because of the agreements I've made with God. Once I made those agreements, God invited me into the terms of each agreement. In short, He started giving me revelation on those subjects. For this reason, I can write a book about either of these topics in a matter of days without outsourcing any information.

Fear. Think of a woman who fears her abusive husband. Because of the world she lives in, she has learned to choose her words carefully. She has severely edited her vocabulary, ridding herself of the words that trigger her husband's rage and/or jealousy. Because she has had to limit her vocabulary, you'll find that she either stutters, won't speak much or she may keep looking at her husband when she's responding to others. Remember, a vocabulary is a body of words and we are words manifested; we are the words we choose, so every time her husband beats her, he snatches another word from her. This is the process of destruction. Destruction isn't always immediate; oftentimes, it's gradual. The same is true for authors. Most of us have been beat up by life, and for this reason, there are some words that we've excluded from our vocabularies, just as there are some words that we've included in our vocabularies. A fearful author will testify about something he or she has endured, all the while, omitting information that is relevant for the readers to mentally form a whole picture. This means that the author confuses the reader. A good example of this that I've witnessed many times reads this way, "It was said of my husband that he couldn't find a decent job because he was lazy. Things were being said about both of us, but we held on to our faith." In this, you'll notice that the author is speaking at the people who hurt her, rather than teaching the readers. Most readers don't personally know the author to understand who said what, when they said it or why they said it. Books written like this are designed to further a conversation that the author still wants to have, but feels that he or she has not been granted the opportunity to have it. So, the author's book becomes a platform for his or her pain. Sadly enough, this is common in the writing world. What you fear will always form, transform or deform your vocabulary. If you fear being sued, you'll choose your words carefully. If you fear being judged by people, for example, who are well-versed with the Bible, you won't write confidently; instead, your book will be littered with statements like, "But that's just what I believe. You may disagree, but that's your right" or "I know some people will disagree, but the Lord told me to write this." These are statements of fear; the author clearly fears criticism, so they give a rebuttal or disclaimer in advance in hopes that it will steer away the critic. Instead, such language only serves to attract critics, after all, a lack of confidence reveals a lack of knowledge.

Limitations. People often criticize what they cannot do and/or do not understand. When you find criticism in a person's vocabulary, chances are, you've met that person's limitations. For example, I grew up in poor. In my world, it was not uncommon for me to hear people say that they would never get on a plane or a cruise ship. As a matter of fact, I used to make this same declaration. The reality was that the people who said this had never been on a plane or a ship and didn't have the funds to travel. This didn't mean that they'd never travel or couldn't travel, it meant that mentally, they've limited themselves to ground travel because of fear and lack of funds, so their vocabularies were limited to that in which they understood. If you ever want to be an excellent writer, increase the size of your world. How do you do this? It's simple. Introduce yourself to new words, new experiences and new people. Go outside of your culture and embrace new things. This will not only help you to increase your vocabulary, but it'll help you to increase your understanding, connections and your finances. A man's finances is always a reflection of his limited understanding!

To build your vocabulary, you need to:
1. Read more books, articles and blogs.
2. Go outside your culture.
3. Offend your fears. For example, when I went to Jamaica in 2012, I held a snake. I have no interest in doing this again, but I wanted to confront a fear of mine. Getting on a plane was another way I confronted a fear; I did this in 2008.
4. Study the world that you want to invade. Learn the vocabulary and culture of that world.
5. Buy a thesaurus or start using an online thesaurus. Study the thesaurus as often as you can.
6. Surround yourself with people who are not like-minded. Like-minded people speak the language of your world—a language that you've already mastered.
7. Surround yourself with or follow wise men and women. Proverbs 13:20 says, "He that walketh with wise men shall be wise: but a companion of fools shall be destroyed."
8. Travel more.
9. Speak less; listen more. This is especially important when wise men and

women are speaking.

10. Open your mouth so that God can fill it (see Psalm 81:10). As a writer, one of the things you'll come to see is that most of the revelation you share in your book will not come from your head-knowledge; it'll fall into your spirit the moment you start typing. This is an example of God sharing His wisdom with you and through you.

AUTHORS COLLECT WORDS BECAUSE AUTHORS ARE WORDS.

Our world is a world of words. The more words we know and understand, the more people we can reach, and the more wealth we can acquire. Think of a man running a clothing store. His company would go out of business if he only had ten tee-shirts and eight styles of jeans available for his customers to buy. He'd garner a few sales, and then, the customers would simply stop coming to his store. To acquire any measure of success, he would have to give his customers a bigger selection to choose from. The same is true for authors. We sale words. Our readers are our customers. They can go anywhere and freely access words, but the words that we bring together helps them to reach certain goals. If your vocabulary is limited and you don't work towards growing it, you'll keep limiting yourself to the same people until they grow weary hearing you say the same thing using different words.

Revealing Your Creativity (Activation)

Study the photo. What do you see? What does it represent to you?

Open a word document or grab a notebook and write what you believe is going on in the image. The goal here is to identify how you ruminate or, better yet, how you break down an image. Remember, God gives us a picture in our minds. We then break that picture down into words; the breaking down of an image is called describing, but the process of transferring the image from one realm to the next is called transcribing. How you break a picture down will always reflect:

1. Your level of maturity
2. How patient or impatient you are
3. Your motives

I want you to challenge yourself. Of course, I won't tell you how many words to write; this is completely up to you. I want you to imagine that you are writing a story, detailing the events taking place in the image. After you have finished, move on to the next section, entitled *Creative Revelation*. **Do NOT read *Creative Revelation* until you've finished this activation.** The reason for this is, I want you to be able to effectively measure yourself as a writer. Again, look at the photo and give your personal assessment of it. You can write it as a non-fictional story, a police report, a diary entry or however you want to write it. You can write it in first person or third person. Dig into your creativity and test your skills as a writer!

Creative Revelation

In the above exercise, you were challenged to look at a picture and break it down into words. In this section, you will learn how to use what you've written to evaluate yourself as a writer.

When you're done, email or print ten copies of what you've written and send or hand a copy to:

- a child or teenager (if the text is age-appropriate. If you're questioning whether the content is appropriate for children or teens, do NOT share it with a child). Make sure you speak with the parents first and let them see what you've written!

- Two young adults (college age students, preferably around 19-25)
- Two of your peers
- Your boss or any non-religious leader
- One leader you admire
- A critic
- An unbeliever
- Your pastor

Do not cheat. Do not revise what you've written. Just challenge yourself by handing or emailing the document to the aforementioned group. You can also take a snapshot of the drawing with your phone and share it with them as well. Tell them what your assignment was and ask them to grade or rate what you've written. If they are familiar with the academic grading system in America, ask them to use it to grade you. If they are not familiar with this system, ask them to rate you using the star system. In the star system, they'd choose a number between one and five, with one representing poor and five representing excellence. Ask them to be honest with you, detailing where they feel you need improvement. Pay attention to how you feel right now about the assignment and how you feel when you hand (or email) the document to every person. If you threw some text together, you've probably already reasoned with yourself to either revise the text or you've decided to not participate in this part of the assignment. Of course, if you revise the text or refuse to share your writing with others, you are cheating yourself out of a lesson. You see, when you sit down to write your actual book, you will become more conscious about how you write. Additionally, this group of people can become your panel of judges; they can become the way by which you measure yourself. Every writer needs to challenge himself or herself. No exceptions. In the future, you won't throw anything together, because you'll know how it feels to hand someone something that does not reflect your true potential (if you rushed through the assignment). What this ought to reveal to you is how you treat, will treat or would have treated your students. You should always write something:

- that's detailed enough for a child to understand
- that's engaging enough to hold the youth's attention
- that's smart enough to motivate *and* teach your peers
- that's thought-provoking enough to change your boss's perspective of you

385

- that's information-rich enough to impress a leader you admire
- that's thoroughly researched enough to silence your biggest critic
- that's sound enough to wet the pallet of an unbeliever
- that's powerful enough to hold your pastor's attention

In which area would you say your writing excelled, and in which area would you say your writing failed? Of course, if you did a great job, you're excited about this assignment and there's no person on this list who you are afraid to share your writing with. Again, this is a reflection of you you'll treat your readers.

The goal of the exercise is for you to find your audience and measure yourself as a writer. A good writer knows how to take, for example, college-level or apostolic-level teachings and break them down until a babe could ingest and digest what they've taught. So, let's reexamine the picture.

Some people would see a woman cracking or, in layman's terms, losing her mind because of stress. In this, they'd see a victim—a woman who has a non-supportive, argumentative husband, a neglected child, and a noisy environment. For this reason, they'd write her a prescription for counseling and toss her away. Others would see a man who was fed up with his wife's inability to manage their home. What if she's an addict who used the bill money to support her addiction? What if her child is suffering from drug withdrawal? What if the husband just came home and the wife is playing profane music, all the while, getting high on drugs? Then again, what if the picture isn't about the two adults, but is instead the story of a young man detailing how he grew up in an abusive home? What if his dad was the abuser, but his mother was promiscuous? What if his dad was promiscuous and his mother was abusive? What if his mother was a saint, but his dad was a lazy, philandering bum who laid around the house all day while his wife worked two jobs? What if the story is about the music the couple is listening to? What if the music is poisoning their minds and destroying their relationship? What if the image is detailing the power and effect of what we listen to? What if the woman is a single mother who was home alone, only to have her delusional, psychotic neighbor break into her home and start ranting about an unpaid bill? What if he's schizophrenic and genuinely believes she's his estranged wife and the baby is their lovechild, conceived while playing their favorite song? What if this picture represents a photo that's being viewed by a recently deceased man in Heaven? What if he's seeing a slideshow of all the evil he's done? This loans credibility to the adage "a picture is worth a thousand words." There were many ways to break the photo down, and if your story is, the woman was going crazy because of her argumentative husband, the truth is, you didn't venture past the outer courts of your creativity. You didn't challenge yourself. A great writer always goes above and beyond the obvious; a great writer can take a simple picture and create a best-selling novel with it.

Regardless of how you did on this assignment, you have the potential to become a great writer. The objective was for you to make your mistakes now so that when you sit down to write your actual book, you will have already experienced what thousands of authors experience everyday. Many authors don't share their books because, quite frankly, they are ashamed of them. Many authors won't tell their pastors about their books; this is because they were so anxious to wear the author label that they pretty much vomited on their pages. Realizing that the content and intent of their hearts are now public, they work harder to keep their books hidden than they do to promote them.

Again, eighty-percent of Christian books flop because people pile words up, wrap them with a cover and toss them across the airwaves, hoping to impact millions of people. Instead, their books become the equivalent of a few pebbles thrown into a large crowd, having little to no impact.

The Weight of the Scribe

We are a manifestation of our own vocabulary. We are a compilation of the words we speak and the words we've received. As humans, our everyday diets consist of words. We spit out the words we don't like and the ones we don't understand, but we binge on the words that confirm what we already believe and the words that affirm us. We wrestle with words, we dance with words and we cry because of words. We are individual books, with each day being another page in the chapter (seasons) we're in. We navigate through words, we get delivered from words, we reach for prophetic words—we are hungry for words. Again, we are individual books; we are a myriad of words brought and glued together through agreement, and as such, there are many pages in our lives that are empty; this is where we are void of information (knowledge), understanding and revelation. It is on these pages of our hearts that the enemy scribbles all manners of lies. It is these pages that attract people to us who have a lot to say, but no room in their own lives to say it. So, they come into our lives, call themselves friends or lovers, and then, proceed to write on the blank pages of our hearts. Lies are weighty, so as we journey more into the heart of God, He rips those pages out of our hearts and we deal with (for a season) what we call a broken heart. Nevertheless, He replaces the ripped pages with more empty pages. He then invites us into His presence, after all, the Bible tells us that God is nigh (near) the brokenhearted. When we are determined to have what we want, we ignore the voice of God and invite more people to create chapters in our lives who shouldn't be within a stone's throw of our hearts. As we mature in the Lord, however, we start believing the Word of God and our lives begin to change for the better. Every time we agree with God, we receive deliverance, impartation and an opportunity to turn a page, rip out a page or edit a chapter in our lives. We then give God the pen and allow Him to draw a picture of His plans for us on those empty pages. Once that picture pops up in our minds as a vision, we are given the assignment to break it down into the words that we understand—the very words that we've filled and surrounded ourselves with—the words that make up our worlds. "And the LORD answered me: "Write the <u>vision</u>; **make it plain** on tablets, so he may run who <u>reads</u> it" (Habakkuk 2:2).

As long as we hold onto these words, we feel heavy. Oftentimes, this heaviness is mistaken for depression when, in truth, it's nothing but a burden for deliverance, a burden for intercession, a burden for evangelism or a burden to write. Understand this: a heavy scribe is a pregnant scribe or a scribe who needs deliverance. As God begins to write on the pages of our hearts, strongholds are broken, voids are filled and demons come running out of us, screaming in terror as we run towards a certain future. We've made it. Another chapter ends and a new season begins.

One of the issues is, we often don't want to break down or understand the vision God has given us. For example, a man engaged to marry the love of his life may find himself having a dream. In the dream, he's standing at the altar, waiting for his bride to arrive at his side. She walks carefully towards him with a beautiful veil covering her face. Once she stands next to him, the two turn and face one another. He then lifts the veil, only to find a donkey staring back at him. He suddenly sits up on his bed as his alarm clock rescues him, yet again, from another nightmare. Believing that Satan is trying to keep him from marrying his soon-to-be bride, the groom-to-be, stands on his bed and screams at the top of his lungs, "Satan, I rebuke you! I will marry Martha! She will be my wife in two weeks and there's nothing you can do to stop this!" One day, a prophet walks up to him at church and says, "I saw a vision of you on a mountaintop. On that mountain, there was a huge bed. Honestly, I've never seen a bed that big before. You were lying in the bed next to snakeskin and a blonde wig. The snake was gone, but it had left its skin behind and the blonde wig was on the pillow next to you." Believing the prophet is a false prophet, the man looks him directly in his eyes and says, "Now, you listen to me. I know who you are! Martha is a good woman and I am going to marry her next week! Is that clear?" Sure enough, a week later, he lifts the veil and kisses his new bride.

Three years into the marriage, he finds himself at a crossroads. He asks himself, "Do I stay so that our children can have a two-parent household, even though I know I'd be absolutely miserable, or should I leave and explain to them, when they are old enough to understand, why I chose to leave?" You see, after seven marriage counselors, a few altar visits and three years of what appears to be unanswered prayers, he has finally come to understand his dream. His wife, Martha, is as stubborn as a mule. No amount of words, counseling or deliverance has changed or will change this fact because she likes being argumentative and arrogant. All the same, he has discovered that Martha is a promiscuous woman, which explains the vision of the large bed on a mountaintop. He finally decides to leave, and years later, he's ready to chew the revelation he once spit out. The pictures God had given him were not to be ignored; they were to be tested, and once they were tested, they were to be chewed until they were palatable enough to swallow and small enough to digest. Howbeit, he carried the weight of that vision around with him until he became strong enough to ignore it. Once he was delivered from Martha, however, he felt a lot lighter and he was ready to turn a page.

WHERE THERE IS NO SUBSTANCE, THERE IS NO WEIGHT.

An author's weight cannot be determined by a digital scale, nor is it measured by the author's title, extensive vocabulary, socioeconomic status or the number of likes he or she gets on social media. An author's weight is measured by his or her faith. Understand that every (truthful) word we release already has weight, but the truth, when released from a doubtful man, has little to no reach. This means if the man doesn't believe the words that come out of his own mouth, it would be hard, but not impossible, for him to find others to believe him. All the same, as teachers, most of us can attest to the fact that God sometimes gives us information with no revelation. Think about the parables that Jesus shared with His disciples. The parables were designed to form pictures in the disciples' minds—pictures that they were not required to decode, but to chew. As they ruminated the parables, they would extract the revelation that they needed to take their next steps in ministry. You see, their loyalty wasn't measured by how many physical steps they took alongside Jesus, after all, Judas Iscariot walked with Jesus for three years, give or take. Their loyalty was measured by how much they believed and obeyed Jesus.

Amos 3:3: Can two walk together, except they be agreed?

Luke 6:46: And why call ye me, Lord, Lord, and do not the things which I say?

A Scribe's Digestive System

As authors, our assignment almost always is to break down the pictures that God forms in our minds, taking time to cast down the images that Satan tosses into the batch. As we do this, God will give us the understanding we need to digest the revelation, but we must first (intentionally) chew the picture. Think of it this way. Most of us eat two or more meals every single day. God has given us help to swallow this food in the form of saliva, but we have to choose to chew the food. After this, we have to make the choice to swallow it as well. Once we do this, the muscles in our esophagus move in wave-like contractions, helping to push the food towards our stomachs. Our help doesn't end there! Once the food enters the stomach, it is met by hydrochloric acid. This acid helps to break the food down. Our bodies then take the nutrients it needs and expels the rest as waste. This is similar to the ruminating process that every teacher and author must master. Sometimes, the pictures (visions, prophecies, words of knowledge, words of wisdom) that God gives us are far too big for us to ingest or digest in the seasons that we're in, so we have to be patient enough to chew them. This means that we consider what God is showing us, pray about it, consult the multitude of counselors and ruminate the information until we can accept it. After this, we can swallow what we now know, but may not necessarily understand. Similar to hydrochloric acid, understanding meets knowledge once it falls into the right place; it helps to break down what we've read, experienced and heard. It then allows us to take what we need from every message and season of our lives, all the while, expelling (as waste) every detail that does not build the story of who we truly are.

When we're enjoying food, we often groan in pleasure, letting those around us know that the food we're eating is pleasant. If we're at a restaurant, this usually provokes other patrons to inquire about the food on our plates. This is called evangelism. We utilize those moments to engage others, sharing the gospel of Jesus Christ with them, whether through a book or in person. This means the groaning sounds are designed to grab people's attention. Nevertheless, as we are eating, a process begins in our bodies to digest the food we are taking in. Once this process is complete, we begin to feel pressure on our stomachs, indicating that we need to visit the nearest restroom and release what our bodies could not use. Again, the groaning sounds draw souls; these are the sounds and expressions that should line the pages of your book. The waste, on the other hand, should come out in the restroom or in the private room of your rest. The problem we see today is that many authors can't tell the difference between their groans and their waste, so they privately dispose of their praises to God, whispering to Him about how good He is, never taking the time to let the world know. All the same, they publish their waste.

WE ARE A WORLD OF WORDS. WE ARE A WELL OF WORDS.

Some of these words are good, while others should be swirling around in a toilet, about to be sent into a bottomless pit. I have learned that, as authors, we shouldn't relieve ourselves on the pages of our books. Sure, that divorce may have been difficult to endure and no one seems to believe your account of what happened, but could it be that your husband didn't necessarily leave you? Is it possible that he was a weapon formed against you, so God drove him out of your life to ensure that he would not prosper? Could it be that you experienced the second level of deliverance (the driving out of the wrong person) after you experienced the first level of deliverance (receiving a new heart and a new mind)? This was, of course, preparation for the third level of deliverance (the driving out of demons). Could it be that you weren't unfairly terminated from that job? Is it possible that your jealous supervisor unwittingly pushed you into your next season? Understand that facts and truth, while similar, are not the same. A book of facts has an expiration date. All it takes is for someone to come along and disprove or cause the public (at large) to question one or more of the facts shared. The point is, it may be a fact that your ex-spouse mistreated you, but when you've only pulled up the facts, you haven't dug deep enough to write. A journey NEVER ends at the facts! You have to get to the truth. To do this, we have to extract the nutrients (wisdom) from the experience and rid ourselves of the haunting details. When we're intentional about obeying God, despite how we feel, the Lord will continue to lead us to the revelation we need to end that chapter of our lives. The fact may be that your ex cheated on you and did a lot of things that ultimately destroyed your marriage, but if you dig deep enough, you'll find the fossil remains of the picture that God gave you. It's a picture of His will for you. It's that picture you threw away to chase after the man who would someday refer to you as his ex-wife. It's that picture you flipped over when Satan showed you the picture of someone else's husband. You didn't divorce because of the other woman, the abuse, the alcohol, the drugs or the in-law interference; you divorced because you married the wrong person! This is the truth! If you'd obeyed God and not married that man, had refused to fornicate (or commit adultery) with him and had heeded every sign that he wasn't the right one, you wouldn't have crashed into that twelve-year storm while running from the truth. This means that your facts, while interesting and entertaining, may very well be crap. Facts have no nutritional value, therefore, they fill readers with surface-level knowledge but no power. God gives us the truth because it is the truth that sets His people free. Facts are good to share, but they have to be backed with the truth, otherwise, your book becomes an interesting read and not a revelatory one.

The above image details what it looks like when an author publishes what should have been expelled (example: attempts to expose people, bitter speech, unsound doctrine, hatred, etc.). The author hasn't given the readers something to glean from; instead, the author is still trying to resolve an issue or gain closure in an event that has long ago passed. This doesn't help the readers, but instead, serves to burden them all the more. This is why, after reading a book, you can either feel invigorated, excited and ready to take on the world or you can feel sluggish, depressed and in some cases, suicidal. As God's scribes, we have the responsibility of carefully stewarding the assignment God has given us. It's great to not bury the talent, but it's even better to use the talent responsibly. You have to filter through your memories and extract only that which is beneficial for teaching. Always remember this: the Bible isn't a journal; it isn't a day-by-day account of what went on in the biblical days. As a matter of fact, it took over 1,500 years for the Bible to be completed from cover to cover. The average Bible has over twelve hundred pages (depending on the dimensions, font and translation). Every man who contributed to the Bible did not give an account for every single day, every single demonic encounter, every single test or every single victory. This didn't mean that those stories weren't relevant to him or the people he ministered to, but God wanted to publish only what was beneficial for His people as a whole. The point is, every event that mesmerized, scared, surprised, hurt or distracted you isn't an event that should be published in your book. This is why it is great and sometimes even necessary for authors to have journals and blogs; this way, we can have outlets to share our thoughts, beliefs and concerns. Authors also need a multitude of counselors who've been where they're trying to go.

Satan Sifts Scribes

Peter was a scribe; this goes without saying, after all, he authored two books in the Bible: 1 Peter and 2 Peter. One thing we know about Peter's life is that, of all Jesus' disciples, Satan specifically asked to *sift* Peter. Why is this? Matthew 16:15-19 may answer this question for us; it reads, "He saith unto them, But whom say ye that I am? And Simon Peter answered and said, Thou art the Christ, the Son of the living God. And Jesus answered and said unto him, Blessed art thou, Simon Barjona: for flesh and blood hath not revealed it unto thee, but my Father which is in Heaven. And I say also unto thee, That thou art Peter, and upon this rock I will build my church; and the gates of hell shall not prevail against it. And I will give unto thee the keys of the Kingdom of Heaven: and whatsoever thou shalt bind on Earth shall be bound in Heaven: and whatsoever thou shalt loose on Earth shall be loosed in Heaven." In this moment, Peter not only received a Word, he received his Kingdom identity. Jesus referred to him as Simon Barjona. Satan wanted to sift Peter because of the Word he'd received. Matthew 5:10 reads, "Blessed are they which are persecuted for righteousness' sake: for theirs is the Kingdom of Heaven." This tells us that we are persecuted, attacked and even killed for the sake of righteousness. Matthew 13:18-23 confirms this in the Parable of the Sower; it reads, "Hear ye therefore the parable of the sower. When any one heareth the word of the kingdom, and understandeth it not, then cometh the wicked one, and catcheth away that which was sown in his heart. This is he which received seed by the wayside. But he that received the seed into stony places, the same is he that heareth the word, and anon with joy receiveth it; Yet hath he not root in himself, but dureth for a while: for **when tribulation or persecution ariseth because of the word**, by and by he is offended. He also that received seed among the thorns is he that heareth the word; and the care of this world, and the deceitfulness of riches, choke the word, and he becometh unfruitful. But he that received seed into the good ground is he that heareth the word, and understandeth it; which also beareth fruit, and bringeth forth, some an hundredfold, some sixty, some thirty." Satan wanted to interrupt the conversation between Peter and Heaven; he wanted to test Peter's faith, hoping he could snatch the prophecy that Peter received. This is because Satan is a devourer. What does his diet consist of? What exactly does he want to devour? The answer-—words.

Scribes eat words; we could start and end the chapter here. Nevertheless, this would be an incomplete statement. Sure, as we've mentioned earlier, not only do scribes eat words, scribes *are* words. As a matter of fact, when people see us, they see a solid picture; they see our flesh. They don't see who we really are, so when we meet people who we're interested in getting to know better, we *describe* ourselves. Remember, the word *describe* can be broken up into two parts: *de* and *scribe.* De means to bring down or break down; scribe, of course, is a person who writes. It also means to write. Another variation of scribe is "script", from where we get the word "scripture."

When we describe ourselves to others, what we're doing is giving them a synopsis of who we think we are, who we want to be, who others have said that we are or who we really are. It's pretty much a preview that allows the other parties to decide whether they want to invite us into their lives or not. This also helps them to determine how intimate their invitation should be. For example, they will determine if they want to invite us into the associate realm or the realm where we house their most intimate relationships.

While people may see the flesh of a scribe, the truth of the matter is, a truly God-established scribe more than likely has experienced some pretty devastating storms in his or her life. This is because the scribe doesn't just copy scriptures; scribes confirm the Word of God. We do this by comparing our experiences with the revelation we received after we got to the truth (not the facts) and publishing it for others to see. Think of the man who once cut himself in the tombs. The Bible says that Jesus cast a network of demonic spirits out of the man who, as a unit, referred to themselves as Legion. After the man was free, he asked the Lord if he could travel with Him and Jesus told him no. He told him to go and tell his friends about the good things the Lord had done for him. Jesus didn't tell the guy to carry around a copy of the Ten Commandments; He told him to share his own testimony with others. The Lord was telling the guy to confirm the Word. The man in question couldn't just tell folks about his deliverance; he had to share a part of his life that he probably wasn't comfortable sharing. How did Legion enter him? The Bible doesn't tell us this, but we can assume that he'd endured some relatively traumatic experiences. Maybe he was molested as a young man. Maybe his father had rejected him. Maybe he'd lost someone he loved and didn't know where to turn. Maybe he'd come from a very twisted family. We can make many assumptions, but what we do know is, the man had a legion of demons. A legion, in the Roman army, was three to six thousand foot soldiers, therefore, it is believed that the man had anywhere between three to six thousand demons possessing him. He had so many devils in him that there was no room for his own personality, sexuality or desires; his entire thought process was fueled by demons. In short, the man likely had to share his story from defeat to victory, and then from victory to victory. This means he had to break himself down. Maybe he had to discuss the embarrassing details about his family life, and this wasn't easy. Maybe he'd been taught that the family's name was more important than his deliverance, but all of a sudden, he found himself in front of strangers, having to detail the events that led to his bondage. Nevertheless, to win a soul for the Kingdom of God, the once deranged man had to pretty much sift himself in front of the people he witnessed to.

Scribes are often said to be transparent, but this isn't necessarily the case. Scribes have been broken down into a fine dust-like material; this allows them to describe their own experiences in life. Remember, we can only feed others at the consistency of what we are or what we've eaten. If you try to shove a hunk of flesh down a man's throat, he'll choke on what you've given him. To be an effective scribe, you have to share every word at a certain consistency; this includes sharing your own personal testimony. Scribes don't just use the words that pop up in their heads; true scribes shop for words, always enlarging their vocabularies so that they can reach a broader audience. When the men and women of God are faced with storms, the problem is often a word that's gotten entangled in their lives. For example, look at the following sentences:

Incorrect Sentence: I not do love you.

Correct Sentence: I do love you.

Now, in the writing world, the first sentence has a grammatical error and my editor would likely think I was trying to say, "I do not love you." Nevertheless, the word "not" could have been a word that I was thinking or hearing while writing. For this reason, having an editor is important. Now, let's relate this to the life of a scribe. A scribe is a world of words and a well of words. We study the Word of God, prophesy to ourselves and do our best to release to others what we'd like to receive for ourselves. Nevertheless, because we are words, we have to be edited and edified. If we're not edited (corrected) and edified (instructed), the people who see us will see a life that does not make sense. They'll see broke, sick and dying Christians! They'll see perverted, bitter and fornicating Christians! But when we're edited and edified, our lives will mirror God's Word. Editing is the more painful and tedious part of the publishing process. This is what Satan pretty much asked to do with Peter when he wanted to sift him as wheat.

Luke 22:31-32: And the Lord said, Simon, Simon, behold, Satan hath desired to have you, that he may sift you as wheat: But I have prayed for thee, that thy faith fail not: and when thou art converted, strengthen thy brethren.

Remember, we are nothing but walking and talking words. Sifting Peter meant violently shaking up his life to separate his fruit from his flesh. Satan was confident that Peter would not be able to endure this process, after all, when farmers sifted grain, they would place the grain on a sieve and shake it violently. This process would cause the dirt and the chaff to fall through the screen to the ground, only leaving behind that which was useful and edible. Satan was confident that all of Peter's good words and prophecies would fall through the sieve to the ground and all that would be left would be his flesh. If this happened, Satan could then devour him. If his flesh fell to the ground, the fruit of the Holy Spirit would be left and Satan

398

would be defeated once again. This was a gamble on Satan's part. Nevertheless, he was confident that he would win this bet if the Lord was willing to let him play his hand. You see, in the demonic kingdom, the sifting process is designed to remove your praise, prayers and faith. It is designed to test your words. If your words have no weight (substance), they will fall to the ground like chaff and be blown away by the winds of doctrine. Sure, we can say that we are prophetic scribes, called to the nations for such a time as this, but the shaking and the sifting will always prove or nullify our declarations. When authors write and find their lives violently interrupted by storms, Satan isn't always trying to get them to stop writing their books. Satan wants them to stain the pages of their books with flesh, opinions and unsound teachings. For example, two of the most fierce storms to ever interrupt my life hit when I was writing books. I was sitting at my computer, finishing up on a book when I suddenly found myself in the midst of a divorce. While writing another book, I had one of the most devastating and longest-lasting storms ever to sweep through my finances. It was so bad that I stopped writing and started panicking. This is the life of a truly God-instituted scribe. It can be ugly at times. It can be difficult at times. It can even be confusing at times. I remember asking the Lord a lot of questions during the financial blizzard. I wondered if I'd offended Him in any way. I wondered if I'd somehow traveled outside of His will without realizing it. I'd prayed a lot and allowed people to pray for me. I wondered if I'd let the wrong person pray into my life. I wondered if returning to tithing had been a mistake, after all, when I wasn't tithing, money seemed to be chasing me. I wondered if I needed deliverance. As a matter of fact, I set up a deliverance session with a powerful deliverance minister, and that session ended with him telling me that I didn't have any demons— my depression and fear were the result of my financial problems. I was being sifted and like Job, I could not figure out what I'd done to deserve so much heartache. I'd forgotten that I would be persecuted for righteousness' sake. I'd forgotten that scribes are oftentimes sifted, and the amount of violence in the shaking is indicative of the size of the Word that has been released into our lives. This isn't to say that you'll endure warfare every time you decide to write a book, but it is to say that every time you decide to write a book that will cause a major paradigm shift, it would be wise to pad yourself with prayer and fasting, and surround yourself with a multitude of counselors.

Satan Robs Scribes

Why did Apostle Paul write more books in the New Testament than any other apostle? Why didn't God use Peter the way He used Paul? Why does God use some scribes more than He uses others? To answer these questions, we have to understand a simple word called "identity." Merriam Webster defines "identity" this way: the distinguishing character or personality of an individual. Your identity is who you are; it's how others identify you and how you identify yourself. If what you believe about yourself does not match what God says of you, it becomes harder for God to use you. Let's consider Peter. There was a moment in history where Peter was having identity issues and Paul rebuked him because of it. Galatians 2:11-14 (ESV) tells the story this way, "But when Cephas came to Antioch, I opposed him to his face, because he stood condemned. For before certain men came from James, he was eating with the Gentiles; but when they came he drew back and separated himself, fearing the circumcision party. And the rest of the Jews acted hypocritically along with him, so that even Barnabas was led astray by their hypocrisy. But when I saw that their conduct was not in step with the truth of the gospel, I said to Cephas before them all, 'If you, though a Jew, live like a Gentile and not like a Jew, how can you force the Gentiles to live like Jews?'"

In this, we see that Peter was having identity issues. Jesus had once dined with tax collectors and sinners. This further infuriated the Pharisees, but this did not stop Jesus from being who He is. He continued to demonstrate God's kind of love to everyone who would receive Him. Now, Peter (also known as Cephas) found himself struggling with right versus wrong. He knew that eating with the Gentiles was okay, but at the same time, he feared the opinions of the Jews. For this reason, he chose to behave like a hypocrite. We can only guess that this behavior humiliated and infuriated the Gentiles who, just moments earlier, had been welcomed by Peter. Now that other Jews had come into the room, Peter put distance between himself and the Gentiles; this behavior provoked the other Jews to behave in the same manner. Remember, in Luke 22:31, Satan had asked to sift Peter, meaning, he wanted to look for error in Peter. When most of us read about Satan asking to sift Peter, we automatically think of what he did to Job. He asked for permission to attack Job, and when God gave it to him, he attacked Job without mercy. God drew a line of demarcation around Job, telling Satan that he could not touch his life, nevertheless, everything that Satan could touch, he attacked. So, it's easy for us to summarize that Satan was not granted permission to sift Peter, but this wasn't necessarily the case. Everybody isn't sifted the same way. Let's look at those moments when we can clearly see Satan operating in Peter's life after Jesus told him about Satan's plans for him.

1. **Matthew 16:21-23:** From that time forth began Jesus to shew unto his disciples, how that he must go unto Jerusalem, and suffer many things of the elders and chief priests and scribes, and be killed, and be raised again the third day. Then Peter took him, and began to rebuke him, saying, Be it far from thee, Lord: this shall not be unto thee. But he turned, and said unto Peter, Get thee behind me, Satan: thou art an offence unto me: for thou savourest not the things that be of God, but those that be of men.

2. **John 18:10:** Then Simon Peter having a sword drew it, and smote the high priest's servant, and cut off his right ear. The servant's name was Malchus.

3. **Matthew 26:75:** And Peter remembered the word of Jesus, which said unto him, Before the cock crow, thou shalt deny me thrice. And he went out, and wept bitterly.

These mistakes didn't mean that Peter was a bad man or that God couldn't use him. We see that God did use Peter many times, but the issue was Peter had identity issues. What Satan went after was Peter's identity. When he went after Job, he killed many of his animals and the servants that were with them. He also killed all of Job's children, stole his camels, destroyed his property, attacked his health and then used his friends to attack his character. Of course, this is what Satan desires to do to all of God's servants; wherever he finds an opening in our lives, he comes in through that window and launches an attack, with his primary target being our identities.

John 10:10: The thief comes only to steal and kill and destroy. I came that they may have life and have it abundantly.

Why do we take out the trash? The answer is simple:

1. We take out the trash because it'll eventually begin to stink.
2. We take out the trash because it'll attract insects into our homes that we don't want to live with.

3. We take the trash out because it'll eventually begin to overflow, thus, robbing us of our precious space.
4. We take out the trash because we have no use for it.

As consumers, we are constantly peeling something, breaking the skin off something, pulling the paper off something or cutting cardboard to get to something. Every day, we find ourselves consuming what we can consume and throwing away the items we feel are useless and worthless—items that, in some cases, need to be discarded in a timely manner. This is especially true with discarded food. Food decays and it attracts everything from flies to roaches which, in turn, attract spiders. It also attracts mice and mice attract snakes. For this reason, most of us empty our trash cans everyday making sure to leave the unwanted trash outside for the trash collector to pick up. This means we've learned the difference between what's trash and what's treasure. None of us would buy a diamond ring, open the box and toss the ring into the trash, all the while, putting the box on display. No. The box, for most of us, would be useless without the ring. This same concept should be applied to our assignments as scribes. We have to know the details, experiences and beliefs to throw away, versus which ones to publish. The truth of the matter is, there are many Christian authors who simply have not forgiven the people who've hurt them, and for this reason, they see their books as opportunities to redeem themselves and clear their names.

In every storm, there is wisdom to be had, just as there are details to the storms that are unpleasant and oftentimes demonic. Everyone goes through the upsets of life. Many of us have endured betrayal, abandonment, rejection, being unfairly judged, and so on. This is just a part of life's menu. Sadly enough, we can't pick everything we want off this menu; we must eat everything that finds its way in front of us, regardless of how it tastes. What happens when an author-to-be does not forgive the people who were involved in the storm or the people who were the storm? Let's revisit the example of the trash. If trash is left in a home, it's almost a guarantee that flies will find their way into that home, especially during the spring and summer months. Flies will feast on the food in the trash and before long, roaches and rats will find their way into the home. These creatures are called pests. This is what happens when a person refuses to forgive the people who hurt him or her. Demons come into that person's heart and life and begin to feed on the negativity in that person's life. Consider what Jesus said to Peter in Matthew 18:23-35 in the parable of the unforgiving servant. It reads, "Therefore is the Kingdom of Heaven likened unto a certain king, which would take account of his servants. And when he had begun to reckon, one was brought unto him, which owed him ten thousand talents. But forasmuch as he had not to pay, his lord commanded him to be sold, and his wife, and children, and all that he had, and payment to be made. The servant therefore fell down, and worshipped him, saying, Lord, have patience with me, and I will pay thee all. Then the lord of that servant was moved with compassion, and loosed him, and forgave him the debt. But the same servant went out, and found one of his fellowservants, which owed him an hundred pence: and he laid hands on him, and took *him* by the throat, saying, Pay me that thou owest. And his fellowservant fell down at his feet, and besought him, saying, Have patience with me, and I will pay thee all. And he would not: but went and cast him into prison, till he should pay the debt. So when his fellowservants saw what was done, they were very sorry, and came and told unto their lord all that was done. Then his lord, after that he had called him, said unto him, O thou wicked servant, I forgave thee all that debt, because thou desiredst me: Shouldest not thou also have had compassion on thy fellowservant, even as I had pity on thee? And his lord was wroth, and delivered him to the tormentors, till he should pay all that was due unto him. So likewise shall my heavenly Father do also unto you, if ye from your hearts forgive not everyone his brother their trespasses."

Because of the sacrifice of Jesus Christ, God forgave us for our sins; we know this, but many of us find it hard to reconcile the notion that we should extend that same grace and mercy to others. For this reason, we often justify staying in unforgiveness. Nevertheless, look at what happened to the unforgiving servant. Because he did not extend the same mercy to his servant as his master had extended to him, he was delivered to the tormentors. The word tormentors here, parabolically speaking, is symbolic for demons. Also note that the man was referred to as the unfaithful servant. As Christians, we are servants of the Most-High God, but this does not exempt us from the rules. We should continue to forgive the people who've hurt us. In this parable, we see that the servant received grace, but would not extend it. For this reason, he was turned over to the enemy of his soul. If you're familiar with the ministry of deliverance, you should know that trying to cast devils out of an unforgiving believer is a waste of time and energy. The believer needs to be counseled. As a matter of fact, if you've ever heard demons speaking out of the mouths of people, you've likely heard them say, "We're not coming out! We have rights to this person!" What rights do they have? In many cases (if not most), they're lying of course, after all, they're demons, but there are some cases when they do have rights to a person. A large majority of these cases were won when the believer chose to forgive the person or people who hurt him or her. When the believer took out the trash (hurt, anger and blame) that accumulated during the event, the flies (devils) had nothing else to feed on. This made it easy for the deliverance minister to take the soul through deliverance. Genesis 15:4-11 reads, "And, behold, the word of the LORD came unto him, saying, This shall not be thine heir; but he that shall come forth out of thine own bowels shall be thine heir. And he brought him forth abroad, and said, Look now toward Heaven, and tell the stars, if thou be able to number them: and he said unto him, So shall thy seed be. And he believed in the LORD; and he counted it to him for righteousness. And he said unto him, I am the LORD that brought thee out of Ur of the Chaldees, to give thee this land to inherit it. And he said, Lord GOD, whereby shall I know that I shall inherit it? And he said unto him, Take me an heifer of three years old, and a she goat of three years old, and a ram of three years old, and a turtledove, and a young pigeon. And he took unto him all these, and divided them in the midst, and laid each piece one against another: but the birds divided he not. And when the fowls came down upon the carcasses, Abram drove them away." The carcasses of the animals attracted the birds of prey, which are also used to represent demonic spirits. The birds wanted to gain access to the carcasses of the animals, so they could devour them. This is what Satan does with scribes.

Every scribe has a story that was birthed in a storm. Now, in every bad story, there is wisdom to be had—the person who experienced it simply must focus on the goodness of God and what He's brought him or her to, versus what the enemy took the author through. What the author focuses on will determine what he or she takes from any given storm. Again, Satan comes to steal, kill and destroy. We are always looking for Satan to come after our material things, but the truth is, he often comes to deform our perspective. He wants to take every storm and make it appear to be another victory for him and his team, robbing us of the wisdom, revelation and information that every storm has. This is why it's necessary to make up our minds in advance to forgive the people who *will* hurt us someday; this way, we aren't so emotionally overwhelmed that we end up inviting the enemy into our hearts. When a scribe's perspective has been deformed, the scribe will release what should have been waste into his or her book. Anytime you release a burden to anyone but Jesus Christ, you share that burden with that person. Do you know that some of the warfare you experienced in life may have been the direct result of a book you read? The author released his or her waste into your life, thus causing the pests and the predators swarming around their minds to come into your life.

Satan uses moments of offense, hurt, rejection, perceived rejection and the like to steal revelation from scribes, after all, a scribe's words are his or her wealth. When Satan successfully robs scribes, he provokes them to parade their pain on the pages of their books. There's nothing worse than having survived a storm, only to come out of it empty-handed with nothing but offense and a warped perspective. In this, the enemy is not only able to rob the scribe of the wisdom, knowledge, understanding and revelation the author needed to set people free, but he also robs the author of his or her freedom. Satan uses bound people to bind people. Let's revisit the story of the unforgiving servant. The unforgiving servant lost everything he had, including his freedom. He lost his wife, children, and his servants all because he chose not to forgive. Imagine if he'd decided to write a book from his prison cell, detailing his ordeal, but never taking the time to take accountability for his role in his own bondage. He'd likely say he'd lost everything because he had servants who owed him money but refused to pay him. For this reason, he could not pay his debts. And he would be sharing facts. Again, facts and truth are not one and the same; facts deal with the fruit of a thing, but the truth deals with the root of it. His book could have been a Christian book filled with blame and laced with pride. This book wouldn't set people free; it would only serve to bind and rob them as well.

Satan seeks to rob scribes of their words, integrity, honor and their good names. He wants to bring an accusation against every godly scribe; this way, he can discredit every person who God chooses to speak to and through. As a scribe, you have to walk in holiness and be intentional about avoiding sin and even the appearance of evil. Satan wants to pervert you so that he can pervert what comes out of you. You should be diligent about remaining free. The unforgiving servant had one assignment after his master had forgiven him and that was to forgive his own servants. Greed would not allow him to do this. Pride would not allow him to do this. Unforgiveness would not allow him to do this. This is the reason we have to wrestle down every ungodly thought and imagination that dares to rise against the knowledge of God and bring into captivity every thought to the obedience of Christ. When temptation comes your way, always remind yourself that Satan is simply trying to lure you, so he can rob you. Don't fall into the trap. The more intentional a scribe is, the more God will use that scribe. Remember, you aren't just a vessel of words; you are words. Pride, unforgiveness, strife and greed are darts that the enemy throws, and if they successfully hit their mark, they will always serve as windows into your heart, thus allowing the enemy to come in and steal everything that is not nailed down. Don't let Satan rob you of your very peace. Don't let Satan rob you of your very identity. Don't let Satan rob you of your assignment. What is your identity? The following scriptures will give you, insight into who you really are.

Genesis 1:27 (ESV): So God created man in his own image, in the image of God he created him; male and female he created them.

2 Corinthians 5:17 (ESV): Therefore, if anyone is in Christ, he is a new creation. The old has passed away; behold, the new has come.

Jeremiah 1:5 (ESV): Before I formed you in the womb I knew you, and before you were born I consecrated you; I appointed you a prophet to the nations."

1 Peter 2:9 (ESV): But you are a chosen race, a royal priesthood, a holy nation, a people for his own possession, that you may proclaim the excellencies of him who called you out of darkness into his marvelous light.

John 15:15 (ESV): No longer do I call you servants, for the servant does not know what his master is doing; but I have called you friends, for all that I have heard from my Father I have made known to you.

The Weight of Your Words

Words have weight. I remember being in a season where it seemed as if everyone around me was far too sensitive to be corrected. I loved the Lord, was teaching His Word and was not in any form of rebellion (that I knew of). Nevertheless, when a friend of mine would do something disrespectful or offensive, I would always wrestle with the offense, pray about it and wait until I'd forgiven that friend before I would correct him or her. Even then, I'd search for the right words, not because I feared my friends, but because I worried that I would shatter them if I didn't sift through my thoughts and choose my words carefully. Why did I think like this? It's simple. Over the course of my life, I had gotten in plenty of trouble for saying the wrong things, oftentimes at the wrong time. I didn't know how to navigate through conflict; I simply went straight to the point. What I'd pretty much gathered from the people closest to me was that I didn't lubricate an interaction before charging in with the hard facts. As a child, I'd gotten in trouble for this a lot. I didn't raise my voice at my parents. I've never run away from home and I have never (intentionally) used profanity in my parents' presence. Nevertheless, I didn't know how to build a conversation or ease my way to a point. If I believed someone was crazy, I wouldn't say that the person needed rest; I'd say they needed a straitjacket. In short, I lacked tact. Not only did I lack tact, I didn't want tact. Tact, to me, allowed crazy folks to stick around for far too long. I just wanted to tell the truth.

Of course, I now know that the truth can be weighty. Evidence of the truth can be weighty. In the American culture, we like to build a foundation of compliments, followed by a few gifts and words of affirmation before stacking the truth on top of all the niceties. We like to remind people that we love them, pretend to be interested in whatever it is they're working towards and then, when they're all buttered up and smiling, we hit them right between the eyes with the truth. While this may seem deceptive today, it can be the most effective mode of navigating our way through offense and conflict. In the Western world, this is called culture.

Scribes release words. Scribes are words. As a teacher and a scribe, you will find that the more you study *and* submit to the Word of God, the more your contact list will thin out. This is the process of ascension. Remember, if a team of hikers heads up a great mountain, the team will begin to thin out over time. Only a few will reach the top, while others will have made great accomplishments by going higher than anyone in their families have ever gone. For them, this is a humongous achievement; it is good enough, but you may be called to the top of the mountain. Nevertheless, every level of ascension requires that you take in more Word. You'll get bolder and you'll get wiser. For this reason, your writings will take on a different tone. The winds of doctrine at the highest levels of a mountain are high. This means that you will need enough Word in you to weigh you down. The higher you go, the more predators you'll encounter. This means you'll need enough confidence in the Word to ground you. This also means that you won't be tossed to and fro anymore; you'll be grounded in your beliefs. In layman's terms, your weight in the realm of the spirit has changed and your words now carry more weight. You can always measure the weight of a scribe's words just by how demons respond to him or her.

The more weight God gives you in the realm of the spirit, the more responsible He expects you to be with your words. You can't just write what you "feel" like writing anymore; you'll have to write what He tells you to write. At the same time, you'll learn to exercise tact. For example, the first line or first chapter in your book shouldn't say that clubbing is a sin. We know this! Most people in the clubs know this, so you'll have to work your way into that conversation in a loving way. You can share your testimony or write a loving poem. The first line or chapter in your book shouldn't say that fornication is a sin. People know this! Sure, those who practice abstinence will cheer you on, but the ones who don't will feel ostracized and judged. You must build the conversation before you invite them into it. Your first book or media introduction shouldn't come off as judgmental; you have to build a relationship and a rapport with your readers before you start trying to have hard conversations with them, otherwise, you can go through what is referred to in the actor's world as typecasting. Google defines "typecast" this way: assign (an actor or actress) repeatedly to the same type of role, as a result of the appropriateness of their appearance or previous success in such roles.

When an author is typecast, people start to control the author's words. How so? For example, I've written a lot of books and recorded a lot of videos about singleness. I noticed that anytime I would try to speak about a different subject, I wouldn't get even half the views or sales I'd normally get. This meant that I had been typecast. To break this, I had to teach about whatever God told me to teach about and just ignore the small numbers. I had to also accept that in the relationship arena, my words weighed more than they did in other arenas. Additionally, another form of typecasting in the writers' world takes place when an author comes off as critical in his or her first book. This is because the author has not built his or her way up to correcting people. Relationship comes before correction. For example, I recorded many videos before I recorded *The Reason for the Wait* on YouTube. Most of those videos were "how to" videos. *The Reason for the Wait*, on the other hand, was more corrective. To date, that video has close to three hundred thousand views and more than 98 percent of the comments are positive. If it had been my first video and if I hadn't had any books or articles out before the video, I may have received a lot of negative feedback because people didn't know me enough for me to be correcting them. Now, the people who follow my ministry aren't offended when I come with a word of correction because they've followed me long enough to know my heart. When someone comes along and gets offended, it's only because that person hasn't followed me for very long. Should that individual leave a negative comment, for example, on a video of mine, many of the people who are familiar with my ministry assignment will give that person a loving word of correction. They'll say things like, "Obviously, you haven't been following her for long," or "You don't know her story." This is because I built rapport before I started trying to correct folks. If my first book or video had been corrective, I could have easily been typecast as just another angry author. Think of it this way. Imagine that you're visiting a church for the very first time. Service is great, and the people seem to be friendly, but at the end of service, you decide to stand in line to greet the pastor. When it's your turn, the pastor looks at you and says, "I appreciate you coming up here to greet us, but next time, please wear looser pants. What you're wearing is not only distracting, but it's distasteful." Would you return to that church? Absolutely not! Why is this? The answer is simple. The pastor hasn't built enough trust and rapport with you to throw such weighty words at you. Why do people think things are different in the author/reader relationship?

As an author, always be mindful of, not just what you write, but how you write. Your tone can make or break your book. Also, be mindful of your target audience. Make sure that your words aren't too weighty for your readers. Books about single living, for example, are generally written for and read by young women who, quite honestly, are focused or overly focused on marriage. These women are oftentimes babes in Christ, with many of them being maturing believers. Talking about jurisdictional lines and measures could be too weighty for them. You can introduce them to the concept, but if you do this, it is always wise to have other books and/or media that they can source from. In other words, you have to give them something to swallow down the information with. You can tell them to check out a specific book that you or another author has written. Additionally, you can introduce them to the spirit realm; that is, if you don't keep them in the subject for too long. You can write a few sentences, detailing the differences between the three levels of a man which are the body, soul and spirit. From there, you could help the readers to understand how the enemy affects every level of a man and how this affects relationships on every plane. Remember, don't take your readers too deep for too long or you'll drown them. Give them just enough information to wet their palettes and then, bring them back to the surface. Your next book or video can take them deeper into the topic of spirituality, ranks, rules and measures, but to do this, you must pay attention to how they respond to your book. Think of it this way. We all introduce our children to meat at some point in their lives, especially those of us who are carnivores. When feeding meat to a baby, parents will often chew the meat until it is at the consistency they believe their babies can manage. Just breaking off a piece of steak and placing it in the mouth of a four-month-old is dangerous because the infant has no teeth to chew what's been given to him or her. So, the parent will chew the meat, reach into his or her mouth and proceed to feed the food to the infant. How the child responds will determine if the parent continues giving steak to the baby at that consistency or at all, for that matter. If the baby seems to have trouble managing the steak and begins to choke, most parents will turn the infant's body until his or her mouth is facing downward. They will then begin to pet or pound on the baby's back until the baby spits the meat out. If the food has gone into the baby's throat, some parents will stick their index finger into the baby's mouth and move it towards the throat area until the food is dislodged and expelled from the baby's throat and mouth. From there, the parent will either choose to chew the meat a little longer, breaking it down even more so the baby can effectively chew and swallow the meat, or the parent will decide that the infant is not yet ready for meat. Lastly, the parent will give the baby something to drink to help him or her swallow down the food, after all, the muscles in a child's esophagus aren't strong enough to push down certain foods on their own. As authors, we pretty much do the same thing with our readers, only it is better to test the market by writing articles and blogs, as well as recording videos before publishing the information in a book. In this, you are not testing the weight of your words, you are testing the appetite and strength of your readers.

God won't put more on us than we can bear. We've all heard this statement, and of course, it's not *exactly* what 1 Corinthians 10:13 states; it reads, "No temptation has overtaken you that is not common to man. God is faithful, and <u>He will not let you be tempted beyond your ability</u>, but with the temptation He will also provide the way of escape, that you may be able to endure it" (ESV)." In short, saying that God won't put more on us than we can bear isn't exactly erroneous; it's simply incomplete, given the fact that God doesn't tempt us with evil. James 4:13-14 reads, "Let no man say when he is tempted, I am tempted of God: for God cannot be tempted with evil, neither tempteth he any man: But every man is tempted, when he is drawn away of his own lust, and enticed." What does this mean?

1. God puts weights on us to increase our strength and these weights come in the form of talents. Remember, a gold talent was typically 110 pounds which was, during the biblical times, the standard weight of a man. Nevertheless, this isn't temptation to sin; it is simply more responsibility (even though some people use it as an excuse to sin). God gave the unfaithful servant one talent, another servant two talents and the most faithful servant received five talents. This is an example of God giving us only that in which we can bear.
2. Temptation comes from the devil.

When God gives us greater responsibility, that weight can feel like warfare when we don't think we have the strength to pick up and carry it, and when we don't think we're smart enough or good enough to balance the weight in the marketplace. In the parable of the talents, the unfaithful servant buried his talent, meaning, he refused to be responsible with what he had been given. He didn't want to carry the weight his master had gifted him with, so he buried it. Words are like talents. They are designed to be heavy enough to get the reader's attention and bearable enough to keep it. This provokes the readers to put down their sins and their burdens and carry their newfound revelation. It is also designed to provoke the readers to dig up whatever gifts and assignments they may have buried. Readers soon learn that if they're strong enough to carry the weight of your words, they are strong enough to carry the weight of the Word of God. This strengthens them and helps them to see how bearable their responsibilities (talents, gifts and assignments) really are. Think about a nine-year-old boy. Imagine that he's your son and you've told him to go into your car and bring in a box that weighs approximately fifteen pounds. He picks it up and carries it into the house. As a parent, you will pay attention to:

1. The sounds he emits while carrying the box. Sounds can be groans or they can come in the form of words. One of the purposes of sound is to notify anyone within earshot of us if and when we are in need of assistance.

2. The expressions on his face while he is carrying the box. Expressions help us to determine if something is bearable or if it's unbearable. When something is bearable but heavy, we will often bite our lips and stretch our necks. Nevertheless, we are still conscious about how we look to others. When something is unbearable to us, quite frankly, we don't care or think about we look. We'll use every muscle in our faces to relay our distress.

3. Your child's body language or the position of his body while carrying the box. If his knees are bent slightly, you'll reason that he can carry 15 pounds, but if his knees are bent to the point where he can barely walk, you will rush over and grab the box out of his hands or send someone who's stronger to assist him.

As an author, it is important that you pay attention to the sounds (response) from your readers, the expressions (ratings) your readers give and the posture (impact) that your book provokes in the readers. People respond with reviews, videos, comments and the like. They also respond by telling others about your book (word of mouth). These are the sounds you'll need to look for. People express their love or disdain for your book by rating it and in some cases, not rating it at all. Lastly, the posture of your readers will help you to see the impact, if any, that your book has had. For example, if a fornicator stops fornicating because of your book, the words were weighty enough to get him or her to bury lust and rejection. If the book is too weighty, most readers won't read it from cover to cover; instead, they'll close the book and keep planning to read it when they have more time. This doesn't mean the book was too much for the reader; it could mean that the reader bit off more than he or she could chew, so the reader needs to take some time to digest what he or she has already ingested. This is the reason you should never rush readers to give you a review. It's great to ask for reviews, but never put pressure on people to give them, otherwise, you may get a negative review from a reader who isn't yet mature enough to chew or ingest what he or she has read.

The Laws of Authorship

For thousands of years, scribes had been writing about the coming of the Christ, but when He finally manifested in the flesh, many of them wanted to kill Him. After all, Jesus was a major earthquake; He shook up their worlds, turned over their tables and brought light to a very dark world. Another moment in creation took place. Mankind found himself in the Genesis of the New Testament, whereas, God was once again declaring, "Let there be light." Darkness had been on the face of the Earth and now, the Day had finally come around. That Light was and is Jesus Christ. He had no desire to pair up with the scribes of that time; instead, He chose His own disciples. He didn't have to be invited into a synagogue to teach; instead, He taught in the streets, He taught from a boat and He taught on a mountain. Of course, He also taught in some synagogues. Jesus didn't need a man-made platform; He simply needed ears that were willing to hear what He had to say. He taught while in the midst of people who envied Him, hated Him and wanted to take His life. He didn't do as Peter did — He didn't secretly hang with Gentiles, but publicly sit with the circumcised Jews. No, He disrupted religious devils by doing things that went against the traditions of that time. He didn't rebel against the law; He came to fulfill the law and give people hope. Nevertheless, many of the scribes of that time, along with the Pharisees and Sadducees, were determined to retain their positions amongst men. They loved the darkness of the night and they loved the praise of men. They felt that Jesus was a threat to the offices they held, so even though they taught, "Thy shalt not kill," they conspired to kill the Lord. Even though they published, "Thy shalt not covet," they coveted His position. They broke every single commandment in the Bible. They broke every single law that they'd promised to uphold.

And now, here you are—a scribe. But you are a Kingdom scribe who's been given the talent (burden) of writing. Who knows? Maybe your books will someday save lives or they may save nations. Your journey starts with a single keystroke. You may be a surface-level scribe, or you may be a fifth level scribe; what's important is that you write on your level and that you are driven by the reverence (fear) of God and love for His people. Additionally, you have to respect every platform that you are assigned to touch. For example, as a scribe and a writer, you should never speak against the pulpit. The general rule of thumb is to teach the people of God in love. If they have been deceived into following false leaders or movements, the words you teach may be enough to open their eyes. Remember, every individual is a compilation of words brought together by agreement and deliverance isn't just casting out devils, it's casting down words. With that being said, it is important that you listen and learn more than you teach.

Levels	Gifts
Crust (First Level)	Teacher
Mantle (Second Level)	Pastor
Outer Core (Third Level)	Evangelist
Inner Core (Fourth Level)	Prophet
Inner Inner Core (Fifth Level)	Apostle

Earlier, we discussed the levels of the Earth and how they relate to our teaching styles. What we learned is that the first level (teacher) is the most common scribe. Nevertheless, what we did not learn was that the teacher can teach on varying levels, including the level of an apostle. This is, of course, if the teacher has studied the Word of God line upon line, precept upon precept and God has invited the teacher into that level of revelation. Additionally, an apostle can teach on the level of a pastor if God hasn't invited him or her into that level of revelation or the apostle simply hasn't accepted God's invitation. Titles don't entitle us to the mysteries of God. God chooses specific people to learn, be tested at and teach on certain levels, and we have to be okay with this. The point is, while this scale helps us to understand levels, it does not mean that someone who has a specific title teaches on the level displayed. You can very well be an evangelist with apostolic insight, however, it is important to note that this doesn't change your assignment. It simply means that God trusts you with certain information or you may be seated under and learning from an apostle. It's important for you to remember to ascend and descend to the level that God has called you to write on. For example, if you are an evangelist and God gives you the assignment to write a book on the fourth level (prophetic), you need to sit under or with some prophets and test every spirit that speaks to you. Your invitation into a new realm has to be respected if it is to remain open. Consider the time when King Saul was in the company of prophets. 1 Samuel 19 tells the story.

1 Samuel 19:18-24: So David fled, and escaped, and came to Samuel to Ramah, and told him all that Saul had done to him. And he and Samuel went and dwelt in Naioth. And it was told Saul, saying, Behold, David is at Naioth in Ramah. And Saul sent messengers to take David: and when they saw the company of the prophets prophesying, and Samuel standing as appointed over them, the Spirit of God was upon the messengers of Saul, and they also prophesied. And when it was told Saul, he sent other messengers, and they prophesied likewise. And Saul sent messengers again the third time, and they prophesied also. Then went he also to Ramah, and came to a great well that is in Sechu: and he asked and said, Where are Samuel and David? And one said, Behold, they be at Naioth in Ramah. And he went thither to Naioth in Ramah: and the Spirit of God was upon him also, and he went on, and prophesied, until he came to Naioth in Ramah. And he stripped off his clothes also, and prophesied before Samuel in like manner, and lay down naked all that day and all that night. Wherefore they say, Is Saul also among the prophets?

Matthew 10:41: He that receiveth a prophet in the name of a prophet shall receive a prophet's reward; and he that receiveth a righteous man in the name of a righteous man shall receive a righteous man's reward.

Layers of the Earth	Gifts	Talents	Tabernacle of Moses	Ascension Process	Man	Power
Crust	Teacher	1	Gate/ Entrance	Enter	Mind	900000 (Minor Earthquake)
Mantle	Pastor	2	Outer Courtyard	Sacrifice/ Cleansing	Body	30000 (Minor to moderate Earthquake)
Outer Core	Evangelist	3	Outer	Praise	Soul	500

			Courtyard			(Moderate Earthquake)
Inner Core	Prophet	4	Holy Place	Worship	Man's Spirit	100 (Strong Earthquake)
Inner Inner Core	Apostle	5	Holy of Holies	Encounter	God's Spirit	20 (Major Earthquake)

The purpose of the above chart is to help you get a better understanding of responsibility. Every scribe has a certain measure of power and with that power comes responsibility. Every (godly) scribe has a certain measure of access to God; some scribes have intimate access into the heart of God, while others rely on the encounters that others have. This mirrors an assembly line at a factory, where one man takes a huge bag of rice and passes it to another man who passes it to another. This continues until the rice is in a box prepared to be shipped to its next destination. This is the very picture of a system. Just like in the body of Christ, everything in a system is designed to work together towards a common goal. Romans 8:28 says it this way, "And we know that all things work together for good to them that love God, to them who are the called according to his purpose." In order for two or more things to work together, they have to agree. "Can two walk together, except they be agreed?" (Amos 3:3). For example, let's say that you are a teacher who's been teaching for 24 years. In your 24 years of ministry, you've never cast out a devil, nor has healing ever passed through your fingertips. Your responsibility for those 24 years was to teach God's people; that's it and that's all. Nevertheless, you hear about a church down the street from your church where people are going to get set free from demonic bondage, plus, a lot of reports of healing have emerged from that church. You don't understand this, after all, God still uses you. You've pastored more than five hundred souls for 24 years and you've followed the very same system your former pastor and your colleagues have followed. You served under your pastor as an armor bearer for ten years before you ever touched a mic. Howbeit, the guy up the street has only been in ministry for three years and he's never served as an armor bearer. Instead, he swept floors at his pastor's church for a single year before he was released by his pastor to start his own church. Everyone says the man is a very energetic prophet who blows on people, openly engages devils while taking people through deliverance and is passionate about the prosperity gospel, all of which are foreign to you. Some of the members of your church have even gone into his church and undergone deliverance. What you're experiencing on your block is an earthquake (revival) with a magnitude greater than the one that God has entrusted you with, and this is okay. Your assignment isn't to look for error in the man or attempt to discredit him; your assignment is to study the Word so that you can show yourself approved. What God wants to do is create a system in that area; He wants you to work with the guy to bring revival to that community, but if you allow your lack of understanding, your church's culture, jealousy or the spirit of competition to bind you, you can easily miss an opportunity to walk at and experience a whole other level of power. God works through cross-pollination, so if you remain prayerful and humble, all the while resolving in your heart to not raise up against another servant of God, a system will be established between the two of you. He will pass revelation and power to you and you can pass the wisdom you've learned in those 24 years of ministry to him. Sure, he may have intimate access to God, but this doesn't mean that you are a heathen. It can simply mean that the prophet could bear more than you can. Let's revisit the parable of the talents. Remember, a gold talent was typically the weight of a small man (110 pounds). The unfaithful servant buried his talent, while the faithful one increased his. Let's look at this from another perspective. The unfaithful servant could not bear his own weight. Maybe he lived with his parents. Maybe he complained about the heat outside and the pain in his back every time his father told him to go and work in the field. It may seem unfair for God to give one man a single talent, all the while, giving another man five talents, but believe it or not, this is called mercy. Understand this: the man with five talents did not have it easy. He had to carry that burden around with him. An apostle's life isn't easy; they have to carry around immeasurable burdens. A prophet's life isn't easy! They have to endure seasons and tests that would kill most folks. The point is, God gave you what you could handle. He understood the warfare that would come with the mantle, and because that warfare would have been too great for you, He decided to use you on another level. Your job is to take the revelation that the prophet up the street shares, ruminate it and feed it to the people God has entrusted you with; that is, if God tells you to do so. Your job is to prepare the people for revival. You get to explain things on a level that the other man of God cannot. It is always an honor to be used by God on any level. Take joy in this.

The Practical and the Spiritual Laws of Authorship

1. Do not speak against God-raised leaders and/or the platforms they stand on.
2. Do not speak against what you do not understand. Just pray.
3. Do not lie to sell books.
4. Do not draw men to yourself; refer them to God.
5. Inquire of the Lord before writing.
6. Always have a multitude of counselors.
7. Don't quit just because you can.
8. Respect the doorkeepers of revelation.
9. Respect your metron.
10. Don't give your readers more than they can chew.
11. Do not run from revelation.
12. Do not cast your pearls (wealth/ wisdom) to swine.
13. Locate the place where God speaks to you the most.
14. Revelation comes out of your belly, not your head.
15. Don't abuse your power.
16. Remain humble.
17. Respect the access that God has granted you.
18. Respect the laws and those who enforce them.

Do not speak against God-raised leaders and/or the platforms they stand on.
In this day and age, it has become common and even trendy for believers and non-believers to speak against God-raised leaders. Of course, this is dishonor, not just to the leader, but to God. The reason God doesn't want us coming up against leaders is because doing so could easily desensitize us to rank and order, thus making it difficult for us to receive correction. We need leaders. As a matter of fact, ungodly leaders help us to appreciate the godly ones. 2 Peter 2:10-12 reads, "But chiefly

them that walk after the flesh in the lust of uncleanness, and <u>despise government</u>. Presumptuous are they, self-willed, <u>they are not afraid to speak evil of dignities</u>. **<u>Whereas angels, which are greater in power and might, bring not railing accusation against them before the Lord.</u>** But these, as natural brute beasts, made to be taken and destroyed, <u>speak evil of the things that they understand not</u>; and shall utterly perish in their own corruption." Government, in this text, comes from the Hebrew word "misrah" and it means: rule or dominion, which are both words used to describe order. The scripture is telling us that there are people out there who despise order, and these are the very people who are not afraid to speak against dignities (people of rank and honor). Nevertheless, even the angels of God—beings who outrank us (see Psalm 8:5)—won't even speak evil of dignities! Another demonstration of this in Jude 1:9, which reads, "Yet Michael the archangel, when contending with the devil he disputed about the body of Moses, durst not bring against him a railing accusation, but said, The Lord rebuke thee."

SOMETIMES, IT'S NOT WARFARE! WHAT YOU SPOKE TO SIMPLY RESPONDED!

This generation has got to understand the power of the tongue! Anything you strike with the tongue has the right to respond to you! The leaders may not respond, but the angels assigned to those leaders may have to defend them from your words. Understand that every evil word spoken is a dart and can only be stopped by another word. The obvious question some people will have is, "What if the leader is in blatant sin? We've all heard about some of the scandalous events surrounding a few men of the cloth!" Satan was guilty of sin when Michael, the archangel, contended with him. Nevertheless, Michael did not overstep his authority, even though he is the "arch" angel, meaning, the chief angel. Even though Satan is a fallen angel, Michael, the archangel, still had to respect his rank. Consider King Saul and David. Regardless of all the evil things Saul did to him, David would not speak evil of Saul, nor would he touch him, even though Saul had been rejected by God. The point is, your goal is to focus on writing what God tells you to write. Don't be distracted by what people are doing, what they have done or what they have the potential to do. Understand this: God knows how to deliver His people better than you can. Use your pen to destroy the works of the devil and be very careful that you don't allow the enemy to lure you into the same trap that Saul fell into.

Do not speak against what you do not understand. Just pray. God uses the foolish things of this world to confound the wise (see 1 Corinthians 1:27). We've all heard it said that God works in mysterious ways. While this isn't found (verbatim) in the Bible, it is true. As a matter of fact, Isaiah 55:9 reads, "For as the heavens are higher than the Earth, so are my ways higher than your ways, and my thoughts than your thoughts." This means that we won't always understand what God is doing, how He's doing it, and who He's doing it through. As a matter of fact, we won't always agree with who God chooses to use, nor will we understand why He chose to use them. With that said, it is important that we don't write or teach against something that God may be for. What's interesting to me is, a lot of people will attack something that God is doing simply because He hasn't taken the time out to explain to them what He's doing. A good example of this is people who teach against the prosperity gospel. While any good thing when done excessively can be overkill, the truth of the matter is, God wants us healed, delivered and living an abundant life; this is what it means to be whole. It is important that we don't box God into our experiences with Him, after all, He can do exceedingly, abundantly above all that we ask or think, according to the power that works in us (see Ephesians 3:20). In layman's terms, don't behave like the disciples when they saw a man casting demons out of folks who they believed should not have been qualified to do so. How did Jesus respond to them? The answer is found in Luke 9:50. "And Jesus said unto him, Forbid him not: for he that is not against us is for us." If you don't understand something, seek to stretch your understanding through prayer and studying, instead of trying to shrink everyone to fit your understanding.

Do not lie to sell books. Lies can be entertaining; lies can and do sell books, but they don't set people free. Instead, they lead people into bondage. John 8:32 reads, "And ye shall know the truth, and the truth shall make you free." If you're patient and you tune in to the heart of God, He will give you fresh revelation for your book. Always remember that God doesn't need your help to sell books; He simply needs you to be obedient. Sure, some lies don't appear to be major, nevertheless, one little white lie has the power to destroy the integrity of a book and the author of that book.

Do not draw men to yourself; refer them to God. Jesus said in John 12:32, "And I, if I be lifted up from the Earth, will draw all men unto me." There are real people with real problems and real devils out there who need Jesus. Don't grab their attention and start entertaining them just because you want to be celebrated. Imagine what would have happened if, after having split the Red Sea, Moses had started feeling prideful. What would have happened if, instead of leading the people of God to safety, Moses had decided to get the crowd to gather around him so that he could talk about himself? Our Bibles probably would have been much thicker. I'm sure God would have still rescued His people, but Moses could have easily been drowned in the Red Sea.

Your book isn't about making you famous. Your book should be all about helping God's people and giving God the glory.

Inquire of the Lord before writing. One of the most effective ways to avoid writers' block is by praying before writing; this way, you don't have to repeatedly tap into your intellect to get the content for your book. Prayer allows us to draw close to God, and if we do this with our hearts, we can tap into God's intellect. You'd be amazed at how much of your book's content will be the revelation that God suddenly shares with you while you write!

Always have a multitude of counselors. Proverbs 11:14 reads, "Where no counsel is, the people fall: but in the multitude of counselors there is safety." A counselor is an adviser; this is someone who tells you that what you thought was a good idea could actually end up destroying your book. A counselor is someone who's been where you're trying to go. The President of the United States has advisers. Most, if not all, kings in the biblical days had advisers. As a matter of fact, King Henry VIII of England is infamous for his decision to separate the Church of England from papal supremacy. During that time, the king had to submit to the Catholic Church and follow the instructions of the Pope. Nevertheless, he passionately wanted to divorce his first wife, Catherine of Aragon, to which, the Pope said no. He then elected himself as the Supreme Head of the Church of England. King Henry VIII hated the word no so much that he changed the laws to get his way. Consequentially, he ended up marrying six times (he had two of his wives beheaded, he divorced another two, one died after childbirth and one succeeded him in death). Additionally, he became morbidly obese later in life so-much-so that devices were created to help move him around. To add insult to injury, he was believed to have gone mad and this madness had once been attributed to syphilis. This belief was debunked by historians who now believed that he may have suffered from scurvy. The short of it all is this ... King Henry made a lot of poor decisions, many of which led to his untimely death at the age of 55. He is a good example of why we need a multitude of counselors. We all need someone to be accountable to.

Don't quit just because you can. God has given us all freewill. We are free to win, and we are free to fail. We are free to obey Him, and we are bound to disobey Him. With that being noted, it is important for us to not abuse the authority God has entrusted us with. How so? It's simple; we don't have the right to quit, even though we have the ability to do so. Writing a book can be mentally, physically and spiritually draining; it can be a very taxing event. For this reason, many authors don't finish their books simply because the process of writing wasn't as glamorous as they'd imagined it to be. Writing is just as much of a spiritual act as it is a physical one. With that said, you can't expect to charge into the devil's camp and start rescuing folks without there being some measure of resistance. Mentally and spiritually prepare yourself for anything the devil might throw your way. You can do this by praying and fasting while writing. Quitting should never be an option for a believer on assignment.

Respect the doorkeepers of revelation. As you journey through knowledge and revelation, you may find yourself bumping into one of the doorkeepers of revelation. Again, this happens when you're going outside of your metron. How do you know when you've encountered a doorkeeper versus when you're just tired? The easiest way to know is by praying and resting when necessary. As for me, I may be writing on a subject and suddenly feel some resistance. In that moment, I find it hard to think. In that moment, I find it hard to concentrate, so I'll skip the chapter I'm working on and start another one. Once I come back to the paragraph that was difficult to write, I'll assess how I am. If I still can't think of the right words to write, I'll back off by hitting backspace. I'll delete the text that was leading to that point and start writing something else. I've found this to be VERY effective. There have been times when, after writing a few lines of text, I've felt extremely discouraged and I simply could not think of the next line to write. After deleting the paragraph or the lines of text that I'd written and changing directions, I've been able to start flowing all over again. Remember, the doorkeeper cannot stop you from moving forward; you have to stop yourself.

Respect your metron. Your metron is your measure; it is your jurisdictional rule. It is the height, width and depth of your God-given assignment. There are boundaries around your assignment, and outside of these boundaries, your authority is severely limited. One of the temptations you'll endure as an author is the temptation to steal another author's idea. Ignore this desire, cast it down and move beyond it! However high, far or deep God calls you, that's the distance you need to go. If someone asks you to write about something outside of your metron, politely decline the offer. Don't try to be deeper than you are or you'll drown yourself and/or your readers. Just be who God has designed you to be and write on the level He's assigned you to write.

Don't give your readers more than they can chew. Remember, revelation has to be chewed, ingested and digested. Sure, your vocabulary may be extensive and your friends, who all happen to be authors, may write some deep, revelatory books. Nevertheless, what they feed their readers may be too rich, too tough or too sweet for your readers. Think of it this way. A mother has twin girls who are three months old. Her best friend also has twin daughters, but her daughters are four years old. Would you feed your daughters what she feeds hers? Absolutely not! Why is this? Because her daughters likely have a full set of teeth, enough power in their jaws to chew whatever their mother gives them, and they have the bellies to digest what they've eaten. Your daughters, on the other hand, need milk and maybe a little cereal in their milk. The same is true for readers. Don't feed your readers the same diet another author feeds his or her readers. How do you know what your crowd can digest? It's simple. Just write the words that God gives you without trying to sound intelligent or deep. Write posts in your blog and on your social media page, and then, pay attention to who responds. Look at the common denominators with all or most of your followers. Are they babes in Christ? Understand that babes often wrestle with fornication, can be emotionally unstable, and are often still in love with worldly music, cultures and people. Feed them at the consistency they need to grow. This means you have to break down what you're teaching until it's at a consistency that they can take in.

Do not run from revelation. Believe it or not, there are some third and fourth level writers who absolutely do not like to teach on their levels. They'd rather teach on the first level because that level is nowhere near as draining as the levels they're called to teach on. For example, they can write a surface-level book about prayer in the matter of a week. Nevertheless, when the Lord instructs them to write about a deep and revelatory book about prayer, they'll keep putting it off because they know this book won't come out of their intellect. They'll have to fully rely on God as they write, and while it may seem easy, it can be rather taxing because they'll have to constantly pull their flesh down to ascend into God's presence. When authors tap more into the spiritual side of writing, they often find themselves mentally exhausted after writing. This weariness finds its way into their bodies, causing the authors to nap more than they usually do. Nevertheless, make up your mind to finish strong. Let God lead you into His mysteries and just ask Him to strengthen, protect and keep you as you write. Again, don't quit just because you can. Continue to ascend with the Lord until you reach the peak (point) of your book.

Do not cast your pearls (wealth/ wisdom) to swine. The enemy often throws everything he can find at authors to stop them from writing. Nevertheless, one of his most effective warfare strategies is to attack the author's finances. Understand this: if God gives you the vision, He will give you the provision, but the enemy knows that if our funds are low, we'll want to guard every penny with our lives. Of course, there are those authors who are so determined to finish their books and get them published that they've decided to throw their last few pennies at the editing and publishing process. For these authors, the enemy employs a different set of weapons. For example, the enemy will often appeal to a single woman's desire to get married. He'll send a man her way who appears to want the same things she wants. This man will speak nonstop about marriage and will be eager to either marry or bed the woman. This is an attack, even though it doesn't look like one. Captivated by the idea that she could be married soon, the aspiring author all of a sudden starts using the funds God gave her to publish her book towards decorating herself. Now, she's determined to impress her beau. The enemy has her throwing all of her wealth and wisdom at a man who, quite frankly, is entertaining the devils of rejection, lust, pride and/or adultery. And throwing wealth at the enemy isn't always direct. Instead, the could-be author is now overly obsessed with her appearance. Every extra dollar she finds will go towards new clothes, getting her nails done, getting her hair styled or doing something to keep the man's attention. This is especially true if the man rejects or threatens to reject her (indirectly or directly). Always remember that every opportunity isn't a good opportunity. Sometimes, what appears to be destiny is just Satan luring you out of your assignment.

Locate the place where God speaks to you the most. For me, I hear Him the clearest when I'm upstairs. When I'm writing, I'll have those times when I decide to take a break and go upstairs for something. It is during those times that revelation starts flowing, so for this very reason, if I find myself stuck, I'll grab a notebook and head upstairs. Your place of encounter may be your car, your closet or your bedroom. I've even met people who've said that they hear God the most in the bathroom. Wherever your place of encounter is, go there, take a notebook with you and wait (patiently) for God to speak.

Revelation comes out of your belly, not your head. The belly, biblically speaking, is the digestive center of your heart. The way this works is, we take knowledge in and ingest it. As it sits in our bellies, the Word of God helps us to extract the nutrients (understanding, discernment) from it. When understanding has matured, it becomes wisdom. Knowledge is taken in, but wisdom is what emerges and goes forth from our mouths. What does this mean to you, the scribe? Stop looking for revelation in your head; it's not there. Authors who sit for hours trying to figure out what to write often abandon their books. When you're in front of your computer (or whatever you're using to write your book), you can tap into your head-knowledge, but you have to tarry (wait) for revelation. How does this look? It looks like someone sitting at a computer and thinking, only the information doesn't come from their heads or their hearts; it simply drops in their spirits. Of course, this isn't for all authors; this pointer is authors who are prophetically in tune with the heart and voice of God.

Don't abuse your power. Every person has a measure of power; please note that power isn't always physical strength or ability. You can be a powerful negotiator, sales rep, dancer, marketing strategist, and the list goes on. Believe it or not, beauty is a power and some people abuse that power. Power is and can be anything you use to lure or repel people. God us to lift Him up; this way, all men are drawn to Him, but some authors use other devices to sell books. If God has given you the charge and the ability to write books, just submit to His voice and write what He tells you. Don't place enticing photos of yourself on the cover or go out of your way to have a controversial title. Taking the controversial route is like throwing a party and inviting nothing but self-proclaimed critics to that party. The people of God just need the truth; that's it and that's all. Books take time to sell (in many cases). You have to be patient and steadfast. You can write twenty books and they not be bestsellers, and all of a sudden, your twenty-first book finds its way to the bestseller's list. In other words, you must to be patient.

Remain humble. One of the strongmen that's attracted to knowledge is pride. 1 Corinthians 8:1 warns us this way, "Now concerning food offered to idols: we know that "all of us possess knowledge." This "knowledge" puffs up, but love builds up." Earlier, we talked about the belly of the believer. Remember, knowledge goes into the belly, matures into understanding and comes out of the mouth as wisdom. But just like food, it enlarges our bellies. We have to work out this knowledge so that it does not swell our egos, thus, making us ineffective witnesses for the Lord. As God gives you access to the vault of wisdom, it becomes easier for you to be prideful than it is for you to remain humble. This means that you have to humble yourself, which means to intentionally and aggressively pull yourself down. The word "humble" comes from the word human; it means that you have the responsibility of reminding yourself that you are human or, better yet, a humbled man.

Respect the access that God has granted you. Earlier on, we talked about our mindsets being like cages, with every man having his own cage. In every cage, there is a Goliath. If you were to look into one cage, you'd find a man slaying his Goliath, in another cage, you'd find a woman pregnant by her Goliath, and in another cage, you'd find a man playing chess with his Goliath. As we discussed, your assignment as a scribe is to shake up each man's cage until he comes out of it. He then enters a larger cage, where he'll find an even bigger Goliath awaiting him. He must then overcome that giant and move on to a bigger cage where he has more freedom. As you continue to elevate in the Lord, you will meet more people like yourself; these will be men and women of God of varying ranks. When you come across these people, God may test you by allowing you to see their nakedness. By nakedness, I mean their flaws. You'll be given a God's eye view of the Goliaths they're struggling with. Now, if you're religious and think that leaders should be perfect, you'll snatch the cover off the cages and try to make a private struggle a public one. Should you do this, you have proven that you do not respect revelation. Understand this: revelation isn't just a fitting word in due season; revelation comes from the word "reveal." This means that God is sharing His mysteries with you. These are the things that God keeps hidden; He only reveals His mysteries to certain people. Your job is to pray, fast and cover. Galatians 6:1 reads, "Brethren, if a man be overtaken in a fault, ye which are spiritual, restore such an one in the spirit of meekness; considering thyself, lest thou also be tempted." If you take your pen, your keyboard or your mouth and use it to expose another believer, you will fall into the same pit that Ham fell into. The reason this is important to note is because many believers think they have the right, the privilege and the responsibility of attacking platforms that they have yet to stand on. Remember, the Bible tells us that one man plants, another waters, but it is God who gives the increase (see 1 Corinthians 3:6-9). This can also be applied to the backslidden and the double-minded believer. Our job is to either plant or water; we do this by restoring or attempting to restore the person through loving correction. We do this by speaking with their leaders. We do this through intercession. If the believer refuses to repent, it is God who brings the increase, meaning, God will deal with the fallen leader. Our job is to shake up the cage, not uncover it! Ham lost his inheritance because he decided to expose the facts, instead of honoring his father enough to cover him. This doesn't mean that you should turn a blind eye to a man's blatant sins; it simply means that you follow protocol by (again) speaking with the man's leader, restoring the man in the spirit of meekness and letting God do the rest. Sure, this may sound like heresy until you thoroughly study the Bible to see how God dealt with high-ranking men who fell into error. For example, when King David slept with Bathsheba, got her pregnant and then arranged for her husband to be killed, God didn't have one of David's servants to expose him. After all, the men who worked closely with David knew what was going on. He was the king, so there was someone with him at all times! Nevertheless, when God wanted to address a king, He would oftentimes send a prophet who the king

429

knew or knew of. God sent the prophet Nathan to rebuke David. Nathan didn't do this publicly; he went in privately to the king's quarters, told him a parable and then related that parable to what David had done (see 1 Samuel 12). When God sent Elijah to rebuke Ahab, Elijah didn't do so publicly. He sent a message via Obadiah, Ahab's servant, that he wanted to meet him. Elijah told Ahab to gather the prophets of Baal and the people, so they could have a battle of the gods. When the people gathered together, Elijah didn't use that time to expose Ahab; instead, he exposed the devil that Ahab worshipped. He challenged Baal and proved that he did not exist. In other words, be responsible with your words. I can't tell you how many books I've come across from authors who did not understand or apply this principle. If you shake the cage, God will deliver His people; if you uncover the people, God will shake your cage.

Respect the laws and those who enforce them. These laws include the laws of gravity, the laws of any given region, spiritual laws and so on. Anyone who breaks a law is subject to imprisonment (in the natural) and bondage (in the spiritual realm). Bondage isn't always seen, but it can always be witnessed. Let me explain. I design seals and logos for ministries. As of right now, I've worked with more than a thousand ministries to date (we've been in business since 2011). Because I've worked with so many people, I've gained insight into a trend. I have some customers who respect all the laws (rules) posted on my site. They never question the rules, and if they request more revisions than their package allots to them, they'll happily pay the revision fees. When I look up their sites and their branding, I can see success written all over everything that they do; they operate in pure excellence and it's obvious that their churches are growing at a rapid rate. For example, some of the churches are relatively new (less than three years old) and they have already amassed anywhere between two hundred to a few thousand members. On the other hand, I've worked with people who did not respect the posted rules at all. As a matter of fact, they would go out of their way to do business with me the way they want to do business with me. I've had people argue with me about the rules, I've had people to try to manipulate their way around the rules and I've had people demand refunds when I wouldn't break the rules for them. Nevertheless, when I look up these ministries, they are oftentimes small, outdated and struggling. Some of them have been in business for ten years or more, and have only amassed thirty to one hundred members, most of which are older. Some people could argue that these smaller ministries didn't respect rules because they were struggling, but this is not true. They were struggling because they didn't respect rules, meaning, they had not decided to trust God wholeheartedly. When we don't trust God, we trust in our own wiles and we'll break every law that we can break just to get by or get over. As a scribe, your job is to study, study and study some more. You will learn about rules, laws and principles that most people are not aware of. God will give you insight into a realm, but again, your job isn't to expose the people in that realm; your job is to come against the mindset. I've learned that two of the keys to success are respect and honor. If you exemplify these two in everything you do, success will chase you and not the other way around.

Exercising Kingdom Authority

Have you ever wondered why some Christian churches cast out demons, while others do not? Mark 16:16 says, "And these signs shall follow them that believe; in my name shall they cast out devils; they shall speak with new tongues." One of the signs of a believer is the casting out of devils! Nevertheless, some churches don't believe that Christians can have demons. We know that this isn't true because Jesus clearly told us to cast them out. Matthew 10:1 states, "And when he had called unto him his twelve disciples, he gave them power against unclean spirits, to cast them out, and to heal all manner of sickness and all manner of disease."

Earlier on, we established the fact that our vocabularies are a body of words that we've used to build our worlds with. These are the words that are familiar to us; these are the words that people associate with us. When exercising authority over devils, we don't wave our hands at people; we use the Word of God. We command them to come out of God's people in the name of Jesus. Remember, the word "author" is in the word "authority." The word "author" is generally described as a writer of a book or article, but this is a limited definition. In truth, an author is anyone who exercises the authority to create. Remember, nearly every man-made item in the realm of the Earth started off as a picture in a person's mind that the man had to ruminate into words. When man could not transfer that picture, he had to describe it. When the picture came from Heaven to the man, God transcribed it, but when it went from one man to another, it had to be described. This means that anyone who creates anything is an author or an artist. Artists can imagine an image and draw it without the use of words, nevertheless, to copyright their works, they have to name and describe them. Remember, nothing is legally protected either naturally, legally or spiritually without a name. Even demons have names.

TO CHANGE LIVES, YOU HAVE NO CHOICE BUT TO SHAKE UP THE SPIRITUAL WORLD.

It doesn't matter if your book is surface-level or one of the deepest and most prolific books ever written. Anytime you mess with the paradigm of a man, a tremor will be released, and in many cases, you may receive a response from the very world that you've shaken up. Again, if I throw a small rock into a crowd, I may get a faint "ouch," but if I throw a large rock off into a crowd, the response will be louder. When you write a book, you have become a modern-day David shooting a rock into a crowd of Goliaths; it's only natural to receive a response, whether that response is the unforeseen reemergence of an ex, the loss of a job or a sudden release of money that's been held up. The point is, as a scribe, you are starting or ending a conversation every time you strike a key on your keyboard. As a reminder, every man's mindset is his cage; it is the manifestation of his limitations. It is a picture of his world. In every cage, there is a Goliath. Jonah's Goliath was the large fish that swallowed him whole. Elijah's Goliath was Jezebel. Queen Esther's Goliath was Haman. Each of these worlds had to be shaken up before they could be changed. David had several Goliaths (King Saul, Absalom, the infamous Goliath, and himself). Nevertheless, despite the many mistakes of David, God still referred to him as a man after His own heart, but to keep David in line, God had to repeatedly shake up his world. This shaking was designed to grow David up; it was designed to get him to outgrow outdated thinking patterns so that God could do more with him. Thankfully, David realized that he wasn't enduring warfare. He realized that he needed to make some changes to his life. In Psalm 4:1, David wrote, "Hear me when I call, O God of my righteousness: thou hast enlarged me when I was in distress; have mercy upon me, and hear my prayer." Notice that he said God enlarged him when he was in distress. As scribes, our worlds are repeatedly shaken, sometimes by our loving Father who simply wants to grow us up, and other times by the enemy who wants to shut us up. But we've come too far to turn around now. There are too many people relying on us to teach them the undiluted, uncompromising Word of God.

We are authors. We speak words. We write words. We are words. We descend with our readers into the deep and we ascend with our readers to the peaks. More than anything, we have to be careful with the people God has entrusted us with, regardless of whether they warm pews or grace pulpits. Our job is to take the many pictures that God shares with us and to ruminate them. From these images, we extract manna, instructions and vision to deliver to our brethren. We cause earthquakes (revivals) with a single keystroke or the stroke of a pen. Satan fears us because our words outlive us. We write on all levels because God wants us to bind the enemy on all levels. We are never insignificant. We are never irrelevant. Nothing we do is wasted. Nothing we say goes unheard. We move mountains, we influence cultures and we destroy the works of the enemy one word at a time.

The End is the Beginning

Genesis 1:1-3: In the beginning God created the Heaven and the Earth. And the Earth was without form, and void; and darkness was upon the face of the deep. And the Spirit of God moved upon the face of the waters. And God said, Let there be light: and there was light.

John 1:1: In the beginning was the Word, and the Word was with God, and the Word was God.

Revelation 20:12: And I saw the dead, small and great, stand before God; and the books were opened: and another book was opened, which is the book of life: and the dead were judged out of those things which were written in the books, according to their works.

Revelation 22:13: I am Alpha and Omega, the beginning and the end, the first and the last.

What does the aforementioned scriptures have in common? They speak of the beginning and the end. God introduces Himself as Alpha (the beginning) and Omega (the end). What God was doing here is introducing us to a principle. Think of it this way. Life is but a book and we are the words scribbled across the pages of that book. Nevertheless, God is the front cover and He is the back cover. Our lives start and end

433

with Him (He covers us); we are simply living in the in between. He knows the beginning from the end because He is the Author and Finisher of our faith! For example, I've discovered that I absolutely love writing fictional books. When writing a fictional book, I can write the end before I determine the beginning. I can decide how I want the story to play out even before I've given the book a proper name. I can then go back to the beginning and start writing, knowing full-well how the story ends. For example, I can write a story and create a good guy and a villain, after all, this is pretty much the standard for fictional writing. From there, I have the pleasure of creating characters, both good and bad, who my star character is going to meet along the way. *Note: most fictional writers LOVE the process of creating villains; we get to be creative when we describe and assign personalities, weapons and voices to villains.* Again, I know where the main character is going; I'm just finding a creative way to get him there. In my masterpiece, I get to write the guy into many scary, funny and frustrating situations. He'll go through storm after storm to get to the breakthrough that he's been longing for. Maybe he desires to be married, but after a nasty breakup with an ex of his, he finds it difficult to trust women. In the story, I can send him to France, cause him to be hit by a car, wake him up from a two-week coma, have him fall in love with a good, godly French nurse and then, cause his ex to fly to France looking to reconcile with him while he's in the hospital. Her reemergence in his life could be centered around the fact that she's been impregnated and abandoned by the guy she left the main character for, and the fact that main character has been accepted into a prestigious medical school in France. I can have her lying, saying the baby is his, even though they'd never had sex. I could use the fact that he's been in a coma and may be suffering from some mild to moderate memory loss to justify him being so gullible. Sure, this sounds like a dramatic romantic comedy in the making, but I can turn it into a horror story. I can have him reconcile with his ex, even though the answer to his prayers keeps walking into his room to check his vitals. After dating his vilified ex for another three months, I could have him to suddenly start getting all his memory back. One day, he recalls the breakup. He also remembers that he has never been physically intimate with his now girlfriend, so he breaks up with her, only to have her to show the world just how crazy and desperate she is. She gets him kicked out of medical school, gets the nurse fired from her job and makes his life a living hell. The final showdown could happen in the parking lot of his apartment after the ex gets into a cab and has the driver to follow him from the nurse's house. She'd emerge from the cab crying and asking for another chance. Stunned, the cab driver pulls off as the woman pleas with her ex for reconciliation. When the star character says no, the ex suddenly pulls out a gun and shoots him in the right arm. She then walks up to him and shoots at his head from a distance and misses. She walks closer, determined to get a better shot and utters a faint, "Goodbye, Jacob." She points the gun at his head and the sound of a single gunshot rings out. Fear and shock cover her face right before she collapses to the ground. Because she's pregnant, I'd be careful not to kill her off; instead, I'd ensure that the bullet grazes her left ear. She'd then be transported to a hospital, where she'd be treated. After this, she'd been arrested and finally extradited back to the United States, having been banned from France. Who saved the star character's life? The cab driver, of course! As it turns out, he not only speaks English, but after having been stalked by a few women, he knew the main character was in trouble. This is where I could introduce some comic relief. The French nurse would end up nursing him back to health, the two would get married and have a huge ceremony where people of different backgrounds and cultures converge for the event of a lifetime. Now, when I started the story, I didn't start at the beginning; I started it with him being in the parking lot of his apartment, staring down the barrel of a revolver. This means that I knew the end before I wrote the beginning. This is the heart and the art of writing; you are pretty much creating a beginning and an end, and from there, you get to creatively connect the two. Isn't this what our Father did? He is the Beginning and the End, but He gave us the power to connect the two by writing the in between. This is the power of authorship; this is the fingerprint of authority!

Hebrews 12:2: Looking unto Jesus the author and finisher of our faith; who for the joy that was set before him endured the cross, despising the shame, and is set down at the right hand of the throne of God.

Knowing the end of your book means to know the purpose of or, better yet, the message behind your book. Your book should be a fresh breath to the reader; you should have already established the goal of your book before you started writing it. When God created Adam, He created Adam for a purpose. "And every plant of the field before it was in the earth, and every herb of the field before it grew: for the LORD God had not caused it to rain upon the earth, and there was not a man to till the ground. But there went up a mist from the earth, and watered the whole face of the ground. And the LORD God formed man of the dust of the ground, and breathed into his nostrils the breath of life; and man became a living soul" (Genesis 2:5-7). Adam was created to solve a problem, and that problem was "there was not a man to till the ground." Everything God does is centered around solving a problem. Remember, problems aren't always bad (think Mathematics), but they are always opportunities. Your book should be centered around solving a problem; again, it should not be centered around making you an author and creating another stream of income for you—these are bonuses, but should never be the motivating factors behind writing. This is because the world of a man is locked up in his mind. The very moment you address the way a man thinks by introducing new information to him, reintroducing old information in a new way or by tearing down old information, you are changing that man by changing his world. Even if the only thing your book is doing is addressing his financial personality, you must understand that his financial personality may be the foundation for many of his beliefs and choices, so once the financial personality is shaken up, there will be some things that fall in his life. This is good if what you're tearing down is ungodly, plus, you're taking the time to give him the Word of God to base his choices on. This is bad if you're just venting and/or sharing your opinion without having prayed or conducted any research. We have to be accountable with the people we lead; we can't just take them where our feelings take us. Instead, leadership has to be intentional and well thought out.

The book of Revelations is interesting because it details the many events that will precede the passing away of the old world and the birthing of a new one. Revelations 21:1-4 reads, "Then I saw a new Heaven and a new Earth, for the first heaven and the first Earth had passed away, and the sea was no more. And I saw the holy city, new Jerusalem, coming down out of Heaven from God, prepared as a bride adorned for her husband. And I heard a loud voice from the throne saying, 'Behold, the dwelling place of God is with man. He will dwell with them, and they will be his people, and God himself will be with them as their God.'" This passage of scripture is so beautiful to read because it forms a picture in our minds of God meeting us in a whole new setting. Every problem we've had is suddenly no more. From that moment on, we'll get to enjoy what Adam and Eve once took for granted. This is our ultimate destination; it's what we have been or should have been chasing. But what if I told you that, as scribes, one of our assignments is to address the many dimensions of a man and cause him to experience a new world of thought in his heart? What does this mean? In layman's terms, a man is like a single world within himself. His world revolves around what he believes, and the atoms of his world are words. These are the words he's spoken and the words that have been spoken to or into him. Nevertheless, because of sin, his world has been divided; every facet of that man does not speak the same language. This is similar to the moment when the people of the Earth tried to build a tower that reached to Heaven (the Tower of Babel) and God confused their languages. This division was centered around separating the wheat (righteous men) from the tares (unrighteous men) so that the two wouldn't continue building together. For this reason, we should never mix or attempt to mix what's holy with anything that is profane.

Every belief system a man has is a region within that man, and just like the many countries of the Earth, every region of a man has a boundary and is established on a series of beliefs. This means that a man can (and often is) divided within himself! "A double minded man is unstable in all his ways." In short, there are some regions in a man where he's not completely settled. In these regions, he's still wondering; this is the mental equivalent of wandering around hopelessly, being led by what he feels. When you visit certain regions of thought within a man, you have to receive his permission; this is the spiritual equivalent of a passport. The man has to invite you in or let you in when you attempt to engage him in a specific area. If you try to access a zone without the man's permission, offense will meet you and the man will say, "You've gone too far," meaning you attempted to illegally enter a territory within the man without first acquiring a passport (his permission). For example, a man's romantic personality is a region within that man. His family is another region; his financial personality is a region, and his career aspirations are a region. You may find that his financial personality conflicts or is at war with his romantic personality. For this reason, his marriage is in danger because two parts of him that directly border one another are at war. He believes that his money is his own money and his wife should make her own money. He believes that he and his wife should split the bills. Nevertheless, within the zone of his marriage personality, he believes that his wife should provide a hot meal for him every day and she should keep the house clean. Do you see why these personalities are conflicting? As an author, your assignment is to address one or both regions of that man, helping them to finally merge. Your goal is to help him receive a new heart and a new mind; this is a new Heaven and a new Earth within the man. In summary, man is constantly being reborn within himself, but as authors and teachers, we are tasked with the assignment of shaking up those regions and then facilitating those new births. I may address the financial side of that man, while God may instruct you to deal with his romantic personality. If we are both hearing from God, we will cause those regions to unite and begin speaking the same language once again. Then again, my assignment may simply be to cause the old world of thought to pass away, while God can and may use you to usher in a new set of beliefs. In this, I would have to give the man enough revelation to sustain him while he navigates from the old system to a new one.

1 Corinthians 3:5-9: Who then is Paul, and who is Apollos, but ministers by whom ye believed, even as the Lord gave to every man? I have planted, Apollos watered; but God gave the increase. So then neither is he that planteth anything, neither he that watereth; but God that giveth the increase. Now he that planteth and he that watereth are one: and every man shall receive his own reward according to his own labor. For we are laborers together with God: ye are God's husbandry, ye are God's building.

Our assignment is to cause a new birth within every region of the man until he comes to the unity of Christ Jesus within himself. In other words, until he becomes whole again. This is when the man will begin to marry his financial personality with his romantic personality, and slowly but surely, every part of that man will begin to unite. This is when he'll be whole in his body, whole in his marriage, whole in his finances, whole in his sexuality—he'll be whole in every aspect of his identity. When this happens, there will be no more division within him; there will be no more regions of thought, divided by misguided beliefs and perceptions. The man will be whole. This is when the man comes fully out of his cage because every limitation (boundary) has been addressed. This is when the world will see the church for what it is!

As an author, you have the authority to change this world one mindset at a time. You will become many things to a man, if but for a few days or a few weeks. You can become his financial adviser, his marriage counselor, his deliverance minister, his doctor, his lawyer, his pastor, his mirror and so on. God has given you a measure of authority and power, but remember, your assignment is to lead the man back to Christ in whatever region of thought God has you addressing. You are a Moses or a Harriet Tubman of your time, leading the captives to freedom one region of thought at a time. Every region of thought is like a vehicle within the man. God has given you the keys and the power to jump-start that vehicle and He's given you the assignment of allowing that vehicle (man) to trail you until he reaches the same freedom that you're enjoying. This is who you are. Now, go shake up the devil's world; go and set the captives free one keystroke at a time! Remember, it is your love for people that legalizes your authority with them. Love will compel you to run into the enemy's camp and snatch as many people as you humanly can. Let the love of God lead and keep you.

God is Alpha and Omega; He is the beginning and the End. We are now living in the in-between. This is similar to what you've initiated in the beginning of this book. You created the beginning and end of your book. Now, you have to fill the "in between."

Imagine this: your heart is a projector and what you see before your eyes is nothing but an illusion; it is one of the slides that you've stored in your heart. In the above image, we see a woman standing in front of what appears to be a wall, and on this wall, we see the issues of her heart. Nevertheless, what if I told you that the wall is just a mirage? It's not physically there. It's the image being cast from her heart because of her unbelief. The woman has a gift and a burden to write, nevertheless, she can't seem to get past her own insecurities; she has had so much trouble getting over herself that she's pretty much ready to give up. What's amazing is, she only encounters this wall whenever she attempts to write her book or do anything that would propel her into her destiny. For this reason, she refuses to do anything that will make her confront her personal Goliath. Because she's been standing and sitting in front of this wall for years on end, she's now magnified the wall, meaning what was once a small hurdle is now a mountain of excuses and doubt. Again, like most authors, she's found her Goliath. Of course, one of her Goliaths is herself. To confront the wall that's confronting her, she must first confront the writing on the wall. She has to confront every excuse and lie, and she must pull them down. But before she can do this, she must take down the images on the wall.

The images represent memories of the past and plans for her future because they justify her keeping the wall up; they give value to a wall that shouldn't even be there in the first place. The images also serve as a distraction; they help her to redirect her attention from the writing on the wall. Taking down the images also means that she must intentionally make herself uncomfortable. Her comfort zone can no longer be comfortable; it has to become more uncomfortable than her perception of the next level. This means that she has to rid herself of her own plans, forgive the folks who hurt her and try to see the past for what it is—a lesson designed to propel her.

You'll notice in this picture, the woman appears to be happy. She's in a relationship and she appears to be content.

In the next image (left), she's alone and miserable. Nevertheless, you'll notice that she's still wearing the same outfit that she wore on the previous picture, and she's still sitting in the same place. What this represents is a mindset and a season. This, along with the first picture, represents a woman who has not changed her mind, nor has she allowed God to dress her for a new season. The only thing she's done is change her position. Howbeit, if you change your position without changing your mind, you'll become religious and bitter.

Above, you'll find every image that she had to pull off the wall of her heart.

In the final picture (left), you'll notice that the woman smiling. She's still in the same place, wearing the same outfit, nevertheless, she's now wearing a smile. This portrait represents a season of religiousness. This happens when we don't change our minds or our positions; instead, we learn to better play the hand that life has dealt us. This won't make our lives better; it simply means we've learned to master seasons that we should have passed through. This means we've become content wandering around the mountain or, better yet, wondering about the mountain. To escape this, we have to pull down every ungodly image or imagination that's making it hard for us to move forward.

Next, she has to confront the wall. How does this look? Confronting the wall requires that she do two things: she has to replace the old words with the Word of God, and after this, she has to humble herself and walk right through that wall.

1. She must confront every lie posted on the wall.

2. After she's pulled down the lies, she must replace those words with the Word of God.

3. After she's digested every scripture on the wall or better yet, taken it into the belly of her spirit (her heart), she must then confront the wall. The wall represents a season of limitation.

Again, the wall simply doesn't exist; it's a mirage. You see, the wall represents her pride, and the writing on the wall is a projection of the excuses and the lies she's accepted. By replacing the words on the wall, she slowly and methodically begins to pull down the wall one lie at a time. By walking right through the wall, she will come to see that it has no true power to hold her back; she'll come to see that the wall simply did not exist. When she walks through the wall, she'll better understand the power that lies within her. This is called renewing the mind. The word "renew" means to make new again. It means to trust God again; it means to allow ourselves to be absolutely vulnerable with God again.

Lastly, she has to confront the devil behind the projector. This is done through a process called deliverance. Remember, we are mountains; we are piles of dirt, filled with caves, and in each cave, there is either darkness or light. Wherever there is darkness, we are in need of truth and we are in need of deliverance. Receiving one without the other only has short-term benefits. This is one of the reasons our minds must be renewed before or immediately after deliverance. The renewing of the mind isn't something that's "cast in." Wisdom has to be invited in. We do this by studying and meditating on the Word of God, going to and participating in church, and intentionally submitting our minds and bodies to Christ Jesus.

Deliverance for the Scribe

We all know that many of the scribes in the New Testament days were wicked, prideful men who plotted to have Jesus killed. It is obvious that they needed some major deliverance. Nevertheless, to get this deliverance, they would have had to humble themselves. Humility is pulling one's self down, all the while, exalting the name of the Lord. Can you imagine what many of their deliverances would have looked like? After all, they were prideful, envious, unloving, hateful liars who were filled with murder. When Jesus came to the tombs, the man who had been cutting himself for years ran up to Him, but the demons in the man spoke out of him. They asked, "What have we to do with thee, Jesus, thou Son of God? Art thou come hither to torment us before the time?" Why is it that a deranged man who was possessed with an army of demons can get set free, but many of the scribes in that day who were brilliant thinkers missed their shot at freedom? The answer is as simple as it is complex. The man in the tombs humbled himself by running over to Jesus. Like the woman with the issue of blood, he pressed through everything that threatened to hold him back. He saw his opportunity and he wasn't about to miss it. First and foremost, how did he know that Jesus could set him free? Because he felt a shift in his being. Suddenly, what had been tormenting him was no longer in control the minute Jesus stepped out of the ship and onto the land of Gadarenes. As a matter of fact, many theologians theorize that the storm spoken of in Mark 4 was the result of demonic activity. Jesus was on His way to Gadarenes with the disciples when a storm broke out. The scriptures tell us that Jesus was sound asleep, but His disciples woke Him up, saying, "Master, carest thou not that we perish?" Jesus got up and rebuked the wind and said to the sea, "Peace be still." This demonic activity was, no doubt, the principalities of that region's attempt to get the men to turn around, but they couldn't touch Jesus or His disciples. Why? Because the storm was just a mirage, meaning, it had no actual power. The goal of the storm was to provoke fear in the hearts of the men and get them to turn the boat around, but they didn't. So, when Jesus placed one of His feet upon the land, a shift happened, and an earthquake took place in the realm of the spirit. When the deranged man saw the Lord, we can safely summarize that he felt a peace he hadn't felt in a long time, and for a moment, what had been in control of him had loosened its grip. He then utilized that opportunity to run up to the Lord and at least get His attention. Nevertheless, the moment he rushed up to Jesus, what was in him spoke up because the man was possessed, meaning, he wasn't saved, and he was rarely (if ever) in control of himself. In that moment, Jesus took control and the man was set free. The scribes of old, on the other hand, weren't interested in serving the Lord. They'd been revered as astute men for so long that giving up that position and everything that came with it was not an option for them, so they tried to change Jesus, rather than asking Him to change them. They wouldn't humble themselves long enough to get set free. The point is, as scribes, we do need to receive regular maintenance in the form of deliverance, and we don't have to wait until we're delirious to do it.

Have you ever seen someone shaking while going through deliverance? For example, some people look like they're having seizures while deliverance is taking place. In truth, what you see happening is the mountain being shaken up. You are witnessing an earthquake take place. You see, demons like to hide in the darkness (anyplace where there is no revelation). By quaking the mountain, God causes many of the stony places to fall away and everything that's hidden in the caves of the mountain to suddenly be exposed. This means that when the person is shaking, deliverance has started, *but* it has not ended. The storm is never over until there is a calm. Of course, everyone doesn't shake during deliverance. Some people yawn, some people vomit, some people cry, some people sneeze, and the most common reaction is coughing. Then again, some people don't manifest at all. Remember, we are personal planets who come equipped with our own storms. Please review the chart below to see how deliverance looks from a devil's standpoint.

Reaction to Deliverance	What Demons Experience
Yawn	Heavy Winds
Spit	Flood
Vomit	Tsunami
Cry	Rain
Sneeze	Volcano
Cough	Hurricane
Convulse	Earthquake
Flatulence	Thunder

During deliverance, the deliverance minister begins to release words, not at the wall because the wall isn't the problem. The minister speaks to the devil operating the projector. As deliverance takes place, the wall begins to shake, but it does not fall. Why is this? Because the projector is simply projecting what the author believes.

The Writing is on the Wall

The wall will disappear once the lies have been confronted with the truth. Again, this can happen before or immediately after deliverance. Once the wall is down, the author has free roam of his or her gift, and will likely finish his or her book in a matter of weeks or a few months. To recap, the following steps need to be taken:

1. You have to take down the pictures on the wall, meaning, you have to intentionally make yourself uncomfortable. You have to drive yourself out of your comfort zone, otherwise, a storm may come along and do it for you.
2. You have to confront every lie on the wall, either before or after deliverance, and replace them with the truth. *Please note that it's better to do this before deliverance.*
3. You need to confront your fear by walking through the wall. This means that you simply need to start writing and stop overthinking the process. You need to prove to yourself that you can do everything God says you can do.
4. You need to confront the devil behind the projector; get him cast all the way out.
5. Finally, it would be wise to tell your leader and/or intercessory team that you're writing. The reason for this is, during the writing process, you may find yourself feeling drained, depending on what level writer you are. It is during this time that you may feel the weakest, which makes it easier for the enemy to attack you. Nevertheless, if you have a team of people standing in the gap for you, you should be fine.

Another thing to remember is, before you can release power, you have to be filled with power; in other words, you must become powerful. This sounds elementary, but it's not. It simply means that you can't release God's power without first experiencing it for yourself. Your book has to be more than you attempting to lead others to revelation; you have to first receive that revelation and allow it to mature in you before you can effectively share it. First, you go through the storm; next (if you don't faint), you'll become the storm. When you become the storm, you can release the winds, the floods, the tsunamis, the rain, the lava, the hurricanes, the earthquakes and the thunder into someone else's life. In short, cast the mote (demon) out of your own eye before you try to perform deliverance on someone else (see Matthew 7:5), whether they received their deliverance in person or from your book. You can't shake up whatever it is that shakes you. You have to cast it out.

To receive deliverance, of course, you need the following:

1. **Salvation.** Remember how Jesus responded to the Canaanite woman who asked the Lord to deliver her daughter from a demon. He responded, "It is not meet to take the children's bread, and to cast it to dogs." Dogs, in this text, is used to represent unbelievers and, of course, bread is used to represent deliverance. The woman's daughter was delivered because of her faith, but Jesus was pretty much saying that it is not meet (right) to give deliverance to an unbeliever since it is a Kingdom benefit that has been reserved for believers. Nevertheless, the desperate mother had faith enough to receive, so her daughter was made whole.

2. **A repentant heart.** Devils love sin; they love pride and they love when the people they are binding refuse to repent.

3. **A church that operates in the ministry of deliverance.** If the church you are a member of does not perform deliverance, please visit a church that does or go to a deliverance conference (at minimum) twice a year. Sure, we can perform deliverance on ourselves, but there are some spirits that you may need help getting free from.

In addition to receiving deliverance, you have to work towards maintaining your deliverance. You do this by remaining prayerful and intentional about living a righteous life. You must also study to show yourself approved.

Please note that deliverance is an important weapon of the scribe. It is very taxing to write while bound because every time you strike a key on your keyboard, you are striking up a conversation in the realm of the spirit. If you're not delivered from whatever it is you are addressing, it *will* respond. What's worse is when it responds from within. Many people who had the talent to write took their talents to their graves with them because every time they struck a key, something struck them. Every time they moved a pen, something moved them. They didn't realize that they simply needed deliverance and, of course, a renewed mind. Don't sit around, waiting on a prophet to call you out of a crowd and take you through deliverance (this is a faint-hearted fantasy of the prideful); do like the deranged man and run after Jesus. Many of the scribes in Jesus' day weren't set free because they wanted Jesus to convince them of His majesty. They missed a very important opportunity because of pride. If you need to be set free, go and get set free without any excuses or delays.

451

You will find that writing is so much easier when the storms that wage up against you aren't coming from within.

Scribal Deliverance

Before we delve into this topic, let's establish one thing: deliverance isn't always the casting out of demons. Sometimes, deliverance is the destruction of ungodly systems, the pulling down of ungodly mindsets, the removal of demonic doctrines and/or debris, and in some cases, it is the removal of seasonal and/or bound people from our lives. For example, God wrote me a prescription for freedom using my own hands. In short, as I wrote books and articles designed to help others, I wrote my way out of bondage. This is the testimony of the scribe. Revelation 12:11 reads, "And they overcame him by the blood of the Lamb, and by the word of their testimony; and they loved not their lives unto the death." God will always cause us to cast the speck out of our own eyes before we address His people. This is the reason so many scribes have their lives shaken up the minute they start writing their books. Obedience is a form of worship, and when a man worships God in spirit and in truth, he engages the supernatural realm. For example, consider the story in the book of Acts detailing the moment when the doors of the prison opened while Paul and Silas were worshipping the Lord. Acts 16:25-26 details the story this way; it reads, "And at midnight Paul and Silas prayed, and sang praises unto God: and the prisoners heard them. And suddenly there was a great earthquake, so that the foundations of the prison were shaken: and immediately all the doors were opened, and everyone's bands were loosed." In that moment, the men were set free, but it was up to them whether they wanted to walk out of bondage or stay in it. Like many believers today, they refused to leave their prisons until they'd been publicly exonerated. Acts 16:36-37 reads, "And the keeper of the prison told this saying to Paul, The magistrates have sent to let you go: now therefore depart, and go in peace. But Paul said unto them, They have beaten us openly uncondemned, being Romans, and have cast us into prison; and now do they thrust us out privily? Nay verily; but let them come themselves and fetch us out." In this, we see that it is possible for God to set us free, but we also have to perform an action; we have to intentionally walk out of our former cells.

And of course, there is demonic deliverance. This is when an ungodly personality (spirit) has managed to lodge itself in our souls or bodies. Scribes who need this form of deliverance often find it hard, if not nearly impossible, to finish their books. This is because the spirit binding them has a specific assignment, and part of that assignment is making sure that the bound soul doesn't effectively help anyone. For example, when I'm coaching bound people, the enemy busies their schedules by distracting them with flourishing relationships, relationship problems, financial problems, opportunities, family issues, depression, hopelessness, perversion or anything that he can send their way. A woman, for example, can find herself suddenly being wooed by the man of her dreams. The relationship can become so distracting to her that she no longer has time to write in her book. The relationship can be so enchanting that she's never sober long enough to hear from God, or it can be so traumatic that she spends most of her waking hours arguing or worrying about her lover. Believe it or not, this is one of the enemy's favorite and most effective distractions!

Think about the Bible. The book of Genesis was completed in or around 1400 BC, but the book of Revelation wasn't finished until around AD 90. This means that it took roughly around 1500 years for the Bible to be completed! Genesis was written more than 3,400 years ago! Nevertheless, these stories have managed to travel through time and make their way to us. What you write may last hundreds, if not thousands of years. I understand that it's hard for us to fathom the idea of the Earth being around for another three thousand years, but it is possible. What will you have left behind? What imprint will you leave on the next generation and the generations to come? It is important for you to look for every area that you're bound in and seek to be free.

Delivering Scribes from Legalism

Matthew 23:1-7: Then spake Jesus to the multitude, and to his disciples, Saying, The scribes and the Pharisees sit in Moses' seat: All therefore whatsoever they bid you observe, that observe and do; but do not ye after their works: for they say, and do not. For they bind *heavy burdens* and grievous to be borne, and lay them on men's shoulders; but they themselves will not move them with one of their fingers. But all their works they do for to be seen of men: they make broad their phylacteries, and enlarge the borders of their garments, and love the uppermost rooms at feasts, and the chief seats in the synagogues, and greetings in the markets, and to be called of men, Rabbi, Rabbi.

In the aforementioned scripture, we witness the Lord describing the hypocrisy of the scribes and Pharisees in that day. One of the Lord's complaints about them was that they ignored the more important matters of the law, which were justice, mercy and faithfulness because they were so infatuated with every letter of the law. They were legalistic lovers of self. They were men who mentally painted and promoted an image of a god who was unmerciful and unloving — one who looked forward to torturing people in hell. They promoted the idea that they themselves held the key to salvation. They were the serial killers of their day — killing the dreams and hopes of many Israelites. It is of no wonder that Jesus said they would receive the greater punishment.

Dictionary.com defines legalism this way:
1. strict adherence, or the principle of strict adherence, to law or prescription, especially to the letter rather than the spirit.
2. Theology

   - the doctrine that salvation is gained through good works.
   - the judging of conduct in terms of adherence to precise laws.

It goes without saying that many of the biblical scribes were legalistic, meaning, they were as tedious and unmerciful when examining people as they were when they copied the Torah. Again, when copying the Torah, the scribes were very meticulous, and if they made one minuscule mistake, they'd destroy the entire document and start all over. Of course, we are grateful that they were cautious when examining and copying the Old Testament, nevertheless, the problem was that they were the same way with people. As a matter of fact, Jesus said they "squinted at a gnat" meaning, they were extremists. They were hypocrites who focused more on appearing holy than actually being holy. In Matthew 23:25, Jesus said, "Woe unto you, scribes and Pharisees, hypocrites! For ye make clean the outside of the cup and of the platter, but within they are full of extortion and excess."

Sadly enough, the spirit of legalism is very much alive and active today. We see it moving in many false religions and Christian denominations, and it has managed to scare many away from the church and into caves. It is a religious spirit that loves to pair up with two other spirits: fear and pride. As a scribe, it is absolutely imperative that you love God and you love His people. You see, love will compel you to examine the heart of God; this way, when you study the Word of God, you'll look at it through the lens of love, rather than through a works perspective.

If you examine the word "legalism," you'll see that it's comprised of two words: legal and ism.

- **Legal:** deriving authority from or founded on law, having a formal status derived from law often without a basis in actual fact.
- **Ism:** a distinctive doctrine, cause, or theory, an oppressive and especially discriminatory attitude or belief.

(Reference: Merriam Webster)

If we combine the two, the word legalism then means an oppressive and discriminatory doctrine that is based on a misinterpretation and/or misrepresentation of the law. Please understand that we have two ways in which we filter information: we filter it through truth (the Word of God) or we run it through our fact filter. Truth and facts are not one and the same. Whatever God says is true, but facts are mankind's version of the truth. Proverbs 14:12 says it this way, "There is a way which seemeth right unto a man, but the end thereof are the ways of death." Notice the scripture says that this way *seems* right to a man. The word "seems" comes from the word "see." We see through our natural eyes, so the word "seems" here references our natural logic or understanding.

First off, what is our fact filter? What we have established as facts has everything to do with what we were taught in school, what we were taught at home and what we've learned over the course of our lives. All of our experiences and lessons converge to form snippets of our belief system. We then get saved and as we study the Word of God, we add another layer to our belief system. In this, we create another filter by which we sift through information, especially anything relating to religion. This is what it means to be double-minded. Every believer starts off as double-minded and unstable; we all start off as babes in Christ. Think about a toddler who's attempting to walk for the first time. The toddler can walk; this is a fact, but the child has to learn to balance himself or herself. Walking is an instinctual act; notice that parents never take hold of their children's legs and place one in front of the other. Instead, the parent stands the toddler to his or her feet and the child instinctively takes a step. Nevertheless, the child is not familiar with the laws of gravity. As a matter of fact, you'll notice that most parents start picking their infants up under their arms, allowing their little legs to rest on the parents' legs. They normally start doing this in the first month of the child's life. As the child develops, especially when the child is between six to twelve months old, the parent will stand the child up, but loosen his or her grip on the child just a little. What the parent is doing is helping the baby to understand his or her part in standing. The child must learn to use the muscles in his or her leg, and the child has to familiarize himself or herself with the laws of gravity. For example, an infant soon learns that if he or she leans back too far that the infant will fall. In short, children don't necessarily learn to walk; they learn to balance themselves as they walk. This means the infant starts off as unstable; the same is true for believers. As babes in Christ, we are accustomed to running everything through our fact filter. For example, we say things like, "That's impossible" or "Prove it," because in school, we were taught the natural laws that govern the earth realm. We didn't learn about the spiritual laws. The truth, on the other hand, is spiritual, meaning, it cannot be disproved; whatever God says will come to pass the minute He speaks it. This explains why it's impossible for God to lie. To bridge our fact filter with our truth filter, we have to study the Word of God all the more; this takes years, determination and consistency. As we begin to factor information through the truth filter, we can then examine some facts and call them what they are: lies. For example, if disease manifests itself in one of our bodies, we can speak the Word of God in faith and the disease has to go. We don't see healing in a lot of our churches because we are still filtering information through our fact filter. The doctor said the man was diseased; this is a fact, but what does God say? Understand this: we've been learning facts for a long time. We went to school for 13-14 years (including preschool and kindergarten); we went to school for nine months out of a year, and we spent eight hours a day at school. This means that we spend close to 19,000 hours in school, and this does not include college, the time spent doing homework and the time spent commuting to school! If you add on a four-year college stint, the average student spends close to 25,000 hours in school learning facts and theories. This explains why it's hard for us to perform miracles; we know more facts than we know truths! This is also why we've given the doctor more reverence than we've given God! This means that many of us have made idols out of doctors, medicine and the many man-established facts that we study. This better helps us to understand the heart of the Lord when He said in Judges 10:14, "Go and cry unto the gods which ye have chosen; let them deliver you in the time of your tribulation." And we have done just this! We run to doctors and anyone who is a keeper of facts, but we rarely lean on the truth!

There's nothing wrong with facts, of course. The issue comes when we filter the truth using our fact filter, for example, the scriptures tell us that Jesus rose from the dead on the third day. It is a fact that a dead man cannot and will not get up out of his grave, especially after three days. Nevertheless, when phenomenon like this occur, we call them miracles, all the while, ignoring the God who performed the miracle. So, according to facts, it is impossible for Jesus to have gotten up on the third day, but the truth is that He did! When we filter truth through facts, we end up confused—we end up wrestling with logic. This is similar to the wrestling match that Jacob had with God. Genesis 32:24-28 tells the story; it reads, "And Jacob was left alone; and there wrestled a man with him until the breaking of the day. And when he saw that he prevailed not against him, he touched the hollow of his thigh; and the hollow of Jacob's thigh was out of joint, as he wrestled with him. And he said, Let me go, for the day breaketh. And he said, I will not let thee go, except thou bless me. And he said unto him, What is thy name? And he said, Jacob. And he said, Thy name shall be called no more Jacob, but Israel: for as a prince hast thou power with God and with men, and hast prevailed." This is how we have to be with the truth. The truth doesn't make sense most times because we run it through our fact filter, but we have to hold on to the truth until it blesses us. Remember, God is Truth.

A legalist is a rigid soul who processes truths as facts, meaning, there is no room for God to be expressive in their hearts. They see the black and white letters on a page; from there, they establish what they've read as laws. There is no room for love in their translations; there is no room in their hearts for God to be the multidimensional and multifaceted God that He is. Instead, they imagine a stiff and unloving God, and they ruminate that image for others to choke on. Anyone who takes in their false doctrines usually becomes just as fearful, religious and prideful as they are.

As an author, how do we avoid becoming the legalistic souls that we have the potential to become? We do this by:

1. Loving God with all of our hearts, soul and strength.
2. Loving our neighbors as we love ourselves. Our neighbor, of course, is any and everyone we come in contact with, even if we see them on a television screen, on the internet or in a newspaper.
3. Meditating on the Word of God.
4. Studying to show ourselves approved daily.
5. Surrounding ourselves with a multitude of counselors and submitting to those counselors. After all, what good is a counselor if we refuse their counsel?
6. Forgiving people. Unforgiveness creates another filter, wherein, unforgiving souls begin to process information through their hurt and their experiences. For example, a woman whose husband has abandoned her to be with someone else could easily write a book about marriage, but when readers dig into the book, they could end up poisoned if the author hasn't forgiven her estranged or ex-husband and his mistress.
7. Remaining prayerful.
8. Fasting often.
9. Not being anxious to share the revelation that God gives to us. Revelation needs to mature before we share it. This is because when we're filtering information (this includes the Word of God, prophecies, words of knowledge), many of our beliefs mix with that information. In other words, it becomes contaminated. We need time to allow this information to overcome our beliefs. In short, the truth we receive often wrestles with the facts we've stored, and we need to allow the truth to emerge as the victor before we open our mouths or share the revelation via our books.
10. Filtering what we allow into our ear and eye gates. Many legalists submerge their minds in conspiracy theories and doctrines created by schizophrenics.

Woe to Ungodly Scribes

Ungodly scribes write God's people a prescription for bondage, but first, let's establish what the word "woe" means. According to English Oxford Living Dictionaries, the word "woe" means: Great sorrow or distress. When Jesus said, "Woe to you, scribes and Pharisees," He was mirroring the moment that Noah cursed Ham. Ham had not covered his father, but had instead, attempted to expose him. When Noah woke up, he'd bless his other two sons, Shem and Japheth, because they'd covered him, but he cursed Ham. Now, it's hard for us to associate the word "curse" with our Lord and Savior, but He didn't curse them in the way that a wicked man would curse someone. He simply took the blessing away from them, and where there is no blessing, there is no empowerment to prosper. He was simply doing what He'd done with the fig tree that had not borne any fruit in its season. As a scribe, it is important for you to understand your role; that way, you don't fall into the same temptation that has bound many of the scribes before you. Below, you'll the eight woes of ungodly scribes.

Scriptures	Scriptural Text
Matthew 23:13	But woe unto you, scribes and Pharisees, hypocrites! For ye shut up the Kingdom of Heaven against men: for ye neither go in yourselves, neither suffer ye them that are entering to go in.
Matthew 23:14	Woe unto you, scribes and Pharisees, hypocrites! For ye devour widows' houses, and for a pretense make long prayer: therefore ye shall receive the greater damnation.
Matthew 23:15	Woe unto you, scribes and Pharisees, hypocrites! For ye compass sea and land to make one proselyte, and when he is made, ye make him twofold more the child of hell than yourselves.
Matthew 23:16	Woe unto you, ye blind guides, which say, Whosoever shall swear by the temple, it is nothing; but whosoever shall swear by the gold of the temple, he is a debtor!

	Ye fools and blind: for whether is greater, the gold, or the temple that sanctifieth the gold? And, Whosoever shall swear by the altar, it is nothing; but whosoever sweareth by the gift that is upon it, he is guilty. Ye fools and blind: for whether is greater, the gift, or the altar that sanctifieth the gift? Whoso therefore shall swear by the altar, sweareth by it, and by all things thereon. And whoso shall swear by the temple, sweareth by it, and by him that dwelleth therein. And he that shall swear by Heaven, sweareth by the throne of God, and by him that sitteth thereon.
Matthew 23:23	Woe unto you, scribes and Pharisees, hypocrites! For ye pay tithe of mint and anise and cummin, and have omitted the weightier matters of the law, judgment, mercy, and faith: these ought ye to have done, and not to leave the other undone. Ye blind guides, which strain at a gnat, and swallow a camel.
Matthew 23:25	Woe unto you, scribes and Pharisees, hypocrites! For ye make clean the outside of the cup and of the platter, but within they are full of extortion and excess. Thou blind Pharisee, cleanse first that which is within the cup and platter, that the outside of them may be clean also.
Matthew 23:27	Woe unto you, scribes and Pharisees, hypocrites! For ye are like unto whited sepulchers, which indeed appear beautiful outward, but are within full of dead men's bones, and of all uncleanness. Even so ye also outwardly appear righteous unto men, but within ye are full of hypocrisy and iniquity.
Matthew 23:29	Woe unto you, scribes and Pharisees, hypocrites! because ye build the tombs of the prophets, and garnish the sepulchers of the righteous, And say, If we

> had been in the days of our fathers, we would not have been partakers with them in the blood of the prophets. Wherefore ye be witnesses unto yourselves, that ye are the children of them which killed the prophets. Fill ye up then the measure of your fathers. Ye serpents, ye generation of vipers, how can ye escape the damnation of hell?

Jesus rebuked the scribes because they made their followers feel like it was nearly impossible for them to enter the Kingdom of Heaven. They were judgmental hypocrites who Jesus said, "squinted at gnats," meaning, they magnified every minute issue and made it bigger than what it was. The scribes often mixed the traditions of men with the scriptures in their attempts to make those traditions laws. Like Judas Iscariot, they were more concerned with the wealth of the temple than they were with the temple itself. They were extraordinary writers who could make even the most foolish arrangement of words read like sound wisdom. They used fear and religion to secure their places in the synagogues. It's important to remember that the scribes weren't just copiers of the Law; many of them were also lawyers. In Matthew 23:14, Jesus rebuked them for having no mercy on widows when they could not pay off their husbands' debts, all the while, praying for widows (in public) just to receive the praise and admiration of men. Every time Jesus said, "Woe unto scribes and Pharisees," He would call them hypocrites and then explain why they would endure the woes that were heading their way. What we have to take from this is that it is possible for us, as scribes, to fall into the very snares that many of the scribes He'd rebuked fell into. This is why so many authors today experience "great sorrow and distress" when they start their writing journeys. Woe isn't reserved for writers; it is reserved for hypocrites. The point is, tell the truth and nothing but the truth. Lead God's people out of captivity and not the other way around.

In the 23rd book of Matthews, we witness Jesus rebuking the scribes. The Lord who had been known for blessing men and setting them free, was now judging the people who'd led many men into captivity. He'd come across many of God's people and had been moved to tears because of what He'd witnessed. The people were sick, distressed, demon-bound and lost. Matthew 9:35-38 reads, "And Jesus went about all the cities and villages, teaching in their synagogues, and preaching the gospel of the kingdom, and healing every sickness and every disease among the people. But when he saw the multitudes, he was moved with compassion on them, because they fainted, and were scattered abroad, as sheep having no shepherd. Then saith he unto his disciples, The harvest truly is plenteous, but the laborers are few; Pray ye therefore the Lord of the harvest, that he will send forth laborers into his harvest." To better understand Jesus' frustration with the scribes, you have to put yourself in His position. Imagine leaving your children in the care of a baby-sitter, only to come back and found that your children are starving, sick and on the edge of their sanity. In the midst of all this turmoil, the baby-sitter has been using your money to buy herself the best clothes, and she's been using your house to impress every man who's expressed interest in her. Additionally, she's been having your children taking snapshots of her just so she can post those pictures to her social media page, even though the children are hungry, cold and scared. Nevertheless, in all of her wicked doings, she's managed to keep every room of the house clean, except for your children's rooms. Can you imagine how upset you'd be? To see the faces of the children you love staring at you with hunger and anxiety in their eyes would upset you to no end. Your love for your children would fuel your anger towards the baby-sitter. This is similar to what happened between Jesus and the scribes. The Lord came down from His holy habitation, only to find that the people who were supposed to be feeding His sheep with the Word and leading them out of their mental bondage were instead starving them and leading them further into bondage. The scribes had so many people convinced that they were too dirty for God; they made the people dependent on them, even though they themselves were not righteous.

When the Master returned, He stood still and watched as herds of beautiful souls rushed towards Him in distress, many of them crying out about their infirmities, their children, their marriages and every other matter that weighed them down. Anytime people heard that Jesus had come into their region, they'd run out of their homes and go to wherever He was. Like the deranged man who'd lived in a graveyard, the people pressed their way towards the Lord with their minds in chains. Think of the parable of the talents. The unfaithful servant buried his talent. Remember, a gold talent was about the weight of a person. The scribes were unfaithful servants, only the talents they'd buried were people, and they hadn't just buried one talent. They'd created a massive above-ground graveyard where they'd buried the hopes and dreams of countless people. In the parable of the talents, when the master came back, he found that the unfaithful servant (or parishioner) had buried his talent (servant). The unfaithful servant started listing off excuses as to why he had not done his "reasonable service," but the master responded by taking the talent from him and giving it to the faithful servant. Ephesians 4:8 reads, "Wherefore he saith, When he ascended up on high, he led captivity captive, and gave gifts unto men." The Lord brought His people out of captivity; He took the talents (people) from the wolves in fancy robes who'd buried them. He then gave them better leaders—leaders who He describes as "gifts." These gifts are God's prescription for freedom. Ephesians 4:11-16 reads, "And he gave some, apostles; and some, prophets; and some, evangelists; and some, pastors and teachers; for the perfecting of the saints, for the work of the ministry, for the edifying of the body of Christ: till we all come in the unity of the faith, and of the knowledge of the Son of God, unto a perfect man, unto the measure of the stature of the fullness of Christ: That we henceforth be no more children, tossed to and fro, and carried about with every wind of doctrine, *by the sleight of men, and cunning craftiness*, whereby they lie in wait to deceive; but speaking the truth in love, may grow up into him in all things, which is the head, even Christ: From whom the whole body fitly joined together and compacted by that which every joint supplieth, according to the effectual working in the measure of every part, maketh increase of the body unto the edifying of itself in love." He brought us from under the bondage of Law and those who bound the people with the Law and He gave us the five-fold ministry! Another interesting scripture is Romans 11:29, which reads, "For the gifts and calling of God are without repentance." As the body of Christ, we've always associated Romans 11:29 with talents, instead of gifts in the forms of men and women. The word "irrevocable" means "impossible to be changed." What if we read Romans 11:29 this way: "For the gifts (apostles, prophets, evangelists, teachers and pastors) and calling (assignment) of God are incorruptible." This doesn't mean that a leader of the five-fold cannot fall into sin; it simply means that if you come across a fallen apostle, he or she is still an apostle, whether the person repents or not! Think about King Saul. When God left him, he was still King Saul. Why is this? Because he had been "anointed" as king. 1 Samuel 19:15 reads, "Now the LORD had told Samuel in his ear a day before Saul came, saying, Tomorrow about this time I will send thee a man out of the land of Benjamin, and thou shalt anoint him to be captain over my people Israel, that he may save my people out of the hand of the Philistines: for I have looked upon my people, because their cry is come unto me." Once a king was anointed by a prophet of God as a king, he would die a king, regardless of what he did. If he did evil, he'd be recorded as an evil king, but he'd still be a king nonetheless. His anointing could not be taken from him, but God could remove Himself from the person. The Lord could also reserve the throne for someone outside of the fallen king's bloodline. David didn't inherit the throne. Like Saul, he was anointed and appointed as King of Israel. Wicked kings often died as kings or were taken into captivity, but they were never dethroned unless the people had appointed them. In layman's terms, the person is corruptible, but the anointing is not. You can cast a king off a throne, but you cannot cast down God's words regarding that king. This explains why David would not open his mouth to speak against King Saul. This is also why Michael, the archangel, did not offer up what the Bible calls a "railing accusation" against Satan when contending with him over the body of Moses. This case was fought in the courtroom of Heaven and it had nothing to do with the evil deeds of Satan; it was about who had rights regarding Moses' body. So, in short, Michael, the archangel, did not deviate from the case at hand. He understood that judging Satan was not his job. His assignment was to carry out the will of God, and he refused to step outside of his assignment. The point is, your job is to focus on whatever assignment YAHWEH gives you. Never use your book to:

1. Bind God's people.
2. Get the praises of men.
3. Impress others.
4. Accuse or attack leaders.
5. Respond to someone who's hurt or offended you.
6. Deal with your rejection issues.
7. Get God's attention.

Sure, it's easy to see a book as an opportunity to grow your name and your income, but when you think like this, your book can easily become an opportunity for the devil to ensnare people as well. Why do you think that more than eighty percent of Christian books flop? It's simple. Because God did not write the foreword in many of them! Some, of course, aren't failures; it's simply not their season for success. Nevertheless, many Christian books were written by authors who weren't concerned with setting the captives free when they penned their books. They were focused completely on themselves, and for this reason, God would not and did not partner with them. If your self-help book is not the result of you being moved with compassion for God's people and wanting to help them, God won't bless the book. If the only self you're trying to help is yourself, God won't promote the book. This is why it is important for you to pray, fast and make a commitment to God that you will lead His people back to Him. This is what He wants. He's not interested in making you a best-seller just because you can grip a microphone and craftily manipulate the sound waves around you. He simply wants His children back. You have to ask yourself this question every time you sit down to write a book ... "Will this book lead people to Christ or will it lead them to me?" While walking my dog one day, I came across a small dog running happily from one side of the street to another. Since the street we were on was a semi-busy street, I knew that it was a matter of time before the dog got hit by a car if it wasn't caught, so I started stooping down and whistling at the dog. That's when I noticed a car that had nearly slowed down to a complete stop, and inside of the car was a woman and her ten-year old son. The mother looked frustrated, but the young boy looked somewhat amused. She explained to me that the dog I was trying to catch was her dog and it had gotten away (once again) after she'd let the dog outside. Both the woman and the young boy were obese, so catching the small, energetic dog had proven to be a huge task. Being a pet owner and an animal lover, I could empathize with her, so I asked her to hold my dog's leash while I tried to convince her dog to come to me. Fifteen minutes into the ordeal, I still hadn't caught the dog. The dog would come super close to me, and then take off the minute I even looked like I was about to reach for it. Another couple walking their dog had joined the rescue party after the loose dog had run up to their dogs in an attempt to make friends with them. They figured that they too had an edge; they had two small dogs who'd obviously captured the loose dog's interest. Ten minutes later, an older guy had joined the growing rescue squad since all the commotion was happening right in front of his house. He brought us two hot dogs, hoping to appeal to the dog's tastebuds. I broke off tiny pieces of the hot dog, dropping them and creating a small trail that led to me. In my hand, I had the bigger piece of one of the hot dogs. The dog ate every morsel, but would not come close enough to get the one directly in front of me unless I took at least two steps back. What's amazing is, the dog didn't mind getting slightly within my reach because it was confident that I couldn't catch it. Five minutes later, two more people had stopped and started trying to use their own techniques to capture the dog. By this time, the dog owner was noticeably frustrated and humiliated. One of the guys went to his house and came out with a comforter and a sheet, hoping to throw it over the dog's head, but this didn't work. Every time the dog would run away from one of us, it would dash onto the semi-busy street without regard for any cars, so we had to be extremely careful. I realized in that moment that the whole rescue had become a competition of sorts, with everyone trying to be "the one" who snagged the dog. We all thought we were dog-savvy, so we all brought our own individual wiles to the party, but we didn't bring those techniques together. Nevertheless, the more frustrated we got, the more we started to partner up in our efforts, after all, none of us could bear the thought of the dog being killed. From that point on, we started advising whoever the dog got closest to, instead of running over and trying to capture the dog ourselves. When we partnered up, we were able to chase the dog into one of the neighbors' fenced-in backyard and close the fence. When the owners came outside, we explained what we were doing, and they joined the party. The wife went into her backyard and grabbed the dog, who by then was not only tired, but was afraid of the two large dogs that had tried to come out of the backdoor with the owner. She brought the dog to the embarrassed owner and she didn't utter a "thank you" or show any form of gratitude. She just took the dog into her car and pulled away. Now, she wasn't ungrateful; I think we all knew that. The problem was, she was frustrated. She wasn't interested in our methods; she couldn't care less who rescued her dog. She simply wanted her dog back. If a pet owner's love for her dog could have her standing next to her car humiliated, frustrated and scared for nearly an hour, while a bunch of strangers worked tirelessly to capture the dog, how much more does God want His children rescued? God doesn't want us craftily manipulating our words in an attempt to prove that we are more effective at winning souls than the next believer. No! When the people worked together to build the Tower of Babel, God said, "Behold, the people is one, and they have all one language; and this they begin to do: and now nothing will be restrained from them, which they have imagined to do." Unity is the recipe for successful evangelism. As a scribe, you will be tested. Opportunities will be extended to you and doors will be opened for you, but in this, it is important that you remember that you are your first talent. Can you carry the weight of your assignment without burying it or burying yourself under it? Understand this—just because you are on a flyer doesn't mean that you are in purpose! The assignment of the scribe is to copy the Word of God, testify, prophesy and to ruminate everything God shares with and through the scribe. The assignment of the scribe is to be a pen-pushing or key-striking evangelist, teacher, prophet, pastor or apostle. The assignment of the scribe is to send a note in the form of a book into the many (mental) prisons that God's people are in and be their literary Moses, leading them to freedom one keystroke at a time. "And at midnight Paul and Silas prayed, and sang praises unto God: and the prisoners heard them. And suddenly there was a great earthquake, so that the foundations of the prison were shaken: and immediately all the doors were opened, and everyone's bands were loosed" (Acts 16:25-26). You have to produce an earthquake in the realm of the spirit in order to set God's people free. Don't try to be the greatest earthquake to ever hit your generation; just move with God and He'll release His power in you, and after His power has hit your life, He will release His power through you.

The assignment of the scribe is to be God's secretary! But the temptation of the scribe is to ignore the cries of God's people, all the while, focusing on the man or woman in the mirror. The temptation of the scribe is to pray eloquent prayers, hoping to impress the multitudes, all the while, ignoring the many sheep who are wandering around without a shepherd and crying out to God for help. Nevertheless, the assignment of the scribe is to shake up the cages that God's people are in until the doors swing open and the people are free. To do this, we must first bind the Goliaths that have been holding them in bondage. Goliath represents a strongman. Matthew 12:29 reads, "Or else how can one enter into a strong man's house, and spoil his goods, except he first bind the strong man? And then he will spoil his house." The spoil of a strongman's house was his material wealth, wives, children (in some instances) and slaves. When a nation would go to war against another nation and win, the victor would often take the spoil of the land. The spoil, in this case, is God's people, only we don't gather them for ourselves; we gather them for Christ.

In Matthew 23, the Lord talks about the evil scribes killing, beating and humiliating some of the good scribes; it reads, "Wherefore, behold, I send unto you prophets, and wise men, and scribes: and some of them ye shall kill and crucify; and some of them shall ye scourge in your synagogues, and persecute them from city to city" (Matthew 23:34). There are some good scribes (obviously), just as there are some not-so good ones. What makes an author good isn't the author's works. In many cases, it's not even the author's intentions, since people can do the wrong things to get the right results. When God blesses an author, it's because the author loves His people and is more concerned with setting them free than the author is with book signings and photo ops. Remember, it is our love for God's people that legalizes our authority with them. Any person who does not love God's people but attempts to lead them by writing a book is on the wrong side of the scribe's spectrum. Some people would be honest enough to confess that they haven't arrived in a place where they can truly say they love the people of God, nevertheless, they still want to write books and they don't want to write for the secular world. While honesty is admirable, it is absolutely important for you (if you are one of those people) to wait until your love has matured, otherwise, your book will only be an expression of who you are and not who God is, even though it may have some Christian undertones. In this, you are still attempting to lead God's people, but you are not desiring to lead them out of bondage; your desire is to get their attention and their applause. This was the same desire that the scribes Jesus rebuked had. It's called temptation. Don't fall into it. Simply let God build your love vocabulary until He decides that you're ready to lead.

A Prescription for Freedom

The Latin roots word "scrib" and its variant "script" both mean "write." The word script also means "a written document." From these words, we get the following:

- Ascribe
- Circumscribe
- Describe/ Description
- Indescribable
- Manuscript
- Postscript

- Prescribe/ Prescription
- Proscribe
- Scribal
- Scribe
- Scribble
- Script
- Scripture
- Subscribe/ Subscriber/ Subscription
- Transcribe/ Transcription

Every one of these words denote writing or something written. To get a better understanding of our job description, please look at the chart below.

Scribal Graces/ Assignments	Explanation
Inscribe	The prefix "in" means "on." It can also mean "not" or "without." In this text, however, it means to write *in* the heart. Jeremiah 31:33 reads, "But this shall be the covenant that I will make with the house of Israel; After those days, saith the LORD, I will put my law *in* their inward parts, and write it *in* their hearts; and will be their God, and they shall be my people." Remember, God often speaks to us in thoughts; we see images, but we identify the words we've learned to associate with those images. Prophets often receive impressions on their hearts to prophesy, but they don't always know what they're going to say before they open their mouths. This is also why God says in Psalm 81:10, "Open thy mouth wide, and I will fill it." You'll notice that even when we dream, we don't see written words; we see images. When we tell others about our dreams, we describe them using words.

As scribes, we have to be sensitive to the voice of the Holy Spirit; we have to pay close attention to what He says and what He reveals to us. We then release whatever He has given us to release in the time appointed to release it.

Subscribe	Hebrews 12:2 reads, "Looking unto Jesus the <u>author and finisher of our faith</u>; who for the joy that was set before him endured the cross, despising the shame, and is set down at the right hand of the throne of God."
	Jesus didn't *physically* write any of the books of the Bible because He is the Word. Nevertheless, He is the Author and Finisher of our faith; He is "the" Scribe Himself. For this reason, we are "sub" scribes. To become a "sub" scribe, we had to submit to the Word of God; we then ruminate what we've been taught until we understand, or better yet, stand under His Word. This means that we finally come into agreement with His Word. After this, we then feed it to God's people.
	Additionally, we subscribe to one another. "And the spirits of the prophets are *subject* to the prophets" (1 Corinthians 14:32).
	Our assignment is to submit to others; we subscribe to one another's teachings and leadership. This is what helps us to remain accountable with what we teach. You should *never* be the most anointed person you know. Understand that there is order in the Kingdom of God, and this order helps us to remain in the will of God.
Transcribe	The word "trans" means to take from one medium to another; it means to cross. Colossians 1:13 reads, "Who hath delivered us from the power of darkness,

	and hath translated us into the kingdom of his dear Son." When we think of the word "translate," for example, most of us think of a translator: a person who bridges the gap of communication between two or more people of differing tongues. What the translator is doing is standing in the gap. Jesus stood in the gap for us; He is our Intercessor and our Translator. He carried us from one medium to the next. Our job is to supernaturally take God's people from one realm of thought to the next. We do this through a process called "describing."
Describe	To describe something is to break it down. Remember, the prefix "de" means "down" or "to bring down." To describe the Word doesn't mean to memorize and explain it using your own intellect. It means to seek the heart of God through the reading of the text, as well as prayer, fasting and submitting to the gifts He's given us (apostles, prophets, evangelists, teachers, pastors). It means to break the Word down until it's sweet enough for the babes in Christ to eat. Let's revisit the example of the mother, the baby and the steak. A mother understands that she cannot place a chunk of steak in her child's mouth. She has to chew that steak until it is at a consistency that her child can swallow. Amazingly enough, in the chewing process, the more the steak is chewed, the sweeter it becomes. This is because most foods contain carbohydrates, which are broken down into sugar. This sweet taste makes it more palatable to the infant.
Prescribe	When we hear the word "prescribe," we automatically think of a doctor's prescription. Doctors normally prescribe medications to people who are sick, diseased or injured. Nevertheless, the prefix "pre" means "before." This means that the old proverb is true when it says, "An ounce of prevention is worth a pound of cure." Our goal isn't just to heal the brokenhearted; it's

> to get to those who are whole before they are broken. Our assignment is to share the uncompromising Word of God with everyone who has ears to hear so that when the enemy comes to break them, they are on the solid foundation of Christ. This way, they are unmovable, unshakable and unbreakable. Luke 6:47-48 reads, "Whosoever cometh to me, and heareth my sayings, and doeth them, I will shew you to whom he is like: He is like a man which built an house, and digged deep, and laid the foundation on a rock: and when the flood arose, the stream beat vehemently upon that house, and could not shake it: for it was founded upon a rock."

Of course, each level involves a certain grace. Some authors aren't that close to God, even though they are saved. John 15:23 reads, "Now there was leaning on Jesus' bosom one of his disciples, whom Jesus loved." This is to get us to understand that there are some people who are closer and more intimate with God than others. Not all of Jesus' disciples were intimately close to Him, nevertheless, they followed and submitted to Him. So, the aforementioned job descriptions are not for everyone. You may operate in any of these graces at any given time, depending on your God-given assignment. 1 Corinthians 3:7-9 reads, "So then neither is he that planteth anything, neither he that watereth; but God that giveth the increase. Now he that planteth and he that watereth are one: and every man shall receive his own reward according to his own labour. For we are labourers together with God: ye are God's husbandry, ye are God's building."

Adam and Eve were evicted from the Garden of Eden because they believed and acted upon the wrong report. While in the midst of perfection, they had been tempted; they had everything they needed right before them, but one of Satan's most effective tricks is to point out what a person does not have. For example, imagine that you were the son or daughter of an earthly dignitary who was incredibly wealthy in both riches and in love. Your father gave you everything! He even requested that the maids prepare a buffet for you every single day; this way, you can have your pick of what you want to eat. One day, you invite a new friend over. She looks at the spread of food that stretches from one end of your father's twenty-two-foot table to the next. "Where's the sweet potatoes?" she asks. You look around and find a bowl of what appears to be sweet potatoes. You then have one of the maids to hand the bowl to your ungrateful friend. She looks at the bowl, sticks her fork in it and tastes the orange delicacy. She then squints, grabs a napkin and spits out the food. "Those are not sweet potatoes," she counters. "They are yams! Why don't y'all have any sweet potatoes?" The maids look around and one of them rushes into the kitchen to get the chef. He explains to your friend that ever since you've been a child, you've always preferred yams over sweet potatoes. For this reason, he always cooks yams for you. Your friend looks at the chef and then at you. "I'm going home," she says. "My Mom cooks the best sweet potatoes and I don't need any maids to give them to me; she does this on her own because she loves me." She then walks out of the kitchen and out of your life.

You go back into the dining hall and look at the delicious spread of food. It doesn't look so good anymore. Suddenly, you don't feel so blessed anymore. Your friend now has you convinced that she's blessed and you are not. She's managed to point out the one thing that you did not have and that is, a bowl of sweet potatoes. She also highlighted the fact that her mother serves the food to her, but your father has a staff of people feeding you. Now, you're feeling robbed and rejected. Frustrated, you begin to mistreat the staff. Your doting father makes his way to the dining hall, looking for you. You're normally in your favorite seat, but when he comes into the hall, you're not there. He calls your name, but you do not answer. Finally, you decide to respond. "What do you want?" you ask. Your tone and choice of words are no longer loving. "Where are you?" asks your father as he frantically searches for you. You wipe away the tears from your eyes and yell out, "I'm under the table! Daisy was over here and she wanted to eat sweet potatoes, but we didn't have any. That stupid kitchen staff of yours didn't put any out! Plus, her mother eats with her! You never eat with me!" Disappointed, your father demands that you come from under the table. He then says to you, "I have given you everything that your heart desired. You have never wanted for anything. But now, since what I have given you is not good enough for you, I'm sending you to live in the outhouse. There, you won't have any staff preparing your food, nor will I provide the food for you. You will have to get a job and buy your own food. Additionally, you will have to prepare your own meals from now on. He then has one of the maids to pack up your clothes and help you to put them in the outhouse. He takes away your key to the main house and tells the security guards around the house to not let you in.

Excited that you now have your own place and independence, you give your jealous friend a call. She's elated that you've managed to sabotage your blessing. "You're a woman now," she says. She then invites you to her house, and when you arrive, you find the house in disarray. The house is located in the trailer park of ghettos and inside of it, you find rotten wood, roaches and a few rotten people. "Come on into the kitchen," she says. "My Mom's sweet potatoes are almost ready." You walk into the kitchen and find yourself nearly face-to-face with a hungry and territorial cockroach. Frightened, you scream, but your friend laughs. She takes a shoe and squishes the insect while it's still on the table. She then grabs a napkin, picks it up and tosses the napkin into the trash. "Butter or no butter?" she asks as she grabs a not-so-clean plate to put your food on. "No butter," you respond, mentally telling yourself to remove the look of utter disgust from your face. She then hands you a plate full of sweet potatoes. "Where's the meat?" you ask. "We don't have any," counters your friend. "What are we drinking?" you ask. Your friend grabs a dirty Styrofoam cup out of the sink and rinses it. She then fills it up with tap water. You ask about bread, other side dishes, dessert ... none of which they have. You decide to humble yourself and eat the sweet potatoes. You place your questionably clean fork into the potatoes and draw out a hefty sized potato. You bite into the vegetable, only to find that it's been loaded with sugar and overcooked.

Frustrated, you head back to your house and look in the refrigerator. It's empty because your monthly bills are draining your finances. You find a package of Ramen noodles in the cabinet and cook it. You then go outside and eat your soggy noodles, and while you're sitting on the steps, you hear laughter coming from your father's house. It's your little sister. To add insult to injury, you can see her through the window; she's sitting in your favorite seat, plus the chef is at it again. He's joking around with her about her big appetite. While he speaks with her, you see a few dishes from the spread of food in front of her. In that moment, you experience the same jealousy that your former friend experienced when she'd visited you. It is then that you realize how foolish you were.

This is a modern-day picture of how Satan deceived Adam and Eve. They wanted for nothing, nevertheless, Satan managed to show them one thing that they did not have, and that was the ability to know good from evil. This was a knowledge that they did not need because they were already perfect. The couple ended up getting kicked out of Eden and having to sweat, dig, plant, water and toil for what they needed. Let's fast forward to the around 2100 BC. The descendants of Adam and Eve were plenteous. They were walking the Earth, trying to figure out how to get back to the paradise that their ancestors had once been expelled from. This was around four hundred years after the great flood that destroyed every living thing on the Earth except Noah and his family. Undoubtedly, the people were still carrying around some of that trauma, given the fact that their life spans, at that time, usually stretched up to nine hundred years. Many of them were frustrated with their lives and wanted to get to Heaven without having to go through all the tests and trials that their ancestors had failed at. For this reason, they decided to build the Tower of Babel. They spent over one hundred years building the Tower, only to have God confuse their language and scatter them across the face of the Earth. They'd obviously heard about Heaven; they'd envisioned a world that was perfect—one where they wouldn't have to suffer anymore. They imagined a picture of Heaven that had been ruminated (in their minds) for hundreds of years. Nevertheless, they didn't know how to take every single word that had been passed down generation to generation about the Kingdom of God, and put those words back together to form the very picture that Adam and Eve had once lived in. Think about it this way. Earlier, we discussed a mother chewing up a steak so her infant can eat it. First, imagine her taking a picture of the steak. Now, think about her chewing the steak vigorously, and then spitting out the chewed-up pieces of the steak onto a plate. She repeats this until the whole steak is chewed up and strewn across her plate. Finally, she carefully attempts to put every granule of the steak back together again. Imagine her attempting to make the steak whole again. She couldn't. This would be an impossible task for her or any human, for that matter. Only God could restore that steak because it has been mixed with saliva and bacteria, and then ripped to pieces by her powerful jaws and sharp teeth. What was on the picture is now contaminated and ruminated; it cannot be put back together again. The Tower of Babel builders didn't realize that their hearts had been chewed up and spit out by sin. God wasn't giving them a complex maze of questions and riddles, designed to help them find their way back to Heaven. He wanted to put their hearts back together again until it formed the picture of Heaven. Heaven is God's will for us, not just in location, but also in essence. Heaven is the mind of God in relation to us! Remember, the pictures that we have in our heads come from our hearts and they dance around in our minds. When we believe those pictures, we begin to ruminate them, either by telling others about them or by doing the work needed to bring those pictures from our heads into our realities. God has a picture in His mind too, and it's called Heaven! But to get there, we have to enter in through the door (not the window) of God's heart. We enter in through God's will. Of course, Jesus is the key that opens the door. Nevertheless, something else is needed. You see, every door has a height and a width, so if you're bigger than that door, you can't get in through it. But this is Heaven's door, right? Most of us believe that we need to grow in stature both physically and spiritually to respect the humongous door that we've envisioned God opening for us, but this is not true. Heaven's door is small. We, on the other hand, have been puffed up by pride and fattened by sin, so the journey isn't about getting us to the door; it's about getting us through the door (see Matthew 19:24)! We are the camels that had trouble getting through the eye of a needle! The journey is about us humbling ourselves and shedding the dead weight of sin, false doctrines and ungodly beliefs until we are small enough to enter in through that door! This is why Jesus said in Mark 10:15, "Verily I say unto you, Whosoever shall not receive the kingdom of God as a little child, he shall not enter therein." You see, our ancestors had it all wrong! They tried to make us grow up when growing up and maturing are not one and the same. God wants us to mature into children; we have to grow out of being grown (independent, prideful and self-willed). This is the lesson that the Tower builders missed. They thought Heaven was up, so God let them build the Tower of Babel for more than one hundred years. Many of us have learned that God will allow us to waste our time building something that He's not in, only for Him to suddenly show up and scatter everyone we've been building with. This is also the lesson that the Israelites almost missed nearly seven hundred years later (est. 1446 BC) when they were led out of Egypt by Moses. They'd watched God do the impossible, including splitting the Red Sea to let them walk across it. Nevertheless, they found themselves in the wilderness going in circles for forty years on what should have been an eleven-day journey. They were heading towards a promise— a land that had been *described* as flowing with milk and honey. They walked and rested for forty years, only to die in their wilderness because they had not realized that their promised land was not ahead of them; it was within them. Like the scattered and fallen men of yesterday, we have to realize that Heaven is not directional; it's dimensional. When God scattered mankind, this was the equivalent of Him scattering puzzle pieces. The goal is not to get to Heaven; the goal is to get Heaven inside of us! This means we have to get a new heart and a new mind. Consider Revelation 21:1, which reads, "And I saw a new Heaven and a new Earth: for the first Heaven and the first Earth were passed away; and there was no more sea." Remember, we are mini-worlds. Let's take the aforementioned verse and make it personal. "And I received a new heart and a new mind, and the first heart had passed away and there was no more me."

The obvious question now is, what's the point of all this? It's to help you, as a writer, understand your assignment. The Bible is a map, and every Word in it is a directive. We are the voices that read those directions; we tell people where to turn and what to turn away from. If you try to lead people to Heaven in works, you'll lead them in circles and have them building structures that they'll eventually have to abandon. If you genuinely want to lead people out of bondage, you have to stop trying to get them to Heaven and start trying to get them into God's will. Remember, Heaven is the shape of God's heart; it is the big picture in His mind for us. We're simply trying to get back in the picture. In order for us to get something in our hearts, we have to meditate on it time and time again until it burns its way into our memory. In order to get in God's mind, we must meditate on His Word until it burns its way into our will. So, study the heart of God; study the very essence of who He is: love. Lead people in love one keystroke at a time. Remember, we are the literary Moses of our generations, and while we may not be leading people physically, we are leading them dimensionally (mentally). This is the prescription for freedom; it's the antidote that God handed Adam when he and Eve fell out of God's will and ended up getting erased from the picture that God created. God wanted them to appreciate what they once had, and He wanted them to make their way back into the picture. Adam and Eve didn't understand this, nor did their children. With each new generation, a memory was lost, only to be replaced by stories shared by the patriarchs who'd once heard those stories from someone else.

JESUS IS THE PRESCRIPTION THAT WE WRITE FOR OTHERS.

Nevertheless, one of the most important lessons you can learn as a scribe is this: you're not always leading people to Jesus. Sometimes, you have to lead them to a set of thoughts; these thoughts will lead them to a person who will lead them to a church that will lead them to Jesus. Understand that many of your readers are scattered around the face of the Earth; you are leading them to a point of agreement, where they can all meet in the will of God. This is the assignment of the scribe. We get people to subscribe to our websites, videos and social media pages with the goal of getting them to submit to God. We do this by describing the picture that God has shared with us, in addition to describing our own journeys. We draw a picture of God's will for them, and we inscribe this picture on their imaginations. We then transcribe them or point them to someone who can help them cross from one dimension of thought to another. Nevertheless, their journeys aren't always short. Some people have watched one generation after another fall as they attempted to find their own personal promised lands, while others have been building towers in deserts for decades. Proverbs 13:12 says that hope deferred (or delayed) makes the heart sick. As scribes, our job is to write them a prescription for freedom, all the while leading them to a person or a conclusion. Understand that a conclusion isn't always the end of a person; it is often the end of a season. Seasons should never overlap because when they do, they produce storms, and storms often produce doubt. Don't rush a reader to a conclusion and don't drown a reader in revelation. Teach each reader to swim in whatever measure of revelation that God has graced you with; teach each reader to ascend into the presence of God, and teach each reader to respect his or her own metron, after all, this is the only way that the reader can eventually become the writer or the teacher God has anointed them to be.

Driving Scribes out of Caves

We all know that caves were used as tombs in the biblical times. They were places where people buried their loved ones. Additionally, earlier on we discussed the parable of the talents and established that we are our first talent, so when the unfaithful servant buried his talent, he (in a sense) buried himself. He did not reproduce himself; he decided to die with everything that his master had deposited in him. So, the parable of the talent is a metaphor describing a gifted man hiding in a cave. He doesn't win any souls, nor does he pass the mantle that God has given him. Instead, he locks himself into a world of self-indulgence, self-pity, self-condemnation and everything selfish.

Most of us have heard about the Dead Sea Scrolls, also known as the Lost Books of the Bible and the Qumran Scrolls. Undoubtedly, these texts were written by scribes, but archaeologists and historians have argued about the origin of the texts, which have been attributed to a religious sect called the Essenes. Before we talk about the Essenes, let's peruse a few historical facts regarding the Dead Sea Scrolls.

1. The Dead Sea Scrolls were found between 1947 to 1956 in a series of 12 caves.
2. The Scrolls were found in the Quarum Caves, which are located in Israel near the Dead Sea.
3. The scrolls were found accidentally by three teenage shepherds named Bedouin Shepherd Muhammed edh-Dhib, Jum'a Muhammed, and Khalil Musa.
4. One of the teenage shepherds threw a rock into what is now known as Cave One and heard a shattering sound. The young men entered the cave and found a collection of clay jars, seven of which contained some of the scrolls.
5. The Scrolls are divided into two parts: biblical and non-biblical. The non-biblical texts are believed to be sectarian, meaning, they enforce the beliefs of a particular sect.
6. The Scrolls are made up of 825-870 manuscripts.
7. The Scrolls were written on documents made from animal skins, papyrus and one of the scrolls was made from copper.
8. There were no punctuation marks in the Scrolls.
9. The Scrolls are believed to be more than two thousand years old.
10. The Dead Sea Scrolls contain fragmented text from every Old Testament book except for the Book of Esther.
11. The Dead Sea Scrolls was written in Hebrew, Aramaic and an ancient paleo-Hebrew alphabet which is no longer in use. Additionally, some of the text features translations of the Hebrew Bible in Greek.
12. In addition to the rest of the Scrolls, there are 19 fragments of Isaiah, 25 fragments of Deuteronomy and 30 fragments of the Psalms.
13. The Dead Sea Scrolls are believed to be the written works of a strictly

religious group of men called the Essenes.

First off, who were the Essenes? Like the Pharisees and the Sadducees, the Essenes were a strictly religious sect of the Jews who lived a communal monastic lifestyle. They left Jerusalem to live in the wilderness; they completely separated themselves from other Jews because they were against the way the Temple was being run. Believed to have been vegetarian, the Essenes were divided up into several groups, and the majority of those groups practiced celibacy. They were a New Testament group of believers who went out of their way to abstain from the pleasures of the world, even subjecting themselves to voluntary poverty. They did not own slaves, were against war, and only carried weapons for protection. They strictly adhered to the Law of Moses, the Sabbath and ritual purity. They were so dedicated to purity that they would not defecate on the Sabbath. The Essenes had been around for about one hundred years when Jesus was born. They separated themselves from the Jews, believing that they were the "chosen ones" who had been called to prepare a way for the Lord, strictly adhering to the Book of Isaiah. Not much is known about this religious group, nevertheless, most evidence points to them being the authors of the Dead Sea Scrolls.

Let's revisit the story of Elijah. Of course, Elijah went on the run from Jezebel and hid himself in a cave. 1 Kings 19:9-10 reads, "And he came thither unto a cave, and lodged there; and, behold, the word of the LORD came to him, and he said unto him, What doest thou here, Elijah? And he said, I have been very jealous for the LORD God of hosts: for the children of Israel have forsaken thy covenant, thrown down thine altars, and slain thy prophets with the sword; and I, even I only, am left; and they seek my life, to take it away." Here, we see that like the Essenes, Elijah believed that he was the only true prophet left. Of course, we know that David hid himself in a cave when he was hiding from Saul. As a matter of fact, David wrote Psalms 57 while hiding in a cave; it reads:

> {To the chief Musician, Altaschith, Michtam of David, when he fled from Saul in the cave.}
> Be merciful unto me, O God, be merciful unto me: for my soul trusteth in thee: yea, in the shadow of thy wings will I make my refuge, until these calamities be overpast.

I will cry unto God most high; unto God that performeth all things for me.

He shall send from Heaven, and save me from the reproach of him that would swallow me up. Selah. God shall send forth his mercy and his truth.

My soul is among lions: and I lie even among them that are set on fire, even the sons of men, whose teeth are spears and arrows, and their tongue a sharp sword.

Be thou exalted, O God, above the heavens; let thy glory be above all the Earth.

They have prepared a net for my steps; my soul is bowed down: they have digged a pit before me, into the midst whereof they are fallen themselves. Selah.

My heart is fixed, O God, my heart is fixed: I will sing and give praise.

Awake up, my glory; awake, psaltery and harp: I myself will awake early.

I will praise thee, O Lord, among the people: I will sing unto thee among the nations.

For thy mercy is great unto the heavens, and thy truth unto the clouds.

Be thou exalted, O God, above the heavens: let thy glory be above all the Earth.

As we can see, the cave has become a hiding place for many scribes. This is largely because most true scribes are prophetic in nature, and of course, the Jezebel spirit hates prophets and prophecies. For this reason, most true scribes have had many encounters with this spirit, and the ones who did not have the right team of counselors around them often retreated to caves. "Where no counsel is, the people fall: but in the multitude of counselors there is safety" (Proverbs 11:14). Nevertheless, let's first address the Essenes. Were they true men of God and are the Dead Sea Scrolls truly lost books from the Bible? The answer is obvious. They were believers, nevertheless, they were religious men who had been driven into their caves by fear. You see, religion makes people fearful. As for the Dead Sea Scrolls, the non-biblical scripts were sectarian, meaning they contained the strict beliefs of the Essenes or whatever sect wrote them. (Again, the origin of these documents is still being debated, even though most evidence points back to the Essenes being the authors). For this reason, they weren't necessarily "lost" per-se; a better way to describe them is the Rejected Books. Remember, the Essenes believed that they were "set apart" to prepare the way for the Lord, but this wasn't true. John the Baptist had been ordained by God to carry out this task. The evidence to this truth is found in Matthew 3:1-3, which reads, "In those days came John the Baptist, preaching in the wilderness of Judaea, and saying, Repent ye: for the Kingdom of Heaven is at hand. For this is he that was spoken of by the prophet Esaias, saying, The voice of one crying in the wilderness, Prepare ye the way of the Lord, make his paths straight." Because they believed they were the chosen ones, the Essenes had gone into the wilderness, separating themselves from the rest of the Jews. Nevertheless, John the Baptist came along a hundred years later and found himself in the wilderness, preparing the people of God for Jesus' arrival. What does this mean? It's simple. The Essenes tried to set themselves apart, not realizing that their works would not qualify them for the assignment that would be given to John the Baptist.

Before we move on, let's consider a few facts about the Dead Sea itself.
1. The cave that David hid in when he fled from Saul is just west of the Dead Sea.
2. Because of the sodium content in the Dead Sea, it cannot sustain life.
3. The Dead Sea is ten times saltier than all the world's oceans.
4. The shores of the Dead Sea are 1,412 feet below sea level, making them the lowest elevation on land.
5. The Dead Sea is 997 feet deep, making it the deepest hypersaline lake in the world.
6. During the rainy seasons, the salinity in the water decreases, making it inhabitable for some forms of bacteria.
7. Water flows into the Dead Sea, but because it is deadlocked by land, water does not flow from it.
8. The Dead Sea is also known as the Stinking Sea because tourists complain of smelling what seems to be rotten eggs when approaching the sea.
9. The asphalt from the Dead Sea is so plenteous that it was once used by Egyptians for mummification.
10. With an annual rainfall less than 50 millimeters, the climate of the Dead Sea is dry.

What can we take from these facts?
1. The Dead Sea is the lowest place. When David ran into a cave near the Dead

Sea, he was in his lowest place. When Elijah hid in a cave near the Dead Sea, he was in his lowest place.

2. The Dead Sea is a lifeless place; it does not sustain life, so it's a graveyard of sorts. Consider the parable of the talents. When David and Elijah hid themselves near the Dead Sea, they were burying their talents (themselves).
3. Even though the Dead Sea is deep, it's too salty (bitter) to consume.
4. The Dead Sea takes water (revelation, wisdom, life) in, but does not give it out.
5. The Dead Sea preserves dead things.
6. The Dead Sea is a dry place.

One city near the Dead Sea is Sodom. One interesting fact is Lot's wife was turned into a pillar of salt when she disobeyed God and looked back at the city as it was being destroyed. Why a pillar of salt? It's simple. She became what she fixed her eyes on. We are all made of dust. Dust contains sand, and sand, of course, is salty. Remember, the Dead Sea is an extremely salty body of water. Genesis 2 tells us that God formed man from the dust of the ground. Genesis 3:19 reads, "In the sweat of thy face shalt thou eat bread, till thou *return* unto the ground; for out of it wast thou taken: for dust thou art, and unto dust shalt thou return." From here, we can safely assume that most, if not all, of the salt in and around the Dead Sea is the remnant of that great and awful day when God rained fire on Sodom and Gomorrah. This is just a theory, of course, but it is more than plausible. Additionally, the smell of raw eggs that tourists complain about is actually the smell of sulfur. Why does that area smell like sulfur? Again, this can be traced back to the day that God destroyed Sodom and Gomorrah in 2067 BC. Genesis 19:23-26 (ESV) reads, "The sun had risen on the earth when Lot came to Zoar. Then the LORD rained on Sodom and Gomorrah *sulfur* and fire from the LORD out of Heaven. And he overthrew those cities, and all the valley, and all the inhabitants of the cities, and what grew on the ground. But Lot's wife, behind him, looked back, and she became a pillar of salt." Here, we see that God caused sulfur to rain on the cities of Sodom and Gomorrah. Again, sulfur smells like rotten eggs and so does the area surrounding the Dead Sea.

Again, the Essenes are believed to be the authors of the Dead Sea Scrolls; they hid themselves in caves near the Dead Sea. As a scribe of God, one of the greatest temptations you'll have to overcome is the temptation to hide yourself in a cave, especially if you are not submitted to a leader or if you are surrounded by the wrong people. It is easy for scribes to think that they are the only true saints left, believing that every other Christian is double-minded or backslidden. This is because the life of a writer is often plagued by loneliness. Please understand that hiding yourself is not the same as being hidden. God often hides scribes, but He doesn't hide them in caves (since caves are dark places), He hides them in plain sight. Nevertheless, a scribe can be surrounded by ten thousand people and still be in a cave of sorts. One of the truths I've stumbled upon is the fact that a cave is not always a place of solitude; a scribe can actually hide himself or herself in a mega church, in a career, in a series of relationships or in a season. Additionally, the way God hides scribes is through revelation. How so? God can set a prophetic scribe in a public place and hide him or her, only revealing the scribe's identity to one or more intercessors, prophets and whomever God chooses to reveal it to. Think about the moment when Jesus asked His disciples, "Who does man say that I am?" Only one of the disciples answered Him. "And Simon Peter answered and said, Thou art the Christ, the Son of the living God. And Jesus answered and said unto him, Blessed art thou, Simon Barjona: for flesh and blood hath not revealed it unto thee, but my Father which is in Heaven" (Matthew 16:16-17). By this time, the disciples had been walking with Jesus for anywhere between one year to two years. Nevertheless, none of the other men answered Jesus' question. His identity had been revealed to Peter by God.

As a scribe of God, you have to be okay with being hidden until God decides to highlight Himself in you. What does this mean?
1. You can write 15 books and still not be known by man.
2. You can go to 75 prophetic conferences and not receive a single prophecy.
3. You can be the most beautiful woman or the most handsome man in a room and still not be noticed.
4. You can reveal your identity to others, telling them your fears, passions, struggles and desires, only to realize years later that the people you've been the most intimate with don't truly know you.

Understand that when God hides a scribe, He does so deliberately. You see, not all scribes are humble enough to stay hidden. Many reveal themselves before the appointed time, believing that their gifts should be on display. Yes, God said that our gifts would make room for us, but He did not say when this would happen! He did, however, tell us in Ecclesiastes 3:1, "To *everything* there is a season, and a time to *every* purpose under the Heaven." There is a season for everything and every gift! A fruit that's consumed before its season will always be as bitter as the Dead Sea. Scribes who prematurely reveal themselves are ambitious, self-seeking and dangerous, not just to themselves, but to anyone who attempts to pastor them. Many scribes leave their church homes the moment they write their first books. Why is this? Because scribes who prematurely reveal themselves are usually salty (bitter), meaning, they find it hard to manage their own weight. These men and women bury themselves, not realizing that the book isn't the talent; they are! They bury themselves under debt and relationships, nevertheless, they reveal themselves in corporate settings and conversations. They endure many unnecessary attacks because of their unwillingness to stay hidden. After they don't get the book sales and the attention they feel they are entitled to, many scribes leave their tribes, often believing themselves to be "set apart" from the rest. This is the very crime that the Essenes committed. Many scribes will hide in their homes, refusing to go to church, whereas, others will hide themselves in careers and in relationships. Many will hide themselves under wigs and tons of makeup, hoping to reinvent themselves. Some scribes even pick up personalities that are not their own; ironically enough, they hide themselves in an attempt to find themselves.

The world of a scribe is a complex place. It is a place of many earthquakes. Consider God's response to Elijah when he hid himself in a cave. "And he said, I have been very jealous for the LORD God of hosts: for the children of Israel have forsaken thy covenant, thrown down thine altars, and slain thy prophets with the sword; and I, even I only, am left; and they seek my life, to take it away. And he said, Go forth, and stand upon the mount before the LORD. And, behold, the LORD passed by, and a great and strong wind rent the mountains, and brake in pieces the rocks before the LORD; but the LORD was not in the wind: and after the wind an earthquake; but the LORD was not in the earthquake: And after the earthquake a fire; but the LORD was not in the fire: and after the fire a still small voice. And it was so, when Elijah heard it, that he wrapped his face in his mantle, <u>and went out</u>, and stood in the entering in of the cave. And, behold, there came a voice unto him, and said, What doest thou here,

Elijah?" (1 Kings 19:10-13).

Notice in the aforementioned text that God first drives Elijah out of the cave before He responds to him. After all the commotion was finished and the dust settled, God asked Elijah the same question He'd already asked him. He asked, "Why are you here?" In verse 14, Elijah gave, almost word for word, the same response he'd given God while he was inside the cave. Verse 14 reads, "And he said, I have been very jealous for the Lord God of hosts: because the children of Israel have forsaken thy covenant, thrown down thine altars, and slain thy prophets with the sword; and I, even I only, am left; and they seek my life, to take it away." Notice here, however, that God does not pose the question to Elijah again. Instead, since Elijah is now outside of the cave, God chooses to give him his next set of instructions. 1 Kings 19:15-18 reads, "And the Lord said unto him, Go, return on thy way to the wilderness of Damascus: and when thou comest, anoint Hazael to be king over Syria: And Jehu the son of Nimshi shalt thou anoint to be king over Israel: and Elisha the son of Shaphat of Abelmeholah shalt thou anoint to be prophet in thy room. And it shall come to pass, that him that escapeth the sword of Hazael shall Jehu slay: and him that escapeth from the sword of Jehu shall Elisha slay.
Yet I have left me seven thousand in Israel, all the knees which have not bowed unto Baal, and every mouth which hath not kissed him." Not only did the Lord give Elijah his next set of instructions, He addressed his fears, letting him know that he wasn't the only prophet left. What if the Essenes had received this same message, letting them know that they weren't the only men concerned with holiness left? They were likely men truly anointed by God, but driven into the depths of 12 caves by fear and religiousness. Now on display in a laboratory in Jerusalem, the Dead Sea Scrolls have become nothing but the subject of discussions, mysteries and conspiracy theories. What can we take from this chapter?

1. Whatever is written in a cave was written in fear.
2. Whatever is written in a cave runs the risk of not being regarded as authentic. Remember, the word "authentic" comes from the word "authority," and it means undiluted power.
3. Fear drives prophetic scribes into caves, but the wind, an earthquake and a fire will drive them out.

Now, the cave that Elijah came out of was a physical cave, but what happened to the mountain was a picture of deliverance. Let's revisit the chart below.

Reaction to Deliverance	What Demons Experience
Yawn	Heavy Winds
Spit	Flood
Vomit	Tsunami
Cry	Rain
Sneeze	Volcano
Cough	Hurricane
Convulse	Earthquake
Flatulence	Thunder

After the wind split the mountains and an earthquake hit, there was a fire. After the fire was lit in Elijah's belly, he heard a still, small voice. After Elijah heard the voice of the Lord, he grabbed his mantle, wrapped his face with it and came out of his cave. It was then that God addressed his season; it was then that God addressed his fears. You see, after deliverance, you need the truth to remain free, otherwise, according to Matthew 12:45, seven spirits more wicked than the ones that came out will come in, along with the one that got cast out.

The problems in your life may very well be God addressing your fears. God drives scribes out of caves, and if at any time you decide that the assignment is too much for you, the Lord just may have you to pass your assignment (talent) to someone else. Matthew 25:28 reads, "Take therefore the talent from him, and give it unto him which hath ten talents." Understand this: Elijah did not lose his anointing. He wasn't less anointed because he hid from his assignment by burying himself in a cave. God didn't love him any less, nor did He turn His back on him. As a matter of fact, along with Enoch, Elijah is the only other man in the Bible who did not taste death. Nevertheless, he had to anoint people to do what God wanted him to do. He also had to pass his mantle to Elisha. Again, this did not disqualify him as a prophet because, unlike the unfaithful servant in the parable of the talents, he actually multiplied his talent by turning the hearts of the Israelites back to God. Nevertheless, while obeying God, he'd found himself up against his own Goliath (Jezebel) and that spirit managed to make itself look bigger and more powerful than it actually was. Howbeit, God had to shake his cage with an earthquake and deliver him from the giant that caused him to tremble. Eventually, to get rid of Jezebel, God sent Jehu to her castle. Jehu didn't lift a finger to slay Jezebel; he simply released a word. "And he lifted up his face to the window, and said, Who is on my side? Who? And there looked out to him two or three eunuchs. And he said, Throw her down. So they threw her down: and some of her blood was sprinkled on the wall, and on the horses: and he trode her under foot" (2 Kings 9:32-33). Jehu understood that the battle was not his; it was the Lord's. Having Jezebel cast off the wall was a picture of deliverance; he cast down the Jezebel principality, but this could only be done after the hearts of the people had been turned back to God, which was a task that Elisha had successfully carried out before he anointed Jehu.

When someone's heart is turned back to God, it simply means that person falls out of agreement with the enemy. Amos 3:3 reads, "Can two walk together, except they are agreed?" To drive a scribe out of a cave, you must do the following:

1. Prove yourself to be trustworthy and address the scribe's fears. Most scribes who are in caves are afraid of being hurt, used or misunderstood. Truly anointed scribes are oftentimes "strange," meaning they stand out in crowds, which is a trait that they do not welcome. To avoid standing out, many scribes simply choose to stay in their caves.

2. After you've gained a small measure of the scribe's trust, explain to the man or woman of God that disappointment is the heartbeat of desire. What this means is, if any person desires to do anything great in the Earth, that person has to acclimate himself or herself with disappointment. Disappointment is not a threat to success; it is a prerequisite for it. The reason this has to be explained is because most wounded scribes will retreat to their caves the very second they endure disappointment, fear or offense; this is because they have a misguided understanding of how church and church folks should be.

3. Show the scribe your scars. Most scribes in caves have lashes on their hearts that you cannot see. They've been whipped by life, false prophecies, false doctrines, false leaders, entitlement, unrealistic expectations, lust and

489

misguided interpretations of the Bible. They genuinely think they are alone in their quests for the truth. Remember, Elijah told the Lord that he alone was left. For this reason, you have to show your scars or, better yet, testify about what God has delivered you from.

4. Teach the scribe how to pray for and/or find his or her own multitude of counselors. Believe it or not, scribes, just like everyone else, desire healthy, beneficial relationships, but because many of them were raised in dysfunctional homes, they tend to gravitate towards dysfunctional people and vice versa. For this reason, many cave scribes simply do not know how to choose godly counsel. Consequentially, they almost always end up submitting to ungodly souls every time they attempt to step out of their caves. This further validates their belief that their caves are hiding places designed for them by God when, in truth, caves are nothing but graveyards for gifted people. When they are surrounded by godly counsel, they'll feel more secure and will wander even further away (mentally) from their caves.

5. Take the scribe far away from his or her cave, and then, release the power of God; in short, release an earthquake to shut the doors of the cave. This means that you must first love the scribe enough to tell him or her the truth. When the scribe has your trust and attention, and when you've received clearance from the Lord, sit the scribe down and help him or her to better understand God's heart in relation to him or her. Do NOT do this when your relationship with the scribe is fresh, otherwise, the man or woman of God will retreat back into the cave. Of course, you have to use wisdom when you reach this stage of the deliverance; you cannot be argumentative, demeaning or display a matter-of-fact tone. Additionally, you cannot and should not embarrass the scribe. Instead, arrange a time to hang out with the child of God. Be sure to meet up at a place that's quiet, serene and comfortable. When the time is right, simply address whatever God tells you to address. If done at the right time, in the right setting and with the right attitude, you'll find that this is a conversation that will be welcomed and even appreciated by the scribe.

6. Never pull a scribe out of a cave; give the prophet a loving nudge or a gentle push. If the scribe resists, please understand that you're either pulling the scribe (going against his/her will) or pushing the scribe prematurely. Attempting to push a scribe into his or her destiny before the scribe's time is

the same as miscarrying your assignment. Lastly, please understand that when we see people from God's eyes, we will often see their potential. It is dangerous to pull on a man's potential when he's not pushing it out because potential is only potent in its right season. If tugged on before its time, it becomes impotent and cannot produce anything.

Microscribeology

"You're grounded! Go to that corner over there and don't you move until you're ready to repent!" The Lord's voice was firm, but loving. Adam and Eve tightened up the strings on their dew-covered skirts and made their way to their new corner of the Earth. They dared not to look back, knowing that they'd disappointed their Father. All their children would be born in that same corner. They wouldn't be born in timeout; they'd be born in time itself, meaning, they would become subject to the Earth's laws. All their children would remain grounded until Jesus paid the price for their sins. We'll talk more about this duo as we go deeper into this chapter.

Microscribeology isn't just magnifying the life of the scribe in general; it is helping you to learn more about yourself as a scribe. What's your depth? What's your latitude? Are you a surface-level teacher or a well-digging apostle? What's your magnitude? In short, how much power is behind your words and what do your words move? I'm not talking about the number or exclamation points you place behind a sentence; I'm talking about actual movement, for example, shifting paradigms and igniting revivals. What's your longitude, metron or better yet, your jurisdictional rule? What and where is your Goliath? You see, the average author does not know the answer to any of these questions, but I am convinced that any author who dares to get to know themselves, their strengths and their limitations is an author who will go far in the writing world.

Authenticity = Authority. The strength of a scribe is in the scribe's ability to be who God created him or her to be. Just like the word "author," the word "authentic" comes from the prefix "auto," which means "self." This means that authenticity is a measure of one's own power. When we're dealing with the word "authentic," it simply means the power of being one's self. Dictionary.com defines "authority" this way:
- Of undisputed origin and not a copy; genuine.
- Made or done in the traditional or original way, or in a way that faithfully resembles an original.
- Based on facts; accurate or reliable.

WHERE THERE IS NO AUTHENTICITY, THERE IS NO LEGAL AUTHORITY.

For example, you've probably come across photos of men and women adorned in colorful bishopric attire. Many of them wear long cloaks, crown themselves with elaborate miters, and firmly grasp brass crosiers, but in those photos, you'll see a group of people who've never cast out a single demon. They can hoop, and they've mastered church politics, but they have no power. Why is this? It's simple. Because demons aren't afraid of religion or cultural uniformity; they are afraid of God-submitted believers who've died to themselves and surrendered wholeheartedly to God. They're afraid of people who have faith, not people who have ordination papers. They aren't afraid of people who have extensive vocabularies, nor are they afraid of Hebrew words; they are afraid of the Word of God. With that being said, the question you must pose to yourself is, "Where is my power?" To answer this, of course, your power lies in your authenticity.

Every person is a planet within himself or herself, but before we go deeper into this, let's visit our own solar system. The sun is the center of our solar system, and everything in the solar system revolves around it. The sun is a star in our solar system; it provides many benefits to us including light, warmth, water, life, food, oxygen and so much more. Of course, the sun is much like the Son of God. Everything in the Earth revolves around Him, even the people who deny Him, and for this reason, He is a star. Let's look at what the sun provides and compare it with what the Son provides.

Sun	Son
Light	"Jesus saith unto him, I am the way, the truth, and the life: no man cometh unto the Father, but by me" (John 14:6)
Warmth	"And we have known and believed the love that God hath to us. God is love; and he that dwelleth in love dwelleth in God, and God in him" (1 John 4:16).
Water	"Jesus answered and said unto her,

	Whosoever drinketh of this water shall thirst again: But whosoever drinketh of the water that I shall give him shall never thirst; but the water that I shall give him shall be in him a well of water springing up into everlasting life" (John 4:13-14).
Life	"And this is the record, that God hath given to us eternal life, and this life is in his Son" (1 John 5:11).
Food	"And Jesus said unto them, I am the bread of life: he that cometh to me shall never hunger; and he that believeth on me shall never thirst" (John 6:35).
Oxygen	"And when he had said this, he breathed on them, and saith unto them, Receive ye the Holy Ghost" (John 20:22).

Knowing now what we know about the sun and the Son, we can better understand our roles as scribes, but before we can do this, we have to understand our roles as servants of the Most High God; we must first understand that we are God's creations and He is our Creator. God produced us and now, we must reproduce ourselves. In Genesis 1:28, God said to Adam and Eve, "Be fruitful, and multiply, and replenish the earth, and subdue it: and have dominion over the fish of the sea, and over the fowl of the air, and over every living thing that moveth upon the earth." That command wasn't just for the couple; it is a commandment for the human race as a whole, since we are all reproductions of Adam and Eve. Additionally, this wasn't just a command to have babies, after all, if you reread the scripture, you'll notice the following words: replenish, subdue, and dominion. To replenish something means to refill it or fill it up again. This means that something that was once full has become empty, and our job is to fill it up again. The word "subdue" means to overcome something or bring it under your control. Lastly, God told the couple to "have dominion." The word "dominion" is a jurisdictional word; it means to have control over a measured space. What's amazing about this command is that it came before the infamous fall of Adam and Eve. Understand this: rules and laws are created when both good and evil are present; they are designed to create a line of demarcation for the wicked, warning them that if they are to cross that line, they would be punished. But if Adam and Eve didn't know sin; they had not yet eaten from the Tree of the Knowledge of Good and Evil, why did God give them dominion over something they were oblivious to? The answer is as simple as it is complex. Because God is Alpha and Omega, the Beginning and the End; He knew their end from their beginning. Evil was present (we see the evidence of this when the serpent made its way over to Eve and deceived her). What God was simply telling the couple is to act like Him. They were to obey Him, serve Him and imitate Him; in short, their assignment was to maintain order. Of course, they were allowed to eat the good of the land, but God told them to replenish what they ate, meaning, don't just consume what comes out of the land, reproduce what you've eaten! But this could only be done if the couple retained their authenticity. For this reason, Satan decided to attack the very source of the couple's power. Genesis 3:1-5 details his deception; it reads, "Now the serpent was more subtle than any beast of the field which the LORD God had made. And he said unto the woman, Yea, hath God said, Ye shall not eat of every tree of the garden? And the woman said unto the serpent, We may eat of the fruit of the trees of the garden: But of the fruit of the tree which is in the midst of the garden, God hath said, Ye shall not eat of it, neither shall ye touch it, lest ye die. And the serpent said unto the woman, Ye shall not surely die: For God doth know that in the day ye eat thereof, then your eyes shall be opened, and ye shall be as gods, knowing good and evil." Notice here, that Satan told Eve that they would be "as gods." 1 Corinthians 8:6 reads, "But to us there is but one God, the Father, of whom are all things, and we in him; and one Lord Jesus Christ, by whom are all things, and we by him."

Satan was introducing Eve to the concept that YAHWEH was just one of many gods. Of course, he was lying to her. He told her that she could be just like the gods, meaning, he was leading her into idolatry and away from her authentic identity. You see, her power was in her identity and her power was also in her ability to identify YAHWEH as the *only* true and living God. This was the only way she could identify with God. Her dominion was found in her authenticity. When he convinced her to bite into the fruit, he simultaneously convinced her to give up her likeness to God (remember, we were created in His image). He convinced her to put on the likeness of "a god" and not the Most High God. We all know the rest of the story. Eve bit into the fruit, gave some to her husband, Adam, and the couple paid dearly for their misconduct. They'd crossed a line of demarcation; God told them not to eat from the Tree of the Knowledge of Good and Evil, but they broke the law. After their fall, they began to reproduce just as God had commanded them to do, but the only problem was, they were no longer a perfect specimen of God. They now had rebellion in their blood. They now had rejection in their blood. They now had double-mindedness in their blood. They were now filled with both good and evil, so they reproduced everything that was good about them, along with their newfound wickedness. They gave birth to a generational curse that Jesus would later come to redeem us from. Like the Earth, they were like small planets, but when they listened to the lies of the enemy, they stopped revolving around the Son, and for this reason, they fell. If the Earth stopped orbiting the sun, it would crash into it, but the "fall" towards the sun would take around 64 days to complete. Nevertheless, before the final crash, all human life will have ceased to exist on the 47th day of the fall because of the rising temperatures (calculations by Aatisha Bhatia/ Wired.com/ What Would Happen if the Earth Stopped in its Orbit).

In Genesis 1, the Earth is created. Later on in Genesis 1, there is a mention about the creation of man, but we don't see any elaboration on this until Genesis 2. When we get to Genesis 3, we witness the fall of man and the expulsion from the Garden of Eden. In Genesis 4, another creation takes place—Eve conceived Cain, and not long after this, she conceived Abel. Cain would go on to kill his brother, and for this reason, he was sent even further away from Eden. Genesis 4:16 says that he settled in a land called Nod, which was east of Eden. From there, Cain reproduced himself and created a son who he named Enoch (not to be confused with the Enoch mentioned in Genesis 5 who did not taste death because he had been taken by God). This system of reproduction continued until God flooded the Earth because it had become full of evil men. Of course, we are all familiar with the story of Noah and the ark. Once the ark rested on the mountain, Noah, along with his three sons and their wives, exited the boat. The boat came to rest on a mountain called Ararat. Scholars have speculated about the location of Eden; of course, it was also affected by the flood, but the truth is, none of these speculations can be backed by irrefutable evidence. Nevertheless, we can summarize that mankind found himself further and further away from Eden.

Out of the ark came Noah, along with his three sons: Ham, Japheth and Shem. Ham was a Cain of sorts, only he didn't kill his brother. Instead, he attempted to expose his father. For this reason, Noah cursed Ham's children, and from there, another generational curse was born. Nevertheless, the people were as one, and all of the brothers' children and descendants continued to roam eastward as one large group.

Realizing that they were traveling away from God and not towards Him, the inhabitants of the Earth decided to build the Tower of Babel. Genesis 11:1-4 tells the story; it reads, "And the whole Earth was of one language, and of one speech. And it came to pass, as they journeyed from the east, that they found a plain in the land of Shinar; and they dwelt there. And they said one to another, Go to, let us make brick, and burn them thoroughly. And they had brick for stone, and slime had they for mortar. And they said, Go to, let us build us a city and a tower, whose top may reach unto Heaven; and let us make us a name, lest we be scattered abroad upon the face of the whole Earth." What the people didn't realize is that "up" is relative, after all, Eden wasn't "up," nor is Heaven beyond the clouds. Let's understand one thing. Adam and Eve didn't fall naturally; they fell dimensionally (Apostle Bryan Meadows). This means that their perception changed. The people were trying to ascend physically, when God wanted them to ascend spiritually. In other words, they were heading in the wrong direction. "There is a way which seemeth right unto a man, but the end thereof are the ways of death" (Proverbs 14:12). We see the concept of up and down, once again, in Genesis 11:5, which reads, "And the LORD came down to see the city and the tower, which the children of men builded." As you can see, the Bible says that the Lord came "down" to see the city and the tower. This does NOT mean that God traveled physically, since He is Spirit; it means He lowered Himself in reasoning so that He could understand the reasoning of man. This is similar to what parents do when their children are lost. A father in a retail store, for example, may try to "think like a child" so that he can find his wandering four-year old. This means that he had to come down from sound reasoning; he had to relate to his son in order to find him. Thinking this way would lead him to the toy section or the candy aisle.

Throughout the book of Genesis, we've watched the descendants of Adam and Eve travel eastward in an attempt to find their way back to the place Adam and Eve had once been evicted from and somewhere along the way, they developed the concept that they needed to go up towards the clouds. The notion that Heaven is up has since traveled thousands of years and is still a common belief amongst Christians to this day. What we're seeing is mankind's desperate attempt to reconcile with God, not realizing ascension isn't about climbing upward; it's about growing up. Sure, the men of old, such as Moses, would ascend mountains to meet with God, but God used this to demonstrate a concept. For example, it was up on Mount Sinai that Moses received the Ten Commandments. Jesus ascended to Heaven from the Mount of Olives. Noah's ark came to rest on Mount Ararat. It was on Mount Moriah that Abraham almost sacrificed his son. It was from Mount Pisgah that Moses got his first and only glimpse of the Promised Land. The mountain represents a high place, not just in height, but in thought. It is a place where man humbles himself; it is a place where the strength of man fails because of the climb. In 2 Corinthians 12:9, the Lord says, "My grace is sufficient for thee: for my strength is made perfect in weakness." The people were gathered together, attempting to build the Tower of Babel, not realizing that mankind had fallen away from God when they'd accepted Satan's lies as truth. The only way back to God would be through His Son who, at that time, had not come into the realm of the Earth yet. Over two thousand years later, the Son of God would come into the Earth and began to draw men to Himself. In John 12:32, He said, "And I, if I be lifted up from the Earth, will draw all men unto me." Notice two words here: up and draw. Up, again, is relative. Nevertheless, what the Lord is saying is if His name is placed above every name (where it belongs), He will cause men to gravitate towards and orbit or revolve around Him, whether they believe upon Him or not. It also demonstrates the manner in which He would be crucified, which was up on a mountain, nailed to a cross. Because He was lifted up on the cross, His name is known all around the world, even in pagan nations. As a matter of fact, you'll notice that even Atheists are drawn to videos and teachings regarding Him. Even though they try to discredit those teachings, they are still innately drawn to the name of Jesus.

The next word we want to focus on is "draw." Remember, the planets orbit or revolve around the sun. This is because of the gravitational pull from the sun. When the Son of God said that He would draw all men to Him, He was speaking of a gravitational pull. The Greek word for "draw" is "helkó" and it means to persuade, pull, drag or attract. This is exactly what gravity does; it pulls, influences and attracts objects.

Again, we are like little planets; we are all in one stage or another. In Genesis 1:1-2, the Bible details the creation of the Earth; it reads, "In the beginning God created the Heaven and the Earth. And the Earth was without form, and void; and darkness was upon the face of the deep. And the Spirit of God moved upon the face of the waters." This is the same state that Adam found himself in at one point. Genesis 2:5-7 reads, "And every plant of the field before it was in the earth, and every herb of the field before it grew: for the LORD God had not caused it to rain upon the earth, and there was not a man to till the ground. But there went up a mist from the earth, and watered the whole face of the ground. And the LORD God formed man of the dust of the ground, and breathed into his nostrils the breath of life; and man became a living soul." God "formed" man, meaning, like the Earth, man was without form, and as we can see in Genesis 1:1, when the Earth was without form, it was void and dark. The same is true for mankind. When we are new converts, we are both void and dark, meaning, we have not come to fully orbit the Son of God because we are still revolving around the world and its systems. During this phase of our lives, we are trying to fill our voids with whatever earthly pleasures we can find. Where do we go to quench our desires? Into the darkness, of course; we head off into sin, hoping to find something to satisfy our ever-growing voids. This means that, as new converts, we're saved, but we're still journeying "downward," or better yet, descending into the depths of insanity. Understand that sinning against God is the result of an unsound mind and there are levels of insanity. What we deem to be normal is nothing but the culturally accepted insanity of our day, for example, homosexuality is becoming widely accepted, but up until 1973, the American Psychiatric Association classified homosexuality as a psychological disorder. Of course, all sins (including fornication between a man and woman) are the result and evidence of an unsound mind.

And this is where you, the scribe, come in. You see, the people thought they needed a king when they needed people to shift their paradigms or better yet, their thinking. Today, we are surrounded by words, some of which are facts, some of which are truths, and some of which are lies. Of course, a fact is anything that can be proven by the laws of the Earth, for example, gravity is a fact; it exists and that's why we're grounded. It holds us in the Earth. Spiritually speaking, gravity is a supernatural law designed to keep us grounded. Let's revisit the modern-day account of Adam and Eve's fall, as described in the beginning of this chapter.

> "You're grounded! Go to that corner over there and don't you move until you're ready to repent!" The Lord's voice was firm, but loving. Adam and Eve tightened up the strings on their dew-covered skirts and made their way to their new corner of the Earth. They dared not to look back, knowing that they'd disappointed their Father. All of their children would be born in that same corner. All of their children would remain grounded until Jesus paid the price for their sins.

Again, gravity grounds us. It has its own set of laws, all of which, were described by a scientist named Isaac Newton. Newton's Law of Gravity pretty much details the relationship between the motion of the moon and the motion of a body. The following information was taken from the University of Illinois at Urbana-Champaign:

> "Newton's Law of Gravity says that gravity is a force that acts between any two objects with mass, and that force increases if the mass increases and decreases if the distance between the two objects increases. This force is always attractive, that is, it always works to pull the objects closer together. This is why objects fall to the ground and the moon doesn't fly away from the Earth. Newton's Laws have been indispensable in our world. They are certainly not all of physics, but the use of them has accomplished much--not the least of which was getting man to the moon!"
> (Reference: University of Illinois at Urbana-Champaign/ Ask the Van/ Laws of Motion and Gravity/John ZuHone)

In short, Newton described the relationship between masses; this means that Adam and Eve were turned over to the state of mind they'd subjected themselves to; their perception had been changed. This changed what they attracted and what they were attracted to. The Law of Attraction, in layman's terms, states that you will attract whatever it is that you focus on. Therefore, people who focus on Jesus will be drawn to Him, and He will manifest Himself to them. James 4:8 confirms this; it reads, "Draw nigh to God, and he will draw nigh to you. Cleanse your hands, ye sinners; and purify your hearts, ye double minded." People who are drawn to other deities, however, will be drawn to false doctrines and demons, and those things will begin to manifest in their lives.

Isaac Newton also penned the Laws of Motion. The following information was taken from National Aeronautics and Space Administration's website:

> "**Newton's first law** states that every object will remain at rest or in uniform motion in a straight line unless compelled to change its state by the action of an external force. This is normally taken as the definition of inertia. The key point here is that if there is no net force acting on an object (if all the external forces cancel each other out) then the object will maintain a constant velocity. If that velocity is zero, then the object remains at rest. If an external force is applied, the velocity will change because of the force.
>
> **The second law** explains how the velocity of an object changes when it is subjected to an external force. The law defines a force to be equal to change in momentum (mass times velocity) per change in time. Newton also developed the calculus of mathematics, and the "changes" expressed in the second law are most accurately defined in differential forms. (Calculus can also be used to determine the velocity and location variations experienced by an object subjected to an external force.) For an object with a constant mass m, the second law states that the force F is the product of an object's mass and its acceleration a:

$$F = m * a$$

> For an external applied force, the change in velocity depends on the mass of the object. A force will cause a change in velocity; and likewise, a change in velocity will generate a force. The equation works both ways.
>
> **The third law** states that for every action (force) in nature there is an equal and opposite reaction. In other words, if object A exerts a force on object B, then object B also exerts an equal force on object A. Notice that the forces are exerted on different objects. The third law can be used to explain the

generation of lift by a wing and the production of thrust by a jet engine."

Before we move forward, let's address the obvious. The church, in general, does not like to marry science with the Word because a lot of scientific findings seem to contradict the Word of God, plus, many renown scientists were atheists. Nevertheless, *all* things work together for good to them that love God, to them who are the called according to his purpose (see Romans 8:28). What does this mean in relation to science? It means that true science will NEVER discredit the Word; it only confirms the Word and explains it on our level. In all truth, science is revelation without the religious undertones. There are, however, some scientific "facts" that are lies. One level of wisdom is being able to differentiate a "mad scientist" from one who's seeking the truth. With that being said, let's revisit the Laws of Motion and see how they affected the people who were building the Tower of Babel.

"**Newton's first law** states that every object will remain at rest or in uniform motion in a straight line unless compelled to change its state by the action of an external force."

Simply put, mankind was "at rest" until Jesus entered the Earth's realm. Man could not save himself, but instead, had to wait for the Savior. For this very reason, man continued to go in a straight line or, better yet, travel horizontally. Our ability to truly ascend into the presence of God was totally reliant on God inviting us into His presence. Before Jesus entered the Earth, He did not live on the inside of mankind, making Him an external force. Nevertheless, once we accepted Him as our Lord and Savior, Newton's first law no longer applied to us.

"**The second law** explains how the velocity of an object changes when it is subjected to an external force."

First and foremost, let's define the word "velocity." According to Google's Online Dictionary, velocity is "the speed of something in a given direction." Remember, the people building the Tower of Babel were attempting to build upward, not realizing that "up" is relative. What we perceive to be "up" is based on our position; this is why some people look *up* to the wrong people. Nevertheless, we're all heading in one direction or another; we're all pursuing a set of ideas, and we're all chasing those ideas or being chased away from them at a specific speed. But when we gave ourselves over to the Lord, we were changed instantly, meaning, we supernaturally defeated the laws of both speed and time.

"The third law states that for every action (force) in nature, there is an equal and opposite reaction."

When building the Tower of Babel, the people built their structure up towards the Heavens, but to counter this, God pulled them down (mentally) and scattered them throughout the Earth (physically). This law pretty much states that for every position, there is an opposition. Opposition is nothing but the opposing of a position. When we're in the will of God, the opposing force will be evil, but when we're in sin, God is the opposing force. This means that as long as we reside in the realm of the Earth, we will experience opposition if we attempt to take any solid position on a matter.

But how does all this tie into your job as a scribe? Your assignment isn't to take men by the hand and lead them vertically; your assignment isn't to lead men to an air shuttle so they can reach new heights horizontally. Your assignment isn't to lead men to submarines where they can explore the deepest places on the ocean or sea. Your assignment is to help man to navigate from his personal Genesis to his Revelation. Remember, we are all little planets, and as such, we all start off "without form and void." As miniature earths, we also have seasons, and each season has a Genesis, just as it has a moment of Revelation. Revelation is the ending of one reality and the beginning of another. In every Revelation season, another one of Satan's lies is cast down and we eventually find ourselves seeing a new Heaven and a new Earth. Nevertheless, the Earth is without form and void, but to address this, God says, "Let there be light." Light is revelation. The moment we come out of the darkness and into God's marvelous light in any given season is the moment that we ascend out of the depths of cultural and religious insanity. Don't get me wrong. I'm not saying you're a madman; I am saying that sin has perverted all of us, and it has placed a cloak over our eyes, making it hard for us to comprehend the things of God. As a scribe, your first assignment is to overcome whatever Goliath you're facing; to do this, you can't wear Saul's armor, meaning, you cannot duplicate the world or anyone, for that matter. Your power lies in your authenticity and your authority is only legalized by your love for God's people. You cannot and will not lead what you do not love to a good place.

MICROSCRIBEOLOGY

Again, Microscribeology is the study of you. What season are you in, and what chapter of that season are you in? Are you in the Genesis of it or are you in the Exodus? Are you running from your assignment or running towards it? Are you hiding from Saul in a cave or are you on a rooftop (high place/pride) somewhere being tempted by your seductive neighbor? Anytime you find yourself in the Revelation of a season, you can teach on that season because you are in the illumination of that season, meaning, the voids and the darkness of that season are no more. Merriam Webster defines "revelation" this way:

- an act of revealing or communicating divine truth
- something that is revealed by God to humans
- an act of revealing to view or making known
- something that is revealed; especially: an enlightening or astonishing disclosure, shocking revelations
- a pleasant often enlightening surprise

A good example of a Revelation season can be seen in criminal court. While this may not be the best example, I believe it will convey the point in a way that's easy to understand. A man sits in criminal court next to his defense attorney. The Prosecutor calls a few witnesses to the stand, and he holds up a few items of evidence for the jury to examine. This is called a revealing; this is the moment of revelation for everyone in the courtroom. The evidence is overwhelming, and a few days later, the man is convicted of the crime. He's then sentenced to prison. What happened with him is all the things he'd done in darkness were brought to the light, and in the presence of two or three witnesses, it was established that he was guilty. After exiting the courtroom, he exits an old season. He's then taken to the prison he'll be housed in and handed a uniform. The uniform is his new garment for the season he's just entered. The moment the prison doors shut, he's just entered the Genesis of a new season. Your assignment is to usher him to the Revelation of that season, but you do this by writing. Scribes lead with their pens, not their feet.

Microscribeology is an examination of your life as a scribe. What are you afraid to share in your book? What have you not overcome? It is important (and necessary) for every scribe to know himself or herself. People who *wonder* mentally are the same people who *wander* around physically because they are scattered in their thoughts, meaning, they have no true position. Sure, they may identify themselves as Christians or identify with Christian beliefs, but they have not submitted to Jesus Christ. "But when he saw the multitudes, he was moved with compassion on them, because they fainted, and were scattered abroad, as sheep having no shepherd" (Matthew 9:36). Genesis 8:11 reads, "So the LORD scattered them abroad from thence upon the face of all the earth: and they left off to build the city." The Hebrew word for "scatter" is "zarah" and it means "to disperse." This means that the people were not united; they were divided in theories, and therefore, divided in their loyalties. First and foremost, if division is bad, why did God scatter the people? The answer can be found in Genesis 1:3-4, which reads, "And God said, Let there be light: and there was light. And God saw the light, that it was good: and God *divided* the light from the darkness." Do you remember Noah's sons: Japheth, Ham and Shem? Ham attempted to expose his father, and for this reason, Noah cursed Ham's son, Canaan, from whom we get the Canaanites. Genesis 9:25 reads, "And he said, Cursed be Canaan; a servant of servants shall he be unto his brethren." As cruel as Noah's response seems, what he was doing was dividing light from darkness, good from evil. Nevertheless, God had given Noah and his family the same command earlier on that He'd given Adam and Eve. Genesis 9:1-4 reads, "And God blessed Noah and his sons, and said unto them, Be fruitful, and multiply, and replenish the earth. And the fear of you and the dread of you shall be upon every beast of the earth, and upon every fowl of the air, upon all that moveth upon the earth, and upon all the fishes of the sea; into your hand are they delivered. Every moving thing that liveth shall be meat for you; even as the green herb have I given you all things. But flesh with the life thereof, which is the blood thereof, shall ye not eat." God was once again drawing a line of demarcation between good and evil. Instead of the Tree of the Knowledge of Good and Evil, the young men were commanded not to eat flesh with the blood still in it. So, the answer is, God scattered the people because the darkness (evil people) were leading the good ones astray.

Matthew 15:14: Let them alone: they be blind leaders of the blind. And if the blind lead the blind, both shall fall into the ditch.

Matthew 13:24-30: Another parable put He forth unto them, saying, The Kingdom of Heaven is likened unto a man which sowed good seed in his field: But while men slept, his enemy came and sowed tares among the wheat, and went his way. But when the blade was sprung up, and brought forth fruit, then appeared the tares also.

So the servants of the householder came and said unto him, Sir, didst not thou sow good seed in thy field? from whence then hath it tares? He said unto them, An enemy hath done this. The servants said unto him, Wilt thou then that we go and gather them up? But he said, Nay; lest while ye gather up the tares, ye root up also the wheat with them. Let both grow together until the harvest: and in the time of harvest I will say to the reapers, Gather ye together first the tares, and bind them in bundles to burn them: but gather the wheat into my barn.

Division, when prompted by God, is designed to unify His people and sanctify or separate us from those who have turned away from Him. Division protects us from those who would go out of their way to usurp our authority and lead us astray. This distinguishes the light from the dark, the day from the night and the good from the not-so-good. This allows us to lead the lost sheep back to the Shepherd (Jesus Christ). By revolving around the Son, we pick up His glory, and this, in essence, draws men back to Him. But to do this, we have to testify about what we were once drawn to. This attracts people to us and ultimately to Jesus Christ.

WE ALSO DRAW MEN WITH OUR GIFTS.

Understand this: Not only does the Lord draw us to Him, He draws our gifts in different seasons. Sure, a gift never lifts or leaves, but each gift comes to the forefront in the season that God is pulling on it because each gift has a season. For example, I can tell when I'm in the Genesis of a gift. During that season, I've just discovered the new gift, or I've suddenly found myself interested in an old gift of mine—a gift that once seemed irrelevant to me. Being immature in that gifting, I'll play and experiment with it. This means that I'm a child in that area of gifting. But when I grow out of that particular season, the gift has increased in value and has become a souvenir of sorts. For this reason, I'll shelf it until I want to show it off or until I need it. Because I've mastered it by then, it becomes a gift that I utilize more often than I did when it seemed irrelevant to me. Additionally, the magnetic pull of that gifting is still strong, even when God has pulled another gift to the forefront. This is similar to what a little boy would do with a set of toy cars given to him by his parents. While he's young, he'll play with the cars because in that season, the cars are valueless and replaceable toys. Nevertheless, once he gets older, the toys become invaluable and irreplaceable to him. He'll then put them on a shelf and store them as souvenirs. They won't necessarily sit around and collect dust; instead, he'll show off his prized collection to the people he loves and the people he wants to impress. A new gift may come to the forefront in his life, for example, his wife may buy him a drone for his photography business. And while this drone is expensive and valuable to him, it does not have the same pull on his heart as the souvenir cars because it is still a new gift. Nevertheless, as he masters using the drone, he'll find himself using it less whenever a new gift surfaces. Over time, the drone will become a souvenir; it will be invaluable and irreplaceable, even though it may not be in use anymore. Again, this is similar to how we treat our God-given gifts.

Why does God pull our gifts to the forefront? Because men are naturally attracted to gifts. When a person is gifted and excellent in a certain arena, that person becomes attractive to certain people. When a creative gets the attention of others, the job of the creative is to then give God the glory. In doing this, the name of Jesus Christ is exalted, and men are drawn to Him. This is why it would be erroneous for a creative to become ambitious, wanting the glory for himself or herself—wanting to be what we refer to in the western world as a "star." A star is a celebrity or, better yet, a largely celebrated person. Sadly enough, this ambition is widespread and it has even hit the church with such a force that it has permanently shut the doors of many religious establishments. But to understand what we see happening, we must first come to understand the life and death of a star in space. According to Collins Dictionary, a star is a large ball of burning gas in space. Stars appear to us as small points of light in the sky on clear nights.

Facts About Stars

1. The more massive the star is, the faster it burns out, meaning, the lifespan of a megastar is shorter than the lifespan of a standard-sized star.
2. Stars tend to orbit one another; they are called Binary Stars. As a matter of fact, most stars are in pairs or are a part of larger associations.
3. The longest living stars are called Red Dwarfs. According to Google, Red Dwarfs are small, old and relatively cool stars. Red Dwarfs are too dim to be seen with the naked eye.
4. The sun is a large star, believed by scientists to be 4.6 billion years old; they also believe that the lifespan of a star like the sun is ten billion years.

5. A Red Giant is a swollen star that's about to die.
6. When a large star dies, it often becomes a black hole, sucking in everything that gets close to what's called its Event Horizon, including light.

You can see how these points relate to what we call "stars" or "celebrities." Now, don't get me wrong; there's nothing wrong with being a celebrity. The issue arises when the "star" does not give God the glory or only gives Him snippets of glory, all the while taking the rest for himself or herself. If we can be honest with ourselves, we've watched megastars implode (self-destruct) before exploding (burning out/ passing away). This is also why it is dangerous and even foolish to covet the glory of God. This is the very sin that Lucifer committed and we all know what happened to him as a result. In Isaiah 14:12, Jesus refers to Lucifer as the son of the morning. Other translations refer to him as the "morning star." What happened to him? When he fell, the glory of God left him, and he became the ruler of darkness. Ephesians 6:12 reads, "For we wrestle not against flesh and blood, but against principalities, against powers, against the rulers of the darkness of this world, against spiritual wickedness in high places." Satan is the embodiment of darkness; he is a fallen star or a black hole. A black hole sucks in everything it that gets close to it. Sadly enough, many people desire to become household names, not realizing the price they'll have to pay to acquire and maintain this fame. This is why Matthew 16:26 says, "For what is a man profited, if he shall gain the whole world, and lose his own soul? Or what shall a man give in exchange for his soul?" The point is, as a gifted person, people are going to be drawn to you. You've likely witnessed this in your personal life. As your name begins to become widely known, it is important for you to give the glory (illumination) back to God. If you do not, please understand that you'll become mesmerized, charmed, bewitched and addicted to the glory. From there, your pride will continue to swell until you implode and eventually explode. Look at the lives of many of the celebrities men have idolized. We've publicly watched them swell in notoriety (and in pride) so much so that people began to publicly worship them. This swelling continues until the star is full of himself or herself; this is what it means to implode. This is because, as humans, we can only hold a certain amount of glory.

Oxford Dictionaries define "glory" this way:

1. High renown or honor won by notable achievements.
2. Magnificence or great beauty.
- A thing that is beautiful, impressive, or worthy of praise.
- The splendor and bliss of Heaven.
3. Praise, worship, and thanksgiving offered to a deity.
4. A luminous ring or halo, especially as depicted around the head of Christ or a saint.

Glory is often depicted as a bright light surrounding Jesus. The Hebrew word for "glory" is "kavod (kabod)" and it means "honor." It is also connected with the Hebrew word "kaved", which means "heavy." On the other end of the spectrum is the Hebrew word "qalon" which is the opposite of glory; it means "shame" or "dishonor." This means that the glory of God is weighty; it is too much for us to bear. There are three things to note about glory and they are:

1. Glory can be seen.
2. Glory is luminous; it has everything to do with light.
3. Glory is heavy.

The more influence a person gets, the more "weight" that person's words is said to carry. For example, when a foolish man or woman is largely celebrated and known in the western world, that person's words, albeit foolish, are highly influential. This is also why we see so much crime in the world. Jesus said that if He is lifted up, He'll draw all men to Him, but when we lift up men instead, they draw the masses to themselves, and then, they begin to scatter, divide and kill them with words. It doesn't matter how much wisdom God shares with us, our hearts, according to Jeremiah 17:9, are deceitful and wicked. This is why the moment we are lifted up, we must strip ourselves of God's glory and give it back to Him. If we do not, we can easily find ourselves experiencing the phenomenon that Lucifer experienced when he watched the angels bow and give glory to God. He became intoxicated with it and wanted the glory for himself. As his pride began to swell, the Bible says that Lucifer said within himself, "I will ascend into Heaven, I will exalt my throne above the stars of God: I will sit also upon the mount of the congregation, in the sides of the north: I will ascend above the heights of the clouds; I will be like the Most High" (see Isaiah 14:13-14). The Bible goes on to talk about Lucifer's punishment, with one of the biggest ones being shame. Isaiah 14:15-18 reads, "Yet thou shalt be brought down to hell, to the sides of the pit. They that see thee shall narrowly look upon thee, and consider thee, saying, Is this the man that made the Earth to tremble, that did shake kingdoms; that made the world as a wilderness, and destroyed the cities thereof; that opened not the house of his prisoners? All the kings of the nations, even all of them, lie in glory, every one in his own house." This scripture speaks about Satan's shame—it talks about the moment men will lay their eyes on him and realize that he is but another creature or creation of God—the moment when he won't look or sound so intimidating.

The angels of God are also referred to as "morning stars." Job 38:4-7 reads, "Where wast thou when I laid the foundations of the Earth? Declare, if thou hast understanding. Who hath laid the measures thereof, if thou knowest? Or who hath stretched the line upon it? Whereupon are the foundations thereof fastened? Or who laid the corner stone thereof; When the *morning stars* sang together, and all the sons of God shouted for joy?" Lastly, Jesus referred to Himself as the "bright and morning star." In Revelation 22:16, He is recorded saying, "I Jesus have sent mine angel to testify unto you these things in the churches. I am the root and the offspring of David, and the bright and morning star." John 9:5 calls Him the "light of the world." What is the light of the natural world? The sun, of course. Here, the scriptures tell us that Jesus is the light of both the natural and spiritual world, whereas, we know that Satan is the prince of darkness. Again, we can compare this with the stars that illuminate our skies at night. We are similar to those stars. We are scattered across the land; we shine ever-so-brightly, even though we cannot mimic the light from the Son, nor can we compete with the moon (the light in the darkness). We all have our own place and we all have our own season—the hour when God calls us forth and highlights our gifts. Nevertheless, it is in this hour that we are to give God the loudest glory. Think of it this way. You put together a musical, and in that musical, you are featuring twelve amazing singers. You know that the event will be packed, so you have the singers and the band come together everyday for rehearsal. Your vision for this musical is to bring more attention to your school. In your school, you train singers to reach within the depths of themselves and pull out their best voices. Every singer on your panel was personally trained by you. During rehearsal, you explain to the singers that they will be called forth during the closing song to sing for thirty seconds. You simply want them to be themselves and not be distracted by the crowd's response. Rehearsal goes great everyday, but on the big day, you notice that one of your singers seems unusually nervous. You've been in business for a long time, so you know what this nervousness entails. It means the singer is focusing on himself and not the unit. He sees this as his opportunity, and for this reason, he's fidgety and cranky. You pull him aside and explain to him that the purpose of the event is to bring more attention to the school. He nods his head and says, "Understood," nevertheless, he remains shaky.

The hour comes, and everything is going well. The crowd is mesmerized by the excellence displayed and there isn't a dry eye in sight. Suddenly, it's the nervous guy's turn, and he steps forward and belches out the loudest sound. He's not singing like he did during rehearsal. It's obvious that he's trying to out-sing everyone else because of the excessive runs he's doing. Thirty seconds pass, and he still hasn't passed the mic to the next singer. He sings for another thirty seconds and then he leans back and lets out the loudest and most profane sound anyone has ever heard. You suspected that he'd pull this stunt, so you'd already devised a plan to counter his antics. You rush to the front, wearing a tailor-made police uniform just seconds before he's ready to give up the mic. He turns to hand the mic to the next singer, only to find you waiting behind him with your hand extended. Ashamed, he hands the mic to you. Suddenly, the music stops, the lights dim and a host of men wearing police uniforms rush onto the stage. In your most theatrical voice, you say, "Officers, take this man away. Strip him of the badge he wears and cast him out of this building." The now humiliated singer begins to swear, but he doesn't have a mic, so no one can hear him over your voice. You then proclaim to the crowd, "This is an example of what can happen if you don't receive training. This is also why our school is about training real musicians who are humble enough to be used by God." You then began to sing while a few dancers and actors come onto the stage, sweeping and dancing around the area where the now humiliated singer once stood. Once the theatrics are over, you continue singing until you reach the bridge of the song once again. From there, you hand the mic to the next singer and things continue to flow smoothly. The audience is left thinking that the man's prideful attempt to captivate them was all a part of the act, so the show goes well. During your meeting with the singers after the show, you explain to them what they saw happening on the stage. The guy was just another good singer who allowed pride to enter his heart. He was just another one whose career, as some would say, "bit the dust." Anything that attempts to get bigger than the Son will swell up and explode with pride. The following information was taken from Windows to the Universe's website:

> "Occasionally, a star bigger than our Sun will end its life in a huge explosion, called a supernova. This explosion happens because the center, or core, of the star collapses in less than a second. The outer layers of the star are blown off in the explosion, leaving a contracting core of the star after the supernova." (Reference: www.windows2universe.com/ExplodingStars/)

When your hour comes, God will bring you to the forefront so that you can give Him the glory. If you get intoxicated and keep that glory for yourself, like a star in the sky, you will begin to swell. The following information was taken from NASA's website:

> "A supernova happens where there is a change in the core, or center, of a star. A change can occur in two different ways, with both resulting in a supernova. The first type of supernova happens in binary star systems. Binary stars are two stars that orbit the same point. One of the stars, a carbon-oxygen white dwarf, steals matter from its companion star. Eventually, the white dwarf accumulates too much matter. Having too much matter causes the star to explode, resulting in a supernova.
> The second type of supernova occurs at the end of a single star's lifetime. As the star runs out of nuclear fuel, some of its mass flows into its core. Eventually, the core is so heavy that it cannot withstand its own gravitational force. The core collapses, which results in the giant explosion of a supernova. The sun is a single star, but it does not have enough mass to become a supernova."

Isaiah 14:12 sums this up beautifully; it reads, "How art thou fallen from Heaven, O Lucifer, son of the morning! How art thou cut down to the ground, which didst weaken the nations!" Lucifer is but a fallen star. This is another reason you have to intentionally and aggressively pull pride down every time it tries to rise up in your life. Please understand that it's not a matter of *if* pride tries to enter your heart; it's *when*. Pride tempts us all, especially when we start mastering our talents or any given skill-set, but it's up to us to pull it down. Remember, the glory of God is weighty; it's too heavy for you. Sure, you can sport it for a season or two, but after a while, it'll bury you before making its way back to its rightful place.

Without going any further into this, the point (once again) is, as a scribe, you have to be smart enough to give the glory right back to God. There is a possibility that your book may become a bestseller. There is a possibility that you'll preach to the nations, but commit right now to giving the glory back to God; this way, more souls will be saved.

How to Build Your Skills as a Writer

Some people think I was born writing, but this isn't true. The fact is, even though writing was and is a talent of mine, it wasn't something I particularly cared for at one point of my life. My sixth-grade teacher (Mrs. Alexander) pulled on that talent, and during my stint in her class, I was a full-blown writer. But once I passed the sixth grade, I stopped writing. I hated writing articles and research papers in school, even though I was good at it. I hated anything that took up large chunks of my time. Over the years, I've watched many of my talents come to the forefront. As a matter of fact, all throughout elementary and some of high school, I wanted to be a Psychologist. I loved any and everything dealing with the mind and the way it worked. I didn't want to be a Psychiatrist, however, because I'm introverted. As I got older, I found myself leaning more towards interior design. At one point in my life, I tried to launch a virtual interior design company. During another season, my love for music and the creation of it came to the forefront, and in another season, I found myself interested in fashion design. Eventually, I grew to realize that it was okay for me to have several talents. Like most people, I thought I needed to pick a talent, master it and build a career around it. This belief was intensified every time I heard people saying things like, "Don't be a jack of all trades, but a master of none." While I get the heart and intent of this message, it can and has confused many multi-gifted and multi-talented people who, quite frankly, don't understand why they are the way that they are. Nevertheless, as an entrepreneur, I've developed a different theory— one that has helped me to tap into whatever talent God is highlighting in any given season, and one that also helps me to master those talents. My theory is this: every talented person NEEDS to focus on the talent that God is highlighting, even if he or she has not yet mastered another talent. The reason for this is, when God stirs up a creative and illuminates a certain talent in the creative, He begins to speak to the creative through the mic of that talent. During this time, the creative hears more from God and learns more about Him, and the creative learns more about himself or herself. This does not mean it's time for that talent be broadcast to the world, however. It means that the creative needs to spend time with God, for example, as a fashion designer because there's some revelation related to fashion design that God wants to share with the creative. He's not necessarily highlighting the creative's creativity in that hour; He's teaching the creative about Himself. When the time comes for that talent to become public, God will illuminate it all the more, causing the creative to become even more attracted to that arena. For example, a man may find himself infatuated with rebuilding cars. He's been building a life as a graphic designer, and he has a somewhat lucrative business. Should he close his business and focus on cars? Absolutely not! When his season as a graphic designer was highlighted, he was supposed to increase his talents, meaning, train others to do what he's doing. He's supposed to expand his business until it gets to the point that it can run without him. This way, when a new season is upon him, he can focus on the talent that's being highlighted, without burying the one that's not. All talents must remain above ground if they are to be effective. Don't get me wrong. I do understand that there are some people out there who are multi-talented, and these people jump around from one talent to the other, never stopping to master one talent. To them, the "jack of all trades, master of none" assertion is true, but to the people who are hearing from God, the process looks a little different.

But how do you build on your writing talent?
1. ***Write daily.*** Even if it's a small article, a short bio or a product description, volunteer to write something everyday. When God highlighted my writing talent, I went online looking for opportunities to write. I found a guy on Craigslist who was paying four dollars for every five-hundred word how-to article. I applied, and he recruited me to be one of his writers. I needed the money badly, so I wrote until I couldn't think of anything else to write about. I ultimately made between $300-$500 writing for him in the two weeks that I worked for him. After this, he simply could not afford to retain me. He'd underestimated the power of a hungry writer.
2. ***Blog.*** Blogging keeps you on a schedule, after all, no one wants to read a rarely updated blog. Blogging is similar to writing a book, but there are some

differences. For example, you can be witty and use strikethroughs and cute little notations in a blog, but this is never good to do in a self-help book. Blogging helps you to learn a whole new style of writing so that you can master authorship as a whole. It also helps you to build your own audience; this way, when your book is published, you'll have a general idea regarding who your target market is.

3. ***Look for and apply to write with a few online magazines.*** I applied to and was accepted to write for Associated Content (now Yahoo) and Examiner (now Ajax). I ended up writing a few articles (maybe ten or more) with Associated Content and over two hundred articles for Examiner between 2011-2015. Be diligent and write even when you don't feel like it.

Because I exercised my writing talent often, it has become one of my strongest talents. I have other talents that I have not exercised, and for this reason, they are weak. For example, when I was younger, I loved everything centered around fashion design. The talent is still there, but nowadays, I'm not into fashion. Nevertheless, I can dig the talent up if I want to and start building on it, after all, I got it from my mother. The point is, this is an inherited talent of mine; it's something I can tap into whenever I want to, but as of today, it is not a strength or interest of mine.

But what if writing isn't a talent of yours? What if you are a writer by trade and not by talent? You can still mature the trade. Some people are better at performing certain trades than the people who are talented in those trades. This is because they've acquired a skill and kept building on it. A few years back, I conducted a survey for business owners. I wanted to tally the results in my book, *Christian & Entrepreneur*. The results were shocking. I asked several business owners if they were gifted to do what they did or if it was a skill they'd acquired. I also asked them how much money they were making in their businesses. To my surprise, the people who said they were skilled (not talented) were making more money, on average, than the people who said that they'd been talented by God to do what they do. I dug a little deeper, of course, and found that the reason for this was the people who were skilled invested more time and money into their businesses than the ones who were talented. This means that they were more determined and they had more faith than the people who'd been gifted to do what they were learning to do. In other words, you don't have to be a talented writer; you simply need to be a diligent one.

Keys to a Successful Writing Career

Life's key chain is full of keys—there are the keys to a successful marriage, keys to starting a successful business, keys to acing an interview, keys to launching a successful blog, and the list goes on. Howbeit, the average person only uses a few of the keys on this key chain.

When we're born, God hands us a set of keys; these keys are called gifts. In the realm of the spirit, we don't lose our keys, we simply have trouble finding the doors for each key on our key rings. The problem with most believers is we waste the majority of our time sticking our keys in every door that's presented to us, instead of paying attention to the neighborhood of thought that we're in. For example, as a single woman, I shouldn't be meeting any man at a hotel, and if a man comes into my life and tries to get me to sleep with him, it's simply because I was in the wrong neighborhood mentally. Sure, I have the Master's key so I could have the man if I wanted him, but I couldn't have the blessing with the man. For this reason, it would be unwise for me to use my key in that season and attempt to open the door of marriage with that guy or any guy, for that matter. Wrong mindset equals wrong door. In other words, he wouldn't be the man for me. He'd be a guy who simply found me in the wrong neighborhood of thinking. So, in that season, I'd waste a lot of my time if I tried to date every man who smiled at me. In that season, I would need to keep my keys in the ignition and just seek the Kingdom of God and all His righteousness, and when I entered into the right mindset, everything else would be added to me. In other words, my husband would come and find me. This is because I'd be in his region of thought.

Earlier in this book, we discovered that we are nothing but a pile of dirt. Each dirt particle represents a letter. Each letter comes together to form a word, for example, one of your strengths may be charity. When Satan got Adam and Eve to sin, he was able to add his two-cents into our makeups. For this reason, sin entered mankind and Satan got to experience fatherhood. When God breathed life into us, every word He has spoken in regards to us came to life. When God breathed life into us, our personalities awakened and we became the unique creatures that we are today. So when we ask God for something, He has to see what's in us before He blesses or, better yet, breathes new life into us. For example, if a woman has been sober for nine months, and yet, the spirit of addiction is still lodged in her, the Lord wouldn't give her more money in that moment, even though she's been praying for it. This is because if the Lord blessed her or, better yet, blew new life into her, He'd have to empower the entirety of who she is. He'd be breathing life into everything that she is, including an addict. So, He would bring people into her life to help her get free from everything that's standing between her prayers and his answers. The distance between a prayer and the answer to that prayer is called agreement. Agreement is what links our walks with God's walk; it is the third fold in the fabric of our relationships with Him. But to walk in agreement, we need the Word of God and we need understanding. So, she'd have to seek the Word of God by seeking the Kingdom of God, and she'd receive understanding along the way. For this reason, the Lord encourages her to use her keys (gifts) whenever she comes in contact with a door that stands between her and understanding. In Proverbs 18:16, He says that those gifts would make room for her and bring her before great men. The room that's made *for* her is made *in* her, meaning, God will increase her capacity to receive more wisdom, knowledge and understanding. When she goes before great men, she'd be going before wise men. These men and women of God would then begin to fill her up with revelation. Eventually, every evil word, including addiction would be dislodged from her character, and she'd be made whole again. It is then that her prayers would link up with God's "yea" and "amen." In other words, God would lead her to the door of her answered prayers. It would then be up to her to use the right key to open those doors and cross over from one realm of thought to another.

So now, we are mountains of words, both good and bad. If our parents dealt with perversion, that perversion probably traveled over into our makeups, and we've had to pray, fast and go through deliverance just to get perversion out of our deoxyribonucleic acid (DNA). But perversion was all we knew. As a matter of fact, perversion led us to a few doors that we didn't even need our keys for. Those doors were always open for us, and we entered them whensoever we pleased. Nowadays, we are new creatures in Christ, trying to live good, godly lives. But this doesn't mean that we're whole. We become whole when we bridge the gap between our will and

God's will.

Again, the Seven Mountain Mandate concludes that there are seven mountains of influence; they are:
- Religion
- Family
- Education
- Government
- Business
- Media
- Arts & Entertainment

Each key (gift) I have gives me a certain measure of access to each mountain. In some of these mountains, I have free roam, but in others, I need a tour guide. In every one of these mountains, there are levels, ranks, rewards and penalties. How I treat each level and the people on it will determine which door I'm led to, for example, if I mistreat the doorman on the second level, I will find myself at the door of penalty, wondering why I seem to be stuck in that season of my life. If I want to get past the second level, I need to find what's lodged in my character so that I can cast it down, cast it out or cast it away from me. These are the three levels of deliverance.

Let's revisit the example I gave earlier on; it read:

> If I were to throw a bunch of rocks into a crowd of people, the people impacted would let out sounds. I'd hear a number of varying sounds every time a rock came in contact with a person. My level of impact could be measured by the number of people I hit, but it is more effectively measured by the sounds that are emitted from the people I hit, the force behind my throw and the distance between myself and the people impacted.

This is a picture of what Satan does. He throws lies and accusations off into the wind to see where they'll land; these words are called "fiery darts." Remember, a mountain is nothing but a homeless pile of dirt and rocks—these materials have not found their way into our ecosystem, so they just pile up and become problems for anyone who wants to go from one region of thought to the next. When Satan releases these fiery darts into crowds, he waits to see who responds. 1 Peter 5:8 tells us that Satan, like a roaring lion, goes about seeing who he may devour. The responses he gets come from the people who are in agreement with him; these people are in the wrong mindsets. When he hears the screams, he releases his bloodhounds (devils) off into those crowds and they rush over to devour any and everyone who has been impacted by Satan's lies and accusations. They look for whining, complaining and gossiping people. As these people are being devoured, they don't lose access to their keys. Romans 11:29 confirms this; it reads, "For the gifts and calling of God are without repentance." Those keys pass through the devoured souls' bloodlines, along with every generational curse that has not been broken. This is why some of the most talented families seem to struggle with addiction, perversion and every sin imaginable.

You have a certain level of access into every mountain of influence, and every gift that God has given you grants you access to a certain level on those mountains. Some people have access to the top level on the Mountain of Government, but can't seem to get past the first floor of the Mountain of Religion. This is because they have not yet learned to access God's heart in regards to that mountain. For example, a man named Bob could make a great governmental official. He could be the governor of his state because he has a great heart for the people of that state. Nevertheless, in the Mountain of Religion, Bob can't seem to get past sweeping floors. This is because Bob wants to see the people financially stable, and he wants them to have access to free healthcare, but Bob doesn't care anything about their souls. Bob is a surface-level leader, and for this reason, in the Mountain of Religion, he would be a sanitation worker. To find success in every mountain of societal influence, he would have to receive God's heart in regards to that mountain. He can't just have a bunch of good ideas, Bob needs to be in agreement with God. If he seeks the heart of God, and resists the temptation to be ambitious, anxious and entitled, God would lead him to the doors of his next level. This will only happen when he is mature enough to bear it.

Of course, like every other author, you want to know the keys to a successful writing career and again, you already have those keys. Right now, you need to find the doors (opportunities) and you need to walk through those doors. Below are seven paths to success:

- **Love God's people.** Remember, love legalizes your authority with people. You cannot legally lead, rebuke or instruct anyone you do not love.

- **Love God with all your heart and mind.** If you don't love the Lord, you won't love His people. This means you'll lead them astray. For this reason, it is imperative that you love God with all of your heart.

- **Seek first the Kingdom of God and all His righteousness.** In your pursuit of the Kingdom of God and all His righteousness, you will find God's heart for His people. You will no longer see them as potential customers, supporters or fans; you'll receive the very compassion that came over Jesus when He said, "The harvest truly is plenteous, but the laborers are few." You will then roll up your sleeves and labor for those souls. Amazingly enough, in this realm, you won't even know you're successful. This is because the world's definition of success simply does not exist in the Kingdom of God. Instead, you'll see your wealth and your time as opportunities to sow into God's Kingdom. Sure, your natural needs will be met, but spiritually, you'll always hunger to do more for the Kingdom; this appetite is unquenchable and it can become a burden if it's not managed correctly.

- **Remain humble.** Every door that God leads you to is small and low. For this reason, if you're high-minded or puffed up, you won't fit through them. Many authors have found the doors of success, but their egos wouldn't let them go through them. You can find authors like these sprinkled around nursing homes, churches, coffee shops, barber shops and just about everywhere you go. They have a lot of stories to tell, and they love to talk about the many celebrities they've met, worked with or dated, but they themselves have never truly tasted success. It is truly sad to see someone who's worked hard, played little and accomplished much, only to have that person ruin every opportunity that's afforded to him because of pride. If you want to be successful, you need to remain humble. Humility is not a feeling; it's a choice you make and it's a path you take. Pride will always lead you to destruction.

- **Be consistent.** I want you to imagine speaking with a millionaire over the phone. He tells you to come by his house so that he can give you a bag of diamonds, valued at $750,000. The millionaire happens to be an eighty-year old man who lives alone. It's clear that he has a hearing problem. You go by the guy's house and start ringing the doorbell. Five minutes later, he still hasn't answered. Would you get frustrated and walk away? Of course not! You wouldn't allow impatience to stand between you and $750,000! Instead, you'd keep ringing the doorbell and beating on the door until he finally answers. If he doesn't answer, you'd call the cops to come and do a welfare check on the guy. This is what success looks like in the writing world. You simply have to keep writing. It doesn't matter how many unsuccessful books you've written, you have to remain consistent in your writing if you want to be granted access to the next level.

- **Excellence is the key.** Anytime you have access to excellence, but choose to go another route because of budget or time constrictions, you prove to all of Heaven that you're not mature enough for the next level. You'll notice that anything God had His people build in the Bible was created in excellence. You can't just pile words up, pack them between a cover and shove them into the mouths of God's people. Presentation is important to God.

- **Give your readers usable content.** I cannot stress this enough. Your book's content is a revelation of the condition of your heart, so before you write anything, conduct a heart check. If you find any word lodged in your heart that shouldn't be there, make deliverance your top priority. If you do not do this, every profane thing in you will sound off in your book. This is why God said in Matthew 12:34, "For out of the abundance of the heart the mouth speaketh." He's not just talking about the mouth on your face; He's talking about every part of you that has the ability to communicate, including your fingers! People don't buy books just to support others; they buy books because they want to eat what's between the covers, so give your readers usable content. Give them something they can feed on. Remember, eighty to ninety percent of your book's content should be usable and editable, meaning, you should have broken it down enough for your readers to understand.

Success is already in you. You just have to partner it up with the right words to form a complete sentence. Sometimes, the right words are the right people, the right experiences or the right responses. Your goal isn't to become the highest paid author in the world. Your assignment is to impact the world by leaving your fingerprints on the walls of every mountain of influence. To do this, you need to start using every key God has given you, but remember, you have to put them in the right doors in the right seasons. If God has told you to write a book, obey Him. Sit down and start the process. Take your time, conduct the necessary research and don't be afraid to share the wisdom that God shares with you. Don't be intimidated by the sound of your own voice. You are a pile of words, and for this reason, you will have a lot of thoughts coming through while you're typing. Pull down the ones that come from Heaven, and cast down the ones that are not. This is how you tap into the best-seller that God has already declared you to be.

Ready. Set. Activate.

You don't have to have an extensive vocabulary to be a good writer. When I initially started writing, my vocabulary wasn't all that impressive. If I were to rate myself as a speaker, I would have rated myself as a standard speaker or maybe just a smidgen above standard. *Why above?* Because growing up, my dad had somewhat of an extensive vocabulary, so I learned quite a few words from him, but when I got out into the world, my friends would laugh and mock me anytime I said something they didn't understand. "Speak English!" I remember hearing one of my friends shouting jokingly after I'd uttered a word that she wasn't familiar with. Slowly but surely, my vocabulary changed to suit my environment, and before long, I sounded just like the people I hung around. I had to learn their language to effectively communicate with them. Many of the words I used to speak fell away and I can't remember half of those words to this day. My vocabulary has since grown by leaps and bounds, but I'm still growing it. One day, I considered all of the prophetic words that had been spoken over me and I realized that I was going to have to prepare myself for where I am going. I needed to expand my vocabulary, learn the difference between a soup spoon and a dessert spoon, and possibly even learn a whole new language. This is how you activate your faith. You have to offend your comfort zone to escape it.

Challenge #1

Below, is a set of questions. You can answer these questions in your copy of this book, you can answer them on a separate sheet of paper or you can email the answers to yourself. The goal is to keep a record so you can measure your growth.

Challenge	Results
Go online and look for a vocabulary tester to see how extensive your vocabulary is. Simply search the term "Test your vocabulary." After this, record your results. This will help you to measure your vocabulary from week to week.	
On a separate sheet of paper or word document, write a 250-word essay about what you learned in this book using your everyday, standard vocabulary. Don't use words that sound professional to you if you don't ordinarily use them. The goal is for you to see your comfort words. Everyone has comfort words, or better yet, words that they use everyday. The goal isn't just to learn new words; it's to incorporate them into your vocabulary until they become standard to you. Note: It is better to use an online word processor for this test; that way, you can check your word count with ease.	
Below are ten words. Write a definition for each word without looking at a dictionary. Remember, don't cheat. You can't measure your growth if you're dishonest with yourself. After you're finished, look up the definition to each word using a credible source and compare your definition to their definition. 1. Sporadic 2. Ingenuity 3. Complacent 4. Metron 5. Apparatus 6. Colloquialism 7. Bashful 8. Attribute 9. Apprentice	

10. Strenuous

Challenge #2

You will need to determine what type of book you're going to write. If you're unsure, it only means that you don't know your strength. What area of expertise do people pull on you for the most? For me, people have always pulled on me for relationship advice, even before I got saved. Even though I was twisted back then, I knew right from wrong, and I knew how to convey a point in a way that most people could understand. So, it goes without saying that I've written a few relationship books.

Challenge	Results
Call three people who you speak with often and ask them what areas would they say you are the strongest in. Record their responses.	

Challenge #3

Next, detail a testimony of yours that you're uncomfortable sharing with others. You can use the box below (if it's short), write it on a separate sheet of paper or record it in a word processor.

Your Testimony

In the previous activation, you were challenged to share an uncomfortable testimony of yours. Was it detailed, or did you give snippets of your testimony, avoiding key details because they made you uncomfortable? This is important in the writing world. Most authors are afraid to share their testimonies in detail because they fear backlash and/or they fear hurting the people they love the most. But as an author, if you are ever going to be effective in helping others, you have to become comfortable with sharing your testimony. The first time that you share it, you will be uncomfortable, but this discomfort will soon lift after you see how many people have been helped by it. Keep repeating this exercise week after week, sharing the same testimony until you're comfortable enough to publish it. Note: I'm not telling you to publish it; I'm challenging you to keep sharing until you're comfortable enough to publish it.

Challenge #4

Now, let's amp up the challenge. Grab your phone or any camera you can find and record your testimony. You don't have to publish it. The challenge is to record it until you're comfortable doing so.

Challenge #5

List three of your favorite foods, and then, break them down. List the ingredients in each food, how those ingredients affect or benefit you, and list the history of that food. The goal of this exercise is to teach you to become a more in-depth writer. Most writers like to state the obvious, but readers really appreciate authors who take the time to dig or, better yet, conduct research.

Challenge #6

Pretend you're in a room with the current president of your country. List ten questions you'd ask him or her. Be sure to detail your response.

The objective behind this exercise is to teach you to spread your wings as a writer. What this means is to explore areas that may not necessarily interest you. Again, writers love new information. One of the biggest mistakes most authors make is by rehashing old, recycled information. Remember, people read self-help books to learn; they want to be helped, and not so much entertained.

Challenge #7

If you know what the title of your book is, this challenge is designed to motivate you to finish your book. Find a graphic designer (be sure to look at several portfolios before picking one) and hire him or her to design your book's cover. Please note that you'll need the following:

- a general idea as to how you want the book's cover designed.
- your book's synopsis. This is just a short overview of what your book is about.
- a very short bio. A bio should only contain relevant information, for example, if your book is a relationship book, your bio should list why you are qualified to write about relationships. A good example is, "Jane Doe is the founder of Jane Doe in Love, a blog designed to help women to love and prepare themselves for their future husbands. She is also a radio personality on DJ & JD Love Matters, a Christian talk show that discusses dating in the twenty-first century. She is a wife, mother and a youth pastor." Bios should not contain irrelevant information like how long you were in school, what you majored in, and all of your accomplishments if none of these accomplishments relate to the book's topic. Of course, you can add this information if you want, but a more effective bio and synopsis is centered around the book's content.
- a professional headshot for the back of the cover. If you're going to have your photo on the front of the cover as well, you'll need that photo. If you do not have any professional photos, look around at some local photographers and set up a session with one of them. Please note that all photographers are created equal, but they are not equally excellent. Be sure to look at several portfolios before choosing one.

Challenge #8

As we discussed earlier, not everyone is an in-depth writer. Some people are more surface-level writers than they are in-depth. Go to Amazon's website and find a book similar to the one you're writing. Using the "Look Inside" feature, read a few pages of the book. Next, determine what level writer the author is based on the tools in this book. You can use the chart below as a measuring stick. If the chart isn't helpful enough, revisit the chapter From Layers to Levels. Repeat this process for at least two or three more books. The goal is to help you measure yourself as a writer.

Levels	Recap
Crust (First Level)	Writes on a level that most people can understand. Surface writers take what's evident and give readers the revelation behind whatever it is that's been obstructing their view.
Mantle (Second Level)	Affects the largest amount of people by affecting the surface-level writers. Can be pretty deep to the point where they can easily be mistaken as third or fourth level writers if given the right opportunities.
Outer Core (Third Level)	Are very, very bold and unapologetic teachers. They are also people who've survived the harshest of conditions, and for this reason, such teachers will not conform to the norm, regardless of what the cost may be.
Inner Core (Fourth Level)	Cannot and will not teach what they want to teach, but are instead, more spiritual in their approach to ministry (think Elijah). Writers and teachers on this level walk in the authority and power of the Son, Jesus Christ. They are potent in their delivery and can easily cast out the most stubborn of demons.
Inner Inner Core (Fifth Level)	They are immovable. Nothing you say or do will change their minds. They live for Christ and have resolved in their hearts to die for Him if necessary. They will not compromise the Kingdom, regardless of what they stand to lose. Usually very

	odd.

Based on what you've read and the exercises you've done so far, what level writer do you believe yourself to be? Explain why.

Challenge #9

Write a long note to your Goliath (500 words or less), detailing how you feel about him (or it). Using scriptures, tell your Goliath what his jurisdictional limitations are and then begin to take authority over your Goliath. The goal of this exercise is to teach you effective problem-solving. You cannot solve a problem if you only deal with it on the surface. In the second part of this exercise, write a note to yourself, detailing how you've allowed your Goliath to control, manipulate and even chase you. Tell yourself how you'll address and correct this behavior in the future.

You'll notice that this exercise, along with a few others, are designed to bring you outside of your comfort zone. This is because comfort zones are oftentimes nothing but beautifully decorated prison cells. You have to become comfortable with your own voice if you are to ever be a best-selling author.

Challenge #10

This is the ultimate challenge. Remember, God is Alpha and Omega; He is the Beginning and the End. We are simply living in the in-between. Your book's cover is a picture of this; it covers and represents your book's content. You should have the cover by now or it should be in the making. Now, it's your turn to go and complete the content or, better yet, the in-between. Don't put this off. Challenge yourself to finish your book within five to seven weeks, and for every week that you do not write, at minimum, twenty pages, give a substantial amount of money to a non-profit organization or shelter. Commit to doing this! This is what true discipline looks like.

No More Excuses

Please understand that writing a book is challenging and the deeper you go, the more warfare you'll experience. Nevertheless, you have to keep on writing and do not allow fear to chase you away from your assignment. While writing this book, I endured one of the biggest attacks on my finances that I've ever seen, plus, my car broke down and was pretty much irreparable. The worst attack, however, was against my mother. She's been battling cancer on and off for years, but she's always won the battle. A couple of weeks ago, she started having breathing problems, and then, her doctor kept insisting that we prepare ourselves for her untimely demise, which of course, was a report we refused to receive. He wanted to put her on hospice, but at first, we wouldn't let him. Throughout it all, I prayed, fasted and dealt with my feelings, however, I refused to stop writing. Why? Because after having written 40 books prior to this, I have been here before. Recently, my mother passed away from lung cancer. These are just a couple of the events that have taken place since I started writing. When I was writing my book *Wise Her Still Too* back in 2013, I underwent a major attack, but I did NOT stop writing. I endured the storm and kept writing. Now, don't get me wrong. I'm not saying that you will automatically go under attack or the attacks will be as devastating as the ones I've endured, after all, the measure of any given attack is predicated upon the level of the minister, the depth of the teacher's teaching and the open doors in that teacher's life. I made the mistake of opening a door on my finances when I took out a loan to get a new car. As for my mother, before she'd passed, she'd started writing her own book, and after she'd endured such a vicious fight with cancer, God was merciful enough to welcome her into His arms. The point is, you can't retreat every time the enemy huffs and puffs at you. You have to meet him head-on, knowing that the victory is already yours. Remember, the Bible says that David encouraged himself in the Lord. The way I do this is by reminding myself that:

1. My testimony isn't for me; my book and my testimony are designed to help others. Someone's deliverance is predicated upon my obedience.
2. No weapon formed against me or my family shall prosper, and every tongue that rises against me in judgment, I have the power and the right to condemn. The devil has no actual power against a believer. His attacks are nothing but him throwing a bunch of temper-tantrums.
3. Storms don't last always. The end of a storm is usually marked by the sun shining down on us, revealing that we've not only survived another day, but it also reveals the tokens or loot we've taken while in the heat of our battles.

So, no more excuses. Just write. Don't worry about how you sound, what you think people will say or what level you're writing on. Just obey God and write. If your book saves one soul or changes one life, you've done more in one book than most believers have done in their entire lives. This is not a numbers' game. Sure, we all want to sell as many books as we can, but always keep your eyes on the bigger picture and that is winning souls and changing lives. When you do this, God will promote your book and write the foreword for it, meaning, He will mark it for success.

Try to write at least four or five times a week, for an hour each day. Every time you have an excuse, write the excuse out in detail. If, at the end of five weeks, your excuse book is thicker than your actual book, publish your book of excuses. Again, you have to challenge and discipline yourself.

Now, it's your time to write the vision and make it plain. Will you start today?